GAS, AIR, AND SPRING GUNS OF THE WORLD

W. H. B. Smith

STACKPOLE BOOKS

Copyright © 1957 by W. H. B. Smith

Published by
STACKPOLE BOOKS
5067 Ritter Road
Mechanicsburg, PA 17055
www.stackpolebooks.com

All rights reserved, including the right to reproduce this book or portions thereof in any form or by any means, electronic or mechanical, including photocopying, recording, or by any information storage and retrieval system, without permission in writing from the publisher. All inquiries should be addressed to Stackpole Books, 5067 Ritter Road, Mechanicsburg, PA 17055.

Printed in the United States of America

10 9 8 7 6 5 4 3 2

First edition

Cover design by Wendy A. Reynolds

Cataloging-in-Publication Data is on file with the Library of Congress

AUTHOR'S PREFACE

THIS is a detailed, documented history and encyclopedia of the air- and gas-gun industry throughout the world. It deals primarily with high-power, high-precision weapons which at short ranges equal or even excel in accuracy the finest powder cartridge arms.

This is the first American book on the subject. It is also the first embracive work ever published anywhere which brings together for the interested shooter, collector, gunsmith, historian, developer, and manufacturer the complete story in text, pictures, and drawings of an industry and a sport which has flourished tremendously in Europe and Great Britain since the beginning of the present century; but which, despite fantastic strides in the past decade, is still in its infancy in the United States, in the opinion of qualified observers.

High-power air and gas arms constitute the one phase of precision target and short-range hunting weapons which have never been dealt with in United States publishing history. As for the industry itself, little is reliably known about its background, its history and development, or even its products. Such data are presented here for the first time.

Nearly 12,000,000 Americans, men and women, purchased hunting licenses in 1955. A very high percentage of these hunters know the "air rifle" as their cherished "first gun," the Daisy which shot "BB's." Today, some 75 years after the founding of the company, over 1,500,000 Daisy air rifles are sold each year; and since today they are precision-made youth trainers, even though they still are in the toy classification because of their controlled low power, they are dealt with in this book. The National Rifle Association of America and the Boy Scouts of America both recognize the value of the "BB" air rifle and even have official shooting courses for its use by boys under supervision.

However, we are concerned here only incidentally with the "toy" variety of rifle. We are directly concerned with those serious, quality rifles and pistols which use either highly compressed air or liquid carbon dioxide (CO_2) gas for propelling small-caliber precision pellets with enough power and velocity to make them ideal short-range sporting, training, and hunting arms; while still limiting the power and the carrying distances so that they may safely be used indoors and outdoors without the long-range hazards, the high cost, or the many other problems encountered with even the .22 powder-cartridge firearms.

The importance of this little-known air- and gas-gun industry economically is indicated by the output of the major British and European manufacturers who have been visited or directly contacted by the author or his qualified personal representatives in the preparation of this work—a project, incidentally, which involved the most intensive tasks of research, personal investigation, and testing ever encountered by the author in some 30 years of close association with all types of arms development and manufacture here and abroad, ranging from small arms to guided missiles.

In Europe and Great Britain, quality high-power guns of this class have been manufactured since the turn of the century, principally by high-quality firearms makers. Such guns have the characteristics of design, production, and quality found in the expensive firearms of those makers. In fact, many are built specifically as companion pieces to corresponding firearms. Thus the owner of a Walther air pistol, for example, may use the arm for an indoor, inexpensive trainer when range facilities for his Walther Olympia .22 pistol are not available. Thus, too, a German, Czech—and even Russian—army group may do indoor shooting with an air rifle which looks, feels, and handles like its official service rifle. Twelve major German manufacturers were contacted, 3 British, 2 Italian, 2 Spanish, 1 Czech, 1 Austrian, and 1 Japanese. All their assorted air arms are dealt with to the degree required by their importance, or by their American availability. Relatively few such arms are exported to the United States, though there is no corner of the world from Chile to New Zealand where German and British air guns in particular are not used for the sport of short-range precision target shooting and for pest shooting.

In the United States, on the other hand, air- and gas-gun manufacture has been developed by a small, highly specialized group outside the firearms trade—although now that the market possibilities have been established, it is to be expected that some members of the firearms group will eventually enter the field, probably via the merger route.

Based on confidential manufacturing and sales data furnished the author, it is possible to state that the combined air-gun production of the foreign makers for export is in excess of 1,500,000 units per year! As to our own domestic market, the major United States manufacturer alone sold a dollar volume at his level of over $2,000,000 in 1955; and the great Sears, Roebuck & Company mail-order house alone recently negotiated one purchase of 50,000 carbon dioxide rifles!

The sport of short-range precision shooting with air and gas guns is rapidly gathering momentum in the United States today; though it has a long way to go before it approaches, as it inevitably must, the acceptance it has achieved in Europe and Great Britain in the fields of recreational shooting, indoor and garden target shooting, hunting training—and even military training.

It is not in any sense a *substitute* for small-bore firearms shooting. It is instead a natural *collateral* sport. It is finding acceptance here today for the same basic reasons that it was accepted abroad 60 years ago. Simply stated, these reasons include: Rapidly expanding population, decentralization of living and the development of suburban home areas, steadily increasing costs of powder arms and of firearms shooting and suitable range facilities, and the difficulty of reaching areas where long-range firearms may safely be used.

In a word, the same human pressures responsible for the development of softball, miniature golf courses, and golf driving ranges are primarily responsible for the rise and the future of air- and gas-gun shooting; for what softball is to baseball, what miniature courses and driving ranges are to golf—that is what this new field of low-cost, accessible precision shooting is to the field of hunting, target, and even military firearms. Aside from training value, it provides all the recreational values of firearms sports at short ranges with a minimum of effort and at a fraction of the cost.

Consider for a moment the factors of population growth and the movement of family life into suburban areas. It is no longer easy for the average American city or suburban dweller to engage in the sport of rifle shooting. The cost and the travel time involved in reaching shooting areas becomes greater with each passing year. Each new residential development, each new suburban shopping center, each new decentralized manufacturing plant adds to the problem.

High-power air and gas arms are the direct answer to this phase. Suitable range facilities can be set up in cellars, backyards, school auditoriums, gymnasiums, meeting halls—in fact, almost anywhere that a range distance of 20 to 75 feet is available. No elaborate or permanent range facilities are required.

As to costs, the arms themselves on the average cost but a fraction as much as comparable firearms, and the ammunition relatively is even less expensive. As to range set-ups, since the propelling force is either compressed air or carbon dioxide gas, only lightweight improvised backstops or portable bullet traps are required to stop safely the specially-designed light pellets used in these precision-rifled arms. The weapons are smokeless, odorless, clean, and for all practical purposes, silent. There are no ventilation problems, no sound-proofing, no expensive backstops, no empty cartridges cases. A school gymnasium, for example, may be used for a gas-or air-gun tournament equal in every practical way to the finest precision short-range firearms course, yet in a matter of minutes the bullet traps, target holders, and other simple paraphernalia may be removed to allow the gymnasium to be used for formal athletic purposes.

Finally, consider the factor of general safe usage. Even the lowly .22 short cartridge today is capable of a degree of penetration which requires the use of expensive backstops. But much more important is the comparison of extreme "carrying ranges." The common .22 short develops a breech pressure of some 16,000 pounds per square inch when fired. Its bullet is ballistically designed

to start its travel at about 1,000 to 1,130 feet per second in a trajectory (or curved bullet flight) which at 300 feet from the muzzle shows a drop of less than 4.5 inches. Should the barrel be held at a high enough angle, the bullet will carry almost a mile with enough force left to injure anything it strikes in its plunging fall. It must be remembered that no projectile, whether an air-gun pellet or a 240-mm. shell travels in a straight line. The instant *any* missile emerges from the firing barrel, gravity begins to pull it down. In other words, it is traveling at all times in a curved flight. Sights on firearms and on air and gas arms are mounted to compensate for this fact. Hence when one lines up his sights on a target, the muzzle is actually tilted up so that the emerging bullet will cross the imaginary "line of sight," will travel in its curved trajectory above that imaginary line, and will come down to enter it at the end of its travel—if the sight setting is correct!

Now consider the lightweight .22 caliber pellet as used in air and gas guns. It is ballistically designed to travel at a starting velocity of 300 to about 780 feet per second, depending upon the arm in which it is used and several variables such as the amount of breech pressure. The breech pressure in an air gun very seldom approaches 1,000 pounds per square inch—it is usually less than half that. The maximum normal pressure in any carbon dioxide gun will seldom exceed 950 pounds per square inch—and will work down to 350 pounds or less.

These air- and gas-gun pellets (they are interchangeable as a rule) will shoot as small a target group as the finest small-bore firearm at 25 feet, and will, in fine arms, group 5 shots in a 1-inch circle or smaller at 60 feet. In Europe they are used up to 50 meters on indoor ranges. However—and this is the all important safety "range" difference between the air-gun and the firearms brand of .22 projectile—because of the light weight and the design of the missile and the relatively low pressures involved, these pellets, which have comparable accuracy at short ranges, lose velocity so fast that their maximum "carrying distance" averages only about 300 feet—as against the nearly 1-mile range of the .22 short! Their remaining energy after traveling such a distance is negligible.

Thus for outdoor shooting with a .22 *firearm* you need a long range of vision to shoot without fear of injuring some person or property. With the comparable .22 *air or gas gun,* if there is nothing within 100 yards, you may shoot in complete safety even without a backstop.

In passing it must be mentioned that the Crosman Arms Company has been primarily responsible for the very rapid growth of this new sport in the United States during the past 10 years. Their sales initiative and constant product development in the compressed-air-gun field, and more particularly their introduction of the carbon dioxide rifle, first really dramatized for American shooters the possibilities of this new field of sport. Other and even more dramatic developments are currently underway, incidentally, both here and abroad.

In searching for reliable historical data, the author turned wherever possible to original records on all early models; and to the manufacturers, inventors, and developers directly on modern arms. The records ranged from authenticated accounts of application of compressed air to missile hurlers by the Alexandrian Greeks of the second century B.C. down through historical, mathematical, and general scientific records of the Middle Ages. As usual in all such research, available early German records were by and large the most prolific and also the most reliable, despite inconsistencies and occasional provable errors which have been duly noted in the text herewith. However British, French, and Austrian archives also proved highly valuable, as the reader can judge for himself.

Research was undertaken personally and through assistants in the historical and patent archives of not only the United States, Germany, and Great Britain, but also of Austria, Canada, Italy, Spain, and Sweden. A generous friend familiar with Russian checked and translated from current Russian works and encyclopedias to see if there were any air-gun inventions of Russian origin—incidentally, this seems to be one field not claimed thus far!

Contemporary historical reactions to various developments are given wherever possible as being more reliable than most current opinions and author's reconstructions. In the matter of recent and current developments, the author visited and spent considerable time with the inventors and manufacturers wherever feasible.

Representative samples of every major world manufacturer were gathered for personal testing to check the manufacturer's varying claims. In some few cases where the makers were stupidly secretive, several of their representative weapons were purchased in the open market to allow averaging the values of their products. For the most part, however, the photographs and data presented are based on samples purchased or borrowed from the makers as being representative of their production, together with comparisons made against similar samples purchased from jobbers or dealers.

Photographs and operational drawings of every important world make are presented for their value to serious students, to gunsmiths, and to developers. Particular pains have been taken to furnish all pictures and drawings necessary to make this work a complete volume of identification of all current and recent air and gas arms. Any such weapon which is or has been produced in quantity anywhere in the world is included in this work. As to pictorial coverage of toy and custom-built guns, every effort has been made to include data and photographs of *representative* types. It is not feasible in a work of this nature to deal thoroughly with hand- and custom-made air and gas guns. The author has personally handled hundreds of individual specimens of this order, and a definitive work is not possible in this field because of the hundreds of gunsmiths through the centuries who have made one, five, or perhaps twenty-five such pieces to special order.

The section of this book dealing with tests (chapter 16) is quite without parallel in the field of arms books. Unless otherwise specified, all test data given herein was developed by or for the author for specific presentation in this book. The most modern electronic testing equipment was employed. The testing for the most part was done under the direct personal supervision of the author, and in all instances was performed by highly qualified engineers and technicians.

In conclusion, it must be emphasized that the findings herein are not what any manufacturer says about his products. These findings are what impartial scientific electronic and mechanical tests indicate about the weapons discussed!

ACKNOWLEDGMENTS

LITERALLY hundreds of manufacturers, dealers, and collectors were contacted by the author during the preparation of this work over a course of many years.

In the United States, appreciation is extended particularly to: Joel A. Gross of Cabot & Webster for photography and for expediting procurement of specimens; to Alan Schreiber; to the U.S. Army Signal Corps for pictorial cooperation; to Messrs. Stoeger and Leinniger of the Stoeger Arms Corporation for use of their collection and facilities; to Continental Arms Corporation; to Abercrombie & Fitch and Mr. L. R. Nichols of that corporation; to Messrs. Wackerhagen and Kraus of the Sheridan Products Company; to Mr. A. P. Spack of the Benjamin organization; to Hy Hunter for his Carbo-Jet data; to Samuel Cummings of Interarmco; and to Andrew Lawrence of Hy Score Manufacturing.

On collections of early air arms available in this country, special mention must be made of Mr. Paul J. Westergaard, not only for use of his personal collection, but for assistance in locating and making available many important and interesting items, and for his cooperation in photography.

The collections of Mr. Robert Abels, Mark Aziz, the noted explorer and lecturer Ivan T. Sanderson, Mr. Harry Wandrus, and a score of others were of special value in checking historical data, mechanisms, and designs.

Special mention must be made of the courtesy and cooperation extended by the West Point Museum of the United States Military Academy, particularly the efforts of Colonel Frederick P. Todd, director, and Mr. Gerald C. Stowe, curator.

For Russian translations, the author is indebted to Mr. W. A. Reichel, a very busy man who still found time to be of assistance.

In the field of British air arms, special mention must be made of the very extensive cooperation provided by Mr. Eric C. Bewley, general manager of Webley & Scott, Limited. Mr. A. G. Scott of B.S.A. Guns, Limited, was also most cooperative.

M. Jacques Bertschinger, president of the Swiss Hämmerli organization, was also cooperative in extending the facilities of his organization. Colonel Rex Applegate of Cia. Importadora Mexicana, S.A., furnished much data not only on Mexican developments but also on those in Japan. Omnipol made available some Czech data.

The list of German manufacturers and authorities is much too long to do more than touch upon, but special acknowledgments are due to Rolf Kriegskorte of Krico, Ernest Pump of Hansa, F. W. Heym, Albert Fohrenbach, and F. Walther, as well as to the firms of Weihrauch, Lloyd, B.S.W., Wilsker, and others.

H. P. White and Burt Munhall and his staff at the White Laboratory were helpful as always. Special mention is reserved for Mr. Cass Hough, Robert Wesley, Ciro Scalingi and his engineering staff at the Daisy Manufacturing Company—and most particularly to Messrs. E. C. Hough and Charles Lefever of Daisy for historical data on the toy division of the air-gun industry.

Finally, acknowledgment is made for the extensive cooperation on American developmental data, for access to all test data, and for the use of research material furnished by Mr. Philip Hahn of the Crosman Arms Company, and by Messrs. Denniston and Merz of the Crosman organization.

TABLE OF CONTENTS

		Page
Chapter 1.	The Blowgun	1
Chapter 2.	The Air Gun	10
Chapter 3.	Other Patterns of Gas and Spring Guns	59
Chapter 4.	Cocking Systems	71
Chapter 5.	Modern Pneumatic Arms	84
Chapter 6.	Carbon Dioxide Arms	89
Chapter 7.	History of Air-Rifle Ammunition	100
Chapter 8.	Shooting With Spring-Air Guns	106
Chapter 9.	British Spring-Air Rifles and Pistols	113
Chapter 10.	German Spring-Air Rifles and Pistols	124
Chapter 11.	Other Foreign Spring-Air Guns	155
Chapter 12.	Current Compressed (Pneumatic) Air Arms	169
Chapter 13.	American Spring-Air Arms	195
Chapter 14.	Carbon Dioxide (CO_2) Powered Arms	206
Chapter 15.	Other Gas Systems	222
Chapter 16.	Air- and Gas-Gun Test Results	226
Index		273

CHAPTER 1

The Blowgun

A BLOWGUN is a simple tube or pipe through which pellets, balls, darts, or arrow missiles are blown by the breath. Lung power alone is the projecting force.

It is still in use today as a serious hunting instrument by many native tribes throughout the world for bird and small-game shooting. It is also used by some ornithologists for shooting birds desired as specimens, as the pellet or dart missile so used will not unduly injure the bird's appearance for purposes of mounting and study.

It is also commonly encountered throughout the world in the form of a short tube of metal, cane, wood, or plastic used by children as a "bean blower" or "peashooter" and as a missile projector for use in games of shooting at targets with darts or pellets.

OTHER NAMES FOR THE BLOWGUN

It is often loosely referred to as a "blowtube," a designation which can be confused with the tube used in glassblowing to gather and blow viscous glass into hollow glassware. Similarly, it is also loosely referred to as a "blowpipe," which in today's usage can confuse it with the instrument used to blow a concentrated stream of air or other gas into a flame to focus and increase heating action.

Thus, while earlier users and writers were quite justified in using these terms interchangeably, the term "blowgun" is more apt and accurate for the missile thrower.

FOREIGN DESIGNATIONS

Older explicit manuscript references to blowguns list them in German as "Blasröhre," in French as "Sarbacane," and in Italian as "Cerbotana."

Among the Indians of Guiana they are known usually as "Pucuna." In South America generally they are encountered under the names "Sarbacan" or "Zarabatana." In the Malay Peninsula they are commonly listed as "Tomeang." The most unusual of all blowguns, that of the natives of Borneo, is known as the "Sumpitan."

Finally, in current civilized usage they are encountered in English as "blowguns," "bean blowers," and "peashooters." In French as "Tubes à vent." In Spanish as "Tubos de viento." In German as "Blasröhre"—or as toys, "Puströhre."

Most people tend to think of the blowgun—if and when they think of it at all—much as the German historian Demmin comments in his definition of it: "As it is nothing but a tube, varying only in length and thickness, it is needless to give an illustration."

However, the researcher today soon finds that even the lowly blowing tube could absorb years of intensive study if one tried to give a definitive picture of its history, and this material could easily fill a thousand pages and more!

A hunting manuscript collection at Angers, France, contains an illustration from a 15th century fresco which shows a hunter high in a tree shooting with a "Sarbacane" at a pigeon resting in the branches of a nearby tree.

In old Chinese, Indian, and Japanese prints we find many illustrations of the use of the blowgun in its various forms, blowing darts, balls, and incendiary devices. In Japan, in particular, the blowgun has been a weapon known and used extensively; some magnificent specimens are to be seen in the Rush collection at Salem, Massachusetts.

In the author's files is material on blowguns throughout the world under the following names: Balsau, Belangah, Belan, Blasröhre, Cerbotana, Damaoq, Fukidake, Fuki Ya, Hengot, Hina, Hung, Ipok, Jemerang, Jowing, Kahuk, Kahuh Isin, Ke Non, Klahulon, Ladjau, Langra, Paser, Penichul, Poeot, Pubu, Pubu Isi, Pucuna, Pungln, Sarbacan, Sarbacane, Sipet, Siren, Sopok, Sumpit, Sumpitan, Taharan, Tanggirl, Telenga, Telep, Tembihan, Tepus, Tolor, Tulup, Tulepan, Ultop, and Zarabatana.

These by no means exhaust the subject—they merely indicate the scope of the material available to the researcher who has the time, money, ability, and interest to apply to finding out the background of the blowing tube so simple that in the mind of a noted writer it "needs no illustration."

ORIGINS OF THE BLOWGUN

Somewhere, sometime in the dim, distant past before recorded history, some native found that he could blow a pebble—or perhaps a thorn—through a hollow reed or cane with enough force to stun, maim, or kill a bird or a small animal. History being what it is and with reeds and canes spread across the face of the earth in some form or other, it is most likely that various men in various corners of the globe made the same discovery at about the same time.

It was thus that the history of ALL firearms, and of gas and air guns too, began. For all guns of these patterns—from single-shot firelocks of the earliest times to the rocket launchers of today—are basically nothing more than tubes from which missiles are discharged by the sudden expansion of some kind of gas in the tube behind the projectile—and air itself is but a mixture of gases, in the case of the blowgun being blasted suddenly by that most efficient of bellows, the human lungs.

HISTORY OF THE BLOWGUN

As an early war weapon we encounter fragmentary reports of blowgun use in various sections of Asia and Asia Minor long before the dawn of the Christian Era. It was used to project small shot, hollow clay balls, or pellets charged with Greek fire or a similar combustible for showering sparks or starting fires, and in some instances for shooting poisoned arrows or darts.

In the annals of the Javanese, written by an historian in 1625 A.D., during the course of a war by Java against the people of Bali, is to be found a bitter diatribe against the "uncivilized" Balinese because they blew *poisoned* arrows through their blowguns. It is indeed an interesting commentary that in nearly all historical periods and in all parts of the world where the blowgun has been used, or is being used, it has been and is still considered permissible to use *poisoned* arrows or darts only against game.

Many instances of this aversion to the use of poison for mankilling can be gathered from the original records of the historians of the Spanish Conquest. Among the best of these is Francisco Lopez de Gomaro (1510-1560). His works might have been classics except for the fact that he was subsidized by the family of Cortes the Conqueror, and as a result his narratives were so loaded with praise for Cortes that his subject matter was often questioned. The most substantial of these old records, perhaps, are those of the author of the Historia General de Indes—the official historiographer, Antonio Herrera y Tordesillas (1549-1625). His major work was written in 1601, drawing upon the earlier manuscripts of Bartolome de Las Casas and Cervantes de Salazar.

Time and later-day research have established Herrera's basic accuracy. Many of his reports were drawn from other and earlier accounts, but even his unverifiable statements are seldom open to question. Among these we find that the Nahuas (the Aztecs) did not make use of poisoned arms because they always sought prisoners in wars to be immolated as sacrifices!

From him also we learn much about the general use of the blowgun among the Indians of Central America and Mexico during the late 16th and early 17th centuries. Herrera is not available in English translation, but the interested reader (if he has the patience and fortitude!) will find various references in the works of such writers as Chevalier Arthur Morelet (*Travels in Central America,* 1871) and H. H. Bancroft, whose monumental *Native Races of the Pacific States,* published in 1874, was written and compiled only after personal travels and after accumulating some 16,000 books, manuscripts, pamphlets, journals, and maps on the subject of those races!

We learn from Herrera and other Spanish historians, confirmed by the later-day investigations of writers such as the Mexican Cartas, many things about blowgun use in both war and hunting. Herrera tells us that among the Chichimick (Central American) tribe blowguns were used with large, hardened-clay pellets and that (in translation): "It is affirmed that with them they can kill a man or a wild beast at a moderate distance." He tells of its use with such pellets by other tribes for hunting birds and says it is popular with children in all tribes.

Herrera deals also in some detail with the various deadly arrow poisons. He mentions the fearful *curare* from the *wourali* vine among others. He also gives details of a fantastic concoction starting with "certain gray roots found along the coast," which were "first burnt in earthen pipkins," then mixed with a species of poisonous black ant, large spiders, hairy caterpillars, heads and tails of poisonous fish, and a dozen other bizarre ingredients; all of which is of interest only in that it establishes that

Native with typical South American blowgun. He is carrying darts in the quiver-like basket slung around his neck. One dart will kill a bird. Three may be necessary to kill a capybara, a huge 4-foot-long rodent. Such a blowgun is efficient up to 60 yards. On electronic chronograph tests by the author, it was found possible to blow darts at a muzzle velocity of 310 feet per second with such a gun! A native with his specialized lung power would doubtless far exceed this.

The oldest known illustration of European use of the blowgun in hunting. From a 15th century fresco.

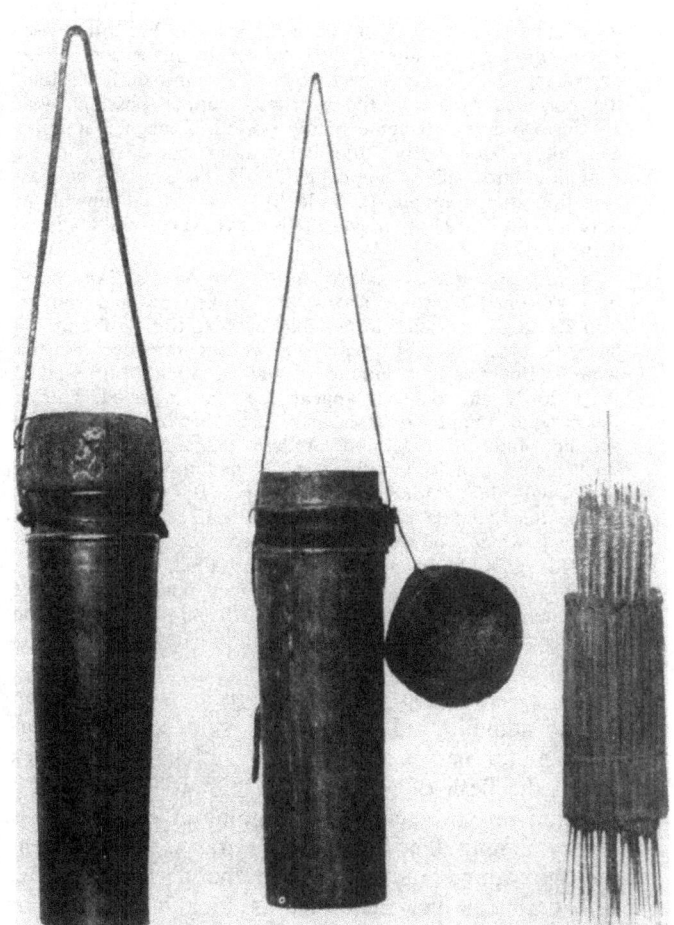

Blowgun poisoned darts wound machinegun-belt fashion ready for use. Waterproof carrying quivers.

blowguns were there and then used with darts and arrows as well as pellets.

As an evidence of the official Aztec interest in blowguns, Herrera and others relate that Montezuma presented Cortes with a dozen of these instruments "ornamented and painted with figures of birds and animals; the mouthpiece of each was made of gold, 5 to 6 inches long; they were also ornamented in the center with gold, and accompanying them were gold network pouches to carry the balls."

Blowguns in North American History

High on the list of the all but unknown historians of 18th century America stands a French marine officer, Jean Bernard Bossu (1720-1792), whose important *Nouveaux Voyages aux Indes Occidentales* in the form of letters sent from America to France was published in 1768. He dealt with the Mississippi Basin—"that part of North America formerly called Louisiana," to quote him.

Since our interest here is in blowguns, we must confine ourselves to Bossu's mention of the use of these weapons, specifically among the Choctaws: "The children," he wrote, "exercise themselves in shooting . . . they are very expert in shooting with an instrument made of reeds about 7 feet long, into which they put a little arrow, feathered with the wool of a thistle, and in aiming at an object, they blow with the tube, and often hit the aim, and frequently kill little birds with it."

All through our southern areas where canes grow, blowguns were known and used by the early Indians. The very names of most of these tribes are unknown to the youth of America today, yet among such southern tribes as the Muskhogeans, the Atticapas, and the Cheti-

3

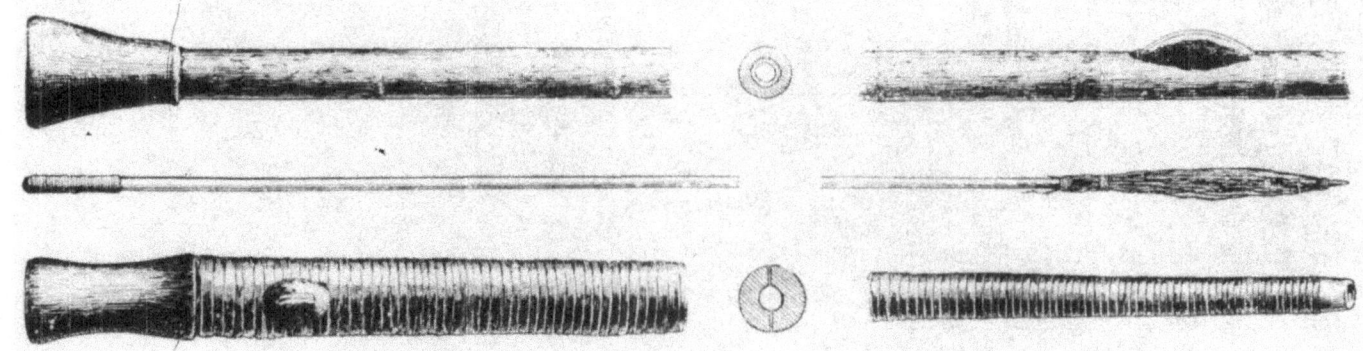

Types of blowguns, showing mouthpiece, "sight," and muzzle views. Also a typical dart. These are standard specimens and may be found in the Museum of Natural History in New York City.

machas ingenuity in the use of the blowgun was developed to the point where groups of reeds were bound together so that they could be loaded revolver-fashion and turned to bring each mouthpiece individually into line for continuous firing!

Blowguns in South American History

By far the most practical and widespread use of the hunting blowgun has been—and still is, for that matter—among the South American Indians in the region of the Orinoco and Amazon Basins. For bird and small-game hunting they have always been favored over that much more powerful missile hurler, the bow.

Of all the company of intrepid 18th century travelers, few can compare with the great Englishman, Charles Watterton, whose *Wanderings in South America, the Northwest of the United States, and the Antilles, in the years 1812, 1816, 1820 and 1821* is the classic from which has come nearly all our early reliable first-hand knowledge of the deadly *wourali* poison and the blowgun. Prior to Watterton, the poison was just a terrifying legend. This amazing man, an observer and reporter of the highest order, was greeted with considerable disbelief at home because of the detailed and explicit reports he made. Time, however, has borne out his complete accuracy.

The present author has hunted over some of the Guiana areas traveled by Watterton nearly a century and a half ago and still finds himself aghast at the courage, strength, and fortitude which must have been required at that time even to reach those areas, much less to live in them and learn some of the natives' innermost secrets as Watterton did.

We know much about *curare* today, the arrow poison made from the deadly *wourali* vine. We know that the involved formulas the Indian poison-brewers disclosed to Watterton (adding to the *wourali* plant extract venomous black and red ants, poison sacs from the *couanacouchi* and *labarri* snakes, *hyarri* root and a dozen other things) had little to do with the terrible efficiency of the basic *Strychnos* and *Chondodrendon tomentosum* plants. The South American Indians doubtless still use the formula patterns disclosed to Watterton and still dip their darts in the mixture and hunt game with them. Meanwhile our scientists have found how to extract *curare* from the *Strychnos toxifera* species of plants, and have found valuable uses for it in physiological and anesthetizing applications for paralyzing or arresting the motor nerves. Drugs of the *curare* family, widely used in hospitals throughout the world today, are the supreme "muscle-relaxants" as used by experts in surgical anesthesia. If the dosage isn't exactly right, however, results are dangerously depressing.

Having seen actual usage in Guiana of the blowgun and poisoned dart, the author feels that the best description of the effect of the poison is again that by Watterton:

> It is natural to imagine that when a slight wound only is inflicted, the game will make its escape. Far otherwise. The *wourali* poison almost instantaneously mixes with blood or water; so that if you wet your finger and dash it along the poisoned arrow in the quickest manner possible, you are sure to carry off some of the poison. Though 3 minutes generally elapse before the convulsions come on in the wounded bird, still a stupor evidently takes place sooner, and this stupor manifests itself by an apparent unwillingness in the bird to move. This was very visible in a dying fowl.
>
> Having procured a healthy, full-grown one, a short piece of a poisoned blowpipe arrow was broken off and run up into its thigh, as near as possible betwixt the skin and the flesh in order that it might not be incommoded by the wound. For the first minute it walked about, but walked very slowly and did not appear the least agitated. During the second minute it stood still and began to peck the ground; and ere half another had elapsed, it frequently opened and shut its mouth. The tail had now dropped, and the wings almost touched the ground. By the termination of the third minute it had sat down, scarce able to support its head, which nodded, and then recovered itself, and then nodded again, lower and lower every time, like that of a weary traveler slumbering in an erect position; the eyes alternately open and shut. The fourth minute brought on convulsions, and life and the fifth terminated together.

Curare, it should be pointed out, is a virulent poison *only* when administered through the skin, since it paralyzes the motor nerves and kills by suffocation. It does not affect the flesh of game killed with it by darts. No putrefaction sets in except at the point of contact. It is customary among the Indians to cut out the segment around the wound and to remove the dart, of course; but the flesh can be eaten just as though the bird or animal had been brought down with a rifle bullet.

One more passing reference to the use of *curare* for

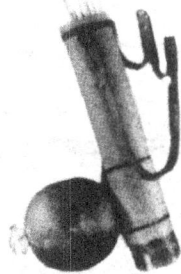

Blowgun dart case with gourd container for cotton.

Yagna hunter with blowgun.

hunting is in order, since many times its effectiveness on big game is questioned by amateur "explorers."

W. W. Greener in the sixth edition (1896) of *The Gun and Its Development* says—without identifying his man: "Dr. Thiercelin invented and used a shell filled with poison and burst by an explosive. Tried on 10 whales, it killed all in from 4 to 18 minutes; 4 out of the 10 were, however, lost by sinking. The poison he used was a soluble salt of *strychnine* and a twentieth part of *curare,* 60 grains of which he deems sufficient to kill the largest North Sea whale." (Note: The mention occurs in a discussion of harpoon guns.)

While there are literally thousands of references to South American poison dart usage for hunting, this author has never encountered any superior to the descriptive works of the writers and explorers who went there in the last century—when all travel was done the hard and thorough way. Besides Watterton, one should mention such other reliable sources as Colonel A. H. Lane-Fox, Grenadier Guards, writing in the *Royal United Service Institution Journal* in 1867; Thurn's *Indians of British Guiana,* published in 1883; Wood's *Uncivilized Races,* published in Hartford, Connecticut, in 1870; and Captain Cochrane's *Journal in Columbia,* where we find the statement "A tiger, when hit, runs ten or a dozen yards, staggers, becomes sick, and dies in 4 or 5 minutes." For this particular statement by the captain, this author cannot vouch, never having seen anything larger than a Guiana waracabas bird hit with a poisoned dart. However, the captain can be substantiated on a statement almost as remarkable; viz., he describes some arrows 8 inches long, with a very sharp point, cut like a corkscrew for an inch up from the point"—a condition occasionally found and which seems to be intended to give a rotating effect to the missile to insure stability in flight.

A closing note on Guiana arrow poisons may be interesting. In Humboldt's *Aspects of Nature* we find the following statement: "In the forests of Guiana there are tribes, such as the Ottomacs, apparently weaponless, but which by simply poisoning the thumbnail with *curare* or *wourali,* at once become formidable antagonists."

From this it will be apparent that the troublemaker is the poison and the man behind it—not the blowgun itself.

TYPES OF BLOWGUNS

While all blowguns used by savage tribes are basically alike, they vary considerably in construction. Thus the blowguns of Central and South America are all based on the use of canes, reeds, palms, and similar natural hollow-tube growths.

At the other extreme are those of the Borneo and Malay areas, the Sumpitans, which are customarily *drilled out of solid hardwood* much like a rifle barrel!

Let us consider briefly the Pucuna of the Guiana Macoushies. They produce probably the best of the South American blowguns. The Pucuna's development was made possible by the fact that there are species of reeds

Dyak blowgun with spear blade attached. Darts shown are hunting and war types. Quiver and wadding container above.

in the Orinoco which while only about one-half inch in diameter grow to a height of 14 feet or so without any bore-distorting joints. This tube is naturally smooth inside, almost polished in fact. Its bore, moreover, is normally astonishingly uniform along its entire length, tending to contract very slightly so that it actually gives the effect of a Gerlach "squeeze-bore," as the dart approaches the muzzle.

This "ourah" as it is known is very fragile, hence it is used as a "liner" and is encased in a more rigid tube of the palm variety which has been hollowed out by steeping it in water which frees the pulp for removal. The outer tube, called "samourah," and the inner tube are straightened by bending much as a rifle barrel is handled. A black wax called "kuramanni" firmly locks the two tubes together. The outside is then scraped, polished, and sometimes waxed.

Several types of mouthpieces are encountered, all being intended to confine the breath as it is blown into the usually cup-shaped unit. This piece is cemented to the breech end, while at the muzzle end a saucer-like piece of an "acuero" nut is bored out to slip over the muzzle where it acts as a ferrule and also as a sort of front sight. Often a rear sight is mounted, consisting usually of the teeth of the rodent, the "acouchi." This arrangement makes an "open" rear sight which compares not too unfavorably with the iron sights provided on some of our modern rifles.

When finished the blowgun (Pucuna) is amazingly strong and exceptionally light in weight. It may be as much as 11 feet long, yet will seldom weigh a pound and a half!

The darts, or arrows, are made from the ribs of leaves of the *coucourite,* a variety of palm, with the point filed down on the razor-sharp edges of the teeth of the murderous "pira" fish as it is known in this area.

A tuft of wild cotton is wound about the rear of the dart and tied in place with a grass fiber. These are woven together so they may be coiled and carried safely on a reel in a waterproof quiver—not unlike machinegun cartridges in a drum magazine.

A variant of the cotton "air seal" is sometimes encountered in the form of a thin piece of bark wrapped cone-fashion around the dart. Blowing into the tube funnels the breath into the cone, expanding its rear so it acts as a seal while the projectile is traveling down the barrel and stabilizes flight.

Zarabatana

A much more common form of blowgun is the South American pattern of the Amazon areas commonly known as the Zarabatana (or Sarbacan). This type is made of two separate pieces of wood, a semicircular groove being cut in each piece, the cuts commonly being made with the incisor teeth of large rodents so that the depth and width of the cuts can be controlled quite accurately. The two halves are brought into contact and bound together with long, winding strips of *jacarita* wood, thereby providing a tube having a circular bore. Variations are encountered, of course. Specimens seen in some museums are made in this same split construction, but have a smoothbore reed, usually rather fragile, laid down in the cuts of the outer sections. Still others are fastened together as units by covering the exterior with smooth, black wax, or even by drawing fresh animal intestines over them and shrinking this covering in place with heat. Some, the least efficient, are merely reeds whose interior pulp has been extracted.

It is common practice to cut the arrow shaft almost in two before inserting it in the blowgun. With this procedure, any hit made will result usually in the arrow shaft being broken off by its own weight or by movement of the bird or animal, leaving the poisoned head completely imbedded in the flesh.

The Malayan Tomeang

The best form of the Tomeang is that of the Malayan Peninsula aboriginal tribes, the Mautras. Made somewhat after the fashion of the Pucuna of the Upper Orinoco, it usually consists of two bamboo tubes, one sealed within the other. The inner tube is bore-scraped and polished for internal smoothness, and the outer one is usually ornamented. The writings of Colonel Lane-Fox already referred to deal at some length with these instruments.

The Sumpitan of Borneo

In many respects the most remarkable of all the native blowguns is the Sumpitan. This is a solid piece of hardwood, carefully and laboriously bored out by hand and with the most primitive tools imaginable. When one considers the difficulty encountered putting a really straight hole through any 7-foot section of even the softest material without the use of elaborate tooling, the Sumpitan rates as a gunmaking marvel.

No better description of it is likely to be encountered than that of the early traveler, Carl Bock, given in his book, *Head Hunters of Borneo,* an English translation of which was published in 1881. Bock had been Commissioner for the Dutch Government in the areas about which he wrote, and one of his drawings from specimens is reproduced herewith.

He writes:

> The Sumpitan is from 6 to 7 feet long and about 1½ inches in diameter, with a bore of about one-half inch. It is made of ironwood, the bore being drilled by means of a long, sharp-pointed piece of iron while the wood is in the rough; the polish, both inside and outside, is obtained by the use of dried leaves of the tree *duan amples* of the Malays. This is used as a substitute for sandpaper in Sumatra as well as in Borneo. The underside of these leaves when dry is rough, resembling very fine sandpaper.
>
> At the upper end the Sumpitan is furnished with a short spear and a small iron hook, which are strongly fastened to the tube with plaited rattan. (Note: This hook according to another author of the period, Hugh Low, is used as a front sight.)
>
> The darts are called "langa." They are bamboo, 9½ to 10 inches long and about 2 to 2½ millimeters thick. The point is dipped in poison. For larger animals they are furnished with a fine barbed-iron blade.
>
> The upper end of the arrow is furnished with a piece of pith (bua) to fit the bore of the tube.
>
> These tiny darts the Dyaks blow with unerring aim to 40 or 50 yards, bringing down the smallest birds without difficulty.
>
> The quiver (talor) is made of a section of bamboo about 13 inches long and 2 inches in diameter, bound with ornamented rings of plaited rattan and fitted with a bamboo lid, and often ornamented on top with a shell (*helix brookeana*).
>
> The quiver is suspended to the belt by a wooden hook, and to it is attached a small gourd (hung) containing the pieces of pith which are fitted to the ends of the arrows when blown from the tube. A wooden stopper is provided for the gourd.

The actual hole drilling in the rough 7-foot length of wood requires the services of two natives. One end of the wood rests on a flat surface. The upper end is attached to a raised platform on which the man to do the boring stands. The tool used is a chisel-type bar, driven by a hammer. As the hole is bored, the helper pours water in to float the chips out. When this slow and tedious job is done, a remarkably straight hole is produced. The hole is brought to a reamed smoothness by polishing with abrasive leaves. The outside of the tube is then worked into shape and polished. The principle, of course, is the same as is used in formal gun-barrel manufacture—first bore a straight hole, then finish off the outside of the tube.

In common with aborigines everywhere, the Dyaks hang their blowguns up by one end when not in use to prevent warping. Theirs differ from most other known types in that they often have a spearhead bound to the side of the tube at the muzzle end in position where it will not obstruct the flight of the dart, yet is usable as a rude front sight as well as a thrusting weapon. The tough wood employed in making the Sumpitan permits use of the tube as a blade carrier of this type.

BLOWGUNS IN WAR

In very early times, blowguns were used to project varying species of Greek fire to touch off flammable thatch roofs and the like. In modern warfare they were at times employed by saboteurs to blow fragile glass ampules of phosphorous compounds into grainfields, a trick picked up from the old I.W.W.[1] terrorists, the "wobblies" who rode freight trains through our western wheat belt and caused much damage and consternation by setting fire to ripe, dried-out field crops.

In times of war certain people with what might politely be called perfervid imaginations always manage to work themselves into positions of importance on the fringes of the not always too intelligent "Intelligence" sections. Thus during World War II, there was the noted motion-picture actor who attracted a great deal of attention to himself by suggesting a submarine dropoff into Japan to "secretly" call upon the Empress—because "He had met her once and knew she would be receptive." There was also the Swedish police official with a "plan" to end the war by capturing Hitler, Himmler, Goebels, and Goering—just a matter of dropping 20,000 British paratroopers in Berlin!

At the other extreme there was Germany's Colonel Otto Skorzeny who actually did land with a party of German paratroopers in Allied territory and freed the captive Mussolini—short lived though the freedom was.

Some agents of this Skorzeny working in neutral zones were known to carry dummy cigarettes loaded with curare-painted darts—a dramatic secret blowgun device, incidentally, used by several novelists in detective stories!

Part of the survival training—some of which is excellent, some of which is not—given in many world-wide intelligence organizations includes the making of impromptu weapons in case of capture or necessity. On the list are various uses of the homemade "zip" gun to combine tubing from lampstands, curtain holders, bathroom fixtures, and the like, with a bent nail and a piece of spring wire or a common elastic band when a loaded cartridge is procurable.

When a cartridge is not, then attention turns to the blowgun made from similar available tubing for firing a sharpened nail or darning needle set in a dowel made from a bottle cork, a piece of any soft wood, a piece of a wax candle, or even a cone of paper twisted to form an air seal. Such devices can, under emergency conditions, be arms of a very serious order where the user has the desperation and courage to use them, as many captured agents have found.

Using a half-inch or smaller diameter piece of seamless tubing and a home-made dart, the user can with

---

[1] International Workers of the World.

some practice kill pigeons or similar birds up to 8 or 10 yards distance, even though normal lung power supplies only about 2 pounds to the square inch blowing pressure. Darts made with heavy needles, or with small nails whose points have been ground and scraped to needle sharpness, can be blown so deeply into soft pine that they can't be extracted with the fingers; and if aimed at the human eye, the ear opening, or the region of the medulla oblongata can be dangerous or fatal to humans or to savage watchdogs.

It might be stated in passing that these are only minor known applications of these principles, that many are much too dangerous for general publication. They point up, however, the fact that the age-old blowgun is still a weapon to be reckoned with in emergency situations, as well as a readily available hunting and foraging instrument.

THE MODERN BLOWGUN

Early in this century blowguns were made, principally in England and Germany, not only as single pieces of tubing but also as canes or walking sticks. They consisted commonly of a piece of 3/8-inch brass tubing encased in a tube of wood, bamboo, or malacca. They were made with knobs and with crooked handles in many styles. Such guns blew hardened-clay balls or darts and were largely used apparently by adults who had never grown up for amusing themselves by stinging unsuspecting friends with the balls and by romantics who carried them for possible "defense" against some attack that never happened, in which case they expected to blow darts at the assailants!

A very unusual specimen with which the author is familiar is in the form of an umbrella, English-made at a guess, though it might have been German. This specimen used special tufted darts which could be blown into a plank to the full length of its sharp shank, some half-inch in length; or alternatively, a blunt-end dart which would badly dent the end of a tomato can (the pointed dart would penetrate the can top or side, incidentally). A rabbit hit in the head with the blunt dart was completely stunned but not killed, and it is reasonable to believe that the same dart hitting a man in the right spot would render him unconscious. This instrument was a custom-made piece, of course.

It was a carefully engineered product, the work of an excellent craftsman. The forward end of the tube had a quick-removable cap—a necessary element since the barrel of any blowgun must be kept dry, clean, and unoiled to minimize friction. The knob handle when drawn back about an inch could be slid out of line of the blowtube without detaching it from the mechanism.

The shooting tube was a polished brass liner of about 5-mm. bore inside the umbrella shaft. Most remarkable was a spring-loaded support plug near the breech end of the shaft and tube, with its inner face supporting the forward section of the dart. This device permitted the umbrella to be carried loaded at all times.

To fire, one pulled off the muzzle cover (which resembles the common umbrella tip), drew back the knob and swung it to the side, brought the umbrella to the mouth, pressed in the spring-plug which was holding the dart in firing position, aimed, and blew.

Umbrella cartridge guns and umbrella air guns (spring-air patterns) are relatively common in collections, as are umbrellas with spring-projected dart-firing mechanisms. Specimens of all have been encountered in Austrian, English, French, and German custom-made arms. There are no records encountered of quantity commercial manufacture. In the period of World War II, several of these turned up in the various "hush-hush" intelligence groups

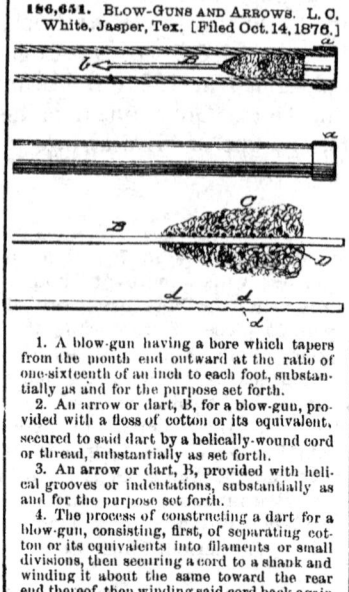

Abstract of original American blowgun patent.

together with the belt-buckle guns, pen guns, pipe guns, and the like.

An umbrella blowgun, however, is certainly not common. This author has encountered only the one described in some thirty-odd years of viewing, inspecting, and designing arms of many descriptions.

Common in Germany at this same period was a jointed brass blowgun used by ornithologists for bringing down small birds without destroying their plumage. These were usually in three sections for ease of carrying, the joints carefully constructed so they gave little drag on the projectile.

At the present time there are numerous short blowguns made in most countries as toys for dart shooting, a variation of the popular English game of dart throwing. These are merely seamless tubes, usually with a protective wood or plastic mouthpiece, and commonly accompanied by a target board. One enterprising California firm markets metal blowguns with 5-foot barrels, which shoot 5-inch steel darts. These darts will travel about 200 feet and at close range will penetrate 1/4-inch plywood. Some hunting use is made of these weapons, which are as accurate at 30 feet as many air guns.

We cannot close this section without some mention of one of the most universal toys—the "bean blower" or "peashooter" as it is commonly called. This device is still astonishingly high on the list of toys without which no boy anywhere can hope to grow to manhood.

Toymakers are notoriously secretive folks. As a result, peashooter sales statistics are hard to come by either here or abroad, though they are known to run high in the millions yearly.

One rather priceless anecdote cabled from London on July 6, 1956 by the highly responsible Associated Press bears recounting in this volume. A 5-year-old English boy, one John Christian Rayner, recently reported to his father a very serious matter—serious indeed to any 5-year-old anywhere. Only 1 dried pea in every 20 he tried to shoot would pass through his brand new peashooter!

Fortunately for 5-year-olds everywhere, John Christian wasn't just any boy. He had the good fortune to be the son of an officer attached to Her Majesty's War Office, one Major John W. Rayner. Calling in the press, the Major issued an indignant (and highly justified) statement. He is quoted directly in part as follows:

> In my youth peas fitted peashooters perfectly. Have peas grown larger or peashooters smaller nowadays?
>
> Whatever it is, it shows a shocking lack of industrial coordination. We are fighting for our export markets and it is a scandal if peashooters are offered for sale which are too small to shoot peas. If such a thing happened in the army it would cause a terrible fuss.

The press, very much upset by it all, queried the head of one of Britain's largest pea-producing firms, Colonel Mawrice Batchelor. As an acknowledged expert, the Colonel immediately denounced as "nonsense" the idea that peas are getting bigger.

The British Toy Makers Association then demanded to be heard, their spokesman hotly denying that the makers had shrunk the size of the shooters to save money!

"They are," said the spokesman, "as fine in quality as they have ever been. Caliber is as carefully adjusted as it was when Major Rayner was a child."

And there, as of this writing, the matter rests. Since you can get an occasional dud in any mechanical product from the finest watch to the most expensive automobile, we would like to think that little John Christian just happened to latch on to a defective peashooter. We can only hope in the interest of all future 5-year-olds that some later historian will check into the peashooter of his day to see!

BLOWGUN PATENTS AND INVENTIONS

Incredible though it may seem, the simple blowgun and dart were at one time the subject of formal patent protection in the United States! In 1877, patent number 186,651 covering both gun and missile was actually issued to L. C. White!

In France and Great Britain several patents were issued at various times for odd patterns in blowguns. One unique type on which the British Patent Office allowed a claim in 1864—the number was 1182—covered a toy rifle which was to be aimed from the shoulder in standard fashion, but in which the pellet or dart was to be projected by air blown from the shooter's mouth into an elastic tube connected to the gun breech to the rear of the missile. This design was the subject of a large number of later applications in England and France.

THE "REPEATING" PEASHOOTER

Of all the amusing oddities encountered in an intensive search of various national patents, none surpasses that of the "repeating peashooter."

While the common boy's system of making a "repeating" peashooter or bean blower is merely to pop 10 or 15 peas or beans into the mouth, inventors have nevertheless offered far more complicated systems. One, a model of which was made for patenting, had a gravity feed tube near the "chamber" end of the peashooter, complete with a thumb-operated control valve! Pushing the valve button allowed an individual pea to pass into the shooter just ahead of the mouthpiece. The reason for the "invention"? It was to prevent a boy from risking "possible strangulation" by swallowing a mouthful of peas when shooting in the common "repeating" manner!

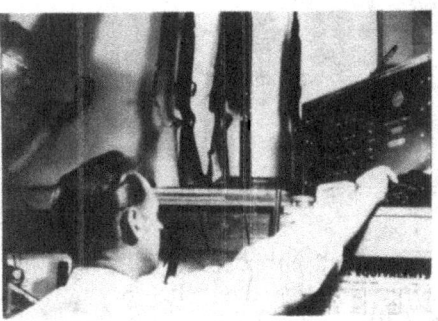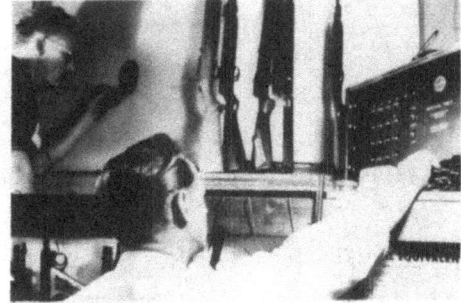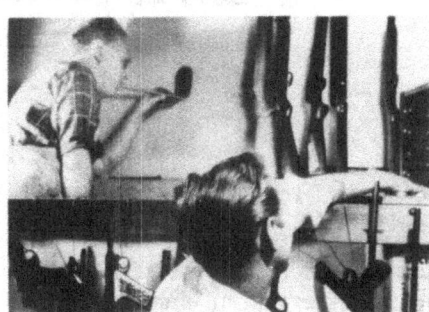

Testing velocity of pea shooters and blowguns on Potter Electronic Chronograph.

CHAPTER 2

The Air Gun

AN AIR GUN is a weapon (or toy), designed to be discharged normally from the shoulder, in which the expanding force of compressed air is employed to propel the projectile. *Specifically,* an air *gun* must have a smooth-bored barrel. The projectiles are commonly either round metal balls, special metal bullets or pellets, or darts. In some few types a *charge* of small shot may be driven by the compressed air as in the common powder-firing shotgun.

An AIR RIFLE *specifically* is a weapon as described above *except* that it must have a rifled barrel. (That is, a barrel in which spiral grooves are cut on the inside to give a rotating motion to the ball, bullet, or pellet as it is propelled by the compressed air. The rotation imparted to the missile helps to stabilize its flight towards the target and increases accuracy by so doing.) Darts and shot charges are not commonly used in a rifled barrel as they may injure the rifling grooves. (Note: As a *toy,* the term "air rifle" is commonly applied to any shoulder arm using compressed air as a propellant, though practically all such toys are smooth bored.)

An AIR PISTOL is a weapon (or toy) as described above, except that it is intended to be discharged normally from one hand. The weapon variety of air pistol may have either a smooth-bored or rifled barrel. The toy variety is not rifled. Missiles used are the same types as for air rifles and air guns.

An AIR SHOTGUN is a smooth-bored shoulder arm using compressed air to propel a small quantity of round shot in the fashion of the common shotgun. In modern breech-loading air shotguns, the charge is packed in a small container of paper or similar fragile material with supporting wads to hold the charge together until it leaves the barrel. In obsolete muzzle-loading air shotguns, this system was also used; but in some types a wad was first rammed down the barrel, the shot charge poured in on top of it, then another wad rammed down to support the charge. Chalk projectiles with very small shot embedded are also encountered.

OPERATING PRINCIPLES OF AIR ARMS

All production patterns of air arms as defined above operate on one of two air-compressing systems. (Note: Collector's freaks, mostly hand- or custom-made, may incorporate parts of both systems.)

System No. 1, Spring-Air Compression Types. In this type of weapon a powerful spring (or springs) operating with a piston or plunger is compressed by manual action. This compression is achieved in various ways through the operation of levers, slides, cams, cranks, or gears as described in the body of this work under the different patterns. The piston and the compressed spring are held by a sear or trigger engagement. (Note: In some uncommon types the spring (or springs) are extended, or expanded types, which furnish power as they are released by drawing together; the opposite of the compression spring which provides energy as it expands).

In all standard types, when the trigger is pressed the compressed spring is released. It drives the attached piston forward in a cylinder (or syringe), compressing the air ahead of it. This compressed air, driven from the

Typical German barrel-cocker, high-power air gun. (Note: This type is not manufactured in the United States.)

large cylinder through a small port behind the projectile, furnishes enough energy to drive the pellet or ball out the muzzle at velocities approaching 600 feet per second. These projectiles will penetrate as much as three-fourths of an inch in white pine 30 feet from the muzzle in a well-made air rifle of this type.

Air pistols have much less power because they must use shorter and lower-powered springs. Air shotguns have less power, of course, because they fire a shot *charge* instead of a single bullet, even though spring compression is the same as in the air rifle.

All *toy* air arms operate on this spring-piston-air com-

Typical German modern high-power air rifle. (Note: This type is not manufactured in the United States.)

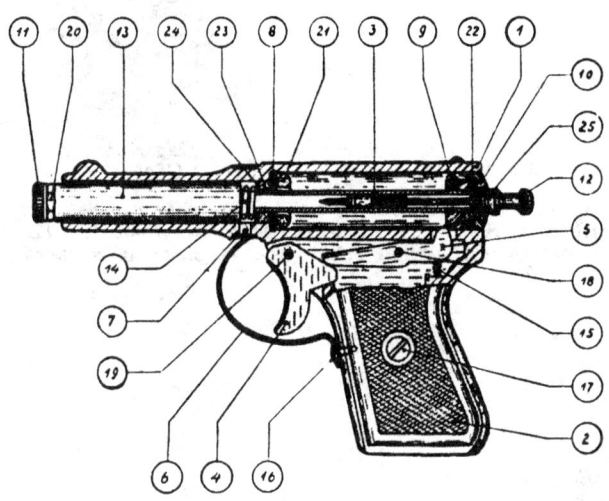

Typical toy type Heym. Barrel is pushed in to cock mainspring. Breech screw is removed and pellet inserted. Breech screw is then replaced. Barrel is thrust forward in barrel casing by spring.

Typical English high-power air pistol.

The Plainsman, a typical modern compressed-air shotgun, shown with striker drawn out to full-cock position. The bolt mechanism above the striker has been turned to unlock and drawn back to expose chamber. A shot shell is in the breech. Bore .280. Barrel muzzle is choked. The "shells" are tubes of cardboard with wads at both ends to hold in the shot charge. When bolt is thrust forward it passes through the tube, forcing both the wads and the shot into the firing chamber. After firing, the shot tube is removed manually to allow inserting a new one. The Plainsman is not currently manufactured. Similar shot shells as made in Europe are commonly solid pieces of chalk with five or six small shot imbedded. The chalk disintegrates as the charge leaves the barrel. These shotguns have very little practical use.

Webley cutaway drawing showing mechanism. The pistol is shown uncocked. Note that a spring guide extends from the muzzle end back into the hollow piston to positively prevent spring kinking. When the barrel is unlocked and raised, the hollow steel piston is pulled forward over the mainspring, thereby compressing it. The sear catches the holding face on the rear of the piston at full cock. This model uses a metal piston ring for prevention of air loss instead of the typical leather or neoprene washer. The simplicity of the design has never been excelled.

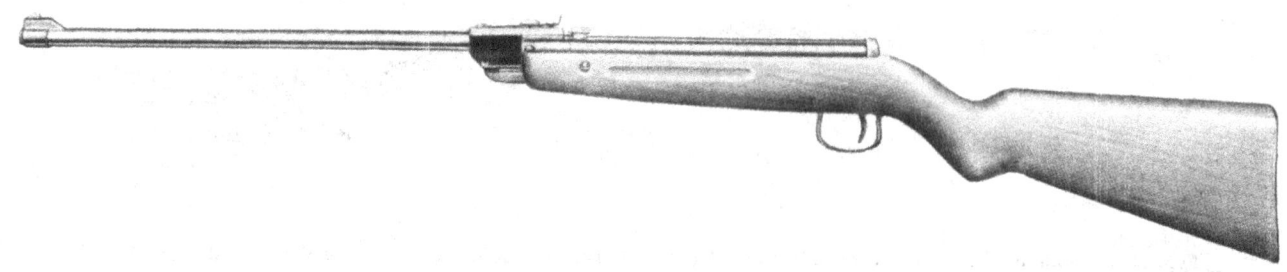

Headlock for
LG54MG

Magazine for
LG54MG

Magazine air rifle, Model LG54MG, caliber .177 (4.5-mm). This air rifle may be used as a repeater with air-rifle shot (5 shots) or as a single-shot rifle with skirted air-gun pellets. The magazine air rifle has been developed from Model LG51Z, featuring in addition the magazine loading device. For single-shot use with skirted air-gun pellets, the magazine is removed and replaced with a headlock as illustrated, in order to insure an airtight seal.

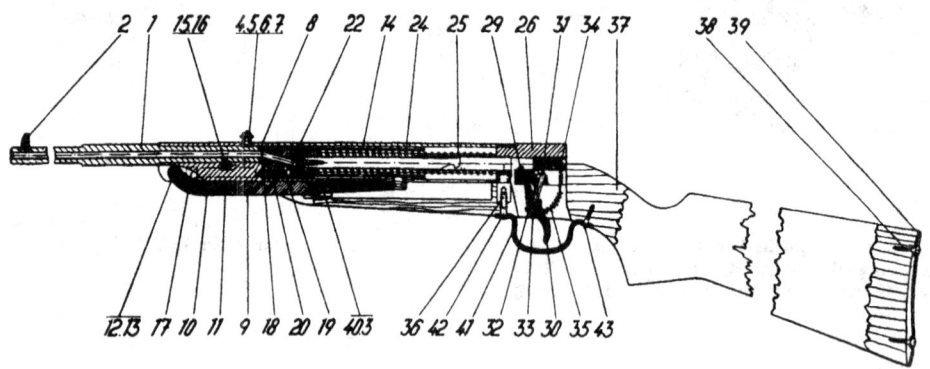

Typical German spring-air rifle, a barrel-cocking Falke. Action is closed, spring and piston forward.

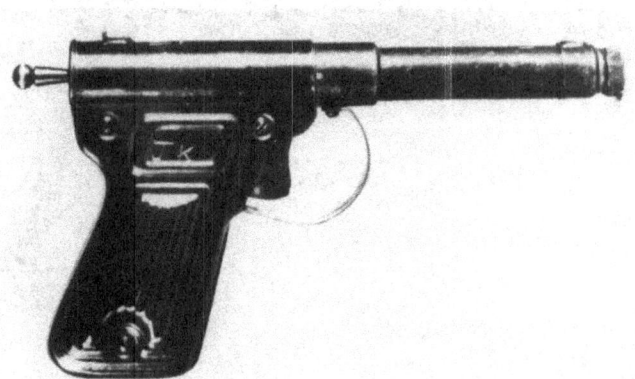

German pistol. Cocked. Note projecting breech screw. This particular model is called "Limit," but it is and has been made under dozens of trade names by many European makers.

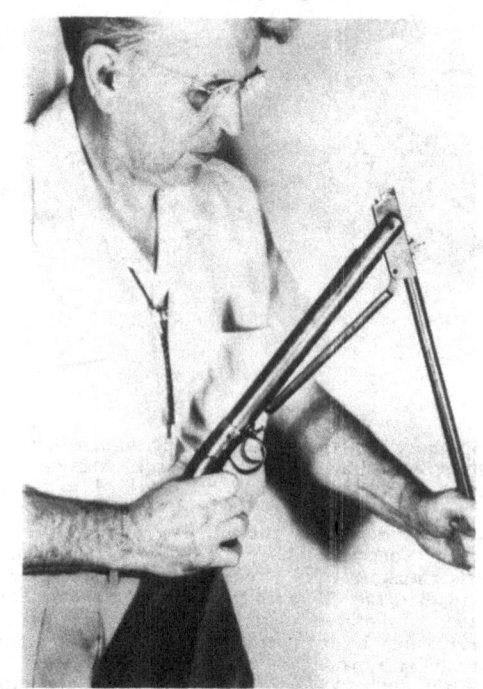

High-power British spring-air rifle, full-cocked ready for loading. This is an obsolete pattern.

12

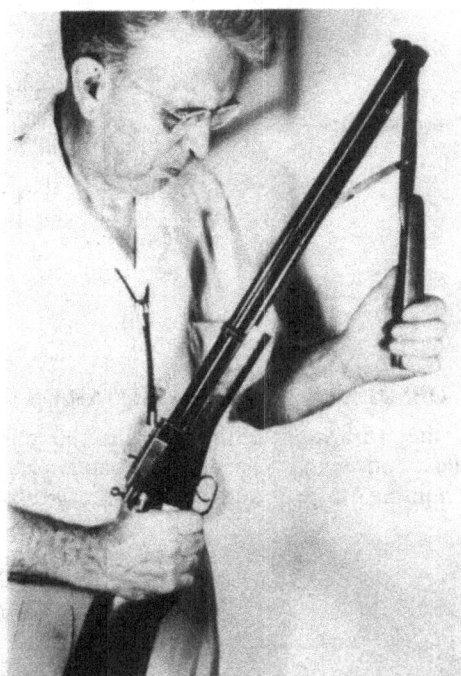

Typical modern compressed-air rifle (American Benjamin) with pump lever full-open for cocking stroke.

pression principle. However, their cheap construction and low-powered springs do not allow real accuracy or much penetration; even though the common pattern shooting the familiar "BB" shot, which are round balls of 2-millimeter or about .08-inch diameter, are occasionally capable of killing sparrows and the like at short distances and may be valuable for training young boys in the safe handling of arms.

IN ALL SPRING-COMPRESSION AIR GUNS, ONLY THE COMPRESSED AIR ACTS AS A PROPELLANT. No mechanical part of the arm is ever in contact with the missile. These must not be confused with SPRING GUNS in which the projectile is actually launched by a plunger which is driven by a spring, the plunger itself being in direct physical contact with the projectile.

The SPRING-AIR COMPRESSION type has four main advantages over the PNEUMATIC type. (1) While loading the bullet requires the same effort as for the pneumatic, *charging* the arm for firing is much easier. This type requires only ONE movement of the charging lever system to bring the spring to full compression. (2) *Consistent power* is obtained; since only one motion is required, the spring gives out the same amount of energy for each trigger pull. In the pneumatic, a different number of strokes, or even a different manner of stroking, will vary the power from shot to shot unless specific care is taken to see that each pumping employs the same number and type of strokes. (3) *Simplicity of action*. Fewer and sturdier parts are usable because no fine valving system is required as with the pneumatic. (4) *Faster delivery of shots*. This is possible because only one cocking or charging stroke is required.

On the adverse side, spring-air compression gives a definite recoil, which must be compensated for by the shooter. This recoil varies even in direction, depending upon position of spring and direction of its thrust. Recoil complexities are discussed under the various arms involved. Also, of course, the common spring-air compression arm allows only *one* power (though there have been exceptions to this in the form of arms allowing different spring compressions).

While most spring-air compression types must be loaded individually, there are some which incorporate tube, drum, or even box magazines. In some of these types each cocking motion automatically loads the chamber also, while in others the magazine must be hand turned or adjusted to feed.

System No. 2, Pneumatic (Pump-Up) Types. In this type of weapon the power is supplied from a reservoir of compressed air when the trigger is pulled. All modern pneumatic types of air rifles, pistols, and guns have built-in pumps which are operated to charge the air reservoir.

Typical modern compressed-air pistol (rifle mechanism is same except for size). Pump lever halfway open to show operation of piston by levers. American Crosman.

13

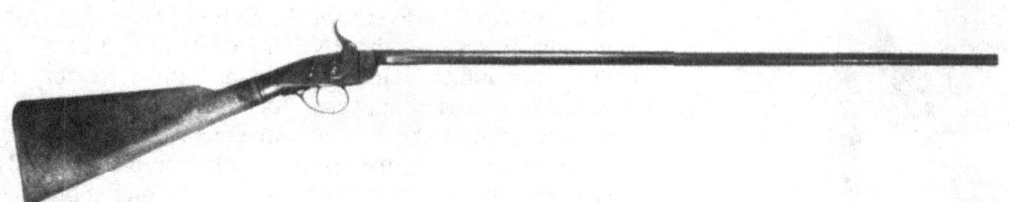

Early 18th century English. Butt is unscrewed. Air chamber in metal butt is pumped up. Will fire about 20 shots before pressure drops off to point of inefficiency. Will kill small game at 80 yards. Caliber of specimen is .36.

These are customarily levers below the barrel, though in early patterns still in use the piston can be drawn forward and then pushed back in to pump up the air in the reservoir or cylinder.

The PNEUMATIC has two advantages over the spring-compression types of air arm. (1) By repeated pumping it can be charged with enough air to give much higher velocities than are possible with normal spring-compression types—up to about 750 feet per second. (2) The pneumatic has no appreciable recoil, hence is easier to shoot accurately. Pressing the trigger opens the valve and allows the air compressed in the reservoir to pass through a small opening behind the bullet. There is no slamming action of a powerful spring being unleashed by the trigger pull, as happens in the spring-compression types.

Some modern pneumatics have been made which release only a part of the air charge stored up at each trigger pull, thereby allowing the arm to be used as a repeater by merely operating the bullet-loading mechanism.

Most patterns, however, are designed to release the entire air charge as the trigger is pressed. This gives maximum power, of course, but requires pumping up the air reservoir for each successive shot as well as loading the projectile.

OBSOLETE PNEUMATIC ARMS

During the 18th and 19th centuries large numbers of air rifles and some air shotguns and pistols were built for hunting, target, and even military use on the

Detachable stock reservoir. Austrian Contriner type. Cast-iron butt. Some butts are made of copper.

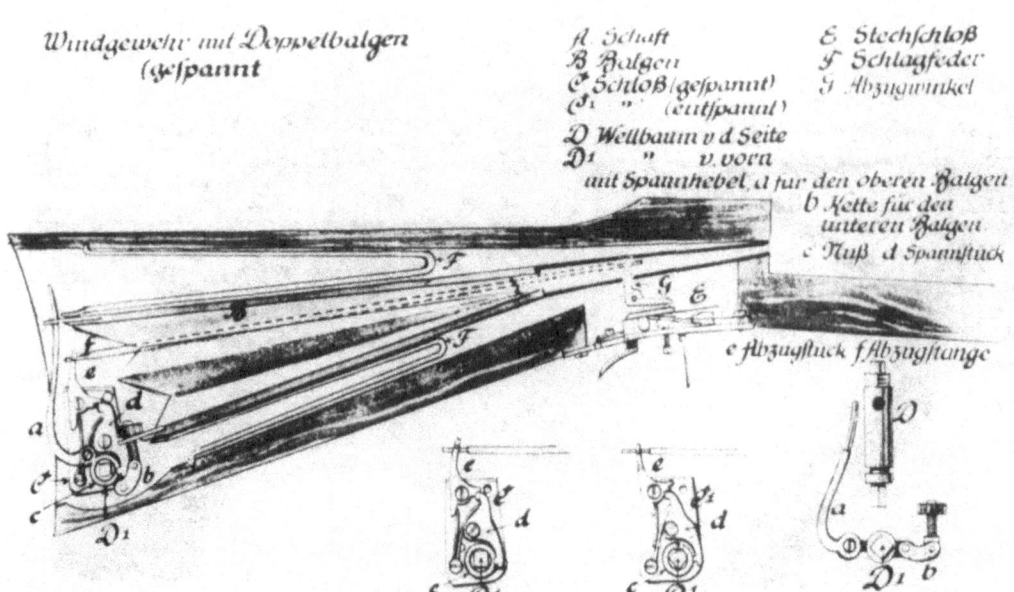

Early German double-bellows air gun. Winding side crank extended two bellows in butt and compressed powerful springs, which were held by a firing sear. Pressing the trigger released the sear. The heavy flat springs violently compressed the leather bellows, forcing the air down the narrow vent behind the missile in the barrel.

pneumatic, or pump-up, system. These are favorite collector's pieces today and are not in manufacture. They are dealt with in detail in the body of this work.

While some of these arms had built-in pumps analogous to modern ones, the very powerful types were all pumped up with separate heavy-duty pumps. These arms fall into three basic classes.

Class 1. Those in which the stock was detachable and contained a strong metal reservoir (or flask), which was pumped up to pressures as high as 550 pounds. When the stock was screwed back on to the breech end of the arm, pressing the trigger opened a valve and allowed compressed air to enter behind the projectile. Such "pump-ups" normally held enough air to allow firing from 10 to 20 shots before more pumping was required. Bullets (or shot) were loaded down the muzzle in some types and into the breech in others.

Class 2. Much the same as class 1, except that the air was pumped into a detachable metal ball, which was customarily then screwed on to the underside of the arm. (In some types the ball was mounted above the barrel, to one side, or even in a hollow in the stock).

Class 3. The least common type had its reservoir in the form of a jacket around the outside of the barrel. It was pumped up as in the types using detachable reservoirs.

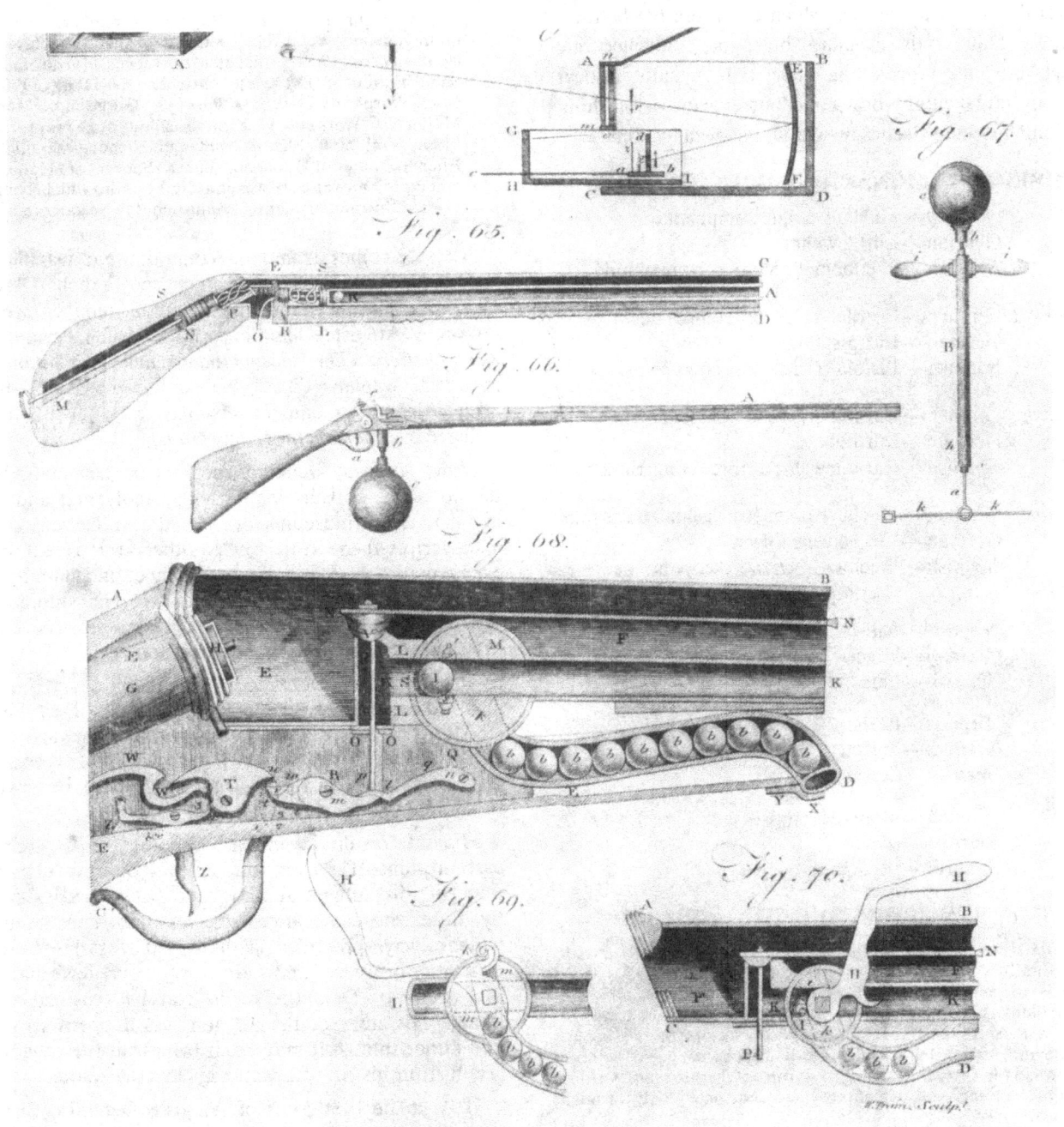

From British encyclopedia of early 1800's. Barrel-jacket-reservoir and ball-reservoir air guns of types then common. Note resemblance, except for ball, which figure 66 bears to the flintlock powder rifle of that period. Figures 68, 69, and 70 show details of a crank-operated magazine air gun with barrel-jacket reservoir. This type of arm was used in shooting galleries early in the 19th century.

15

FREAKS—THE BELLOWS-SPRING COMPRESSION SYSTEM

Only one freak system is of any particular importance. This type may well be the earliest form of air gun, as some very old pieces exist. It was made extensively for indoor target use in the 19th century, and is still made by custom builders in Europe.

This is the bellows type. In the common form, a powerful bellows is contained in the butt of the arm—even pistols were made on this system. A separate crank is used to wind or expand powerful springs inside the butt and to expand the bellows. When the trigger is pressed, it releases the powerful springs, which compress the bellows violently. This sends a sharp blast of controlled air through a vent to drive the projectile (usually a dart in indoor target guns) down the barrel with astonishing force and extreme accuracy within its distance limits.

FOREIGN DESIGNATIONS FOR AIR ARMS

Air Gun. French—Fusil m à air comprime
German—Lüftgewehr
Spanish—Escopeta f de aire comprimide

Air Pistol. French—Pistolet m à air comprime
German—Lüftpistole
Spanish—Pistola f de aire comprimido

Air Rifle. French—Carabine f à air comprime
German—Lüftbuchse
Spanish—Carabina f de aire comprimido

Air Dart. French—Fleche f pour fusil á air comprime
German—Lüftgewehrbölzen
Spanish—Flecha f para escopeta de aire comprimido

Bullet. French—balle
German—kügel
Spanish—bala

Dart. French—flèche
German—bölzen
Spanish—flecha

Pellet. French—plom de chasse
German—schrot
Spanish—perdigan

THE "INVENTION" OF THE AIR GUN

> It is a sad thing to say that though archeological investigators in vain turn over the dust of centuries and pass their lives in pointing out, with evidence in their hands, all these involuntary errors, these childish jugglings, the band of compilers continue to manufacture books out of old books, copying afresh that which already has been copied without examination, and so going on from father to son, writing about subjects with which they are acquainted only through books.
>
> Translated from *Die Kriegswaffen in ihren geschichtlichen Entwickelungen von den altestan zeiten bis auf die Gegenwart.*
> **AUGUSTE FREDERIC DEMMIN** (c1823-1898)

Who Invented the Air Gun? When? Where?

In the course of doing research for the preparation of this book, the author was struck by the fact that all encyclopedias and works consulted, regardless of when or where published or in what language printed, gave almost the same information in about the same form. The data was just too pat. It was never documented. It had the ring of material prepared by a compiler taking for granted the statements of some earlier writer, not that of the true researcher who digs, and works, and checks the background of the statements. As to the invention of the air gun, practically all references said with more or less directness:

> The air gun, invented by Guter of Nuremberg in 1560, and improved on successively by Gerlach and Sars of Berlin, by Contriner of Vienna, Fachter of Liege, Martin Fischer of Suhl, Futter of Dresden, Schrieber of Halle (1760-1769), C. G. Werner of Leipzig (1750-1780), Gottsche of Merseburg, Muller of Warsaw, Valentin Siegling of Frankfurt-on-the-Main, Vrel of Coblentz, John and Nicholas Bouillet of St. Etienne, Bate of England, Facka Speyer of Holland, and others, is an explosive weapon fired by air, which being compressed by an air-pump, is allowed to escape rapidly . . .

All this comes from one common, but usually unacknowledged source—the English or French 1870 and 1877 translations of the monumental study of arms and armor by Auguste Demmin, published in German as *Die Kriegswaffen, Eine Encyclopadie der Waffenkunde*. In an 1893 German edition, the data is the same—but the alleged invention date *is advanced to 1430!* Guter still is listed as the inventor, however.

Now, Auguste Demmin spent years traveling through the countries of Europe, studying, analyzing, and checking the actual museums of war, the collections and the manuscripts then available. No other arms researcher has ever equalled him in energy, diligence, and intelligence of approach. He was a great debunker. His studies paved the way to all later accurate presentations of data on arms and armor from the earliest times.

Unfortunately, Demmin often failed to give any precise documentation on many subjects which required it. Many of these, like the invention of the air gun, require further investigation in the light of records and knowledge not known in Demmin's time, but available to us today.

His data on the invention of the air gun is a particular case in point. It is truly ironical that Demmin's own writings on this subject should have been used uncritically by those who came after him, very much in the manner which always provoked in that great historian bitter and cynical attitudes. There are very, very few matters in the works of Demmin which can be reasonably questioned. His story of the air gun just happens to be one, and minor though it may be, it brings up the cogent paragraph from his magnificent encyclopedia quoted above.

It is in the best spirit of Auguste Demmin, then, that the present author essays here a fresh approach to the matter of the history of the air gun—that of going to sources which must not in many instances have been available to Demmin.

THE EARLY HISTORY OF THE AIR GUN

Before we can intelligently study the early history of air arms, we must first consider a few elementary facts about them.

Now, the number of makes and types of hand-operated air arms runs high in the thousands. They include toy patterns, low-powered types for short-range target shooting and indoor use, types powerful enough for use against small birds, rodents, and vermin, ultra-precision types bolt operated—as pump or trombone designs—as lever actions. They have appeared as tube action and box-magazine repeaters.

They have been among the crudest of the crude. They have been among the most ornamented of collection pieces. Plain triggers, single set and double set triggers—name just about any of the myriad refinements found through the centuries in any firearm and it will be shown to have occurred also among air arms.

But when this bewildering array of types and com-

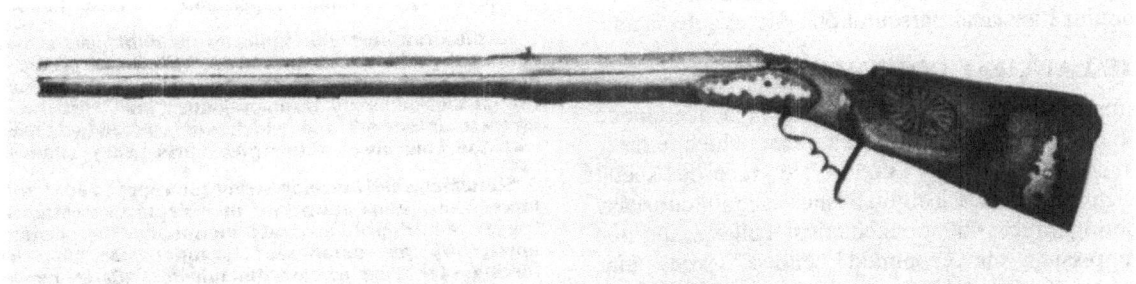

One of the earliest known authenticated air guns. German crank gun about 1560 A.D.

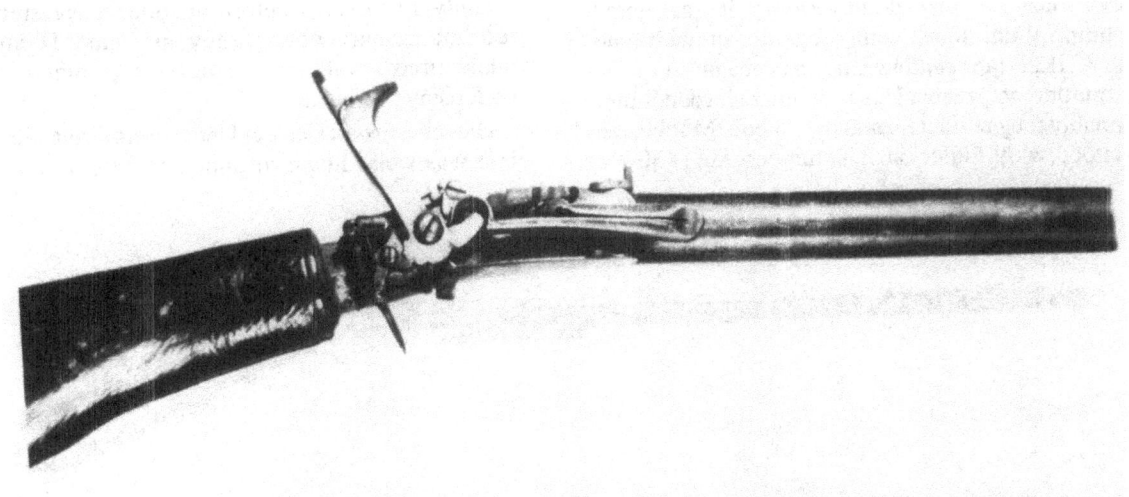

Early English butt-flask type. Similar crude specimens, as well as elaborate types, were also made in Europe generally during the late 18th century.

rivalling the accuracy of the best cartridge weapons at short distances, and finally, types powerful enough for deer and boar hunting—and some actually used in the 18th and 19th centuries for military sharpshooting!

They embrace the field of smoothbores, used with ball in the fashion of the early musket—true rifles with any conceivable type and depth of rifling (including the shallow grooving currently popular in target firearms!) firing balls and bullets of nearly every pattern—shotguns firing a cluster of small shot backed by a wad—pistols both smooth-bored and rifled. Calibers have run from .12-inch to as high as .775-inch! although today it is customary to confine them to .177-, .20-, .22-, or .25-inch.

They have been made as muzzle loaders—as breech loaders—as single shots and as double-barrels, both side-by-side and over-unders. They have been made as turn-

binations made through the centuries has been examined and studied, we find that ALL fall into one of three simple operating classifications:

First the principle of the bellows. Tradition ascribes the invention of the bellows to Anacharsis the Scythian, that troubled philosopher and traveler befriended by Solon some 600 years before Christ—but it unquestionably antedates him. A bellows was used on many very early European short-range precision rifles, and it is made in some few forms even today.

Second, the principle of the condensing syringe, a principle used by the Alexandrian Greeks 200 years before Christ as *an already familiar tool!* Modified little except for the valving and spring-loaded pistons, it is the principle of some 99 percent of all modern air arms.

Third, the independent air cylinder or flask pumped up by hand or machine to store air under pressure some times as high as 500 pounds per square inch. This system was known and used in the late Middle Ages at least. It is still the basic principle of the types currently manufactured in huge numbers under the classification of "pneumatic" or "pump-up" guns.

We shall now examine in cursory fashion only (since each type could readily support a 1,000-page book) the highlights of what this author has been able to establish as authentic, or probably authentic, in this vast field. Since no adequately documented books or basic literature have ever before been attempted in this field, the following is intended as a research instrument as well as a popular historical presentation of provable facts.

THE EARLIEST DOCUMENTATION

The first mechanical air gun may well have been one operating on the bellows principle, a form which exists even today. Nobody really knows. No records spell out the design for us. Basically all such a gun consists of is a shooting tube with a mechanical bellows in the stock. Compressing the expanded bellows forces air under pressure to drive a ball or dart down the tube.

The principle of the *bellows* has been used since the early days of mining and working metals—a time lost in the murky haze of unwritten history. It far antedates the pump. Who, then, can hope to say with authority just WHEN the *bellows air gun* began in principle? As a matter of practical use within recorded time, it unquestionably began in Germany. When? Maybe, as Demmin stated, with Guter in Nuremberg in 1430 or

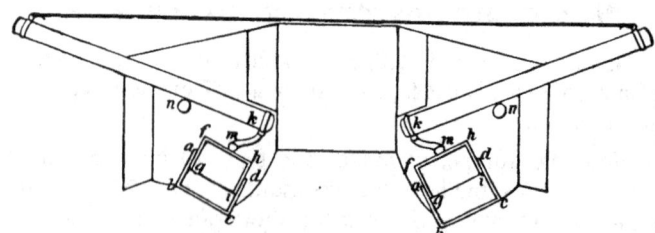

Ctesibius' compressed-air gun (pneumatic spanner). This device was specifically described and praised by the military engineer and historian, Philo of Byzantium. A reconstruction was made and tested by Schramm in Germany in recent times.

In the drawing "fghi" indicates air-tight pistons which move in and out within cylinders "abcd." When the pistons were forced down into the air cylinders they compressed the air within. The two pistons hook up through joints "km" with two arms which turn on axles "n," and which are secured at their upper ends with the launching string which hurls heavy missiles.

Stretching the launching string (or rope) to load a heavy missile forced the pistons down into their respective cylinders. When the trigger was tripped to release the missile, the pistons were forced upward by the compressed air and passed on a terrific thrust, forcing the string against the missile with tremendously violent force to hurl it a great distance.

of that discovery, too, is subject to question; but it was certainly 1500 years before anyone in Nuremberg undertook the construction of any air gun! Today the most widely used of all air-gun designs is that of the simple condensing syringe.

The best historical evidence establishes that this principle was well known to and used by Ctesibius of Ascra,

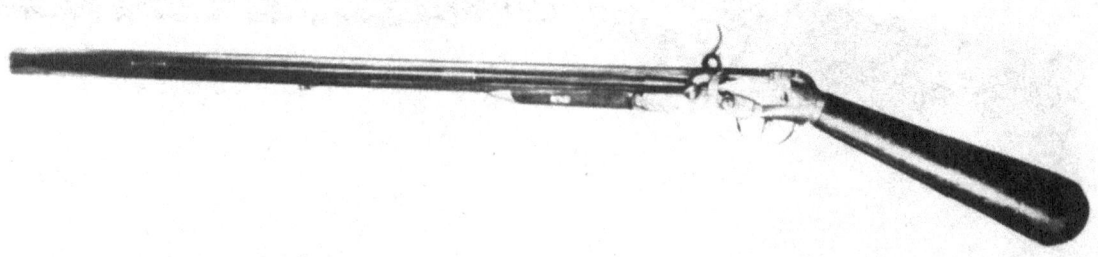

Typical European (Austrian shown) over-under with detachable butt flask. The butt shown is typical of hundreds made by independent Austrian gunsmiths who bought surplus Army parts after the Austrian Model 1799 (Girardoni) air rifle became obsolete.

1560, depending on the edition you favor, though the weight of evidence is much against it, as will be pointed out as we proceed. Certainly the bellows was widely used and known in the Nuremberg area at that time. But a "Guter" was not! It must here be noted that while the bellows was the first practical means of compressing air, it could have had but a very limited application to hurling serious projectiles because of its bulk and low compressive power. Still, guns on that principle, old and new, are available in many museums and collections.

The principle of the *condensing syringe* was known and in use in the second century B.C. Obviously, the first serious air projector could start ONLY when this principle (the use of the elastic force of air compressed by a piston close-fitted in a tube) came to be understood in relation to its use as a motive power. The actual date

a contemporary of Archimedes. Ctesibius started life as a barber in Alexandria in the golden days of Ptolemy Philadelphius and Ptolemy Euergetes, when mind was king, and when the mathematician and the mechanician were given full rein to develop arts and knowledge and sciences.

We know little of Ctesibius today. What we do know stems from Vitruvius, Pliny the Elder, Trifone, Milone; and from his "pupil" Hero of Alexandria and Philo of Byzantium, himself a noted mechanician, who lived a generation after him. We do know that Ctesibius developed a remarkable device, based on the syringe principle, for increasing threefold the power of some of the huge stone-throwing military siege equipment of the early Greeks. This "Machine of Ctesibius" is well known today (one was reconstructed in Germany during the last century from known details). The common early Greek "artillery" utilized the elasticity of wood or rope in various forms (some on the simple principle of the bow or crossbow). The Machine of Ctesibius utilized a huge "air-booster" at either end of the machine, tubes in which pistons were closely fitted so that as the machine was "cocked" ready for hurling, air was compressed in the booster cylinders. When the device was triggered, the air under compression developed about three times the force of the mechanical hurler. The device is described in considerable detail by Albert Neuberger in his *Die Technik des Altertums*.

Some Greek historians, drawing large on Byzantine tradition and translations from early Arabic, have contended that Ctesibius actually invented an "air gun." If so, it is lost to history. Indeed a manuscript published in Athens in 1868 by one M. Rhodios, and drawing largely on such sources together with some early drawings, contends that the pre-Christian Era Greeks actually used forms of explosive air cannons much like the submarine mine throwers in use in all navies today! Such devices would have required knowledge of the air pump and huge compressive machines, and we have no historical data indicating such knowledge at that period. But, who can truly say what has been and what has not, in a time when so much that is old is constantly being rediscovered?

Some have contended that Hero of Alexandria also developed air-powered arms. Hero, who lived probably about 125 B.C., while still a shadowy figure like Ctesibius, has left us some written records of his works which at least establish positively that the Alexandrian Greeks of his period understood the nature and uses of the elasticity of air for furnishing motive power. Vitruvius, himself one of the great architects of all time and a military engineer of note, gives us no references to Hero but ascribes to Ctesibius many of the devices we find in Hero's surviving *Pneumatica*, which may indicate that he was a sort of "interpreter" for Ctesibius.

Strangely enough, we know nothing personal today about Vitruvius—or Marcus Vitruvius Pollio to give him his full name—except what he tells us and what little we can extract from his writings. He recounts that he was appointed a superintendent of balistae (missile throwers or early artillery) during the reign of Augustus, in the 1st century A.D. A genius, yet a modest and humble man, Vitruvius credits most of the theory and history in his works to the early Greeks. Most of his sources have been lost to history except for his references to Ctesibius as we have noted. (Note: An excellent English edition of Vitruvius is that of Morgan, published by the Harvard University Press in 1914).

Taunery's *Athénée sur Ctesibios el l'hydraulis*, published in 1896, is perhaps the best detailed coverage of the known facts about the master Greek scientist and his works.

The Arabic translation of the *Mechanica* of Philo of Byzantium executed by the Mohammedan scholar Kosta ben Luka about 888 A.D. is also a great source of data concerning Ctesibius.

The *Mathematica Veteres* (Ancient Mathematicians), edited by Melchisedech Thévenot (1620-1692), king's librarian to Louis XIV of France, contains several treatises on ancient siege operations from the known works of Apollodorus, Biton, Hero, and Philo—but the only direct air device mentioned is that of Ctesibius.

Hero of Alexandria

While we know that Hero spoke and wrote Greek and that he was born at Alexandria, the evidence which has come down to us of his methods, phraseology, and thinking processes has led many eminent researchers to believe that he was an Egyptian. Much of what he did bore directly on the earlier work of Egyptian "mechanicians," as the "doers" were then classed to distinguish them from the teachers or thinkers who were classed as "mathematicians."

While in the surviving section of Hero's *Pneumatica* we find detailed descriptions of nearly a hundred small machines and mechanical toys, the truly important sections are those dealing with practical engines which came to world attention and use again only after centuries of loss to the world because of the vicious destruction of the Alexandrian Library. These were the double-forcing pump used as a fire engine, a design originally outlined by Ctesibius and actually used in the 16th century in Italy after the rediscovery of Hero's manuscript data; and, even more remarkable, a stationary steam engine!

This steam engine appeared in England in the 19th century where it became noted as the "Avery's Patent" engine and was very widely used throughout Scotland until the opening of the present century! Since Hero's *Pneumatica* was known in Latin translation since the 16th century (and the English Woodcroft and Greenwood translation with drawings was published in London in 1851) one wonders to what extent Mr. Avery might have drawn upon the knowledge of those pre-Christian scientists of Alexandria! If he never had heard of them—as certainly the British Patent Office had not! —then about the most that can be said is that Avery's 19th century thinking exactly paralleled that of the men who lived some 2,000 years before him!

In the face of correlative evidence of this sort, the unprejudiced researcher may be excused if he demonstrates skepticism with writers who arbitrarily name a date, and a place, and a man in Germany in the year 1430 as having invented the first arm to hurl projectiles pneumatically!

It might be noted in passing that while many classical writers refer to Hero as a "pupil of Ctesibius" it is by no means established that the two even lived at the same time! It is entirely likely that Hero thought of himself as a "pupil" in the sense that he *applied* knowledge promulgated by Ctesibius perhaps long before Hero's time; and that later writers, seeing the connection between the ideas of the two men, incorrectly related them to each other.

Indeed, Hero of Alexandria has even been confused with Hero of Constantinople, a later-day scientist (about 900 A.D.) often called "the Younger" because much of his work paralleled that of the earlier Hero. Hero of Constantinople applied much of his time and knowledge to the development of mechanical principles as applied to engines of war—siege equipment and the like. (Note: References are to be found in Greek and German, but very little has been translated into English. See *Die Geschichte der Textüberlieferung griechises Wortregister*, published 1899 at Leipzig.)

Alexandrian Library

No man can say how many ages the history of the world was set back by the brutal "book burning" of the ignorant zealots and despots following the advent of Christ. In the pre-Christian days of Alexandria, the thinker who originated theories and the doer who could apply them formed a combination which only now is beginning to be achieved again. The dissemination of knowledge was widespread and was not hampered by religious and ecomonic prejudices and intolerances of later periods —nor by the political and national economic stresses of today.

Much of the great book and manuscript collection of early Alexandria was destroyed by the early Christians, but it fell to the followers of Mohammed to complete the blight of early learning. It happened not long after the death of Mohammed.

About 641 A.D.—the date cannot be established with certainty, but is probably accurate within two years— Alexandria was stormed by the Mohammedans. The captive residents became increasingly restive under restraint, and after one attempt at revolt the Caliph Omar ordered the Library, the pride of Alexandria, to be destroyed as a punitive measure.

"If the books," pontificated Omar, "contain what is agreeable with the Book of God, then the Book of God is sufficient without them; and if they contain that which is contrary, there is no need for them." Since even in our own time we have experienced similar burnings and restraints, we can picture the horror of the powerless Alexandrian Greeks as for six terrible months they watched, so tradition has it, while the entire contents of their priceless Library was burned day by day in the public baths of the city.

Hero's Pneumatica

Hero's treatise on pneumatics (*Pneumatica*) comes to us through time and many translations. In spite of the inevitable loss and distortion as it passed from Greek to Arabic to Italian to Latin, the simplicity and detail of his known writings become genius of the highest order— yet Hero himself claims little more than the application to special devices of pneumatic and mechanical principles developed by thinkers far beyond his own sphere!

An Italian translation of his work by Aleotti was published at Bologna in 1547, followed by a Latin version first published by F. Commandini at Urbino in 1575 and soon thereafter reprinted in Amsterdam and Paris. The effect of Hero's knowledge on the scientific thinking of the Middle Ages can be established through those publications. There were many later Greek and German versions, but the first English translation was made in London in 1851, edited by B. Woodcroft, Professor of Machinery in University College, London.

Among other things, Hero gives a detailed description of a syringe. He calls it a "puylcus." It needs only a spring behind it to be the prototype of the air system of a dozen varieties of modern European air gun. In another device listed as "an altar organ blown by manual labor" he substitutes a syringe for the common bellows as an instrument for compressing air by an attached lever. The air being blown into pipes opens and closes valves and produces musical sounds. Still another device is a miniature windmill set to drive a syringe piston which blows air into an organ to operate it. He mentions as already "well known" a marine torpedo which can penetrate steel— but doesn't feel it necessary to describe it!

It will be seen from the foregoing fragmentary documentary descriptions that the ancient Greeks COULD have had air guns or similar air military machines. They knew and used most of the required *principles* involved. But the actuality is still a matter of speculation and conjecture. In passing, mention might be made that in the 19th century the English Patent Office issued a patent for use of a windmill or steam engine to pump air into containers for use as air cannons, and the Duke of Wellington experimented with a steam engine as a power unit for hurling musket balls. Hero, in addition to using a small windmill as described above, also detailed a steam operated fire pump as noted. The only reference to steam as a motive power which has thus far been found in ancient writings is that in the *Pneumatica*.

THE AIR GUN IN EARLY EUROPEAN RECORDS

On the basis of all available evidence, there can be little question but that the air gun as a small arm to be used and carried by one man was invented and developed in Germany. However, the probability is that there was a long period of time between the conception and the actual development of a truly usable weapon. Let us rapidly sketch in merely the supporting highlights which the present researcher has been able to unearth, and which are not to be found in any of the standard encyclopedias or arms books heretofore published.

First, let us examine the Guter story propagated by Demmin. There where two great chroniclers of Nuremberg. One was Siebenkees. His *Little Chronicle of Nuremberg (Kleine Chronik Nurnberg)*, published in 1790 tells us that in 1429 A.D. rifles were used there for target shooting—yet he makes no reference of any kind to either Guter or to an *air* rifle! Von Murr was the other. In his *Description of the Curiosities in Nuremberg (Beschreibung der Merkwurdigkeiten in Nurnberg)*, published in 1801, this great authority is also completely blank on the subject of Guter (or "Gester," as he is sometimes listed).

The French *Dictionnaire de l'arme de terre*, a huge 4-volume work prepared under the supervision of Baron Etienne Alexandre Bardin, was published in Paris in 1851. In this work is a passing mention claiming that a Frenchman named Bontemps *invented an air gun in 1430!* There is no documentation. No serious modern French scholar gives any credit to the Bontemps story or date.

In all the early (1870 and 1877) editions of Demmin's work on arms, he gives Guter as the inventor *in 1560*, but in his later enlarged and somewhat amended edition published only in German in 1893 *he advances the Guter date to 1430!*

The 1560 records of the *Nuremberg Chronicle* do *not* disclose any mechanic of note named either Guter or Guest. There is some ground for believing that Demmin altered his discovery date to conform with the Bardin date in the 1893 edition of his work, because he learned this fact and because the 1430 date had come to receive popular acceptance by then.

The first traceable mention of any "Guter" is found in Vollbeding's *Archives of Useful Inventions (Archiv der nützlichen Erfindungen)* published at Leipzig in 1792, merely a fragmentary notice by a chronicler who cannot be compared to the distinguished Siebenkees and Murr. The "evidence" for Guter is very, very sketchy. As to others, Musschenbrock in his *Introduction to Natural Philosophy (Introductio ad philosopiam natural)* tells of the existence of an air rifle dating from 1474 to be seen in "the armory of the Lord of Schmettau." It is stated that the rifle is not perfect in its operation—but no mention is made of either when or where the said armory was located!

When we come to the matter of Hans Lobsinger, on the other hand, the picture is considerably clearer. He was a noted mechanic at Nuremberg, and it is recorded that he invented *an improved form of bellows*—an item which could well have formed the basis for an early air-gun design, as we have already pointed out.

Johann Gabriel Doppelmayr in his *Historical Reports on Mathematicians and Artists of Nuremberg (Historischen Nachrichten von Nürnberger Mathematiken und Kunstlern)*, published in Nuremberg in 1730, tells us that about 1550 this Hans Lobsinger turned over to the municipal administration a long list of the artifacts (or useful objects) made by him.

Siebenkees verifies this and tells us specifically that Lobsinger invented an air rifle about 1560—the *first recorded report* mentioning a specific person, time, place and object to establish real credibility!

Since no one nation ever has a monopoly on thinking, every development whether air gun or atomic bomb has seen every advance soon duplicated in other than the originating countries. In fact, it seems almost a law of nature that any important development will be the subject of simultaneous international discovery.

Thus in connection with the air gun we find M. Mersenne in his *Phenomena Pneumatica,* a part of a treatise published in Paris in Latin in 1644, tells us that Marin Bourgeois of Lisieux in Normandy built an air rifle for King Henry IV, who reigned 1589-1610. This rifle, incidentally, fired many projectiles on one charging of the air reservoir—and may have been the forerunner of many later types.

The Dutch, too, have a claim. Zedler in his *Universal Encyclopedia (Universal Lexikon)* under "Büchse," the early German and Dutch term covering guns and rifles, attributes the air gun to Bartholomew Koes, a mechanic at Amsterdam who lived about 1600.

Even more to the point is that an actual description of an air rifle is given by the Italian, B. Crescentio, in in his *Nautica Mediterranea,* published in Rome in 1607!

Von Guericke's famous "air gun" as set up on the grounds of his famous laboratory. This was the prototype of all the later detachable-air-reservoir air guns. From contemporary drawing.

Among the scores of others to whom the air gun has been credited, without, however, well established facts to back up the claim, might be mentioned a man identified as "Douson" by Paul Marperger in a treatise published in Hamburg in 1704 in *Odd Reports on Inventors and Inventions (Curieuse Nachrichten von Erfindern und Erfindungen).*

The important factor in the development of the truly powerful air gun, the pneumatic or "pump-up" as differentiated from the bellows or syringe-spring types of relatively lower power is the efficient *air pump;* a fact which leads us to a great German scientist of the past who directly, and indirectly, had much to do with the increased efficiency of the air arm—undoubtedly the least important of all his developments, incidentally, but the one we are concerned with in this book.

He was Otto von Guericke, born at Madgeburg, Germany, November 20, 1602. To him is credited the discovery and invention of the air pump, and samples of his design are still to be seen in museums. We get a considerable sidelight on this genius from just the outline of his scholastic background: University of Leipzig in 1617; Helmsted, 1620; Jena, 1621; Leiden, 1623. He traveled to England also in the course of his studies. His *Experiment of the Madgeburg Spheres* in 1641 revolutionized much scientific thinking which had been unchanged since the days of the early Greeks.

Placing together two close-fitting halves of a copper sphere sealed only with grease, he attached his air pump to a valve in one of the halves and drew out the air within the sphere thus formed. In short, he thereby established the principle of the vacuum. He dramatized the discovery by harnessing six horses to pull on each side of the device, demonstrating that the atmospheric pressure was so great that the horses pulling in opposite directions could not wrench the halves apart until he opened the valve to allow air to enter. From this it was just a step to utilizing the pump as a compressor, just as one blows up bicycle tires today. Thus it is entirely reasonable that those who credit von Guericke with being the inventor of the "unterdruck lüftbusche" are correct, even though we do not know of the existence of his rifle today.

We do know that von Guericke constructed what has come to be known as "The Madgeburg Air Rifle," which is pictured herein as it appeared set up on the grounds of his famous Works and which is reproduced from Ostwald's *Classics* (Ostwald's *Klassikern*). This "air rifle" on its mount is a "rifle" pretty much in the sense that the modern recoilless rifle is! That is, it is more a piece of artillery than a hand arm. Indeed it is recorded that later mechanics at Nuremberg built such "wind chambers" to throw 4-pound iron balls with enough force that they are said to have penetrated a 2-inch board at 400 yards! (Note: Because of the trajectories involved, the balls would plunge under conditions where the penetration stated is quite within reason).

One thing seems sure—the literally scores of later-day air gun makers who used the principle of charging a sphere with air and attaching it to a rifle for use as a propellant all merely followed in von Guericke's footsteps. This system was used throughout England and Europe in the 18th and 19th centuries, as will be noted further on.

There are scores of others whose names have been linked with the invention and development of the air rifle. Paul Weber is named as the inventor by Fabricius in his *General History of Learning* (*Allegemeine Historie der Gelehrsamkeit*) published in 1752, though documentation is lacking.

A much more substantial case can be made out for Denis Papin who lived 1647 to 1712. A scientist who followed in the footsteps of von Guericke, and a French citizen by birth, Papin worked on an air pump with Huygens and with Boyle in England on steam experiments. He developed a steam engine of his own, which was not very successful, incidentally.

While his scientific stature was such that he held the chair of mathematics at Marburg for several years and his inventions and developments were many, he died in obscurity.

While at Marburg University he collected the most important of his own papers which were published there in 1695 under title *Fasciculus dissertationem*. In these papers we find the two air guns he invented, the second being but an improvement of the original. So far as can be traced, they were never generally produced.

Papin made a mark on his time with the introduction of his widely heralded "steam digester" as he described it, in 1679. This device, complete with automatic safety escape valve, has come down to us under many names—and amusingly enough under many patents also! The device makes millions of dollars yearly in our time for its manufacturers. We call it a "pressure cooker," the steam cooker common to countless homes throughout the world.

In his *Philosophical Transaction* in 1686, Papin first described an air-rifle construction. While the author has never found them listed in any English publication, actually the two air-rifle designs by Papin, one in 1684 and the improved one in 1686, are shown in the *History of the Art of Physical Experimentation* (*Geschichte der physikalischen experimentierkunst*) of Gerland and Trautmuller, published in 1899.

Gropp (in *Reichs-Anzeiger*, 1793), Lieberkuhn (in *Jacobson's Technolog Worterbuch*), Mathey (in *Memoires de l'academie*, Paris, 1737)—these are but a sprinkling of those who improved the forms of the air rifle.

Demmin cites air rifles of the copper ball reservoir type by Sars and others then in the Artillery Museum in Paris. It is noteworthy that in the early editions of his works he recognizes *only two basic types*—those with the air compressed *in a detachable ball* screwed to the rifle barrel (both below and above) and the Austrian Contriner type (based on the official Austrian Girardoni about which Demmin indicates no knowledge), where *the reservoir forms a detachable stock* to the rifle. However, in his late editions (1893) he added a sketch and comment on the then new American Quackenbush Air Rifle—not the common type generally encountered here, but a powerful lever actuated spring-air gun we shall touch upon later, for Quackenbush was truly the father of the mass-produced air gun.

The *Nuremberg Chronicle* mentions Peter Dumbler's air gun of 1607 as being too powerful and silent to allow it to be sold. George Fehr as early as 1655 was building both rifles and pistols with air reservoirs in the form of jackets around the barrel, with built-in pumps in the stock. However, it is not until the beginning of the 18th century that we find *widespread* manufacture of powerful air guns.

The range of air guns, rifles, and pistols of this era examined by the author can be but a very small fraction of the types actually made, since air-gun collections as such are few and far between; and almost every noted 18th- and early 19th-century gunmaker built a few special air guns to order. Yet to present even a fragmentary description of these would require hundreds of pictures and pages of type!

As a general indication of their scope, however, some mention must be made, but we shall confine it to a few documented specimens only.

In the Army Museum collection in Paris are numerous piston and ball reservoir types as well as some with built-in pumps. There are specimens signed Bate of London, Stephen of London, Nicolas Everard of Verdun, Contriner in Wien, Carl Starrk in Wien, Lorenz Paur in Linz, May in Salsburg. Others are signed P. J. Kornfield, Joseph Kuehenreuter, L. P. (probably for LePage), I. C. Aperlin, Ehresbretstein, Berlin-Darmstadt-Fack Steyr.

The Copenhagen Museum has numerous specimens, including a barrel-jacket reservoir pump-up type signed and dated "George Fehr of Dresden," unusual in that the pump is built into the stock as shown herein in an illustration from Thornton's travel book published in England early in the 18th century.

Still others encountered in private collections include many originally in the old Erbach and Lobkowitz collections, as well as several European museum collections which were dispersed or destroyed during World War II. Among these might be listed some magnificently inlaid and engraved pieces by G. B. Guettner of Basel, Facka Speger (or Speyer) of Holland who built stock-flask types, T. C. Sars of Berlin, J. and N. Bouillet of St. Etienne, Werner of Leipzig, Siegling of Frankfurt-on-Main, Kuhlman of Breslau, Gerlach of Berlin. The list is all but endless!

Pistols, while never as commonly encountered as rifles, were still made in any number of calibers, though very

AIR-OPERATING SYSTEMS OF THE EARLY PERIODS

Some writers have ascribed the "invention" of the air gun to Guter in 1430 as we have seen—others, to a "Guest" at the same period; yet the weight of existing evidence, as has been pointed out, is strictly against this conjecture, and there are no reliable records or descriptions of any air guns of that period.

Likewise the statement has occasionally been made that the earliest air types were pumped-up designs with air reservoirs in the stocks. The weight of evidence as we have pointed out is against this also.

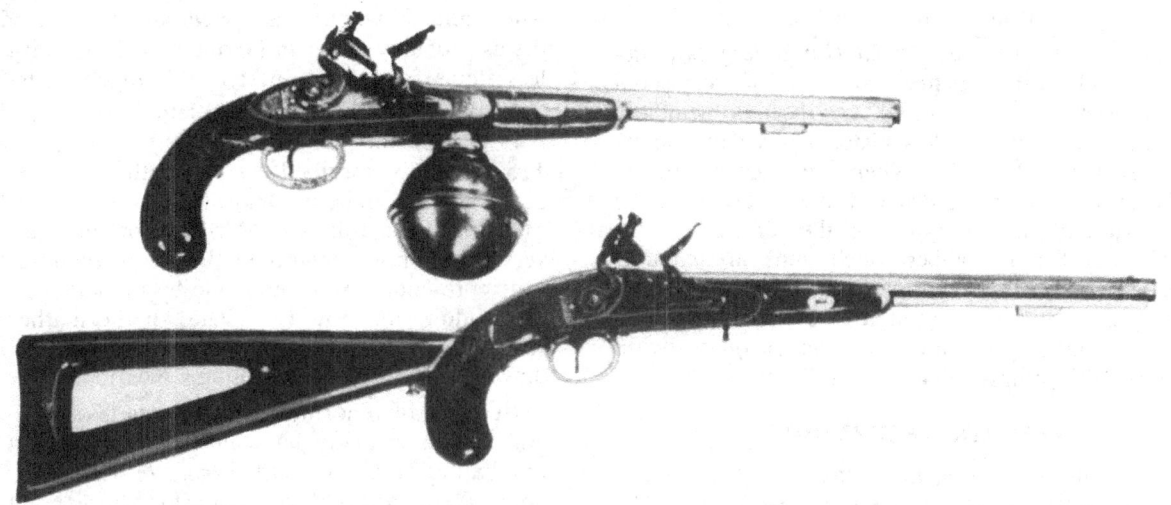

Austrian-made "Russian" air pistols. Early 19th century. One shown with round detachable ball. The one with detachable shoulder stock is the same; the two are a pair.

seldom are there two *exactly* alike, indicating that manufacture was basically on a "custom-made" basis, not as a standard production type such as we encounter about the year 1800 in some Austrian patterns.

Some very unusual air pistols encountered were marked "Joseph Oesterleinsche Fabrique, Wien." These, curiously, were usually called "Russian models," apparently because many had been purchased by Russian travelers. A typical pair were about 7.65-mm. (.32) caliber with the magazines on the right sides of the barrels. Magazines loaded through a capped opening on top of the barrels, and individual bullets were chambered by pressing a loading bar on the right side—the downfeed being gravity. Outside dummy hammers controlled the air release valves. The iron butts were detachable and were unscrewed for pumping up by an independent pump.

Huhlman also made air pistols at Breslau about 1760, specimens of which have been encountered in 9- and 10-mm. calibers! These were single-shot patterns in which the entire air load was released to fire a single bullet and had very considerable power.

Air canes of the period are also encountered, though most of these are of a later date and were made in England. Some German patterns (unmarked) were 9-mm. caliber with 23-inch barrels. Those encountered were commonly muzzle loaders. The pumped-up air chamber was screwed to the barrel breech for firing.

The oldest specimens with reasonably authentic backgrounds which this author has ever personally examined are Nuremberg-area guns which combine the bellows principle with that of the crank-wound spring. This wound-spring compressor occurs in several forms, one of which is but an extension of the clock-spring idea which was developed and raised to perfection in and around Nuremberg, and which at a period about 1510 appeared in Germany as the new gunpowder ignition system, the "Wheel lock" (Radschlöss). Turning an axle in the rear of the air gun stock wound a heavy chain which in turn opened the bellows and compressed an extremely powerful spring. The relationship is obvious, and a bellows-crank air system at this time was at least a mechanical possibility. In other versions the crank opened the bellows and tensioned opposed flat springs which slammed the bellows closed when the trigger was pulled.

The old United States Cartridge Company collection of firearms contained one of these specimens which was subjected to special study by the technicians of that organization. Every detail of the gun manufacture, from materials and design to actual workmanship, indicated manufacture by German artisans of the early 16th century period.

In any event, this crank-wound, spring-compressed bellows gun combined the features of *the bellows of that period* and *the spring-wind lock of that period*. It was a weapon of amazing power; this author has seen only two others like it.

There is some reason to believe that this design was not made in quantity at the time because of a fear of its silence and power. It is not to be confused with similar bellows designs of much later periods—and even of today—which are common dart throwers or subcaliber guns (Bolzenbüchsen) often used for indoor shooting because of the amazing accuracy which can be built into them. The early calibers encountered were, as in the United States Cartridge Company specimen mentioned, about 9-mm. (or .38).

The French Marin gun mentioned was a crank-wound "wheel-lock" pattern, also, with a stock air reservoir.

At a much later date, but also at Nuremberg, was developed a stock-syringe pattern air rifle of very considerable power in which a crank was used to wind up a stock axle which drew back a piston against the power of a very strong coil spring. When the trigger pull released the piston, the spring drove it ahead just as in the most modern patterns, compressing the air behind the bullet of 8- or 9-mm. caliber. Such guns are capable of velocities of 500 feet per second or more with a good sized slug, and were (and are) serious arms, not toys. Common later types often pull the piston forward, volute "ribbon" springs being used generally.

EARLY AIR RESERVOIRS

These fell into two categories generally, if we judge by the guns which have survived as specimens. The commonest forms were those with detachable stock reservoirs. These required a separate compressor (commonly called a pump) which was used to charge the reservoir, made generally of malleable iron, brass, or copper.

If we judge by the available literature of the times (which is very scanty indeed), a common form was that of the barrel-jacket reservoir as found in the Fehr and similar guns. In these the compressor was often built into the stock and the air pumped into the jacket around the barrel. A few specimens exist.

"FLINTLOCK" AIR GUNS

Numerous guns have been made to resemble closely the flintlock firearms then in common use. Such arms are encountered in a bewildering number of variations. Many were constructed from flintlock gun parts by custom arms makers; others from parts purchased from large arms makers, much as Belgian, German, and Spanish guns of the early part of this century were often made from basic parts purchased by small family groups and added to or altered to provide "individual" makes. (For example, since the close of World War II, well over 100,000 Mauser rifle actions made by the F. N. factory in Belgium have been sold to individual small companies and custom gun builders who have altered, stocked, and barreled them to personal specifications of the purchasers!)

Some of these air guns which are commonly called by collectors "flintlock air guns" have all the external parts of the true flintlock firearm, even to the point of being equipped to discharge priming powder in the pan! None that this author has seen had any communication between the flash and the air mechanism; but since at a later date the explosion of gunpowder was used to compress air in military pneumatic cannon, it is possible that this system was investigated. In most such guns, however, only the cock (hammer) and trigger were part of the operating air release system; though there are exceptions where the cock also is purely for visual effect, all the air release mechanism except the trigger being housed within the lock frame or plates.

THE DETACHABLE BALL AIR RESERVOIR

Again it is impossible to establish precisely where, when, and by whom this system was first introduced, but it was probably either in Germany or England; and doubtless stems from von Guericke's Madgeburg Rifle.

Writing in his fascinating letters (published later in book form) the English Colonel Thornton (who lived 1757 to 1853) ascribed the ball pattern to one B. Martin of London, England. Thornton wrote in 1802 of the Martin gun as follows: "Air-guns of late have received very great improvements in their construction. Figure 10 is a representation of one made by the late Mr. B. Martin of London, and now by several of the mathematical instrument and gun makers of the metropolis." He shows drawings of the gun and pump mentioned.

Because of Thornton's background, ability, and general accuracy, many have taken this statement to prove the ball-reservoir pattern *began in England*. However, noted German and Swiss collectors have pointed out to this author specimens of similar patterns made in Germany well before Thornton's time. C. H. Werner, for instance, who appears in the Leipzig records as a gunmaker in the 1750-1780 period made some. Specimens examined had below-barrel reservoirs of iron, sphere shaped, caliber about .45 and bore the stamp, "C. G. Werner, 1752." Several ornamented specimens of these are known, apparently having been made for the German sportsmen counterparts of Colonel Thornton. Dozens of other makes could be cited and documented and there is no question that the ball reservoir air gun, rifle, and pistol were all in wide European use at an early 18th century date.

Colonel Thornton's detailed description of the functioning of the barrel-jacket reservoir air gun, the ball-reservoir air gun, and the air cane, together with his illustrations, from his book, *A Sporting Tour Through France* (1802) are reproduced on pages 26 and 27. These constitute an excellent contemporary explanation for interested collectors.

THE AIR GUN AS A MILITARY WEAPON

Around the turn of the present century the actuality of the use of the air rifle as a military weapon was treated with extreme skepticism by many German experts of both arms and military subjects. Very little was known about such use. Most of the proponents of its military use could quote only Auguste Demmin's statement (undocumented, as was the case so often with him) that "It (the air rifle) was used in the Austrian war at the end of the 18th century and became the special weapon of many regiments." It was widely pointed out that Demmin didn't even show a drawing of such an arm, one said to be a repeater, also! Since Demmin had died a few years before (in 1898) there was no one who could defend him.

Yet there were some available proofs that the Austrians had used such air rifles at the Battle of Wagram against Napoleon Bonaparte. Most records were buried in military archives.

It is understandable that the learned German experts hadn't read Colonel Thornton's account, as his book had not been widely circulated. It is even understandable that the skeptical souls wouldn't believe this rather arrogant Englishman, who gave no facts nor sources to back up his statements, even if they knew his book! Here is the tale Thornton told in his *A Sporting Tour Through France in the Year 1802*, published in two magnificent volumes in the year 1806, a story whose highlights and accuracy have since been borne out:

> I saw, in the course of the day, several well-informed men, some of them members of the senate, with whom I conversed on the subject of the law which renders a 10 years residence in France necessary to naturalization; and they unanimously declared that the restriction was impolitic and absurd.
> I proposed that all persons buying estates to the value of ten thousand pounds, and paying the taxes for that amount, should, from the time of purchasing such property, be eligible to places of trust, and become Frenchmen.
> By order of the First Consul, I was introduced to General Mortier, who is commander in chief of the first military division. In his person he is about 6 feet 3 inches high, being nearly 50 years of age, and altogether a remarkably handsome man. His manners denote him to possess a quick and penetrating mind, and, as an officer and a gentleman, he is certainly entitled to peculiar respect. From the period of my first introduction, we were on the most intimate terms, frequently visiting and dining together. I had also an *entré libre* to his house and table, which fully enabled me to judge of his character.
> When the conversation turned upon the events of the late war, in Germany, or elsewhere, it is impossible to describe the entertainment I received; and the officers who conversed with him upon this favourite topic spoke in the most eager manner respecting the nature of the country they had fought in. Thus, for instance, they would exclaim—"This was *delicious* for cavalry, that for infantry, etc." so that they seemed to enjoy the remembrance with all the keenness of a fox-hunter who relates the tale of an extraordinary chase.
> One day in particular, General Mortier, in speaking of air guns, recalled to the recollection of some officers in the company a circumstance which happened after the retreat of the enemy, but where I cannot precisely call to mind. He said, "do you not remember when I had ordered the cannon to cease firing that an orderly sergeant who was standing close to us leaped up very high into the air and then fell down? We supposed, at first, that he was in a fit, and we were greatly astonished to find him dead, as nothing had been heard or seen to injure him. On his being undressed, however, a ball was found to have struck him, which must have been shot from an air-gun in the adjoining field and aimed at some of us."
> "Yes," replied one of the officers, "I remember it well, and I think we had a fortunate escape." They then stated,

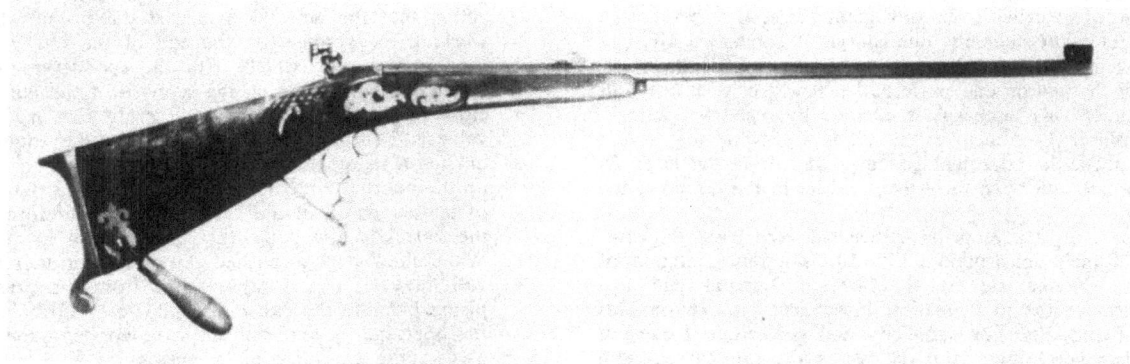

Typical Bolzenbüchse. Crank opens bellows and compresses spring. Crank is then withdrawn. When trigger is pressed the springs force the rear of the bellows violently together, compressing air down the narrow mouth of the bellows to drive the missile down the barrel.

> that on account of this treachery they hung up all that corps that fell into their hands, considering them not as soldiers, but assassins, and never after gave them any quarter. They acknowledged, at the same time, that they lost many fine men by that corps of Austrians, which they stated to consist of about five hundred men."

Perhaps Colonel Thornton's account requires some little contemporary comment at this point:

England in the year 1802 had a tremendous variety of taxes in effect. Thornton and many other wealthy Englishmen traveled to France with the hope of obtaining dual citizenship, so they could take advantage of the lower French taxes and still retain their full English privileges. The situation was similar to that today where many "operators" deal in Monaco, Tangier, Lebanon and similar areas where tax collectors are more lenient than at home. They want the national protection without the cost.

While France at that period was a far easier tax collector than was England, it is to Napoleon's credit that the good Colonel Thornton (and others) was not able to sway him.

Another comment is necessary to establish the authority of Thornton's source for his air-gun-in-war note; viz, the "General Mortier" to whom he refers was Edouard-Adolphe-Casimir-Joseph Mortier, in 1804 made a maréchal of France. He was duc de Trévise. Thornton speaks of him as then being "nearly 50 years of age." Actually Mortier was only 34 years old in 1802—but his experiences may have aged his appearance. He had

25

[FROM *A SPORTING TOUR THROUGH FRANCE*]

... The next was my air-gun*, at ninety-three yards, against their rifle. I shot within an inch of their mark, though it was not fully pumped. The day was extremely sultry, and yet my next shot was still more exact.

---

*It may not be improper, in this place, to introduce some account of the air-gun; which instrument, of the common description, is usually made of brass, and has two barrels; the inside barrel A, fig. 8. which is of a small bore, from whence the bullets are exploded; and a large barrel ECDR on the outside of it. There is a syringe SMNP fixed in the stock of the gun, by which the air is injected into the cavity between the two barrels through the valve EP. The ball K is put down into its place in the small barrel, with the rammer, as in any other gun. At SL is another valve, which, being opened by the trigger O, permits the air to come behind the bullet, so as to drive it out with great force. If this valve be opened and shut suddenly, one charge of condensed air may be sufficient for several discharges of bullets; but if the whole air be discharged on one single bullet, it will drive it out with great force. This discharge is effected by means of a lock, fig. 9. placed here as usual in other guns; for the trigger being pulled, the cock will go down and drive the lever O, fig. 8. which will open the valve, and let in the air upon the bullet K.

Air-guns of late years have received very great improvements in their construction. Fig. 10. is a representation of one made by the late Mr. B. Martin of London, and now by several of the mathematical instrument and gun-makers of the metropolis. For simplicity and perfection it exceeds any other heretofore contrived. A is the gun-barrel, with the lock, stock, ram-rod, of the size and weight of a common fowling-piece. Under the lock, at *b,* is a round steel tube, having a small moveable pin in the inside, which is pushed out when the trigger *a* is pulled, by the spring-work within the lock; to this tube *b*, a hollow copper-ball *c* screws, perfectly air-tight. This copper ball is fully charged with condensed air by the syringe B (fig. 7.) previous to its being applied to the tube *b* of fig. 10. It is then evident, if a bullet be rammed down in the barrel, the copper ball screwed fast at *b,* and the trigger *a* be pulled, that the pin in *b* will, by the action of the spring-work within the lock, forcibly strike out into the copper ball; and thereby pushing in suddenly a *valve* within the copper ball, let out a portion of the condensed air; which air will rush up through the aperture of the lock, and forcibly act against the bullet, driving it to the distance of 60 or 70 yards, or further. If the air is strongly condensed at every discharge, only a portion of the air escapes from the ball; therefore, by re-cocking the piece, another discharge may be made; and this repeated to the amount of 15 or 16 times. An additional barrel is sometimes made, and applied for the discharge of shot, instead of the one above described.

The air in the copper ball is condensed by means of the syringe B (fig. 7.), in the following manner: The ball *c* is screwed quite close on the top of the syringe at *b,* at the end of the steel-pointed rod: *a* is a stout ring through which passes the rod *k:* upon this rod the feet should be firmly set; then the hands are to be applied to the handles *ii,* fixed on the side of the barrel of the syringe. Now by moving the barrel B steadily up and down on the rod *a,* the ball *c* will become charged with condensed air; and it may be easily known when the ball is as full as possible, by the irresistible action that the air makes against the piston when you are working the syringe. At the end of the rod *k* is usually a four-square hole, which with the rod serves as a key to fasten the ball *c* fast on the screw *b* of the gun and syringe close to the orifice in the ball *c.* In the inside is fixed a valve and spring, which gives way for the admission of air; but upon its emission comes close up to the orifice, shutting up the internal air. The piston-rod works air-tight, by a collar of leather on it, in the barrel B; it is therefore plain, when the barrel is drawn up, the air will rush in at the hole *h.* When the barrel is pushed down, the air therein contained will have no other way to pass from the pressure of the piston but into the ball *c* at top. The barrel being drawn up, the operation is repeated, until the condensation is so strong as to resist the action of the piston.

Sometimes the syringe is applied to the end of the barrel C (see fig. 11,): the lock and trigger shut up in a brass case *d;* and the trigger pulled, or discharge made, by pulling the chain *b.* In this contrivance there is a round chamber for the condensed air at the end of the syringe at *e,* and it has a valve acting in a similar manner to that of the copper ball. When this instrument is not in use, the brass case *d* is made to slide off, and the instrument then becomes a walking-stick; from which circumstance, and the barrel being made of cane, brass, &c. it has received the appellation of the *air-cane.* The head of the cane unscrews and takes off at *a,* where the extremity of the piston-rod in the barrel is shown: an iron rod is placed in a ring at the end of this, and the air condensed in the barrel in a similar manner to that of the gun as above; but its force of action is not near so strong and permanent as that of the latter.

The air guns described by Thornton and reproduced on the opposite page are pictured as follows: Upper right, figure 10. Detachable ball-reservoir pattern. Note resemblance to flintlock guns of the same period except for the ball. Figure 7. Pump with ball ready for charging. Figure at lower right. The air cane. Lower left, figure 8. Barrel-jacket-reservoir air gun with built-in pump in butt.

Figure H. Bullet mold. Note that all good air guns of the period were supplied with individual bullet molds as required for that specific arm. As a result, literally thousands of calibers appear in early air arms. Any attempt to recondition and use these old-timers will be difficult and it would be impossible to get good shooting results uoless the original bullet molds were available.

(Note: Other items shown are powder arms or sporting accessories. Figure A—three-barrel pistol Thornton gave to Napoleon. Figure D—freak 14-barrel gun Thornton had made. All 14 barrels fired simultaneously. Figure F—barrel arrangement from muzzle view. Figures K and L show a simple takedown double shotgun design.)

(See opposite page)

27

served in the Netherlands and on the northern frontier. He commanded a French and Polish corps in the Ulm campaign and had particularly distinguished himself at Dürrenstein where he first encountered the air gun sharpshooters. In 1812 and 1813 Mortier was commander of Napoleon's "Young Guard." When Napoleon fled exile, Mortier was among the generals who rejoined him; but he was not at fateful Waterloo, having been taken strangely ill just before that campaign began. Mortier along with 11 others was killed at Fieschi in 1835 by a bomb hurled at Louis Philippe with whom he was riding to attend a review.

It is also quite understandable why these German experts even in the year 1900 did not know that the

published at Vienna in 1896 and drawn by him from personal contacts with members of the Girardoni family as well as from official sources; from Hauptman (Captain) Halla's *Bulletins of the Military Archives for the Year 1890* (*Mittheilungen des k.k. Kriegs-Archivs, Jahrgang* 1890); and from personal studies of these old archives by the present author many years ago.

The Austrian Repeating Air Rifle (System Girardoni) M. 1799 (Repetier Wind-Büchse (Sistem Girardoni) 1799)

This rifle, officially the Model 1799, was used in battle to a considerable degree as a sharpshooter's weapon; and specimens made in 1780 are often cataloged

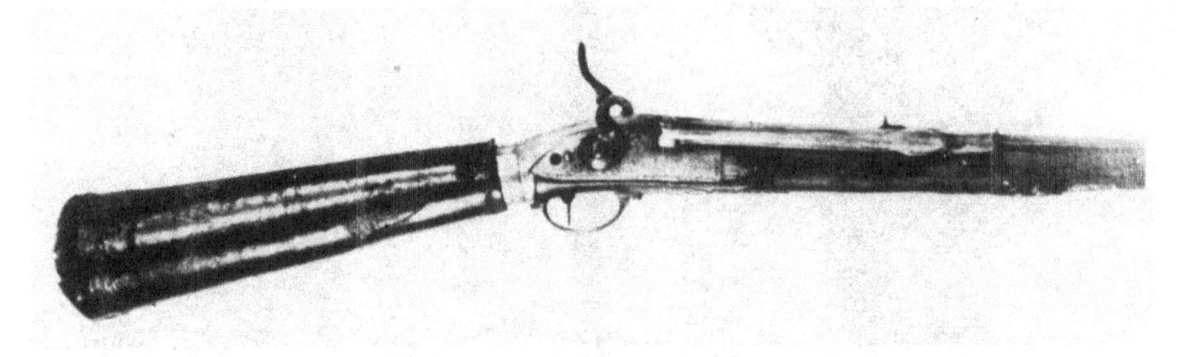

Austrian repeating air rifle, Model 1799. Originally made by the designer, M. Girardoni, it was later made under maximum security by Contriner and several other Austrian gunmakers.

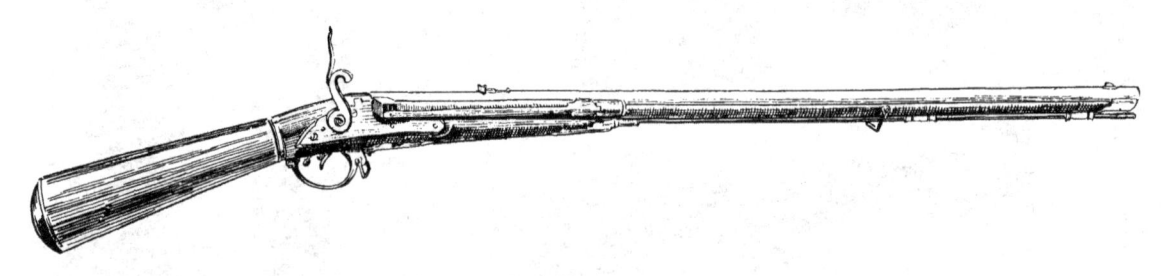

Original Austrian service drawing of the Model 1799 Austrian service repeating rifle used against Napoleon at the Battle of Wagram. This was a secret weapon issued only to sharpshooters who were under top security regulations.

French in 1799 and 1780 had been under instructions from the First Consul (that is, Napoleon Bonaparte) to execute all enemy soldiers found in possession of air guns. After all, that was still by way of being a French "military secret" even though it had happened a good hundred years before!

Evidently the learned German arguers had never heard of Poe's *Purloined Letter*—for right under their eyes was proof positive that air rifles had been military arms, officially adopted. For the Berlin Armory (Das Berliner Zeughaüs) had at that very time a group of cataloged air arms which included an Austrian weapon bearing the service designation "Repeating Air Rifle M. 1780"!

This rifle, designed by Girardoni, is still little known and less understood. As a matter of historical record, therefore, the general background will be set forth here. For sources we have drawn on A. Dolleczek's little known *Monograph of the Imperial-Royal Austro-Hungarian Weapons* (*Monographie der k.k. oster. ungar. Waffen*),

by museums and collectors as "M. 1780" because of manufacturing date.

The caliber was officially 12.8 mm. (.499 inch). Barrel was 122 cm. (47.58 inches) and was rifled with 12 grooves in what today would be called "microgrooving." The rifle weighed 3.8 kilos. (8.36 pounds). It cost 33 gulden.

To the rear of the barrel was the action and valve housing made of brass. The screw type cast iron or sheet metal butt was leather covered and was actually a hollow "flask" which formed the air reservoir. In later models the front of the flask is brazed, the shoulder section folded over, and the unit copper plated against rust.

The tube magazine for the bullets was positioned on the right side of the receiver forward of the cock (hammer). Bullets were loaded into the magazine from its front end through a swiveled spring cover.

The magazine was fed by gravity. When the muzzle

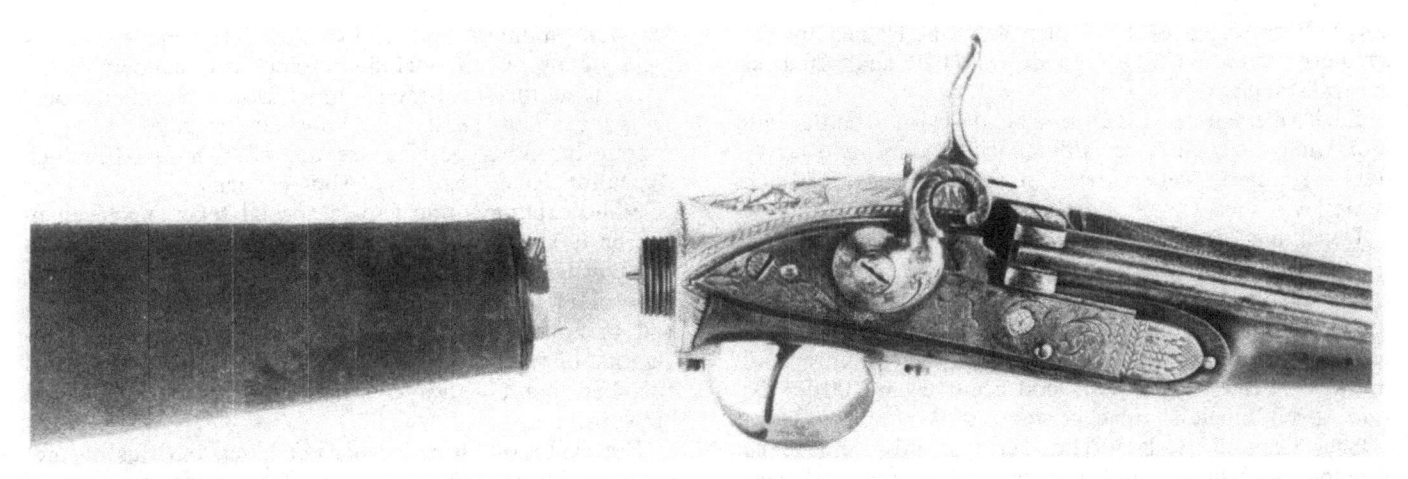

Austrian Model 1799 made and decorated by Contriner. This is an officer's rifle. Butt flask is detached. Valve stem seen projecting from rear of lock.

was held in up position, the first ball rested against a cross-sliding breechblock held normally to the right by a support spring. The hammer was now drawn back to full cock. The breechblock slide was pushed in against its spring to the left. It carried with it the first ball nesting in a hole in the block. (Note: This hole passed through the block so the soldier could see that the gun was ready for chamber loading; but was tapered to the rear to prevent the bullet dropping out the rear of the breechblock.)

Pressing the trigger released the hammer to momentarily open the escape valve and allow a blast of high pressure air to drive the bullet out the barrel. As the tight fitting sliding breechblock was automatically spring-locked when in barrel line-up position, air escape was negligible at first. (Note: Later the difficulty of maintaining the tolerances rendered the weapon comparatively useless. This and valve trouble eventually outmoded the design.)

The breechblock release on the left side of the receiver was now pressed. The return spring moved the breechblock back to the right in line with the magazine. The muzzle was again raised to allow the balls in the tube to move down by gravity, the first one seating in the tapered hole in the breechblock. The arm was again ready to be cocked and to have the block pressed to the left for line-up for the next shot.

(Note: It is interesting to note here that in recent years the Crosman Arms Company marketed a pneumatic repeater somewhat on this principle! The tube magazine was on the left side, the block was operated by the cocking piece and was moved over to pick up successive bullets, gravity fed.)

The maximum pump-up pressure was of the order of 33 atmospheres (an atmosphere being a conventional unit of measure equal to about 15 pounds at sea level). This required about 2000 strokes of the conventional pump, usually by two men. Pauses had to be made due to the heat generated. The wagon pumps, heavy duty affairs, had a water-coolant device and a spoked-wheel pumping arrangement.

The butt-flasks were normally hand pumped up to pressures as high as 400 foot-pounds. This air charge was normally sufficient for some 40 shots, but pressures fell off so rapidly that in actual field use the flasks were replaced after 20 shots had been fired.

Initially 4 men in each company were armed with these "secret" weapons. However, they proved so successful for close-range fighting where cover was available that in 1790 the Army set up a special air-rifle

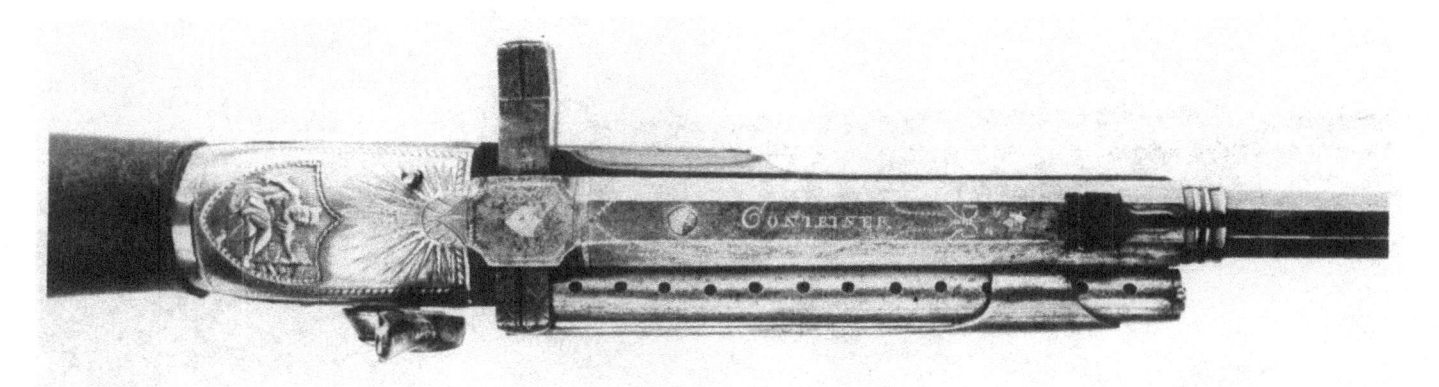

Austrian Model 1799 officer's rifle made and decorated by Contriner of Vienna. Holes in top of magazine allowed check on number of bullets at all times. Bullets fed down by gravity to the cross-slide. Pushing the slide to the left fed a bullet into line for firing. When slide lock was released a spring returned the slide and magazine tube to feeding position. Hammer was thumb-cocked for each shot.

corps. It consisted of 1300 men and was trained by the Freiherr von Mack, a captain on the quartermaster general's staff.

Each rifleman carried 2 to 4 air flasks into battle with him, while carts carrying additional flasks and two heavy duty air pumps were carried in support carts for each company.

Depending upon pressures and types of shooting required, the rifles are said to have been used at distances from 150 to 400 paces. As to their effectiveness, there are few records but many traditions. (Contemporary tests with two reconditioned rifles of this type, a Girardoni and a Contriner, gave very good accuracy at 100 yards; but proved hopelessly inaccurate at 200.)

Says Captain Halla: "The fact that this remarkable weapon nevertheless did not remain in use and was removed as expendable supply to the fortress of Olmutz in 1815 was due not only to the changed tactical principles, but chiefly to the circumstance that there were no adequately trained riflesmiths available to take care of the delicate component parts of the locks and valves, and therefore the percentage of unusable air rifles shown in the reports was frighteningly high."

It is interesting to note, however, that in 1848 and 1849, during the Czech and Hungarian revolt, the serviceable air rifles at Olmutz Armory were withdrawn by order of Emperor Franz Josef, then 18 years old, and issued for temporary service. (Note: In this connection it might be pointed out that even today there are very few general gunsmiths who are capable of servicing the common American varieties of compressed air guns. Most of the factory repair men with whom this author has discussed the subject, all stressed the fact that most of their troubles stemmed from owners misusing the arms or from average gunsmiths butchering them! "Keep screwdrivers out of the hands of owners and we'd have very little trouble with returns," is the way one manufacturing expert succinctly expressed it. We can well understand, therefore, the troubles the Austrians encountered 150 years ago!)

The designer, C. G. Girardoni, was a most efficient and prolific maker of all types of firearms and air arms for both military and civilian use. He made various types of air pistols, including some with bellows in the grips, used for short-range target work. He made some shotguns about 1814, and sporting air rifles in 1815. Among his other designs are the 1776 model Flintlock Repeating Rifle, also of 12-shot capacity.

While experimenting with a special repeating mechanism on a 15-mm. hunting rifle, the priming flash ignited the powder magazine. (This remember was before the days of metallic cartridges, and each propelling charge had to be set off by an individual flash which the inventors of the time tried to confine to the individual chamber charge—always with eventual powder magazine blowups.)

The explosion shredded his left hand, but this did not deter the inventor. With the aid of an artificial iron hand he had attached to the arm stump, Girardoni went back to work on the magazine principle; but applied it now to use with compressed air. Girardoni's great-great-grandson wrote to Dollcezek: "This was the origin of the air rifle which, with its smokeless and almost soundless shot, was used by the Austrian army for more than 35 years."

The Austrians treated the development as a real "secret weapon." A special shop was set up for Girardoni, and workers were specially selected and sworn to a secrecy about equivalent to that required for an H-Bomb "Q" clearance today.

It should be mentioned in passing that the Girardoni pattern was produced by other makers on contract. Then, even as now, Austria was a hotbed of *small* gunmakers who were good at duplication. In 1956 the giant Steyr works has two factories operating with an employment roll of some 20,000 men—and that plant, to the average American shooter who knows the fine quality of their Mannlicher-Schoenauer rifles, is the epitome of firearms quality. However, Steyr today is basically a roller bearing and farm equipment maker, and this author is constantly amazed at finding so many American gunmakers so ill-informed that they are frightened at the size of the Steyr payroll.

As a matter of record, fewer than 200 men are employed in manufacturing firearms there! At the same time,

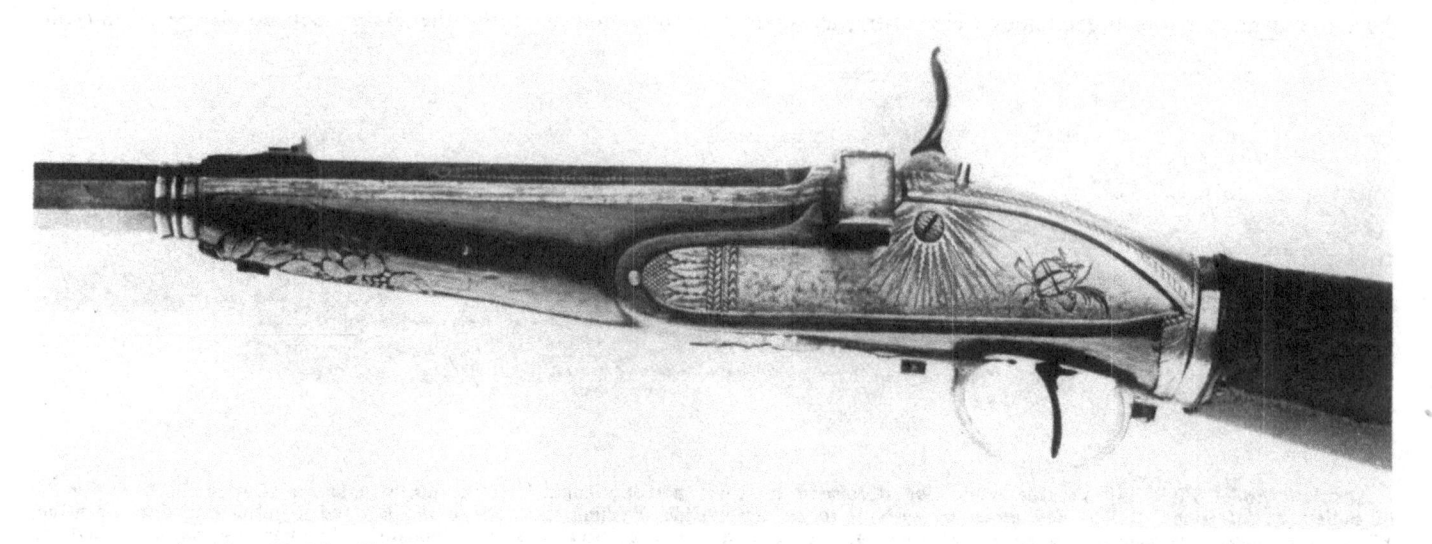

Austrian Model 1799 by Contriner. Pin in line with trigger is the feed and breechblock release catch.

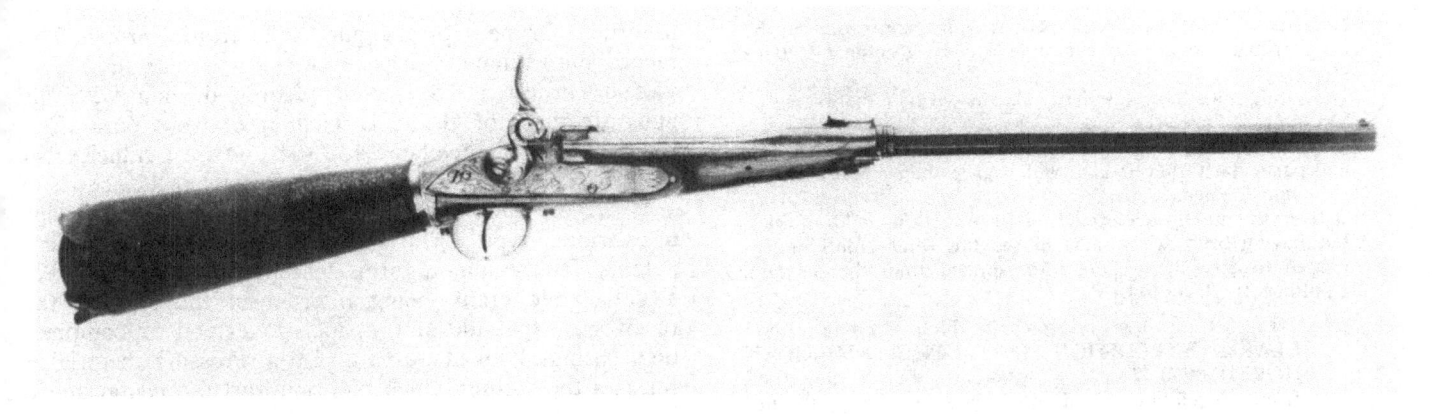

Austrian Model 1799 officer's rifle by Contriner. The butt flask is leather covered.

there are literally scores of fine, small gunmaking and gun-decorating plants in operation in Austria.

The Girardoni 1799 pattern air rifle was also made by Contriner (later noted for his magnificently ornamented arms), Fruwirth (later the developer of some dozen weird magazine rifle systems), Lowenz (noted for fine hunting arms), and many others. For years after the government contracts expired, all these makers produced air arms in various calibers and styles of decorations—single-shot, over-unders, and repeaters; but all borrowed heavily from the first Girardoni.

As we have learned from Colonel Thornton, General Mortier encountered the Girardoni about the year 1800. The next time Napoleon's men faced it (and recognized it) was in the Tyrolean campaign in 1808-1809.

Marshal Lefebre, apparently panic stricken by the discovery that silent rifles were being employed against him, reported the fact by courier to Napoleon, who immediately issued an order to shoot or hang without trial, and with no pardon given, any man found armed with an air rifle.

Actually the toll of the air rifle was probably insignificant, but the strain of the terrible blood letting finally panicked most of the soldiers and officers engaged; and, indeed, except for the stony presence of Napoleon himself on the field of Deutsch Wagram on the momentous 5th and 6th of July, 1809, it is doubtful if the French would have continued the fight.

The psychological impact of the announcement of the use of silent guns on Napoleon's soldiers at that time cannot be underestimated.

In this day and age few pause to think of that deadly campaign and the crucial battle fought just 11 or 12 miles from Vienna. That was the day of massed charges and McDonald's French hollow square which the Austrians slaughtered. The Austrians spread 120,000 men along a 12-mile front which was compacted to six. Napoleon threw in 181,700 men against Archduke Charles' numerically inferior forces. When the battle ended, the French counted 23,000 dead and wounded and 7,000 missing. The Austrians lost 19,110 and 6,740 missing according to reliable statistics. No modern battle approaches that percentage of casualties.

These facts are set forth not to "debunk" the value of the air rifle in this war. Psychologically at least it had a considerable impact at the moment. But the interest in air guns is steadily growing in the United States, and inevitably some well-meaning but ill-informed legislator is going to point with alarm to the "dangers" of a type which was once a military weapon. This author hopes that the presentation here made will be accurately informative.

Literally scores of air rifles of the Girardoni pattern have been encountered by the author. They range from simple copies to the most elaborate alterations imaginable. The famous Austrian gunmaker of the day, Contriner of Vienna, in particular, produced magnificently made, inlaid and engraved specimens.

Often the Girardoni action will be encountered used on an air shotgun, or on a rifle different from the military caliber. Sometimes it will be used as a single-shot air rifle or gun.

The explanation gained by the author from a study of Austrian records, and the arms themselves, may clear up some misconceptions on the subject. It is basically the "war surplus" story. Just as at the end of our own wars obsolete guns and actions found their way into used-gun dealers and export channels, so with the Girardonis. In our own day we find Springfield and Enfield and Mauser actions made up into various types and classes of rifles by everybody from Griffin & Howe on down. Besides the hundreds of gunsmiths who made stocks and supplied special caliber barrels for such arms, thousands of ex-GI's "built their own" on these actions.

Exactly the same thing happened (on a lesser scale, of course) with the Girardoni rifles and spare parts—they were bought up and assembled by later makers. In addition to this, as pointed out elsewhere herein, Contriner and many of the other good gun makers of that day also duplicated the Girardoni from government supplied prints when the Austrian army needed rush supplies which the original maker could not turn out—just as Rock Island, Remington, and others made "Springfield" rifles when needed.

EARLY HISTORY OF THE AIR GUN IN AMERICA

They had indeed abundant sources of surprise in all they saw, the appearance of the men, their arms, their clothing, the canoes, the strange looks of the Negro, and the sagacity of our dog, all in turn shared their admiration, which was raised to astonishment by a shot from the air gun; this operation was instantly considered as a great medicine, by which they as well as the other Indians mean something emanating directly from the Great Spirit, or produced by his invisible and incomprehensible agency. (Volume I, Page 409-410.)

The air gun, too, was fired, and astonished them greatly. (Volume I, Page 41.)

In the evening we exhibited different objects of curiosity, and particularly the air gun, which gave them great surprise. (Volume I, Page 51.)

Everything they see excites their attention and inquiries, but having been accustomed to see the whites, nothing appeared to give them more astonishment than the air gun. (Volume II, Page 144.)

> Entries in the records of THE LEWIS AND CLARK EXPEDITION INTO THE AMERICAN NORTHWEST IN 1804-5 AND 6. Direct quotations from the edition edited by Paul Allen, and published in Philadelphia, Pa., in January, 1814. References to the effect of an air gun carried by the expedition upon the Indian tribes encountered.

Curiously enough, the records of the Lewis & Clark expedition, while they carried all the foregoing entries, at no point identified or described the gun as to make, caliber, or operating system. In recent years some attempts have been made at identifying the gun; but the record above tells about all that we really know concerning it.

The Indians at that time were quite familiar with firearms and their use, having purchased them from traders. The air gun used obviously approximated the outward appearance of the guns of the time, and the Indians expected it to make "thunder and fire." Astonished and frightened when the bullet struck without benefit of noise

to order. Or perhaps the gun came from Europe. The record unfortunately gives us no hint or clue.

The earliest U. S. patent records dealing with air guns are those of G. W. B. Gedney of New York City, No. 33344 of September 24, 1861 and E. Lindner, also of New York City, No. 37173 of December 12, 1862.

However, there are known American-made specimens of various types which considerably antedate these patents. The common forms tend to be crank-operated, a detachable crank being inserted in the side of the receiver or the side of the stock to extend or compress dual springs hooked up to a piston. Pressing the trigger releases the springs which pull or thrust the piston ahead into an iron or brass syringe cylinder, compressing the air and giving a velocity of several hundred feet per second to the bullet. Such types are usually based on older German forms, knowingly or not. Calibers encountered range from .28 to as high as .40. Most of these arms are breechloaders. In the common form, the barrel and attached fore-end swing to the right for loading. Many such guns are products of the percussion period, though most are of a later date. Some are occasionally encountered with magazine feeds. All are fine examples of gun art.

Most early American air arms were spring operated— the "pump-up" system was just too much work in the era of rapid cartridge development in this country. And it still is, for that matter, as we shall see further on.

On June 1, 1869 a patent was granted to E. H. Hawley of Kalamazoo, Michigan, for what was probably the first successful American compressed-air arm to see

Austrian Army Repeating Flintlock Rifle. One of these blew the right hand off its designer, Girardoni. The Austrian Model 1799 Air Rifle was developed from this flintlock.

and flash, the simple Red Man immediately saw in the air gun the hand of the Great Spirit. What hunting use was made of the arm as they traveled through hostile country or what pacifying effect the gun had on Indians to whom it was demonstrated, the journals unfortunately do not tell us; but if the imagination is allowed to wander, one might see great value to the Lewis & Clark expedition in their air gun.

This Lewis & Clark air gun may have been American made, for we had many expert custom gunmakers at that time who were capable of building such arms—men who had learned their trade in Germany, Austria, and England, where high-powered air guns then had considerable vogue. Philadelphia, Boston, Albany, Geneva all had small shops where any type of known gun could be made

production. Usually in pistol form with offset sights, the Hawley could be fitted with a metal shoulder stock for use as a rifle. While it had considerable power, it was basically a dart-type arm for amusement, not a serious air weapon. However, it was accurate enough for short-range indoor shooting, and its use as a trainer was recommended by various Army officials.

Pope pistols on a spring variation of the Hawley pattern were made in Boston as early as 1870, as witness photographs of the specimen herewith, though patents were not applied for for several years after manufacture was undertaken. Even today this Pope is a rugged, easy-cocking, hard-and-straight-shooting pistol of its type. It, too, has a butt hole for a wire shoulder stock, by the way. Pulling the barrel forward compresses the piston

American Hawley compressed-air pistol with hammer down and breech open for loading chamber. The sleeve around the breech is turned and pushed forward to expose the chamber.

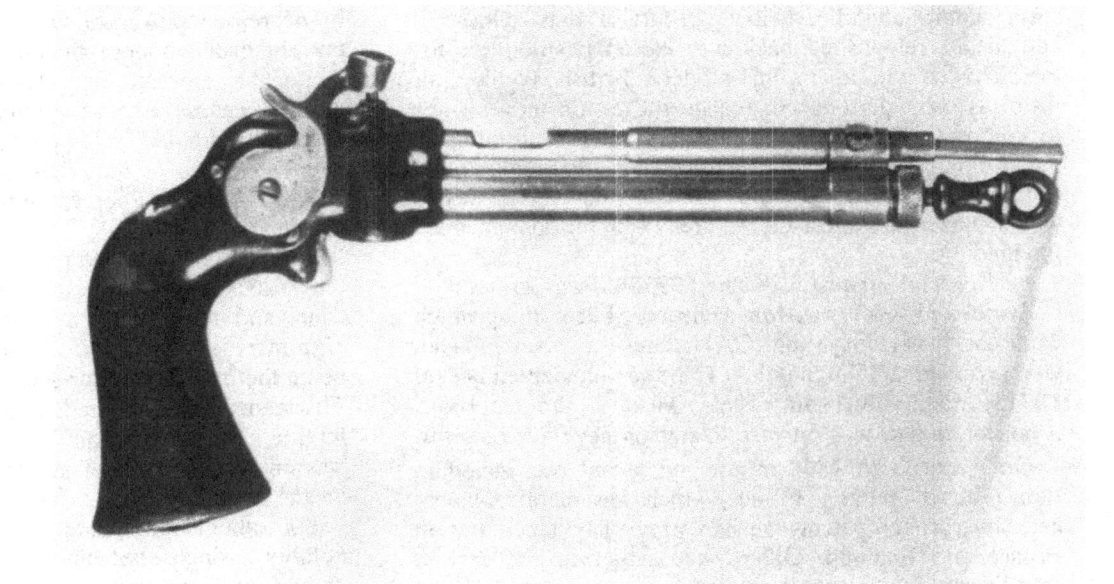

H. M. Quackenbush, Herkimer, N. Y. Patented July 19, 1881. This is representative of all the Quackenbush line except the barrel cockers. This is cocked by pushing in the barrel as in the earlier Pope pistol.

American Pope. Breech closed ready to fire. This pistol was one recommended for military training use by General Sherman after the Civil War.

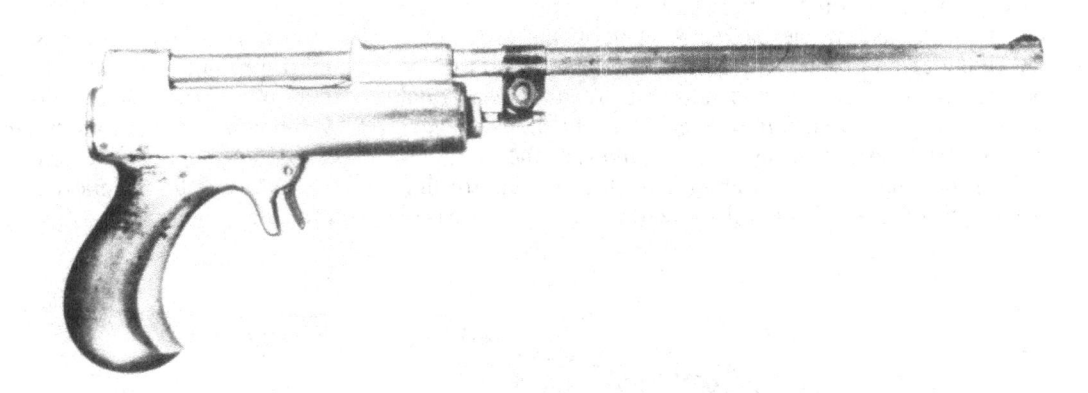

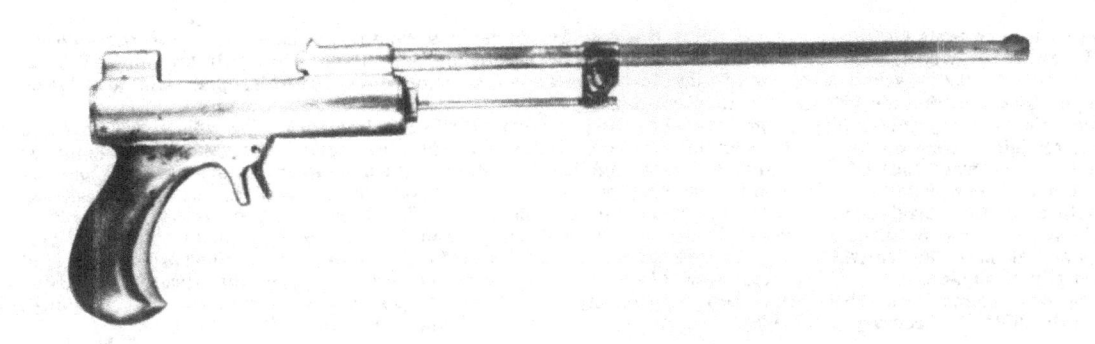

American Pope. Barrel pulled forward to load. Pushing barrel in cocked the mainspring which powered the air piston.

33

spring in the chamber below. A dart or ball is inserted and the barrel pushed back into closed position for firing. The action, as in the modern British Webley air pistol, is a bit disconcerting since the piston moves *back* to compress the air in the cylinder, giving an unusual recoil effect. It has several features not commonly found even in expensive air arms today, such as a design which makes it impossible to fire when the gun is open for loading.

In 1870 an air-pistol patent (99754) was granted to R. Brooks of Rockport, Massachusetts, but nothing much came of it. Hawley and G. H. Snow of New Haven were granted a joint patent (118,886) in September of 1871 for still other air pistols. Most of the emphasis, it will be noted, was on *pistols,* not on air *rifles* or *guns.*

On February 9, 1864 an air gun patent was issued to Paul Giffard of Paris, France, which was merely American coverage of patents he had previously taken out in France and England. Giffard, the father of the carbon dioxide gun, as we shall see later, was a pioneer in the field of general pneumatics at this period, though none of his arms were manufactured here or achieved any success in our market.

Nevertheless, Giffard's ideas in several instances were forerunners of things to come; some were impractical while others were just too advanced for the technology of his time to be successful. The U. S. patents granted him February 25, 1873 (No. 136315-16) are a case in point.

These deal with several items. First, a pneumatic (pump-up) breechloader, single-shot, a type which did not see production here until the 20th century. The breechpiece rotated by lever quite as in most of the strictly modern pneumatics and CO_2 guns. The air chamber was below the barrel. A valve in the end of the air chamber controlled the air release. The valve spindle passed through guides and was hit by a conventional hammer (which was manually cocked) when the trigger was pressed. An adjustable stop allowed the hammer fall to be increased or diminished, thereby controlling the length of time of the valve opening—giving increased or decreased power at will. Most of these features are current in all modern pneumatic rifles, guns, and pistols in one form or another. They are successful today primarily because of our ability to hold closer tolerance than Giffard could in his production, and also because we have better valve materials than were available to him in 1873. Just another example of an inventor ahead of his time!

Another device covered was "a compressed-air defense stick." This was a somewhat *unconventional* air cane, and this author has seen only one specimen. As customary, it unscrewed into two sections, the front being the barrel, the rear section housing the air chamber. This cane, however, had a "built-in" pump, an unusual feature. The valve from the air chamber to the barrel was operated by a bolt actuated by a small thumb lever on the barrel section.

Still other Giffard patents covered a few weird items—notably a single-shot air "cartridge" which is of interest in its loose resemblance to the CO_2 "cartridges" of today. Air was compressed into a metal thimble which was inserted in the gun and was needle pierced as the hammer fell, allowing the compressed-air charge to propel the bullet. Unlike the modern CO_2 device, of course, it gave up its entire charge at each hammer fall. A CO_2 cartridge will give from 40 to several hundred discharges depending upon its "cartridge" capacity, but is initially pierced by the first hammer fall.

In 1871, in patent 115,638 issued June 6th, we encounter for the first time another remarkable American inventor and business genius upon whom we must dwell for a moment, H. M. Quackenbush.

The Quackenbush Air Guns

Henry Marcus Quackenbush more than any one man is responsible for the earliest development of toy air guns and pistols here and abroad, and also for the development of mass-manufactured serious air guns for short-range target and small-game shooting.

Like so many pioneers of his time, little is known of him today—and less of what he made and what he ac-

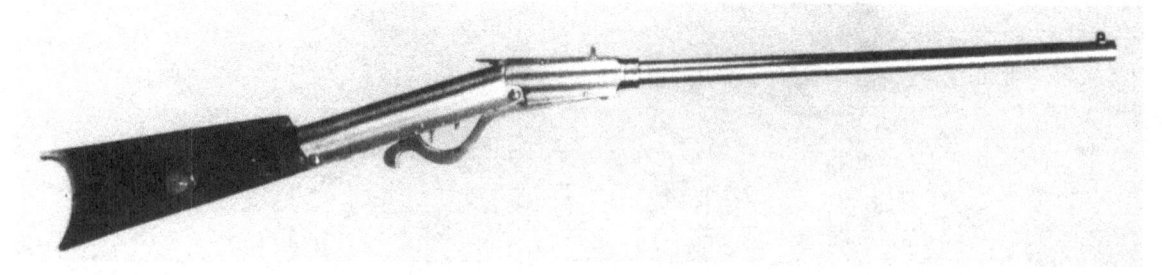

Typical Quackenbush combination air-and-cartridge rifle originally designed by Haviland & Gunn. Specimens are from the author's collection and are dated 1871 and 1878. Models vary only in minor details. As a spring-air gun, these rifles will fire old TT shot, No. 21½ darts, or felted slugs. Due to the powerful spring used, they will penetrate about one-inch of white pine and at 60 feet are as accurate as any average modern spring-air rifle in the medium-price groups.

To use as a .22 cartridge rifle, a heavy metal plug is provided in a hinged receptacle in the buttstock. The rifle is broken down on its hinge for cocking and a retaining screw on top of the standing breech is backed off. The plug (which serves as a firing hammer) is inserted in the air opening in the forward face of the standing breech and the top screw tightened down. A standard .22 powder cartridge is then inserted in the chamber, below which is an extracting pin, which is mechanically elevated as the gun is opened. The action is closed, the snaplock on the barrel closing automatically into its seat in the standing breech. When the trigger is pulled, the piston and spring are released in standard air-gun fashion. However, the air compressed by the moving piston plunger drives the floating hammer plug forward to strike the cartridge case over its entire head. This striking system is very efficient in firing, but since the hammer plug is basically unsupported, the empty .22 case blows back violently enough to swell the case head. Using modern high-velocity .22 long rifle ammunition, these guns proved perfectly safe, though the cases were sometimes swollen enough to make opening the gun a little difficult. Accuracy is excellent, as the barrels were well-rifled even in 1871.

34

complished. We can merely touch here on the highlights of his air-gun work.

With the granting of his patent, Quackenbush started manufacture of toy air pistols in the little New York town of Herkimer. The first factory was in a one-story building. The working force was Quackenbush and one helper. He was his own sales force, too. The "factory" was 10 by 15 feet. By the fall of 1871 he had so many orders on hand that he was able to borrow $1500 as capital—quite a feat in itself in those days. He took larger quarters, bought a 4-horse steam engine, upped his working staff to 4 men, improved his product, and widened his sales.

By 1874 he had built a new factory, a two-story frame structure, 70 x 30 feet, across from the operating one and there undertook manufacture of air-gun ammunition as well as guns and pistols. This was a stroke of genius. Like the later Gillette, whose blades fit scores of razors, his slugs and darts fitted most of the air arms of the time.

His darts and slugs were so superior, as were his methods of manufacture, that he was granted patent protection in England and on the Continent. English patent 3448 of October 4, 1875 covered his darts. But far more important was No. 765 of February 23, 1876 which covered slugs *and their manufacture*. Mass produced slugs then were poor in themselves and dies were costly. Even more important, barrel dimensions varied so much that a "universal" slug was needed. Quackenbush had a trick here which made him master of the precision slug until years later when the Germans developed the current "Diabolo" pattern of spool shape and until mass barrel drilling, reaming, and rifling became the nearly exact operations they are today.

These early slugs were pointed, cylindrical, and made of lead. Upon the periphery of the slug body were a series of thin, shallow burrs or ribs. His patents covered use of these ribs for longitudinal, spiral, or oblique direction to the axis of the slug. These ribs did more than merely make an air tight fit to improve velocity and striking energy of the slug itself. They actually allowed use in *off-dimension barrels* which were then common.

His method of manufacture was by compression in steel dies, which were expensive to use on standard slugs because they wore in and gave off-size slugs with metals then used. By employing ribs, he was able to make his dies of smaller bore than the gun barrel to start manufacture; and as the dies wore in and the bodies of the slugs correspondingly enlarged, the ribs flattened down when inserted in the air rifle to compensate accordingly. The ribs gave a dimensional flexibility which allowed them to be used successfully even in poorly bored barrels, and for a time he enjoyed a near monopoly. Later felted slugs were introduced for further sealing. Quackenbush's patent protection was so sound that it was very nearly a violation for any other air-bullet maker to even look at a lead pig.

Meanwhile two remarkable mechanics and designers —but poor businessmen—had developed some worthwhile air gun and pistol designs on which everybody but they made money. These two, Benjamin Haviland and G. P. Gunn, had sold rights to Quackenbush on a toy air pistol developed in 1865. Then they had tried to market, under their own names, a very powerful break-open rifle which was quite revolutionary at the time. It achieved through leverage and the positioning of the syringe, piston, and spring an ultra-compact design equaling in power the best crank-and-lever air guns of the day. The basic design trick lay in positioning the spring and piston in a long tube which formed an oversized pistol grip, giving a very ungainly appearance but allowing spring compression which is not surpassed by the finest modern designs made in England and Germany today! (No such high-power spring types are made in the U.S. at the time of this writing.)

This rifle has been so often erroneously attributed to German designers and to Quackenbush personally that the author feels some documentation is required at this point to establish the true identities of the developers. Reproduced herewith, therefore, is a page from the

ILLUSTRATED CATALOGUE   65

SPRINGFIELD MUZZLE-LOADING MILITARY RIFLES.

Calibre 58, with bayonets, ... $5 00
Same, calibre 69, with bayonets, ... 2 00

HAVILAND & GUNN'S AIR RIFLE.

No Crank! No Lever! No Pumping!

LOADS AT BREECH BY LETTING DOWN BARREL.

No. 1. Using cartridges, darts, or shot, ... $25 00
" 2. Smooth-bore, same style, for darts or shot only,   22 00
" 3. Same style, brass-lined barrel, " " "   20 00
" 4. Parlor Air Gun, all metal, skeleton stock, brass-lined barrel,
    for darts or shot, ... 7 50

Length of gun, 29 inches. Calibre of all the above is 22/100. Darts, per doz., 75 cents. Felted shot, $1 per 1,000. Target for shot or darts, with bell, $6.

The No. 1 uses the regular 22/100 rim-fire cartridge, and is a very accurate rifle for 100 yards. The barrels of these rifles are made by Remington & Sons. The beauty of this rifle is that it can be used in the parlor with darts or shot, which it throws with great accuracy from 50 to 75 feet, and also as an out-door shooting gun, second to none of that calibre.

QUACKENBUSH'S AIR RIFLE.

The best Air Rifle made for the money, shoots darts or slugs. Loads by pushing in the barrel. Just the thing for shooting galleries, or practicing in the parlor. Each gun is neatly boxed with 6 darts, 6 paper targets, 100 slugs, with dart claw and wrench.

PRICES.

Browned Frame-plated Barrel, ... $7 50
Full Nickel-plated, ... 8 00
Extra darts, per doz., ... 0 75
" Slugs, per 1,000, ... 1 50
" Paper Targets, per 100, ... 0 50

This gun was later produced under the name "Quackenbush 1½." It was sold under the Haviland & Gunn name as shown by this catalog in 1876. British patents were granted to a German firm covering the design in 1886 (British patent 4413). Quackenbush licensed several German firms to manufacture. Evidently, the foreign patent offices knew nothing of Haviland & Gunn's prior invention.

original 1876 catalog of James Bown & Son of Pittsburgh—a firm still in business, by the way—showing and describing the gun clearly under its original name, the Haviland & Gunn. Below it is pictured a typical Quackenbush, a gun which really established the air rifle in the United States. Not quite a toy. Yet not quite a serious target air gun.

The H&G gun later appeared under the Quackenbush name when the two sold out their patents and assets to him. It will be noted that the rifle was also advertised as using "regular 22/100 rim-fire cartridges." This was then a popular name for the .22 short cartridge which Smith & Wesson had developed.

Unless one has actually examined the rifle or is familiar with German and English patents involved, the method of operation is a puzzle. How does one fire powder cartridges, air darts, and air slugs all in the same gun?

The answer is simple, when you know it! The gun is opened by releasing the top catch and "breaking" the barrel down on its hinge to cock the powerful piston spring in the grip area of the stock. If it is to be used as an *air rifle* for slugs or darts, a steel chamber liner is inserted in a space in the receiver to the rear of the barrel, while a plug with an air passage vent is inserted in the standing face of the breech section. Leather washers give an airtight fit. Pulling the trigger releases the spring. The spring drives the piston ahead in the cylinder. The air compressed ahead of the piston is driven through the vent to propel the dart or slug inserted in the liner.

To use as a *cartridge rifle* (with bullet or shot), the gun is opened. It is of course cocked thereby. The liner is removed. It is replaced by a unit which resembles the so-called "supplemental chambers" used early in the present century. This chamber carries, however, a loose firing pin. The air plug with vent is removed. When the trigger is pulled, the head of the spring-driven *piston* hits the firing pin to discharge the cartridge.

This device was granted an English patent (4413 of March 29, 1886) in the name of Flurscheim & Bergmann, trading as "Eisenwerke" who made the gun in Germany for some time under license from Quackenbush, hence much of the confusion. Other German makers also operated under license.

It will be noted in the accompanying reproduction from an international German arms catalog of 1910, that even there it was in this form sold under the Quackenbush name. This was a stipulation of the license.

Haviland & Gunn were unable to sell their powerful rifle because the price was too high, for one thing. Twenty-five dollars in 1876, a date well before income taxes and when day laborers were lucky to get two dollars a day pay, was a *very* high price. Another strike against them was the fact that cartridge .22 rifles were cheap, restrictions were few, and, except in the largest cities, one could fire a .22 without danger to the rest of the scattered population.

The gun under the Quackenbush name was made in Germany under license and sold under that name, as

4413. Arbenz, A., [*Flurscheim & Bergmann*, (trading as "*Eisenwerke*")]. March 29. [1886

Pneumatic small-arms.—The gun is made to fire darts and projectiles, or ordinary shot and ball cartridges. The general construction of the arm is of the ordinary drop-down kind, but in the action face a recess is made for a plug. When firing darts and projectiles, a lining-tube A is fitted into the barrel, and a plug B, with a small central opening for the passage of the compressed air, is placed in the recess in the action face. Leather washers C make the joints tight. For firing ordinary cartridges, the liner is removed and the plug is replaced by another with a loose firing-pin, which is struck by the piston in the air chamber when the trigger is pulled, and so fires the cartridge.

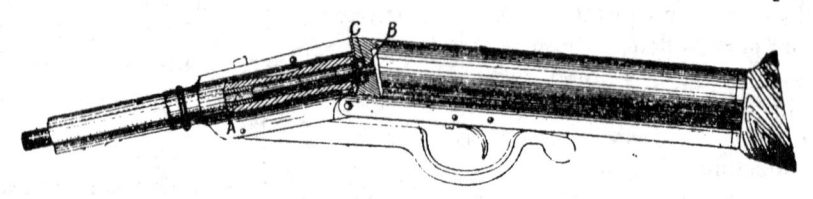

Abstract of original British patent.

has been stated. Why did it sell abroad? There at the time factories were better tooled than here, and wages were even lower. However, the matter of range of the .22 powder rifle was even then a worrisome factor, and a production-pattern, reasonably high-powered air gun, with range short enough for safe general shooting and indoor use, met an immediate European acceptance. There were laws against powder arms, but these precision air rifles were acceptable. All German air guns prior to that had been either Nuremberg toys or expensive hand-crafted rifles, which the average little man could not afford.

By far the most important maker of serious target air guns in the world from 1900 to 1915 and both before and after World War II was the "Diana" manufacturers, von Mayer & Grammelspacher at Rastatt. At this time they are again in the forefront, production-wise at least, in that field. This firm, and in fact the entire German air-gun industry, on a *production-gun basis* stems directly from the development and merchandising genius of H. M. Quackenbush and his long-forgotten inventors, Haviland and Gunn with an assist from the later American "Daisy." The earliest serious "Diana" guns were made on a slight variation of Quackenbush's patents. The early Diana toys follow the Daisy pattern. Much of the production know-how he later developed in the drowsy little New York town of Herkimer—and it was considerable—Quackenbush passed on to German licensees.

Quackenbush began manufacture of the H&G design under his name late in 1876 and personally handled marketing both here and in England and Germany. The

"Diana" works was founded in 1890. The dates and early catalogs tell the rest of the story.

The *History of Herkimer County, N. Y.* published in 1879 tells us that "The business was begun by H. M. Quackenbush, in whose hands it has always been and remains." That sentence might almost be his epitaph. Quackenbush rifles were still listed in gun sales catalogs in the early 1920's, though during World War I the production facilities had been turned in other directions. The business was the type that could function only under the control of one iron-willed man; and that, Henry Marcus Quackenbush certainly was!

The Dutch Quackenbush family, among the old settlers of early "Niew Amsterdam," had a family motto to which H. M. constantly aspired. It translates from the Latin "Peace of mind through prosperity." We know he enjoyed prosperity. We hope he also enjoyed the peace of mind. But mottoes to the contrary, the two don't necessarily go together.

The period 1870 to 1900 saw a rash of patents in the air-gun field in the U.S., most of which were of the toy or low-power varieties. One C. Robinson from Boston patented a "gun arrow for spring or air launching." A St. Louis man named Sperry dreamed up a "toy" harpoon gun! Bedford, Carey, Cross, Bye, Pope, Quackenbush, Walker—those were a few of the inventors. Iver Johnson and M. Bye from Fitchburg, Massachusetts patented here and abroad various air pistols, some of which were just too far ahead of their time for acceptance.

Iver Johnson, still an honored name in the field of low priced firearms, had air-gun models which were forerunners in many ways of the successful English air pistol first introduced by Webley & Scott in 1924, still one of the best of the spring-air arms. It was barrel cocked, the barrel hinging up from the breech to cock and to allow loading. One of Bedford's 1876 designs had a push-type plunger, a tapered chamber and bolt; and was in many ways the forerunner of some of the cheap Quacken-

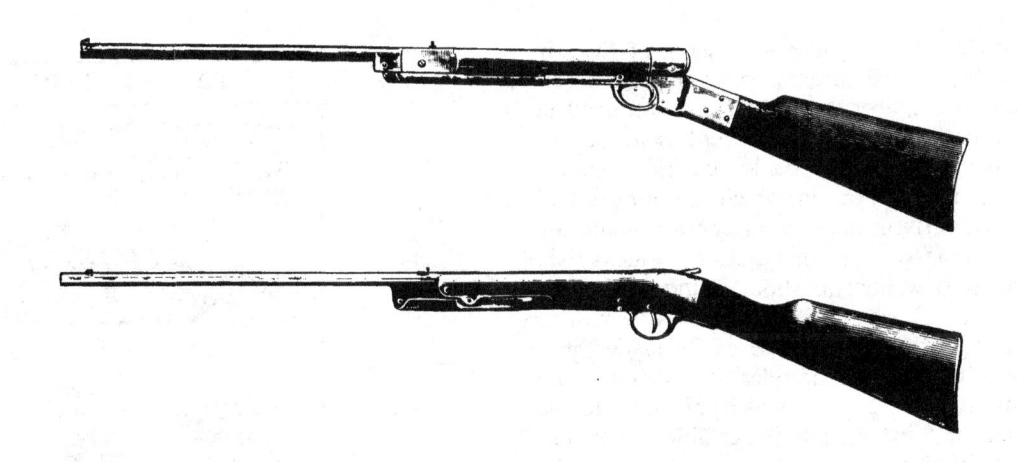

"Diana" rifles are still made at Rastatt by Mayer and Grammelspacher. The American Quackenbush, as indicated, really started this firm on its way to being the world's largest maker of air guns.

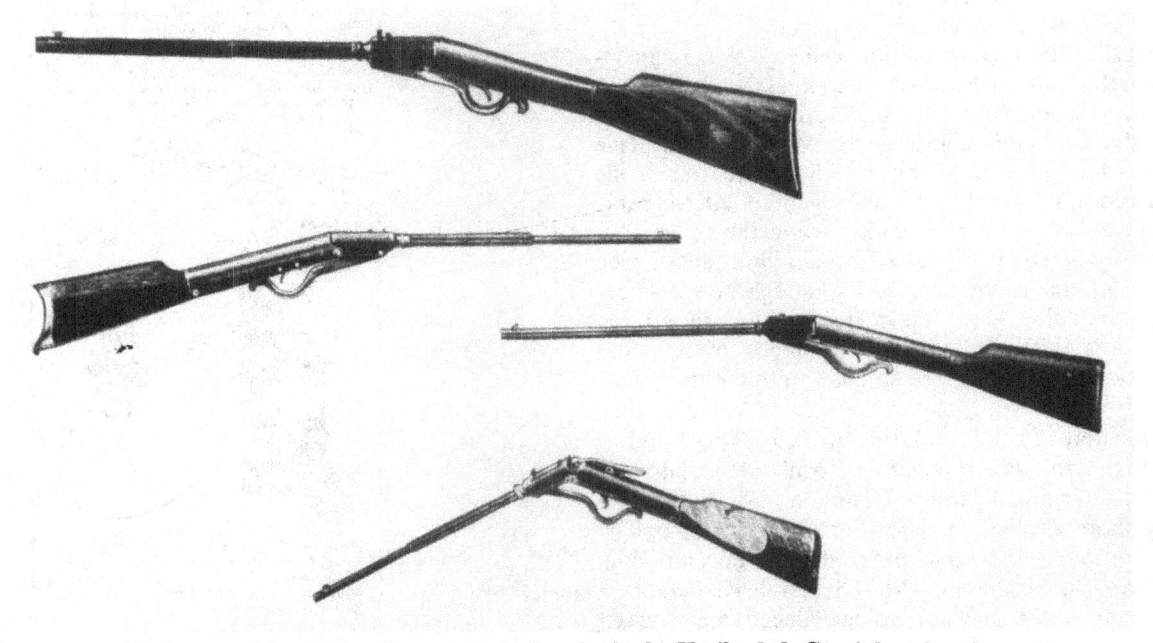

Various models of the German-made Quackenbush (Haviland & Gunn) barrel cocker.

37

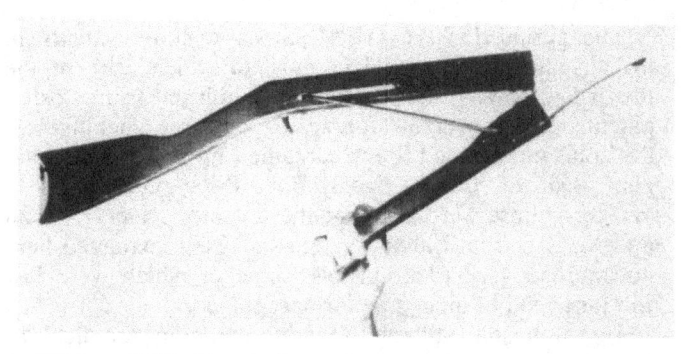

"Chicago" (Markham) all-wood construction except springs and trigger. This BB rifle still shoots hard and accurately. This was the design which started C. Hamilton on all-metal air-rifle construction. It is 32 inches overall. Barrel is 9.75 inches, precision drilled in hardwood.

bush guns and of the modern Benjamin air rifles and pistols. G. Walker's design of the same year forecast the turnbolt Haenel air-rifle military trainer of pre-Hitler Germany—a type again currently in production in East Germany at the old Haenel works, this time as a Russian trainer!

Some notice must be made here in passing of the *toy* air-gun field. High-powered arms using compressed air pumped up in an air chamber were not mass produced in the United States until comparatively recent years, as we shall see. The low cost of .22 powder cartridge shooting, and the wide open spaces in which shooting could safely be done even early in the present century made the development of compressed-air arms a poor business risk. Youths and men who wanted to shoot found it cheaper and easier to buy a .22 rifle where a low-cost cartridge with very considerable power could be easily loaded into the breech, than to bother with air rifles at that time. The much lower powered air gun in which air had to be manually pumped up, just wasn't marketable. In recent years high ammunition costs, plus the dangers from the great carrying distance of a .22 powder-driven bullet (as much as one mile under some conditions) has developed a market for compressed-air guns, and more particularly for CO_2 arms, which is steadily expanding.

However, at the turn of the last century, American ingenuity in the air-gun field was concentrated on the toy variety for training young boys. One of the first of the mass producers in this field was the Markham Air Rifle Company of Plymouth, Michigan. Their rifle was made almost entirely of wood, yet was a gun of considerable power, accuracy, and dependability within the range of a nonlethal toy. About 1885 Markham introduced the "Chicago" air rifle as they named it. Though no sales records are available today, it evidently really started the trend towards this form of toy. Specimens of this mahogany colored old timer are still in good shooting condition.

Unfortunately for the Markham firm, they had a fellow townsman who thought in terms of metal—not wood. That man was Clarence Hamilton about whom we must say more further on. Hamilton conceived the idea of an *all-metal* air gun and proceeded to develop one. When it was in production, Markham received another jolt. The star salesman who had introduced the wooden "Chicago" to the trade became dissatisfied with his relations with Markham company and proposed to Hamilton's concern (by then called the Daisy Manufacturing Company in Plymouth) that they make a metal rifle he could sell. The result was the "Sentinel," a rifle which started the chain of events which compelled Markham to produce metal air rifles also, models later to become famous as the "King" brand—which in due course were taken over by Daisy.

Space does not permit us to deal even lightly with most of the developments of this period until near its close, when we come to one of the most remarkable and least known stories in an industry which through the years has done much to bring joy and healthy sports training to countless millions of growing boys everywhere in the world, with one country excepted. That country? Russia! The company? The Daisy Manufacturing Company of Plymouth, Michigan, a little town 24 miles west of Detroit.

U. S. PATENT OFFICE.

176,003. SPRING AIR-PISTOLS. Iver Johnson and Martin Bye, Worcester, Mass.
[Filed Mar. 15, 1876.]
Brief.—The barrel tips up at the rear, and serves as a cross-handle to depress the spring piston.

1. The combination, in a spring-piston and air pistol or gun, having the barrel B, and chamber A, of the cap G, having a seat, D, fitting the end of the barrel, and forming a guide for the rod C, the rod C pivoted to the barrel and provided with a spring-head, E, for forcing the barrel B against the seat D, all constructed and arranged to operate substantially as and for the purposes set forth.
2. The combination, in a spring piston and air pistol or gun, of the spring-compressing slotted rod C, with the guiding-cap G, having a spline or projection fitting the slot in the rod C, substantially as and for the purposes described.

176,004. SPRING AIR-PISTOLS. Iver Johnson and Martin Bye, Worcester, Mass.
[Filed Mar. 15, 1876.]

The combination, in a spring piston and air pistol or gun, of the screw pin F, threaded socket C, and the movable end A of the barrel, arranged to be elevated for inserting the projectile, all constructed substantially as and for the purposes set forth.

Abstract of original patent.

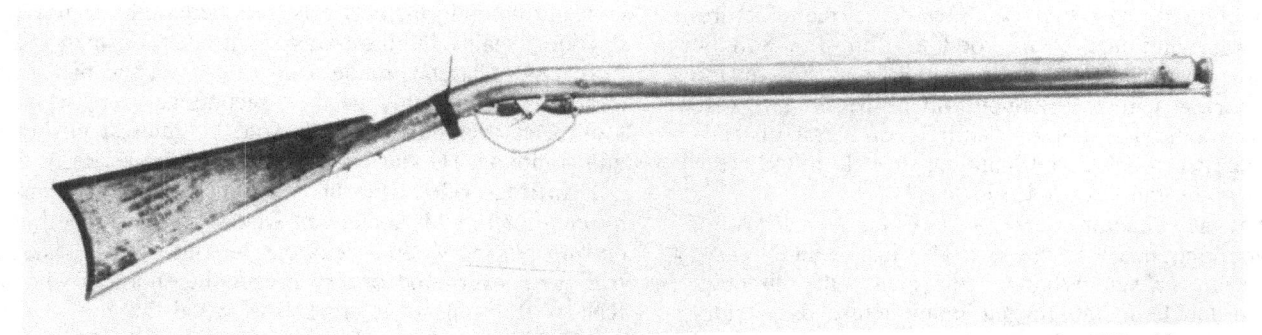

Remarkable low-cost early American compressed-air gun. Made by St. Louis Air Rifle Company in 1899. Air compression tube is bent tubing. Shot barrel below is also tubing. Piston is split-wood construction on the principle of a clothespin to give air seal. Leather washer at forward end of piston compressed the air in a small reservoir formed behind the trigger. Pushing the trigger forward sealed off the air exit. When rifle was pumped up and then loaded at muzzle, pulling the trigger released the stored air. The cheap design is still capable of considerable power. Rear receiver peep sight is an effective stamping, straddling the tang.

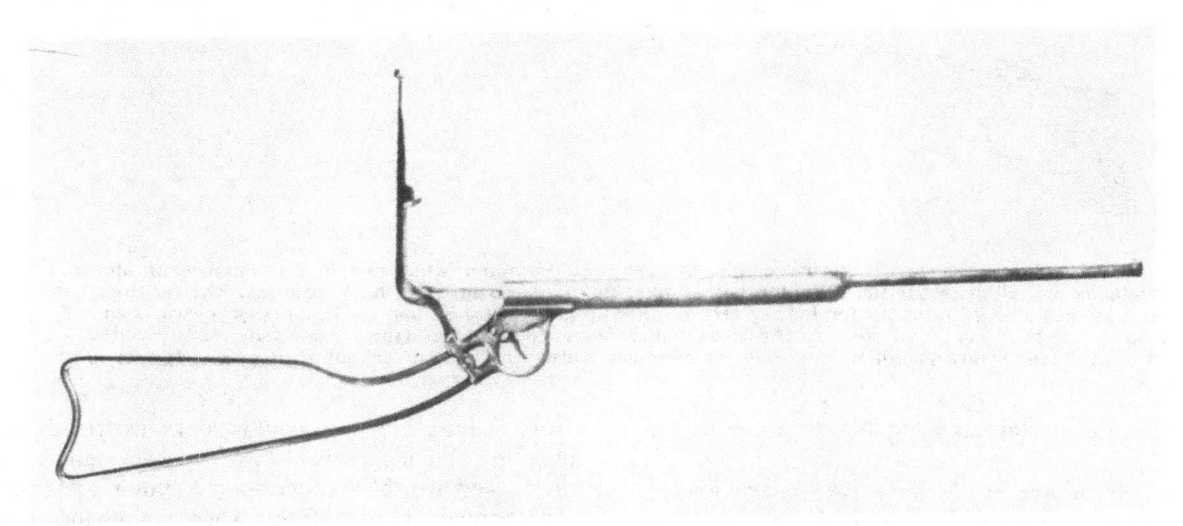

Daisy Model 1888 single shot. BB. 31 inches overall. Barrel 15 inches. Cocked by lifting and pulling back lever folded down into the top of receiver. Skeleton stock. Rear sight is integral part of cocking lever.

The Early Daisy Air Rifle Story

Well over 1,500,000 lucky boys—with a sprinkling of girls, too!—are given Daisy air rifles each year by parents, relatives, or friends. They are gifts from those who want the children to know the joys and benefits of the outdoors and how to get off on the right foot as a sportsman, or perhaps as a soldier in the service of his country and the world. The joys, the sporting value, and the military training uses of the Daisy from generation to generation since 1888 are hard to conceive.

It all started in a typically American fashion. In this day when industries are constantly diversifying their activities we wouldn't give the development much thought. But we are talking now about the year 1882—and not about air guns. Not at all. The subject is windmills! For the Daisy Manufacturing Company, the world's largest makers of air guns, started life as the Plymouth Iron Windmill Company!

It started, like all real businesses, with an idea. In the front window of R. L. Root's Drug and Jewelry Store in Plymouth, Michigan, Clarence J. Hamilton worked away mechanically repairing clocks and watches for the town folks, dreaming of bigger and better things.

Willow Run, Henry Ford, and General Motors were not then names to conjure with, and the area near Detroit as well as faraway had farms and livestock dependent largely on windmills to pump all-essential water. Windmills to the average man then had always been made of wood in this country, and presumably always would be. But Clarence Hamilton wasn't just an average man. Why couldn't they be made better, cheaper, and stronger, he asked himself, of iron?

The Patent Office agreed that Clarence had an idea worth protecting. Mr. Root agreed that such an idea was worth risking his money on. Other friends caught the fever—or more probably Clarence infected them. A stock company was formed. On January 9, 1882 the Plymouth Iron Windmill Company became a corporate reality, blossoming out with a 2-story factory which some of the founders later described as "pretentious."

Under the unrelenting drive of Hamilton and his far sighted board of directors the company mushroomed. Business boomed. Farmers from one end of the United States to the other spoke of the "Hamilton Mill" as a friend well known. Hamilton spent his time operating the manufacturing plant and developing improvements on the original windmill. The company prospered.

39

The restless Mr. Hamilton had a mind that seemed to have an antipathy for the use of wood in manufacture. First it was windmills, from wood to iron. In 1888 he had another brainstorm: All the toy air guns then on the market starting with the Plymouth-made Markham, were made of wood. Why not one entirely of metal instead? He had learned much about handling sheet iron and steel. Why not apply the knowledge to toys?

Maybe the directors were a very far-seeing group. Or maybe Clarence was the sort who just wouldn't take "No" for an answer. Whatever the cause, the directors agreed to tackle metal air-gun manufacture as a sideline. Their heirs all lived to be happy about the mental leap that must have startled many—from windmills to wind guns!

The best description of the first Daisy invented by Hamilton perhaps is that of Mr. Edward C. Hough, long-time treasurer of Daisy and son of one of its founders:

> Until the advent of the "Daisy," previous air rifles had been made almost entirely of wood, and the increased strength and improved design resulted in an immediate increase in demand.
> The air chamber and shooting barrel were made from drawn-brass tubing joined together by a molded section of lead, tin and antimony that provided the cone-shaped holder for the BB shot when dropped from the end of the shooting barrel.
> The plunger was made from tempered steel wire that was formed in a hand-operated die and hardened at the point where it engaged the trigger sear by grinding on an emery wheel until hot, then dipped in water. This plunger wire then went to the iron foundry where a section was molded on that provided a place that, when wound by hand with well-oiled candle wicking, made a joint that was sufficiently tight to compress the air behind the pellet when the spring was released.
> The spring was compressed by pulling a malleable iron lever that rested on the main barrel section and was connected with the plunger by a wire link.
> The stock was made from wire and was attached to the barrel by cast-iron plates held in place by a machine screw. All parts were nickel plated, and the gun presented a very handsome appearance to boys who up to that time had only slingshots and home-made bows and arrows to test their marksmanship.

The gun was named the "Daisy." It was one of those natural things that take from the very start. In no time at all sales hit such a peak and brought such a profit that the company proceeded to forget all about windmills and concentrated all their efforts on increased air-gun production. Again Hamilton was the production man.

In 1898 Clarence made a mistake—not too bad a one, and one evident only to the "second guesser" who can look back over the years. He sold his interest in the air-gun company. He started manufacture of a series of boys' .22 cartridge rifles—the first of which, naturally, was an *all metal* item with a skeleton wire stock. True, he had to end up putting wood stocks on the rifles, but at least he *tried* to convert that ornery breed, the shooters who just KNOW that unless the stock is of wood the gun isn't any good! For years the Hamilton rifles were the pride of

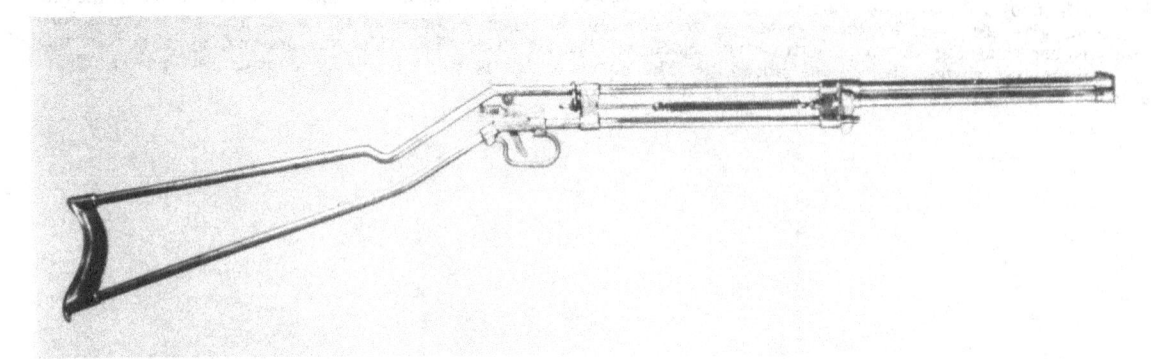

First Hamilton all-metal .22 cartridge rifle, made by C. Hamilton who was the first maker of all-metal windmills and all-metal air rifles. Pulling back on cocking piece compressed the mainspring. The cartridge barrel was then free to pivot up for loading. Hamilton was ahead of his time in this design which used only tubing, stampings, and coil springs. His later models were conventional types, principally drop-barrel types of which tremendous quantities were sold by premium houses. The first model shown is extremely rare today.

every country boy who could cajole his friends and relatives into buying bluing, salves, seeds, and other over-priced and worthless junk so the junior salesman could get a "premium" rifle "free." Then as now the "premium" business was a big business; and no man can say today how many Hamilton rifles brought the premium houses ten times their value in goods sold thereby. Most were sold that way—relatively few were merchandised through regular channels. Here we must leave the dynamic metal-minded Mr. Hamilton.

The name of the company, understandably, was quite a business problem, and since windmills had long ceased to be a product anyway, the name was changed to Daisy Manufacturing Company in 1895.

Every successful business has to start with something of value to sell. The Daisy Company, as their steadily increasing growth and success establish, had the right product in their concept of a toy which would help to shape good citizens from growing youth. But a good product alone is never enough.

Every successful business must have, in addition, masterful financial and business guidance, plus real sales drive. In these respects, too, Daisy was under a bright star. In 1894 Lewis Cass Hough was made manager and treasurer, a post he retained until he passed on in January of 1902. The ethics, the sound and realistic business policies, the unwavering honesty, and the long-range business vision instilled by Hough set the pattern, which has ever since been adhered to. On the sales end, Charles H. Bennett not only laid but actually built the nucleus of the sales acceptance which has made the trademark

"Daisy" known throughout every corner of the world except, as we have said, Russia!

Bennett in 1899 started selling the line to hardware and sporting goods outlets in the United States. Soon he spread the scope of his sales, making many trips around the world to establish outlets. Even in his early days he was unable to sell a single American-made air rifle in Russia! First, the reactionary Czarist officials were suspicious. The Bolsheviks followed suit. And the Communists, even while giving detailed instruction in handling of firearms in the elementary schools, still resist the entry of these air guns! Perhaps they just don't believe in youngsters having fun. Perhaps they are afraid that a people short of the absolute necessities of life in so many cases would react badly to the import of metal goods whose principal aim is just fun and sport. We really don't know. But Daisy had a very early knowledge of the fact set out so well by Sir Winston Churchill in his definition of Russia: "A puzzle within a mystery within an enigma!"

Another "first" in establishing the Daisy product was the appropriation of $3,000 in 1897 for "advertising" in the form of a lithographed banner, which proved so effective in sales stimulation that each manufacturing year since then the custom has been continued and expanded. In the best American manner, Daisy learned early that no matter how good the item, it isn't worth anything until people know and recognize it. Many firms both here and abroad might in the early years have rivalled Daisy on a basis of product quality and manufacturing efficiency; but those who could just didn't have either the American ingenuity or the courage to invest money in such an intangible as "advertising." Throughout the world "Daisy" has come to mean an air rifle just as automatically as "Winchester" conjures up pictures of a rifle or "Colt" makes one think of revolvers.

Still another factor in the steady Daisy growth was its facing up to real competition—not getting "buck fever" every time some newcomer entered the field, but not failing to recognize a product or an organization which might affect it adversely, either.

When the "Warrior" air rifle made by Dubuar in the nearby town of Northville gave evidence of becoming a disturbing factor in the trade, Daisy bought the company out in 1903 and the following year consolidated Dubuar with Daisy. Similarly they bought up the "Atlas" air rifle manufacturers whose plant was at Ilion, New York, and in 1906 withdrew that rifle from the market.

The success story of Daisy is linked, too, to its enlightened labor relations, a definite policy dating back to 1906 with the introduction of a "Daisy Day" picnic and excursion for employees. Daisy then established a policy in World War I of paying to the dependents of any employee who entered the armed forces the difference between what he was earning at Daisy at the time and what he would receive in the service, and later established a workers union which led to one of the most successful profit-sharing systems devised by American industry.

This plan divides profits fairly between employees and stockholders and has afforded a production and efficiency incentive which has had much to do with Daisy's continuing ability to hold down manufacturing costs and increase product quality to meet all legitimate competition through the years. Several generations of many families have worked, and still work, in the plant.

While much of the foregoing may appear a bit afield on the subject of air guns, it is introduced here to afford a slight picture of what went into the development of the product from its date of introduction and to point out that the growth has been based on merit, effort, energy, value, and service. There is nothing haphazard about the development of any of the successful air-gun companies, either toy or serious match varieties. And even the most common of them are the result of years of painstaking and efficient work at great expense.

If we contrast the Daisy sales in 1889 when some 86,-

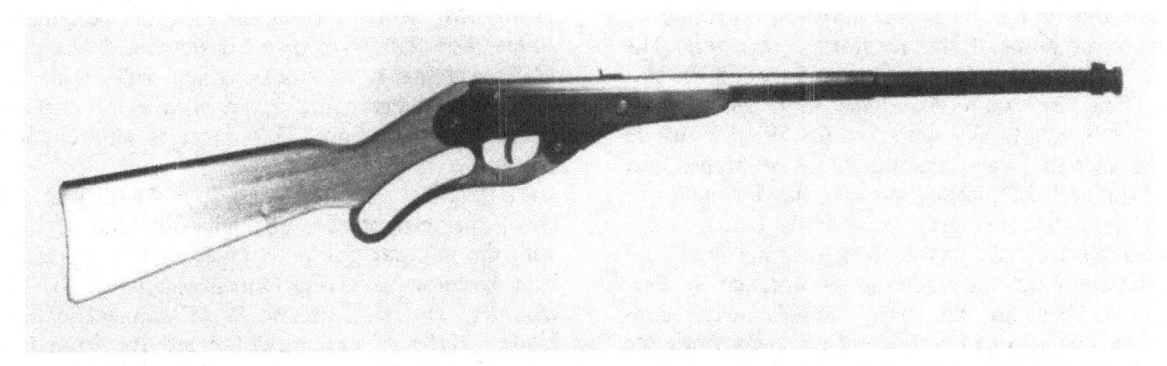

Mexican Mendoza triggerguard-lever repeater. This is a BB gun, a variant of the Daisy. Sr. Mendoza is famous for his light machinegun, one of the finest lightweight, high-power guns of the B.A.R. type ever designed. This is his only air rifle, Model V-45 "Ti-Men." Overall 33 inches. Barrel (insert) 12 inches.

400 pieces were sold, with those in 1952 when sales included 1,285,001 air rifles, we see a part of the magnitude of the picture!

Before 1930, the largest foreign market was China, strange as it may seem; while in the 1930's, export, which by then accounted for 25 percent of the total business, was spread across Great Britain, South Africa, and Australia in about equal volume.

Study of the valuable old catalogs of the great German export houses of the early years of the 20th century show graphically not only the place held by Daisy, but the extent to which their designs were copied and even pirated throughout the world, as those houses sold not only the Daisy line but all the European copies as well.

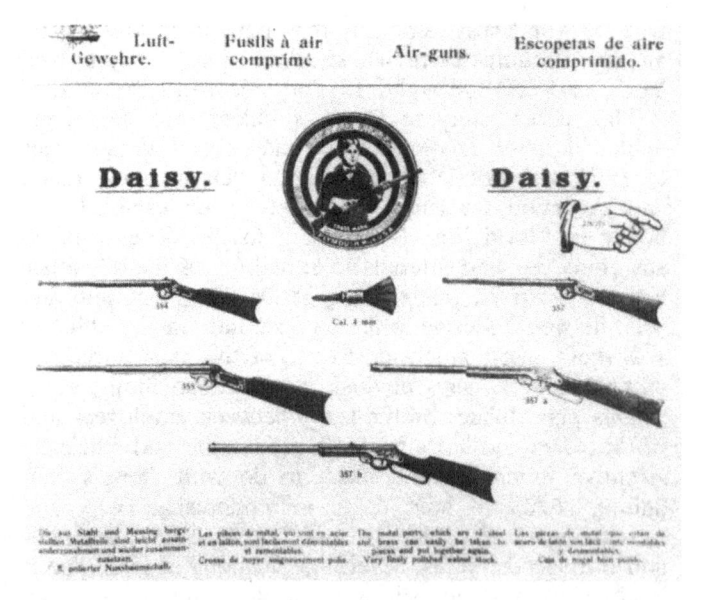

Daisy rifles were sold by leading German exporters wherever German gun salesmen traveled.

Other U. S. Air Guns

In 1882 W. R. Benjamin of St. Louis, Missouri, introduced the first of the long line of "Benjamin Pump" air rifles, manufactured for him by the Wissler Instrument Company of that city.

The Benjamin was not—and is not—in the toy category. It was from its inception a high-powered "pump-up" compressed-air arm with a built-in pump piston housed in a tube below the barrel. Its power can be controlled by the amount of air pumped into its storage reservoir. The story of the Benjamin will be found in the section on current arms. The Benjamin Air Rifle Company, today owned by the Spack family who bought Wissler out in 1926, is the second largest manufacturer of high-power compressed-air and CO_2 pellet guns in the business.

Benjamin was the only firm aside from Daisy which survived through the early years when air guns were laying the foundation for their present acceptance as firearms trainers. They are the only manufacturers consistently in the business of *compressed-air* arms since the beginning of the century.

EARLY HISTORY OF AIR GUN IN GREAT BRITAIN

As we have seen, many of the finest examples of high-power compressed-air guns and rifles—with a few pistols of equal quality—which have ever been made were the products of English gunmakers in the 1780 to 1830 period. The coming of the metallic powder-loaded cartridge brought compressed-air gun activities and interest to a general halt except for the production of air canes we have noted.

Early English patent records, while they carry a wealth of interesting data on scores of toy and serious air devices, have little which has been of lasting value except for certain United States and French filings. Ever slow to move on to something new, British manufacturers took a long time to do anything more than merely patent improvements. Many of these were for guns which were never made! Others for genuine advances which were never put into production for reasons too numerous to deal with here.

John Shaw was granted patent No. 12728 in 1849 for locks for air guns, but nothing much came of it. The 1872 records show Giffard's compressed-air gun, cane, and cartridge. A. Bedford's patent of 1876 covered an ingenious turn-bolt breech plug. In the same year the American Iver Johnson patents on air pistols received attention. In 1884 we find the American Quackenbush rigid barrel, pull-back cocking model, which was not produced in quantity. Giffard's compressed-air cartridge in new form is back in 1886. G. P. Gunn, who with Haviland developed the forerunner of all later day successful barrel-cocking spring-air guns already noted, in 1886 received a British patent for an ingenious tube magazine above the barrel of the gun—a design capable of development in English and German-made match arms of that type today. Flurscheim & Bergmann were covered on darts, balls, and cartridges they had licensed from Quackenbush.

In many of the early British patents we find elements of later air arms which were and are successfully marketed. For example, in 1877 No. 190,893 granted to O'Connor and Dinnan there is provision for a below-barrel push-piston somewhat related to the German Tell of the early 1900's and the later American Benjamin first models. Quackenbush's No. 188,028 of that same year cocks by pressing in the barrel, a form which, together with its system of removable breech pin loading is common to two recent German low-powered "patented" air pistols. M. Weber of Zurich, one of the greatest of the single-shot .22 target pistol designers, developed in 1877 (No. 198,061), a stock-syringe rifle with set-trigger, cocked by triggerguard lever, with a forward ratchet for helping compression. This form is still encountered in Europe.

Hertzfeld's patent 208,016 of 1878 was for an air cane, spring-operated, not powerful enough to compete with the popular pump-up types then being made. American inventors receiving British patents in 1879 and 1880 included Myron Coloney, W. Chamberlain, and A. G. Hyde—Hyde developing a top gravity drum feed, which was a forerunner of the later Haenel and now appears in more finished form in the latest Walther air rifles in Germany. Turning the magazine chamber piece allowed the shot to drop into the chamber, but the air could propel the bullet only when the turning motion was completed and the breech fully closed.

AIR CANES

Air canes have not been commercially manufactured since the period of World War I. They have been almost completely a British monopoly. They received some attention on the Continent, but little in the United States. Basically they are just collection pieces, but enough are encountered that some representative types require our attention here.

Early in the century, Germany, Belgium, and France made a rash of *sword* canes. They came with short blades and long blades, triangular blades—and even saw-toothed blades. Another German staple was the cane or walking stick "mit Gummischlager." This cute little gadget was a quick-draw flexible rubber cudgel with which one could beat the daylights out of an enemy, real or imagined, without marking him up too much.

But the production of *air* canes met with fast police suppression on the Continent—with considerable justification, since many of the canes could be pumped up enough to be deadly at a not inconsiderable range; and being released, as in the common European modern air gun.

Cane Calibers

Air canes may be encountered in a bewildering range of calibers, usually to shoot round balls. However shot shells were also made for some of these; and indeed there were forms of air canes with smooth-bored barrels for shot which carried insert rifled barrels for firing lead balls, giving the owner a shotgun and rifle in the same

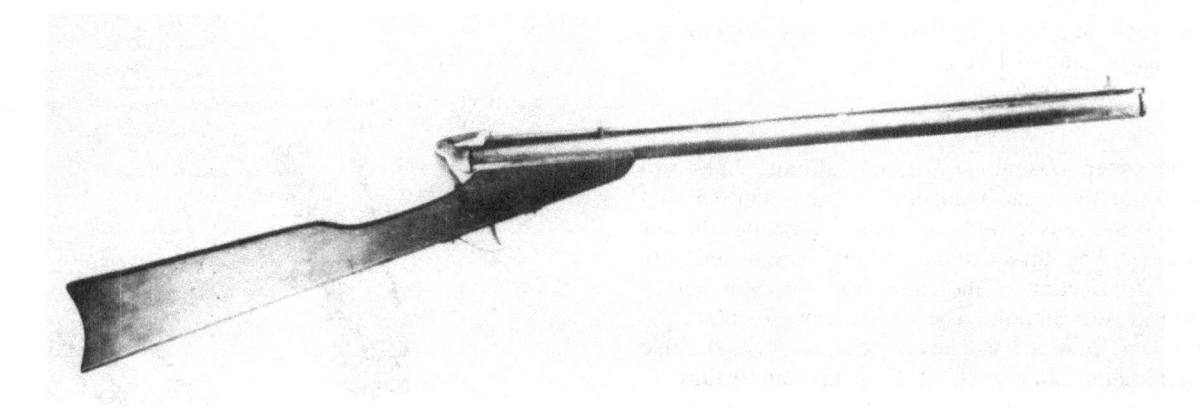

Earliest model Benjamin compressed-air rifle. Push piston below barrel. Single shot. 36 inches overall. 21-inch barrel. BB. Trigger-lever valve release.

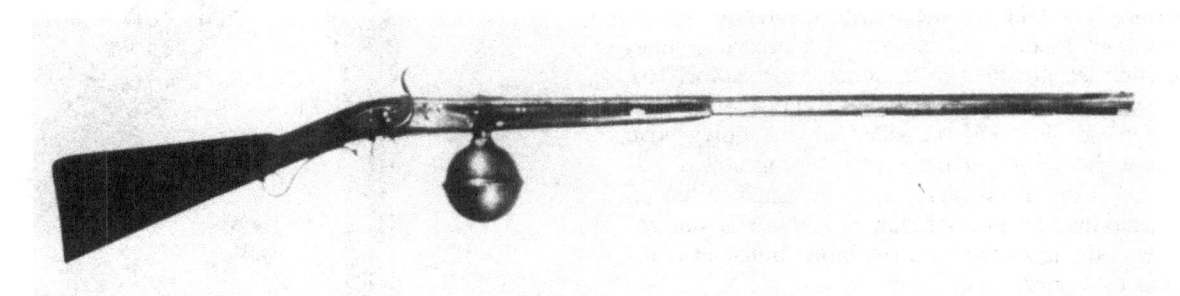

Early 18th century British high-power air gun with detachable-ball (copper or iron) air reservoir. This is a typical specimen. Dozens of instrument makers as well as gunmakers produced similar rifles.

in that day of walking-stick users, they constituted a highly concealable weapon.

Early English catalogs by Blanche, Cogswell & Harrison, Greener, Reilly, and others all deal with pneumatic (that is, "pump up") designs in which the upper section of the stick houses the air chamber which is charged with an independent pump. The lower section, of course, houses the barrel and the lockwork.

Inventors models and custom models of air canes with built-in pumps are encountered, but there is no evidence that any quantity of this pattern was ever made for commercial distribution, as is the case with the pneumatic cane with separate pump. This variant, when encountered, is usually pumped up by repeatedly forcing the sliding pumping element against a solid surface until the air chamber is charged; although some specimens exist where a section of the handle is operated in and out to pump up—this pattern having relatively little power.

Finally, there are occasional models seen in which the air is compressed syringe fashion by a compressed spring

weapon. Calibers ran from about .177 to .750 (that is, up to ¾-inch diameter!). The diameter of the cane itself may be up to 2 inches. Canes weigh up to 8 pounds!

W. W. Greener in his monumental *The Gun and Its Development* makes no reference whatever to air arms in the early editions of his work. In the 6th (1896) edition, however, he gets around to some slight mention, telling us only that the form resembling the common walking cane is the most popular form. He tells us that since these are pump-up weapons, the propelling force becomes less after each shot; and that while *shot* is of no use beyond 15 yards, that the *bullet* can be relied upon up to 25 yards or more. He illustrates, without explanation, what is known as the "Bent" air cane.

Both muzzle and breech loading types are common. A typical Greener advertisement at the turn of the century for instance reads: "Bent air canes with rifle and shot barrels complete with pump and key—55, 60, 80, and 98 shillings. If breech loading, 8 shillings extra." (If we remember that at the time a shilling was worth 25

43

cents, the cheapest Greener cost a lot more than the average Englishman or American of that day earned in a full 6-day work week!)

The "Bent" Air Cane

These followed in common the shape shown in the Greener illustration herewith. They were intended to be sighted from the shoulder, rifle fashion—not held out awkwardly as in the common cane. On the other hand there was no disguising the "Bent" types—they were just what they appeared, air guns. They were widely used by ornothologist of the time and to some slight extent for rook shooting, though here they lacked the requisite "reach" and power as a rule.

Operation

With the exceptions already noted, all air canes operated in about the same manner. The air chamber and barrel halves are unscrewed, the latter carrying the air release trigger. The threaded pump end is screwed into the air-chamber section of the cane. Both feet are placed on the pump-piston handle. The air-chamber is held with both hands and pumped with even strokes. Considerable heat is generated, and even strokes are important to (relative) ease of compression. These guns if of large caliber will take about 500 pounds pressure. They will stand much more—with the strength, will, time, and enthusiasm to pump hard and long enough.

To operate, first take off the muzzle protector. Screw the cane sections together. If the gun is a muzzle loader, the ramrod will be attached to the muzzle protector. Use the rod to press in and seat the bullet, then withdraw it. As most of these air canes are rifled on the polygroove principle now being popularized as "microgrooved" or "multigrooved," the fit is tight and the patch used in normal muzzle-loading powder gun procedure is not required. If the cane is a breechloader, insert bullet in loading port and close port.

The cocking key shown is inserted in the hole near the chamber. Turning the key will bring the trigger out within reach, and the sear will spring into engagement. This is brought about by the action of the key compressing a leaf spring, which is held in position by the trigger-stud lever. When the trigger is pressed, the leaf spring reacts and hits the head of the valve through a tripping device. The valve opens to permit a jet of compressed air to escape down the barrel behind the bullet. The spring-loaded valve automatically closes as in common practice, assisted by the pressure in the air chamber; but the valve-opening blow, because it is spring delivered, does not vary as does the steadily falling air pressure. This results in the valve closing at a slower rate as air compression diminishes, a factor which tends to roughly equalize the projecting force for the first 15 or 20 shots.

The valve itself is quite an elementary device— spindle-shaped, spring-loaded for rebound, a washer or disc usually of horn, the unit fitting into a tapering recess. To neutralize dust, which inevitably works into pump-up chambers, the air chambers have an inside grease coating, the grease preventing the dust from being blown into the valve. (Incidentally, the few specimens found in good shooting condition have been fitted with neoprene valves by their owners.)

Pressing the trigger will now fire the projectile in the barrel. It is necessary only to repeat the bullet insertion— not the pumping—for further shots until the air pressure drops unsatisfactorily. A fully charged air chamber will allow 15 to 20 shots before too much bullet drop is encountered.

Most specimens carry fixed sights set for about 30 yards at the normal operating pressures, but small game can be killed up to perhaps 100 yards if hit properly,

337,395. AIR-GUN. GEORGE P. GUNN, Herkimer, N. Y. Filed Aug. 12. 1885. (No model.)

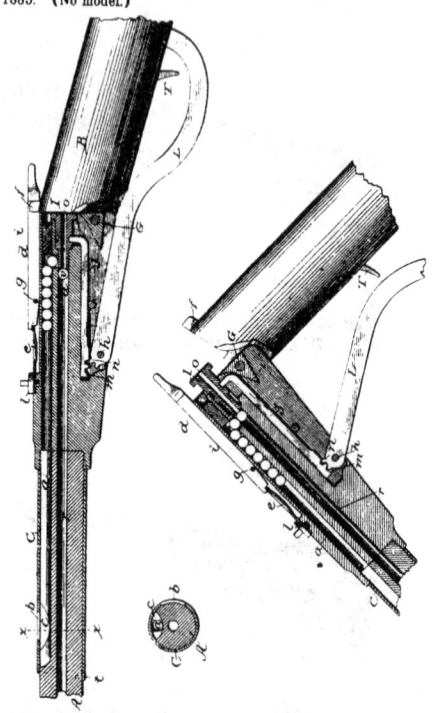

Claim.—1. In combination with the barrel A, the magazine *a*, more or less of which shall consist of an open groove, and the rotating sleeve C, provided with a hole, *b*, said sleeve being arranged to turn on the barrel and open or close the magazine, substantially as shown and described.

2. In combination with the magazine *a* and the rotating sleeve C, having a hole, *b*, therein, the concave chamber or enlargement *c* in the magazine, arranged to register with the hole *b* of the sleeve when the latter is turned into position to open the magazine, substantially as and for the purpose set forth.

3. The combination, in a gun, of the magazine *a*, connected to the bore of the barrel by a transverse passage, *i*, and the reciprocating plug I, connected to lever L by the slide J, said parts being constructed and arranged to operate substantially as described, whereby the passage from the magazine to the bore of the gun is automatically opened and closed in the act of swinging the barrel to compress the spring in the stock, as set forth.

4. The combination of the barrel A, having a magazine, *a*, arranged thereon, and connected with the bore thereof by a transverse hole, *i*, with the reciprocating plug I, the slide J, connected to said plug and provided with the teeth *m*, and the lever L, provided with corresponding teeth, *n*, all constructed and arranged for joint operation, substantially as described.

5. The combination, in an air-gun, of a magazine and a barrel with a transverse opening leading from the magazine to the bore of the barrel, and the reciprocating tubular plug arranged to close and open the passage from the magazine to the barrel and admit the air for propelling the projectile, substantially as set forth.

Abstract of original patent.

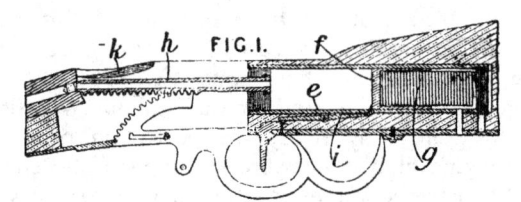

M. Weber's patent 3376 of September 5, 1877. An unusual triggerguard-cocking air-rifle design using a ratchet system to give maximum spring compression with minimum effort.

though allowing for the trajectory in the face of pressure and range imponderables is quite a trick.

A few specimens which the present author has been priviliged to test, models which were original except for the valving, would penetrate about 1.5 inches of pine at 50 feet; while the larger ones would get through 1 inch. In all instances, however, the balls, while making clean entry holes, would punch long slivers of wood out of the back of the boards they penetrated. Shot cartridges proved almost useless for penetration; but one gun fitted with an old Roper-type muzzle choking device (the forerunner of all the modern shotgun adjustable chokes) held a surprisingly good pattern at 50-foot range.

Stocked Air Canes

There are two general classes of stocked air canes, the English and the Continental.

Class 1 (English). In the common English versions, they are the same as the air canes and Bent air canes of the same makers so far as barrel, lockwork, and actual air reservoir are concerned. The forward half carries both the barrel AND the lockwork; the rear half is the air-reservoir mechanism only. The trigger is normally released by the key.

They differ from the others in that the rear half resembles a reasonably *conventional rifle butt!* In short, if you build a rifle-butt hull around the rear half of most English air canes, you have a "stocked air cane." In spite of appearances to the contrary, the air reservoirs, for example, are not the entire interior butt area as in equivalent-pattern air rifles or guns.

Except that they are designed for shoulder sighting and for rifle appearance, all *production* models of this pattern are as similar to the canes by the same maker as a Ford 2-door sedan is to a 4-door.

Class 2 (Continental). In the regular European Continental fashion, stocked air canes are an entirely "differ-

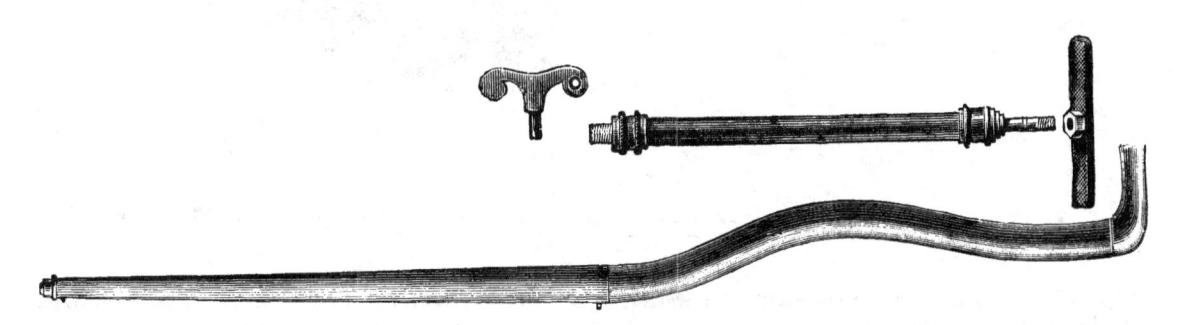

British air-gun stick with pump and key.

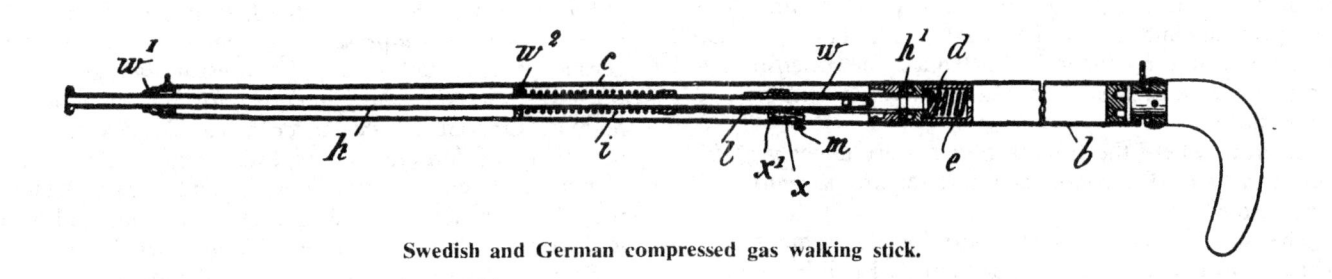

Swedish and German compressed gas walking stick.

This walking-stick shotgun operates with any compressed gas; e.g., compressed air. Illustration shows such a "walking-stick air shotgun" in longitudinal section, ready to fire. The letter b designates the gas container, in which gas; e.g., compressed air, is stored; d is the outlet valve and h the barrel which slides on the ring bearings of the walking-stick jacket c. The spiral spring i, which is slipped on the barrel and rests against the ring bearings, w^2 of the walking-stick jacket, tends to press the barrel back. The tapered rear end of the barrel, whose tapered inner bore serves to prevent the loaded bullet from slipping out, is equipped with a canal for admitting the compressed gas behind the bullet. This rear end slides air-tight in a guide box w, which is joined to the outlet valve of the gas container. The trigger m, which fits into notches in the barrel and thus holds it back, prevents the barrel, when the weapon is cocked, from sliding back against the opening valve of the gas container. When the trigger is operated the stretched spring i hurls the rear end of the barrel against the opening valve of the gas container; this opens, and the compressed gases enters the barrel behind the bullet and expels it. Since the barrel is at the same time pushed forward by the pressure of the compressed gas and prevented from recoiling by the trigger which is caught in its notches, any sudden, unnecessary emptying of the gas container is thereby made impossible.

ent breed of cat." They follow the pattern of the one pictured here which was manufactured by Rochus Wastl in Vienna. Like the English patterns, the Continental varieties may be encountered either muzzle or breech loading; and either smooth bored or rifled in many gauges and calibers. They were never made in quantity production.

The "cane" section in these types was actually intended to be used as a walking stick of very elegant design—though on occasion the lord of the manor could

It is believed that Continental arms of this pattern were built primarily for ease of carrying—the fancy walking stick as shown being one mark of the "gentleman" in that day, he could parade about with it and always have instantly ready the protection of a good, solid, swinging club if he were set upon. If he chose to swing the rear section on a strap across his chest, the common greatcoat would conceal or protect the stocked firing mechanism. In this Austrian version, the rear stock section measures 24 inches.

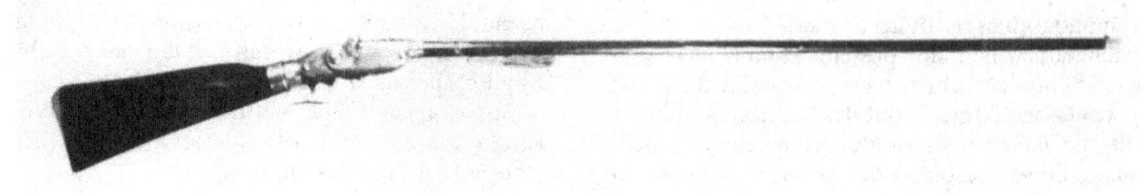

Wastl cane gun assembled ready for firing.

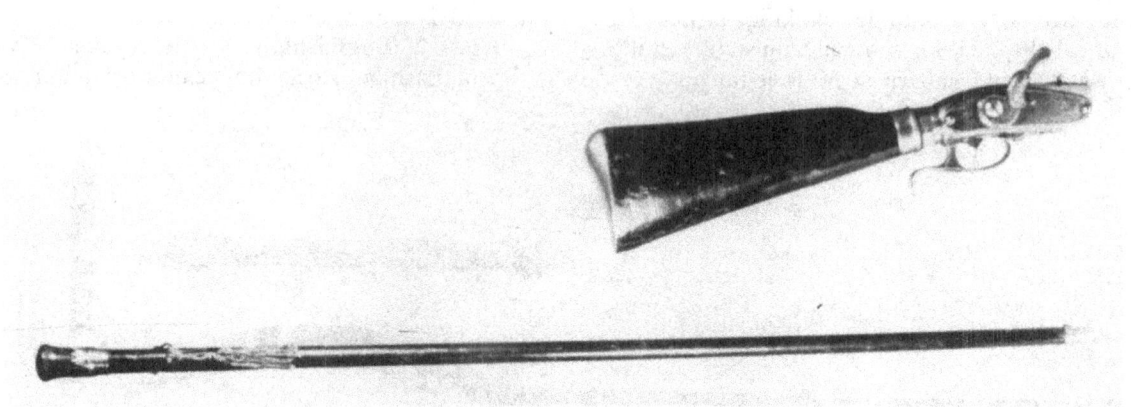

Wastl of Vienna cane gun. Cane used as a walking stick. Stock section was to be carried under greatcoat ready for quick field assembly.

also beat someone to death with it. Barrels were commonly brass, leather or skin covered; though occasionally they are encountered with a wood veneer covering.

The "cane" section in the specimen shown measures 36 inches overall with caps at each end. The front brass cap protects and hides the front sight. The rear cap holds several .36-caliber balls. Unlike the English patterns, the cane section does NOT contain the trigger and firing mechanism.

In short, where the English patterns are *air canes with false gunstocks,* the continental patterns are *air guns with false "cane" barrels.*

The stock reservoir is standard for the same gun—which is to say markedly larger than its English counterpart. When the two halves are screwed together in the English pattern, the key is used to release the trigger (or stud in some models) for firing.

When the two halves of the Continental pattern are screwed together, you merely cock the hammer of the regular gun type lock and fire exactly as for a gun.

In the muzzle-loading varieties, in practice common to both types, the ramrod is housed in the barrel when not in use.

These guns customarily shoot either large caliber balls or light shot charges against poachers.

CAUTION TO COLLECTOR-USERS

Old pneumatic canes and guns can safely be used when adequately tested and if fitted with new valves, usually of neoprene, for best results.

Some owners have practiced charging from underwater (diving) compressed air cylinders—a very dangerous practice unless a good pressure gauge is used. Most old air guns were intended for use at about 500 pounds. Oxygen should *never* be used because of the possibility of forming an explosive compound when in contact with ever-present gun oil and grease. (This is roughly equivalent to loading a rifle cartridge with priming compound—the entire air chamber can let go!)

Some collectors use the ever-available "bottled" carbon dioxide (CO_2). This gas is bottled as a liquid at about 850 p.s.i. pressure—the pressure will increase with changes in the outside temperature to as much as 1000 p.s.i. If your air cane or gun has been adequately tested and will stand 1000 pounds, it may be charged from the regular CO_2 cylinders with entire satisfaction. A good CO_2 servicing mechanic (NOT the average gunsmith!) can readily alter many early compressed-air guns to receive an easy-fill CO_2 tube or cylinder. After all, that's all that ANY modern CO_2 gun is—just the old compressed-air type simplified to take a CO_2 tube!

One further word of caution! Unless you are a capable physicist, don't fool around with nitrogen or any other gases! With air you have only the matter of *pressures* to worry about. CO_2 being both nontoxic and nonexplosive can also be properly discounted. You are inviting trouble with most other gases. Even liquified vapors of the butane, freon, or propane school *should be left strictly alone by the amateur!*

THE COMING-OF-AGE OF THE AIR GUN IN GREAT BRITAIN

Near the close of the 19th century a great wave of interest spread over Britain in connection with serious target shooting at short ranges with air guns. The first *mass produced* British-made product was the "Gem," a break-open model which was really little more than a toy with an overpowered spring. It soon proved too fragile for serious shooting.

At about the same period the Diana works, Langenhan, Steigleider, and numerous other Continental makers were turning out large quantities of rather high-powered arms based largely on the American Quackenbush designed by Haviland & Gunn. These were marketed under many names and not only expanded German interest in target shooting with air rifles but also soon became an important export item, bringing marks to the Fatherland from Britain as well as other places.

The firm of Martin Pulverman & Co. then at 26, the Minories, London E. C. introduced the first of these German-made patterns into England. They called it for English consumption "The Millita." It was different from the Quackenbush largely in that (as in most modern designs) the spring and piston were housed in a long tube extended forward from the trigger to the barrel jointure. It had a catch on the side (or top in some models) of the tube which when pressed allowed the barrel to be pulled down on its axis pin fastened to the receiver (or tube). The barrel carried an attached underlever with it in standard fashion to cock the powerful spring and bring the piston to firing position. The pellet was inserted in the barrel and the action snapped shut ready for firing. The materials and workmanship were excellent, and because of the use of a tube forward of the shoulder stock (instead of in the stock as in the Quackenbush and some others) it was reasonably cheap to make. Barrels were made with gunmaking precision, and the rifles were amazingly accurate. Their main drawback was the overall length required because of the tube position, a factor which also put the rear sight at too great a distance from the eye for many shooters.

In their advertising well into the 20th century, Pulverman laid claim that their rifles were directly responsible for the tremendous development of rifle clubs which speedily followed—several thousand in the Birmingham area alone. No one ever challenged this Pulverman claim.

The Birmingham Small Arms Company, then as now Britain's largest arms works, became interested in the air-gun market potential, both domestic and export. They fully realized the time, cost, and genius that goes into even such a relatively simple mechanical development as an air rifle. Instead of spending years on development, B.S.A. therefore bought the patents of a fully developed rifle, the Lincoln-Jeffries.

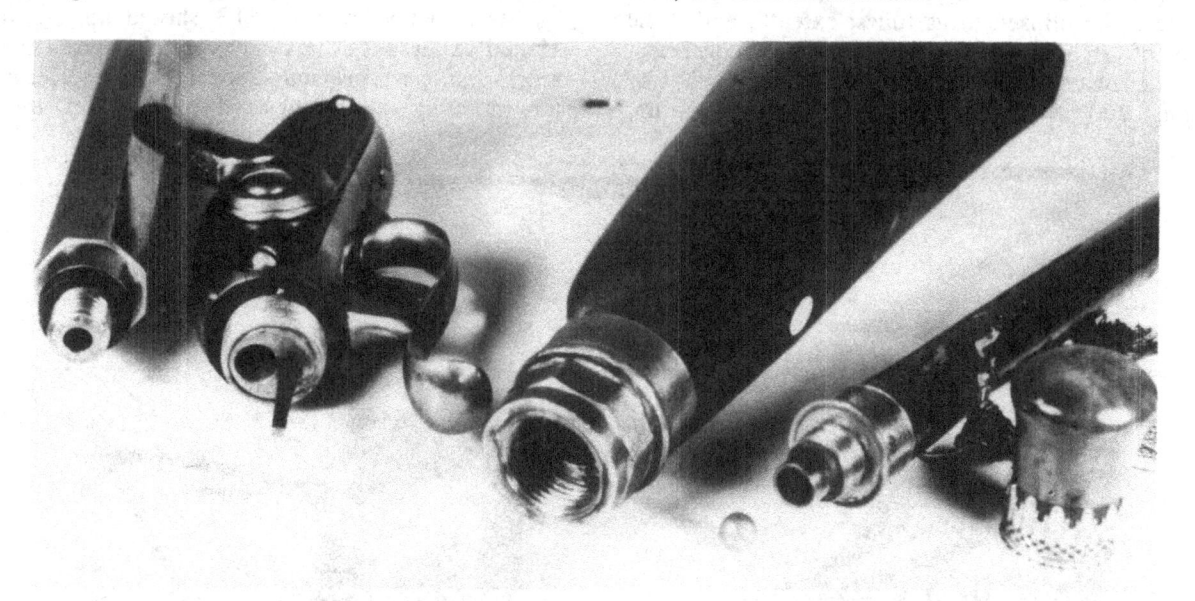

Wastl gun dismounted. Left to right: (1) Regular rifle barrel. (2) Lockwork. (3) Air-reservoir butt. (4) Cane barrel and sample bullet. (5) Cane cap which held 5 bullets.

This Lincoln-Jeffries was a departure from previous manufacture. Having studied closely the factors of joint wear and air leakage on most of the breakdown pattern air guns, the inventors set out to develop a solid breech-barrel design of comparable power. (Note: Today's powerful German air rifles are in most cases still the breakdown or hinged-frame construction, but means have been found to provide perfect air seals, and the leverage available allows use of ultrapowerful springs for maximum air compression.)

The new B.S.A. rifle had an adjustable trigger. A loading tap was provided at the area of the barrel breech. The rifle, instead of being cocked by the barrel being bent down as in the Millita, was cocked by a powerful lever below the barrel which, when pulled down and back, carried the spring and piston back to full-compressed position, where the sear held them. The tap lever was drawn back and a pellet inserted in the breech—a clumsier system than the breakdown, but then giving a better air seal. The tap was then closed.

As B.S.A. made the rifle, it was provided with a barrel of finest quality. The manufacturers displayed the new rifle, later to be designated the "B.S.A. Mark I," at the Stanley show at Islington, in November of 1905, where it attracted great attention. One of the targets shot at that show with this rifle tells why: the bull shot at 10 yards has 7 shots in it!

The B.S.A., like any good gun then or now, was costly. Its original price was 2 pounds 10 shillings in a day when that was really a lot of money.

Not long afterwards the "Britannia" rifle appeared at a somewhat lower price. It was made by C. G. Bonehill of Birmingham. It was actually a modification of the old American Haviland & Gunn system made by Quackenbush. This rifle was a breakdown pattern with air cylinder, piston, and spring housed in the stock. The maker summed up the features thus: "A combination of moderate and convenient entire length, with ample length of barrel to enable the extraordinary power of the rifle to be utilized to its fullest extent"; and "The provision of an extra-long and powerful mainspring, which lies at rest when the rifle is not cocked ready for discharging, and which requires only a trifling amount of compression when being put into the rifle." Truly valuable features!

The "Britannia" had many other good points. With a 21-inch barrel, its overall length was only 35½ inches. It had a limit-screw which allowed two different compression sets to be taken on the spring to give power changes. It was advertised in .17, .22, and .25 caliber. With the long, powerful spring housed in the stock, it was truly one of the hardest hitting designs of its day—or of now for that matter! A breech catch was pulled back to allow the barrel to be hinged down for cocking, giving tremendous leverage and allowing use of both hands if needed.

With all due respect to its makers, however, the "Britannia" was British principally in its manufacture! The design itself was so close to the old American Haviland & Gunn of 1876, and the later Quackenbush and its German variants, that one wonders why the gunmakers of that day didn't spot it!

Some may ask, "What about patents involved?" Here's what W. W. Greener had to say on that subject in 1881: "We can assure amateur inventors that neither the patent laws nor the patent agent cares that '— is possessed of a new and useful invention' as long as the necessary fees are paid, and the very same invention *may* and *has been* patented several times by different parties in a few months! This should not be so. In the United States, the patent commissioners institute a search amongst previous models and specifications before granting the patent, and yet the fees are not half

The Pulverman air rifle.

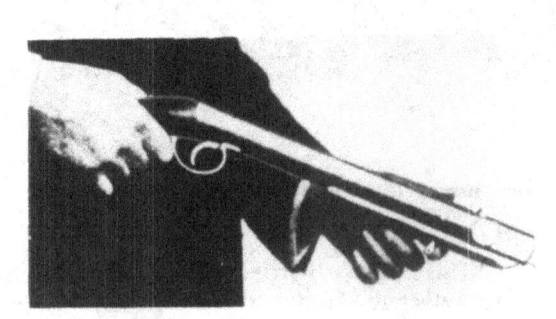

Method of loading the Pulverman air rifle. Pressing catch to release the barrel.

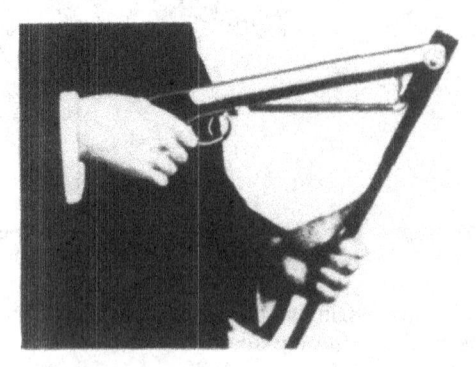

Compressing the spring.

The barrel released.

Inserting the pellet.

B.S.A. No. 1.

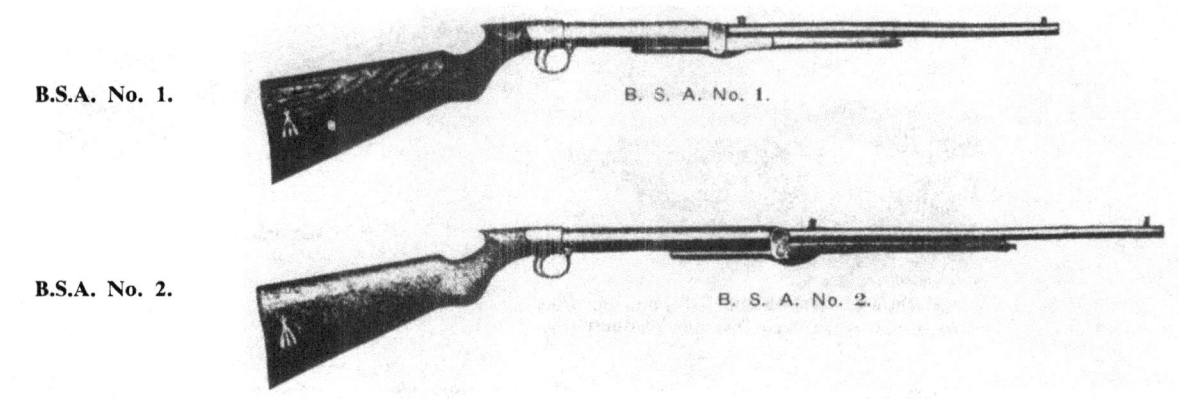

B.S.A. No. 2.

B. S. A. No. 1.

B. S. A. No. 2.

so high, whilst the patent is of longer duration, and the patentee far more secure from infringement than in England, where one may patent almost anything, and we very much regret to say, *where direct infringements* may be patented; and so defective are the patent laws, that infringements are declared valid, whilst the original patent is not secure." Greener had a good deal more to say on the subject on page 428 of this second edition (revised and enlarged) of his book *The Gun and Its Development,* but the quotation above is sufficient here for our purpose.

AIR ARMS DEVELOPMENT IN GREAT BRITAIN, 1900 TO THE PRESENT

During the early part of the 20th century the Birmingham Small Arms Company had almost complete control of the serious (that is to say, target type) air-rifle market. The Britannia could not find enough of a market, even in the face of a tremendous popular interest in air-rifle target shooting. Except for German imports, B.S.A. had the field to itself because of the excellence of its product and the relatively reasonable price at

Method of loading the early B.S.A. air rifle. The cocking-lever catch is unfastened by pressure of the left thumb against the barrel.

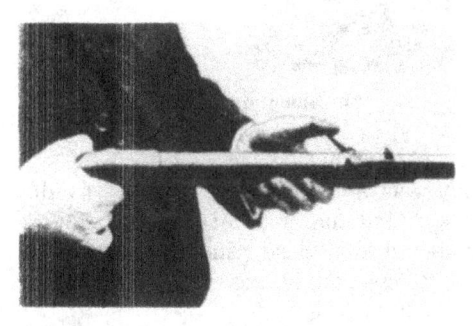

Opening the breechblock for loading.

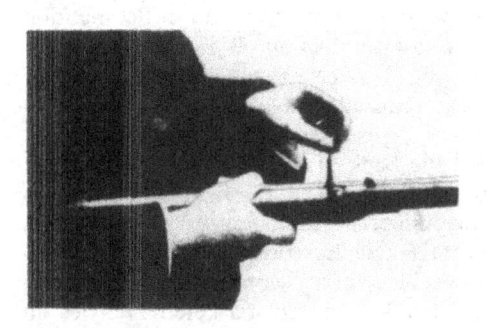

Inserting the pellet.

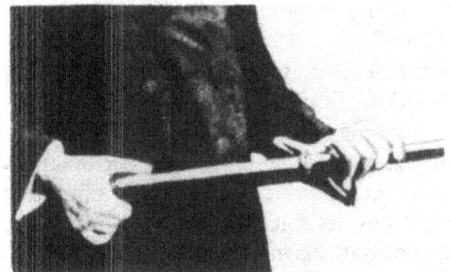

The lever pulled down to compress the charge of air and cock the rifle.

Closing the breechblock.

49

The Britannia air rifle

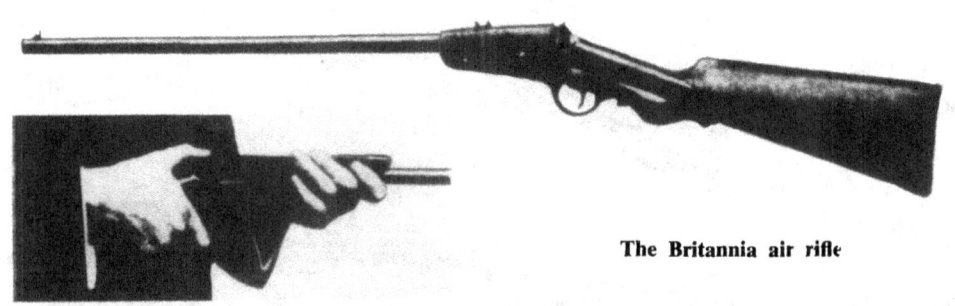

Method of loading the Britannia air rifle. Drawing back breech fastener to open rifle.

"Breaking open" the rifle.

Inserting the pellet.

which the company was able to sell it, which was due in turn to its background and manufacturing facilities. It must be remembered that these rifles are and were precision products, often costing more to manufacture than equivalent powder-cartridge rifles.

The Patent Office was flooded during the first and second decade with all sorts of toy and serious air-gun specifications, but we have room for very little mention here, since few ever saw production. Whiting's No. 4213 of 1910 for an air pistol to be cocked by lifting the air chamber section was unusual. Jeffries & Co. No. 10,250 of the same year was a pistol cocked by pulling out the lever which formed the back of the grip, the air chamber being in the grip as in the latest German Walther patterns. It was a forerunner—in some ways of the recent Acvoke. The leverage, while complex, offered possibilities for considerable spring compression, meaning added power; but this was never marketed. Jeffries in the same year also patented No. 25,783, a solid-barrel design with a bolt cocking mechanism and a safety sear system of merit (30,338). The American designer of the old Savage automatic pistols, E. H. Searle, patented a Daisy-type lever-action air rifle. (Note: Savage Arms about that time was considering entering the air-gun field in the United States, which accounts for Searle's patent coverage here and abroad. While this company did not produce air rifles for the market, they did turn out a toy shotgun shooting harmless rubber balls.)

In 1911 Jeffries patented a drop-barrel pistol with air chamber again in the grip (No. 1405) followed by another modification and a rifle specification (No. 15,823). B.S.A. and their designer, G. Norman, received patent 12,692 covering an air pistol cocked by pushing in the barrel, but it was never marketed in quantity.

The year 1912 saw E. Coke's spring-air design, No. 26,329, and a number of freak air-use patents ranging from a pneumatic cattle-stunning pistol to a constant drum compressor by B.S.A. But the prize of that year for hopeless air arms goes to No. 4676 and 77! These patents to J. Holloway and J. Howden covered *pneumatic guns for use on airplanes to be operated by a compressor attached to the motor which turned the propeller!*

B.S.A.'s patent No. 5564 of 1913 was the first approach to a real improvement in air rifles since the introduction of the old Lincoln-Jeffries, now known as the B.S.A. Mark I. This provided for spring compression on *both the opening and return strokes* of the compression lever, a system capable of use today in either increasing power (which the British do not want to do because of legal restrictions) or to ease the problem of cocking (which apparently they did not then believe worth the effort and expense).

In 1914 B.S.A. patented an air rifle with a sliding barrel and Norman's trigger and safety for it. No. 4313 to J. Mayer in 1915 covered an air gun with bolt cocking as in the current German "Sportmodells," a device curiously long ago used and forgotten in Germany itself. W. Baker's No. 5045 covered a barrel moving

Early British underlever swung down to cock spring.

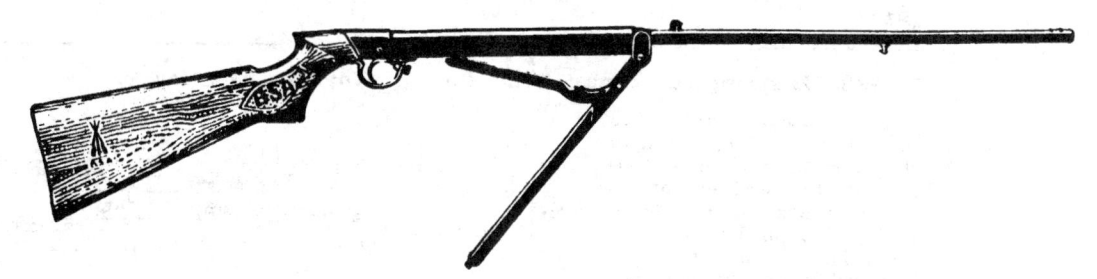

both longitudinally and down when cocking to give a complete air seal—another principle as old as early French shotgun design! But the weirdest item in British 1915 patents of the type is No. 15,914, G. J. Gawley's proposed propulsion of air pellets by utilizing the kinetic energy of air entering a vacuum!

The period of World War I slowed down air-gun patents, naturally, as it also slowed down interest in air-gun shooting. In 1920 a Firearms Act was passed which prohibited the free sale of firearms in Great Britain, and the licensing requirements were such that they gave a big boost to air-gun interest once more. One result was an added interest in the subject by inventors, qualified and unqualified! Most of them, as always, were unduly optimistic, and most of them just wasted time, energy, and money on patents they could not market and nobody would buy. That is the old, old story that inventors in all lands never seem to learn—that in any closely controlled industry with a long manufacturing background, the newcomer has very, very little chance of gaining an entrance.

Even established and knowing gunsmiths like Parker-Hale did some patenting; their No. 166,759 patent covering an air pistol along general lines which Webley & Scott had patented (but not produced) in 1911, but utilizing a rack-and-wheel cocking system. E. J. Anson's No. 178,048 for an air pistol with a jacket-around-barrel, rearward-moving piston, and cocking by a pivoting handle had elements of several pistols later marketed and was an interesting design indeed. L. Jeffries appeared again with Nos. 181,277 and 181, 640 and 41 encompassing pistols with compression springs and pistons in the butts. One pattern was cocked by a drop barrel and rod from the triggerguard; another by grip backstrap lever.

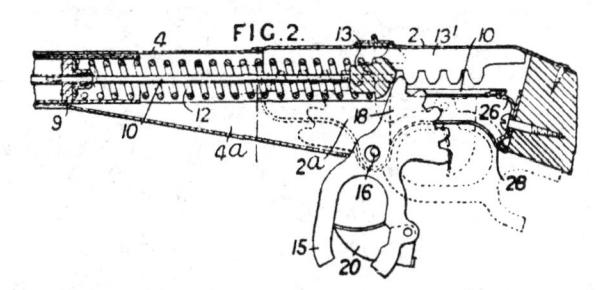

E. H. Searle's British patent 12,723 of 1910 for a trigger-guard-lever air rifle, ratchet operated. Searle was the inventor of the Savage automatic pistols. Savage never made this rifle, though they did produce a double-barreled toy spring gun at a later date.

1405. Jeffries & Co., L., and Jeffries, L. Jan. 19.

Pneumatic.—Relates to air-pistols in which the air cylinder is located within the handle or grip, and consists in cocking the plunger by a link detachably connected at one end to the drop-down barrel and at the other to the plunger. In the form shown, the barrel 3 is hinged on the pin 5 to the body 1, and is pivotally connected to one end of the cocking link 12, the other end of which carries a guide head 13 which slides in a slot 14 in the air cylinder 2, and, when the barrel is broken down, engages with the bottom of a slot 15 in a tubular extension of the plunger 16, depressing the latter and compressing the spring 11 until the spring-actuated sear 17 pivoted to the barrel engages the recess 17ª in the plunger. The barrel 3 is secured to the body 1 in the firing position by a spring-controlled lever 19, pivoted at 20 on the body 1, which snaps into engagement with a recess 23 in the side face of the rear end of the barrel, and may be released by pressing the rear end 19ª of the latch. The trigger 26 is pivoted at 27 to the barrel, and carries a projection 29 which trips the sear 17 when the trigger is pulled. The cocking link 12 acts as a trigger guard, and is detachably connected to the barrel 3 and the plunger 16 in the manner set forth in Specification 15,823/11. The pull required on the trigger may be adjusted by a screw 47, Fig. 11, passing transversely through the slotted part 30 of the body, and having a conical head 48 engaging the chamfered surface 49 of the sear 17 and adapted, on being screwed further home, to cause the sear to engage more lightly with the plunger 16, so that a lighter pull of the trigger will cause the discharge.

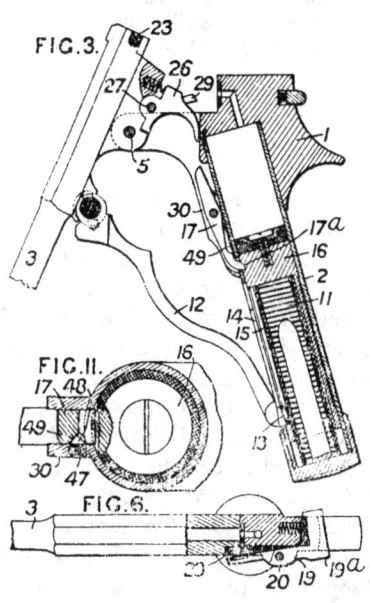

Abstract of original patent.

12,692. Birmingham Small Arms Co., and **Norman, G.** May 26.

Pneumatic. — Consists in forming the sliding piston in the form of a chamber embracing the breech end of the barrel. The invention is shown in Fig. 1 applied to a pistol. The hollow piston 3 fits on the enlarged breech end 1^a of the barrel, and is impelled forwards by a spring 6 acting on a shoulder 5 at its front end. The handle 14, Fig. 2, of the loading-plug 12 conforms to the outer diameter of the barrel when the plug is in its loaded position to allow the piston to slide over it, and recesses are formed in the outer casing 2 and in the hollow piston to allow the handle 14 to be reached when the weapon is cocked.

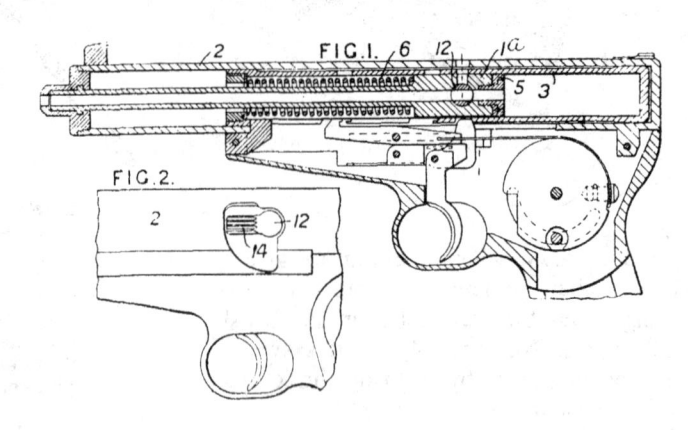

Abstract of original patent.

In 1922, E. C. T. Marks of the English Markham Air Rifle Co. was granted patent 191,291 on a breakdown air rifle with barrel pressed to the rear and sliding to make a better air seal—another old principle newly discovered! (Webley used it too.) E. E. Miles' No. 202,106 was for a very unique lever-action rifle, utilizing several independent springs, one compressed on opening the arm, another was engaged for compression on the closing action. Here was the nucleus for a powerful triggerguard-lever rifle, but it was never produced. Clark's No. 298,341, while approved, was not granted because the patent fee was not paid—another common enough occurrence in British patent history. Here a cocking rod folded down against the back of the grip, a system which met with some success on low-priced German makes later. Safeties, sears, breech sealers, and other "improvements" galore were patented, many of them really worthwhile, but useless to the inventor because there just were too few manufacturers, and they were not interested. (Note: Such lack of interest is not necessarily to be held against the manufacturers. They know their products, their costs, and their problems; and if they added every improvement suggested or offered on their arms, the tooling costs alone would often drive them out of business. All design and manufacturing is a matter of compromise.)

We must now confine ourselves because of lack of space to the successful, or reasonably successful, British air arms actually marketed from 1920 to the present time.

Birmingham Small Arms Air Rifles

The prewar B.S.A. Models 1 and 4 air rifles are identical in either .177 or .22 calibers (known in Great Britain as No. 1 and No. 2 bores, respectively), except for barrels and loading taps as required. These are clumsy-looking underlever cockers with spring and piston elements contained in a straight tube to the rear of the breech. They are cocked by drawing the lever housed in the fore-end down and back to the limit of the stroke. They are loaded by pushing back the loading tap lever and inserting a pellet, then closing the tap. They have adjustable triggers. These arms are well made and powerful as air rifles go and are extremely accurate. If in good condition, these rifles except for their ungainly appearance are the equal of any made today.

These models were followed by the modern streamlined designs demanded by users throughout the world following World War II.

The current models fall into two classes: First, the "Cadet" and "Cadet Major," lightweight breakdown types (cocked by breaking the barrel down) in caliber .177. Second, the heavier fixed-barrel, underlever cockers listed as the "Club Model" (cal. .177) and the similar but more powerful "Airsporter Model" (cal. .22).

As current production these rifles will be found pictured and detailed in the later section of this work, dealing with modern designs.

B.S.A. does not make air pistols.

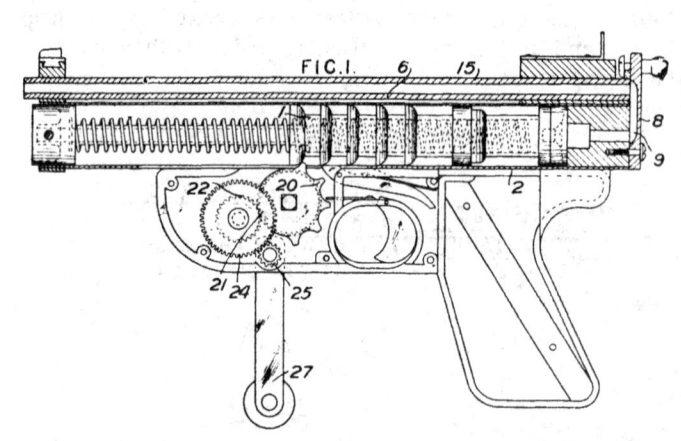

Parker & Hale patent application. Patent was never issued. Unusual ratchet-cocking pistol operated by underlever. Breech plug swung aside for loading. Parker & Hale is the largest mail-order gun house in Great Britain and is noted for quality accessories of their own design.

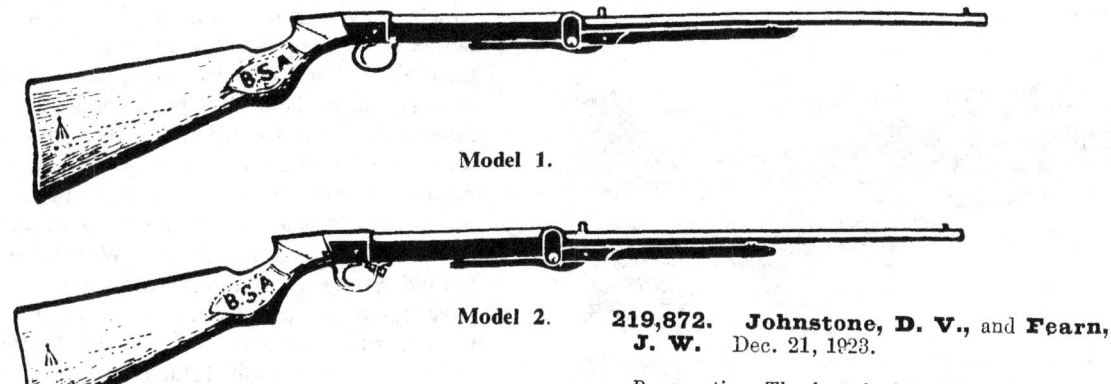

Model 1.

Model 2.

B.S.A. prewar underlever air rifles.

Webley & Scott Air Rifles and Air Pistols

Webley & Scott are world famous as makers of British service revolvers and pistols. Their air rifles and pistols are of the same high quality always found in their government production and firearms generally.

The firm's history goes back to 1790, when William Davis (later father-in-law of Philip Webley) set up business in Weaman Street in Birmingham, on the site of the present Webley & Scott factory. Philip Webley at the age of 14 was apprenticed to learn the art of gunlock filing, and some of the details of his indenture give an idea of how and why gunsmiths of that day became the master craftsmen they did. He was signed up for 7 years by his father. The first year he received 5 shillings per week. Each year thereafter his salary was increased 1 shilling per week progressively—in other words, he received the princely sum of 11 shillings per week when in his seventh year! His working hours? Six days per week, he worked from 6 o'clock in the morning until 7 o'clock at night in the summertime. In the winter it was a bit different: then he worked from 7 o'clock in the morning until 8 o'clock at night. When he was late for any reason whatever, his salary was "docked" accordingly! A hard system, true. But it laid the foundations for Britain's industrial greatness.

After his apprenticeship, Philip joined his brother, James, then making percussion guns and gunlocks, in 1835. Philip married William Davis' daughter and the two firms merged. When Philip's two sons were old enough to be taken into the firm, the name was changed to P. Webley & Sons. Their production ran all the way from gunmakers' tools to tomahawks, handcuffs, and boarding pikes.

Meanwhile, in 1834 the firm of W. & C. Scott & Son was founded in Birmingham, a firm which produced so many worthwhile gun and rifle designs and patents that it soon made a name for quality. The name "Scott" appeared alone on some guns as late as 1925.

Webley & Son admittedly had their interest in revolvers excited by Sam Colt's showing at the Great Exhibition in the Crystal Palace in London in 1851, and when Colt set up a factory in London two years later, Webley was ready with a percussion revolver on

219,872. Johnstone, D. V., and Fearn, J. W. Dec. 21, 1923.

Pneumatic.—The barrel of an air pistol or rifle is mounted above and parallel to the air cylinder, and is hinged thereto to serve as the cocking lever. As shown in Fig. 3, the air cylinder a is fixed to the handle a^1 and forms the body of the weapon. The barrel d is hinged to the front of the cylinder by a depending swinging bracket h and at the breech end normally engages a fixed bracket i^2 which is formed with air passages c, c^1 leading from the rear of the air cylinder to the barrel. The piston is pressed rearwardly by the action-spring and is cocked by a slide f connected by a link k to the barrel so that it is drawn forwards when the barrel is raised, as shown in Fig. 2. The slide f engages a collar b^2 at the front of the piston and forces it forwards until the sear e springs into bent with a collar b^1 towards the rear of the piston. In a modification, Fig. 8, the barrel d is hinged at the breech end, and is adapted to displace the piston rearwardly for cocking purposes. Air from the front of the cylinder a reaches the breech of the barrel through a tube m fixed axially in the cylinder.

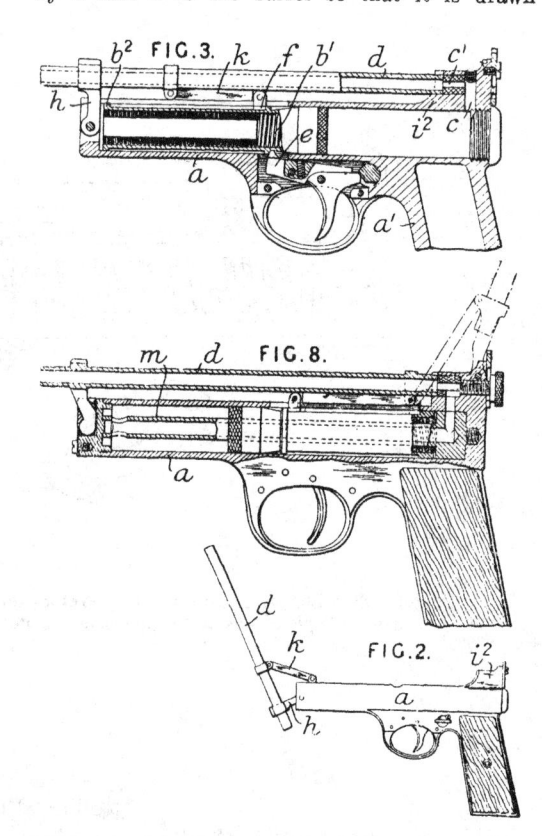

Abstract of original patent assigned to Webley & Scott.

53

Very early Webley Mark I pistol. Though over 35 years old and not well cared for, the pistol is still in good shooting condition. The somewhat clumsy turning trigger safety does not appear in current production. The grip has been altered on later models to afford better pitch and holding qualities. However, the basic sturdy design remains. The Webley is a "lifetime" manufactured precision air pistol.

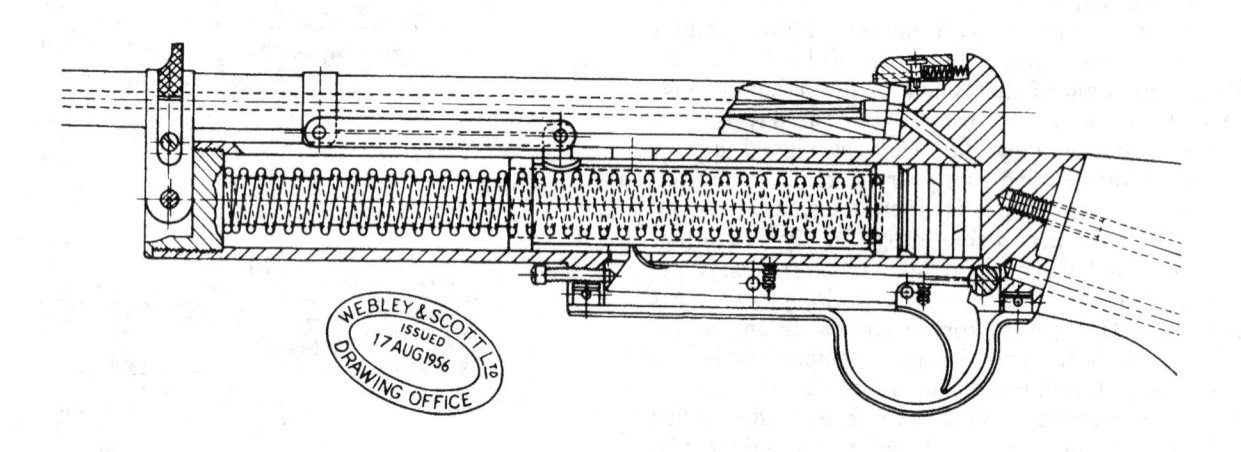

Factory drawing of action of first Webley air rifle, the Mark I. The design was based on the same patents as the Mark I pistol, as a comparison of details shows. Action is shown fired.

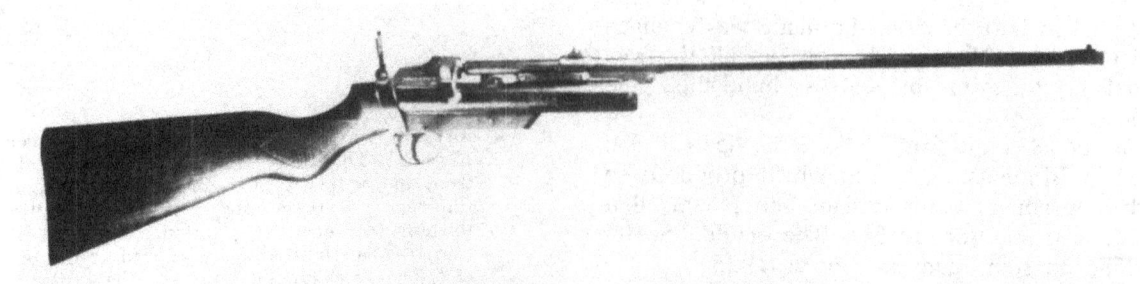

Webley Mark II, one of the finest air rifles ever designed. Rifle was too costly to make to be a financial success. It was used to some extent as a British service rifle trainer. Raising the army-pattern bolt handle frees the barrel, allowing it to rise at the breech end without effort. The barrel is then used as a lever, exactly as in the Webley pistols to cock the mainspring with very little effort for the power involved. A pellet is inserted in the breech, the barrel snapped down, and the bolt handle turned into locking position. As the bolt handle is turned down, a face cams the barrel back solidly against the breech face giving a positive air seal.

---

which they received Patent No. 734 of 1853. They dodged some of Sam'l's patents by substituting a detachable bullet rammer (these were muzzle-loading revolvers, remember) for his hinged ones and by various other expedients for which we have no space here. Later they even worked out a way to improve an attached rammer without giving the American any grounds to hit them with a lawsuit. When they couldn't meet Sam's low-cost production, T. W. Webley was sent to the United States to purchase production equipment which gave them an equal footing with Colt. Philip Webley worked out a double action (The Webley Self-Cocker) in 1853. When Colt folded up the London Works—quite a story in itself!—Webley was the only firm able to mass produce revolvers in England. Webley now set out for government business.

Many Webley's were sold to the Confederate States during our Civil War, a period which saw the coming of the first successful metallic cartridge revolver, the Smith & Wesson. Daniel B. Wesson, bothered by all the foreign (including English) pirates who were duplicating his new revolver, licensed Webley to make the design in .30 caliber. Thus, old Daniel, a most formidable antagonist, was able to muzzle the Birmingham attempts to steal his design, while he concentrated on slapping restraining suits on any American patent-jumpers. He graciously presented a revolver, dated 1863, to Mrs. Emma Webley, incidentally.

Webley's own first breechloader came in 1865. A monster revolver shooting the .577 Boxer cartridge was introduced soon after, an arm surpassed in power today only by the new S&W .357 and .44 Magnums. Then followed a series of powerful "Bulldog" revolvers, the Webley-Pryse hinge frame; and then the Webley-Kaufman of 1880, which led the way to the long line of British the barrel was raised, being pivoted at the muzzle end to the air cylinder. Linkage from barrel through a slot in the top of the air cylinder provided great leverage for forcing the piston and compressing the spring *towards the muzzle* within the air cylinder. A pellet was loaded into the breech. The barrel was brought down to closed position, where the spring catch engaged. Pulling the trigger released the piston which was driven to the rear by its spring, compressing the air ahead of it and forcing it through a small vent to propel the pellet. The design met with instant success at the Wembley exhibition and production started.

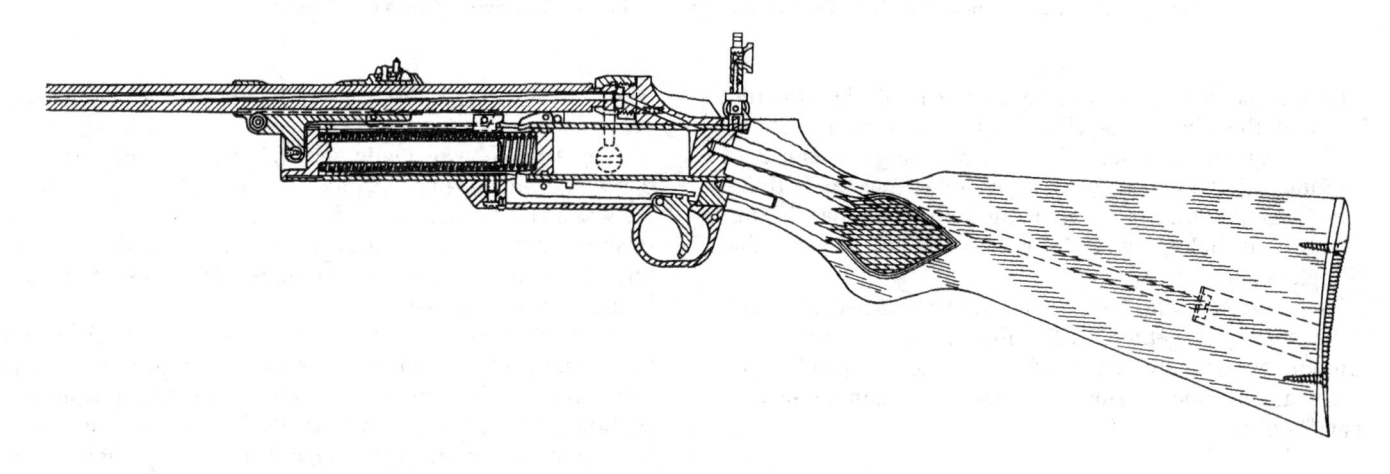

Webley factory detail drawing of the Mark II service air rifle.

service revolvers, police and target hinge frames, used right on through World War II. In 1898 Webley picked up rights to the "Mars" auto pistol developed by an Englishman (Gabbet-Fairfax) leading to the W&S pocket autos (made and sold in the U.S. under license by Harrington & Richardson) and to the huge Navy Model .455.

It was in 1897 that P. Webley and Son amalgamated with W&C Scott and Son and Richard Ellis and Son to form the Webley and Scott Revolver and Arms Co., Ltd. In 1906 the name was changed again to the current "Webley and Scott, Limited."

While the products of both name members of the firm are generally well known to shooters and collectors, few know that Webley made some 75,000 French Chassepot rifles used in the Franco-Prussian War and that they have also manufactured modern Austrian Mannlicher-Schoenauer rifles under license. So much for the Webley & Scott background.

All Webley & Scott air rifles and pistols are commonly known as "Webleys." They are sold throughout the world.

While Webley patented an air pistol as far back as 1911, it was not then marketed because of apparent small demand. When the restrictions on firearms in 1924 came into being, Webley moved swiftly to fill the gap for shooters. The Mark I Air Pistol appeared in both .177 and .22 calibers. It was quite similar in general design to the improved current models. A rear catch was drawn back to free the barrel, which was mounted above the air chamber and grip. The rear of

An improved form with a metal piston ring instead of the previous leather washer, which gave higher velocity through better air sealage, was introduced as the Mark II. In 1930 a cheaper version, the "Junior," with easier cocking, and less power, was introduced for use by boys. The "Senior" superseded the Mark II, incorporating the famous Webley revolver stirrup lock.

Details of all these current models are shown and discussed in the section dealing with today's air arms manufactured by Webley & Scott.

The first Webley air rifle did not appear until 1926. It was the Mark I, an unusual rifle based on the earlier pistol patents, utilizing the cocking principle of the pivoted superimposed barrel as used in the pistol. In a word, it was the Webley pistol altered as required to mount in a rifle stock for shoulder shooting. Manufacturing cost was so high that the price was correspondingly high, and the Mark I did not sell well.

The so-called Mark II Service Air Rifle of 1929 was unquestionably one of the finest target-type air rifles ever made. It was an improved version of the Mark I. Its barrels were quick-detachable, so three calibers could be had in one rifle merely by changing barrels. Calibers were .177, .22, and .25. To prevent loss of air at the jointure of barrel and air outlet, this model utilized a bolt-handle system with a screw nut having a quick-action thread. When locked down, the bolt *pulled* the breech end of the sliding barrel firmly against a fiber breech washer so no air could escape except directly into the chamber behind the bullet. It was a

British Greener air rifle, Model 1939. Caliber .177 was rated at 650 f.p.s. and caliber .22 at 590 f.p.s. velocity. The high power of this barrel-cocking design comes from the heavy-duty spring plus an unusual hermetic breech seal, the type being original with Greener though the principle is old. A lever attached to the barrel pivot actuates a cam which draws the barrel back against the washer at the breech as the action is closed. Note that the earlier Webley Mark I and II rifles produced a similar effect by different means. The cam is adjustable, allowing takeup when necessary to positively prevent air loss at breech, as can develop in ordinary barrel cockers. Weight about 6.4 pounds. Barrel approximately 20 inches. Overall 44.5 inches. Screw-adjustable trigger.

very ingenious way of overcoming one of the inherent faults of the hinged-barrel air-gun construction systems.

Here again, however, the cost was high because of manufacturing costs. You can't *get* something for nothing; and W&S couldn't *give* something for nothing. Manufacture was halted in 1946 because of poor sales due to high costs.

The current Mark III is an underlever, rigid-barrel type which, together with the cheaper breakdown "Junior" model, are described under current production. There are no finer spring-air rifles made than these current Webleys.

Greener Air Rifle

The old-line firm of W. W. Greener Ltd. of Birmingham made a powerful breakdown pattern air rifle for several years, production halting about 1940. Like all Greener products it was well designed and constructed, but for some strange reason was built along the ugly lines of the early B.S.A. rifles. Its very appearance was a block to sales. Like most breakdown patterns, it had a very short sight base because of the cocking system; the barrel being about 20 inches long and the overall length about 45 inches. Both sights were carried on the barrel. The piston and spring, of course, were housed in the cylindrical tube to the rear of the breech. It had good sights and the standard screw-adjustable trigger. As usual with Greener arms, the designers went out of their way to furnish at least one improvement. In this case it was the employment of a special lever on the barrel pivot pin, which automatically operated an adjustable cam to draw the barrel firmly back against the washer in the standing breech to give a positive air seal when the action was closed. The adjustment, of course, allowed tightening to take up any slack which might develop as the rifle wore in through usage. The gun has so much required hand-fitting that it is understandable why it had to be withdrawn from the market; but any owner who has one in good condition has a rifle of fine design and performance.

The Acvoke (Accles & Shelvoke) Pistol

This is another Birmingham product no longer in production. It was made by a firm long noted for the manufacture of cattle-stunning pistols in which a bolt is driven by blank cartridges, a slaughtering accessory much in favor in Great Britain.

The Acvoke was made in .177 caliber only. Its appearance was against it, too. Ugly and junky looking (it was made to sell at a low price), it nevertheless had several good design features—not particularly unique, but good copies and adaptations. Its cocking action borders on the fantastic!

A rifled barrel is mounted in a cylindrical barrel jacket, passing through the center of the piston and the coil spring. The spring is quite powerful, giving exceptional power for this type of design as here employed. It is cocked by pressing down on the opening lever, a feature the manufacturers stressed as being "easy." The beginner will find it otherwise. However, when one learns to apply simultaneous pressure with both hands, one against the unfolding lever, the other against the barrel jacket, it is quite easy. The makers touted this cocking system as avoiding the risk of bent barrels— an apparent disparaging reference to the Webley, where the barrel is used as the cocking lever. However, this author has handled dozens of Webleys and has never seen a bent barrel, though deliberate abuse by a very strong man can undoubtedly do it—and for the matter, the same abuse could ruin an Acvoke cocking lever! Parts requiring it were heat treated (sear, trigger, etc.). A good feature was the elimination of leather washers often used as seals. For the price, the Acvoke was a very

British Acvoke (for Accles & Shelvoke) .177 pistol. Concentric piston and spring system. A robust but rather clumsy design. Cocking lever forms grip back strap.

British Acvoke pistol. Cocking lever started.

good air pistol, penetration and accuracy being equal to nearly all the higher-priced ones. (As a cost index, it might be stated that in 1950 when this pistol was selling in England for 69 shillings 6 pence (plus the inevitable tax) the Webley price for their cheapest model was only 63 shillings, but the Senior model brought 6 pounds (120 shillings) plus tax. While the Webley is worth the additional money, the point is made merely to indicate why the Acvoke just couldn't be compared on a basis of manufacture and quality to the Webley Senior.

The Abas Major Air Pistol

The Abas Major formerly made by A. and A. Brown & Sons of Birmingham was also an interesting air pistol in the low-priced field. A weird looking, bulky arm, reminiscent of the Acvoke lines but of entirely different construction, this pistol had several unusual features to recommend it in its class.

Caliber .177, barrel well-rifled, overall length 7¾ inches, and weighing 2 pounds, the Abas Major was another example of the spring-driven piston air pistol where the barrel runs the length of the piston and spring—a system which allows maximum spring length and compression in a pistol, with consequent maximum power for its type.

In this pistol the barrel length was 7 inches, a factor which taken with its cocking system and spring-piston mounting system, allowed quite remarkable velocities to be developed. (Note: This author has seen only a few of these pistols, but tests for velocity showed the specimens unusually good in this respect.)

The long and powerful cocking lever begins at the butt, forms the triggerguard, and pivots at the muzzle end of the casing. A ratchet mechanism prevents the weapon being fired until the lever is in full closed position—an important item with such a leverage system, where the fingers could be pinched by any accidental closing movement.

Utilizing a fixed barrel, this pistol also incorporated a loading tap similar in principle to that found on high priced underlever rigid-barrel rifles, a system which not only allows ease of loading but also provides an excellent air seal.

Except for its ungainly appearance, the Abas Major is a better air pistol than most of the designs currently being made in Germany today for world export.

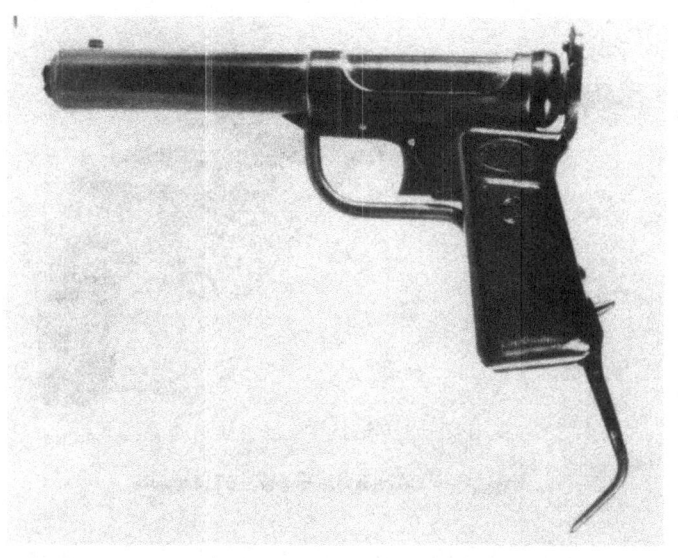

British Acvoke pistol. Back-strap lever full down ready for compression stroke. (Mainspring is around the barrel, which is positioned inside the barrel casing.)

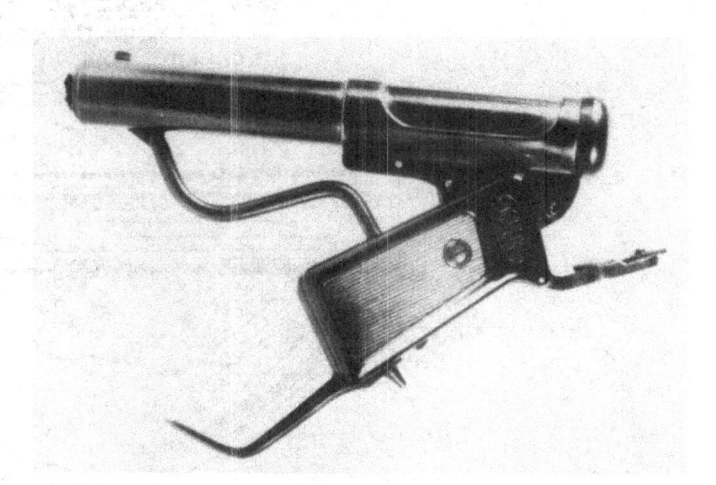

British Acvoke pistol. Cocking stroke. Note that as in the old German Haenel and the current American Hy Score, the grip actually is the true cocking lever. The Acvoke uses the back strap to furnish added cocking leverage, however. Also, as in the Haenel and Hy Score, note that opening the action for cocking does not expose the barrel breech for loading. This requires a separate action in all three.

British Abas-Major air pistol (A. & B. Brown Brothers). Concentric design. Cocked by pulling out lever which forms triggerguard and front grip strap. Loads at breech through loading plug (or tap) as in underlever rifles.

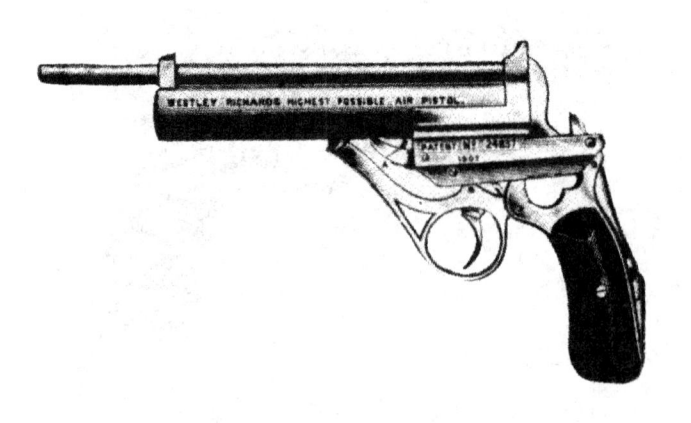

Obsolete Westley-Richards air pistol.

Westley Richards

The obsolete Westley Richards "Highest Possible" air pistol is of interest only as a collector's item, though in its day we are told it was an accurate and powerful pistol of its class. Caliber .177, length 12 inches, weighing 44 ounces, and with a 9¾-inch barrel according to old catalogs, it had rifled barrel and adjustable trigger. A clumsy and ungainly pistol with superimposed barrel above the air cylinder and a revolver-type grip, it operated on a form of the breakdown system. The pistol never achieved wide sales and will seldom be seen except in collections. This author has never shot one, but examination of a collection piece indicates that for power and accuracy it should have been the equivalent of any made today. All products of the W-R firm have been noteworthy for quality and accuracy.

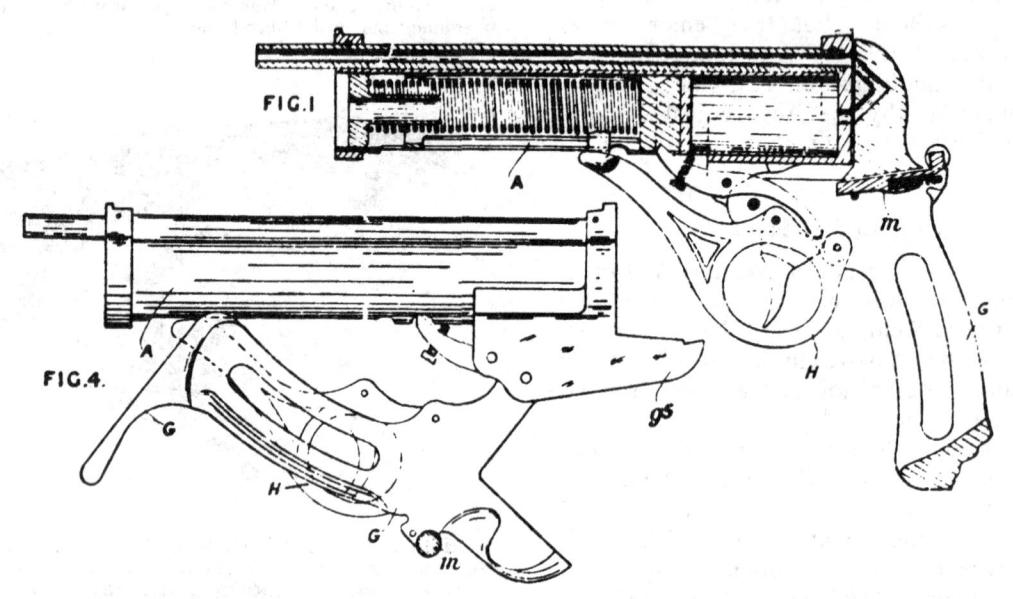

The drawings illustrate clearly the operation of spring compression in this ungainly but powerful spring-air design.

58

CHAPTER 3

Other Patterns of Gas and Spring Guns

> If Mr. Perkins's steam guns were introduced into general use, there would be but very short wars; since no fecundity could provide population for its attacks. . . .
> What plague, what pestilence would exceed, in its effects, those of the steam gun?—500 balls fired every minute . . . one out of 20 to reach its mark—why, 10 such guns would destroy 150,000 daily. If we did not feel that this mode of warfare would end in producing peace, we should be far from recommending it. . . .
> We have heard, but we do not vouch for the fact, that the Emperor of Russia, who has more knowledge of the importance of steam than some of us Englishmen, has sent an agent to procure a supply of Perkins's steam guns, which that gentleman's patriotism will not allow him to offer. . . .
> Opinions on steam guns, warfare, and Russia as expressed by the learned editors of *The London Mechanics Register,* November 1824.

ALTHOUGH the fact is very little known today, there have been many steam-operated guns and cannon and steam-powered centrifugally-discharged arms of amazing power and speed of fire.

Since this book deals with all pellet throwing arms other than powder types, some slight indication of these off-beat patterns is in order here.

Leonardo da Vinci left us a drawing of a "steam cannon" he dreamed up which is pictured here. There is only tradition that the idea ever went beyond the crude drawing stage, but at least he did toy with the idea. Many writers who have credited the great Leonardo with inventing an "air" gun, have confused this steam-gun drawing with an air cannon. In his lifetime (1452-1519) Da Vinci sketched out many ideas too advanced for the technology of the period. This was one of them.

Early in the 19th century, Watt and Bolton in England and Murray in America gave some attention to utilizing the new steam engines (which had been made possible, incidentally, by Denis Papin's application of the piston) in an artillery form. Later both the French and the Russians claimed to have done work on this order. *All, however, were failures* primarily because they could not control steam at high pressures—10 atmospheres (roughly 140 pounds) then being the maximum their boilers would then hold.

About 1804, one M. Jairy brought to the French minister of marines a model of a steam gun he proposed to use aboard warships, where the necessary engine, boiler, fuel, water, and ammunition could all be made readily available.

M. Jairy's gun was really a triple-threat weapon as he visioned it! First, it would throw solid shot to sink the ship itself; next, it would hurl small shot at a terrific rate to annihilate the personnel in case the ship proved unsinkable; and finally, it would flood the enemy decks with high-pressure water at close quarters to put their guns out of action by wetting down their powder supplies in case it didn't kill all the crew with bullets!

The gun never got beyond the model stage—but apparently the model worked. However, when the usable steam gun finally did emerge due to advanced technology, the Jairy device (as so often in history) allowed national face-savers to take the superior "we knew it all the time" attitude.

French records also indicate that in 1814 an engineering officer in the French army, one M. Gerard, developed a steam gun for use in the defense of Paris. It was a 6-barreled affair, crank operated somewhat in the fashion of the later Gatling gun of the metallic cartridge era. (It is to be remembered that in 1814, firearms were still muzzle loaded, either with separate priming, ball, powder, and wad, or with a paper or similar "cartridge" carrying the powder and ball, which still had to be rammed down the barrel and the outside pan then primed in order to ready for flint firing.)

A large boiler mounted on a carriage accompanied the firing section. When the steam line was hitched up to the firing mechanism, turning the handle brought each barrel successively into line for feeding and then for a steam injection. It is said that the gun fired 180 balls per minute. A cart with fuel and ammunition followed the bulky apparatus.

Used from behind fortifications and fired at close range against infantry, the device might have had some military value. It was intended for use in defending Paris, but the war ended and the city fell without a struggle. Soon afterwards the device was destroyed. In view of the low-pressure steam available at that time, we know that it could not have had either long range, reliable operation, or great power; but it showed imaginative military thinking.

It was not until the appearance in England of the Perkins steam gun, however, that the device really became a potentially important military arm—and only the advent of the metallic cartridge finally prevented its utilization.

THE PERKINS STEAM GUN

The inventor, Jacob Perkins, is all but unknown in American history today—yet his genius contributed greatly to our present day comfort and to mechanical and even social developments.

He was born at Newburyport, Massachusetts, at the mouth of the Merrimac River, on July 9, 1766. His ancestors had landed at Ipswich in 1630. At the age of about 12 he was apprenticed to a goldsmith. His master died 3 years later, and young Perkins continued to operate the business! While still only 15 he invented a process for plating shoe buckles—a good business in that day—and the business prospered. He was so remarkable a craftsman that when he was barely 21, the State of Massachusetts commissioned him to make the dies for the State's copper coins! At the age of 31 he invented a machine for heading and pointing nails and tacks in a single operation, a most remarkable invention in its day; but he fell in with promoters who ruined him, while others profited from the invention.

He moved to New York and later to Philadelphia where he developed probably the first steel plates for banknote engraving, a system of preventing banknote forgery which was widely acclaimed and used, methods for hardening and annealing steel, and a wide variety of other items.

Unable despite his ability and energy to get proper financial backing here, he moved to England in 1818 taking a group of his craftsmen with him. America's loss was Britain's gain. In England he received financial support. He started a successful banknote business and went on to develop instruments for measuring ships' speeds, for determining diving depths, and a score of other devices.

When he turned his attention to steam development, this amazing man really hit his stride. He developed a single-cylinder steam engine with a boiler capable of holding the then unbelievable pressure of 800 pounds. When pistons didn't stand up, Perkins produced a special alloy which gave a machined finish requiring no lubricant, together with all the other required physical properties. Then he produced his steam gun.

The Duke of Wellington became very interested in this Perkins gun, but even with this support Perkins had two strikes against him in trying to deal with the professional military minds. First, he was a "Colonial" not far removed from Concord, Lexington, and the year 1776. Second, he was trying to convince a professional military body, a group which in any age has been, is, and probably always will be slow to accept the new. Like Texas Judge Roy Bean's approach of "Let's give him a fair trial and then hang him!" the military bodies approached the Perkins gun convinced it just wouldn't work anyway! Due to Wellington's interest they at least had to listen.

In the first trials before the Iron Duke and his engineering officers, Perkins streamed volumes of lead musket balls against a ¼-inch iron plate to demonstrate close quarters accuracy and destructive force. His steam pressure was now up to some 900 pounds, low by comparison with any gunpowder even of that day, but unbelievably higher than had ever before been achieved; and sufficient to completely shatter the projectiles against the iron target.

When the penetrating power was *still* questioned, Perkins fired at a set of eleven 1-inch planks spaced for testing. All 11 were penetrated. Tough iron projectiles punched through a ¼-inch iron plate! All the penetration tests were at 35 yards from the muzzle, then a good musket distance. If we remember that a penetration of ¼-inch in pine is considered equal to a dangerous human wound, the significance of the tests stands out; particularly in that day of muzzle-loading, single-shot weapons.

Perkins then screwed a tube to the gun barrel which would feed the balls in by gravity to make a sort of

Steam gun (small). This gun was discharged by steam pressure created by water flowing into the barrel kept at red heat by live coals. (Model of invention by Leonardo da Vinci.)

machinegun. This device worked. The next step was a wheel mounting carrying several such tubes, spoke-fashion, which could be brought into play for rapid fire. The fantastic firing rate of 1,000 shots per minute was thereby obtained—all this remember in the year 1824!

By attaching a movable joint to the barrel, Perkins sent bullets down a 12-foot plank, spacing them to show that a military company charging in the approved fashion of the time would have had every soldier in the line down with a bullet in the brisket! Another attachment allowed *shooting around corners*—a device introduced by the Germans for block-fighting in streets and for getting at blind corners from inside tanks during World War II!

Some of the military objections raised were really interesting; as for example, the steam pressure would deform the musket balls in firing them! Accuracy penetration, rate of fire—those were not questioned. But—deforming the projectiles was a very serious consideration!

The French became interested, and at Greenwich Perkins conducted exhibitions for Prince Polignac and a group of French military engineers. They specified a design to fire sixty 4-pound balls a minute. Perkins agreed to adapt the gun. Then they wanted it to shoot musket balls, machinegun style also. Perkins obliged. When it came to spending money to buy the guns, however, all dragged heels, and nothing eventuated.

The Greeks wanted a couple to chase the Turks out of Patras—an old story still new. "The Russian Autocrat," as one writer of the day put it, "has been vainly negotiating for a park of them." That word "vainly" stands out. Perkins was a man of principle as well as ability.

Meanwhile cartridge development was moving ahead —thanks to civilian sporting development for the most part. Percussion caps had come into being and the era of the "fixed" cartridge was in sight. These developments, together with the practical difficulties of working with steam under high pressure in the field, canceled out any acceptance of the steam gun. True, cannon were still muzzle-loading, and the French now toyed with the idea of Perkins steam cannon on warships because of rapid fire, close-quarters, and boarding value; but warfare too was changing rapidly.

So Perkins patent 4592, British, of May 15, 1824 came to naught as a gun; but from its development the inventor and industry learned much about handling high-pressure steam which was incorporated into home and industry usage. We have no space here to pursue those collateral developments, however.

Later Steam Guns and Centrifugals

Perkins's guns projected *entirely* by force of steam, using it as the motive power by *direct* application just as gunpowder is used.

Many of his successors used steam to *generate power* for spinning what was in effect an enclosed flywheel onto which metal balls were spilled. The balls were thrown by utilizing *centrifugal force* and a nozzle which imparted direction to their flight.

The London MECHANICS' REGISTER.

"He that enlarges his curiosity after the works of nature, demonstrably multiplies his inlets to happiness." JOHNSON.

No. I.]   SATURDAY, NOVEMBER 6, 1824.   [Price 3d

Mr. PERKINS's EXTRAORDINARY STEAM GUN.

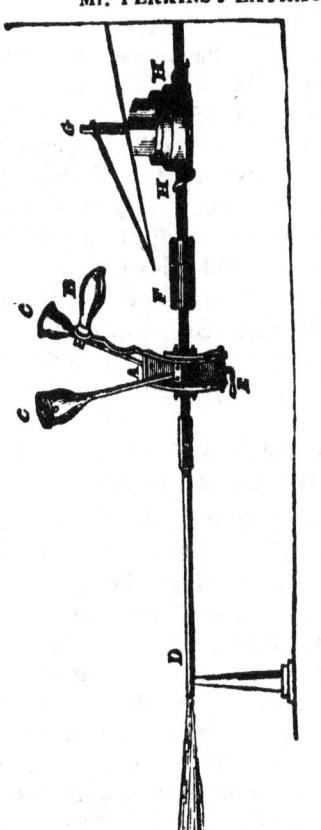

Description of Mr. Perkins's Steam Gun.

A.—The Chamber of the Gun, from which the Barrel is charged.

B.—The Handle which directs the piece working in the Chamber, and by means of which the Balls are conveyed from the Hoppers (C) into the Barrel.

C.—The Hoppers, into which the Balls are placed, and from which they drop one by one into the Chamber, when the Handle (B) is moved to its extent.

D.—The Barrel, which is about six feet in length.

E.—A Regulating Screw, by means of which the Handle is kept tight.

F.—A Swivel Joint, which allows of the Gun being elevated or lowered to any point, and by means of which the Barrel may be moved in almost any direction.

G.—A Throttle Valve, by which the Steam is admitted from the Generator of the Engine, and into which the Pipe, communicating with the Barrel, is introduced.

H. H.—Mr. PERKINS's admirable mode of uniting Pipes so as to resist any pressure. This represents the junction of the Pipe from the Generator with that from the Chamber.

Vol. I.   A

Original announcement of successful Perkins steam-gun tests.

Description of the Ball.

A.—The Ball before it is placed in the Barrel; the exact size is described.
B.—The appearance of the Ball on the side nearest to the Gun when discharged against an Iron Plate on the wall, at a distance of 100 feet from the Barrel, and flattened by the force of the concussion.
C.—The appearance of the Ball on the side which strikes against the Plate.

Original drawings indicating great penetrating power of the Perkins steam gun.

Numerous patents were granted on such devices in the United States just about the period of the Civil War. Thayer in Boston was first in 1858, followed by Joslin, Dickinson, Eaton, and Turner—all the latter in Cleveland, a city something of a hotbed of such development. The original work on these lines, incidentally, appears to have rested with two earlier engineers, de Parville and Kinderhook, who constructed a centrifugal gun as early as 1837. At the time, the Scientific American Magazine gave considerable backing to the idea.

However, Dickinson's seems to have been the first really efficient gun of this type. One was being built for use by the Confederate forces, but delivery was headed off by General Benjamin Butler—a political general, not a professional soldier, who also headed off delivery of Gatling machineguns to the South and who had enough foresight that he tried (ineffectually) to get the North to invest in both Gatlings and Dickinsons.

In 1870, one H. Kahn of Troy, New York was granted a patent on a spring-actuated centrifugal gun; but by now the metallic cartridge was an established fact, and the Kahn gun was never produced.

HISTORY OF MILITARY AND NAVAL USES OF COMPRESSED-AIR PROJECTORS

From the works of Philo of Byzantium, the second century B.C. military engineer, we learn much of the "Beleopeacca" of Ctesibius, a form of heavy rock-throwing machine in which the force of compressed air was used, it is stated, by the Greeks before the time of Christ. Here, however, we find the air compression acting through mechanical thrusting heads—the compressed air is *not* used directly against the projectile as in standard compressed-air arms. Of the Greek uses of air as an explosive force, we know little except what can be gathered from the Rhodios treatise already referred to.

All notice of use of compressed air as a direct projectile force seems to have vanished with the burning of the records in the Alexandrian Library, if indeed it was so used, and it is not until we reach the 15th century that we have even any traditions of such use; and not until the 16th century that we have any actually verifiable ones!

In this connection, though, we should not lose sight of the fact already pointed out, generally, that Hero of Alexandria left *positive* records of a stationary steam engine, another device which was greeted as new and original when it reappeared in the 18th and 19th centuries, and which shows that forces other than the purely mechanical were known very early.

From the 16th century French *Elements de l'artillerie* by the Sieur de Fleurance Rivault, we learn of a simple and rather efficient rampart gun on the compressed-air principle. Air for this gun was pumped up in a cylindrical container to the rear of the breech. The arm fired a heavy dart-type slug Rivault called a "flèche." Little use was made of the device, apparently because of the superiority of powder arms even at that period.

About the year 1883, Lieutenant Edmund L. Zalinski began work in the United States on perfecting pneumatic dynamite-throwing guns. Born in Prussian Poland, Zalinski was brought to the United States by his parents while still a child. He fought with great distinction in the Union Army during our Civil War, earning a commission. After the war he was enrolled as an officer in the Regular Army and served for a time as a military scientist at the Massachusetts Institute of Technology. His story merits our attention here.

The So-Called "Zalinski" Guns

> The gun is generally spoken of as Zalinski's Gun and as being my invention. This I have deprecated and repeatedly denied. I claim however that I have given direction to its development as a practical military appliance, indicating in a general way the requirements to make it such.
>
> I am not a mechanical engineer and could not properly have worked out the mechanical details and design unassisted. Mechanical Engineer Mr. Nat. W. Pratt of the Babcock & Wilcox Company, and Mechanical Engineer of the Pneumatic Dynamite Gun Company worked out the details.
>
> The electrical fuse, alone, I claim as my personal invention. But in its development I have received very material assistance from others.
>
> Direct quotation from a lecture in 1887 at Fort Hamilton, New York, by First Lieutenant E. L. Zalinski, U. S. A., Fifth Artillery.

The quotation above, it is hoped, will assist future writers in treating more accurately than in the past the subject of the huge U.S.S. *Vesuvius'* pneumatic guns used in the War of 1898, whose invention have been ascribed by biographical, encyclopedical, and popular writers to Lieutenant Zalinski. His modest disclaimer never caught up with the erroneous stories originally peddled by overly enthusiastic journalists and hazy observers.

Anywhere the subject of compressed-air guns arises, the name of Zalinski appears—and rightly so! Without his drive it is questionable whether the dynamite guns would ever have been truly developed. Indeed, the artillerist owes him a debt for bringing into the open not only their possibilities, but also their deficiencies; and his work on fuses did much to advance the study of detonation.

The present author found that published reports usually encountered came under the criticism so ably expressed by Auguste Demmin—they were written by compilation, not by study and research, the only reliable channels when, as in this case, direct observation is no longer possible. Research was undertaken in the musty collections of old American, English, and French army and navy files; in the records of Babcock & Wilcox; in engineering reports of the Royal Engineers; and in the original statements of Zalinski and those of Lieutenant Hamilton, his superior, who first assigned him to study the ORIGINAL pneumatic dynamite gun.

The real story is far more interesting and provocative than the myths which surround the guns. Since the subject would require books to cover thoroughly only a few of the highlights can be touched upon here.

The First Test Dynamite Gun

In 1883 a Mr. Mefford from Ohio manufactured a special pneumatic gun which was delivered to Fort

Hamilton, New York Harbor, for testing as a new form of weapon. The post adjutant, Lieutenant William R. Hamilton, assigned Lieutenant Zalinski the duty of conducting the experimentation.

The Mefford gun was basically a seamless brass tube 28 feet long mounted on a tripod. The internal diameter was 2.00 inches. Its wall thickness was about ¼ inch. Its reservoir held 12 cubic feet of air at a pressure of about 500 pounds. The air supply was connected with the gun breech by a simple flexible rubber hose. The "firing-valve" was a simple 2-way cock turned off and on by hand, not satisfactory, but adequate.

This crude first model was intended to fire the then new explosive dynamite or one of its minor variants in the explosive gelatine field. The new explosives packed nearly double the power of the same weight of the best powders then in use, but safe fusing had not been developed for using dynamite in standard powder-propelled gun missiles.

The Mefford design, because of the lack of shock in projecting missiles with compressed air, was intended for hurling relatively large quantities of sensitive high explosives in offensive actions, particularly at shore installations. Zalinski also felt the principle had some value for fortress defense.

In the initial Fort Hamilton demonstrations under Lieutenant Zalinski's control, this crude model fired projectiles with reasonable accuracy some 2100 yards distance across the harbor, a remarkable record for compressed-air propulsion.

Results were so satisfactory that larger models of improved design were immediately undertaken. A 4-inch model built by the Delamater Works from the improved design of G. F. Reynolds gave a quite remarkable test performance. The gun tube (barrel) was made from 3 sections of seamless brass tubing with an internal dimension of 4 inches and a 3/16-inch-thick wall. Special reservoirs and efficient valves were provided. This model was actually a finished product. Pressure was kept at 2,000 pounds by a steam pumping engine; but the ideal *launching* pressure came to only 1,000 pounds. It must be noted however that unlike powder arms where usually the maximum pressure generated is gradually diminished as the projectile moves down the barrel, in this pneumatic gun the air pressure *was maintained* so that the pressure remained constant—a big factor in the performance of these huge air guns. It is also to be remembered that *no air hand or shoulder arms* work on this *sustained-power* principle; all being fed air or gas under conditions which approximate a firearm's discharge because of the valving complexity. This factor is desirable in such arms, for while it reduces their power, it lowers manufacturing costs and makes for simplicity of design and reduction of number of parts.

This 4-inch model was not, as reported in English military engineering journals, tested at Fort Hamilton, but actually at Fort Lafayette. The pentration tests in particular were interesting. Six iron plates of .8-inch thickness were backed up at 60 yards. These plates, by the way, as well as other metal targets used, were taken from the English ship *Nankin,* which had been sunk in the New York harbor and raised by our Department of Engineers for salvage study! All English reports pass over this sidelight. Zalinski, of course, was merely trying to establish penetration against metal of foreign proof.

A projectile made up of an iron and brass casing loaded with sand, having a total weight of 30 pounds, was fired at the iron plates from the 40-foot launching tube. It penetrated 3 plates—a total of 2.4 inches! This remarkable result was achieved with a pressure, as stated, of 1,000 pounds of air which gave the missile a muzzle velocity of about 800 feet per second!

Larger models were built starting with 8-inch, and Zalinski experimented with one of 15-inch bore! Babcock & Wilcox were responsible for most of the production.

Special ships were designed to mount these new guns —the *Vesuvius* class. The original *Vesuvius* used in the War of 1898 was equipped with 3 of these guns in improved form. The tubes were about 40 feet long— though Zalinski's experiments had established that almost equal performance could be achieved with a 24-foot length. They were made of bronze. The guns could launch at the rate of one projectile per minute. They were fired fore and aft, incidentally.

Their record of destruction at Santiago Harbor, where they were used under optimum conditions, was interesting, but very highly overrated in the popular press. They were rejected by both military and naval authorities as inadequate for the purposes intended soon after the war ended. No more *Vesuvius* class ships were built.

It should be remembered that the use of compressed air for heavy-missile throwing was not original with Mefford, though the concept of its particular use was. Hero of Alexandria, as we have seen, made passing mention of a submarine torpedo long before the time of Christ. When Zalinski started experiments with the Mefford model gun, all important navies were using compressed air either directly, through pneumatic rams, or with black powder or cordite "boosters." Accuracy range, and control were all poor, however, and it was Zalinski's hope to outmode the torpedo with the new pneumatic guns.

The compressed-air launching provided a way to cushion the shock of discharge when hurling projectiles carrying highly sensitive warheads. He checked windage by use of wads and stabilized his flying projectiles by mounting wings at an angle to a tail which served much as arrow feathers do.

The experimental 8-inch guns were tested by the English at Shoeburyness in March 1891. These had 60-foot tubes, and operated on a 1,000-pounds air pressure, delivered from 8 steel reservoirs positioned below the trunnions. They were fired without warheads in an accuracy test with quite remarkable results. At over 3,000 yards range, two landed in the same hole, the third less than 30 yards away!

However, these and other tests all seem to have overlooked one very elementary fact: the shooting was from a stable land position. When shooting from the rolling decks of the little *Vesuvius,* the accuracy could not be so perfectly controlled. *When* they hit anything, naturally 500 pounds of gelatine scarred things up a bit!

63

One very interesting sidelight is furnished by reports of our Chief of Ordnance in 1890, dealing with the use of subcaliber projectiles developed for these pneumatic guns. An experimental gun of 15-inch caliber was used for close ranges, the subcaliber projectiles from the same gun being employed for longer-range firing.

The 15-inch projectile weighed 1,000 pounds, the 10-inch sub weighed 500 pounds, and the 8-inch sub weighed 300 pounds.

Muzzle velocity of the 15-inch was 625 feet per second. The 10-inch was up to 865 feet per second. The 8-inch reached 1049 feet per second! All with an air pressure of 1,000 p.s.i.

With a 30 degree elevation, the 15-inch dropped 2 shells at 2,445 and 2,541 yards, while the 8-inch sub at the same elevation ranged 5,007 yards with little dispersion.

Lieutenant Zalinski in particular took over the ticklish task of developing satisfactory fuses, both contact and time, finally producing an electric unit. In the course of studying the explosive effects of the missiles, Zalinski —and all other military and naval experts through the world, all of whom eventually had access to Zalinski's findings—missed one item which might have had momentous value: the method of achieving extreme penetration with missiles.

He soon found that when the explosive was in the head of his missile, most of its effectiveness was wasted on contact. The major effort blasted back to the rear in line of least resistance. So Zalinski moved his charge *to the rear* of the projectile for improved penetration. These experiments were actually forerunners of the Monroe Effect, the so-called "hollow" or "shaped" charge—the "secret" weapon of World War II which gave the bazooka its devastating ability to punch through armor. Had Zalinski by research, design, or accident followed through on the lines of his penetration experiments, the next progressive step would have led him to the answer, shaping the charge to give the greatest direction of the explosive effect straight ahead!

The "Rough Riders" Pneumatic Cannon

There are many old-wives' tales circulated about these guns also. In the first place, they were not used by the beloved Colonel "Teddy" Roosevelt. They were owned and operated by the Cuban insurgents who were supporting his charge at San Juan Hill.

Furthermore, they were not straight compressed-air guns operating from pumped-up air reservoirs. These were Sims-Dudley field guns (though some were also mounted for naval use). Instead of the cumbrous air tanks and compressing equipment, these guns fired a smokeless powder blank cartridge into a chamber to compress air for launching.

Too many popular writers have drawn upon the per-

Pneumatic cannon shooting torpedo explosives.

fervid Richard Harding Davis and other good, exciting, but unqualified reporters of the era—good in that they knew how to write to attract public attention, unqualified in that they knew nothing about the technicalities of compressed-air guns.

Simon Robin, a French gunmaker who lived 1769 to 1842, developed a gun in which the explosion of powder gases was used to compress air, which in turn hurled a projectile. Others might be mentioned, but the development doesn't warrant the space here.

In any event, the so-called pneumatic guns of the Cuban War period, except for the Mefford type, were Sims-Dudley guns utilizing the general principle of Robin. After the war, the New York firm of Francis Bannerman, the originator of the "war surplus" business, purchased the entire stock of seized and obsolete equipment from our War Department.

Francis Bannerman, one of the great selling copywriters of all time, described them in his early catalogs as the " 'Rough Riders' Dynamite Guns attached to Colonel Roosevelt's command and which caused consternation to the Spanish Army—one shell destroying a large building." Going on to quote Richard Harding Davis, he adds: "Our dynamite gun hit one of the enemy's big guns under the lip and threw it 30 feet into the air. The Spaniards may be able to stand rifle and artillery fire, but dynamite is too much for them—after the third shot from the dynamite gun, the Spaniards were in full retreat." This from the New York Sun in 1898.

Bannerman got 11 of these field guns in his "grab bag" purchase of equipment—a commentary on what the qualified military experts thought of the design, by the way! Bannerman quotes an army officer as telling him that "He personally never would have sold him the particular gun which had backed up the Rough Riders" (the gun was operated by Cubans). Bannerman goes on to say that in reply to a request from Colonel Hayes, son of President Hayes, some years later that he donate this gun to be used in decorating a battlefield memorial at San Juan, Cuba, he said: "If we ever make a donation of it, it will be to send it to President Roosevelt's home at Oyster Bay!"

As a matter of record, Francis Bannerman has long since gone to meet his Maker, leaving behind him on Poloppel or "Bannerman's Island" in the Hudson, the decaying hulk of an enormous "castle" he constructed to serve as an arsenal; and a little home there in which over lintels and fireplaces and in sundry other places he had carved in stone or concrete biblical quotations attesting to his rock-ribbed religious beliefs and his charitable nature.

But the present author, having seen the graven quotations, must add that Mr. Bannerman did *not* give the "Rough Rider" gun to the Roosevelt Museum; and that if memory is correct, he saw the self-same gun in the famous arms collection of Fuad, King of Egypt, some few years before that worthy fled from the throne— a long distance indeed from Oyster Bay and American history!

Bannerman listed 10 of these guns, complete with field carriages and limbers. To order he would mount them on naval or other types of support. They were bronze, 16 feet long, and weighed 480 pounds for the gun. The carriage weighed approximately another 600 pounds. The loaded projectiles weighed about 11.5 pounds, the stated range (extreme) being about 3600 yards. They were lightweight metal casings filled with H.E. and carried either time or contact fuses.

These guns had an upper tube or barrel for launching the projectile and a lower tube about 7 feet long and about 12.5 inches in diameter which formed the combustion and air chambers. The explosive, loosely identified as "dynamite," was an explosive gelatine.

To fire the gun, the firing chamber was loaded with a cartridge which contained from 7 to 9 ounces of smokeless powder—an interesting commentary in itself, since most of our infantry were then armed with black-powder rifles, cartridges for which (.45-70's) the Bannerman firm is still selling, from their original purchase!

The explosion of the smokeless powder immediately generated gases which compressed the air in the air chamber, forcing it through a vent into the space behind the projectile and launching it.

In later catalogs these Sims-Dudleys were enthusiastically offered by the redoubtable Bannerman (and

Rough Riders' dynamite gun.

sold by him, incidentally!) as being usable from "field carriage, naval cone carriage, or flat carriage *for firing aimed shots from airships*"! Of this gun the New York World wrote: "It threw earthquakes into the Spanish trenches terrorizing the Spanish soldiers"—a statement which sober history doesn't substantiate very well in light of the few casualties inflicted thereby. When General Funston got around to describing this 1898 "Hydrogen Bomb," writing in Scribner's Magazine in 1910, he said of this gun: "When it gave its characteristic cough, we saw the projectile sail through the air and strike the blockhouse squarely in the center; the shell penetrated and burst inside killing the 16 defenders. The structure was all but demolished, portions of the roof being blown a hundred feet in the air." Hardly a famous victory!

In offering 10 of these guns on field carriages with projectiles, the owner proferred the services of "the inventor, Mr. W. Scott Syms [sic] who will inspect and pass guns and projectiles as in serviceable order for use before delivery." Offering the guns "at bargain prices to responsible parties," the sage Scot added: "No revolution will be attempted against a government armed with such destructive, terrorizing guns"! Since *every* nation to which Mr. Bannerman supplied equipment has since gone through various and sundry revolutions —they run all the way from China to Nicaragua—his gift of prophecy may be subject to question; though certainly his knowledge of salesmanship never could be!

The powder charge in a brass blank shell was fired in the combustion chamber when the lanyard was pulled. The gases in turn compressed the air to "cushion" the shock of propulsion. This gun was about 14 feet long and weighed about 1,000 pounds. The projectile, with a velocity of about 700 feet per second, was a 36-inch torpedo-shaped affair with a warhead of some 4 pounds of explosive gelatine. A "rudder" projected from the rear of the projectile to impart rotary motion to it while in flight.

Mention might also be made of the pneumatic gun used on the Brazilian ship *Nichtheroy* during the Brazilian War of 1893. This monster was of 15-inch caliber with a tube (barrel) some 50 feet long. It was a powder-compressed-air type.

In actual war usage, none of these guns proved to have sufficient accuracy or range to meet requirements as serious guns.

During World War I, the Germans used some compressed-air weapons based on the naval minethrowers, projectiles which threw terror into all those who heard the "cough," watched the projectile sail through the air, and waited for the deafening explosion that followed.

Compressed air, as is commonly known if one stops to think about it, has played a very important part in war since the turn of the century. It is the force which has been commonly used at sea for minethrowing, for launching submarine torpedoes, and even for launching aircraft from carriers.

Today it is being supplanted as an aircraft launcher, the jets being hurtled off deck in modern navies by high-pressure steam.

Note On Contemporary Military Uses

Early during World War II both our Army and Navy Air Forces made some training uses of compressed-air machineguns for aerial training. One such was the McGlashan Air Machine Gun made at Long Beach, California. Originally it was fitted with dual handles with a thumb trigger between them as in the Vickers British guns and in our Browning .50's. Compressed air trainers of this type later appeared (many are now in use in shooting galleries) as imitations of our regular infantry Browning .30's and even as Lewis aircraft guns!

They used common BB air rifle shot and were fired by compressed air fed through a hose from a tank supply (some were used with CO_2 cylinders also). Rate of fire was as high as 500 per minute with an air pressure of under 200 p.s.i. The McGlashan used an electromagnetic valve release and feed mechanism. Adaptations in gallery use commonly are simpler.

In the author's observations at aerial gunnery centers during the War, these guns had a certain value in pre-training *complete neophytes!* It was soon observable, however, that when these men were advanced to .22 trainers, they completely lost the proficiency they had picked up in target following—they had learned to compensate for air gun trajectory! Even when illuminating beams gave a tracer effect, the net training result was not good.

The .22 trainers, followed by automatic-shotgun trap shooting on an extended scale, did prove of great value in aerial shooting training, however. The value of free aerial guns today is very limited indeed because of new high-speed ships and electronic "fix" developments. The day of the aerial compressed-air trainer is over.

THE STORY OF THE U.S.S. "DYNAMITE CRUISER" VESUVIUS

The *Vesuvius* is little known in real history but well known in legend as the "compressed-air dynamite gun cruiser" used at Santiago, Cuba in 1898.

She was an experimental ship of 930 tons built by the Cramps and was originally assigned to Rear Admiral Walker's "White Squadron."

The "dynamite guns" projected from the deck near the bow at an angle of 18 degrees. Most of their 54 foot length was housed below the deck. The tubes (barrels) were of ⅜-inch cast iron with ⅛-inch brass liners. Little wall thickness was required because the propellant was compressed air at a pressure of 1,000 p.s.i., which gave little shock effect in launching.

The projectiles were 14.75 inches in diameter. They measured about 7 feet with their spiral rotating vanes. They had brass casings and a 12-inch conical cast-iron head. The high explosive charge was 250 pounds and could be hurled about a mile and a half.

Intelligence records indicate that it was a toss-up who were more fearful of these shells—the crew who fired them, and who were always expecting the then new explosive to let go in the tube; or the Spanish land gunners who never got hit but always worried about the visible "flying fish" and the terrific blast when it landed within hearing distance!

There were three of these guns on the *Vesuvius*, with 10 projectiles for each gun. However, what made them valueless (except psychologically) was the fact that they were aimed by *pointing the ship,* watching the pitch and roll of the little vessel, and trusting in the Lord! Captain John E. Pillsbury ordered the firing from his bridge. These guns were fixed.

As to their effectiveness, it is a matter of who was talking—and when! Captain Chadwick of the *New York* the big ship engaged with the *Vesuvius*, wrote: "The shells ploughed great pits in the earth, and had they fallen fairly in a battery must have put the guns hors de combat for a time, at least."

Rear Admiral S. S. Robinson, U. S. N., in his *Battleships in Action,* published by the U. S. Naval Institute in 1942 says: "From the night of June 22 (1898) onwards a novel weapon was employed by the gunboat *Vesuvius* which carried three pneumatic dischargers for throwing shells loaded with high explosive to a distance of some 2,000 yards. They were so erratic that they caused the garrison little concern." Hardly surprising when we remember that the little *Vesuvius* was actually a floating gun carriage!

Orders for additional ships of the *Vesuvius* class were canceled as a result of studies of the Santiago siege.

The Brazilian ship *Nichtheroy*, used by Brazil in its Civil War in 1893, as pointed out elsewhere herein, used dynamite guns on a variation of the straight pneumatic principle by compressing air *through a powder discharge* rather than through mechanical compressors.

The United States Navy bought the *Nichtheroy* and renamed it the "U.S.S. Buffalo," incidentally, as we were in the process of developing our Navy at that time.

WHY COMPRESSED AIR CANNOT SUPPLANT POWDER CARTRIDGES

Very little use has ever been made of *individual* air arms in warfare, except for the Austrian experiences already pointed out. The principal "reason why" is because "fixed" cartridges (that is, cartridges which have projectile, powder, primer, and case assembled as a unit) came into being in time to make further military air-gun development unprofitable. Regardless of the compression involved, air as a propellant cannot approach the expansion rate of exploding gunpowders.

Since the subject is but little understood by the average citizen, if we can judge by the rash of nonsensical laws and ordinances against air guns in France during the 19th century, and even developing in the United States today, it might be well to interpolate here a few general remarks on compressed air as applied to small arms.

First and most important is the matter of pressures. The common little .22 rim fire short powder cartridge can develop pressures as high as 16,000 pounds per square inch when fired, because of the volume of gases generated when the primer ignites the powder. The common U. S. .30-06 rifle cartridge normally develops a pressure close to *50,000* pounds per square inch and with proof loads can easily be run up to double that pressure!

Remember that these pressure potentials are *safely* dormant and ready for release in every cartridge in the belt or box. Metallic cartridges are easy and safe to carry and to store. They take up little room. They are truly dangerous only when in a firearm and when the primer is hit to fire the powder, thereby generating high-pressure gases instantaneously, for all practical purposes.

Consider now the large-bore compressed-air gun. It can *under some circumstances* be pumped up to a pressure of 500 pounds per square inch *after much effort* or by using very heavy-duty compressing equipment, which is both bulky and clumsy. With a good double-action hand pump, bringing the obsolete Greener air canes to 500 pounds pressure requires about 300 graduated strokes—a very much tougher job in fact than pumping up the heaviest duty auto tire. This poundage, incidentally, will fire about 15 to 20 balls at a velocity approaching 500 feet per second. Contrast this to the 3,000 and more feet per second of many powder rifles!

For comparison it might be pointed out that American makers of *modern* pneumatic .177 and .22 caliber rifles advise 10 or 12 strokes of the pump (which is built into these arms) as being the maximum advisable and usable. And even that is very hard work! These modern rifles are of much smaller caliber than the old British and German types, and their missiles weigh only a fraction as much. They normally require pump-up for each shot, the reservoir being exhausted at each trigger pull, unlike the old large-reservoir patterns. Air repeaters thus far produced have not been particularly successful, except for the spring-toy varieties which are not pneumatics—that is the air storage type.

If lawmakers were required to use even the modern pump-ups on an extended basis, they would soon come to feel that the physical effort involved makes any more "anti" legislation impractical. It is an unfortunate part of our life today that those who make the laws often seem to have little real knowledge of the subject on which they happily legislate, so often to the detriment of the individual and of society as a whole.

One will often hear about the possibility of pumping up a pneumatic rifle to some fantastic pressures. Heavy-duty pneumatic industrial equipment seldom operates at over 75 pounds pressure, and enormous air drill compressors seldom generate over 200 pounds! The normal *maximum* air compressions possible in heavy duty cylinders of finest construction is of the order of 3,000 pounds per square inch. It might be noted in passing that in the laboratory *on a purely experimental basis* a pressure of 60,000 pounds has been obtained on occasion—a pressure which is *easily and safely duplicated by powder cartridges* used in modern elephant rifles without effort!

For ballistic efficiency one needs bullet weight, shape, and mass plus velocity, which simply cannot be achieved in any long-range air gun. This factor should be clearly understood. *Small caliber pneumatic rifles* have their own place in the field of arms—as trainers, particularly for indoor use, and for outdoor use where their light 16 to 20 grain bullets can be used up to perhaps 120 feet. Large caliber, obsolete air guns of calibers from .30 to .75 are merely freak or museum pieces, not worth the trouble, expense, and effort to utilize for target or field purposes.

The maximum test velocity the author obtained with any modern air rifle was 782 feet per second with a heavily pumped-up Sheridan .20 caliber. At 75 feet, it was deadly accurate; but velocity fell off fast after 125 feet, and the bullet hit the ground at less than 300 feet. A powder-driven .22 long rifle with double the bullet weight started at 1376 feet per second, was traveling at 1085 feet per second at 300 feet, and reached nearly 5000 feet extreme range.

No air arm is in any sense a *substitute* for a modern cartridge rifle—nor do legitimate makers intend to so represent it. It is a valuable trainer intermediate between the toy gun of early youth and the boy's first powder-cartridge rifle, pistol, or shotgun. For adults, too, it can be a source of arms training and a safe, short-range target or plinking arm; but it has neither the long-range qualities nor the danger factors of true firearms.

VARIOUS GAS PROJECTION SYSTEMS

As we have seen, the great Leonardo da Vinci proposed using steam in a cannon in the early 16th century. Since steam is water in the form of invisible gases or vapor, some enthusiasts see in Leonardo therefore the

Dynamite cruiser, U.S.S. "Vesuvius." Muzzles of two of its compressed-air guns are seen rising near the bow. The guns were fixed and most of the barrel areas were below deck where the guns were loaded. The entire ship was aimed at the target when firing the guns.

Figure 1.

Figure 2.

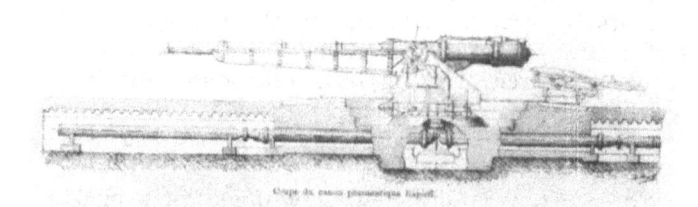

Figure 3.

Figure 4.

NOTE ON GIANT AIR GUNS OF THE 19th CENTURY

The pictures on this page were located in French artillery archives after this book was on the press. It is for that reason that they are not included in the section dealing with the so-called "Zalinski" guns.

Figure 1, looking very much like the modern Nike guided-missile launcher which currently guards our important military installations, shows one of Lieutenant Zalinski's early models and its missile. Using a warhead of 25 kilograms (about 55.5 pounds) of gelatine, Zalinski, with this gun, blew up the old schooner "Siliman" in the presence of foreign military and naval observers.

Figure 2 shows the Rapieff coast defense pneumatic gun, while figure 3 shows details of the operation of the Rapieff and its missile ready for breech loading. The designer, after whom the gun was named, was a former Russian artillery officer residing in the United States. He was chief engineer of a American company formed to exploit the potential of the pneumatic launching principle after Zalinski had established its value at that stage in arms development.

Figure 4 is a cross-section of the original American Dudley gun, forerunner of the Sims-Dudley pneumatic cannon. Originally designed as shown to fire a conventional missile, it was later adapted to hurl vaned torpedoes. Unlike the Rapieff, which used stored compressed air as a propellant, the Dudley gun compressed air in a special chamber (A) by firing a powder charge—just as a modern spring-air rifle compresses air by a spring plunger. This system, like the true pneumatics, made it safe to hurl the sensitive explosives of the 1890 period.

Figure 5 shows details of the U.S. dynamite cruiser "Vesuvius." Its pneumatic guns were loaded below decks, and its torpedoes were launched by compressed air, which was stored in the tanks by the compressors shown. These guns were "aimed" by pointing the ship, since all tubes were fixed.

The development of stable high explosives, together with advanced fuses of Zalinski and other designs, made it possible to fire high-explosive warheads from big guns powered by conventional naval powder explosives; and since these gave better velocities and trajectories than can be obtained by air pressures, the early pneumatic giants passed into history with the close of the Spanish-American War.

Figure 5.

"inventor" of the gas gun. This is really stretching out definitions!

Who first proposed the use of any form of gas as a propellant is a matter of conjecture which would be both useless and purposeless here. The thought came to many scientists in many lands as the nature and usability of gases were demonstrated.

Carbonic acid was a natural thought to the early experimenter, but it falls into a special "liquified gas" classification with which we shall deal separately. It is the only successful gas arms system except for compressed air thus far marketed in quantity; though an ether system is currently under development in Germany.

In 1849 John Charles Edington (Spec. No. 549, British) proposed use of carbureted hydrogen and atmospheric air to be exploded in a cylinder to drive a piston; and on the heels of release of that suggestion, various inventors tried to apply it to weapons without success. Ten years later Henry Francis Cohade (British, 1859) proposed using oxy-hydrogen to be exploded by electricity, and experimenters promptly tried that too, also without success. Thomas Meekins had similar proposals.

In 1864 Isaac Evans (No. 775) had a plan for "carbureted hydrogen transported in strong bags of gutta percha" to be used as a propellant! De Penning and Smith in 1887 (British 2864) suggested propulsion of projectiles "by combined vapours of water and oil or fats having higher evaporating points." E. H. C. Monckton was granted a patent in 1876 for using "gases under high pressure for propelling shot from small arms"—but again nothing came of it because of technical problems.

Ronnebeck's No. 203,076 in the early 1920's was an interesting forerunner of a type which the Germans are currently trying to develop, though with more volatile gases than that inventor had in mind—the system of using a spring plunger to generate heat which will explode a mixture of oil and air in Ronnebeck's proposal. The spring power necesssary for such a purpose is formidable, though actually the idea is merely an attempt at doing what comes naturally in many high compression air rifles: utilizing the "diesel effect."

This means merely that as in the common diesel engine, the heat generated by the tight-fitting piston being driven down in the smooth-walled cylinder and compressing the gases in its path explodes them. In air rifles quite often this effect is produced (increasing the power twofold or threefold in some instances) when the heat fires the mixture of air and petroleum compounds such as gun oil and grease in the gun. If firing happens to be in the dark, this "diesel" firing will be visible in muzzle flash. Ronnebeck's was one of the earliest attempts to capitalize on this elementary and well-known fact. Many other tries at introducing oil spray injected into the air chamber have since been attempted.

Aside from the very high compression required, meaning heavy springs and consequently hard cocking, utilization of the "diesel effect" is difficult to achieve satisfactorily because of *lack of firing consistency*. Any gun requires stability of performance—the velocity and energy must be relatively constant factors if accuracy is to be achieved. While not impossible to attain, these factors would require tremendous amounts of experimentation before commercially sound models could be produced; and when achieved, the result would be added complications, mechanically. There is no substitute in sight for the powder cartridge *if power and range are desired*. Air and gas arms are practical for short-range, low-power use, where they fill a real need.

203,076.   Ronnebeck, H. R.   June 10, 1922.

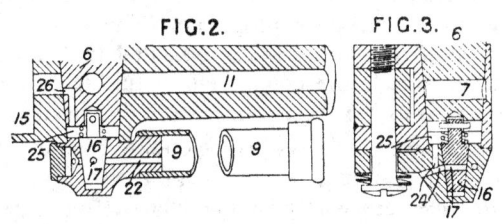

Pneumatic.—Guns of the kind in which a spring plunger compresses an explosive mixture of air and vapour or gas which is fired by the heat due to compression, are provided with a fuel reservoir 9 and a measuring device 16 which is connected with the loading mechanism or the like so that it is operated, during the actuation of the gun, to isolate a measured quantity of the fuel and place it in communication with the compression chamber. The invention is shown applied to a gun having a barrel 11, a compression chamber 15, and a loading plug 6. The measuring device comprises a plug 16 having a hole 17 which forms the measuring chamber. The plug 16 is connected to the loading plug 6 and is rotated during the actuation of the loading mechanism from a position in which the boring communicates with a passage 22 leading to the fuel reservoir to a position, shown in Figs. 2 and 3, in which the boring 17 communicates with the compression chamber 15 through passages and recesses 24, 25, 26.

Abstract of original patent.

But they are not in any sense *substitutes* for powder arms.

On the subject of use of other gases (except the low pressure liquifying types to be discussed separately), none of the explosive group nor of those requiring a very high compression are desirable, as has already been pointed out.

Ether-Air Guns

In recent years considerable experimentation has been done in Germany in adapting the use of an ether atomizer as a "booster" on the common spring-air type of gun. The principle is simple. Ether is fed in controlled amounts directly into the air chamber ahead of the cocked spring-piston. When the piston is driven forward, friction and the resultant compression of the air-and-ether mixture, results in explosion by the heat generated, just about doubling the velocity. This system will be covered more thoroughly in the section on current German arms.

The "Dry Ice" Gas System

Dry ice, or carbon dioxide snow as it is technically called, is common carbon dioxide (CO_2) gas **solidified** under great pressure. Its preparation is merely a matter of using higher pressures than are required to liquify the gas.

Its common usage, of course, is as a refrigerant, since it passes directly from the solid to the gaseous state, and in the course of so doing is a most efficient heat absorber.

Back in 1943, Mr. R. J. Monner of Denver visited the National Rifle Association of America's headquarters in Washington, D. C., with a very remarkable rifle which used dry ice as a propellant. The rifle was subjected to numerous tests which indicated that the system might have some future commercial value. Unfortunately, nothing has thus far been done with this system.

The rifle was a heavy bolt-action repeater with a magazine tube running the full length of the barrel and with a dry ice reservoir positioned below the barrel. Its caliber was .22.

Mr. Monner said that the rifle as presented had been filled with dry ice some 4 months earlier and had been used for thousands of rounds of firing. As tested it gave a much higher velocity than the CO_2 liquified-gas rifle (Crosman) then available. Velocity was well over 700 feet per second, and with its heavier bullet it gave quite remarkable penetration. Unfortunately, press of business at the time prevented the author from checking more thoroughly into the rifle. Most of the N.R.A. testing was done by the late Al Barr, one of the most thorough and competent technicians of the time. Since there seemed to be a possibility that the rifle would be produced and would be available for further testing, its potentialities were not as thoroughly checked as they might have been.

In principle, of course, the rifle was merely a modified form of the standard liquid CO_2 pattern, merely substituting a solid for a liquid propellant, but functioning on the basic gas-rifle system of trapping gas in a chamber with valve controls. Chamber-loading of the bullet was by the common turn-bolt system, though the magazine was an obvious improvement. When the trigger was pulled the striker hit the escape valve, opening it against the valve spring and gas, which then automatically closed the valve. The gas not only helped to close the valve but also exerted pressure to hold it closed.

The rifle was usually accurate for a gas rifle. Much of this added accuracy was probably due to a fine barrel; but it was undoubtedly aided by more uniform gas pressure than is commonly encountered with liquified-gas propellants.

Mr. Monner had set up an organization called the "Denver Air Rifle Company," and expected to try to produce a semi-automatic action instead of a bolt loader. Adequate financing was not available, and he tried to sell the idea of the gun to numerous arms companies. At the time, the subject of air and gas guns had not received the attention and sales acceptance which has since developed; and since modern American arms makers are notoriously slow to tackle any new venture, Monner was unsuccessful.

The gun was not perfected by any means—but for that matter no gas rifle made today has reached a development plateau where its performance can be compared with that of either the .22 cartridge rifle or the .22 spring-air rifle systems! Monner just was ahead of his time.

If fired steadily and rapidly, the Monner gun acted like a refrigerator. It cooled off very perceptibly and in damp air the gun actually frosted up! It had other faults, including servicing problems. Nevertheless, it offered many potential advantages over the liquified-gas system. So far as the author has been able to determine, nothing further has been done with this principle.

CHAPTER 4

Cocking Systems

IN the **crank operated spring-air arms** commonly encountered, the barrel is octagonal, the air cylinder is of large diameter (often 2-inch), the lockwork is to the rear of the cylinder, the stock is secured in shotgun-fashion by a bolt through the butt, and a separate wooden forearm is secured to the forward end of the air cylinder. Springs are sometimes spiral, sometimes volute.

All these designs have in common the fact that a detachable crank is used to extend or compress the springs, which are often attached to a piston which works in the air cylinder. The crank is inserted into either the lock or the stock section, again depending upon the design, and turned as required. The cranking effort may be from one-half turn to two-and- a-half turns customarily, though an occasional freak will be encountered where an abnormally long design allows overlength springs requiring three or even four turns. These patterns often have very unusual power for arms of their type. Since all true spiral or volute springs have greater elasticity (and consequently, power) than the common helical coil spring, unusually long or heavy ones are of even greater power. The elastic deflection which the spring can take under load determines the power, as springs conform fairly exactly to Hooke's Law that deflection is proportional to the load.

Operating the Crank System

The principle of operation is essentially simple. The crank is inserted and turned to its limit. At that point the spring has been extended (or compressed in some few types) to its limit. It has also brought the piston, which is secured to the springs in various ways, back to full position, where a sear element engages the piston and holds it back ready for firing.

Normally these types are breechloaders—though muzzle loaders are in existence. The usual system of loading is pushing the muzzle end of the barrel, which allows the breech end to rise from its juncture at the air cylinder for loading. The barrels usually slide enough on a steel rod to allow the breech to rise; but at times some will be found operating on standard pivots. The bullet or dart is inserted. The breech is closed.

Pressing the trigger pivots it (and its sear where one is present) out of piston engagement. The springs drive the piston ahead in the air cylinder. The close-fit piston compresses the air in the cylinder. The opening in the cylinder being a small vent to the rear of the bullet chamber, the highly compressed air drives the bullet ahead of it out the barrel.

The Oldest Crank Types

Just when the crank system originated is not known. Since it stems from the mechanical principle of the winch, it is most likely that either it or the crank-bellows design was actually the first variety of air gun.

Examples of this system of Nuremberg origin can definitely be traced to the middle of the 16th century. In fact a few guns of this general type are occasionally encountered in the exterior form of wheel-lock guns. The collector should be warned, however, that such designs do not necessarily mean that the air-gun specimen was actually made by a wheel-lock maker in the heyday of that form of arm! Some specimens were altered by experimenters from powder-firing wheel locks to air-compression wheel locks using either springs or bellows. Some specimens encountered by this author on close examination proved to have springs and bellows made of materials available only in recent years, though the guns themselves were unquestionably original! the moral: Don't jump at conclusions!

The Bolzenbüchse

This is a crank-wound pattern dating certainly to the beginning of the 18th century. The name means literally

Typical crank-operated spring-air gun. Crank is withdrawn before firing.

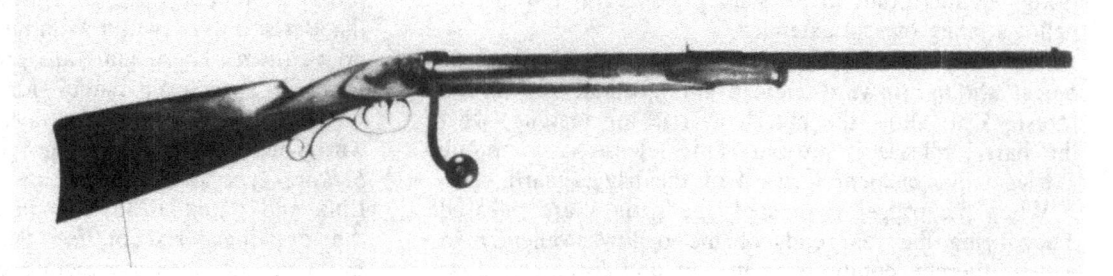

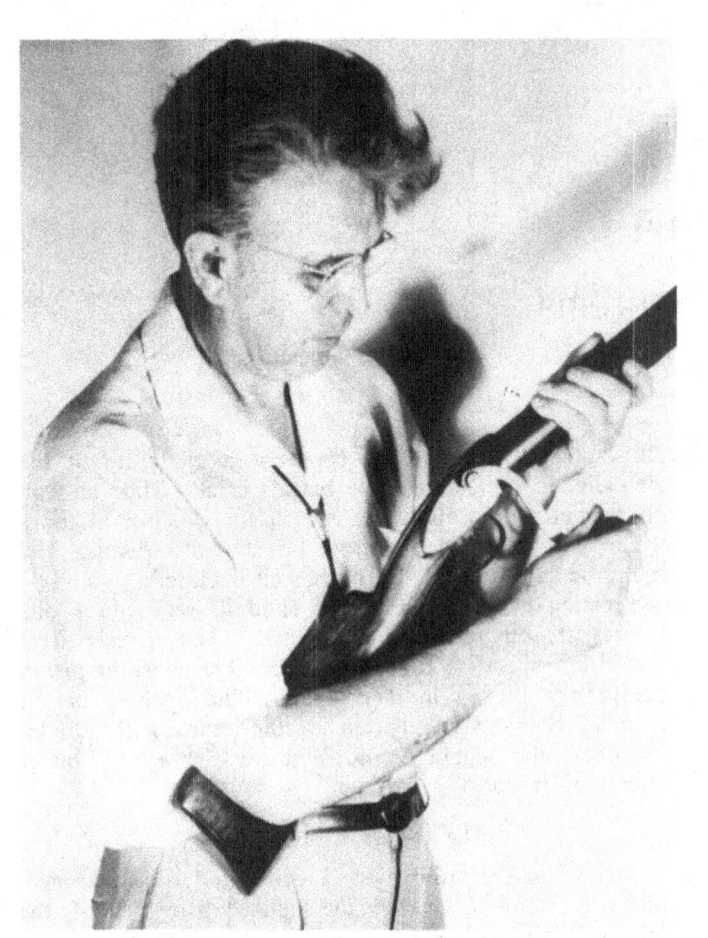

Cranking the gun.

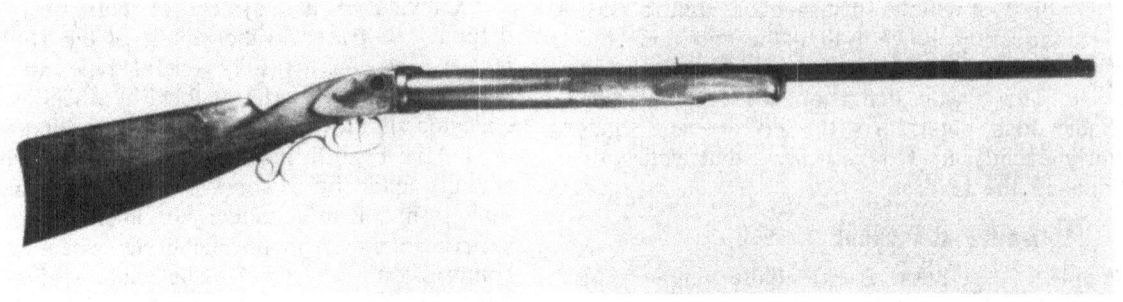

Rifle with crank removed ready for firing. Caliber of specimen shown is .36.

the cone to the air vent behind the bullet. The true Bolzenbüchse usually has a real "hair" trigger—one which dimensionally *looks* like a hair, and which can be *blown* off!

The Bolzenbüchse has been made by many German and particularly Austrian master gunsmiths. While all conform pretty much to the description given, they do vary in detail. The specimen shown here is the standard form.

These guns were expensive to make even in the early 18th century and are not common. Even today they are used in Europe by shooting enthusiasts, however. In former times clubs would often organize to purchase one for the common use.

Specially made darts were the rule, quite expensive in the early days. Often a specially colored hair was provided to give the shooter a setting mark for placing the dart in exactly the same position for each shot. The darts are so accurate that it was (and is) customary for the shooter to pull hairs carefully from the tail to "zero in" each dart! Today these darts are produced as "Präzisionsbolzen" in calibers 4.5-, 5.5-, 6.27-, 6.28-, 6.29-, 6.30- and 6.33-mm. as *standard* manufacture. However, old calibers as high as 7.5-mm. are encountered.

These fine arms whether 17th, 18th century or later are smooth-bored and intended for indoor dart shooting only. They usually weigh about 9 pounds, but are so balanced that they seem much lighter. From one-half to one turn of the crank completes the windup, depending upon the type and manufacture.

"Dart Gun," from the missile (Bölzen) it was designed to shoot, a special dart, and the German common word then for a gun (büchse). The true Bolzenbüchse form has a crank inserted in the rear of the stock (commonly on the right side), which when turned tensions flat springs within the hollow stock. These springs are attached to the rear of the parchment bellows (Bläsbag), which are spread full open as the springs are tensioned ready for firing. At this point there is no pressure on the air, the bellows being merely extended.

The common Bolzenbüchse is a breechloader, the barrel sliding forward enough on a metal rod in the forestock to allow the breech to rise for loading, when the barrel release is pressed. This release is commonly a trigger-like element forward of the triggerguard.

When the trigger is pressed, the springs are released. They bring the rear ends of the bellows violently together, thereby compressing the air and forcing it down

Their accuracy is well-nigh unbelievable at short range (about 10 meters). Many of the old ones have handmade diopter tang sights rivaling the finest of today's makes. The usual Austrian target for this arm is a 12-circle one, whose total diameter is only 1.375 inches. An expert with this arm can outshoot most powder riflemen at 10 meters! Power is deliberately kept low in these arms to permit recovery of the darts uninjured. If power is stepped up even a little, it is quite a job to pull the darts out of wood without using pliers, which will injure them. These guns are probably the most accurate shooting arms ever made—for short-range work!

Of course, there are always exceptions. Shown elsewhere herein is a contemporary drawing of a *double-bellows* type of Bolzenbüchse made by Anton Pell of Linz and dated 1735, together with an explanation of the drawings. Except for the *double-bellows* system, this gives an accurate picture of the Bolzenbüchse.

It must be noted in passing that it is *possible* to build this design with enough power to allow use of fairly heavy balls, but its true purpose is for close-range dart shooting.

Crank Guns in America

A very wide group of such guns were manufactured by small gunsmiths in the United States in the 18th century. They were made in both single-shot and in repeater designs.

The specimens shown herewith are representative of the best types. Many makers did not put any identifying marks on their production, some because of danger of real or imaginary patent infringements; some because they were just copying old German types brought here from the old country. Philadelphia, Albany, Geneva, and New York City all had gunsmiths who made at least a few of these.

The best American types have barrels which swing over to the right on a pivot for breech loading, as in the ones pictured here. A common caliber is .28—seemingly adapted to the early Colt's .28 caliber ball, which they handle perfectly. Customary cranking calls for 2 to 3 turns, and the springs are so powerful that you can get a bad knuckle rap if the crank gets away from you! These designs are infinitely more powerful than any air guns on today's market and are actually capable of short-range hunting use. Barrels may be smooth or rifled. Bullet molds were usually sold with such arms, so you could make your own bullets.

As the crank is turned, springs are extended. The piston is usually leather covered and works in an iron or brass cylinder. Air cylinders are of uniformly large capacity for shooting power. Sights are usually hunting types, open and bead. Barrels are commonly octagon or half-octagon and are generally short (21 to 24 inches) because of the length of the air cylinder behind it. Fits and finish are excellent.

The most remarkable crank specimen ever encountered by the author is the American 13-shot revolving Bunge repeater shown herein. Combining the crank-air system with the 1851 Colt loading system, it is both ingenious and magnificently crafted.

Crank Guns in Germany

Doubtless the oldest air-gun maker in the world is—or was until recently—the firm of Oscar Will, founded in 1844 at Zella Mehlis in Thuringia, the site of the Will "Venuswaffenwerk" long noted for precision air and firearms. This plant is now in East Germany under Russian control. However, since crank air guns of their original design (called "Kürbelspanners" in Germany) are still available from some of the major European gun exporters, the firm is doubtless carrying on business in one fashion or another. (Note: Most of the major Zella Mehlis firms such as Carl Walther, H. Weihrauch, and Anschutz are now operating their factories in West Germany.)

A favorite arms designation in Germany has always been "original." The term has been abused and misused quite a little one way and another.

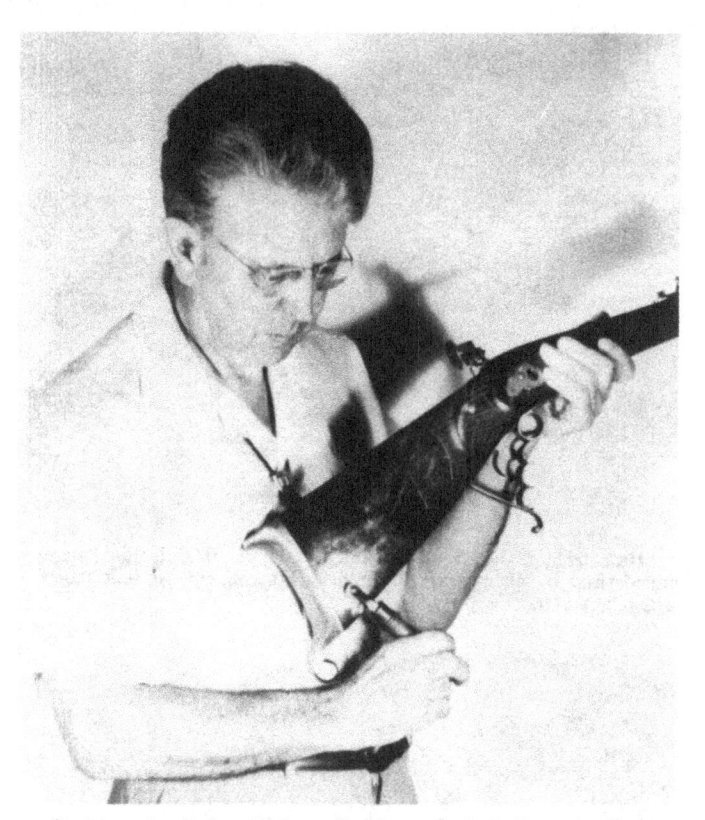

Cocking the Bolzenbüchse. Crank expands bellows and compresses springs. Crank is removed before firing.

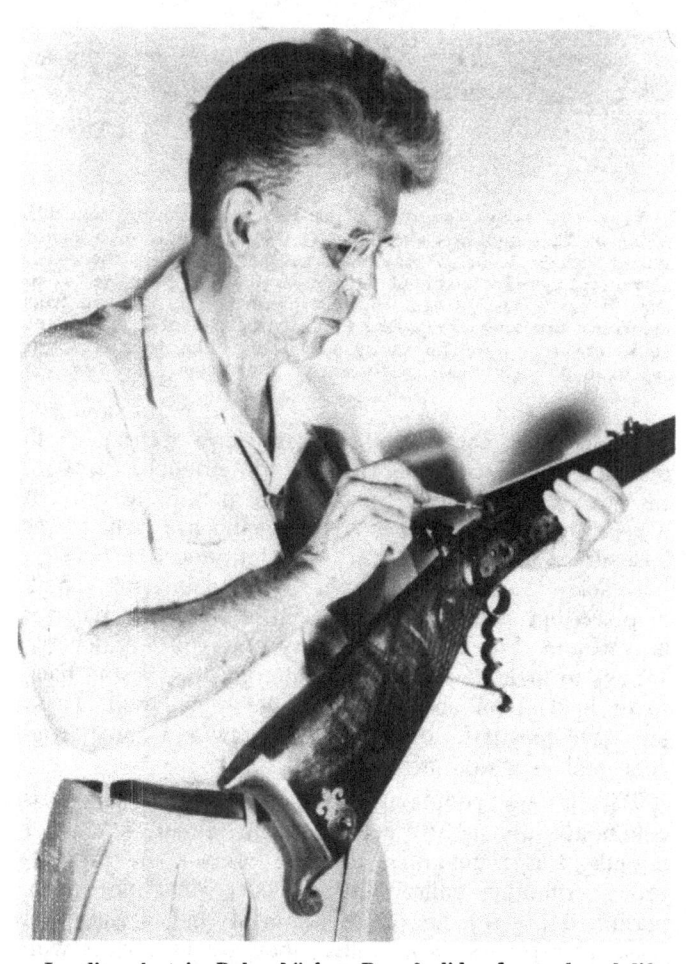

Loading dart in Bolzenbüchse. Barrel slides forward and lifts at breech for loading.

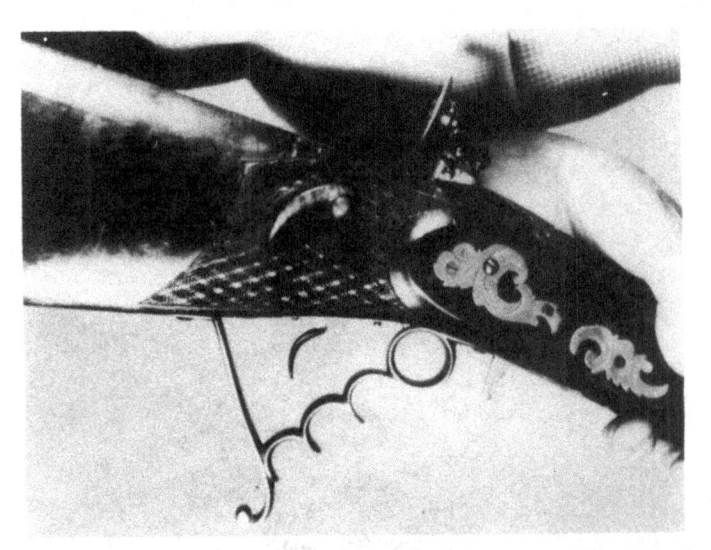

"Hair trigger" is almost as thin as a hair. It is inside trigger-guard ring. It can actually be fired by blowing on the hair trigger when it is set.

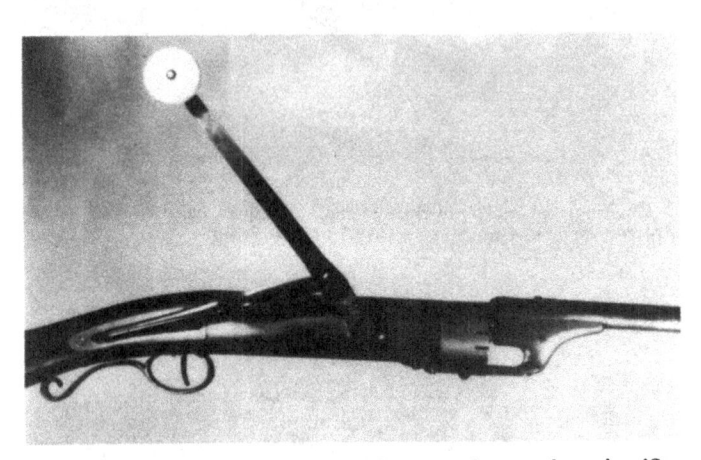

Very rare early American crank-operated repeating air rifle. Made by C. Bunge at Geneva, N. Y. Overall length, 42.5 inches. Barrel 18.25 inches. This remarkable rifle uses the basic barrel and cylinder design of the comparable Colt's revolver of its day. It has a 13-shot cylinder, the chambers being loaded from the front end with .28-caliber Colt's balls. Actuating the crank cocks the very powerful spring and piston. This is a very rare specimen of early American ingenuity and design.

In air rifles, Oscar Will used the term "'Original" to indicate that he sold the original Bolzenbüchse type of air gun, for one thing. Later, in an attempt to put out a *production* equivalent of the Bolzenbüchse (which was basically a rich man's gun), Will introduced his "Kürbelspanner Schiessbudengewehr." The detachable crank is placed in position on the right side of the receiver and wound. This extends the very powerful spiral block springs to their limit and carries the attached piston back to be held at full-cock ready for the trigger pull. These are breechloaders, have simple screw-adjustable triggers, and as a rule are not rifled.

Barrels are commonly octagon. Overall length is commonly about 36 inches, weight about 6.5 to 7 pounds. Large quantities of these were made for European shooting gallery use (powder rifles not being permitted). They are quite powerful and accurate at reasonable ranges. When rifled, they are in a class with the finest of the later designs for accuracy and are usually much more powerful. The common caliber is 6 1/3-mm. The customary projectile is a pointed, bullet type lead design, like the current American Sheridan in shape.

This gun design was pirated extensively in Germany and unless the Will name or the Venuswaffenwerk name or trade-mark appears, it is not an original.

Crank Operated Pistols

These are uncommon. However some were made by the O. Will Venuswaffenwerk and others, the only *production* types being German. Caliber is usually 4.5-mm. (.177), weight about 2.5 pounds, length about 20 inches. Darts, slugs, (and later) Diabolo pellets were used in these pistols, barrels being smooth-bored. Power of one sample tested was better than a recent German "Zenit"-make pistol, based on penetration.

TRIGGERGUARD-LEVER SPRING-AIR SYSTEMS

Here again we have no accurate historical proof of when or where the design was originated. The triggerguard-lever design has never been favored in Europe. The reason is that any use of such a system was never favored by the military. It is true that practically all precision air-rifle shooting is from a standing position, where any underlever operation is satisfactory. Nevertheless, the fact remains that the military tradition that

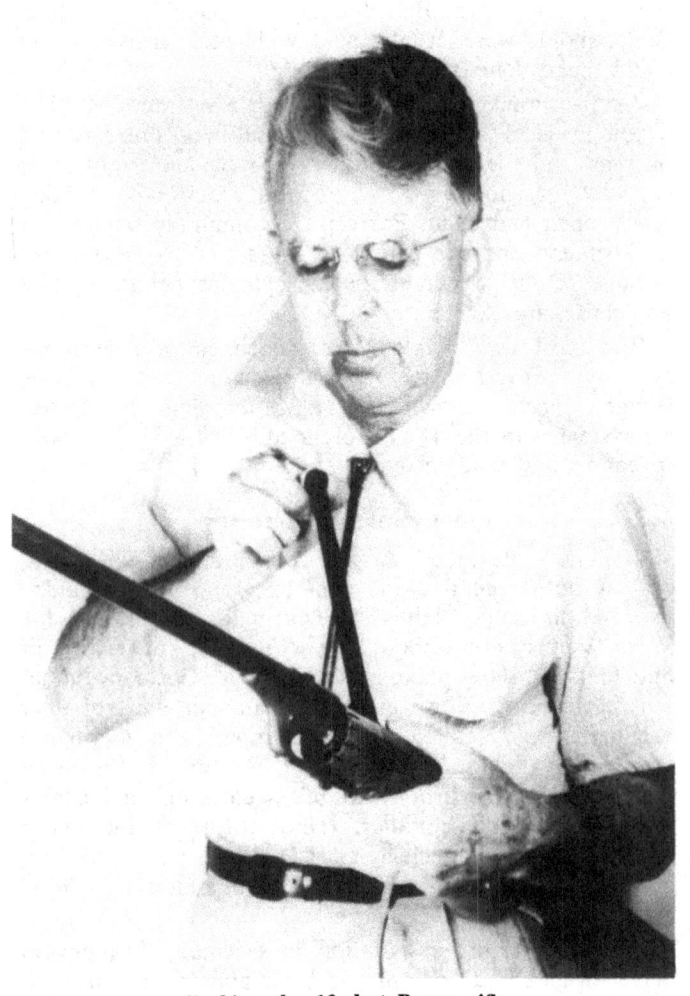

Cocking the 13-shot Bunge rifle.

shooting is normallly from a position where the lever could interfere influenced all early air-gun design in Europe.

However, there is little question that the first *production* design at least originated with Oscar Will at Zella Mehlis. Even in the period of the middle 18th century, air-club and gallery shooting was a business to be considered. The ease of mislaying a crank (his earliest design) led Will directly to the application of the built-in triggerguard lever.

These "Bügelspanners" as they are known in Germany are still obtainable, though not carrying the O. Will name. Recent versions are in 5.5-mm. (.22) caliber and have 20-inch round barrels, but otherwise are the old prewar Will guns.

Pre-War I and War II patterns usually had octagon barrels and commonly used the same pointed bullet as the crank guns—the 6 1/3-mm. In general they are not as powerful but except for adapting the triggerguard to levering the springs and pistons into firing position (instead of key-winding) they were the crank types.

The triggerguard is pivoted at the rear. On its front face is a projection for the hand to grip, an opening.

The guard is pulled down to extend the spring and cock the position. The trigger is adjustable by an outside screw in standard fashion, the length of bite of the screw determining how much pull must be exerted to free the piston. The barrel slides and elevates for breech-loading in standard fashion for the type. While the cocking unit (the triggerguard lever) is self-contained, it does not have the cocking power of the crank, obviously.

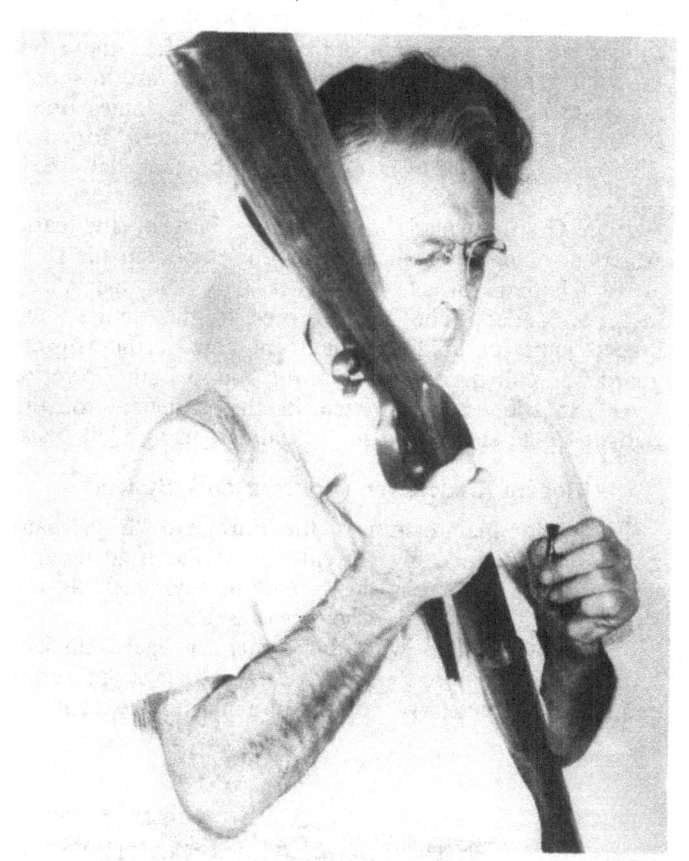

American Underlever Types

After the appearance of the Will guns about the middle 18th century, several small American makers produced rather similar guns in small quantities. John Zuendorf, a gunmaker at 106 Houston Street in New York City, during the Civil-War period made such guns with brass cylinders and leather-covered pistons. Some were used during the Civil-War draft riots, a nasty page in New York City's history. His guns were about .30

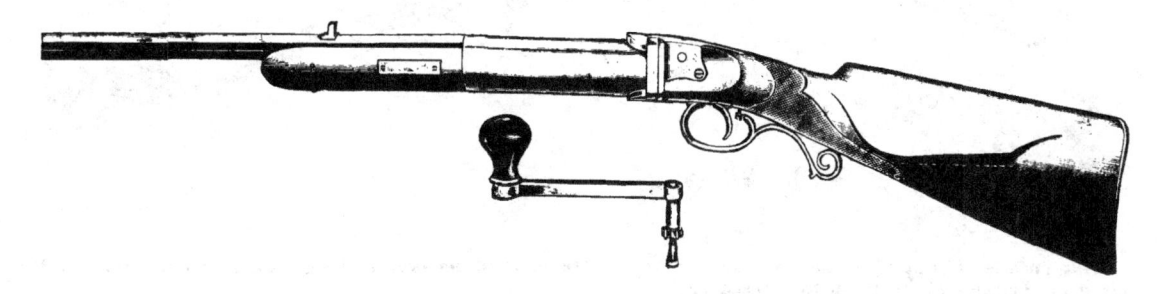

Loading another American crank-type by G. Fischer of New York City. This rifle is also .28 caliber and will fire either the Colt's ball of its day or special darts. The barrel swings out on a pivot to permit direct chamber loading. The workmanship is unequalled today.

Typical German crank gun. These are again in limited production.

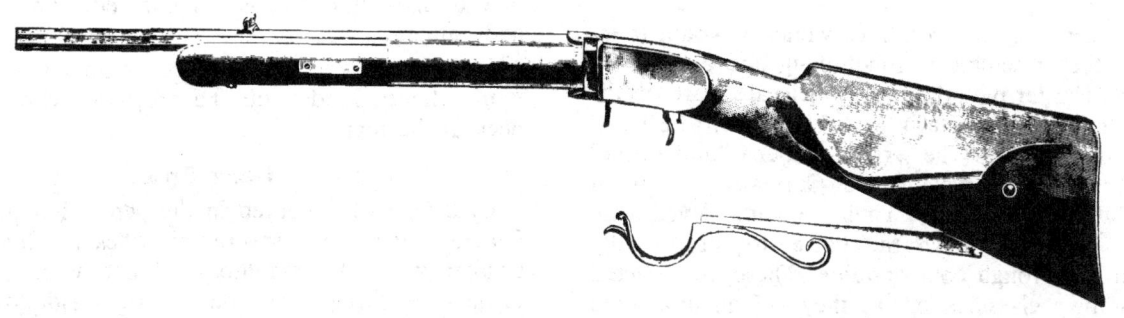

German triggerguard-lever design. These have relatively low power and are not in current production.

caliber and were smoothbored. Shortly after the Civil War this general type was manufactured for use in shooting galleries of the day and for use at fairs. James Bown & Son's catalog of 1876 offers one pattern for dart shooting. The price was quite high for that day—$30 each!

John G. Sims made some of the best of the early American underlever air rifles of this period in his shop at 44 Chatham Street, New York City. He specialized in breechloaders. The barrel turned to the right at the breech joint for loading. The front end of the triggerguard was pulled down to cock the gun, a long, powerful lever extension being housed in the underside of the buttstock. He specialized in .28 caliber, using Colt balls.

Modern Underlever (Triggerguard) Systems

Except for manufacture of the European "Bügelspanner" as noted, the only current use of the triggerguard-lever cocking system is that found in toys such as the Daisy rifle described elsewhere in this book.

It is not possible with this system to get sufficient leverage to compress (or extend) springs powerful enough for true target or small-game use except by leverage compounding which would require a bulky and costly design.

The toy varieties, however, have value for youth training in that they resemble in functioning and appearance the old Winchester-pattern rifles which are part of the American heritage and which are still our favorite hunting-rifle design. (Note: The serious modern "underlever" rifles made in Great Britain and Germany are in an entirely different category. Their cocking levers are commonly positioned under the barrel to furnish adequate leverage through compounding. These are covered under their own classification, as they are manufactured by several foreign makers. These are serious target arms, capable of maximum short-range accuracy. Some can kill vermin or even rabbits at ranges up to 60 yards.)

MISCELLANEOUS OLD SYSTEMS

The more widely produced semi-standard systems have all been dealt with herein.

However, there have been literally dozens of variants made in model form and a few for production. We do not have space to deal with them here except in passing. They are of interest and value only to collectors.

Push Lever Lock

This "Hebelscheiber Verschluss" as it was classed in Germany where it was designed about 1905 never met with any commercial success. It had a pivoting barrel to be tipped for breech loading. Its spring system resembled the crank types but was lever-cocked by opening the action. This design was actually an attempt to utilize parts and equipment to manufacture a gun on the lines of the "breakdown" barrel system, which was pioneered by the American Quackenbush version of the Haviland-Gunn patents, and which by the opening of the present century was being widely made in Europe. This "push lever lock" system could not compete in price with the new designs and it soon disappeared from manufacture and catalogs.

Its pellet is worthy of passing comment. It was a 6.2-mm. caliber round knob-like projectile with a projecting neck at the rear.

Other Freaks

C. Bunge who worked in the percussion period in the United States made several air rifles at Geneva, N. Y. Caliber was .28 smoothbore. Some were 15 shot repeaters. A lifting lever on the right side of the stock (or top of the stock in others) cocked the firing spring.

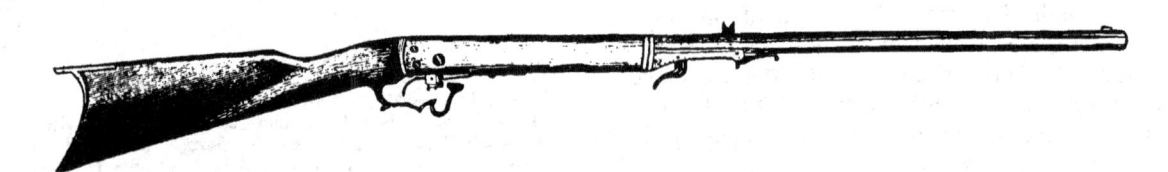

American underlever, period of 1870. Used largely as a gallery gun in model pictured.

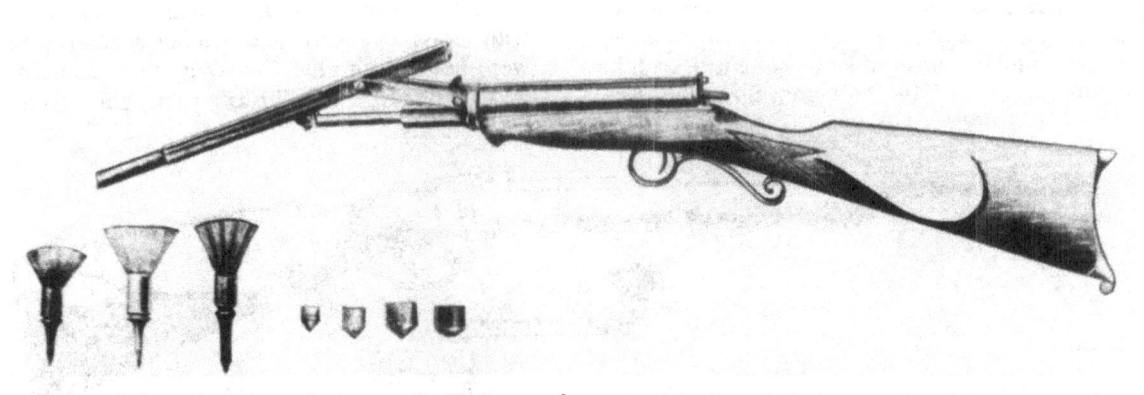

This push-lever lock is no longer made. However, elements of its breech design are found in some modern air arms because of its hermetic breech seal.

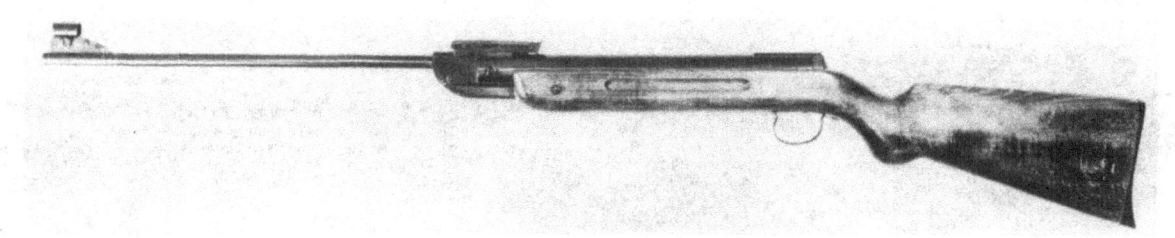

Typical German Diana high-power barrel cocker.

The Swedish "Excellent" firm also made guns on this pattern about 1905.

Occasionally one encounters an American or German type (generally without identifying markings) in which the lever forms triggerguard and extends to the butt plate. The length of this lever permits cocking an unusually powerful spring.

Another version has a cocking lever extending the full length of the top of the stock back from the air cylinder to the butt.

Except for the leverage features in an attempt to gain power, such types have nothing to offer in advantages over standard systems.

MODERN BARREL-COCKING TYPES

Over 90 percent of all the serious spring-air rifles and guns manufactured throughout the world are of barrel-breakdown construction. In these arms the act of forcing the barrel down on its pivot or hinge to expose the breech for loading, also serves to operate levers which either pull or push the piston and compress the coil spring which powers it. At the end of the stroke the trigger (or sear, depending upon individual design) engages the piston, holding it cocked ready for firing.

A pellet (or at times a dart in smoothbores) is inserted in the chamber and seated. The barrel is snapped shut. The arm is now ready for firing by pulling the trigger.

Operational Principle

Basically all makes and patterns on this system are alike. Specific differences and variation from the norm will be mentioned under description of the varying makes and models.

The barrel is movably attached to the receiver which houses the air cylinder. The hinge point may be a screw or cross bolt. When the action is closed, the barrel is held securely in position by its construction design and by a spring-loaded detent bolt. This detent bolt is by its mechanical nature *not* a positive lock. It is mechanically a "latch," a device to hold the action firmly closed against any accidental opening, but requiring only a stiff downward movement of the barrel sufficient to overcome the latch in order to open it. This construction is thus differentiated from the true "locked" pattern. Note that because of the low breech pressures involved, there is no need for anything more positive than the detents employed on arms of this design. (Some systems, as we shall see, employ a lock in addition, but except for precision match rifles of the highest order these additions are of questionable value. Others have a sliding *and* tilting barrel for added air seal; their value is inconsiderable.)

Detent bolts are always slidably mounted and furnished with required cam surfaces to allow their springs to push then automatically *into* engagement when the action is closed; and to permit them to be cammed *out of* engagement against their spring compression as the action is opened.

The cocking-lever arm is hinged under the barrel at its forward end. At the rear it interlocks through a shaped projection with the piston inside the air cylinder.

Thus as the barrel is broken down on its receiver hinge, the cocking lever brings the piston straight back in the air cylinder, thereby effecting compression of the heavy spring. In simple designs (the lower priced ones) a projection on the trigger catches and holds the piston at full cock, the trigger being urged into contact by its

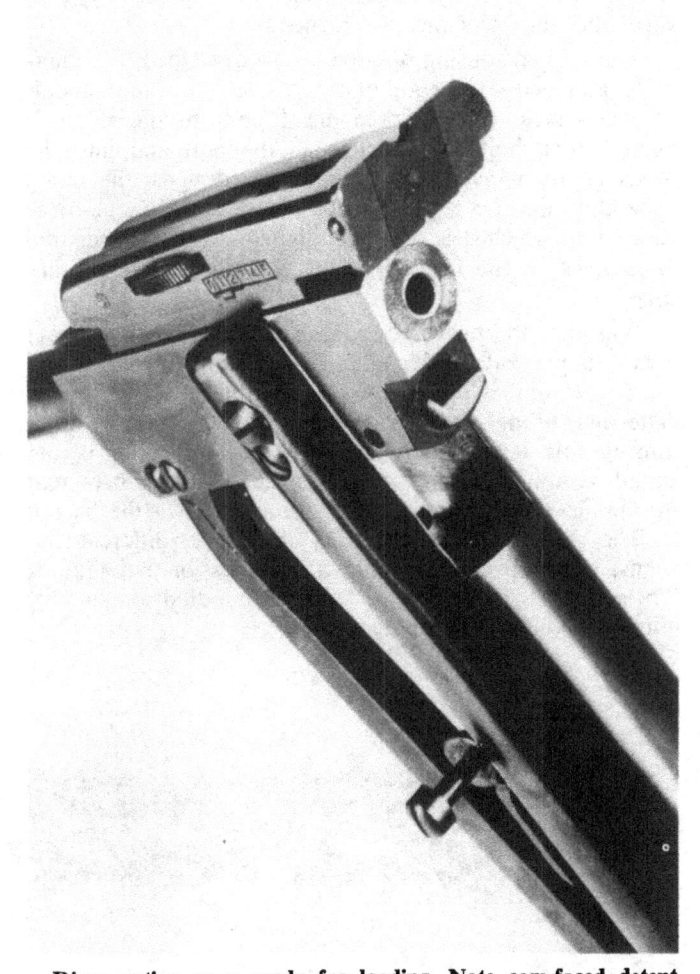

Diana action open ready for loading. Note cam-faced detent below chamber. Barrel has thrust back the cocking lever to carry piston back and compress powerful mainspring.

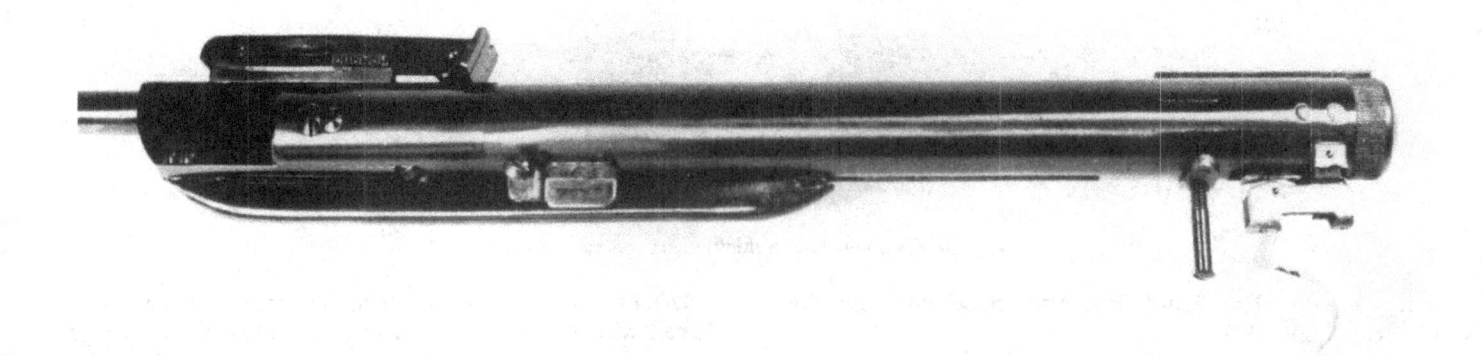

Barrel cocker with stock removed to show detail of cocking lever and compression tube.

spring after the piston has overridden it in rearward travel. In such designs the trigger usually has an adjusting screw which regulates the depth to which the trigger nose engages in the piston holding notch—the less the grasp, obviously, the easier the pull needed to release the piston.

More expensive models often have sears of standard rifle design. These are merely intermediate holding devices in which trigger pressure is working through increased leverage to make for easier and smoother pull. These vary in every major model as required by construction, but principles are identical.

The trigger housing may be screwed, welded, or otherwise attached to the tubular receiver. In some models it also serves to secure the metal units to the stock, a heavy stock bolt passing through the butt and into the housing. In many of the more recent designs, the metal assembly may be withdrawn as a unit from a one-piece stock into which it is dropped, and to which it is secured by screws, in the fashion of the typical modern military rifle.

Washers are provided at barrel and breech contact faces to prevent air leakage. The piston when released by trigger pull is driven forward by the powerful spring. The tight-fitting piston compresses the air in its cylinder during this forward travel. The only air outlet is the small vent behind the bullet. Since the bullet bars exit to the air, the pressure built up forces it down the barrel.

The springs and piston vary in size in different designs, some springs reaching a compression strength of 75 pounds. These develop several hundred pounds of air pressure in the cylinders.

Locked-Breech Variations

In some of the early German designs, crossbolts and locks were used to prevent (or at least to slow down) joint and breech looseness. In such patterns it is necessary to press in the spring-supported crossbolt (usually from the left) before the barrel can be broken down on its hinge for cocking and loading. In current, well-made English and German arms of this design, crossbolts are of questionable value. The barrel and receiver being of good quality, with the necessary contact surfaces properly hardened and fitted, the amount of play is controlled about as well by a detent as by a lock. Bushings and washers are required in either case, and these are replaceable when they wear.

Some recent heavy-duty German makes do require the pushing or pulling of a release lever at the breech to unlock the action for breakdown, but these are in the minority. It any event, there is no factor of *safety* involved, merely a rather theoretical consideration of wear and air-sealage factors, plus the ease of starting the opening action.

MODERN UNDERLEVER COCKING SYSTEMS

The underlever system as applied to serious air-rifle design offers several good features. Such rifles are commonly too expensive to manufacture to permit them to be sold in the low-price category. As a result, they are all expensive match (or sport) type rifles.

It is commonly believed that underlevers are much more powerful than barrel cockers. This was so originally. It isn't any more. However, power for power, it is still normally easier to *cock* the underlever pattern.

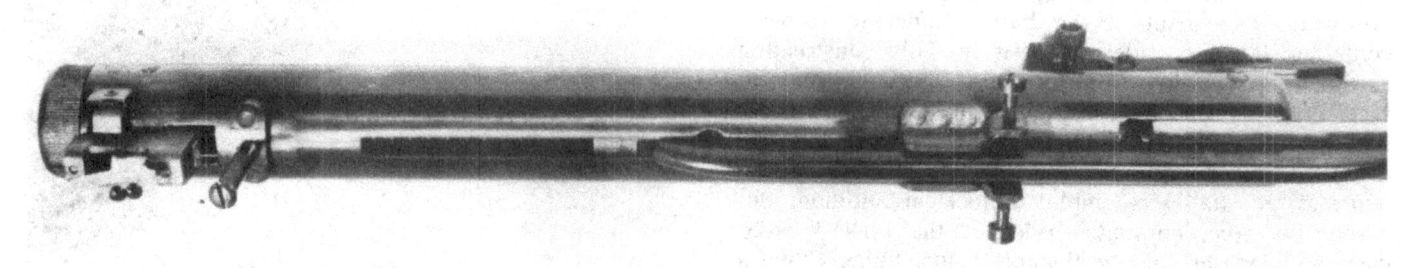

Underside of typical barrel cocker. Pistonhead is just to rear of cocking-lever tip. Tip of lever acts on piston to compress spring as barrel is broken down to thrust lever back.

The modern underlever rifle folds into the stock fore-end, or forward of it below the barrel, adding to the beauty of line as well as the balance of the rifle. The barrel of course is secured firmly to the receiver in this pattern.

To operate such a rifle, the cocking arm of the lever is pulled out of its seat in the fore-end or under the barrel as the case may be. In any event it is housed towards the muzzle end (not in the trigger area), except in the British new B.S.A. and German Falke 80 and 90 models. (See index.)

The positioning of the fulcrum of the arm is regulated to require but a relatively short throw of the arm to provide maximum leverage to *push* (or in the new B.S.A., to *pull*) the piston and spring back to full cock. The rigidity of the solid rifle construction plus the great leverage allows application of adequate cocking force while holding the rifle in natural position across the chest.

Except that it substitutes a mechanical pivoting lever arm to provide the actuation of the cocking lever, the mechanics of this system and those of the barrel cocker are the same.

Loading, of course, is quite different. Solid-frame underlever designs require a top loading plug (or tap). When the loading lever (which may be on either right or left side) is pushed or pulled, it exposes the plug cavity to allow insertion of a pellet. A few types open automatically as the gun is cocked. When closed it provides a positive, air-tight seal behind the pellet, the compressed air passing through a hole in the crossbolt or plug, which is actuated by the lever. This hole (an air vent) is lined up with the pellet in the chamber and the vent in the air cylinder when the plug is closed.

Some designs have "self-opening" taps or plugs which require no manual manipulation. In these the act of working the lever to cock the rifle also opens the breech tap for loading, and the closing stroke of the lever automatically closes the breech also.

SYSTEM EVALUATIONS—BARREL COCKING vs. UNDERLEVER

Ease of Cocking. Power for power the underlever is easier.

Efficiency of Air Seal. In theory at least the underlever is superior and stands up better.

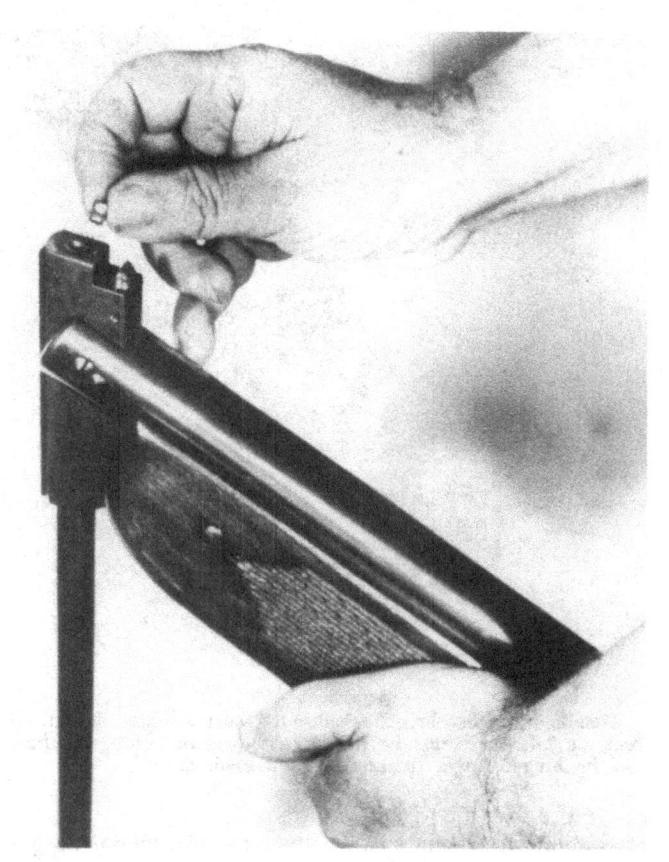

Loading barrel-cocker design. Note spring-loaded detent bolt and washer.

Strength and Rigidity. Weight for weight, the underlever is superior.

Ease of Loading. The barrel cocker is superior. Even though some taps are designed for "drop-in" loading, it is generally simpler to position the small pellets in the open barrel breech type.

Safety. It is easier to check *loading* in the barrel cockers. Otherwise one is as safe as the other.

Accuracy. A well-made barrel cocker selling for the approximate price of the underlever will be equally accurate. Low-priced barrel cockers will not, since they lack weight and the careful fitting of the higher-priced varieties.

Power. Same comment as for Accuracy above, except that the breech-sealing feature of underlever may require

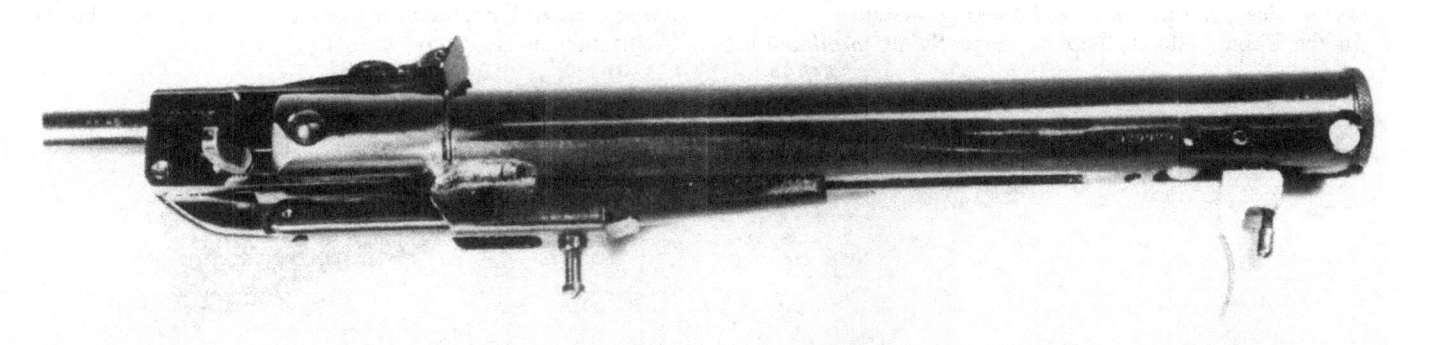

Current heavy-duty German Weihrauch barrel cocker with positive lock. Note trigger adjusting screw. The barrel-lock catch is the serrated piece at forward end of the frame.

Details of locked-breech Weihrauch barrel-cocker design. The lock on left side must be deliberately pressed before the barrel can be hinged down for cocking and loading.

less attention to air leakage than barrel-cocking designs.

In England there are only two firms making precision air rifles. They are Birmingham Small Arms Company and Webley and Scott, Limited. Both of these firms make *underlever rifles* of the highest spring-air power consistent with relatively easy cocking and reasonable weight. For lower power rifles intended for boys, both firms manufacture lighter rifles of the *barrel-cocking pattern*. In Scotland, Messrs. Millard Brothers of Lanarkshire make prewar German "Diana"-type rifles.

In Germany, on the other hand, where air-rifle match shooting is a most serious sport, most of the major manufacturers still concentrate on the barrel cockers, even for precision shooting—firms such as Carl Walther, Herman Weihrauch, Heym, Wagria, Krico, etc. The "Diana" line, largest of all, has barrel cockers from the lowest priced to the highest, as does Falke. Each makes an underlever type in small quantities, but they also make heavy barrel cockers of *equal power and precision*.

Spain, Italy, Japan, and Austria make only low-powered designs on the barrel-cocking system.

In the United States there is currently no *production*

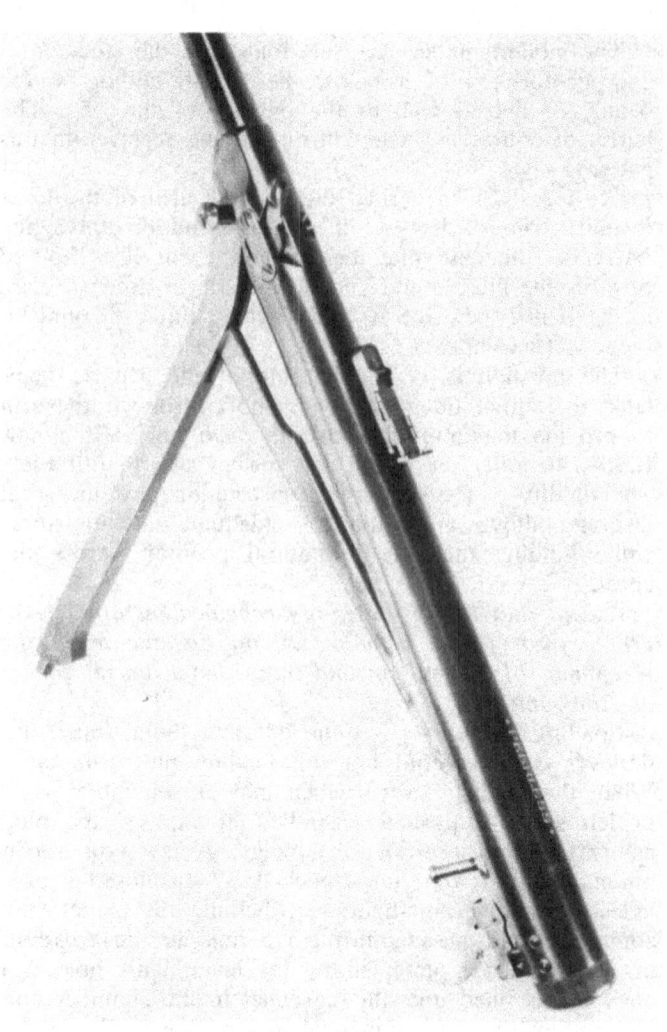

Diana underlever cocker with stock removed and action open to show operational details. Lever is at end of cocking stroke. Spring catch at front end supports lever when closed. Thumb-piece operates the loading plug (or tap). In this model it must be pushed to expose the port. A pellet is dropped in and the plug is closed.

on serious spring-air guns. Rifles are marketed by the Hy Score Manufacturing Company of Brooklyn, N. Y., but these are actually imported barrel cockers of the low-priced variety made by the "Diana" firm at Rastatt in Germany. *High-grade* barrel cockers and underlevers made by the "Diana" firm are marketed in this country by Stoeger Arms Company of New York City under their own trade name "Peerless," as well as some *high-grade* match barrel cockers made for this firm by H. Weihrauch in Germany.

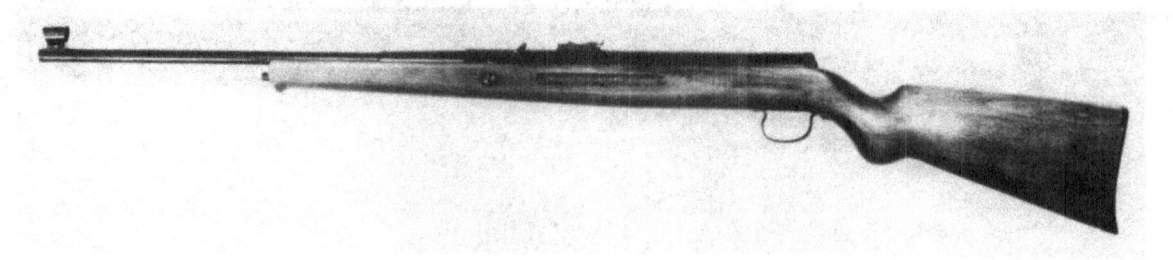

Typical modern underlever German Diana. Note that lever is concealed within fore-end when rifle action is closed.

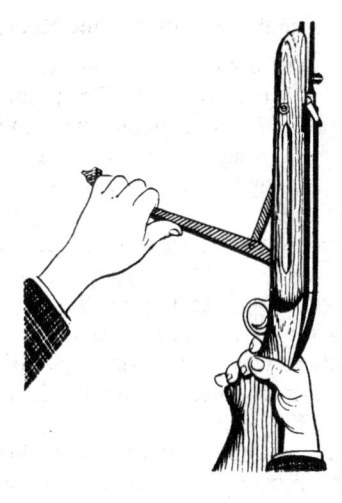

New B.S.A. with new rear-stroke lever system.

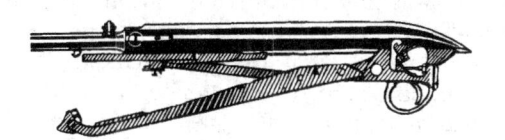

B.S.A. action with second cocking-lever system newly positioned. This design is also used by the German Falke.

German-made rifle for United States sales.

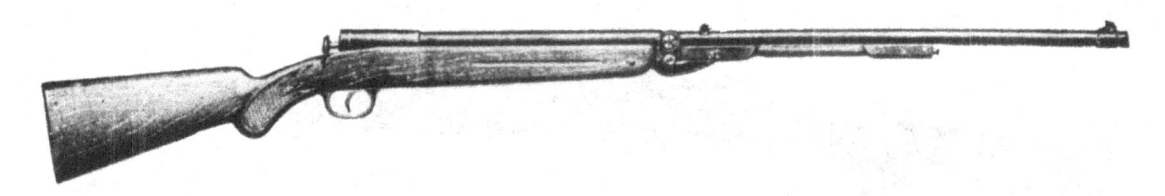

German-made Peerless underlever with independent cocking system for safety. This design has not been widely used.

(Note: Hy Score makes spring-air *pistols,* which are dealt with under a separate heading. As stated above they do not manufacture guns or rifles, however. There is some popular confusion on this point in the trade.)

MISCELLANEOUS UNDERLEVER RIFLES
The Peerless Model 3104-05

This was a German-made rifle imported by the Stoeger Arms Company of New York City, before World War II. The arm was furnished in .177 and .22 caliber. Weight about 7 pounds. Overall length about 46 inches. This was a well-made rifle about equivalent in design and power to the B.S.A. No. 2, which it rather closely resembled. It retailed for $48.

The Peerless Model 3106-07

This model closely resembled the 3104 in internal construction, but had one unique feature. Unlike other underlever patterns either British or German, this design was *not* ready to fire when the lever was returned after cocking the piston spring.

As a safety factor, this design featured a special bolt or plug positioned in the rear of the receiver. Pulling back the knurled head drew the bolt back to serve as a cocking indicator and to set the trigger ready for the firing pull. Aside from the safety factor (with this design you always knew if the piece was ready to fire), an exceptionally fine trigger pull was available, as the let-off was through leverage which connected to the piston, not by direct contact. Weight was nearly 9 pounds, length about 48.5 inches. Made in .177 and .22 calibers, this model was prewar priced at $70. Its high price militated against wide sales.

TURN-BOLT SYSTEM SPRING-AIR RIFLES

The earliest application of the military turn-bolt (or Mauser) system applied to spring-air rifles appeared as toys in Germany about the turn of the present century. Similar designs were subjects of patent application in the United States and England, several patents dating back to the 1880's.

Mayer & Grammelspacher about 1905, however, produced a boy's model with turn-bolt of a more serious type on this system. It shot 4.5-mm. slugs or darts and was powered by a spring which was cocked as the bolt was turned up and pulled back in standard military fashion. It was much more difficult to cock than the barrel cockers then in fashion, and its power was too low. It soon disappeared from the market.

In the period after World War I when arms manufacture was not allowed in Germany, air-rifle manufacture again took a spurt. One of the developments was a so-called "sportsmodell" intended, so the story went, for the sport of gallery shooting.

It so happened that this design was also a first-class military trainer. It approximated the new German Mauser pattern rifle in looks, weight, length, sights, and general handling. It was, incidentally, a repeater.

The Schmeisser Bolt-Action Repeater

In 1933 this arm appeared in two styles—a "Senior" model, 44 inches long, weighing 7.5 pounds, and using an 8-shot, detachable box magazine; and a "Junior" model, 40 inches long, weighing 5.25 pounds, and having a 6-shot magazine. Both had Mauser pattern "wing"-type safeties.

The magazine was inserted through the stock just below the line of the military-type rear sight. It was a box type, with numbers and holes in the side to allow an instant check on the number of rounds in the magazine.

The ammunition was a precision ball of special hard lead, 4.45-mm. caliber to stack into the rear of the magazine well.

Turning up the jointed bolt handle to line up with its travel slot in the receiver, the bolt was then rocked back

Very early German youth trainer based on the original Model 1871 German service rifle. Turning the bolt handle up unlocks action. Pulling it back cocks the firing spring. Chamber is loaded directly. Face of bolt is recessed to enclose the barrel chamber when gun is locked. Similar types but based on later German service models are made today.

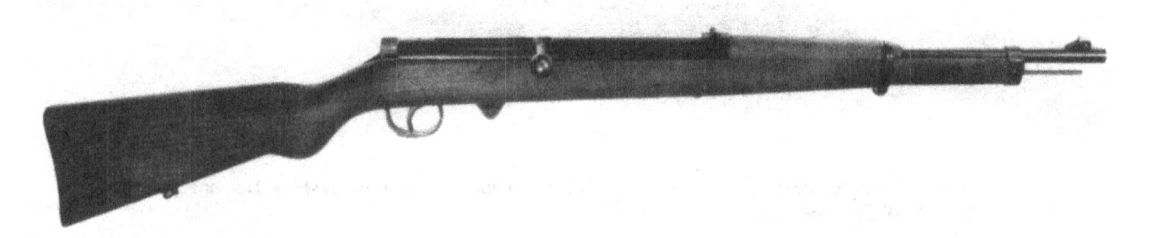

Formerly the "Schmeisser Model 33," this pattern is again in production by several European factories. It is currently popular in shooting galleries.

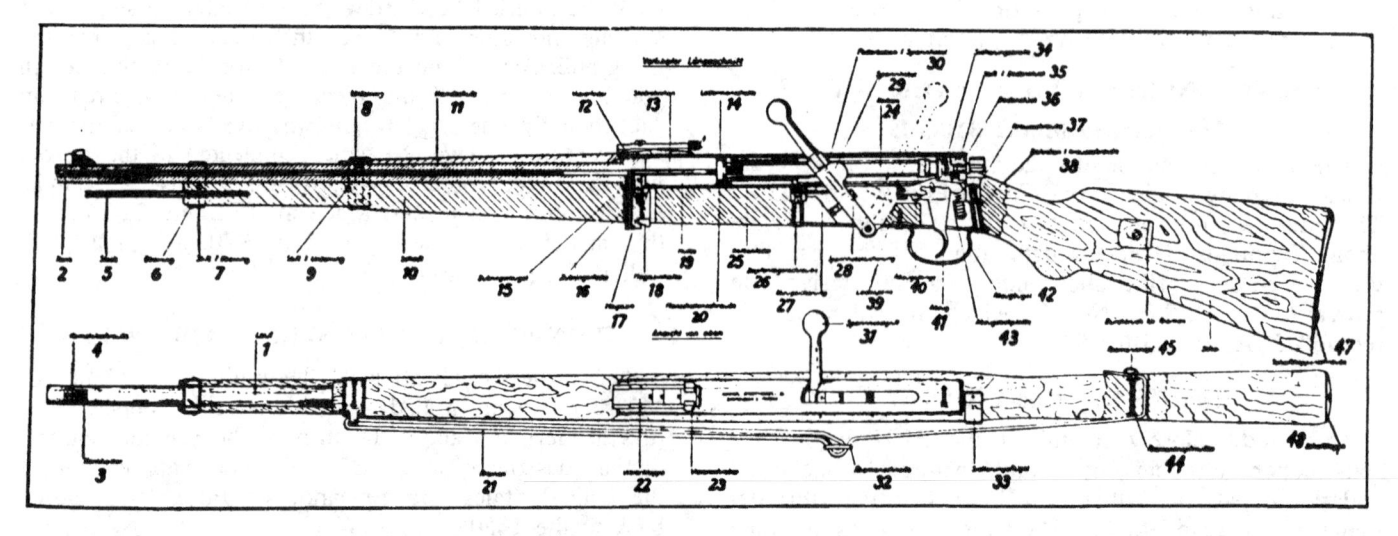

German Schmeisser 33 (and current manufacture) turn-bolt army air trainers. Originally used for German troop training. Now being utilized by Russians. Drawings show all details of parts operation.

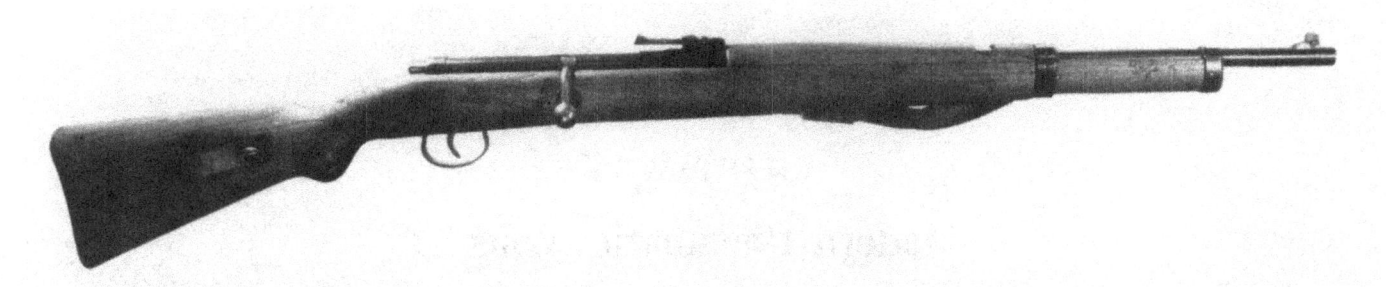

Detail of Russian air-rifle trainer made at seized plant of former B.S.W. (Berlin-Suhler-Waffen) plant at Suhl, Eastern Zone, Germany. Bolt handle operating in cam slot allows power for very considerable power compression for this design. Military-type "wing" safety.

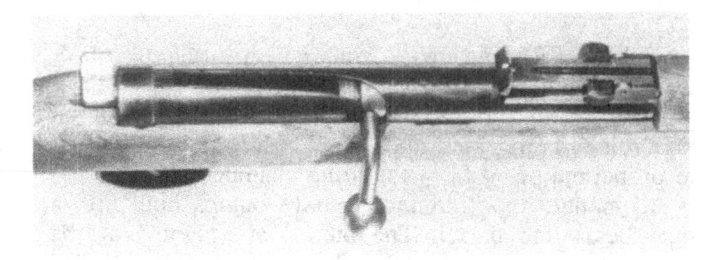

to length of the stroke. This cocked the piston and compressed a reasonably strong spring whose power could not, naturally, compare with that of the typical barrel-cocker design because of leverage and space limitations.

H. Schmeisser, who designed and originally manufactured this interesting short-range precision rifle, is noted as the designer of the German M.P. 38, one of the most efficient submachineguns ever mass manufactured. He is also noted for auto pistols and for machinegun design.

Rifles of this pattern were later manufactured by Haenel and others at Suhl for military training purposes and for commercial sale. At this time, when the Suhl area is under Russian control, similar rifles still are being manufactured. Some bear Russian markings indicating use as trainers.

Under the design of "Blitz" Repeating Air Rifles ("Blitz" Repetier Lüftgewehr) these bolt-action air rifles are also sold in Germany with sporter-type stock. The projectile is the usual special 4.45-mm. round precision ball. The magazine holds 6. Exactly similar rifles are also sold under the Haenel name, curiously enough, though some of these may represent a carry-over from prewar days by the large export houses. (Note: These are all identical to the Schmeisser except for trademarks.)

A different type, but on the same military bolt-action pattern and appearance, is produced under the "Bonna" trademark. The Bonna design, however, uses still another projectile—a round steel ball of 4.40-mm. The magazine below the barrel is the *tubular* type and holds either 75 or 100 balls, depending upon the model length.

Still another pattern of a serious bolt-action military trainer was made in Czechoslovakia. (Described in this book under current types.) The original design was made at Strakonice, a government small-arms center. It is a departure from the German types in action and loading.

CHAPTER 5
Modern Pneumatic Arms

A MODERN pneumatic arm (whether rifle, pistol, or shotgun) is a mechanical device in which air is pumped up *and stored in* an air-pressure chamber or reservoir to be released upon pressure of the firing trigger to propel the pellet from the firing chamber.

All modern types commonly have pumps built into a tube below the barrel. The pumps are pivoted at the forward end near the muzzle. These arms are first cocked and loaded to seal off the air-release valve. They are then pumped up by actuation of the pump lever. Air is compressed in a small chamber below the pellet chamber and may reach a pressure as high as 1,500 pounds per square inch. When the trigger is pressed, usually a hammer or striker with a powerful spring is released to strike a blow against the impact valve controlling the air release. Basically this approximates the elementary poppet valve familiar to motorists in which a spring reacts to close the valve immediately after actuation. *All* air in the chamber should be released behind the bullet by the original valve opening. When this does not occur, an "air lock" results.

(Note: Instead of the familiar "impact"-type valve, however, the Crosman designs utilize an improved air-type release system operating off the trigger and sear mechanism. See under Crosman for details.)

The sole exception to the above currently in production is the Benjamin Model 720, using round or air-rifle shot from a magazine feed. By heavy pumping, this model will discharge several shot before repumping is necessary. Only a portion of the air is released by each trigger pull. This system, however, is neither powerful nor efficient.

FEATURES OF THE PNEUMATIC DESIGN

Because the pump, which is the power-charging mechanism, and the air reservoir are housed below the barrel, pneumatic designs are short and compact in relation to their barrel length, a most desirable feature in any arm. This is opposed to the spring-air type of design in which the spring is normally housed together with the piston in a tube which is usually a prolongation of the barrel. The stroke thus required makes for a very long overall length in relation to the barrel length.

All pneumatics as currently manufactured permit a pre-selected variation of power depending upon the number of pump strokes used to charge the air reservoir. Normally *two strokes* are necessary to give an initial velocity sufficient to propel the bullet out of the barrel. In the better grade of rifle this requires about 200 feet per second. By increasing the number of pumps progressively, this velocity may be raised to as high as 770 feet per second without injury to the valves in the rifle. This additional velocity of course gives tremendously increased penetration. The principal feature of this design is that it allows flexibility of use. Thus it may be used for indoor or short-range target shooting with two or three pumps and may be used outdoors for vermin shooting by increasing the pressure.

The spring-air design on the other hand is limited to one power as ordinarily manufactured, though occasional freaks are known in which compound springs allow variable powers. These designs have never proved efficient, however. The spring design is such as *to pre-set the velocity,* which is normally between 400 and 600 feet per second depending upon the quality of the arm, the weight and type of the spring compressed, the general efficiency of the arm, and the leverage involved.

When the *pneumatic* arm is fired, the air release does not produce any noticeable recoil. This type has therefore the added value of preventing flinching when used as a training rifle. This factor also permits excellent aiming control, which allows the absolute maximum of accuracy in a weapon of the air type.

Spring-air designs, on the other hand, are subject to jarring effects as the springs move to drive the piston forward to compress air ahead of it for propelling the bullet. *Each design of a spring-air actuated arm reacts differently in the manner of its recoil.* Thus a weapon in which the spring action is directly forward, as in the case of the standard B.S.A. rifle, will act differently than one designed like the Webley pistol, where the spring compression is such that the piston is driven to the rear to fire. The Walther upward thrust produces still different characteristics. Varying compression-tube lengths also alter recoil.

While heat is generated in pumping up the air in compressed-air types, resulting in a normal loss of efficiency, this is discounted somewhat in the ultimate pressure pumped up in the air reservoir. Pneumatic arms operate on the principle of *decompression*. The act of air *release* is a cooling one and can produce moisture in the barrel, producing rusting effects with common steel barrels.

Spring-air arms, on the other hand, are operated on the principle of *compression* of air. In other words, they compress the air as the piston moves forward, resulting in heat being generated during the movement of the piston, which also limits the efficiency of the air-pressure development. This compressive action occasionally produces a temperature high enough to ignite oil and give a "diesel" effect which gives added velocity to that particular bullet. Such uncontrollable pressures account for "flyers" in an otherwise normal target group (though

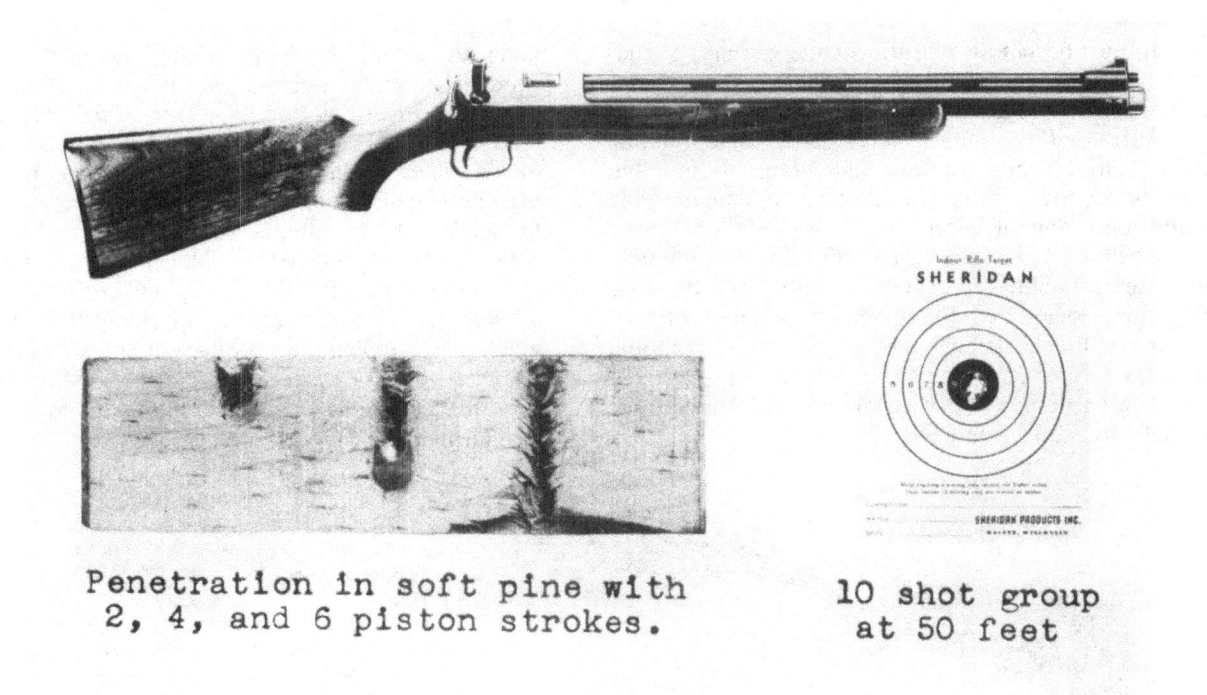

Penetration in soft pine with 2, 4, and 6 piston strokes.

10 shot group at 50 feet

Typical modern compressed-air arm—Sheridan rifle.

other factors may also be at work). As a result, despite the popular desire to utilize the diesel effect, serious manufacturers usually try to prevent or regulate it by recommending special oils and oiling procedures for the compression chambers in particular. It must be remembered that the combination of a powerful spring, close-fitting piston, a tight fit in the compression chamber, and particularly the very small air escape hole compared to the large pistonhead can result in very high compression-chamber pressures and temperatures.

THE HISTORY OF MODERN PNEUMATIC ARMS

While there has been considerable recent experimentation in pneumatic arms in Great Britain and in Europe, in the present century there have been no important *production* developments along this line in those areas.

The reason for this is simple. Both Europe and Great Britain regulate the power of air arms by law. In Great Britain the regulation is done somewhat negatively. For example, a determination is made whether an air arm should be classed as a *toy* or *"lethal" weapon*. The test consists of determining the number of 3/64-inch strawboards which can be penetrated at a range of 5 feet, distances between them being specified. Any air pistol capable of penetrating 7 such boards would be illegal. For this reason pump-up *pneumatic* arms are not desirable, since they have the potential penetrative force to make them come under regulations. For practical short-range air shooting, pneumatics do not have enough added accuracy to warrant the licensing difficulties, since the additional power is a legal hindrance. Spring-air types have their power "pre-set." Pneumatics cannot.

In this connection it must be remembered that outside the United States, firearm regulations even for the elementary .22-caliber rifle design are usually quite stringent. In the United States, therefore, since no pneumatic begins to approach the penetrative or the carrying power of the .22, most local legislation against air arms may be considered oppressive, misguided, or stupid.

The story of the modern pneumatic arm actually begins with the Wissler Instrument Company, predecessors of the present Benjamin Air Rifle Company of St. Louis, Missouri. In 1882, Walter R. Benjamin arranged with the Wissler organization to manufacture his newly designed compressed-air rifle under patents granted him for a pump-up design in which the long piston below the barrel was withdrawn to full stroke, then pressed against some solid surface and forced home. Three or four strokes gave a relatively high velocity and penetration; and the power was, of course, controllable by the number of pumping strokes. It was marketed as the "Benjamin Pump." It fired round BB shot or darts.

Starting with the manufacture of this first crude version

How to handle the Benjamin air rifle. 1. Catch knob on end of pump rod under soles of shoes and pull out the pump rod. 2. Place one hand on breech end of gun, other hand on stock. 3. Then push down with a strong, quick movement pushing the rod way in every time by applying weight of body on breech end of gun. 4. DO NOT pump the gun as shown above. It is awkward and the weight of the body cannot be used in this way.

85

of a pump-up rifle before the turn of the century, Benjamin has remained consistently in production through the years. They have not achieved the sales success that their designs warranted for numerous reasons, some relating to design and business policies and some to national shooting trends. It is only now that the pneumatic rifle is coming into general acceptance in the United States, largely because of the increasing difficulty in obtaining shooting-range facilities for the .22-caliber powder-type cartridge and because of the increased accuracy obtainable today with short-range pneumatic rifles. National growth and economic conditions (including the increasingly high cost of powder-rifle shooting) are principally responsible for today's interest.

financial instability of the original manufacturers. However, it must be pointed out that the manufacture of pneumatic arms of any type is a much more complex matter than appears on the surface. Air is a combination of extremely "thin" gases which will leak past any but the finest quality and the finest fitting valves. As a result, the *design* of a pneumatic rifle is only a small part of its actual operating efficiency. The *quality* of the material and more particularly the quality and *constant supervision of manufacture* is far more important. It is indeed very much more difficult to produce a good pneumatic rifle than it is a .22-caliber powder arm of equivalent grade! Few formal gunmakers could hope to compete in the air-gun field.

1924 Model Crosman compressed-air rifle.

Simco compressed-air magazine rifle, caliber .22. This rifle was made in California. A similar type of magazine system is currently in use in the Carbo-Jet CO_2 pistol, consisting of a spring-driven magazine follower. The Simco, like the Apache, Kessler, and Plainsman, was not a commercial success. All modern compressed-air designs made in the United States are common in operating principles.

True, the Benjamin Company is the *pioneer* in this field. However, the Crosman Arms Company of Fairport, New York, must be credited with developing a major interest in air- and gas-gun shooting for training and short-range sport use because of their aggressive advertising and developmental policies. Their sales drive focused attention on air-gun shooting at the popular level in the United States.

On the other hand, Sheridan Products, Incorporated, of Racine, Wisconsin, must receive credit for producing the first pneumatic arms to provide really maximum penetrative ability combined with maximum *target* accuracy. In all fairness to the other manufacturers, however, it must be pointed out that Sheridan rifles cost rather more than their competitors'.

Through the years a very large number of manufacturers have sought to enter the pneumatic rifle field in this country. Over 30 have entered this business and failed since the close of World War II alone. The reasons are many. Some stem from poor design and some from

Among the unsuccessful types which may be encountered are the Apache, which was made in California for some time after the war. This arm was produced as a rifle and also as a pistol. The Apache was a novelty in that it used an exterior barrel of .250 caliber with an insert, removable barrel of .177 caliber, thus furnishing two different velocities with the different bullets. It was supposed to be used as a target arm with the smaller caliber or as a vermin-shooting arm with the higher caliber, in theory at least! The Apache line of rifles and pistols developed noticeable valve trouble. Other difficulties were in the stocks used on the rifles, many of which were plastic at a time when plastic was not nearly as dependable a material as it is today, resulting in easily broken stocks. The best plastic gunstocks are still impractical, since when used in very hot or very cold areas they are subject to warping and bending on the one hand, or shattering on the other. The history of the Apache manufacturers commercially was somewhat less than successful. The guns are no longer made and should be purchased only for possible collection value, since repair services would be too costly.

Still another advertised line which showed initial promise included a line of rifles, pistols, and shotguns of the pump-up variety under the trade name of "Plainsman." Originally these were also manufactured in California after the war and marketed by the Challenger Manufacturing Company. The same designs were also sold under the "Challenger" brand name. The design under the name of the "Plainsman" was also marketed by the Goodenow Manufacturing Company of Erie, Pennsylvania. (Goodenow later offered a line of CO_2 pistols and rifles called "Plainsman.") These arms had much in common in their reasons for failure with the Apache, with particular reference to valving trouble, manufacturing operations, and fits. In short, the manufacturers, because of the pricing situation in this field, were forced to try to produce arms at a price which was not feasible with good pneumatic quality, except by established firms which have worked the "bugs" out of their designs and have established both markets and proficient manufacturing methods.

The Kessler pneumatic rifles manufactured in New York State were initially successful, though they, too, were manufactured down to a price rather than up to a quality. This organization was formed by a group of financial interests in Rochester, New York, then the home of the Crosman Air Rifle Company, after the Crosman interests refused to sell their business. The Kessler organization sometime later entered the manufacturing field on standard shotguns because of the low-profit range possible in the pneumatic field, and because of costly manufacturing difficulties encountered in pneumatic-type production. Kessler eventually terminated in bankruptcy. Ironically, some of their finest equipment, including high-speed stock-making machinery, was picked up by Crosman at bargain auction prices which allowed Crosman to still further increase manufacturing efficiency and reduce costs!

It must be stressed that *any* pneumatic arms which are not in current production are subject to troubles which will cost more to repair than the arms themselves are worth. Anyone buying pneumatic arms should seek to purchase *new ones* or at least to buy *standard makes* which are currently in manufacture and where repairs can be made by the original makers if necessary.

In passing it might be noted that the average gunsmith is not capable of properly repairing most of the pneumatic arms available. In the first place, the cost of the arm itself is so low in relation to that of fine firearms, that the normal amount of gunsmithing time necessary merely to disassemble the rifle would make prohibitive any actual extensive alterations or repairs by him. The Benjamin Company has consistently adhered to a wise

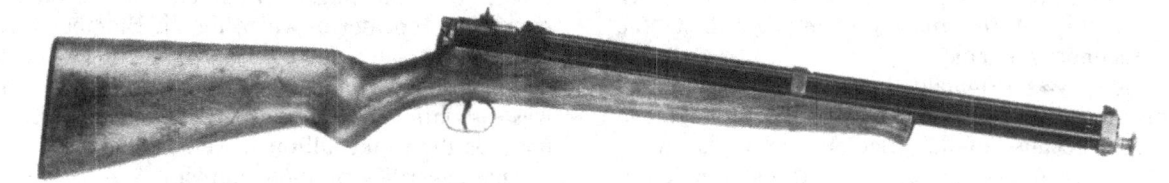

The first Crosman compressed-air rifle, Model 1923. Note that it used the pull-out push-in system of air compression found in earlier rifles by Benjamin.

The second Crosman compressed-air rifle, Model 1924. This is the first modern design to employ this form of underlever compressor. The hand grip was very practical, preventing hand pinching during operation as can happen with current models of all makers. However, its appearance was against it, and in later models the front section of the forearm itself is used as the compressor grip.

policy of requiring most dealers to send rifles or pistols of their make to the factory for repair. This is normally a long-drawn-out process and ordinarily quite expensive because of the minimum repair and transportation charges involved. In this author's extensive experience, it is cheaper to buy new ones than to repair old.

On the other hand, the Crosman Arms Company has at great trouble and expense set up a very comprehensive group of organizations across the country capable of repairing their arms at set prices. Parts are stocked. These organizations have been trained by Crosman personnel, and repair service is available in practically all parts of the country. Benjamin followed with a system along similar lines, though not nearly as comprehensive as the Crosman. This is not to be construed as a recommendation by this author in any sense. It is merely an observation presented for the general information of the potential air-gun buyer who doesn't "know the ropes."

Incidentally, the Sears-Roebuck organization and other mail-order houses have sold quantities of various pneumatic rifles made to their specifications. Normally, mail-order-house specifications are *those of the manufacturer except* that cheaper stocks, sights, and incidental hardware are furnished. In other words, the *basic quality* of the arm is that of the name brand of the manufacturer himself. These rifles are normally sold at a lower price than the standard factory production because of these factors and because of merchandising savings possible through very large purchases by organizations such as Sears-Roebuck. The Sears brand name is "J. C. Higgins." Montgomery-Ward often sells under their controlled brand name of "Western Field."

The Sheridan rifles on the other hand have never been made in large quantity. However, the numbers which have been produced and which have been sold at prices substantially higher than the Crosman and the Benjamin are of a very fine order of workmanship and fit. In the observation of the current author relatively few of the Sheridan rifles have been returned for repairs, except where the arms have been particularly abused. In other words, the quality of the rifle is maintained first, the price is a secondary factor.

The Sheridan was originally introduced in a "super grade" only at a price of $56.50. This did not achieve market success because of the price. It was replaced by successively lower priced lines. The current production type sells for $23.95. As a basis for cost comparison, the Benjamin .22 sells for $20 and the Crosman for $16.95. Again it must be pointed out that because of large sales and highly efficient manufacturing organizations, both the Benjamin and the Crosman actually give very much more in dollar value than the prices indicate. Dollar for dollar, all American air guns are a very big value. However, anyone seeking a pneumatic rifle should personally look over all available types before purchasing.

Benjamin and Crosman also manufacture pneumatic pistols. There is a possibility that Crosman will soon manufacture a pneumatic shotgun. Benjamin and Crosman have also produced repeating air rifles, some of which require individual pump-up for each charge, but which carry a number of pellets in a magazine so that each one does not have to be individually fed into the breech with the fingers. Benjamin also produced a true pneumatic repeater in which the air chamber was pumped up and specially valved to allow firing repeated shots without added pump-ups. This was the Model 710. It was discontinued because of the effort involved in pumping plus the rapid fall-off in velocity.

Characteristics of these individual arms will be found under the names of the makers.

Sheridan Blue Streak, late model.

CHAPTER 6

Carbon Dioxide Arms

IT IS seldom indeed in the course of the most exhaustive study of arms history that the researcher is able to pinpoint the time, place, and development of any specific variety of weapon. The use of carbon dioxide in small arms as a propellant happens to be one notable exception!

Fortunately, the patent records of Great Britain, the United States, and Germany are all clear and in general agreement on the matter of the carbon dioxide (CO_2) rifles and pistols. Even more important, engineering journals, manufacturers' records, distributors' sales catalogs, advertising literature, the best shooting and sporting journals of the late 19th and early 20th centuries, and usable examples of the guns themselves all bear out the origin of the CO_2 arms.

PAUL GIFFARD

The father of the carbon dioxide gun, a design only now beginning to come into its own in the sport of short-range target shooting, was Paul Giffard (1837-1897), a noted French engineer and inventor whose brother, Henri, is noted in history as the man who flew the first powered aircraft on December 21, 1852.

Paul worked with his brother at times. However, in his own right he developed scores of worthwhile inventions. Some were immediately successful, others being technologically ahead of their time benefited only those who followed in his footsteps at later dates. His "pneumatique" or compressed-air system for fast delivery of mail via tubes is well known. Other developments included a pneumatic telegraph system and a series of compressed-air rifles and pistols. The list is much too numerous to detail here.

His British patent No. 2931 of 1859 covered *compressed-air guns* with built-in pumps below and parallel to the barrel. Similar designs have been marketed in the United States by the Benjamin and Crosman Arms companies in quite recent years. In fact, these push-pull types actually started the trend of American manufacture in the compressed-air gun field and were the forerunners of our current CO_2 rifles and pistols.

Paul Giffard's British patent No. 41,500 of 1864 was followed by a series of others in various countries. When he turned his attention to the use of gases other than air, and *included mention of CO_2 in his patent specifications,* a rash of applications for CO_2 coverage soon appeared in patent offices throughout the world.

Thus in England in 1873 we find in No. 3194 a proposal to use carbonic acid as an explosive "for military purposes, etc." In true "shotgun" fashion it sought coverage for use of the liquified gas also for "producing motor power for use in locomotives, factories, etc., driving sewing machines, extinguishing fires, freezing, making soda water, etc." Curiously it did not *specifically* mention use as a propellant for arms!

EARLY MODELS

Early models of Giffard's single-shot pneumatic guns are not rifled. Made in caliber 6- and 8-mm, they use round lead bullets. The valves are controlled by the sear without benefit of springs, and when the trigger is pressed the entire compressed-air charge is instantly released. When heavily pumped up, such arms have very great penetrating power; but unlike silent, spring-controlled types, the air blast gives off a report comparable to a powder rifle. Pistols of the same calibers were also made up on this system by Giffard, and like the guns were breech-loaded through a tap.

As we have previously mentioned herein, Giffard's idea of a self-contained compressed-air cartridge was also the subject of patent imitation. Though quite powerful, these 8-mm air cartridges could not of course compare with powder cartridges for power and efficiency and were foredoomed to failure. However, a repeating rifle was designed to handle them but was never out into production.

When Paul Giffard turned to the design of CO_2 arms, he naturally adapted his guns and pistols as originally made for compressed air, since only relatively minor changes were required. (Note: This same procedure was followed recently in the United States by Benjamin and Crosman in altering their compressed-air arms to CO_2 designs.)

After patents had been granted in 1889 covering weapons using CO_2 as the propellant, Giffard induced France's most noted arms makers, Manufacture d'Armes et Cycles de St. Etienne, at Loire, to manufacture the designs as rifles, smooth-bore guns, and pistols.

From the accounts in French periodicals of the day, one gathers that Giffard and many military experts actually expected the new CO_2 rifle to be a sort of 19th century hydrogen bomb! There was much talk of its "silent deadliness" and what a revolution it would bring in warfare! In view of Giffard's standing as a scientist and technician, it is indeed difficult to conceive how he could have so overrated the potentials of his design! Then as now it was an interesting and valuable *training system,* excellent for match and vermin shooting up to about 50 yards. But it was not and is not by any stretch of the

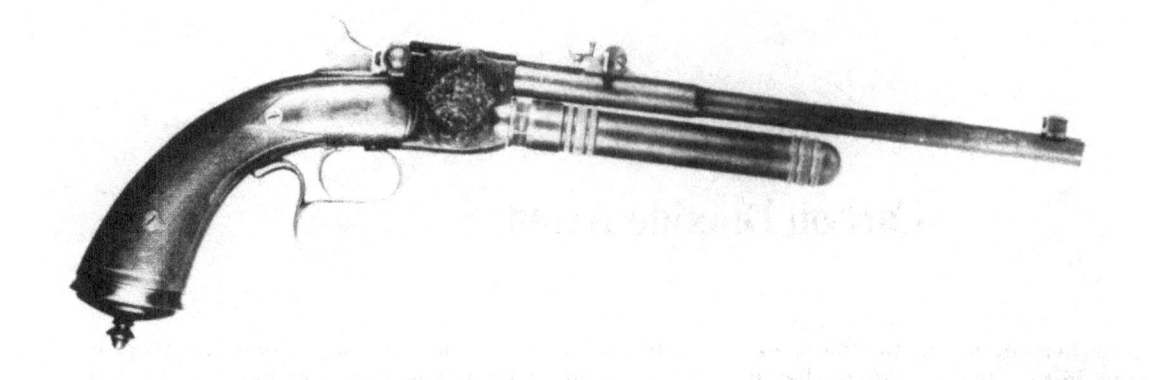

Giffard gas (CO$_2$) pistol. Construction same as for rifle.

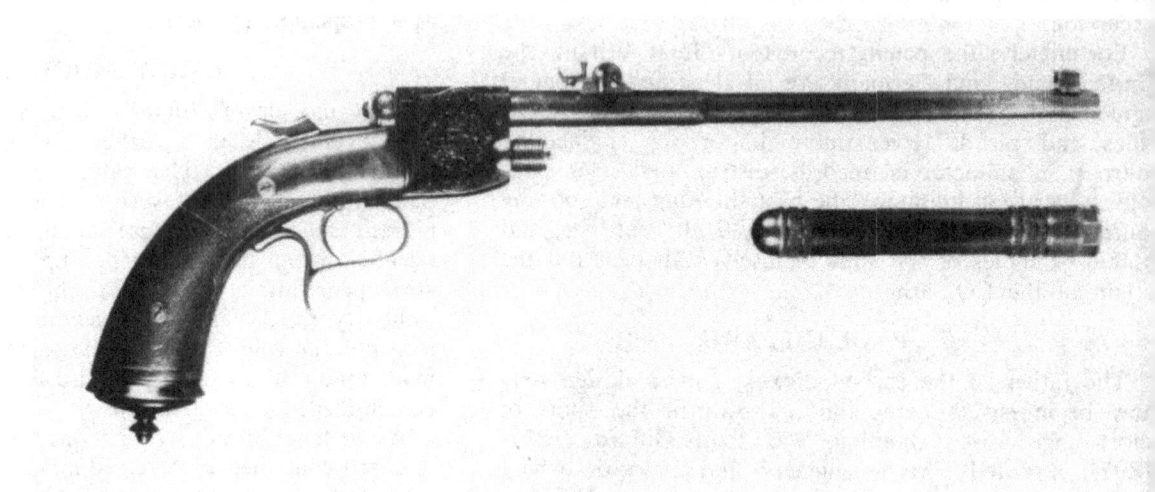

Giffard CO$_2$ pistol with gas cylinder detached and hammer cocked. Hammer fall can be regulated to open valve slow or fast, thus increasing or decreasing power.

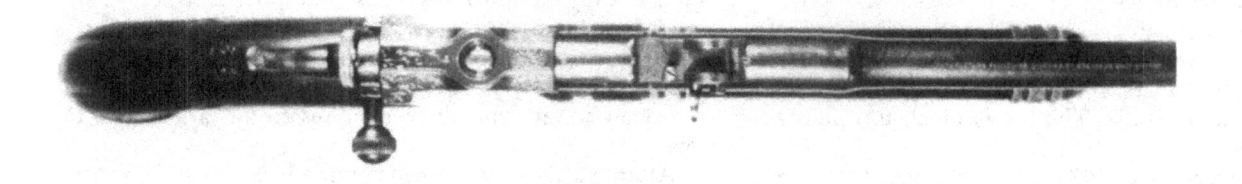

Giffard CO$_2$ gas pistol, top view, to show detail of loading tap.

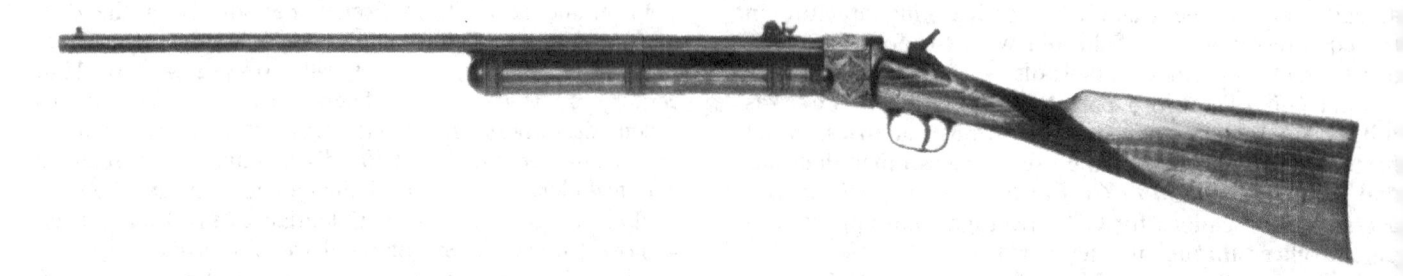

First Giffard CO$_2$ gas rifle. Caliber 8-mm. Made at St. Etienne, France. This is the first successful gas-operated arm.

imagination a substitute for even the lowly .22-short powder cartridge, much less the high-power military rifle with its 50,000 pounds breech pressure!

Giffard's scientific standing was such that even the learned editors of the best scientific journals of the time went easy on unmasking the fallacy of many of his claims. In fact, some even managed to see in the design potential use as a *machinegun!*

A discussion of this arm by *Engineering News* of August 9, 1890 is reproduced here for its historic value. It is based on a translation from the *Revue Industrielle* and is much more restrained than most of the laudatory reports given to Giffard's modest invention at the time. Seldom has such a relatively minor arms development been the subject of so much overrated praise in engineering circles.

THE GIFFARD LIQUID-GAS GUN

We reproduce from the *Revue Industrielle* the accompanying drawings of the Giffard gun which has lately been attracting so much attention, largely perhaps on account of the high reputation of the inventor, and the great value which he attaches to the invention. M. Giffard is best known to the world as the inventor of the Giffard injector, but his inventions are almost numberless, and many of them highly meritorious. He has publicly claimed himself that this gun is destined to revolutionize warfare, and to make war almost impossible. The one grave defect of the gun, however, seems to be lack of adequate range.

In principle the gun is simplicity itself. Carbonic anhydride (CO_2) liquifies at 36 atmospheres or some 540 pounds per square inch and is the explosive so far used. A steel cylinder 9 inches long, shown in detail in figure 3 and in place in figure 1, contains enough liquid for 150 shots. The reservoir is easily detachable, as will be seen, and as nearly as we can judge from the imperfect description, the impact of the hammer drives back the piston closing the chamber against the pressure of the gas and of a spring far enough to permit a small part of the fluid to escape; the chamber then instantly closing in spite of the resistance of the trigger spring. The conical ball, as nearly as we can judge, is inserted vertically at A, figure 1, the round plug in which it rests being then revolved through 90°, making the hole through the plug, with the shot in it, a part of the barrel. The gun is a very much cheaper one than those for powder, and firing it, of course, produces intense cold instead of heat, with no tendency to fouling. On the other hand, the work done in expelling the ball through the rifled barrel will produce no little heat, so that the piece may maintain a sufficiently equable temperature.

The gun is very cheap and there is, of course, no smoke. There is also very little noise; it is compared to the popping of a soda-water bottle. *Industrielle* states that some Birmingham firms have offered to manufacture them for $4.86 each, and have been underbid by a Belgian firm. The cost of the "explosive" is said to be only one cent for 50 shots. The entire weight of the arm is only 4½ pounds, the charging chamber weighing 9 ounces charged.

The one difficulty which seems to be fatal is lack of sufficient range; 540 pounds per square inch is a very low initial pressure, most modern rifles having 30,000 to 35,000 pounds. The range would not be reduced in the proportion of these pressures, of course, nor in anything like it, but it is difficult to see how its effective range could be much, if any, over half a mile. Something might be gained in this respect, should the principle of the gun be established as successful, by using a gas which requires a higher pressure to liquefy.

Another difficulty which occurs to us in the gun as now designed is that the muzzle must be elevated above the horizontal or there is danger that no fluid at all will escape from the chamber, but merely gas. Unless the fluid entirely covers the aperture, it is obvious that no fluid at all is likely to escape, for gas escapes from the orifice at so much greater velocity than a liquid that it would entirely fill the small space left for the liquid, and create a back pressure against it, before any had escaped. Ordinarily, the muzzle is slightly elevated, but should it chance to be necessary to depress it, to hit an attacking foe, the consequences might be awkward.

On the other hand, the gun is particularly well adapted for development into a machinegun, for obvious reasons, and such a gun, even if of short range, might well do terrible execution. On the whole, the next great war, if it holds off long enough, is likely to bring out some remarkable developments in the art of scientific slaughter.

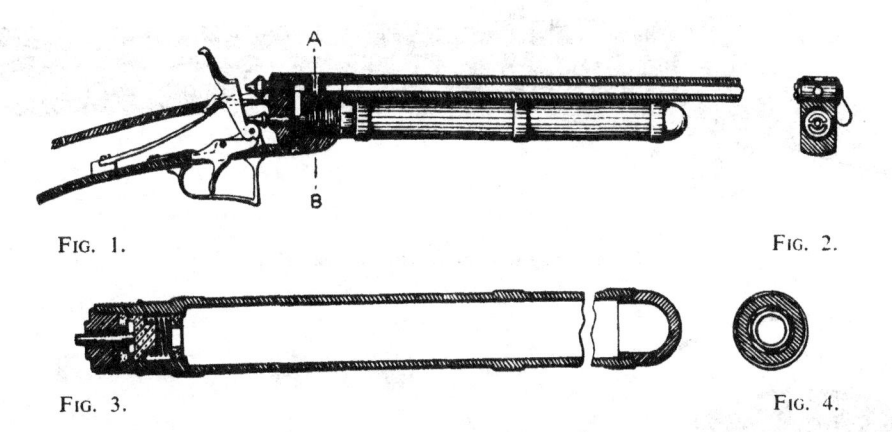

These first Giffard rifles and pistols are magnificently made weapons. Glowing reports of low cost to the contrary they were actually *much more costly* to build than were comparable powder arms. Their savings were in propellant and bullet costs not in the price of the arm itself. The French have seldom produced *any* guns of comparable quality except in the very high-priced fields.

Charged CO_2 cylinders were available on an exchange basis quite as in recent times. The loaded rifle cylinder cost 1.25 francs, the smaller pistol size cost 75 centimes. (Note: 100 centimes equals 1 franc.) The 6-mm.-caliber lead balls sold for 2 francs per 1,000, and the 8-mm. were 4 francs per 1,000.

The present author has in the past used various Giffard arms to some extent and is familiar with their design and their potentials. The accompanying explanatory drawings, targets, and bullet photos were originally published early in the century by an independent testing station near Neudamm (Die Versuchsstation Neumannswalde bei Neudamm). They are reproduced here together with the author's English translation as an accurate coverage of the original Giffard rifles and *their actual capabilities,* as seen through the eyes of contemporary German gun experts.

THE GAS RIFLE

Rifles with liquid carbon dioxide as a propulsive agent have been manufactured in France for quite a number of years already. These are the so-called gas rifles of the Giffard system, made by the Manufacture Française d'Armes et Cycles in St. Etienne. Since these rifles, and pistols of the same construction, are now marketed also in Germany, a description of the system may be of interest. The rifle factory of Ernst Friedrich Büchel in Mehlis, which sells these weapons, kindly put at our disposal such a rifle of 6-mm. caliber with a rifled barrel for testing purposes; we thus had an occasion to form a judgment of the performance of these weapons.

Illustration No. 1 shows the central part of the rifle. The carbon dioxide container has been unscrewed and detached. Illustration No. 2 shows the mechanism of the rifle.

The gas container consists of a steel tube about 30 cm. long, with a valve, closed by a strong spring, screwed into the open end. The simple hammerlock operates a pin which, on snapping forward, opens the valve for a moment, so that a little carbon dioxide can escape and enter the barrel above through an inclined canal. The shooting strength can be regulated by turning the adjusting screw S; when this is tightened, the hammer pushes the valve bolt in more strongly, the valve opens consequently somewhat more, and hence more carbon dioxide escapes, so that the bullet at-

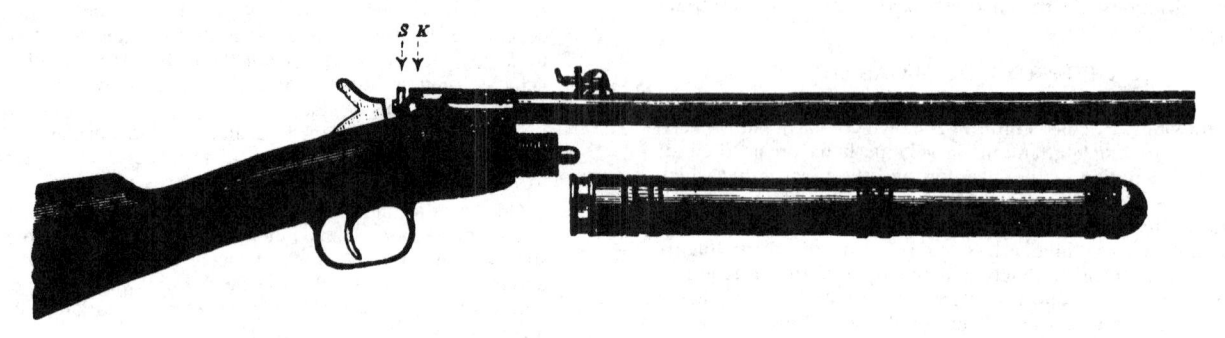

No. 1: Gas rifle, Giffard system, with gas container detached.

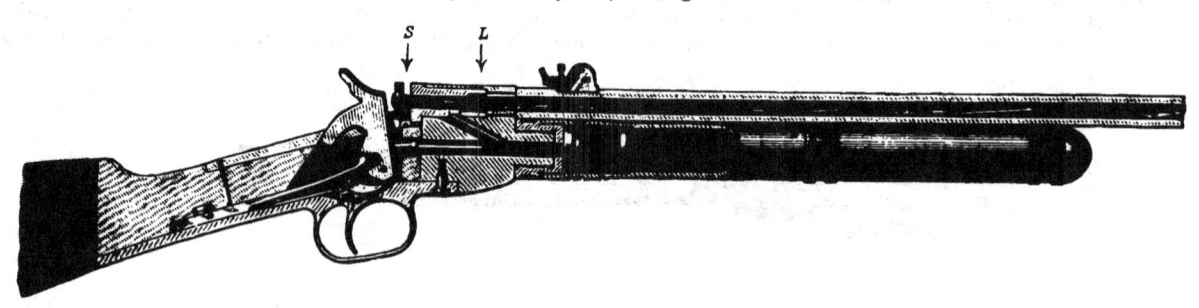

No. 2: Longitudinal section of gas rifle.

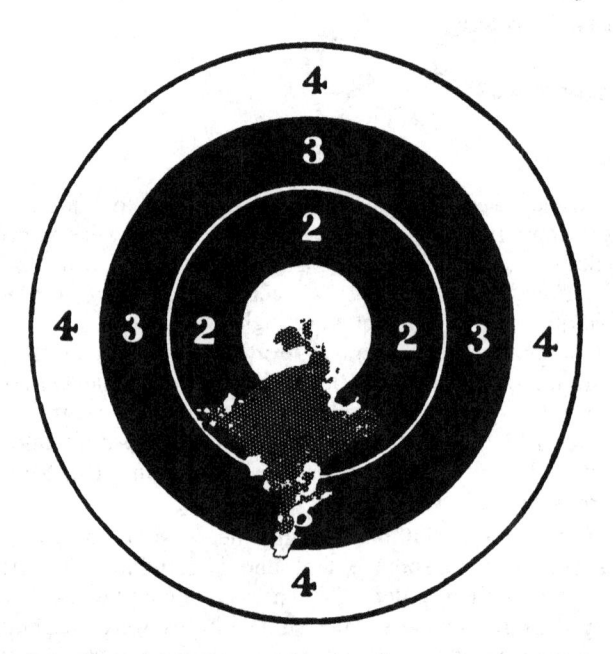

No. 4: Bullets of 8-mm. caliber shot from gas rifle at a distance of 8 meters, with charges of different strengths. (Actual size.)

tains a higher velocity. When the screw is loosened until it touches the pressed-down hammer, the latter does not open the valve at all; the rifle is then put "at safe." The adjusting screw S is fixed by tightening the bolt knob K. At 6-mm. caliber the hammer should be at a distance of 1½- to 2-mm. from the adjusting screw. One charge of carbon dioxide gas is then sufficient for 200 to 300 shots. At 4½-mm. caliber this distance should be about 1-mm., and then one charge of gas is said to suffice for about 800 shots. A caliber of 8-mm., of course, consumes the largest amount of gas; the charge is then consumed by about 120 shots.

The rifle is very easy to handle; in this respect the gas rifle is far superior to the air rifle. The bolt knob K is turned upward 45 degrees, a round bullet is put in the cartridge space L, the bolt knob is turned downward, and the hammer is cocked.

The rifles are manufactured with a smooth bore (for small shot) of 8-mm. caliber, and with a rifled barrel of 4½-, 6-

No. 3: Twenty-five shots with a gas rifle, 6-mm. caliber, at a distance of 8 meters.

and 8-mm. caliber, as well as pistols of 4½- and 8-mm. caliber.

Since one gas charge costs 1 to 1.25 marks—to which postage must be added because the gas containers are not obtainable everywhere—and 100 bullets cost 25 to 45 pfennigs (darts cannot be used), shooting with these weapons is considerably more expensive than with air rifles.

The rifle tested by us of 6-mm. caliber, shot very well, as is shown by the hit pattern, illustration No. 3, p. 105 (25 shots at 8 meters). The penetrative power is sufficient to shoot sparrows, etc. The bullets shown in illustration No. 4, shot with charges of different strength against an iron sheet, prove that the velocity approaches that of a Flobert small-bore rifle. However, the rifles tested did not quite equal the performance of such a small-bore rifle.

—*Experimental station at Neumannswalde near Neudamm.*

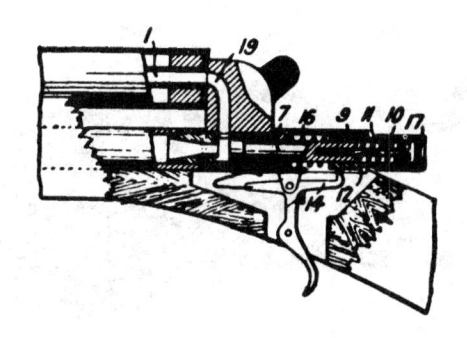

Valve detail of the Swedish "Excellent" system. This is one of the earliest forms of the blow-open valve.

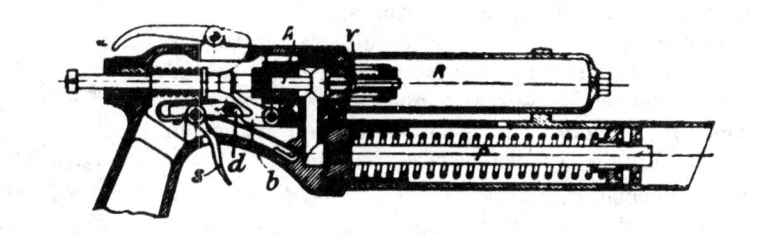

Morini (British) CO_2 pistol with liquified gas cylinder positioned about barrel. The form shown was used as a cattle stunner. This is an impact-valve type, the sliding hammer hitting the valve "v" to allow escape of gas to drive the plunger below forward against the forehead of the animal to be slaughtered. As in the latest Crosman type, the gas escape produced also a self-cocking hammer action. The bolt was withdrawn by spring ready for the next operation.

Giffard later developed an improved *hammerless* rifle on the CO_2 system, and a special company was set up in London for its manufacture. It was produced for a few years to shoot a conical .295-caliber bullet. A combination of valve troubles (even today the major headache in CO_2 guns) and the difficulty of obtaining refills prevented its achieving any real popularity. About the time of the introduction of this improved Giffard, Germany was already far along on the production of spring-air rifles which sold at relatively low prices and which required only one opening movement of the barrel to provide power.

Fritz Langenhan at Zella Mehlis was manufacturing such rifles for Pulverman, who was importing them into Britain as the "Millita" rifles, which his advertising claimed started the original British interest in air-gun target shooting. (Note: Though Langenhan was founded in 1842 and made fine precision firearms and cycles, their air-gun business was based on original deals with H. M. Quackenbush of Herkimer, New York.)

When the first of the fine *underlever* spring-air rifles appeared (the Lincoln-Jeffries) and manufacture was taken over by Birmingham Small Arms Company, the Giffard gun was doomed in England. It never did sell very well in Germany for many of the same reasons it failed to succeed in Britain.

In the London-made Giffard, the hammer was internal, not subject to thumb cocking as in the original St. Etienne manufacture. Pulling down the triggerguard lever opened the breech and cocked the concealed hammer. At this point the tip of the lever rotated the breech bolt to allow insertion of a ball in the breech opening. A numbered disc was revolved slightly by the same movement. On the tenth opening movement of the lever, the number 10 was visible, and so on in units of 10, the numbers being seen through a hole in the side plate, until 90 was reached. This device offered a reasonably positive check on how much liquified gas remained in the cylinder at any given time. It was a sort of early-day "Veeder-Root counter."

A safety was also applied automatically by the opening movement of the triggerguard lever. It had to be pushed off to fire much in the fashion of today's common shotgun tang safety.

Returning the lever to place closed the breech for firing by rotating the breech bolt. When the trigger was pressed it dropped the hammer, which was of the rebound type. This system required use of a hard valve material which inevitably leaked gas, but was the only way in which adequate power could be achieved with the valving materials then available.

GIFFARD'S CO_2 SUCCESSORS

Giffard's U.S. patent No. 452,882 was granted May 26, 1891. It was followed by Hubbard's (471,176) in May 1892, Calkins' (614,532) in 1898, Harvey's (632,526) in 1899, and a host of applications both here and abroad. None of these are of any particular value here since they were not the subject of commercial production, but interested researchers may find some value in those original patent papers.

The "EXCELLENT" CO_2 Rifles

One line which merits passing notice however is a Swedish development. The operational principles were unique in that the arms were intended to be operated on gallery shooting tables, from special lockers, or otherwise direct from a major CO_2 supply. The gas supply, in other words, was NOT contained within the rifle as in the Giffard, but in a container to which the rifle could

Swedish Excellent rifle. Made as both a compressed-air and a carbon dioxide rifle. Special valve system operated by pushing in button at extreme end of bolt to close valve. Rear breech assembly swung to side for chamber loading. CO₂ model fed from a hose line in shooting galleries.

be attached. (The same system was later used for gallery rifles by Crosman.) (See under Crosman.)

This system was introduced as a rifle trainer by the Swedish Ministry of the Navy about 1910. A special variation of the device was also made as a big-gun attachment for gunnery training and was considered an important military and naval "secret" for some time!

Sweden's official *Budget Estimate for 1914* carried a breakdown on the operating costs of these arms as a justification for their continued use.

While the original design was Swedish, most of the gun parts were actually made in Germany, so of course it was no secret to the German army! After some consideration by German authorities the design was passed over. However, it was later introduced in *shooting galleries* in Germany and Austria, where powder-cartridge firing was not permitted!

The rifle could be made to any exterior form desired, and various models appeared as bolt-and-block designs for instruction in both military and sporting marksmanship.

Used on a table, box, or shooting platform, the rifle was secured by two pins which fitted into table sockets. One of these served as a movable mount. The other was a hollow stem leading to a valve. When the stock was pressed down slightly, the hollow-pin pressure opened valves allowing a charge of CO₂ from the loading container in the box or below the table to pass into the rifle gas chamber. Loading was at the breech, caliber 6-mm., round lead ball. To charge the rifle for each shot it was necessary only to press the stock down on its pin. The gas container for service use weighed 8 kilos (about 17.6 pounds) and serviced the rifle for about 8,000 shots at approximately the same power level.

This Swedish device was, of course, a forerunner of the subcaliber training devices and pneumatic "machine-gun trainers" developed and used in most armed services at much later dates. It was *really* unique only in its early appearance and in its use of CO₂. (Note: The rifles themselves are occasionally encountered in collections where they are seldom recognized today. Rifles of similar appearance but with a long-stroke pump below the barrel were later made in Germany and will often be confused with these CO₂ arms.) The rifling was unusual, thought not unique, in that it was smooth bore at the rear, only the last few inches towards the muzzle being rifled.

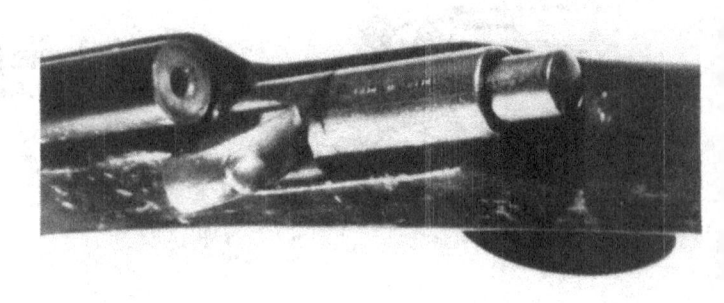

Swedish Excellent carbon dioxide rifle (1909 to 1915). Breechblock swung aside for loading. An early "blow-off" valve variant.

Except that the rifling ran further up the barrel, it was an imitation of the weird British "Paradox" gun design, and an approach to that used in many types of German cap-fired parlor rifles (Zimmerstützen).

Special CO₂ Weapons

The picture below shows an ambitious attempt at utilizing CO₂ in a variety of arms. The devices are of historical interest only. They were not commercially successful.

A translation is given of the only data published (in Germany early in this century).

A WALKING-STICK SHOTGUN FOR COMPRESSED GAS

The advantages of the old air rifles are utilized again in the construction of a compressed-gas rifle invented by C. H. Böhm. Carbon dioxide under a pressure of 50 atmospheres is used as a propulsive agent. The air rifles used hitherto operate with a pressure of 3 or 4 atmospheres. Böhm's walking-stick shotgun can be disassembled and assembled again without any tools within a few seconds. The shotgun has the following special advantages: no report, no smoke, no cartridges, cheap ammunition, and simple handling. The use of carbon dioxide guarantees a constant pressure of the gas, so that the trajectory remains uniform from the first to the last shot. One carbon dioxide charge suffices for 100 to 120 shots, and costs about 50 pfennigs. A special oiling device ensures the automatic oiling of all sliding parts at each shot. Böhm's shotgun is made in the form of a walking-stick shotgun, a pistol, and also as a repeating rifle. (See illustration.) In the case of the pistol the cocking occurs simultaneously with the loading, so that shots can be fired at extremely short intervals. It is reported that at a distance of 20 meters a board of 3 to 4 inches thickness can be pierced.

(Note: Small arms with carbon dioxide as a propulsive

94

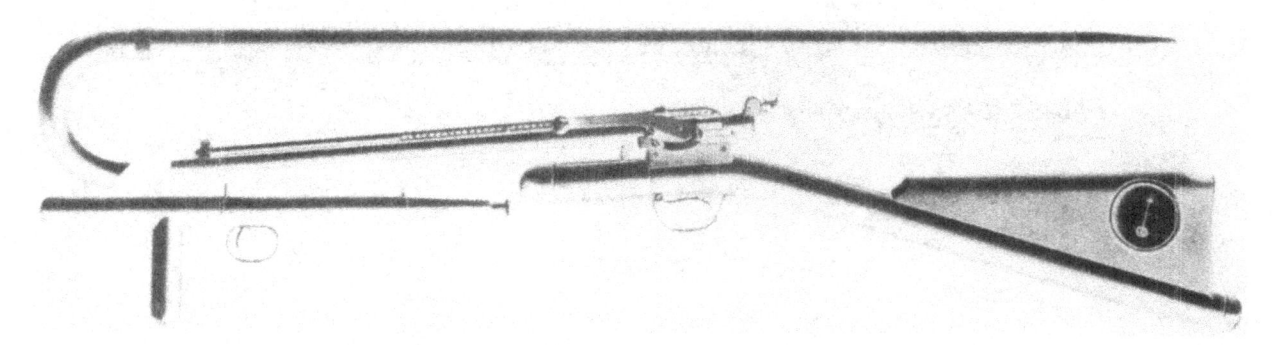

Swedish and German CO₂ gas cane, rifle, and pistol.

agent have been patented in many models, but no results worth mentioning have been achieved with them up to now. Despite our efforts, we have not been able to get one of the small arms described for testing purposes. Hence we cannot say whether this system is superior to Giffard's which, though known, has not proved to be adequate, and is just sufficient for shooting practice within a room.)

—*The Experimental Station at Neumannswalde.*

MODERN CO₂ ARMS

The modern line of CO₂ arms is *principally* an American development. Such weapons whether pistols, rifles, or smooth bores for shot are manufactured ONLY in the United States at this time.

(Note: Hämmerli, the noted Swiss arms makers, will soon introduce improved CO₂ guns, details of which have been released to the author. Other manufacturer which cannot yet be announced is also contemplated.)

To Paul Giffard belongs the credit and honor for launching the *first successful* pistols, rifles, and shotguns using CO₂ as a propellant, as we have already established for historical purposes.

The first modern CO₂ production arm to see the U.S. market was a pistol—the "Schimel"—made in California, about which more will be said later.

Crosman CO₂ Guns

To the Crosman Arms Company of Fairport, New York, however, and more specifically to the imagination, initiative, and drive of its present president, Philip Y. Hahn, Sr., goes full credit for *modernizing* Giffard's principle and for financing the improvements which made wide sales possible. It is also due to his personal sales, publicity, and advertising drive during the past 10 years that the CO₂ gun has finally come of age.

We have no space here to dwell upon the years of effort Hahn put into raising the position of the Crosman Arms Company from that of a small-time manufacturer of compressed-air guns to the largest manufacturer in that field and also in the field of CO₂ guns.

Suffice it to say here, that from his first connection with Crosman Arms he foresaw the inevitable expansion of short-range, low-cost, safe target shooting as a coming necessity on the American scene. The constantly increasing population was—and is—steadily making the sport of rifle and pistol shooting difficult for the average man to engage in. But the healthy interest of American youth in outdoor sports, as well as the ever-continuing need for pre-military arms instruction, pointed the way to a business which still has tremendous expansion possibilities.

The original Crosman compressed-air rifles were a step in the right direction. The pioneers in this field, the Benjamin Air Rifle Company of St. Louis, had established that fact long before Crosman Arms was formed. Such rifles provide more power than the European spring designs. Being more powerful, they can be used against vermin and bird nuisances with safety because of their relatively short range but adequate power. The shooter can easily judge when it is safe to shoot at such targets without wondering, as with the long-range .22 powder rifle, where the bullet will land if he misses.

But the compressed-air design has one drawback for the average American—it requires quite a lot of effort (6 or 8 pump strokes) to bring the air compression up high enough for the kind of shooting it does best.

Up to the point where Hahn turned his attention to this problem of work involved, no one in the United States had done anything about it.

The answer was simple to anyone who knew the history of air guns and gas guns. However, there were no

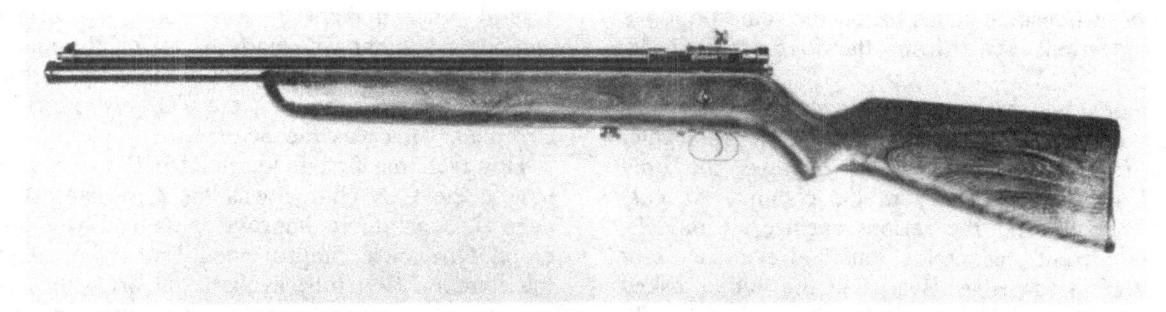

Gas rifle. CO₂ was transferred from 10-ounce cylinder (refillable). Each refill averaged about 70 shots—produced approximately 500 shots from 10 ounces. Models 113 and 114. This is an early Crosman.

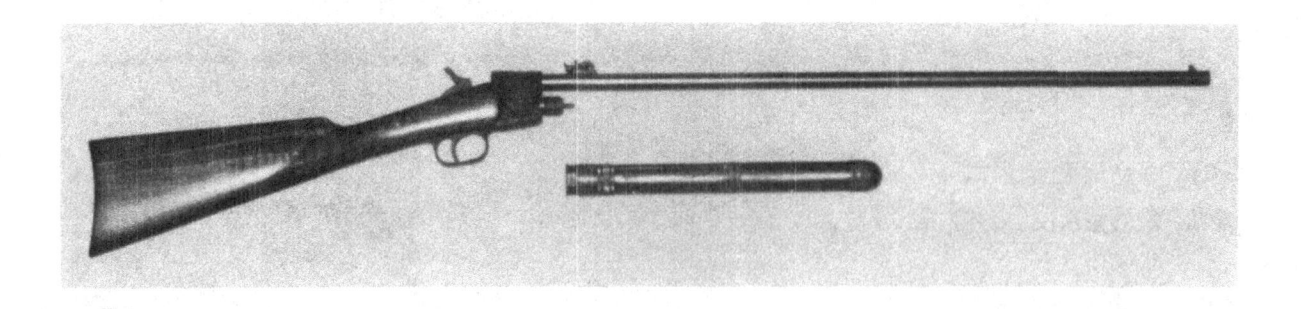

First model Giffard CO_2 rifle, from Crosman Arms Company collection, shown with gas cylinder detached. These rifles were very much more powerful than today's CO_2 types. Giffard's power was achieved through using the gas-vapor head to force liquid CO_2 into the expansion chamber in exactly controlled quantity. It didn't always work, but it still gave more consistent maximum power than is encountered in current models where the vapor rather than the liquid CO_2 is the power source, since power and hence velocity drop off as pressure in the accumulator lowers.

books on the subject, and what literature existed was very difficult to come by. It is a very strange fact to anyone with a research background, but it IS a fact, that no major United States arms maker has any clear idea of what arms developments have been tried, adopted, or discarded in Europe! German arms manufacturers have always made it a point to keep abreast of world developments in their field, even though they seldom make any use of them. The Germans, for example, knew all about the possibilities of CO_2 use; but they did not attempt manufacture for a variety of reasons. For one thing they knew they were too weak for military use; and for training use, they already had impressive air-gun and small-bore powder-rifle industries well developed.

The Development of Crosman CO_2 Guns

Anyone who has even seen and handled Giffard guns can not fail to note many similarities in today's design, After all, there are just so many mechanical ways of achieving any given results! Giffard, originally a specialist in pneumatics, had first developed a pump-up air gun. Then when he had acquainted himself with the characteristics of liquified CO_2, it was a simple step to alter his design from a difficult-charging compressed-air rifle to an easy-charging CO_2 design. There was little to it except to supplant the pump with a simple gas cylinder!

Phil Hahn of Crosman Arms hit on the same principle with an inadvertent assist from the long-departed M. Giffard!

This author's first visit to the Crosman factory was in company of a mutual friend, Colonel Rex Applegate, on a visit from Mexico, where he operates the only commercial small-arms factory in the country. As customary, we looked over the various engineering models. None of the current engineering staff had ever heard of Giffard to their knowledge. But when the author asked specifically if Crosman had an early specimen of the St. Etienne-made Giffard rifle, Mr. Hahn was able to remind his staff that they *did* have a specimen which he had stumbled upon at Abercrombie & Fitch's Madison Avenue store many years before! The rifle was located, a fine specimen as pictured herein, lightly engraved, with the name inlaid in gold on top. Its right side had been milled out to disclose the operating principles.

When, years later, the Crosman Company was working on producing an experimental compressed-air gun to *fire shot charges,* they soon discovered that it took 40 to 50 pump strokes to chamber enough pressure for practical use because of the weight and mass of the shot container.

At this point Hahn turned his attention to the possibility of using an already compressed gas to replace the hand pump. Curiously enough, at this time there were available at low cost from Government war surplus large quantities of gas cylinders generally similar in appearance to the old Giffard. The relationship was obvious.

Hahn took a sales trip across the country to sound out his jobbers on their reaction to a rifle with power equaling or surpassing his compressed-air design, which would sell for about the same price, yet would require no manual effort except that necessary for loading and cocking. The reaction, subject to his being able to lick the refill problem, was excellent. The trouble with such sales surveys is that they *always* leak secrets! His sales discussions started several other makers thinking along his original lines, and some attempt was made to get on the market ahead of Crosman. One maker, quite possibly through sheer coincidence, did actually get a CO_2 *pistol* out before the Crosman. This was the Schimel.

However, the first modern RIFLE to be produced to handle the CO_2 charge was the Crosman. It has since gone through many improvements and will go through more. One such "improvement" was the adaptation of the common CO_2 tube available at drugstores across the country as a power supply. This obviates the original necessity of making trips to service stations to obtain refills. (Note: This idea was pioneered by Schimel. Crosman uses a more practical, larger-than-standard tube, giving extra power. Independent testing by the author has already disclosed deficiencies in the present CO_2 power supply systems which will eventually require changes.)

Building sales acceptance and dependable CO_2 arms through continuing development, publicity, and promotion was a long and costly task. Only a man with much energy, vision, and belief could have seen it through. Those who follow in the field will benefit of course from Hahn's efforts; but his trade acceptance and product developments are such that it will be a long time before anyone can challenge the Crosman hold on the CO_2 arms field, barring the entry of a major competitor from the arms or toy field, or of an aggressive importer.

Crosman CO₂ Rifle

Single Shot Models 113, 114.

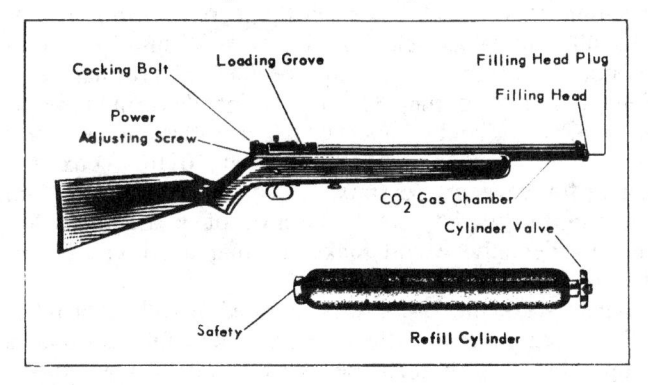

TO CHARGE RIFLE

1. Make sure there is no pell in barrel.

2. Cock rifle. (See step 1 under "To Shoot").

3. Screw cylinder into gun as shown. Hold handwheel with one hand, turn cylinder with other until valve is fully open. Transfer of CO_2 automatically stops when pressure is equal between gun reservoir and cylinder. Close valve and unscrew cylinder BY HANDWHEEL. Light blow-off of CO_2 thru vent is normal escape of excess as cylinder is removed.

4. Always replace filling head screw plug, after charging rifle.

TO SHOOT

1. Cock rifle. Turn bolt knob to unlock and draw bolt back until trigger sets with an audible click. Push safety "on".

2. Lay Crosman Super Pell in loading channel, blunt nose forward, and push into breach firmly until bolt knob can be locked.

3. When conditions are safe, push safety "off", aim and shoot.

4. Cock load, and shoot again. Rifles have CO_2 storage capacity for 75 shots at full power.

Crosman CO₂ Rifle Instruction Card.

The Schimel CO₂ Pistol

The Schimel pistol was the first American-made *production* pistol to use CO_2 as a propellant. It was also the first *production*-made arm to use the common CO_2 metal gas bulb in its construction.

This Schimel pistol was made in California. Unfortunately, its designer went bankrupt before he could achieve market acceptance. It reached the market before the Crosman pistol did and was indeed an improvement over that weapon in the *form of charger it* originally used. (Note: Current Crosman and other CO_2 arms all use this form of bulb, though made to their own specifications as a rule. It is by no means a completely satisfactory answer to the CO_2 power problem incidentally.

It is to be noted at this point that the author has personal knowledge of several *custom-made* pistols which were designed to use CO_2 before the Schimel appeared on the market, the power supply being the same. Since these chargers were used not only for carbonating water but also for powering model airplanes and motorboats both here and abroad, their application to model pistols could have been anticipated. However, credit for the first *commercial application* goes to the developers of the Schimel pistol.

This pistol was an impressive die-cast piece very closely approximating the appearance of the famous German Luger pistol. The appearance was intentional, to capitalize on the world-wide acceptance of the Luger lines. It was 9.25 inches long, and had a 6-inch barrel of .22 caliber with a rifled liner. Its height was 5⅜ inches, maximum width 1.25 inches, and it weighed about 40 ounces. It will be seen that it was not just the Luger outline which was sought, but a good approximation of the general dimensions, hang, balance, and weight. Sights were a fixed Luger-pattern front and a windage-adjustable rear.

To load, a movable block at the top rear of the arm was pulled back. This forced the gas cylinder down in the butt exposing a screw plug, which was taken out to allow insertion in the butt of a charged CO_2 bulb, the small end going in first. The plug was then screwed in tight. Next a valve button on the right (rather resembling the takedown-lever piece on the Luger) was pushed ahead to close the valve. When the breechblock was shoved home, it broke the seal on the gas container. Another back-and-forward movement of the block allowed a propelling charge of CO_2 to enter and be trapped in the expansion chamber.

A very bad feature of the design was that *at each gas charging*, the valve button had to be pushed forward before pulling back the charging block. If you forgot to do this, when you pulled the block back the entire contents of the gas bulb was exhausted! No danger—just annoying and costly!

The bar resembling the Luger toggle knobs was raised to allow a pellet to be inserted in the barrel. Pressing it down forced the pellet into the chamber and locked the breech. A trigger safety could be applied if wanted.

When the trigger was pressed, the expanded gas in the chamber was released through the outlet hole behind the pellet. Velocity was standard for CO_2 guns of the type up to 580 f.p.s. Balance and accuracy were good.

First model Benjamin CO₂ pistol, the Super CO₂ model.

Power was stable for most of the shots because of the liquified gas employed. There was only one power available.

The Schimel pistol was a good design which received a somewhat bad reputation because of the gas-escape feature, principally, though it had some lesser faults. Its manufacturers, unfortunately, did not have the capital to hang on until they could work out the "bugs" and establish a good selling organization: an old, old story in all undercapitalized businesses, unfortunately!

The manufacturing dies and tools were later purchased by a California sales group. Some alterations were made to correct the gas trouble, and to incorporate a repeating feature, and the Schimel was again offered, this time under the name of "The American Luger." It happens that the Stoeger Arms Company of New York City controls a trade-mark on the name "Luger" applied to a pistol, and they promptly turned the matter over to their attorneys. With advertising halted, the pistol was again

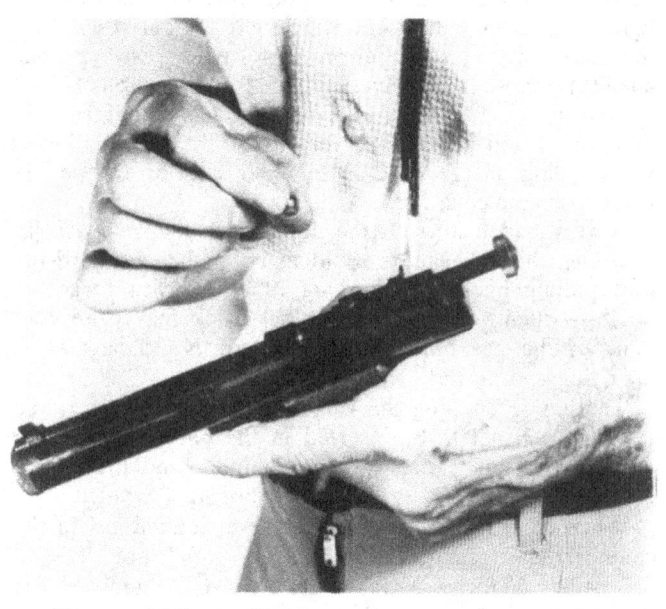

First model Benjamin CO₂ pistol. Breech open. Loading.

withdrawn from the market, but it remains an interesting page in the developmental history of CO₂ arms.

(Note: This pistol, now offered under the name "Carbo-Jet," is described in detail later in this work.)

Early Benjamin CO₂ Pistols

The Benjamin Air Rifle Company followed the Crosman with a CO₂ pistol they called their "Super CO₂". Like Crosman, Benjamin adapted tools, parts, and designs as far as possible from their original compressed-air pistols to meet the threat from the new, easy-charging CO₂ system.

Unlike Crosman, who was in the midst of tooling when Schimel came on the market, Benjamin had time to study the situation and make certain advances based on its competitors' first-trials with observable errors.

The result was a nice little pistol of the rather Spartan Benjamin lines, but charged like the Schimel with a gas bulb. The bulb was inserted in a tube below the barrel, not in the grip. However, the Benjamin Company has been in business a long time and has learned many, if by no means all, of the tricks of the trade. Instead of contributing to the well-being of the corner drugstore for gas-bulb supply as Schimel did, or furnishing a clumsy cylinder refill service as the originator Crosman did, Benjamin utilized the "Gillette" principle with a modification: They sold "Super CO₂" cartridges under their own name—throwaway bulbs packed 10 to a box and selling for 95 cents per box, which would do more than the drugstore variety would because of greater capacity; and, incidentally, would make the manufacturers a continuous profit!

They made the pistol with a rifled barrel for caliber .177 or .22 pellets as did Crosman (matching Crosman's "Super Pells" with their Benjamin "High Compression" Pellets). But they went a step further. As old hands at selling round shot and darts, they also furnished this new pistol to shoot lead or steel BB balls! (.175-inch-diameter round balls.) This shot retails at about 75 cents per pound (a pound equals about 1,200). .22 pellets of the "Diabolo" or hour-glass shape cost about $4.30 per 1,000. This is an important fact to the man who likes to "plink" but does not have the interest in extreme accuracy, penetration, and hitting power that the more expensive pellets give.

To prepare the Benjamin for firing, the muzzle cap below the barrel is first unscrewed as in the Crosman. Instead of the early and now obsolete Crosman gas reservoir, this Benjamin tube is designed to receive the special gas bulb, which is inserted in the tube narrow end first. Benjamin calls it "a cartridge."

The muzzle cap is then screwed back on tight. With the insertion of a new bulb (in any such pistol design regardless of make), one complete firing manipulation is required to *pierce the bulb*. In this Benjamin, the projecting bolthead is turned and drawn back to cocking position, then pushed closed. Trigger is pulled. When the bulb seal is thus pierced, controlled gas enters the pressure chamber where it is valve-locked. The bolt is again turned and withdrawn to open the breech and automatically cocks the pistol. A pellet is inserted in the breech. The bolt is pushed forward and turned to locked position.

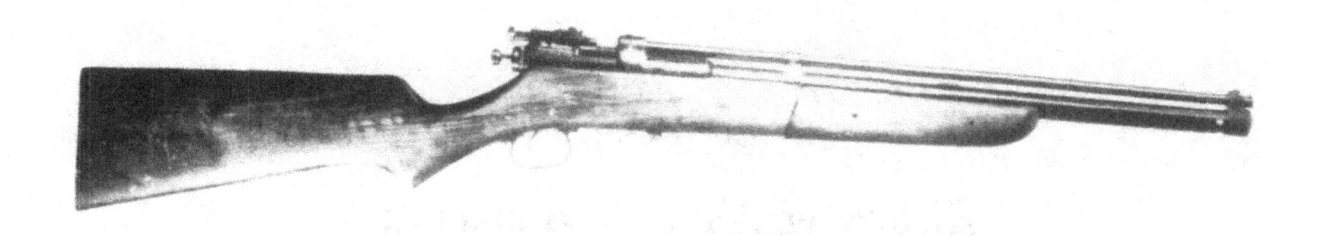

American Plainsman compressed-air rifle. This rifle also appeared under other brand names such as Challenger. It was not a commercial success in this highly competitive field. It is an elementary form, a variant of the Benjamin and Crosman. This design was later altered to use CO_2 cartridges and appeared in both rifle and pistol form. These also were not commercially successful.

The pistol is now ready to fire when the trigger is pressed. Firing is by internal hammer which momentarily opens the gas-chamber valve as it strikes.

Sights are the customary Patridge type, the rear being adjustable for windage. The distance between the sights is only 6½ inches and overall length 7⅞ inches, the pistol having a short, 5-inch barrel and plain wood stock. The finish is usually quite good. A special feature of several Benjamin specimens used by this author was that they had very good trigger pulls for arms of this pattern. The manufacturer claims a trigger pull of 2 to 3 pounds.

The gas "cartridges" are expected to give about 40 shots. As in all such pistols due to relative constancy of power and a well-rifled barrel, if good pellets are used this Benjamin is supposed to shoot 1-inch target groups at 10-yards range when fired from a rest. (Note: The author's independent machine-rest tests seldom achieved such accuracy.)

The smooth-bore BB type was listed as No. 250 in this series. The rifled .22 was No. 252. The rifled .177 was No. 257. Prices ranged at retail from $13.50 to $15.00, constituting one of the most remarkable trainer pistol values ever offered. When one considers the number and complexity of parts, the close tolerances and fits required, the sale of such pistols at such low prices is a most favorable commentary on the manufacturing organization and on American precision production. No European organization could possibly exceed this value.

Plainsman CO_2 Arms

Late in 1954 the Goodenow Manufacturing Company of Erie, Pennsylvania, offered a line of well-made CO_2 arms embracing a pistol and a rifle. The trade name for the line was "Plainsman." The design bore a close resemblance to the Benjamin pistol. The name was used earlier by unsuccessful manufacturers in California, incidentally, the Challenger Arms Corporation.

The Plainsman Pistol. This pistol achieved a pretty fair approximation of the lines of the familiar Colt's Government Model .45 Automatic. Adjustable rear sight, 9½ inches overall in length, and about 34 ounces in weight, it was well finished and reasonably priced at $14.95.

For power supply it followed the line taken by Schimel and used the standard seltzer-gas bulb which can be purchased in the average drugstore. Two stages of power were provided, the lower being approximately half that of the maximum and resulting in about double the number of discharges possible.

Preparing to Fire. It was loaded with the bulb from the front end of the tube below the barrel as for the Benjamin. A cocking knob directly below the bolt knob provided an *independent* cocking system, the first firing stroke breaking the gas seal as in standard practice. The bolt here was not the cocking unit also, as in the Benjamin, but was turned to release and drawn back to expose the chamber for loading. A pellet was inserted and the bolt pushed home and turned to lock. The cocking knob was then drawn back to first or second stage according to power desired, and the sights adjusted accordingly. No safety was provided.

The Plainsman Rifle. The caliber, like the pistol, was .22. The barrel was well rifled. The mechanism was exactly the same as for the pistol described above. Power was from the same gas bulb. An adjustable aperture rear sight was a feature. Trigger pull was a bit on the stiff side, but otherwise functioning was good. The rifle was priced at $18.95.

(Note: This firm previously made a pump-up compressed-air shotgun. See under compressed-air arms.)

99

CHAPTER 7

History of Air-Rifle Ammunition

THE following are the basic types of modern air- and gas-gun ammunition:

"BB" shot.

"Air-rifle" shot.

These are balls of either lead or steel. Steel "BB's" as made for Daisy rifles are copper-flashed for rust prevention. The average diameter of this "BB" shot is .175 inch and is held to very close tolerances. (Note: While Daisy calls this "BB", others list it as "air rifle shot" to distinguish it from the shotgun "BB" which is of .180-inch diameter.)

This shot is used in the famous line of DAISY toy and youth training rifles, as well as in Benjamin and some other serious short-range target air and CO_2 rifles and pistols.

DAISY MANUFACTURING COMPANY is the largest maker of this steel "BB" shot, Daisy having absorbed the original large maker, the American Ball Company of Minneapolis, Minnesota, in 1939.

MANUFACTURE OF DAISY "BB" STEEL SHOT

It always comes as a surprise to those who do not know the Daisy manufacturing background to find the astonishing tolerances held in their lines of toy and training air guns and ammunition.

The average diameter of their steel "BB" shot is .175 inch. However, they will not accept any shot below .172 inch because of velocity loss in their guns due to air slippage; and, conversely, they will not accept shot with larger diameter than .176 inch because of velocity loss through barrel friction!

The finest precision makers of European high-power air arms selling for $50 and higher do not exceed such specifications on normal production!

These shot weigh about 1,276 to the pound. Popular opinion to the contrary, *steel* shot in accuracy tests comes out about on a level with *lead* shot. The original lead shot was soft and when oversized would often still feed into the barrel but would jam when fired. Soft-lead shot is subject to damage and deformation in handling, which steel is not.

Manufacture is completely mechanical. Steel wire whose diameter is two-thirds that of the finished shot is "cold-headed" and then sized, an elementary and completely automatic process analogous to nailmaking in many ways.

The wire is fed into a swaging machine, which automatically (1) cuts it to a predetermined length; (2) moves it into position between two dies having matching semi-spherical die cavities; (3) closes the two dies together, compressing the wire cutoff into the cavities to nearly fill them; (4) ejects the rough balls. No hand touches the balls during any of these operations.

The balls go to automatic rolling machines where they are mechanically rolled into nearly perfect spheres of the required diameter within the tolerance limits allowed. Washing machines which will handle 2 tons capacity at a time clean the balls, after which they enter the automatic copper flasher. An electrolytic deposit of .0002 to .0003 inch (that's ten-thousandths of an inch!) is applied. The plated balls are passed on within the same automatic machine to be rinsed through several waters and then are dried by steam-heated air shot through the containers by centrifugal fans.

The final step is to the automatic packaging machines.

The tremendous Daisy investment in time, money, experimentation, and special shot-making machinery alone makes it possible to produce at low cost and sell at such low prices.

LEAD SHOT MANUFACTURE

Modern shot is a direct descendant of the original "grapeshot" used in the 15th century in artillery. Records show that it was used in *hand guns* as early as 1510 A.D.!

Shot in ball form was the subject of British patent No. 725 of the year 1758; but modern lead shot pouring methods (as distinguished from the recent "cold-header" system of swaging from steel wire fed from a reel) dates back to British patent No. 1347 of 1782. The first "shot tower," incidentally, was constructed in Austria in 1818.

The principle itself is simple. Lead is mixed with a very small percentage of other metals to assist flow and provide more hardness than pure lead allows. In small shot this alloying material is usually arsenic to the amount of about .2 percent, the shotmaker buying the alloy in blocks to his own specifications. When very hard shot is wanted, as much as 2 percent antimony is often added to the alloy.

In the original shot-tower process, the alloy is melted and poured through a sieve arrangement high in a tower. The distance the drops fall from the tower into a cold water filled tank, and their initial size as determined by the sieve gauge, determines their final size. The drop for small sizes is generally about 100 feet, but may be as great as three times that for larger shot.

Modern alternative methods allow melted alloy to fall on a rapidly rotating metal plate from which the resulting balls are hurled by centrifugal force against a stop or apron, thence into water. Here the speed of the *plate rotation* controls the shot size.

The shots are rolled down an incline over graded openings which sort out sizes, and are afterwards tumbled in barrels with a mixture of ground graphite to protect them from oxydation by giving a graphite coating to each shot. As in steel shot, hard lead is occasionally copper flashed (lightly plated) instead of graphited to further increase hardness.

While air-rifle shot is commonly called "BB," in today's precision manufacture it is more correctly called "air-rifle shot." Its controlled size as we have seen gives an average diameter of .175 inch (running about 55 to the ounce in lead). The customary lead "BB" shot for *shotgun use* was originally used in air rifles also, but its average diameter is actually .180 inch (about 50 to the ounce). A matter of plus or minus five one-thousandths of an inch in shot size means little in a shotgun, but in a precision air rifle, even the boy's Daisy type, that difference can give low velocity or jam in the barrel depending upon whether it is under- or over-sized!

OTHER LEAD BALL SHOT FOR AIR GUNS

No. 6 chilled shot (caliber is .11) is used in Daisy and other very short range parlor shooting pistols and games.

.22 caliber round shot is used in some arms, the obsolete Schimel CO_2 pistol and its successor the Carbo-Jet pistol, for instance.

A wide range of sizes is made in Germany for current or recent arms. Popular sizes in lead are (in millimeters) 4.3, 4.35, 4.4, 4.45, 4.5, 4.55, 4.6, 4.65, 4.7, and 4.75. Popular sizes in steel balls are 4.4 and 4.38-mm. (Note: 1-mm. equals .039 inch approximate).

Large-caliber round balls for early compressed-air guns were commonly produced from hand molds, which were supplied with the arms. Making these balls constitutes a bit of a problem for anyone but the enthusiast.

A feature of round balls is that they may be used in either smooth-bored or rifled barrels, though they do not equal the accuracy of other shapes, except at very close ranges.

WAISTED (DIABOLO PATTERN) PELLETS

The second most common form in all air-gun ammunition today is the so-called "Diabolo" pattern, a soft-lead pellet capable of extreme precision shooting, which is shaped somewhat like an hour glass. This is the most recent development (pointed cylindrical bullets were actually the second stage of development for production air-gun projectiles, as we shall discuss next).

The name "Diabolo" by which it is generally known in Europe, where it originated, comes from its resemblance to the juggling or throwing spool used in the very ancient European game of "Diabolo," a game so old that its time of origin is not accurately known.

In England and Europe, dimensions of the Diabolo pellets are pretty well standardized, though even there they vary enough that air target shooters usually size individual pellets before shooting. (Most important dimensions and drawings will be found herein.)

In the United States the shape has been altered a little

Section of Daisy shotmaking department. There are 60 of these "cold headers" operating automatically in this one division of the shot manufacture. Air rifles and ammunition are definitely big business.

Daisy "cold header" shotmaking machine. Wire is fed automatically. Balls of steel come out ready for pouring into polishing machines. Sizing, washing, copper-plating, and gauging are also done automatically.

here and there, sometimes in the honest belief that ballistics have been improved thereby; sometimes for sales reasons. Crosman Arms, for instance, makes Diabolos on their own special swaging machines and markets them as "Super Pells." Benjamin Air Rifle Company sells theirs as Benjamin HC (High Compression) Pellets. Hy Score Arms, whose pellets are actually made in Birmingham, England by I.C.I. (Imperial Chemical Industries), calls

101

theirs modestly enough just "Hy Score Pellets"—with a thoughtful sales line added "for all air guns"!

In Germany as produced by Geco, RWS, Dynamit A. G., and H&N they are merely "Diabolo"—Lüftgewehr kügeln (air rifle bullets).

In England today, as in the United States, brand names have been developed even when the ammunition is made by a common maker to set standards (though it must be said that some makers *do* specify better tolerances than average)! Hence we have air rifle pellets No. 1 bore (.177 caliber), No. 2 bore (.22 caliber), and in a few makes the nearly obsolete No. 3 (.250). Good brand names are Webley, "Beatall," Pylarm (B.S.A.), Marksman, and Wasp.

In England and the United States we have only a few serious air-gun makers, and they must oversee the quality of the pellets used to be sure that their products perform, since no gun is any better than its ammunition. England has standards. Officially, we do not.

Germany, on the other hand, has a huge domestic and export air-gun market for serious air arms—the number of makers runs to about 20, compared to 3 currently in Great Britain and only 4 in the United States. German ammunition therefore is well standardized.

What is a 'Diabolo' Pellet?

It is the bullet which made possible the world-wide sport of precision short-range air and CO_2 shooting. At short ranges it is one of the most accurate shooting projectiles ever developed!

The dimension drawings herewith show its design clearly. The front edge fits the bore and is designed to ride on the rifling lands as a guide, with a minimum of friction. The bullet is waisted at the center and the base is hollow, the design idea being to move all possible weight to the head to give maximum flight stability. The rear edge is flared out to engage the rifling and seal off the air behind the pellet. This flare (or skirt) is carefully dimensioned to give minimum friction because of the inherently low power of air arms; at the same time it must be husky enough to prevent the pellet from being driven down the barrel without a turning motion being imparted, as can happen with undersized or inadequately skirted projectiles. The hollow runs almost to the head of the bullet.

The extremely light weight produced thereby is so low in comparison to the air resistance during flight that the ballistic coefficient is correspondingly low. In short, the pellets lose velocity (speed) so fast during flight that they are rendered harmless when less than 100 yards from the muzzle! This is a very important factor in an air or CO_2 gun which is designed for short-range shooting in areas where close-range accuracy is demanded; but which must be coupled with short-range bullet flight under any circumstances to prevent accidents. (Compare this maximum

Types and calibers of prewar air-rifle and gun ammunition made in Germany.

British average air-pellet dimensions.

range, for instance, with the .22 long rifle bullet which will often carry a full mile!)

Diabolo pellets on an average weigh about 8.2 grains for caliber .177 and about 15 grains for caliber .22. Air and CO_2 pressures are normally the same in pistols or rifles regardless of calibers. Hence the .177 gives greater velocity and flatter trajectory because of low weight, and therefore in Europe generally is the caliber used for match target shooting. Correspondingly, the heavier .22 moves slower but hits harder, and is more generally used for short-range outdoor vermin shooting.

Diabolo design pellets today are universally made on varieties of either punch or automatic swaging equipment. Lead, which should be virgin and about 99 percent pure for the finest pellets, is fed from rolls or strips into the machines automatically. It is cut off, moved into dies, formed into shape in the die cavities, and expelled automatically. Quality control of the machines and of the metal is the one requisite for manufacturing the best ammunition.

Regardless of quality, some pellets will have injured skirts due to packing and handling if nothing else. As a result, the knowing air-rifle match shooter always pushes the Diabolo *into the rifling* so it will encounter the least possible starting resistance. In arms having ports or loading plugs, the pellets are pressed down into the bottom of the tapered hole to size them all equally before firing. In most U.S. designs the conical bolt face usually takes care of this automatically. Some arms (like the British Acvoke pistol) *have a gauge built into some part* of the weapon, so that pellets can be pressed in for accurate sizing for the particular bore involved). Dimensional tolerances are all closely held, but many variables can occur—particularly if the lead is not virgin, but is a re-melt which may have impurities that harden it in spots.

The current price for .177 pellets in the United States is about $3.50 per 1,000 and for the .22 caliber is about $4.30 per 1,000.

(Note: The .25 caliber as made by Webley & Scott was never popular, as its greater weight than the .22 was offset by its lower muzzle velocity. The English "Triumph" brand heavy .22 Diabolo slugs are not common. They have good hitting power due to the added weight, however.)

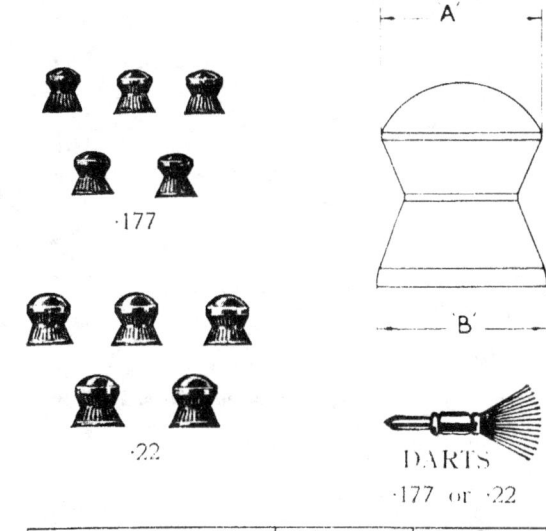

MAKE OF PELLET	A LOW	A HIGH	B LOW	B HIGH
WEBLEY .177	.177"	.179"	.186"	.190"
WEBLEY .22	.218"	.220"	.227"	.231"

Webley special pellets and darts with dimensions.

MODERN POINTED CONICAL AIR BULLETS

The pointed bullet (Spitzkügeln in German) in terms of development followed the round ball as an air-gun missile. It was first used early in this century in production guns. It appeared in many calibers.

In the United States the Sheridan compressed-air rifles all use a special .20-caliber bullet of this type with a hollow base. It has a special 75 percent hardened point to give it better penetration than is customary for use against small game. It has a hollow base which expands to seal the bullet in the barrel. This is unlike the Diabolo, which is designed hollow for lighter weight, *not* for base expansion, although some does occur. (See under Sheridan.)

No other American and no British arm uses this caliber of bullet. In Germany, however, Spitzkügeln are standard production in calibers 5⅓ mm., 5½ mm., and 6⅓ mm. Before the war, the range of calibers was still greater.

AIR-GUN DARTS

Steel darts in calibers .177 and .22 are used in some models of the American Benjamin single-shot compressed-air rifles and pistols and in some models of the Hy Score spring-air pistol. Note that darts should *never be used in RIFLED barrels!* They may injure the rifling. Darts are for use only in smoothbored arms.

They may be used in smoothbored English and German weapons, of course.

In Germany darts intended for indoor shooting are

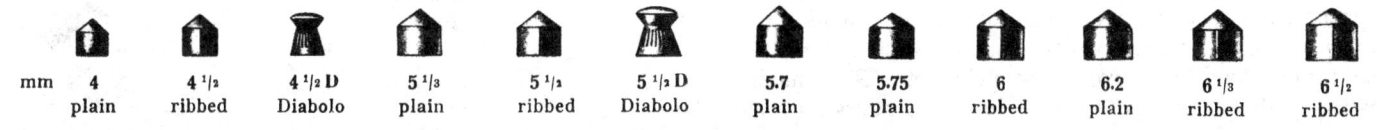

| mm | 4 plain | 4½ ribbed | 4½ D Diabolo | 5⅓ plain | 5⅓ ribbed | 5½ D Diabolo | 5.7 plain | 5.75 plain | 6 ribbed | 6.2 plain | 6⅓ ribbed | 6½ ribbed |

German Diabolo and pointed air pellets as made by R.W.S. (Rheinisch-Westfälische Sprengstoff-Actien Gesellschaft at Nuremberg, currently controlled by Dynamit A.G. of Nuremberg.)

Typical air-gun darts. Used in standard smooth-bore arms. Bores Nos. 1, 3, and 2.

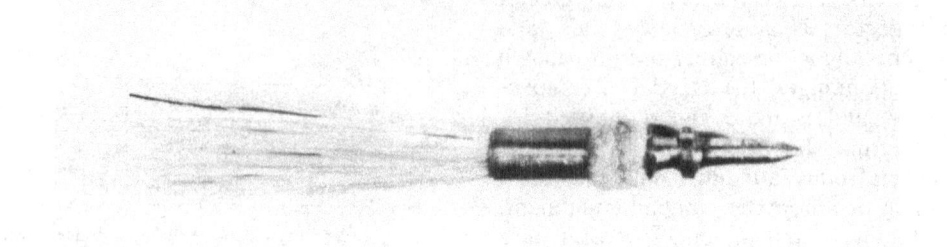

Precision dart used in Bolzenbüchse. Very expensive. Such darts are "zeroed in" by the individual shooter by removing hairs as required. A colored hair is used to mark the exact lineup of the dart in the gun breech. The most accurate short-range arm in existence is the Bolzenbüchse.

commonly made in calibers 4.5, 5.5, and 6⅓ mm. Special darts are produced in a tremendous range of calibers, the common ones being 4.5, 5.5, 6.25, 6.27, 6.28, 6.29 and 6.33 mm.—these are all, naturally, precision calibers of the highest order only.

Darts are expensive anywhere. The common U.S. .177 for instance cost about 5 cents each and the .22 about 12 cents (they are usually sold only by the dozen). They can be used over and over again, of course, provided they are shot against targets which don't allow them to imbed so firmly that they have to be pried out. Shot against wood at short range, you may have to use pliers on them.

MISCELLANEOUS

Old Quackenbush-type slugs with felt glued to the base to lessen friction and provide an air seal are about obsolete, though occasionally found in old dealers' stocks.

Shot shells rather like the early Giffard type were used in the Plainsman air shotgun, and are being experimented with by CO_2 makers at this time. The ammunition is in the form of a small cardboard tube with felt discs at each end and shot in between. At this time these constitute novelties only, though they may be developed later.

Some air "shot shells" consist of several (usually 6) small lead shot sunk into a piece of chalk of proper bore size. The chalk disintegrates as the gun is fired.

EUROPEAN VS. AMERICAN PELLETS

As a general rule, as has been pointed out, it is usually wise to start with ammunition recommended by the maker of an air (or CO_2) rifle or pistol.

This rule is general only, and it must be pointed out

Original shot shells used in Giffard compressed-air and CO_2 guns from 1890 to 1910.

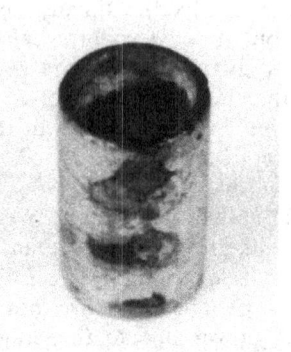

Modern Challenger or Plainsman shot shell, .250.

that independent tests by the author indicate that some manufacturers have a lot to learn about ammunition designs and manufacturing controls.

In the case of the Sheridan, there is no alternative since the caliber is unique with the manufacturer.

Crosman manufactures its own pellets on automatic equipment. While it is to its benefit to sell ammunition, it should also be realized that as the largest manufacturer in its field, it also has a big stake in the rifles it produces. Since it directly or through service stations knows about any ammunition complaints, Crosman endeavors to control quality.

Benjamin is the oldest firm in the compressed-air gun field. Its background is a guarantee that it knows its own products best. The ammunition it sells under its own brand name is held to the specific tolerances which it has found by experience to give best results with its arms.

Hy Score imports pellets from Great Britain, where they are made at Birmingham to good standards. It is to be assumed that in its opinion the standards and dimensions are best suited to its own pistol as made in the United States; but since it is also to be used in German-made rifles which they import, it is obvious that they cannot hold the restrictive dimensions specified by American manufacturers. Such ammunition may give as good results as the American, and then again, it may not.

Similarly, pellets imported from Germany by Stoeger Arms Corporation are also to finest standards and qualities for all general air arms; but again it must be pointed out that the standards involved are *average* for foreign-manufactured guns of many types, makes, and qualities.

It must be kept in mind that in Europe and Great Britain, air arms and ammunition have long been coordinated to very good average standards. When, as in U.S. manufacture, those standards are even slightly altered to meet specific product conditions, they can be expected to give finest performance in the arms for which they were designed; and theoretically at least other makes should not equal their performance.

As a general rule, German pellets will function best in German-made arms. Also as a general rule, in British arms pellets made by the individual arms maker will be best suited to his weapons, though most standard pellets made there are good. In the United States, because of the lack of the German and British degree of standardization and control, it is better to start with the gunmaker's recommendations.

CHAPTER 8

Shooting With Spring-Air Guns

THE only spring-air rifles manufactured in the United States today are those produced by the **Daisy Manufacturing Company** of Plymouth, Michigan. These are classed as toys. Nevertheless they do form a part of rifle target *training* as well as *hunting training* for boys between the ages of 6 and 15.

In recognition of this fact, the National Rifle Association of America has set up a special classification for use of this type of spring-air gun.

Official 15-foot Junior Air Rifle qualification targets are issued by the National Rifle Association for use by individual boys associated with the organization or clubs under its control. It should be clearly understood that this is not done in the belief that target use of the toy-type spring-air rifle classifies it as a target arm. The specific purpose behind the program conducted by the National Rifle Association is to train boys in the *correct and safe handling of all types of firearms. The primary purpose is "safety" education.* What they learn in the course of youth training in handling the Daisy-type air rifle, shooting BB shot, can be carried over into later high-power air-arm use and thence into the field of other ammunition shooting, which is the National Rifle Association's main objective.

THE NRA JUNIOR QUALIFICATION COURSE FOR AIR RIFLES

SHOOTING INSTRUCTIONS FOR DAISY CLASS AIR RIFLEMEN AT HOME—CAMP—SCHOOL—CLUB

Here are the official, iron-clad rules under which such Air Riflemen will shoot—as an individual NRA Junior Member at home—or with any NRA-Affiliated group or club.
1. Official NRA 15-foot, single bullseye targets for spring-type air rifles must be used. NO OTHER TARGETS WILL BE ACCEPTED. **2.** Distance or range must be no less than 15 feet from firing point to target. **3.** Any spring-air rifle (Daisy, King or similar types) using spherical steel or lead shot, commonly known as "BBs," may be used. PNEUMATIC OR "PUMP-UP" TYPE AIR GUNS MAY NOT BE USED AT 15 FOOT RANGE. **4.** Ten Qualifying targets are required for each rating or stage. Qualifying targets need not be fired consecutively. **5.** No time limit is specified for qualification firing. **6.** All qualification ratings must be earned in order of listing. A shooter must first win his Pro-Marksman rating then Marksman rating, etc. **7.** Prone, Sitting, Kneeling or Standing positions (with no artificial support or rest) may be used competing for ratings from Pro-Marksman to Sharpshooter inclusive. Specific positions are designated for Sharpshooter Bar Stages. **8.** Five shots must be fired at each single bullseye target; targets to be fired one at a time. Only bullseyes having required qualifying score will be counted. **9.** Shot holes which touch or break a scoring line or circle score the higher value. If more than 5 shots appear on one bullseye, five lowest count for score. **10.** Individual NRA Junior Air Rifle members must do all firing in presence of adult witness who will testify all these rules were complied with. Such individual members must submit complete sets of 10 qualifying targets, in one mailing, for each qualification stage. All targets must be filled in completely with this information: *shooter's name, complete address, position fired, score, qualification rating for which targets are submitted, and signature of the witness.* Targets not containing this information may be disqualified. **11.** To obtain awards, an individual member will send his set of qualifying targets to NRA Headquarters, accompanied by his NRA membership card. If a medal, pin, bar or brassard award (diplomas and seals furnished without charge) is desired, he must specify decoration wanted and enclose proper remittance. Membership card will be returned with appropriate diploma. **12.** Members of NRA affiliated Junior Air Rifle Clubs or Summer Camps will submit their qualifications through their Instructor. He will report the member's qualifications on affidavits furnished by NRA Headquarters. Do not send targets to NRA for such club qualifications.

While no extravagant claims are made for accuracy, the fact remains that a good marksman with one of these rifles can pretty consistently group five shots into a space the size of a dime at the 15-foot official range! The velocity of the pump-model Daisy is surprisingly high, 330 to 340 feet per second. The lever-action Daisy gives 275- to 280-feet-per-second velocity. Because of the extremely close tolerances to which manufacture is held (in many instances as close as plus or minus .001 inch), the resulting accuracy is relatively good and uniform at rather close ranges. When one knows that the sales of air rifles of this type are in excess of 1,500,000 per year, the tremendous value of the training program under National Rifle Association direction can be more fully appreciated. Incidentally, every Daisy air rifle is actually shot for function and target grouping just as the finest hunting rifles are!

Anyone interested in this aspect of the use of this classification of air rifle may obtain full information by writing to the National Rifle Association, 1600 Rhode Island Avenue N.W., Washington, D. C., or to the Daisy Manufacturing Company, Plymouth, Michigan.

In passing, it might be mentioned that it is quite possible to use these Daisy air arms very efficiently for training boys in shooting at flying targets to simulate bird shooting. With arms of this type, it is possible to repeatedly hit small tin cans, such as the standard No. 2 can, thrown high in the air. Indeed as an early trainer for shotgun handling it has very valuable uses.

The very limited range of this type of rifle is one of its prime safety characteristics for training. The bullet even when fired at a high angle at an aerial target will dissipate its force and drop harmlessly to the ground in the average back yard. Daisy rigidly controls at the factory level not only the quality but also the power and range of these guns.

THE HY SCORE SPRING-AIR PISTOL

This is the only serious spring-air pistol manufactured in the United States. (Note: Daisy manufactures a toy variety, and there are several others in this general type of classification with which we are not concerned here, since they are not serious target arms.)

An analysis of these pistols is to be found under the proper designation in this book. We are concerned here only with target aspects of the Hy Score pistols.

The manufacturers claim accuracy of 1-inch groups fired from a machine rest at 30 feet. As in all spring-air arms, the construction produces a recoil peculiar to the arm itself. Anyone shooting this pistol can become quite expert with it at ranges up to 30 feet. However, the spring driving the piston to compress air produces a down-and-up recoil which may be compensated for but cannot be overcome. In common with arms of this type, the pellet in the chamber is moving down the barrel before the piston has fully completed its power stroke. As a result, the recoil is further conditioned by this fact, as well as by impact of the piston when it hits its breech stop.

It should be noted, however, that as in all spring guns the spring pressure is relatively *constant*. If the pellets are of stable and uniform quality, once compensation has been made in the sighting arrangement, quite accurate shooting can be done within the limitations of the weapon involved. In this connection it should be added that the trigger release and sear system of the Hy Score is such as to provide a rather good target-type trigger pull.

The muzzle velocity of the .177 caliber will normally range about 25 percent higher than that of the .22 caliber, the basic reason being the difference in weight of the bullet and added friction because of the contact area. It cannot be emphasized too much that accuracy in shooting arms of this sort, at ranges in excess of 30 feet, depends very largely on the quality and measurements of the ammunition involved.

It should be noted that variables in ammunition of the Diabolo pattern used in pistols such as the Hy Score *are not necessarily* the result of poor manufacture or poor lead, though a 99 percent purity is an essential factor in the lead used. Thus if any re-melt lead is used in production, the result may be very bad from a standpoint of airgun accuracy, hard spots often developing in the pellets.

This ammunition is normally packed loose in round metal cans. Distortion during transportation and handling can affect the pellets enough to interfere with accuracy. When targeting arms of this sort to establish group "possibles," it is customary to micrometer each pellet and to make sure that its insertion in the breech is done very carefully.

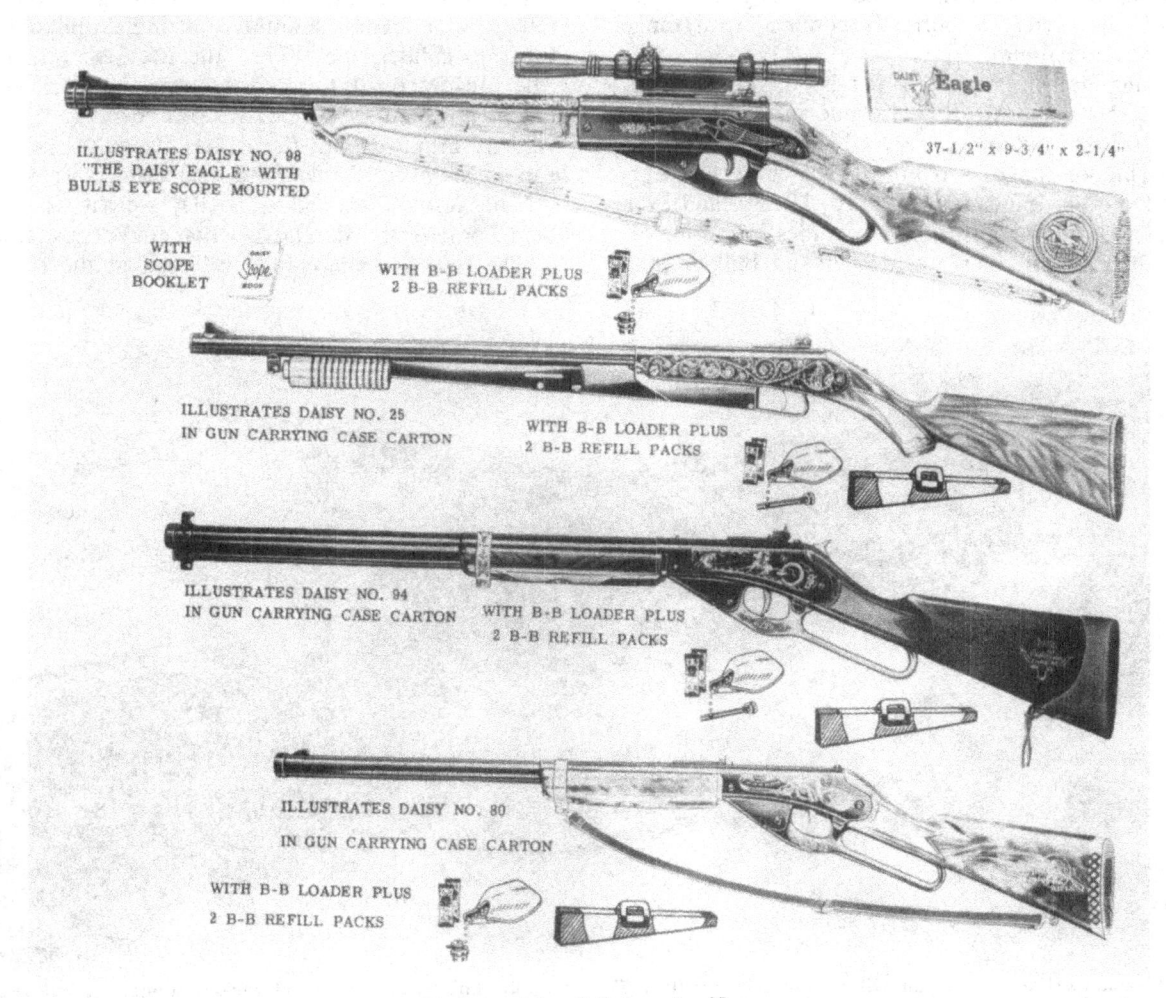

Four models of Daisy air rifles.

Hy Score air pistol, single-shot model. This is one of the most powerful air pistols made.

In fact, serious shooters use a short rod with a stop to force each pellet into the rifling to a uniform distance. This gives some added velocity as well as accuracy, since this manual action frees more of the developed air energy for pellet propulsion.

SHOOTING WITH EUROPEAN AND BRITISH SPRING-AIR ARMS

Because of power limitations and accuracy, air-pistol shooting of this variety is normally confined to a range of 10 meters, maximum.

With spring-air rifles, on the other hand, the distances range in the National Air Rifle League in Great Britain from 6 to 10 yards indoors to 15 yards for outdoor shooting. In the indoor range, it is normally 6 yards. In Germany, on the other hand, ranges of 10, 20, 30, and even 50 meters are shot with the better grades of spring-air rifles! German match rifles are heavier and bulkier than British. Many have elaborate sights and triggers. Recoil control is helped by this greater weight. However in the observation of the author 20 yards is maximum range for really accurate air-rifle shooting.

It must be kept in mind at all times that shooting with a spring-air rifle is entirely different than firing with a pneumatic or a powder-operated arm. The Germans of late have done considerable experimental work with making very heavy rifles with exceptionally large target-type stocks, into which the metalwork is securely bedded. The attempt here is to overcome many of the otherwise difficult-to-control recoil factors in spring-air arms.

Air rifles should be fired with as little shoulder support as possible. When trigger pressure releases the compressed spring, the expanding spring pushes the piston forward to compress air in the chamber ahead of it. Hence a disturbing recoil action commences before the air pressure built up in the chamber is sufficient even to start the bullet down the barrel. This of course is the direct opposite of high-velocity, powder-driven bullets. In a rifle of this spring pattern, the piston normally has completed its travel and jarred against the breech before the bullet has left the barrel. It is obvious, therefore, that no two makes of rifles will function exactly alike. Indeed the individual spring characteristics of each individual rifle of a given make will vary somewhat! It is necessary therefore for the true air-rifle marksman to know thoroughly the individual arm and ammunition he is using. (Note: We are talking of *precision* shooting, not mere plinking.)

As to caliber, the .177 is the specified target-shooting rifle for practically all indoor ranges and most outdoor ranges in Great Britain and Europe because of the higher velocity attained with the lighter weight bullet. However for ranges over 10 meters the difference is in favor of the .22 because of the added bullet weight, the trajectory being practically identical in both calibers at that range.

The type and amount of oil used in the rifle are also

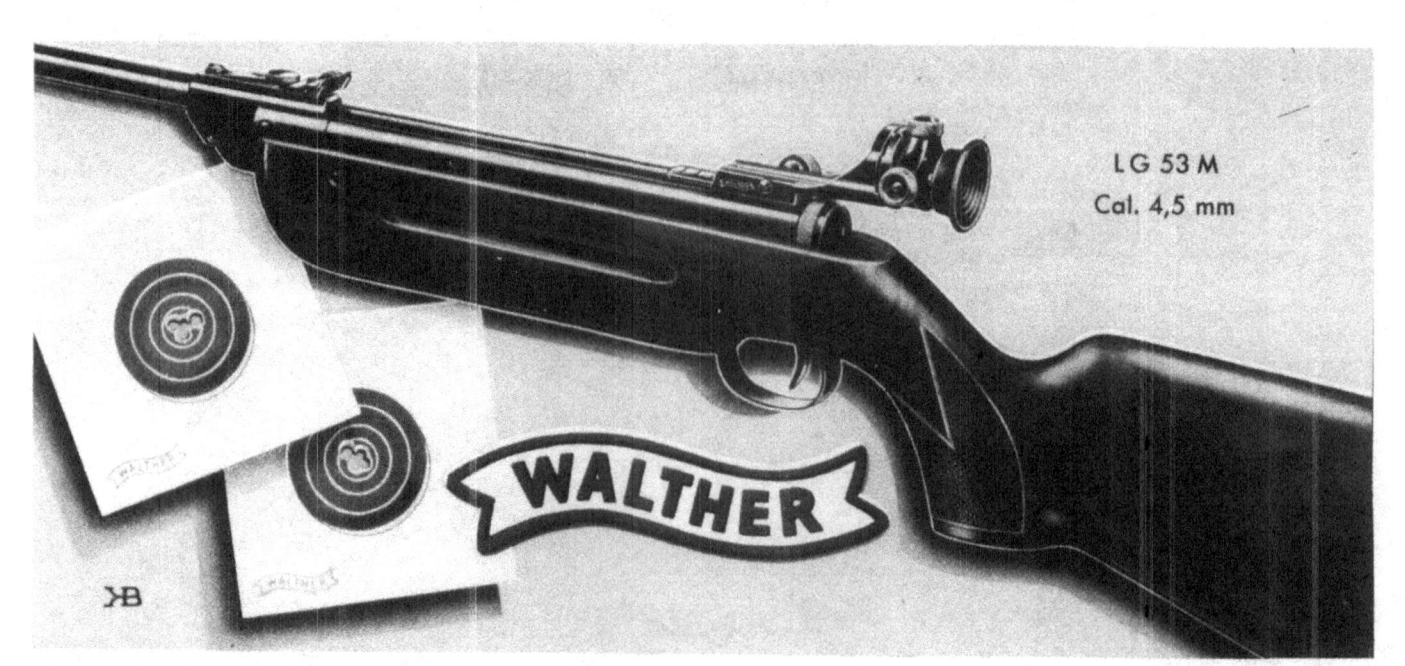

Typical German ultra-precision air rifle. Caliber is usually .177 (4.5-mm.). This type is a barrel cocker, though underlevers are also used. Targets shot at factory are always enclosed with each rifle to show what it can do.

Rear sights alone usually cost more than a complete American air or gas rifle does. They are made to gun standards for precision shooting. Note features of Walther rear sights shown. The peep may be fitted with optical glass ground to the same prescription as the shooter's glasses. Telescopes are also available.

factors in arms of the spring-air design. Varying thicknesses of oil will produce different effects. The oil must be very light, of the order of SAE 30. In general it is best to use the oil developed or recommended by the specific manufacturer whose rifle is used.

The so-called "diesel effect" has a considerable influence also on the velocity achieved in a typical spring-air rifle. While it is not always in evidence, it nevertheless is a potential which must be considered. Good manufacturers who seek highest accuracy try to limit piston oiling (and resultant occasional diesel firing).

Electronic velocity and machine-rest accuracy tests run with a number of standard spring-air rifles indicate that up to a distance of 30 feet, the rifling is not necessarily a basic accuracy factor. Over that distance, however, appreciably better results are found with well-rifled designs. This is not commonly realized, but is stated here on the basis of electronically controlled tests and firing tests from both machine rests and supported positions.

In the section of this book dealing with bullets will be found dimensioned illustrations showing various types of *standard* Diabolo pellets. It will be noted that in general the front end which rides the lands is to be held between a low of .176 and a high of .178 of an inch. The rear section which must engage the rifling is allowed a low of .183 and a high of .186 of an inch. These are optimum dimensions and frankly are not too often held in actual manufacture. The greater the resistance to starting encountered by an oversize rear section, the lower the velocity is likely to be and the more friction that will be encountered. This is a major reason why experts deliberately force each pellet into the rifling.

To offset this, the qualified air-gun enthusiast will start the pellet directly into the chamber, pushing it in far enough for the rear section of the Diabolo to engage in the rifling, thereby decreasing the starting resistance to the air pressure when the trigger is pulled. In underlever rifles where a loading port is provided (since the gun is not broken down for the chamber to be exposed), the pellets must be pressed to the bottom of the tapered hole which sizes them equally. (Note: In some arms such as the Acvoke pistol, a special, small sizing die is incorporated in the gun frame to allow pre-sizing of the pellets.)

Specific velocity and accuracy tests made with electronic and machine equipment will give a clear picture of just how important this bullet factor is in the very low-power (comparatively speaking) air arms. For instance, a brand new caliber .177 pistol of a standard make was tested against the manufacturer's claim of very high velocity. Groups were fired using ammunition supplied by the maker as being best for his product.

A 15-shot group fired at 5-foot range on Potter screens, with an electronic interval timer, and with the shots fired 4 inches above the photo cell, showed an average velocity of only 52 percent of the maker's advertised claims! Using competing pellets, curiously enough, gave better velocity!

When these particular pellets were accurately sized to overcome the starting friction in this same pistol, experiments made on the same standard Potter electronic equipment showed that the velocity had been stepped up an average of 27 percent. Since these tests were conducted consecutively, the factors of oiling and temperature variables can be discounted. This test establishes that with proper ammunition, properly started, velocity increase can be considerable.

As to accuracy, the group fired with the sized pellets gave about a 30 percent smaller group than those fired with the standard ammunition.

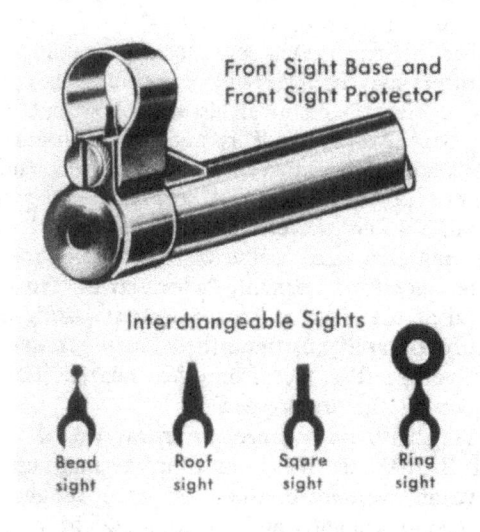

Front sights shown are interchangeable by removing the fixing screw (Walther rifle). Such rifles are capable of remarkable group shooting at 20 meters indoors, despite light bullet weight.

109

EUROPEAN AIR ARMS

It must be pointed out here that there is a considerably greater diversity in the recoil action of air pistols than in air rifles, due to weight and spring factors.

Each pistol design is an entity entirely in itself. Thus the British Webley has its spring below the barrel and its piston moves in a rearward direction to compress the air when released by the trigger pull. It will give entirely different recoil effect than that of, say, the Walther 53 Model, in which the spring-compression mechanism and piston are housed in the grip, and the piston thrust is straight up rather than to the rear. Various other European types, such as the Wischo, have recoil springs positioned as in rifles in prolongation of the barrel, giving a direct forward thrust which again requires special compensation in holding or in sight adjustment.

There is no set rule for the proper handling of these various air arms. Each type must be studied by its owner to achieve best effect. Regardless of claims by the average maker, it is seldom that any .177 air pistol (except when an unusually strong "diesel" effect is encountered) will register better than 365 feet per second on an electronic chronograph. The corresponding model in .22 caliber will run an average of about 330 feet per second. Claims for higher velocities than these made by the manufacturers may be the result of special tests conducted with less efficient mechanical testing equipment. Or they may be pure advertising. This author has found a tendency in some manufacturers to exaggerate considerably.

The most powerful types of spring-air *rifles* in .177 caliber will seldom exceed 600-feet-per-second velocity, the corresponding .22 producing about 540-feet. Note that while velocity is normally expressed in terms of feet per second at the muzzle, it is customary, using an electronic chronograph, to time them at distances which actually average 2½ feet from the muzzle. This is an inconsequential factor, however.

Test-firing with an average group of two of the most powerful British air rifles and four German equivalent types gave an average for the .177 group of about 525-feet-per-second velocity and for the .22 of about 410 feet. Individually compared, the British W&S and B.S.A. rifles were about equal. Comparable velocity in the German makes was less uniform, and also lower than the British, lowering the group average. The Webley .177, for instance, was of the order of 570 f.p.s., and the .22 was of the order of 510 f.p.s.

The customary accuracy tests with a good air *pistol* are at a 10-yard range in a good factory, at which distance the 5 shots are expected to group in a 1-inch circle. However, it is possible to shoot a ½-inch or even smaller group with some of these pistols under some conditions! As in powder-pistol shooting, curiously enough, individual shooters will often fire better average groups than will a machine rest.

Current Walther M53 air pistol. While not very powerful because of grip-spring system, it is extremely accurate at 20-foot range.

With reference to the better type of match air *rifle,* at 10 yards all shots can be held within a ⅜-inch circle. At 30 yards the .177 caliber will often group 1.25 and the .22 caliber will group about 1.75 inches. Again individual shooters may better these averages. British makers expect their higher-priced models to group 5 shots in 1 inch at 20 yards range.

The various sight combinations provided by better manufacturers are listed under their individual arms. In the Germans versions, in particular, the range of special sight equipment is equivalent to anything provided for the finest .22 match rifles. Some German match sights cost more to make than a complete, popular-priced rifle does in the United States!

As a matter of theory, an air arm should have better potential accuracy *at close ranges* than powder-fired weapons, since they are not affected by varying loads, powders, and primers. The velocity should be more constant also, since the principal factor involved is that of a spring which is compressed to the same degree each time the arm is opened. (Note: This does not apply to pneumatics where a varying number of pump-ups may be employed.) When shooting these rifles it is important to avoid any pressure of the butt against the shoulder, as has been mentioned. The rifle should be properly supported at the center of gravity or balance by the left (or supporting) hand. The right (or firing) hand should be used to support the rear section of the arm with the butt nearly against the shoulder. Any alteration of hold or even of shooting position will vary the point of impact of the bullet in a spring-type air rifle. As to outdoor shooting, it must be kept in mind that while good target work may on occasion be done up to 50 yards, even a mild wind can move the very light weight bullet as much as 5 or 6 inches out at that distance. No air-rifle pellet has sufficient weight for "wind bucking." If care is taken to minimize the uncontrollable power variations where "dieseling" occurs, the spring-air system is capable of an amazing degree of consistent velocity and consequent pellet trajectory with resultant accuracy.

THE SPRING-AIR RIFLE IN HUNTING USE

The use of air-operated arms in hunting should be extremely limited because of the danger of wounding the animal painfully without killing it.

Indeed it is better to confine its use to employment against birds of the sparrow or starling variety, which are basically farm pests, or against rats or similar rodents.

The normal penetration in strawboard is an aggregate of about 11 inches for the typical well-designed pistol of .177 caliber, while the penetration of the .22 caliber is slightly more because of the bullet weight.

In the best of the high-power spring-air rifles, a penetration of ⅝ to ¾ of an inch in soft pine or equivalent is about the best that can be expected. These penetrations are an average at a standard 20-foot testing range. They fall off rapidly as range increases. It is possible, if a head shot is effected, to kill a rabbit at 50 or even 60 yards with such a weapon. However use of this sort is neither contemplated nor recommended by the manufacturers. In general the maximum range at which these arms should be used against even vermin is something on the order of 25 yards.

If we keep in mind that most efficient powder-pistol shooting is done at this range as a normal maximum and that the normal maximum shotgun effective range is only 40 yards, it will be apparent that we should not expect too much in the way of hunting performance from spring-air type arms. They are fine for sparrows, starlings, and general barnyard pests. For serious small-game hunting, use a powder rifle.

The muzzle velocity of the typical .177 spring-air pistol is of the order of about 3 foot-pounds per square inch. The average muzzle velocity of the typical highest-power type of spring-air rifle is of the order of perhaps 6.5 pounds per square inch. For a rough comparison, the muzzle energy of the .22 short powder cartridge is about 60 pounds per square inch and of the same caliber in a "hi-speed" load is about 81 foot-pounds. The common .22 long rifle powder cartridge has a muzzle energy of approximately 111 foot-pounds and the "hi-speed" va-

riety of the same caliber will develop a muzzle energy of about 158 foot-pounds!

In conclusion, we may reiterate that for short ranges up to about 15 or 20 feet, the air arm will do anything the powder arm will do *in the way of accuracy.* As a trainer for target use indoors or outdoors it has its place in the scheme of shooting. As a hunting weapon it is not advisable to use it except in case of emergency against any but very small game. Its use should be confined as a rule to shooting vermin and destructive bird pests; though in exceptional cases close-range brain shots have been effective against various animals.

USE OF THE WEBLEY AIR RIFLE FOR ZOOLOGICAL COLLECTION

The following evaluation of the Webley Mark II air rifle was made 30 October 1956 by Mr. Ivan T. Sanderson, world noted zoologist and collector for museums and scientific institutes, the British Museum among others. Mr. Sanderson is the author of a wide series of books including the best-selling *Animals of the World, Natural Treasure, Animal Treasure,* etc. He has lectured throughout the world on natural history, has conducted programs on the Mutual Broadcasting Company's National Network, and currently has a television program on the CBS Network.

> For many years of scientific collecting, mostly in the Tropics, we were faced with a peculiar technical problem. This was simply that many small animals—notably lizards, birds, small mammals, and fish—cannot be trapped; and if hit even with the smallest shot (such as dust) are useless as specimens for preservation.
>
> Then we found the Webley Mark II Air Rifle. This proved to be so accurate and powerful, yet "clean," that even such a bad marksman as I, appeared rather miraculously to be able

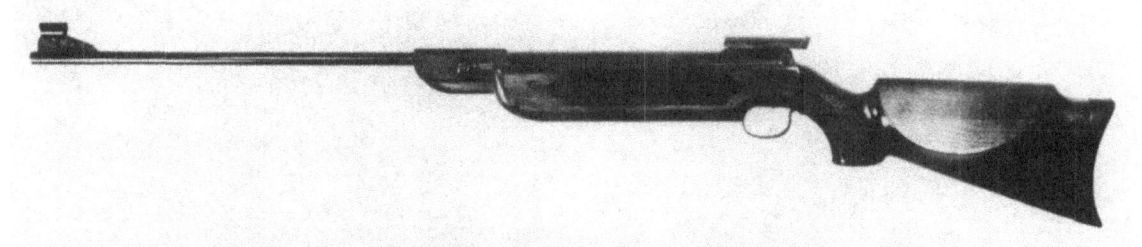

Typical modern high-power German spring-air gun powerful enough for short-range vermin work. Because of light bullet, no air rifle should be used on small game except where head shots are possible.

> to hit small lizards and frogs at night at the limit of my vision. From then on, this remarkable gun became standard equipment for the collection of all the smaller, rarer, and otherwise more or less unapproachable species.
>
> The extreme simplicity of construction of this gun, combined with ease of loading and more especially the fact that it is possible to load it in almost complete silence, added very greatly to its value. The relative absence of noise on firing compared to the smallest powder gun makes it, in my opinion, a "must" for all professional collecting of the smaller vertebrates.
>
> I may further add that it proved a remarkable weapon for obtaining rare fish both in the sea and in rivers by day and night when they are feeding or swimming within as much as two inches of the surface. In some twenty years of use none of these guns ever once required return to the factory, and all normal wear and tear due to the excessively rugged treatment they received could be made good in the jungle with

the very limited and simple materials at hand, such as bits of wire, tin, and old shoe leather and sealing wax.

The guns are, in fact, still in perfect operating condition and pack their original punch in marked contradistinction to all the many other makes of air rifles that we have tested. I see no reason why they should not last another 20 years, and I really don't know what we will do if they don't!

The gun is definitely not obsolete, even if it is no longer manufactured, and I only hope that Webley will continue to produce instruments of this quality for future generations engaged in our specialized and like pursuits.

NOTE ON AIR GUNS AND DARTS

Darts should be used *only* with smoothbore, that is, unrifled, barrels whether in pistols or shoulder arms. The bearing surface of the darts is customarily steel and may injure the rifling as the dart is driven down the barrel. In many instances if the dart is not perfectly formed it can jam in the barrel, causing serious trouble and difficult removal.

It must be pointed out that darts are intended normally for indoor shooting at ranges of 15 to 18 feet. A really expert marksman using the finest quality darts can put darts consistently into a ¼-inch area at this distance with a good gun. Darts should never be fired into hardwood because of the danger of deforming the darts in removing them. The particular value of the dart is in the fact that it is re-usable if the target against which it is aimed is a relatively soft material.

Under no conditions, however, should lead air-rifle *pellets* be re-used once they have been fired. Should they be caught in a bullet trap, they will be deformed and unless completely re-sized are almost certain to cause eventual damage or stoppage in a fine rifle barrel. While this is less true of round balls than of Diabolo pellets, it is still a good rule to adhere to if you value your rifle.

Some people—not all in juvenile age groups!—will try to shoot the weirdest projectiles from air guns! Kitchen matches, paper wads, pebbles, and even spitballs are commonly found fouling up barrels returned to factories as "unsatisfactory." Usually such "experimenters" finally get around to shooting a pellet down the barrel to try to clear it. It very seldom works.

In general it is best to be guided by the manufacturer's recommendation as to the type ammunition to use, particularly if he happens to make ammunition as well as air guns. However, as the author's tests show, that does not mean that you should not use some other brand of that particular type of pellet for best accuracy.

CHAPTER 9

British Spring-Air Rifles and Pistols

THE "Britannia" air rifles made by Bonehill of Birmingham and the British Greener air rifles are occasionally encountered. However, they represent rifles which were never particularly successful commercially. Their principal current value is to collectors.

The only air rifles currently in manufacture in Great Britain are manufactured by three organizations.

The first and still probably the largest selling of all the British precision air rifles are those manufactured by Birmingham Small Arms Guns, Limited. While their famous underlever operating air rifle, which will be described below, is their prime development in this field (B.S.A. having introduced this system after purchasing the design from Lincoln and Jeffries), their line of lower-priced barrel-cocking rifles is also of an excellent order. Incidentally, the current underlevers developed and produced after World War II are vastly improved over the prewar types, though millions of the latter are still used.

The noted firm of Webley and Scott, Limited, also of Birmingham, manufactures both highest quality underlevers and medium-priced barrel cockers. All W&S products are of the best quality, British designed.

The third brand of air rifles manufactured in Great Britain is a very sore subject of conversation with German manufacturers. Due to an original arrangement between Millard Brothers of Lanarkshire, Scotland, and the German firm of Mayer and Grammelspacher, the line known as the "Diana" rifles originated by the German firm are manufactured under that same trade-mark in Great Britain at the present time.

At the close of the war the entire plant fixtures and tooling from the Diana works at Rastatt were apparently moved to Great Britain, where a factory was set up to continue production of the prewar group of Diana rifles. These rifles are merchandised throughout the world by this British firm under the Diana name today.

As a result the German "Diana" firm when shipping their air arms into Great Britain and its dependencies and dominions for sale must list them under a different trade name! They appear in such areas under the name "Original," meaning the original German Diana rifles. In the United States, higher-priced models of the Diana rifles are sold under the trade-mark of the U.S. importer, the Stoeger Arms Company of New York, "Peerless," while cheaper forms are marketed under the name of Hy Score, the brand name of another firm which imports the lower-priced rifles of this group. In other places the rifles will be found under the original German name of Diana, a factor giving considerable confusion to buyers.

(Note: It is common practice in Germany to manufacture under any suggested brand name provided the order is large enough to warrant it, except in the case of a few organizations like the Carl Walther firm. Hence, "Diana" pistols alone are sold under a score or more "brand" names.)

At the present time the only line of air pistols being made of British design are the Webley group discussed below. The Diana-type pistols as made in prewar Germany are also manufactured under that name by the Millard Brothers organization already mentioned.

Pistols of the "Gat" and "Thunderbolt" type are actually in the toy classification equivalent to the Daisy American air pistol and are not serious target arms. They are immediately classified by their sheet-metal construction—in a word, toy-style stampings.

Early in this century an air pistol with considerable power and precision for a spring-actuated arm was manufactured by the famous British gunmaking firm of Westley Richards under patent 24837 of 1907. This pistol is obsolete today and is seldom encountered except in collections.

A later pistol which did achieve some success, some 20,000 having been sold, is the Acvoke, also made at Birmingham, England. This pistol because of its unusual, almost freakish design is pictured and discussed below. It has several unusual features.

The one other British pistol of comparatively recent manufacture to achieve any success in this group is the Abas Major, which is also covered in the text following.

It might be noted here that under the British Firearms Act of 1937, air arms of all types are classified as to the velocity and penetration allowable. *Because of this factor, no high-power pneumatic or carbon dioxide type arms have been manufactured in Britain, either as pistols or rifles.* Development work has been done with a view to possible export markets, but no production is as yet underway. The great British Teddington organization, for instance, did develop a magnificent compressed-air rifle which was brought to the United States and shown to manufacturers. On actual comparison tests to which the author has had access, it proved more costly to manufacture and less efficient than our American Sheridan.

ACVOKE PISTOL

This pistol consists basically of a barrel casing which houses the rifled barrel and the piston and spring. Piston and spring in turn position around the barrel within the barrel casing. This is a so-called "concentric" system.

Obsolete Webley Mark II air rifle. Operating the bolt handle freed the barrel, which hinged down. The barrel was then used as a lever to cock. A powerful design replaced by the current underlever type because of manufacturing cost.

This arrangement of the spring and piston allows the greatest possible spring compression within the limits of the space available. In this respect, it is theoretically much more efficient than the Webley type in which the barrel is superimposed above the casing which contains the spring and piston. (This concentric system is also used in the American Hy Score pistol, incidentally, an American production air pistol which borrowed basic successful principles, added some improvements, and was production designed.)

This design while clumsy in appearance, is mechanically very efficient. The barrel runs the entire length of the casing and is surrounded by the compression spring and the piston, which compresses the air in the chamber ahead of it after being released by the trigger pull.

The Acvoke cocking arrangement is quite unusual in that the lever is pivoted at the muzzle of the pistol and forms the triggerguard as well as part of the grip backstrap! This idea of using an extension of the triggerguard lever to form a part of the grip is not original with the English manufacturer, having appeared in various German pistols. Basically similar patents are common both in England and Germany.

A ratchet keeps the cocking lever from sliding back to jam the fingers at any time during the cocking motion and also provides a safety factor in that it serves to prevent the trigger from being pulled until the cocking lever is completely closed.

Another very unusual and excellent design feature in this pistol is the incorporation of a loading port or plug at the breech similar to the type employed in the fixed-barrel high-power air rifles.

The photographs herewith were taken expressly to show in detail the various essential features, and no amount of explanation can take their place. Curiously enough, in spite of its involved and theoretically excellent leverage, the Acvoke as tested did not prove particularly efficient in velocity.

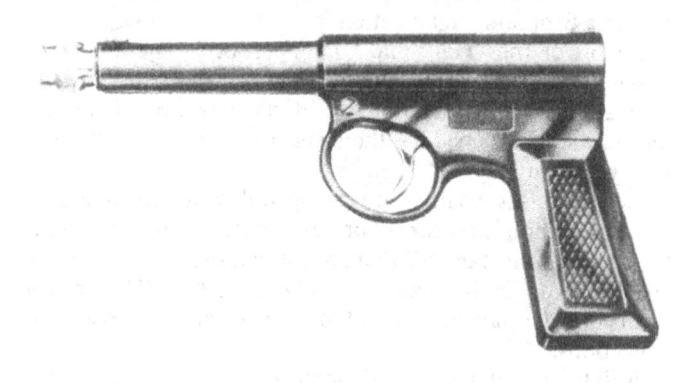

Current British Gat spring-air pistol. This is almost in the toy category, but has some close-range training value.

Acvoke pellets. Pictures and details of the Acvoke pistol will be found elsewhere in this book.

WEBLEY & SCOTT

Webley Air Pistols

The accompanying photographs, data, and drawings illustrate in detail the general construction and the design of this line of fine pistols. Webleys cost more than most other pistols. They are worth more.

The barrel and receiver are forgings. The Mark I receiver alone requires some 50 machine operations, including milling, drilling, reaming, grinding, tapping, and profiling. Unlike most other pistols of this classification, the barrels are deep-hole drilled and are not common steel tubing. The barrel as produced by Webley requires some 30 machining operations, though it must be pointed out that the barrel also functions as the cocking lever.

All barrels are individually checked for concentricity and are handset for straightness.

Rifling in the .177 caliber, because of small size, is done with standard rifling cutters, taking a cut of .0005 inch. The .22 calibers are precision broached. The grooves are .002-inch deep. Grooves are very wide in relation to the narrow lands between them. Rifling is 7-groove, right-hand twist, one turn in 15 inches.

The groove width is deliberately designed to minimize the power necessary to start the lands cutting into the rear skirt section of the Diabolo pellet, thereby materially reducing friction and increasing velocity.

These pistols as manufactured by Webley are precision arms entailing over 200 separate machine operations.

Operation. The operation is basically very simple. When the barrel catch is released at the breech, the rear of the barrel may be lifted up. The barrel acts as a cocking lever, being pivoted at the forward end of the receiver piston casing. The attached link on the barrel engages the mouth of the hollow piston, drawing it to the forward end of the pistol, thereby compressing the spring which lies within the piston. At the point of full compression, the sear engages the grooved end of the piston at its rear

British Webley .177 pistol, Junior model. This pistol is built on a lighter frame than the more expensive Webleys. Its spring is lighter to make it easier for the youngsters to cock. Sights are fixed in the Junior. Operation is the same as the Mark I model, however, except for lack of adjustable rear sight and adjustable trigger.

Current Webley Senior, the aristocrat of air pistols. No stampings are used. This is firearms quality throughout. Over 280 separate operations and inspections go into the production of this pistol.

where a 360-degree holding surface is available. A pellet is inserted in the barrel breech and the barrel pushed down to locked position. Pressing the trigger draws the sear out of engagement, allowing the spring to drive the piston to the rear. This compresses the air in its path in the chamber. The air is forced through a vent into the breech behind the bullet. The bullet in this type of design of course serves as a form of valve, keeping the air compressed during the period of travel of the bullet down the barrel. The resulting compression and bullet friction produces considerable heat. When a light oil is present in the barrel, under some conditions (specifically when a pressure ratio of 15 or 17 to 1 is established) there may be a mild diesel discharge, which aids the velocity.

This effect is common to all spring-air pistols and rifles, but is most efficiently handled and controlled to maintain uniform performance in finely made arms where close tolerances are held as in the Webley. Fine tolerances and fits account to a considerable degree for the better velocity often obtained with the Webley than with similar pistols of other manufacture. Incidentally it should be noted that the new double linkage of the Senior model allows nearly 50 percent easier spring compression than is possible with the earlier designs. However in the independent tests conducted by the author, the greatly extended leverage "throw" was considered to be a rather undesirable factor.

Webley uses the dual linkage primarily to make cocking easier, as added power is not desirable because it would invite restrictive legislation and would not add materially to accuracy at air-pistol ranges. A study of the photographs will show the added leverage provided by this special linkage when compared with earlier and less powerful Webleys. Barrels are sturdy enough to prevent bending (unless very deliberately and senselessly abused). This is one of the most efficient air-pistol cocking systems yet devised. Webleys were specifically designed as air pistols of highest quality to last a lifetime—or longer. Forgings and machinings were designed to eliminate need for many fragile parts. There is no simpler nor stronger pistol made.

WEBLEY JUNIOR AIR PISTOL

Manufacturer: Webley & Scott, Limited, Birmingham 4, England.
Overall Length: 7.75 inches.
Weight: 24 ounces.
Caliber(s): .177 only (4.5-mm.) British No. 1 bore.
Type(s) of Ammunition Used: Webley (or equivalent) Diabolo-type pellets. Also darts.
Rifled: No. Smooth bore only in this model.
Operating System: Spring-air.
Cocked & Spring Compressed by: Unlocking breech catch and lifting barrel to open position.
Loaded: Directly into barrel breech when action is open.
Number Rounds: Single shot only.
Stock Type: Grip plates. Screw attached to grip frame.
Front Sight: Blade.
Rear Sight: Fixed.
Velocity (Approximate): 290 f.p.s.
Normal Accurate Range: 10 to 15 yards.
Normal Maximum Range: 100 yards approximately.
Official Penetration Test: Seven 3/64-inch strawboards, placed .5 inch apart, penetrated at 20 feet from muzzle.

REMARKS

Note: This is the lowest-power Webley. It is designed for training young boys in pistol shooting. Smooth bore permits using .177 darts if desired. Barrel release catch is spring-supported serrated thumbpiece above and behind barrel breech. Single-link cocking lever. Operation otherwise as described for Webley "SENIOR."

This model is built as sturdily as any expensive firearm. Frame and barrel are heavy-duty forgings, machined. Over 200 distinct operations and tests are involved in making this pistol! It is precision manufactured for long life and parts interchangeability.

WEBLEY MARK I AIR PISTOL

Manufacturer: Webley & Scott, Limited, Birmingham 4, England.
Overall Length: 8.5 inches.
Weight: 30 ounces.
Caliber(s): .177 (4.5-min. or No. 1 bore). Also .22 (No. 2 bore).
Types(s) of Ammunition Used: Webley (or equivalent) .177 or .22 pellets as required.
Rifled: Yes. 6.5-inch barrel.
Operating System: Spring-air.
Cocked & Spring Compressed By: Unlocking breech catch and lifting barrel as in JUNIOR.
Loaded: Directly into open barrel breech.
Number Rounds: Single shot only.
Stock Type: Grip plates. Screw-attached to forged frame.
Front Sight(s): Blade, integral with barrel.
Rear Sight(s): Screw-locked, adjustable elevation.
Velocity (Approximate): 177, 350 f.p.s. .22, 314 f.p.s.
Normal Accurate Range: Targeted to group 1 inch at 30 feet.
Normal Maximum Range: 100 yards approximately. (Not effective.)
Official Penetration Test: As stated for JUNIOR: .177, 10 boards; .22, 11 boards.

REMARKS

Broached rifling. Screw-adjustable trigger. Barrel release catch same principle as for JUNIOR. Rear of barrel serrated for better grip when cocking. Single-link lever. Heavier construction and piston spring than in JUNIOR.

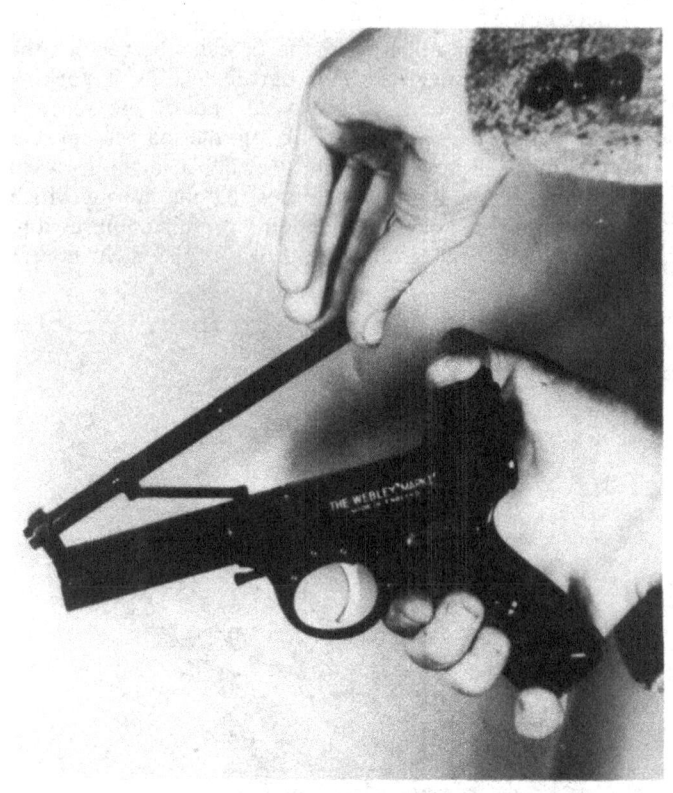

Webley Mark I model. Cocking. Barrel catch drawn back to free barrel at breech. Barrel raised to start mainspring compression.

Webley Mark I model as currently manufactured. While the basic design is unchanged, the current manufacture is improved over earlier versions, particularly in the pitch of the grip, heavier barrel, and barrel corrugations, to give a firm cocking grasp.

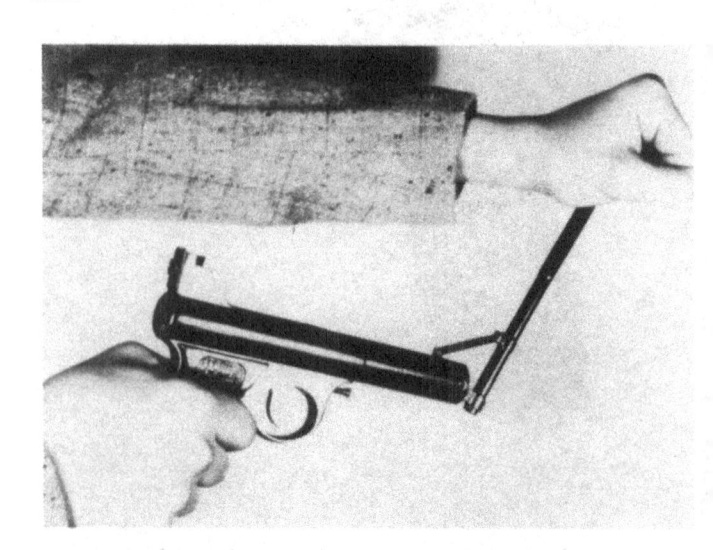

Webley Mark I model. Full cocking stroke. Note position of barrel in relation to that of the Senior, which uses the new double-joint levers.

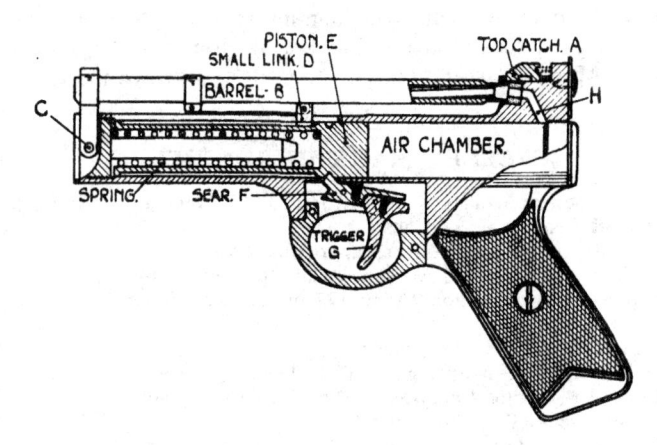

Section of the mechanism of a Webley Mark I air pistol.

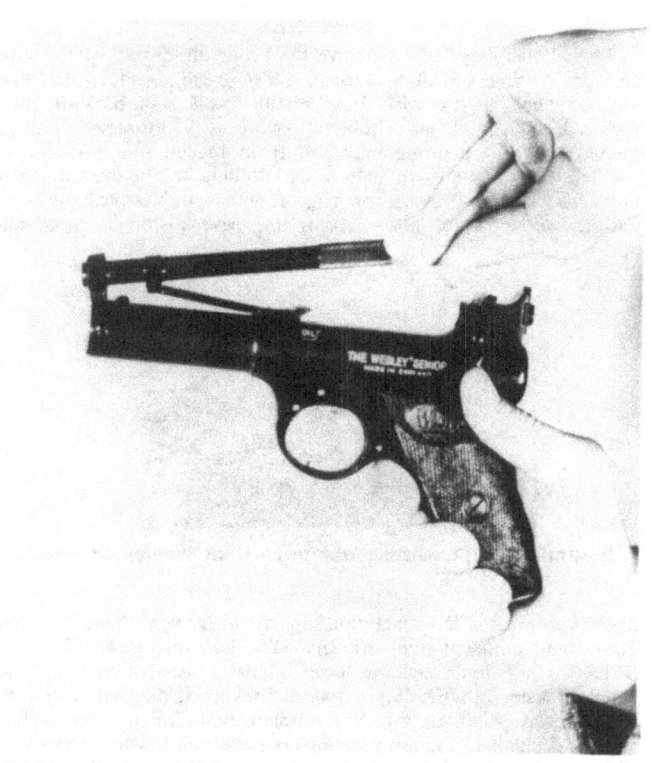

WEBLEY SENIOR AIR PISTOL

Manufacturer: Webley & Scott, Limited, Birmingham 4, England.
U. S. Distributors: Griffin & Howe, New York City.
Overall Length: 8.5 inches.
Weight: 33 ounces.
Caliber(s): .177 or .22.
Type(s) of Ammunition Used: Webley & Scott suitable caliber pellets (or equal).
Rifled: Yes.
Operating System: Spring-air barrel cocker of unique design.
Cocked & Spring Compressed By: Unlock barrel at breech. Raise barrel on breech pivot.
Loaded: Directly into barrel breech when action is open and cocked.
Number Rounds: Single shot only.
Stock Type: Pistol grip, plastic, checkered.
Front Sight(s): Blade.
Rear Sight(s): Screw adjustable for elevation and windage. No clicks.
Velocity (Approximate): .177, 360 f.p.s. .22, 330 f.p.s.
Normal Accurate Range: Standard for air pistol. (Targeted at factory, 1 inch at 30 feet.)
Normal Maximum Range: Standard for design and power. (Effective target, 75 feet.)
Approximate Retail Price: $30 (in U. S.).

Webley Senior model. Cocking. Barrel stirrup lock is pushed forward to free barrel at breech. Barrel raised to start mainspring compression. (Note: Position of opening is posed to show the action. For easy cocking, see picture on next page.)

Webley Senior model. The aristocrat of modern air pistols. The famous Webley revolver "stirrup" lock is easier to operate than the lock catch on other models. Push forward with thumb to unlock barrel. Double-joint cocking levers in this model give the cocking stroke an additional 25-percent throw, which makes cocking very much easier than in many other makes and models of air pistols.

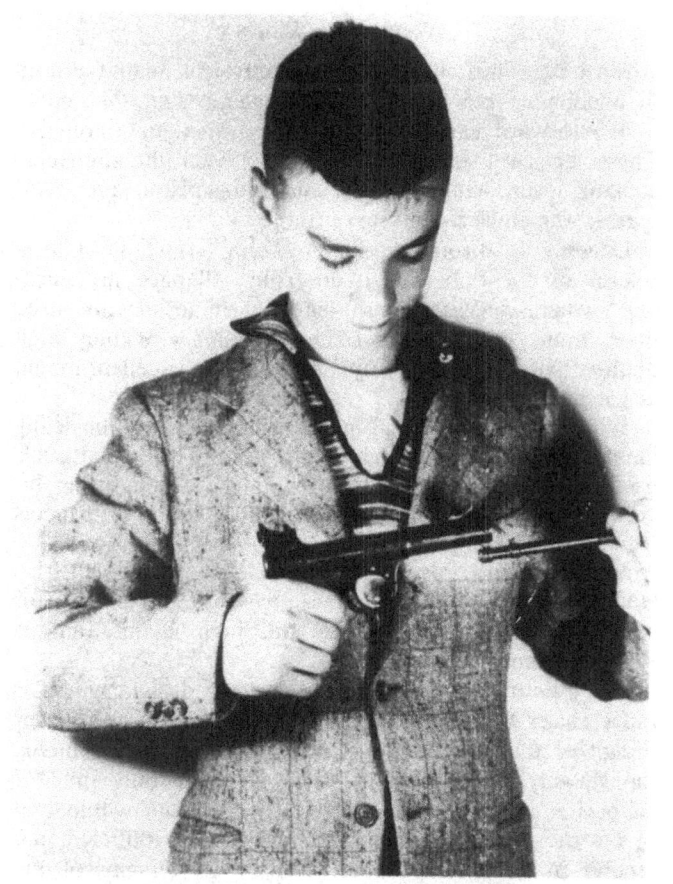

Webley Senior model. End of cocking stroke. A boy can often cock this powerful pistol because of the improved leverage. Note the position of barrel in relation to that of the Mark I at end of its single-lever cocking stroke.

REMARKS

This model has W&S revolver-type stirrup barrel catch. Push forward to free barrel at breech. Raise barrel on forward pivot and attached levers will draw piston inside compression tube forward. Spring inside hollow piston is compressed and is guided by rod extending rearward from breech plug. At end of cocking stroke, sear will engage on holding lip on piston. Load and close barrel. Pressure on trigger, which moves straight back, will lower sear and allow spring to drive piston to rear and

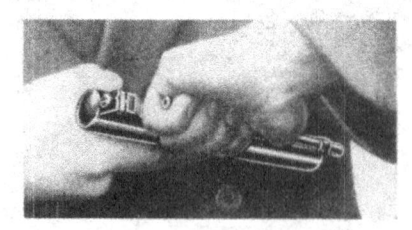

Illustration of the correct way to cock all Webley air pistols.

drive compressed air back and up through vent behind pellet. Note that unlike lighter models JUNIOR and MARK I, the SENIOR has dual cocking lever. This is used here to make cocking easier by affording a longer cocking stroke, not to obtain more power. Pitch of grip is a studied evolution to achieve best hang and balance. The only spring-air pistol made which compares with this for materials, workmanship, design, and fits is the new German Walther M53; and that pistol does not have the power nor range of the Webley SENIOR. On independent tests by the author, this pistol exceeded all manufacturer's claims for velocity, accuracy, and range.

Webley Air Rifles

Mark III. This rifle is the most powerful manufactured by Webley. It is a standard underlever design. The catch at the forward end of the lever is pushed in to release. The lever arm is drawn down to force back the connected cocking lever, which in turn cocks the piston and compresses the powerful firing spring.

Loading is through a loading plug (or tap) with a release on the right side of the rifle. All parts are hardened where necessary and the best materials are used throughout. The rifling is of the customary Webley high quality. The trigger pull adjustment allows excellent match target possibilities.

While all conventional underlever rifles are basically identical in operating principle, the quality of the materials used and the quality of the workmanship and fitting involved is a matter of major importance. In these respects Webley has no superiors.

Junior. While this is a relatively low-priced rifle intended primarily for trainer use by boys, the quality of workmanship and material is still high in the famous Webley manner.

The Junior is a simple barrel-cocking design, which is much easier to manufacture than the precision underlever design of the Mark III. As a comparative power index, the velocity of the Junior, which is made only in .177 caliber, is approximately 405 feet per second while that of the more powerful Mark III approaches 600 feet per second in the same caliber. The lower velocity of the Junior is accounted for, naturally, by the lower-priced construction of the barrel-cocker system, and particularly because the spring power is carefully determined to enable boys to cock the rifle with a minimum of effort. Barrel-cocking the special heavy-duty springs found in the underlever Mark III would tax the strength of a grown man.

WEBLEY MARK III AIR RIFLE

Manufacturer: Webley & Scott, Limited, Birmingham 4, England.
Overall Length: 43.5 inches.
Weight: 6 pounds 13 ounces approximately.
Caliber(s): .177 or .22 Webley pellets (or equivalent).
Type(s) of Ammunition Used: .177 or .22 Diabolo-type pellets as required.
Rifled: Yes. Barrel 18.5 inches.
Operating System: Spring-air. Fixed-barrel pattern.
Cocked & Spring Compressed By: Underlever pivoted at end of fore-end. Pull down and back.
Loaded: Loading tap on right side of receiver. Manually opened.
Number Rounds: Single shot only.
Stock Type: One-piece-butt and fore-end construction. Walnut.
Front Sight(s): .177, bead, .070 inch. .22, blade, .070 inch.
Rear Sight(s): .177, V standard. .22, U standard. Receiver sight available.
Velocity (Approximate): .177, 600 f.p.s. .22, 540 f.p.s.
Normal Accurate Range: Targeted, 40 yards. 5 shots .177 in 1¼ inches, and .22 in 1¾ inches. Targeted 5 shots in ⅜-inch bull at 10 yards, both calibers.
Normal Maximum Range: Effective about 60 yards. Normal maximum about 300 feet.
Official Penetration Test: On 3/64-inch strawboards, spaced .5 inch apart, at 20 feet: .177, 16 boards; .22, 18 boards.

REMARKS

Distance between sights 17 inches. Adjustable trigger. Special aperture-adjustable target sights to order. Six-hole eyepiece if desired.

This is one of the finest and most powerful spring-air rifles made. It is easier to cock than most barrel cockers of comparable power. Materials, fits, and workmanship are of the highest order.

Operation is standard for classical underlevers.

WEBLEY JUNIOR AIR RIFLE

Manufacturer: Webley & Scott, Limited, Birmingham 4, England.
Overall Length: 37 inches.
Weight: 3.25 pounds.
Caliber(s): .177 ONLY. (No. 1 bore or 4.5-mm.)
Type(s) of Ammunition Used: Pellets in rifled barrels. Pellets or darts in smooth bore.
Rifled: Optional. Barrel length 18 inches.
Operating System: Spring-air.
Cocked & Spring Compressed By: Barrel cocker. Break barrel down on joint to cock.
Loaded: Directly into barrel breech when action is opened to cock.
Number Rounds: Single shot only.
Stock Type: One-piece butt and fore-end. (Stock length 13.25 inches.)
Front Sight(s): Semi-bead.
Rear Sight(s): Adjustable wheel type for elevation.
Velocity (Approximate): 405 f.p.s.
Normal Accurate Range: 30 to 45 feet.
Normal Maximum Range: Accurate to about 50 feet. Maximum about 200 feet.

REMARKS

Strawboard penetration as per Mark III rifle—12 boards.

Accuracy of this rifle is usually better than most similar rifles in its price range. Probably due to Webley's careful attention to rifling.

Webley Mark III high-power underlever air rifle. This rifle is capable of extreme short-range precision shooting. It, too, is made on the methods of high-priced firearm designs. Over 500 manufacturing and inspecting operations are required.

Aperture sight. For attachment to the Webley Mark III air rifle. If required, sight should be ordered when purchasing the rifle as it is necessary to drill and tap the metal portion of the body. The framework of this sight is strong and protective of the working parts. It has lateral and vertical clicking movements by half-minute clicks, and is equally suitable for target or sporting purposes.

COMPARATIVE DATA

	Senior Air Pistol ·177	Senior Air Pistol ·22	Mark 1 Air Pistol ·177	Mark 1 Air Pistol ·22	Junior Air Pistol ·177	Junior Air Rifle ·177	Mark 3 Air Rifle ·177	Mark 3 Air Rifle ·22
Number of Strawboards $\frac{3}{4}$" thick placed $\frac{1}{4}$" apart penetrated at 20 ft.	11	13	10	11	7	12	16	18
Velocity Foot/Seconds	360	330	350	314	290	405	600	540
	Range 20 ft.					Range 30 ft.		

Pellets fired at Steel Plate (actual size)

Range 20 ft. — Range 30 ft. — Range 120 ft.

A few specimen pellets fired from the Webley Junior .177 rifle at a steel plate from 10 yards range indicate its muzzle velocity.

119

BIRMINGHAM SMALL ARMS GUNS, LIMITED, AIR RIFLES

Birmingham Small Arms Guns, Limited, has for several generations been Great Britain's largest production manufacturer of sporting guns, rifles and shotguns, and air rifles.

Before the war it was "Birmingham Small Arms, Limited" or just "B.S.A." Today the gun division is a separate entity.

The trade-mark B.S.A. on any firearm or air rifle is a guarantee of the finest production quality available. In this connection it should be pointed out that most of the British manufacture is of a type involving a very considerable amount of hand labor. These types are customarily very much higher priced than the B.S.A. *production-type* of arms.

From the standpoint of research facilities and modern manufacturing techniques, B.S.A. today is the equal of any arms manufacturer in the world.

In the field of spring-air rifles B.S.A. was the first British firm to achieve major production. As we have already pointed out in our historical section, B.S.A. purchased the original design for their first high-power, spring-air rifle, the original Lincoln-Jefferies. This was the first *production model* of a fixed-barrel, underlever-operated air rifle of high-power design. It was extensively copied, in Germany in particular. Almost exact duplicates of the old Mark I and Model 4 are even today manufactured in Germany in both East and West Zones. A comparison of some of the types featured in our German section with the early B.S.A. will show the striking resemblance. Millions of these rifles have been manufactured and sold throughout the world since the turn of the century. They will be encountered in every clime, and even after years of service many will be found to be in excellent shooting condition.

Current Models of B.S.A. Spring-Air Rifles

At the end of World War II, B.S.A. recognized the necessity for a new design in the field of spring-air rifles. They were not content, as were the Germans, merely to duplicate pre-World-War-II patterns or merely present minor modifications in the way of special sights or special trigger mechanisms, as is currently being done on the Continent generally.

The ugly, clumsy, rather muzzle-heavy prewar B.S.A. types were completely abandoned. New designs were developed not only to permit mass manufacture, but also to present ease of dismounting for repair. In addition, most of the notable deficiencies of the earlier models were corrected in the new designs.

The B.S.A. Cadet and Cadet-Major

The Cadet. This is a lightweight, barrel-cocking design intended for very young boys. It is easily handled. While it has many of the characteristics and failings of the original barrel-cocking models, it is a metal unit suspended in a one-piece wooden stock. As an instance of the type of safety thinking built into the rifle, a deliberately heavy trigger pull is incorporated, requiring the youth to exert considerable deliberate pressure on the trigger to prevent accidental discharge.

Special filter disks have been provided to filter dirt and dust out of the air sucked into the cylinder, a factor of some importance in African and Australian sales areas. Permanently positioned between the barrel and the air cylinder, it prevents the passage into the air chamber of dust and grit, which would impair the efficiency and operating life of the air-compression unit.

The Cadet-Major. This is also a breakdown or barrel-cocking design, but is built with a longer and heavier barrel than the Cadet model. It is designed with an adjustable trigger which can be made heavier or lighter by a screw adjustment. While the cocking design is that of the general earlier types, the cylinder and piston designs are entirely novel.

The High-Power Club and Airsporter

These two rifles are nearly identical except that the Club is .177 caliber, which is the caliber favored in Great Britain and in Europe generally for air-rifle target shooting because of the additional accuracy of the lighter-weight, higher-velocity bullet at short ranges.

The Airsporter is .22 caliber and the spring and tube are slightly longer. Because of the heavier bullet, this design is better suited for small pests and vermin. The manufacturer claims usability up to about 60 yards. It must

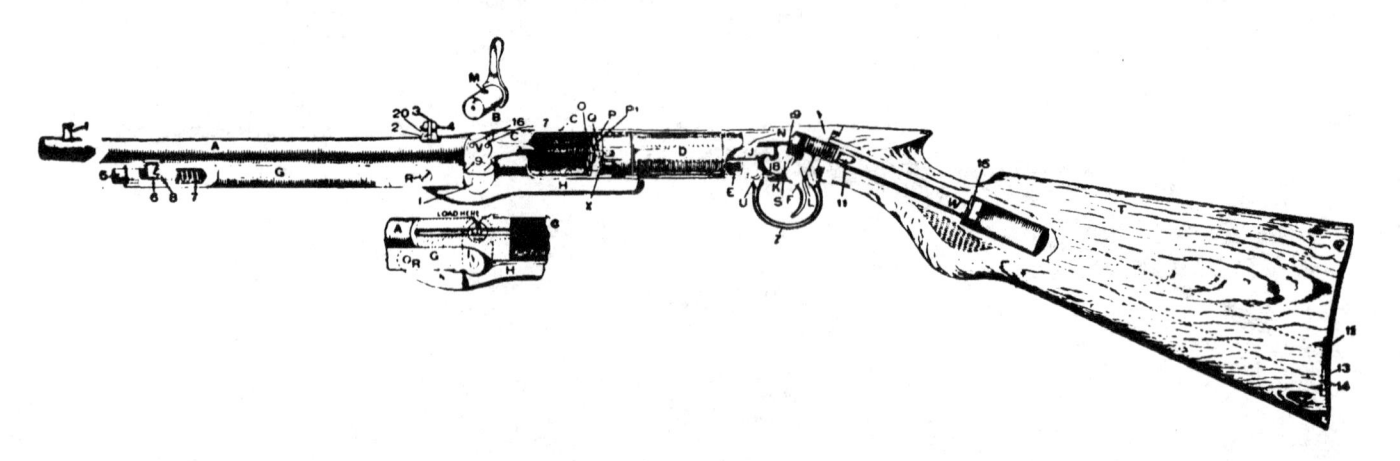

Obsolete British B.S.A. No. 2 air-rifle drawing. Shows details of pre-World War II type with underlever far forward. Action shown in cocked position. Details show loading plug and port design.

B.S.A. Cadet.

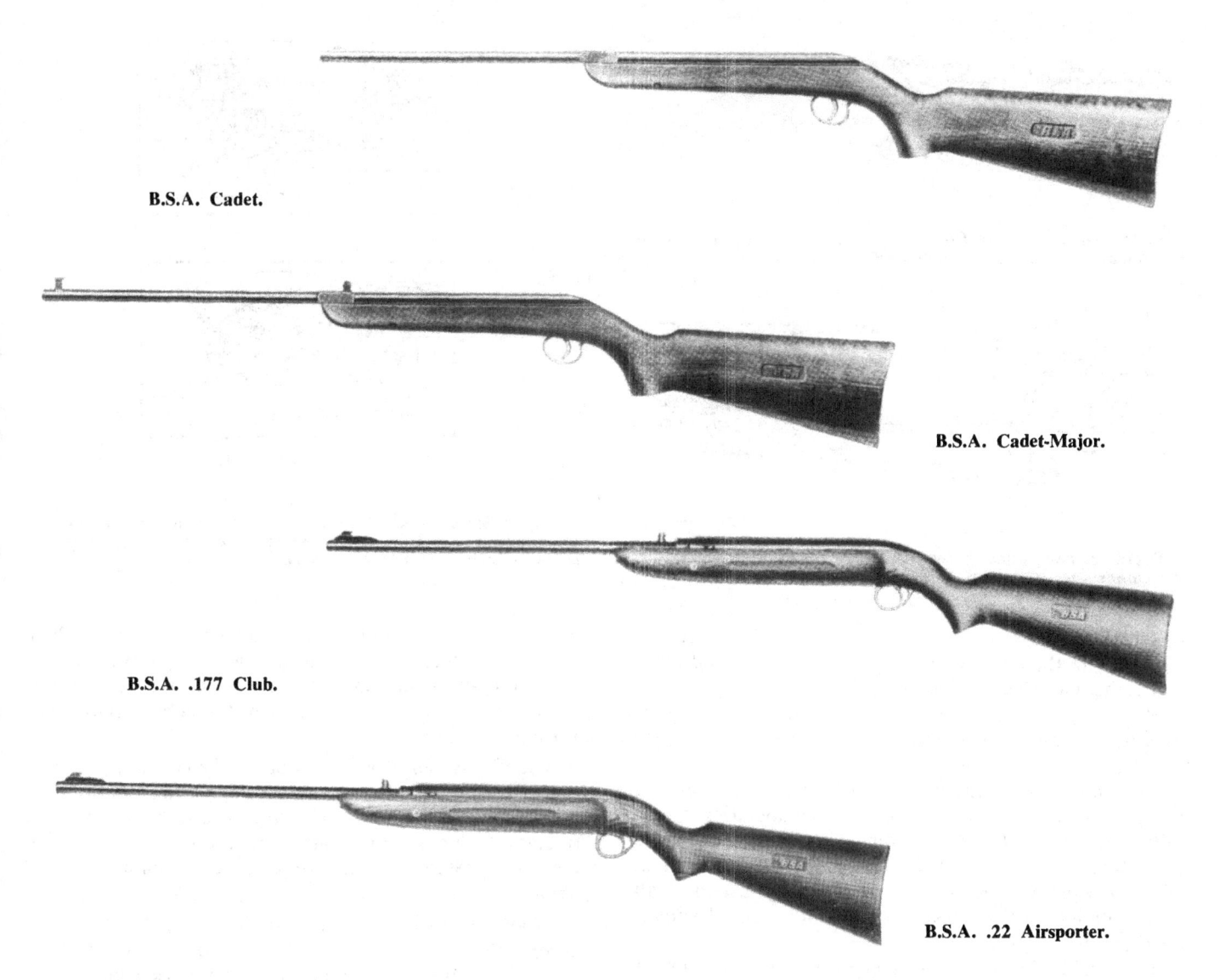

B.S.A. Cadet-Major.

B.S.A. .177 Club.

B.S.A. .22 Airsporter.

be noted that in the observation and tests of the author, the statement seems rather broad. Because of the very light weight of the bullet involved, it is not felt that velocity, accuracy, and penetration of *any* spring-air rifle of this design are such as to warrant its use even on vermin at ranges much in excess of 30 yards, although it is true that an expert shot or a lucky one will occasionally kill game at double that distance.

New Designs

These rifles have a new form of underlever cocking design, found also in certain postwar German patterns. The rifles have a simple one-piece stock somewhat reminiscent of the stock on the United States Army Carbine M1. The cocking arm folds up into this short stock in the fore-end. The spring and piston compression tube is in direct prolongation of the fixed barrel as customary. Pulling down on the tip of the lever catch allows the lever arm to be swung down. This new rearward positioning of the lever completely removes the muzzle heaviness and clumsy cocking effort necessary to cock B.S.A. rifles of earlier designs on this system.

A study of the cutaway drawing and the exposed-mechanism photographs following will show at a glance the reason for the superiority of this design over earlier types of B.S.A. underlevers and most of those currently manufactured and used in Germany.

The cocking arm has been so designed that the distance between its fulcrum and the pivot of the second cocking lever is very short. The action is to *pull* the piston into the fully cocked position where it is held by the sear. In most other underlever rifles the action is to *push* the cocking mechanism, the piston, and spring back.

The air chamber of the Airsporter model is somewhat longer than that of the Club model to permit greater air compression.

The new power-piston unit is also an exceptionally important factor in design. The conical pistonhead is designed to give maximum compression and to concentrate the airflow into its funnel-shaped seat in direct line of prolongation of the rifle bore. This design also lessens the inevitable and customarily severe rebound action of the piston, a factor which causes much disturbance of aim in many typical spring-air operated rifles.

Still another important feature built into the rifle is that of an automatic operating "loading tap" or plug. When the cocking lever is pulled down to cock the arm, the breech is opened *automatically* to permit insertion of a

B.S.A. Airsporter (and Club) mechanism. New leverage system. Self-opening loading plug. Simplified dismounting.

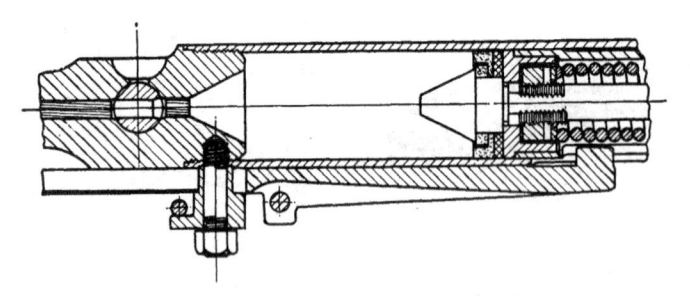

Details of new piston system. Piston is in firing position within the compression chamber.

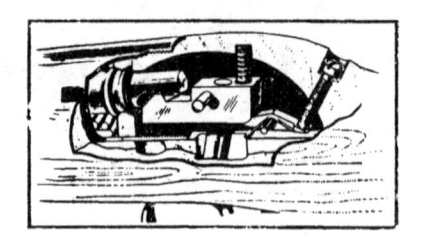

Upper: Special filter disc between barrel and compression cylinder excludes grit. Lower: New sear design. Adjusting trigger screw only in Cadet-Major model.

pellet. When the lever is returned to its position of rest in the forearm, the plug closes the breech securely and automatically. The rifle is then ready to fire.

However, the finger lever operating the plug may be used to examine the breech at any time to check for loading.

The entire metal assembly is easily removed from the stock as a unit. A screw adjustment on the trigger permits setting the pull for whatever weight is desired by the individual shooter. This is the first design of this sort in which it is practical to remove, clean, and re-assemble all parts without special tools or fixtures or a special knowledge of air-gun mechanics.

The positioning of the sear element allows maximum trigger leverage to give a smooth let-off for the release of the extremely powerful compressed spring. It must be remembered that only *one cocking stroke* is required to cock this rifle ready for loading. The velocities developed are the maximum allowable under British regulations. Because the operation is entirely through the spring, the velocity is generally constant, and the rifle may be accurately sighted-in for fine target shooting.

It is normally necessary with a *compressed*-air gun to pump 4 or 5 strokes in order to provide the amount of velocity developed in the Airsporter or Club by a single compression stroke of its spring. However, with all the improvements built into it, and particularly the factor of new compression thrust, the fact still remains that spring-

air rifles *do* have individual recoil characteristics which differentiate them entirely from powder-type arms. If one keeps this distinction in mind, it will be found possible to use these air rifles for most efficient target and short-range vermin shooting.

The B.S.A. air rifles are not marketed in the United States because of the necessarily high price. In spite of their production design they still require so many hand operations and so much fitting that the price landed in the United States would require a retail selling price of about $55.

When this price is contrasted to that of the American *compressed-air* or CO_2 *rifles,* which sell from $13 to $25, it will be seen that it would have little market here. Only a person who has need for the special features of the B.S.A. or who particularly appreciates its combination of quality and design, would buy such a weapon in this country.

As a group, we Americans tend to buy air arms for short-term use, and our large production manufacturers can meet our requirements at far lower prices than European firms can.

Conversely, in Great Britain, because of the legal requirements which force a power-control limit, compressed-air and CO_2 arms of the American types are not acceptable to the authorities. Also the British tend to buy such items for long and lasting usage.

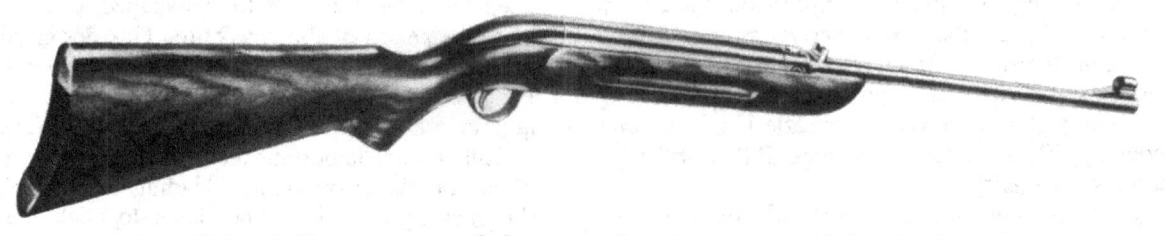

B.S.A. Club and Airsporter new underlever operation. Lever is concealed within fore-end.

Front Sight(s): Bead type on streamlined ramp.
Rear Sight(s): Screw type, elevating by finger wheel.
Velocity (Approximate): .177, 600 f.p.s. .22, 550 f.p.s.
Normal Accurate Range: Targeted to group 1 inch at 20 yards.
Normal Maximum Range: Maker claims 60 yards for .22 and 50 yards for .177.

REMARKS

New position of cocking lever and the pulling action to cock the piston is quite effective in reducing cocking effort for power involved. Automatic opening of loading tap as gun is cocked is a definite improvement. Note that in all such designs the loading tap actually forms a barrel chamber for the pellet. New design of power piston should, theoretically, be particularly efficient in air compression; but independent tests do not demonstrate it. This is one of the most advanced spring-air designs on the market.

B.S.A. CADET (CAL. .177 LIGHT CONSTRUCTION) AND CADET-MAJOR (CAL. .177 HEAVIER CONSTRUCTION) AIR RIFLES

Manufacturer: B.S.A. Guns, Limited, Birmingham 11, England.
Overall Length: CADET, 37.75 inches. CADET-MAJOR, 42 inches.
Weight: CADET, 4.75 pounds. CADET-MAJOR, 5.25 pounds.
Caliber(s): .177 only.
Type(s) of Ammunition Used: .177 Pylarm (or equivalent) Diabolo-type pellets.
Rifled: Yes. CADET barrel, 15 inches. CADET-MAJOR, 18.5 inches.
Operating System: Spring-air.
Cocked & Spring Compressed By: Barrel cockers. Break down barrel on its hinge.
Loaded: Directly into barrel breech when opened for cocking.
Number Rounds: Single shot only.
Stock Type: One-piece butt and fore-end.
Front Sight(s): Bead.
Rear Sight(s): Wheel adjustable for elevation. Sight bases 12.5 and 16 inches, respectively.
Velocity (Approximate): About 405 and 450 f.p.s., respectively.
Normal Accurate Range: 30 to 45 feet.
Normal Maximum Range: Maker claims 30 yards with CADET and 40 yards with CADET-MAJOR.

REMARKS

CADET-MAJOR has an adjustable trigger. Filter and trigger mechanisms in both models are improvements over prewar equivalents; but it must be noted that postwar German trigger systems, as well as several of the earlier Diana types are equal or better.

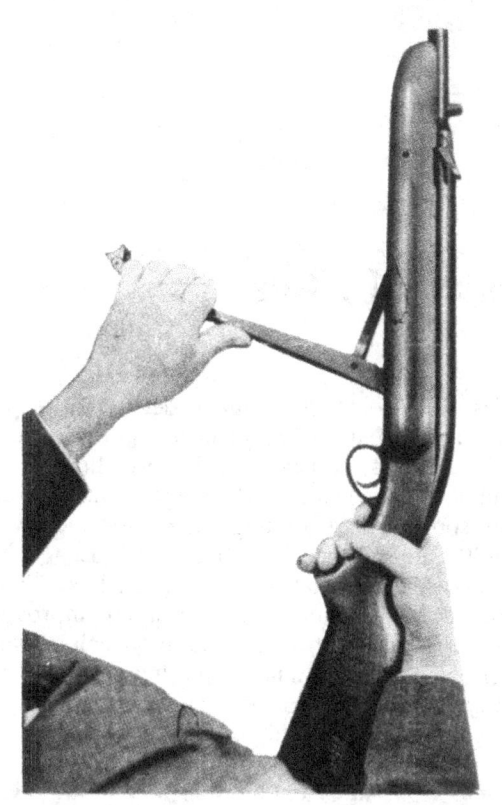

B.S.A. Club and Airsporter. Note improved cocking position of the design.

B.S.A. CLUB (CAL. .177) AND AIRSPORTER (CAL. .22) AIR RIFLES

Manufacturer: B.S.A. Guns Limited (Division of Birmingham Small Arms), Birmingham 11, England.
Overall Length: 44 inches.
Weight: 7.5 pounds approximately.
Caliber(s): Either .177 (the CLUB) or .22 (the AIRSPORTER).
Type(s) of Ammunition Used: .177 or .22 B.S.A. Pylarm pellets (or equivalent).
Rifled: Yes. Barrel 20 inches.
Operating System: Spring-air.
Cocked & Spring Compressed By: New type underlever in forearm.
Loaded: Loading tap (or plug) in breech opens as action is cocked.
Number Rounds: Single shot only.
Stock Type: One-piece walnut. Somewhat resembles U.S. carbines M1 and M2.

B.S.A. Cadet and Cadet-Major. These are breakdown barrel cockers for boys and youths.

123

CHAPTER 10

German Spring-Air Rifles and Pistols

SERIOUS air guns for target shooting, sporting uses, and military training purposes have been a major item of commerce in Germany, both for home use and for export, since the turn of the century. Except when war requirements halted production during the period of the two World Wars, German air-gun manufacture has long been big business.

This production falls into three classifications. The first class concerns manufacture from the year 1900 to the beginning of World War I. Large numbers of those early guns are still in use.

Major production at the beginning of the century was in the hands of the firm of Mayer and Grammelspacher in Rastatt. This firm was then manufacturing large quantities of barrel-cocking air guns on the general pattern of the American Quackenbush, on whose original patents they were manufactured. However the firm early developed a variety of its own which evaded the Quackenbush patents and which simplified the design by moving the compression spring from the stock to a tube directly behind the barrel. Under the trade name of "Diana" these guns became world famous for quality. The firm of Fritz Langenhan at Zella St. Blasii manufactured very large quantities of a somewhat similar design for export. In conjunction with export-import firms, they produced very large quantities of air rifles which were shipped to England and its dependencies, where there was then a considerable sporting and training market for such weapons.

In 1900, M. Pulverman, acting for F. Langenhan, an air-gun and bicycle maker at Zella Mehlis, Thuringia, was granted British patent 15802 for an improved barrel-cocking design. While the basic principle was that of the German "Laufspanner," in which the act of cocking and spring compression is brought about by breaking the barrel down on its hinge, there were enough new features in the design to warrant a patent.

The important new feature was that of the design of the cocking lever, whose nose passed through a notch in the underside of the receiver to contact a piston. This design permitted the lever to lie close to the stock at all times. This is the basic principle of *all* the Laufspanners today. The secondary design feature on which the patent was granted was a spring lock positioned on the top or bottom of the receiver; this top lock also incorporated the rear sight. Pulverman marketed this rifle in Great Britain under the name of the "Millita." In his advertis-

Upper pictures: Pulverman Millita type. Late designs are improved but no more powerful. Lower pictures: Mauser type. These are low-power designs. Latest production is substantially unchanged.

ing in British magazines early in this century, he made claims (which were never contested) to the effect that his rifle had initiated the tremendous interest in the sport of precision air-gun shooting in the British Isles.

The Millita was produced originally only in smooth bore, but later appeared rifled. The original calibers were Nos. 1, 2, and 3 bore, which are the British equivalents of calibers .177, .22, and .250.

During this early period, there were numerous small German manufacturing concerns producing rifles of the general Diana type. However, except for those already mentioned, the early sporting and trade journals in Germany disclose only two other *major* producers of such rifles. These were Ernst Steiglider with factories at Berlin and Suhl and Wilhelm Endter. The latter was a prime manufacturer for the export organization of Adolph Frank Gesellschaft, a Hamburg firm with worldwide connections specializing in arms and military goods.

During this period the old and respected firm of O. Will of Zella St. Blasii was manufacturing relatively small quantities of triggerguard-cocking air rifles (Bügelspanners) for shooting galleries and Kürbelspanners or crank-winding cockers for shooting clubs. These designs never at any time reached even an approximation of the high production output of the barrel-cocking types, however.

The "Venuswaffenwerk" founded by O. Will at Zella in 1844 also manufactured bolt-action air rifles which were basically intended for training use by children. These rifles followed the general design of the German military rifle of then and of today, the Mauser pattern. Marketed under the trade name of "Tell," they were commonly known as "Mauserverschluss" or cylinder locks. These were the German toy-rifle-trainer equivalents of the Daisy air rifles manufactured in the United States, except that their designs lent themselves to a military training application rather than to the sporting application of the typical American lever-action rifle of the day. They were 4.4-mm. caliber, shooting steel round shot. In addition under the Tell name, barrel-cocking rifles of the higher order were also produced, but the quantity was not large in relation to those of other makers.

All such production was halted during the course of World War I, naturally. In 1920 when German armament making was strictly controlled, former rifle and pistol manufacturers generally turned to the production of serious air guns.

During the period between World Wars I and II, the manufacture and export of precision air rifles for target and small-game shooting again became a major business. The Diana organization of Mayer and Grammelspacher forged to the front in this industry. They had as many as 12 different models, ranging from the elementary air rifle for a boy of 7 to the serious target models capable of the utmost short-range precision shooting by the best adult marksman.

In addition to their expensive line of barrel-cocking guns, the Germans introduced a version of the Birming-

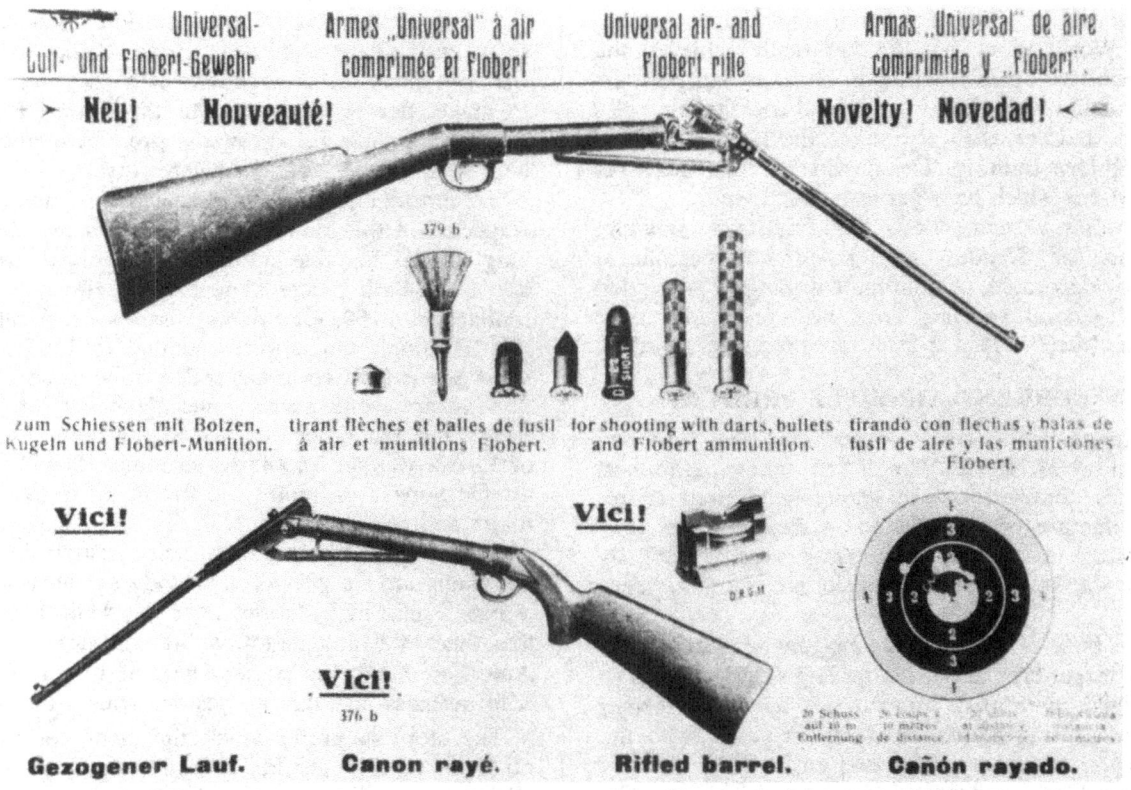

Upper: Early Langenhan gun made on principle of Haviland & Gunn's original design sold under "Quackenbush 1½" designation. Fires air-rifle pellets or darts. When special floating firing pin is inserted, the air piston will hit it and fire BB and CB caps, .22 shorts, or .22 shot shells. Not rifled.
Lower: Same as above except it is purely an air rifle. First rifled German design. Target indicates accuracy. Introduced in 1909.

ham Small Arms' famous fixed-barrel, underlever cocking arm, called in Germany "Hebelspanner." This was intended to meet British competition in the field of ultra precision arms of its type. It was followed by the weapon ironically known in Germany as the "Sportmodell." This design externally was a duplicate of the German Karabiner (Kar.) 98, the official German military rifle operated by a turnbolt. However, it had a detachable box magazine so that continuous military-type firing training could be simulated using an air gun.

The firm of Von Moritz and Gerstenberg at Zella Mehlis also forged to the front during this period. They manufactured barrel-cocking rifles and an unusual line of pistols of the air type, including the "Zenit," which will be found herein and a standard barrel-cocking type.

The firm of C. G. Haenel of Suhl produced serious barrel-cocking rifles of the finest order, as well as a group in the toy variety for youth training. They also manufactured a wide range of air pistols for short-range target shooting, both single shot and repeaters. Haenel air pistols are known and used throughout the world.

Hugo Schmiesser also developed an excellent form of the bolt-action rifle which almost exactly simulated the design of the German Mauser Kar. 98 which was manufactured by him and by various other firms for military training purposes before the German Army was permitted to be equipped with powder-cartridge rifles.

The familiar brand names of Tell, Will, and Venuswaffenwerk again reappeared on their familiar lines of converted rifles as well as on the military-pattern variety.

This period also saw the rapid rise of the remarkable firm of Carl Walther Waffenfabrik at Zella Mehlis. Although founded in 1886, it was not until the period between the World Wars that Walther really achieved the high position it is again reaching in both air and powder-arms production. In addition to barrel-cocking air rifles of the highest order, they also made the bolt-action pattern for military training. The quality of their arms set world standards which have yet to be surpassed.

At the other extreme, firms like Friederick Wilhelm Heym, who for decades were noted for magnificent examples of decorated, custom-built drillings (3-barreled guns) and general sporting arms also re-entered their field at the close of the war by turning out fine air rifles.

GERMAN CURRENT AIR-RIFLE PRODUCTION

All weapons production was prohibited in Germany after the close of World War II, of course. However, various arms companies were gradually allowed to resume manufacture of air rifles for domestic commercial and export use as the armistice terms were realistically modified in the face of world political and economic conditions.

Since the bulk of the German air-gun production was for serious target-type arms, the tooling skills and equipment available permitted manufacture by many former arms manufacturing plants. In short, in contrast to the United States, where air rifles are basically in the toy category, the German production has, with the sole exception of the Diana works, always been linked with the production of formal military and sporting arms manufacture. Thus the air-gun industry of today can almost overnight become the source of large-scale military production in an emergency.

GERMAN MANUFACTURERS

At the close of World War II, the traditional German gunmaking area of Thuringia was placed under Soviet control. Many of the world's finest small-arms factories there were either destroyed or uprooted. The heads of most of the best known firms escaped to the American Zone at the first opportunity. A few plants were kept in production on sporting arms by the Russians.

Except for the famous Dianawerk plant of Mayer & Grammelspacher situated at Rastatt, a small town near Baden-Baden and Karlsruhe, most of the fine air-rifle design and manufacture had been conducted by the better powder-arms manufacturers in the Thüringer Wald (Thuringia Forest) district, particularly at Suhl, a town with a population of some 25,000 and Zella Mehlis, whose population was only about 17,000.

This "Arms Chamber of Europe" as it was called has an arms-making history running back into the Middle Ages. The nearby mountains provided great mines of iron ore, the forest furnished wood for stocks and for charcoal. Before the dawn of gunpowder the "Suhler Brustpanzer" or steel "breastcoats" were the armor of many of the ruling dynasties. With the arrival of gunpowder, Nuremberg became the seat of firearms production, but it soon overlapped into Suhl and Zella Mehlis.

Down through the centuries some of the finest designs, qualities, and decorations of arms have come out of this area where arms trades were passed down for generations from father to son.

Many of the best of these old-line firms, as we have seen, entered the American Zone. Since air rifles were the first items in their line which they were permitted to make, nearly all went into this form of production. Because of their backgrounds, product quality has been kept at a rather high level generally.

To consider just one typical example, one of the most respected of the old names was that of the Heym family, long known for fine inlaid and engraved arms as well as custom-built pieces. The firm of Heym Brothers was founded in 1750. One of its best known developments is the "Drilling" which they patented in 1891. The 3-barreled gun is favored in Central Europe as an "all around" hunting arm; one barrel generally being for a rifle cartridge and the other two for shot shells. The last Czar of Russia was an important customer. Some of the finest double guns ever made are products of the Heym factories and artisans.

The Heym family and their best technicians fled Thuringia after a period of custody by the Russian secret police. Again in a district near the Thüringer Wald, but this time at Münnerstadt, a little Bavarian town in the American Zone, the present firm of Friedr. Wilh. Heym is in business making fine custom arms—and air rifles!

The story is pretty much the same for most of the other makers. In general all are making air arms of the classical types, principally because air guns are very close to their ultimate in design and performance by European standards. However, since the companies are no longer crowded into a small community of interest, it is possible that *individual* developments in the field of air weapons manufacture in Germany in the coming years will be of interest. In fact, this tendency is already being exhibited, as witness the new Walther repeating air rifle design, the new Falke short-stroke underlever cocking system on their Models 80 and 90, and the new Barakuda air-gas rifle, all described herein; and there are other developments which the author is not free to discuss here.

Interesting developments may be expected if the German air-gun industry turns to carbon dioxide and compressed-air arms manufacture, a field which until now has been exclusively American.

We shall consider here in alphabetical order the major German manufacturers currently making air arms of various types. The list is comprehensive, and the author has contacted directly or otherwise all the factories cited. Small subcontract groups who do solely *assembly* have not been included, since their products are merely duplicates of standard types.

Details and drawings are included to give a thorough understanding of all the classical types, as well as all the advanced designs.

GERMAN DIANA AIR RIFLES

These guns are manufactured at Rastatt, Baden, at Mayer & Grammelspacher's Dianawerks. This very old-line air-gun firm manufactures a complete line from toys through the finest quality precision air rifles. Most of their business is done through major distributors, notably G. Genschow (Geco) of Hamburg, Akah and Waffen-Frankonia.

In the United States Diana Models 16, 22, 23, and 27 purchased through Genschow are imported and sold by the Hy Score Arms Corporation of Brooklyn under the designation "Hy Score Models 805, 806, 801, and 807." Model 807, the highest priced, is one of the best buys in the Diana field, being a serious rifle with good power and excellent trigger mechanism.

The Diana model series 35 and 50 are imported by Stoeger Arms Corporation of New York City and are sold under the trade name "Peerless" with the added Diana model designation; and little attempt is made to disguise the fact that they are German Dianas. The latter are the most expensive of the Diana line and rank very high among the best spring-air rifles made, though many seasoned shooters prefer other German makes. On independent tests by the author, however, they fell below British performance on both velocity and accuracy.

The German "Diana" line is sold in Great Britain under the name "Original." A competing line of "Dianas" also marketed under that name, and all practically identical with the German, is made by Millard Brothers at Lanarkshire, Scotland.

It should be noted that imitations of the original "Diana" types are also made in Austria, Japan, Italy, and Spain. In the opinion of the author who has examined all types, only the Scotch-made rifles approximate the German manufacturing quality in this group.

Finally, it must be remembered that these arms are also often made under private brand names for export.

The following is a complete list of all current German-made "Dianas." Special photos, drawings, and details are included where they are considered of real or potential value to the shooter, collector, gunsmith, historian, or developer.

Much of the other German air-gun production is merely an adaptation of the principles found in the Diana line. Where outstanding advances have been made, the individual manufacturers have been duly credited.

Models

Diana No. 1. This is the simplest and cheapest form of the Diana line. It is the single-shot sheet-metal design for boys and in effect is little more than a toy trainer. This low-priced design is based on the very earliest form of the obsolete Daisy American, single-shot, top-break air gun. The inner tube must be withdrawn to load.

Diana No. 1.

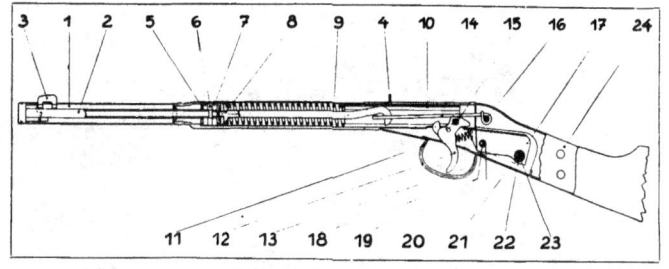

Elementary breakdown barrel, toy-type construction.

127

Diana No. 15. This is the second step in a progressive advance of the Diana line in furnishing trainer air guns for youth purposes. It, too, is a basic sheet-metal construction, more of a toy than a serious trainer because of its lack of accuracy. However, it has much better leverage and considerably more power than the No. 1 and is intended for older and stronger boys. The receiver section is sheet metal.

Diana No. 15.

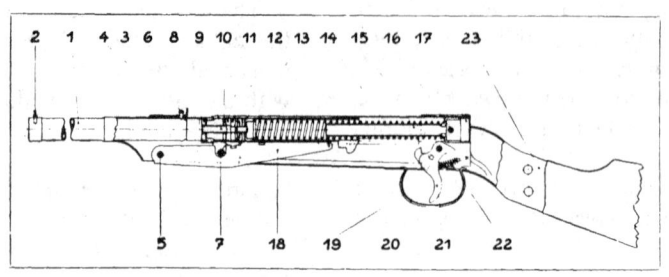

Leverage principle as in expensive types.

Diana No. 16. This is the third step in this progression. The design follows that of the No. 15 but the gun is provided with a wood stock, which allows better lines and better balance for the growing shooter.

Diana No. 16.

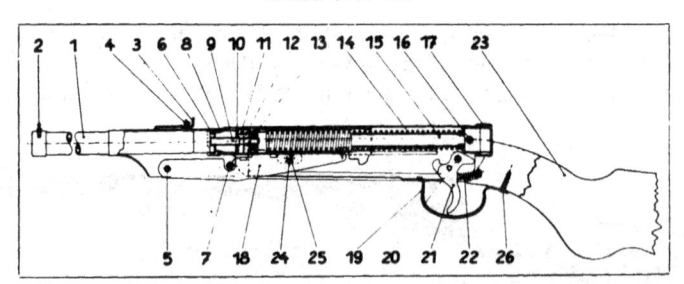

Action at rest. Note lever point ready to pick up piston as barrel is hinged down.

Diana No. 22. This model is a superior form of the "Jugend" or boy's model. It has most of the features of the later rifles, including the most efficient form of barrel detent based on camming faces on the lugs. However it is light in weight and designed for young boys.

Diana No. 22.

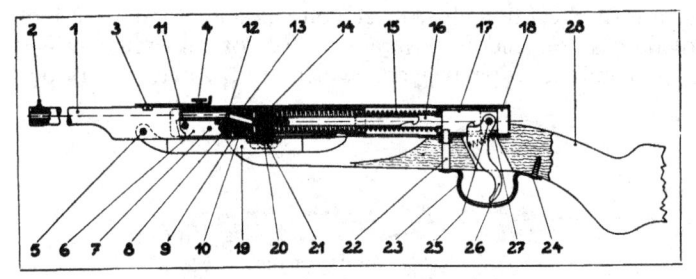

Diana No. 22. Improved air-vent system.

Diana No. 25. While still a rifle for the growing boy, this model is again of sturdier construction than the previous models and is also adapted to either the 4.5- or the 5.5-mm. calibers.

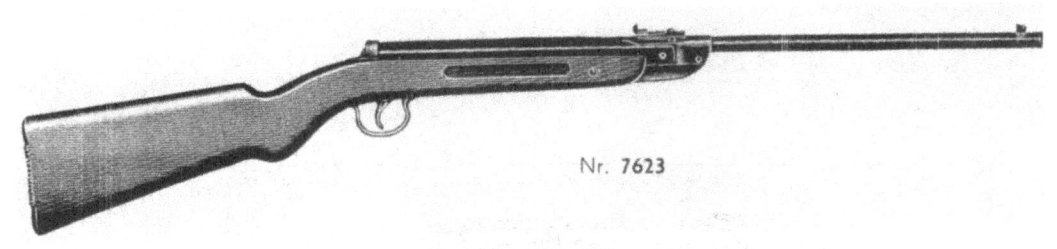

Diana No. 25.

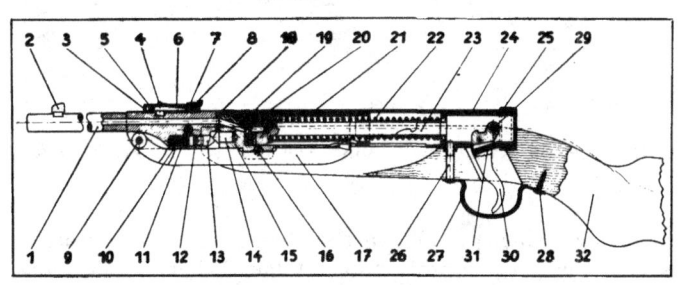

Improved trigger and detent bolt.

Diana No. 27. This is a considerable departure from all the earlier types. It incorporates a new design, two-stage trigger pull, which allows a very considerable degree of accuracy because of the smooth let-off. The trigger is adjustable, and the entire design stronger than that of the earlier types.

There are several variations of the Model 27 Diana. However the difference is only in sights, stocks, and similar externals. These are the "best buys" in the Diana line judged by the author's velocity, accuracy, and penetration tests.

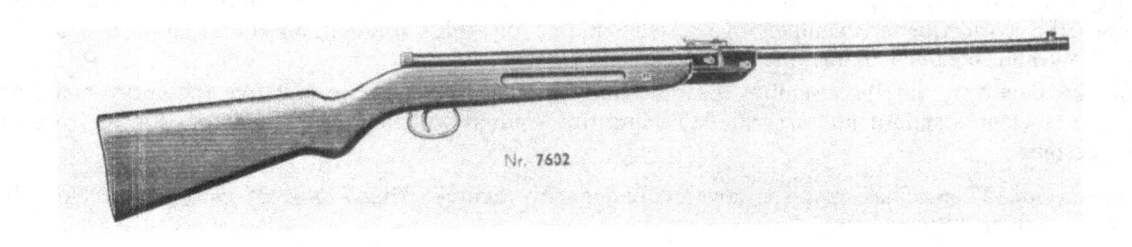

Diana No. 27.

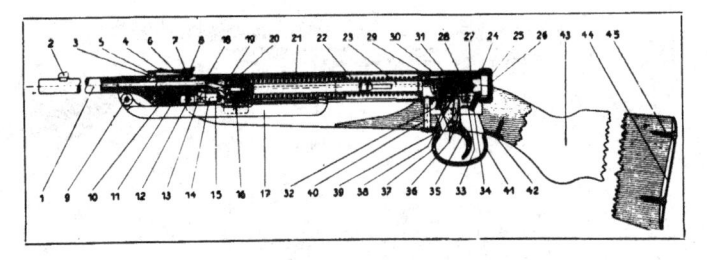

New adjustable trigger system.

Diana No. 35. These rifles are of exceptionally robust construction, though still of the barrel-cocking type. The barrels are 20 inches long, providing a tremendous leverage factor for maximum weight of spring compression. They are fitted with excellent double-pull military-type triggers, which are favored in Europe.

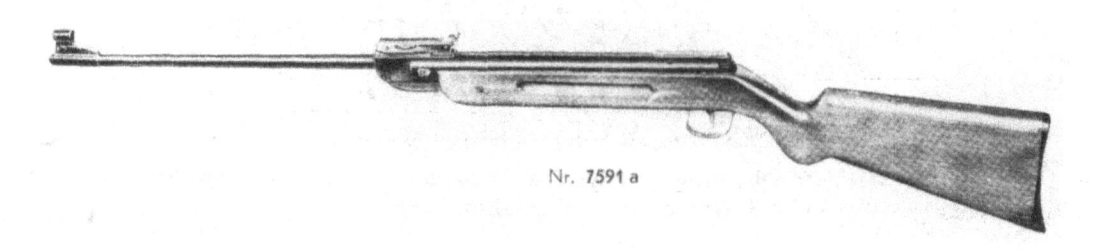

Diana No. 35.

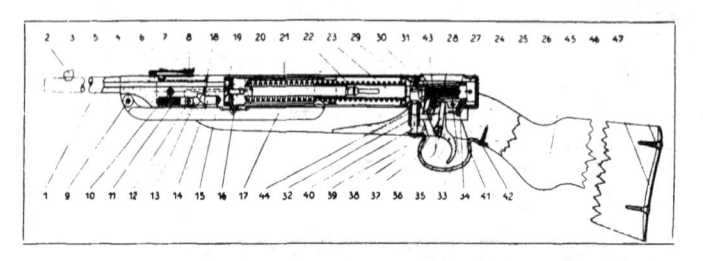

No. 35 series. Heavy duty. Improved bolt and trigger system.

Diana No. 48. This is an underlever rifle, the first in the Diana series so operated. Its general design is quite close to that of the prewar British B.S.A., with the conformation of the earlier B.S.A. stock line. The stock is attached to the rear of the receiver by a through bolt as in regular shotgun design.

The barrel being fixed, the design requires a separate loading cap or port at the breech. This design is also fitted with an adjusting screw for trigger adjustment. While of considerable power, its lines are somewhat ungainly. However the quality is equal to that of the standard Diana production.

The Diana 50. This is the improved and streamlined version of the earlier Model 48. The principal differences in the designs of the various models are again primarily those of the stocks and sights.

These are underlever rifles with a fixed barrel, having a maximum spring compression for the general design used. They are among the world's better examples of precision match air rifles; though on impartial tests they were found inferior in velocity and accuracy to the British Webley.

Mechanically they very closely resemble the mechanism of the Model 48, except that the entire metal assembly is dropped into the stock in standard military rifle style and not secured with a through bolt passing in from the butt as in the earlier designs.

(Note: Diana No. 27 as a basic type is covered under "Hy Score"; Diana No. 35 and Diana No. 50 as basic types are covered under "Peerless.")

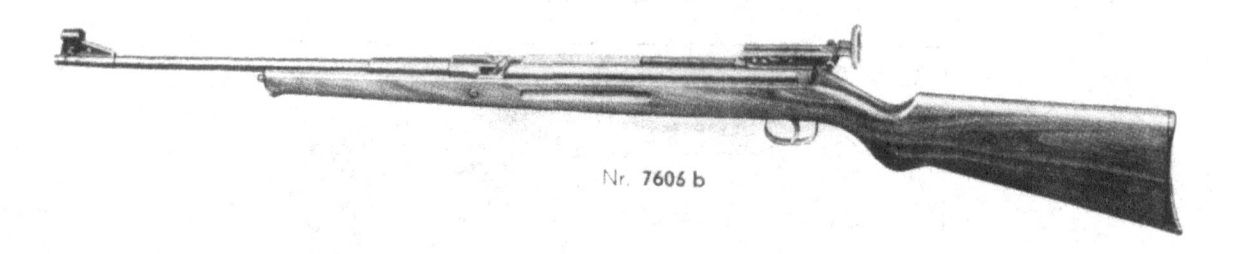

Diana No. 50.

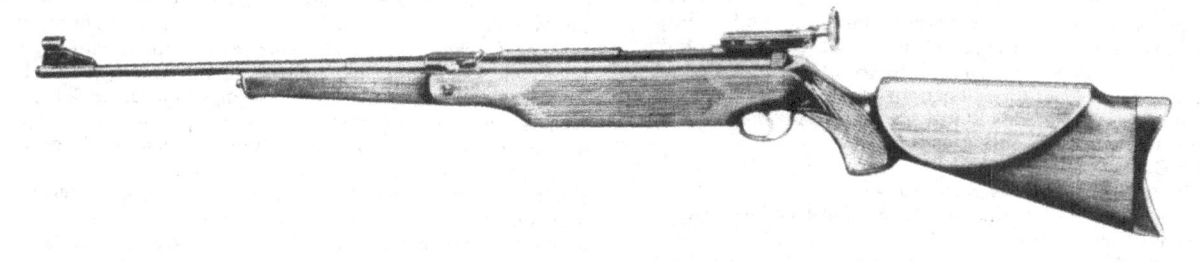

Diana No. 50M.

Diana low-price design sold by importers, Hy Score Arms Corporation, as Hy Score Model 805.

HY SCORE MODEL 807 AIR RIFLE

Manufacturer: Dianawerk—Mayer & Grammelspacher, Rastatt, Baden.
U.S. Distributor: Hy Score Arms Corporation, Brooklyn, New York.
Overall Length: 41.75 inches.
Weight: 5 pounds 14 ounces.
Caliber(s): .177 or .22.
Type(s) of Ammunition Used: Suitable caliber Hy Score Diabolo-type pellets (or equal).
Rifled: Yes. Barrel 17⅜ inches.
Operating System: Spring-air.
Cocked & Spring Compressed By: Breaking barrel down on its hinge opens and cocks action.
Loaded: Directly into breech while action is opened after cocking.
Number Rounds: Single shot only.
Stock Type: Wood, one-piece. Well finished. No checkering.
Front Sight(s): Blade.
Rear Sight(s): Adjustable elevation. On barrel, short sight line.
Velocity (Approximate): Distributor claims 600 f.p.s.
Normal Accurate Range: Average for type.
Normal Maximum Range: Average for type.
Approximate Retail Price: In the United States about $30.

REMARKS

This is an elementary barrel-cocker design. Barrel is secured by detent and spring, all that is necessary in way of a lock for the design and power involved. Materials and workmanship, Diana quality for price. This is an intermediate grade. Piston is thrust back and its spring compressed as barrel is broken down,

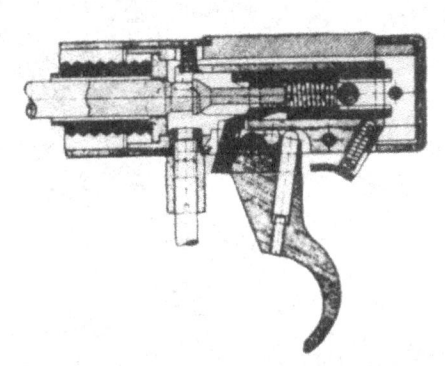

Hair-trigger mechanism of Model 807 Hy Score pellet rifle, in fully cocked position. In the conventional type trigger the full force of the compressed spring (about 165 pounds) is released by the trigger. In this new patented design, a hammer mechanism replaced the trigger. This hammer is actuated by a sensitive spring, giving a trigger pull similar to that of the highest grade target rifles. This trigger can be regulated from stationary to a two-stage military pull.

Cocking Diana medium-priced rifle sold in the United States by importers under trade designation Hy Score Model 807.

131

forcing attached cocking lever to act through piston engagement. Relatively easy to cock for power involved. Special sear design is one of Diana's best, allowing very good trigger-pull adjustment. Adjusting screw in trigger. May be set for single-stage (sporting) or double-stage (military) pull, as desired. While not to be confused with true target-type air rifles of heavier construction and higher price, this sturdy design is adequate for all plinking and short-range shooting in its class.
(Note: Other Diana models marketed by Hy Score are as follows:
M805—about $9. Cheap boy's breakdown type.
M806—about $15. Boy's rifle of better construction. Breakdown (barrel cocker).
M801—about $20. (Heavier and better grade, as indicated by price.)

PEERLESS M35 AND 35B AIR RIFLES

Manufacturer: Dianawerk-Mayer & Grammelspacher, Rastatt, Baden.
U.S. Distributor: Stoeger Arms Corporation, New York City.
Overall Length: 45 inches.
Weight: 7¼ pounds approximately. (Slightly heavier in B model.)
Caliber(s): .22 ONLY. (Note: Under "Diana" name, also in .177 caliber.)
Type(s) of Ammunition Used: .22 Stoeger Hornet Diabolo-type pellets (or equal).
Rifled: Yes.
Operating System: Spring-air.
Cocked & Spring Compressed By: High-grade barrel cocker. Breaking barrel cocks action.
Loaded: Directly into breech when action is opened for cocking.
Number Rounds: Single shot only.
Stock Type: One-piece, wood. Good bedding. No checkering. Pistol grip.
Front Sight(s): Bead on M35. Special hooded "star" type on 35B with 4 blades.
Rear Sight(s): M35, fixed on barrel, elevation. 35B, micro-peep, sliding.
Velocity (Approximate): Claimed 600 f.p.s. (See test section.)
Normal Accurate Range: Used for match shooting up to about 20 meters.
Normal Maximum Range: Average for air rifle.
Approximate Retail Price: M35, about $35. 35B, about $46.

REMARKS

These are among the finest Diana barrel cockers. (In Germany an M model is fitted with a finer stock at a higher price.) This is a real match-quality air rifle when fitted with sights as in the B model. Action and loading is standard for barrel cockers. Action is held closed by detent, springs, and close fits. No formal lock is necessary for power involved. Special sear and adjustable trigger mechanism allow match-type trigger pull. Special barrel rear sight combinations include detachable four-aperture disc-click sights. Rear sight may be slid along rib on top of receiver (compression tube) to adjust distance between sights as desired by individual shooter. Front sight is a four-point-star design common in Europe, but little-known here. Turn control button on side of ramp and star can be turned to bring 2 types of bead and 2 types of post fronts into sighting line as desired. This rifle has ultra-heavy spring and requires considerable force to cock. It is not a boy's rifle in any sense.

PEERLESS M50E AND 50M AIR RIFLES
(Stoeger Trade Name)

Manufacturer: Dianawerk—Mayer & Grammelspacher, Rastatt, Baden.
U.S. Distributor: Stoeger Arms Corporation, New York City.
Overall Length: 45 inches.
Weight: M50E, 8 pounds, 6 ounces. 50M, 9 pounds 8 ounces.
Caliber(s): .22 ONLY. (Note: Under Diana name, also in .177 caliber.)
Type(s) of Ammunition Used: .22 Stoeger Hornet Diabolo-type pellet (or equal).
Rifled: Yes. Fixed barrel with breech loading tap.
Operating System: Spring-air.
Cocked & Spring Compressed By: Underlever housed in fore-end. Pull down and back to cock.
Loaded: Press spring-powered loading-tap release. Open tap. Insert pellet. When tap is closed, bullet lines up.
Number Rounds: Single shot only.
Stock Type: Wood, one-piece, but with fore-end extension for lever.
Front Sights(s): M50E, hooded post. 50M, hooded ramp with special star and 4 sights.
Rear Sight(s): M50E, adjustable, rear of breech. 50M, special match designs.

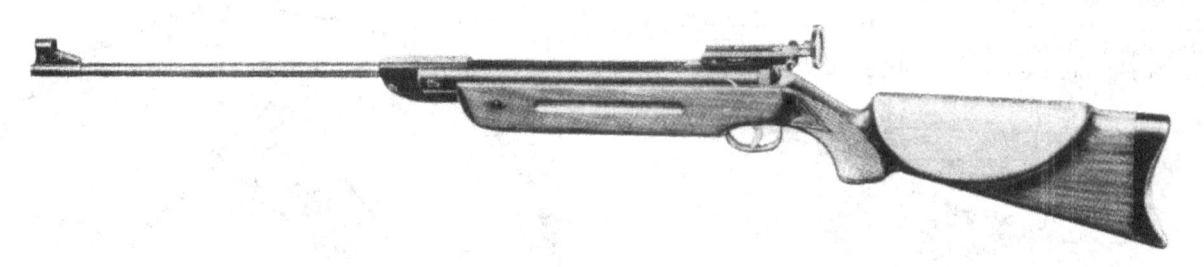

Diana No. 35M.

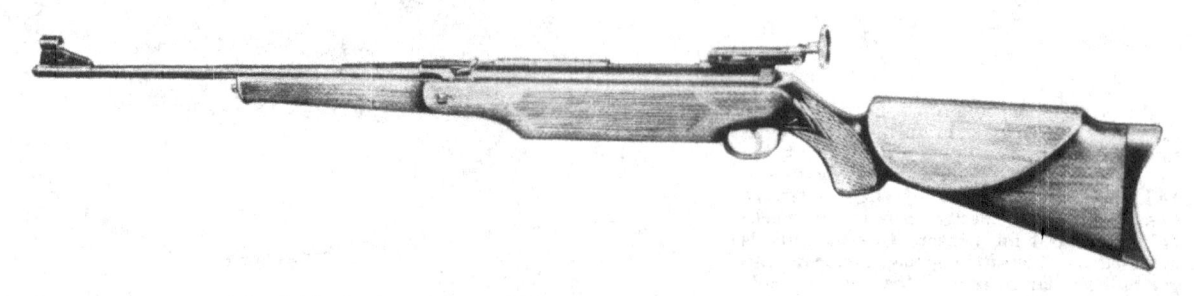

Diana No. 50M.

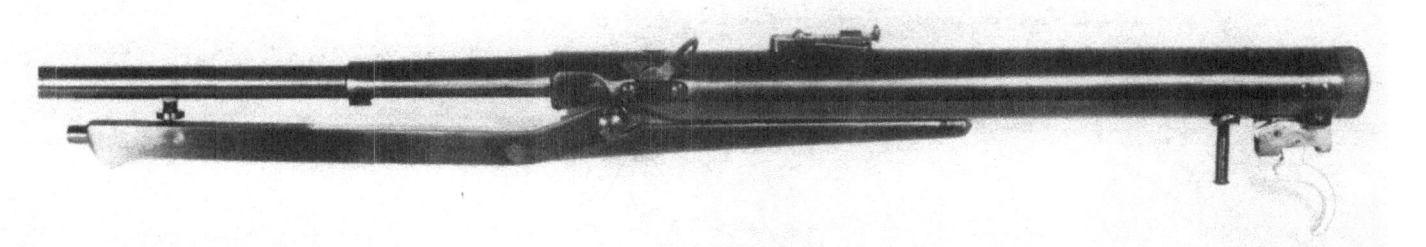

Peerless (Diana) Model 50. Note that all metal parts are removable as a unit. Projecting button at forward end of cocking lever is spring-loaded and must be pushed in to release lever. Loading tap must be opened manually by operating thumb lever seen at breech.

Velocity (Approximate): Claimed 500 f.p.s. (Note: This is one of the most powerful made.)
Normal Accurate Range: Most precision air-rifle shooting is done at 10 to 20 yards. Used in German match shooting up to 50 meters, however.
Normal Maximum Range: Standard for bullet and velocity.
Approximate Retail Price: M50E, $50. 50M, $85.

REMARKS

The M50E is one of the better grade air vermin rifles made. 50M is one of the best grade match target types to compete with the British Webley and B.S.A. Sight combinations are pictured. These are high-grade micrometer sights. The underlever operation allows easier cocking for the powerful spring used than does corresponding barrel cockers. Loading through tap is not as easy as in barrel cockers. Very high quality materials, fits, and finishes; but not quite up to Walther in this respect.

It must be noted that most British air-rifle shooting is done with underlevers; but in Germany it is only recently that this trend has been developing, most match shooting being done with heavy barrel-cocking types. Trigger system is excellent, an improved version of the old Model 27. The 50M has checkered pistol grip and fore-end, high cheekpiece, target-type butt plate. (Note: These rifles are often represented abroad as capable of 50-meter shooting; but realistically, 20 yards is about maximum for average work.)

THE "FALKE" GERMAN LINE OF AIR RIFLES

In common with the Diana system, the Falke organization (the name means "falcon"), provides an entire line of air rifles to start the youngest boy with a toy pattern and to carry him progressively through the various stages of advanced design as his ability and age allows.

Model 10 is a light rifle of the barrel-cocking type of single-shot design. It is in many ways related to the earlier Haenel rifles which were produced on the same basic system before the war.

Model 20 while still a boy's design is somewhat heavier in construction though it still retains the short one-piece butt stock. It is provided with a fore-end.

Model 30 is a full-stocked type of more advanced design with a stock of actual rifle shape to interest the older boys who are beginning to appreciate quality.

Model 40 fits into the junior classification although still a barrel-cocking arm relatively easy to cock. It is equipped with an improved trigger and better sights, allowing for more careful sighting and better let-off and

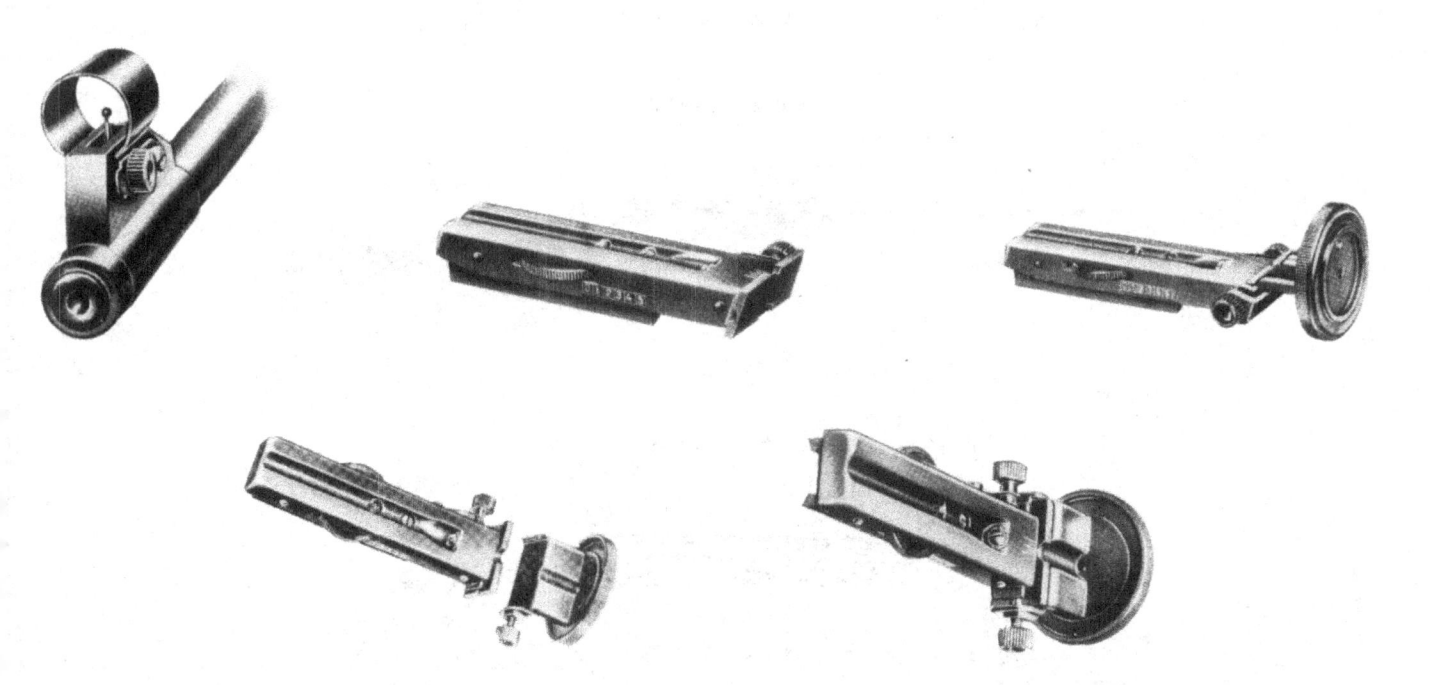

Front and rear sight combinations available for match target shooting with heavy-duty Diana rifles. Front sight has four different posts on a rotating "star." Turning button will bring them into position as desired. Note that some slide (tangent) open rear sights have attachable peeps. No United States firearms maker produces a sight of equivalent quality.

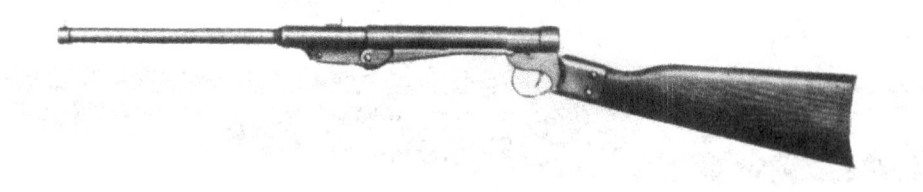

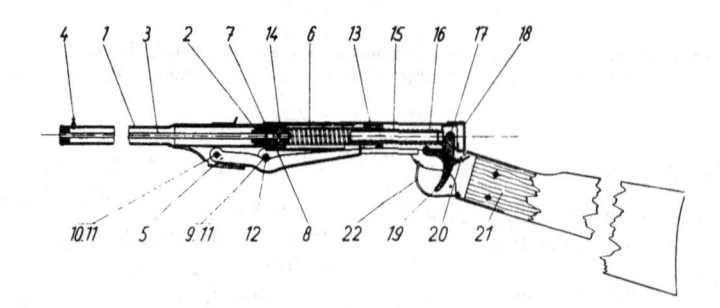

Falke Model 10.

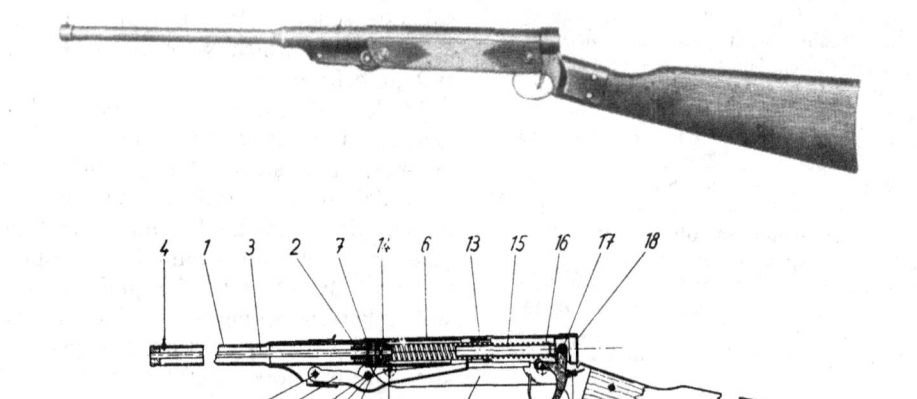

Falke Model 20.

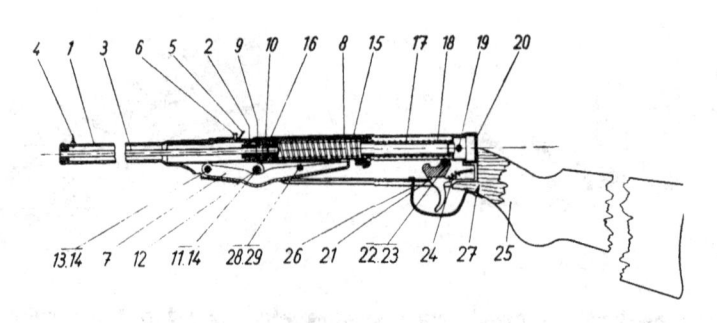

Falke Model 30.

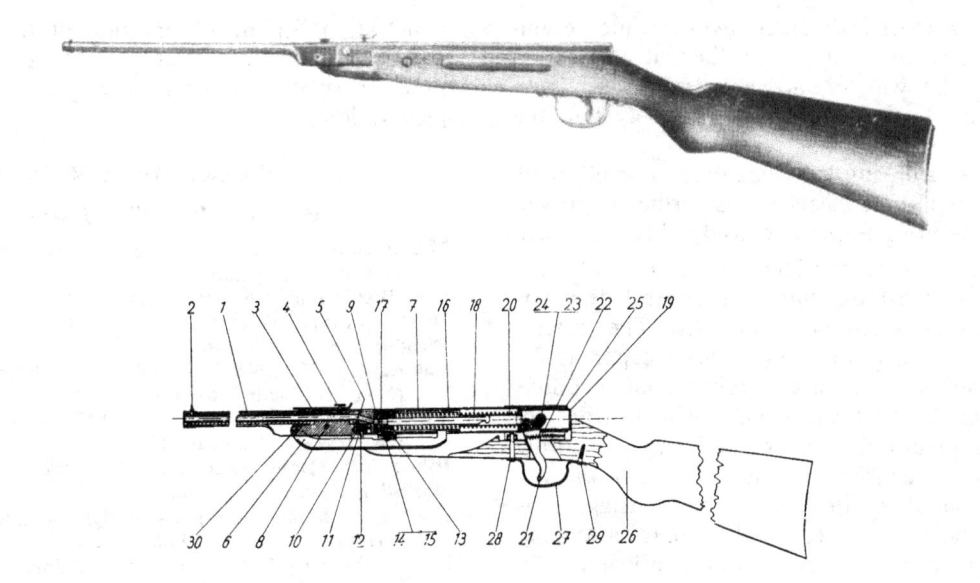

Falke Model 40.

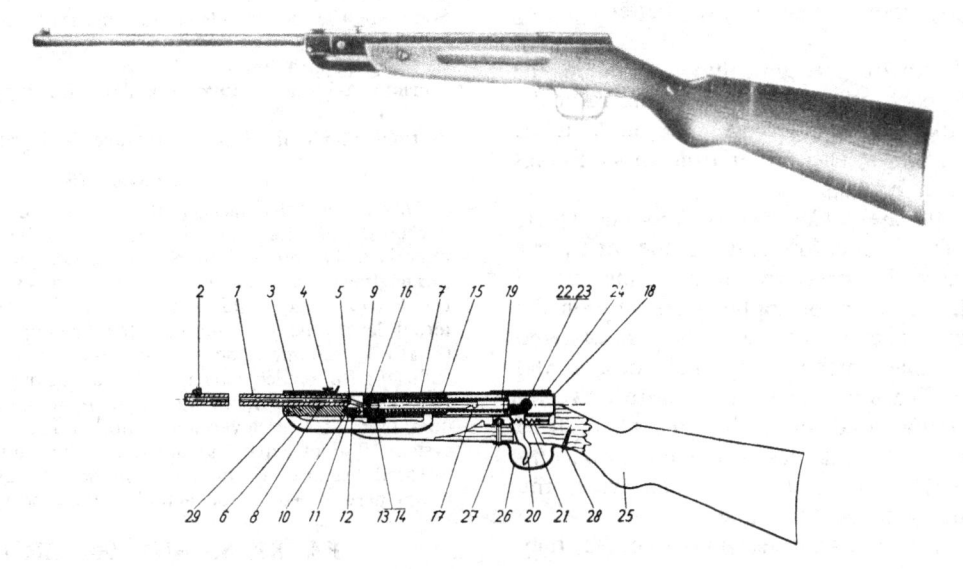

Falke Model 50.

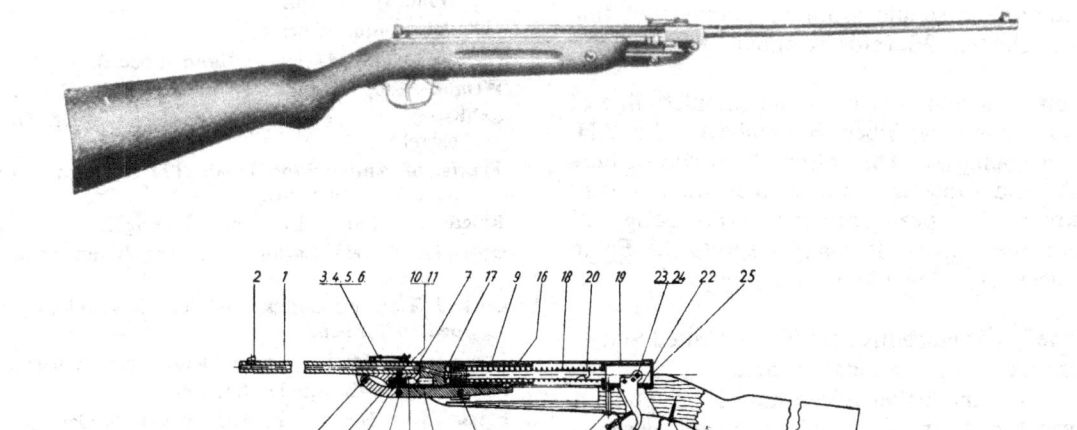

Falke Model 60.

135

tending towards increased accuracy. Also, while resembling the M30 externally in its general lines, it has several improvements in the way of air vents and trigger and sear arrangements. These all fit it more closely into the advanced types of air guns.

Model 50 is of still sturdier construction, employing a solid, seamless steel-tube barrel and a further-improved trigger system. The firing power is considerably increased.

Model 60, while usable by older boys is basically the first adult model in the Falke line. The general design is excellent. An adjustable trigger is provided. The general construction and spring power allows this weapon to be used for vermin shooting and not merely for target plinking. Serious target shooting can be done with this design.

Model 70 is a precision rifle for good target shooting use. Not only is it considerably heavier than all the previous models but it is fitted with a better trigger adjustment. It also has a side lever which actuates a locking bolt to provide a more perfect breech seal than is normally found in barrel-cocking systems, since these normally depend upon detents and washers alone for tightness of breech closure. Easy breech opening gives better cocking leverage.

Models 80 and 90 are mechanically very much the same in relation to each other, though differing radically from all other Falkes. The differences are in weights, stocks, sights, and fittings. They differ from other Falkes in NOT being barrel cockers.

Models 80 and 90 are *underlever* cockers the levers being housed in the heavy fore-end of the one-piece stock. When released by pressure on a spring-control lock button, they hinge down for applying pressure on the actual cocking lever. The use of very heavy levers and powerful springs is made possible by their design and heavy construction. There are no finer or more powerful spring-air guns manufactured today than the 80 and 90 series of the Falke. (Note: The design has much in common with the postwar British B.S.A. underlevers, the fulcrum position being much the same.)

As is customary in fixed-barrel designs, of course, they are provided with loading ports at the breech.

These rifles are capable of accuracy at maximum ranges for air guns, actual match shooting being done up to 50 meters, although it should again be pointed out that for the average shooter 20 yards is about maximum for air rifles.

Falke (falcon) is a trade name for the complete line of air arms manufactured by Albert Fohrenbach, G.m.b.H. at Bennigsen in Hannover. The entire line is shown here in photographs and drawings because they offer a very complete study in European spring-air arms design of the newest and finest order. In many respects the Falke line are advances over the old Diana group of similar arms.

Since this line is not currently sold in the United States, only representative types are detailed here.

Special features in the higher-priced models are pointed up. The lower-priced arms are all common designs, though quality of workmanship is good throughout.

Note, however, that the heavy-duty design, large-diameter piston tube, and oversized springs do not produce much, if anything, in the way of added velocity or penetration. In the observation of the author, frictional and spring factors offset possible gains; and in actual practice smaller designs may give better velocity and penetration.

FALKE 70 AIR RIFLE
(Best Grade Falke Barrel Cocker)

Manufacturer: Falke, Albert Fohrenbach, G.m.b.H., Bennigsen, Hannover, Germany.
U.S. Distributor: Currently none.
Overall Length: 37 inches.
Weight: 6 pounds 9 ounces.
Caliber(s): .177 ONLY (British No. 1 bore. German 4.5-mm.) (Note: .22-caliber to order.)
Type(s) of Ammunition Used: .177 German pellets, Diabolo-type RWS or equivalent.
Rifled: Yes. (Note: Smooth bore to order.)
Operating System: Spring-air.
Cocked & Spring Compressed By: Breaking barrel. Standard barrel-cocker system, but has positive barrel lock.
Loaded: Directly into breech when action is open after cocking.
Number Rounds: Single shot only.
Stock Type: One-piece, wood. Checkered. (Note: Walnut stained.)
Front Sight(s): Bead.
Rear Sight(s): Screw elevating type with finger wheel. Rear of breech.
Velocity (Approximate): 450 f.p.s.
Normal Accurate Range: Standard for type. Usually not over 20 yards.
Normal Maximum Range: Average for spring system.

REMARKS

This is basically just another version of the classical barrel-cocker design. Its merit lies in its excellent workmanship and materials. Trigger system is very good, giving fine adjustment.

The breech is positively locked by a spring-supported bolt at the barrel breech and compression-tube jointure. A small external lever operates the bolt for opening. In view of the low (relatively) compression of air arms of this type, latches are sufficient for breech closing; but the locking bolt here used does have certain value in taking up wear at the closure point. While operating the lock lever adds another motion to cocking in this system, it does have the advantage that initial opening motion is eased because of the common detent bolt and spring thrust is not here added to the actual cocking stroke of the lever.

FALKE 80 AND 90 AIR RIFLES
(Same Mechanism. Stocks and Sights Differ)

Manufacturer: Falke, Albert Fohrenbach, G.m.b.H., Bennigsen, Hannover, Germany.
U.S. Distributor: Currently none.
Overall Length: 44 inches (both models).
Weight: M80, 8 pounds 13 ounces. M90, 9 pounds 7 ounces.
Caliber(s): .177. (Note: .22 to special order. Only difference is barrel.)
Type(s) of Ammunition Used: .177 standard German (or British or U.S. equivalent).
Rifled: Yes. (Note: Fixed-barrel design.)
Operating System: Spring-air. Spring-driven piston compresses air in path.
Cocked & Spring Compressed By: Close-fulcrum underlever bedded in fore-end.
Loaded: Automatic-opening loading tap at barrel breech.
Number Rounds: Single shot only.
Stock Type: Heavy, one-piece wood. Model 90 has high comb, special stock.
Front Sight(s): On ramp. Removable beads or blades. Hood available.
Rear Sight(s): M80, fine adjustable open type. M90, special micrometer adjustable peep.

Falke Model 70.

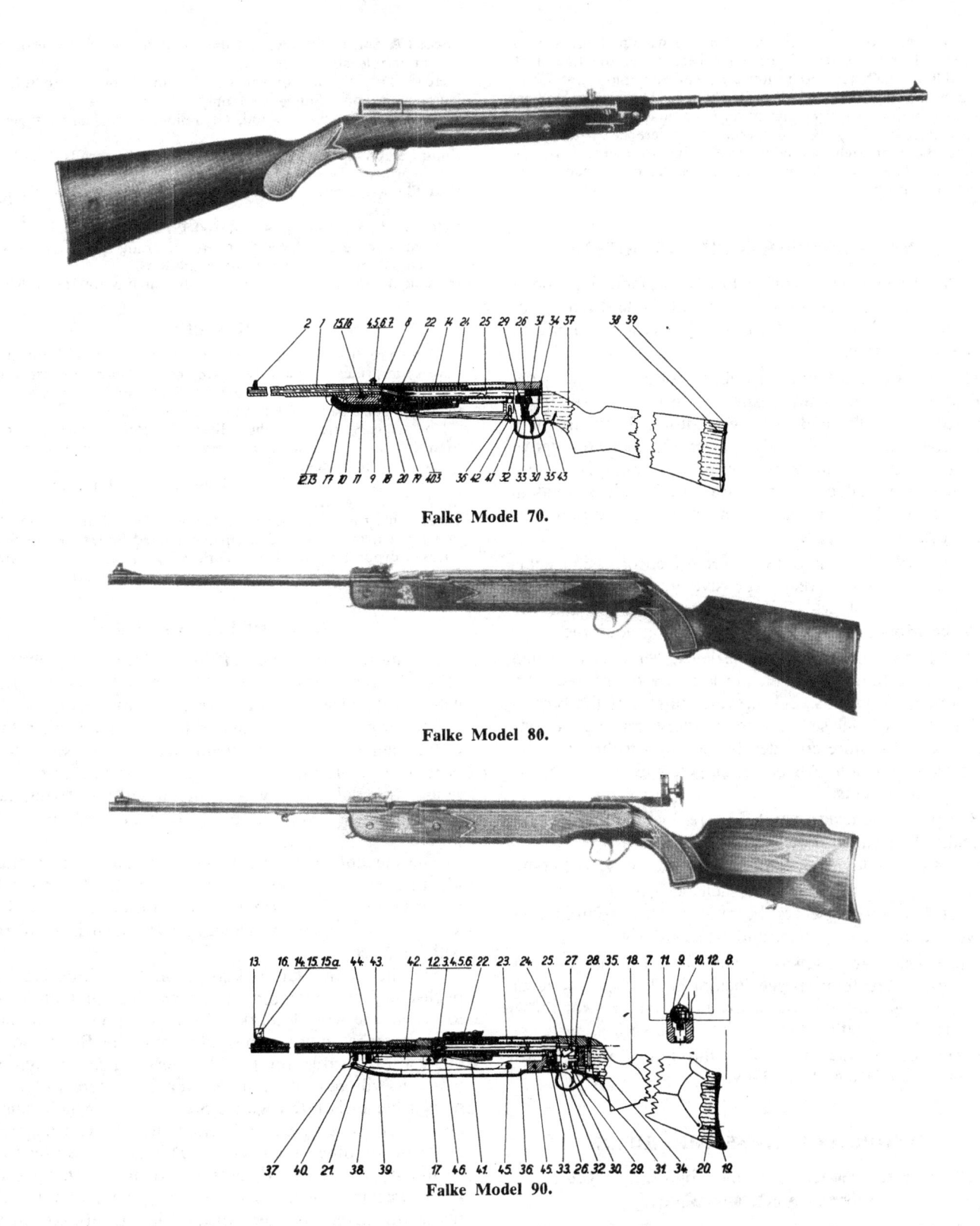

Falke Model 80.

Falke Model 90.

Velocity (Approximate): 600 f.p.s. (Note: No more powerful design made.)

Normal Accurate Range: Because of weight, power, and design, up to 50 meters. Twenty meters normal.

Normal Maximum Range: Stated to kill vermin at 60 yards. Light bullet limits maximum range.

REMARKS

There are no finer nor more powerful spring-air rifles made than these. Quality throughout is that of fine firearms manufacture. The new underlever-cocking system is similar to that of postwar B.S.A. In many air rifles, the piston is commonly hollow, the forward end of the compression spring being housed within it. In the common underlever pattern, the first lever is positioned below the barrel towards the muzzle and is designed to work on the actual cocking lever to push the piston back and compress the spring. In these designs (Falke), the starting lever and its release catch are placed well to the rear within the fore-end, preventing any muzzle heaviness. The distance between the lever fulcrum and the pivot of the second (cocking) lever is very short, resulting in a positioning wherein the piston is *pulled* rather than pushed into position for the sear to catch and hold it cocked.

137

M80 stocks are commonly of elm; M90 are walnut. Sling swivels are supplied and are actually of value because of the fine stock and bedding which tend to neutralize recoil, an important factor in match shooting with light air-rifle bullets. The sight combinations, as pictured, are very elaborate. Combinations are available for any degree of eyesight or shooting preference. The ability to slide the rear sight along prismatic fins to increase or decrease sight line is a valuable feature. The trigger is capable of the finest adjustment.

HERMANN WEIHRAUCH AIR RIFLES

H. Weihrauch was another firm manufacturing sporting and high-class small-bore rifles at Zella Mehlis before the war. Their new factory is in West Germany at Mellrichstadt, Bavaria.

The line of high-power air rifles produced by this organization are in many respects reminiscent of those produced by Falke and also by Walther. They are of a high order and of the utmost power for their respective systems. They are all of the barrel-cocking type. However the more effective ones are fitted with individual barrel-release locks instead of the usual spring-powered, cam-faced detent bolts.

Model HW35 is one of the lower-priced precision items in the line, but still very expensive in relation to most air rifles. Model 50 while differing very little mechanically from the Model 30 has additional sighting equipment.

Models 55S and 55M are the latest versions provided with positive barrel locks on the left side of the receiver. The actions in both cases, however, are still of the barrel-cocking variety. These rifles are all very massive in construction and require considerable strength to bring to the full-cocked position. All are equipped with good adjustable-trigger systems.

Except for the lever-operated barrel lock, all models are basically classical barrel-cocking designs.

The 55 models are very husky rifles with exceptionally large and powerful springs for such designs and are capable of fine target scores because of the combination of weight, balance, power, and trigger designs.

These rifles are shown in accompanying photos and drawings, where their special locking and trigger systems are clearly shown to afford pictorial comparisons for those interested in the detailed mechanics of the various systems.

Some models are obtainable through Stoeger Arms Corporation of New York City.

WEIHRAUCH HW55 AIR RIFLE

("M" Indicates Target Stock and Sights. "S" Indicates Sporting Stock and Sights)

Manufacturer: Hermann Weihrauch, Sportwaffen-fabrik, Mellrichstadt, Bayern (Bavaria), Germany.
U.S. Distributor: Stoeger Arms Corporation, New York City.
Overall Length: Approximately 43 inches.
Weight: 7 pounds approximately (varies with stock type).
Caliber(s): .177 (4.5-mm. or No. 1 British bore).
Type(s) of Ammunition Used: German .177 pellets (or equivalent British or U.S.).
Rifled: Yes.
Operating System: Spring-air. Barrel cocker.
Cocked & Spring Compressed By: Breaking barrel down on hinge after releasing barrel catch.
Loaded: Directly into breech when action is opened to full cock.
Number Rounds: Single shot only.
Stock Type: One-piece wood. Olympic sport or target types ("S" or "M").
Front Sight(s): Hooded ramp. Removable beads, blades, or apertures.
Rear Sight(s): Both adjustable barrel and removable receiver peep types.
Velocity (Approximate): About 500 f.p.s.
Normal Accurate Range: Standard air ranges, 10 to 20 yards. To 50 meters under some conditions.
Normal Maximum Range: Normal for high-power air rifle.

REMARKS

These are the highest priced and best of the Weihrauch line. Few better rifles of their type are made. Thumb-release breech-lock is easy to operate and efficient. Sight combinations are equal to any requirement of air match shooting.

The triggers used are the adjustable "Rekord" pattern, details of which may be seen in the drawings shown. There is no better trigger system made.

Materials, workmanship, and fits are all of the highest order in the higher grades.
(Note: This rifle with added explosive-gas attachment is marketed under the name "Barracuda" in the United States by the Stoeger Arms Corporation of New York City. The German name is "Barakuda." Gun is pictured and detailed herein.)

JUNG ROLAND RIFLES

During the early years of this century, high-power barrel-cocking air rifles were sold extensively in export, together with targets, under this trade appellation.

The original Jung Roland rifle was very similar to the Pulverman barrel cocker manufactured and sold for export by Fritz Langenhan. However this rifle in the 1909 model was sold only with a metal self-registering target and was extensively used in shooting galleries of the period.

The current postwar rifles of this make are practically identical with the common run of similar barrel-cocking air arms made in Germany. The stocks are streamlined. The arm is of medium accuracy and finish in conformity with its price.

The heavy model is known as the "Meisterschaftsbüchse." This "champion rifle" was the first of its type to reach the world market from West Germany under arrangements between the Allies and the Bonn Government. It is usable up to 50-meters range, though normally it will not be shot at over 20-meters range. The hinged barrel is fitted with a positive lock which must be pushed out of engagement before the rifle can be broken down on its hinge for cocking. This is in addition to the customary cam-faced detents found in the cheaper rifle. It also has an indicator showing when the action is cocked ready for firing. A steel piston ring is utilized instead of the typical leather washers, though the added efficiency may be subject to some question. Most manufacturers after trying the automotive-type steel pistons have reverted to leather washers as producing the better air seals. The piston in this design is operated by two pressure springs which are wound in opposite directions, thereby allowing the use of lighter springs than customary. This was a feature incorporated in many machineguns during the war by the German armed forces.

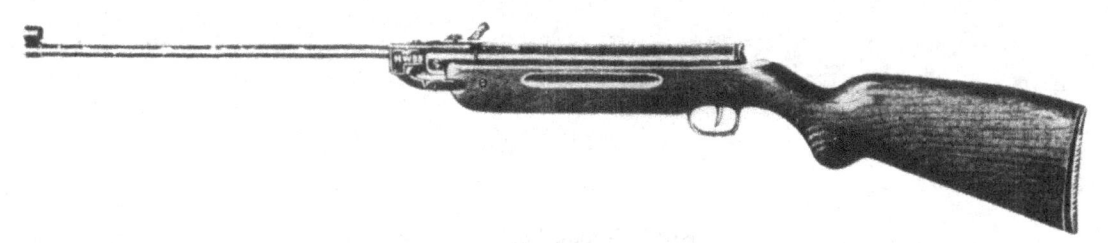

German Weihrauch standard M35 heavy-duty barrel cocker.

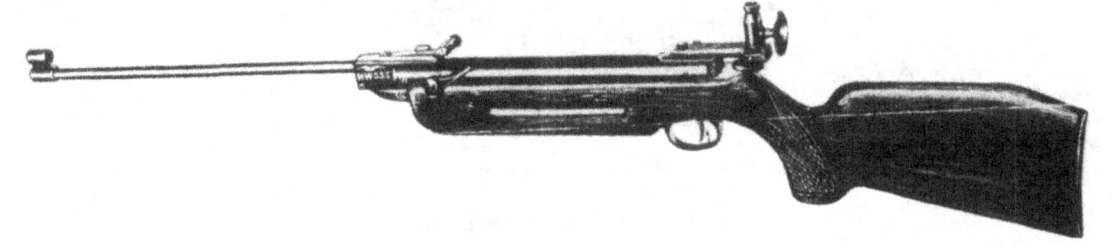

Weihrauch Model 55S.

Weihrauch Model 55M.

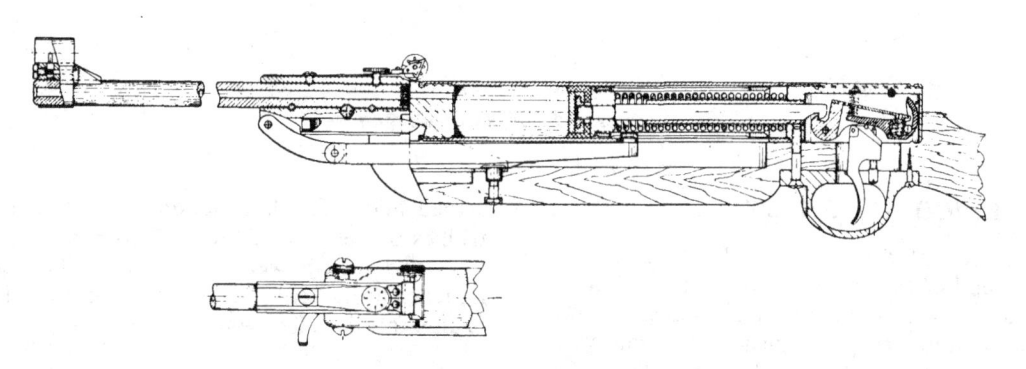

Weihrauch 55S and 55M gun is shown uncocked. Note special match trigger and sear. Top detail of locking bolt. This is a locked breech—not a detent type.

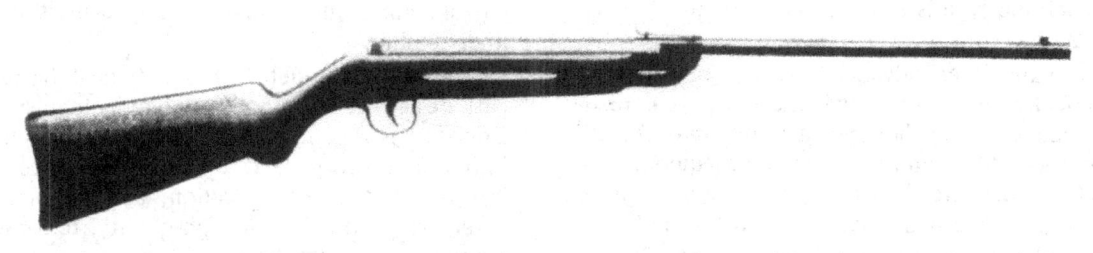

Jung Roland. Standard barrel-cocking design.

Krico air gun, Model LG1.

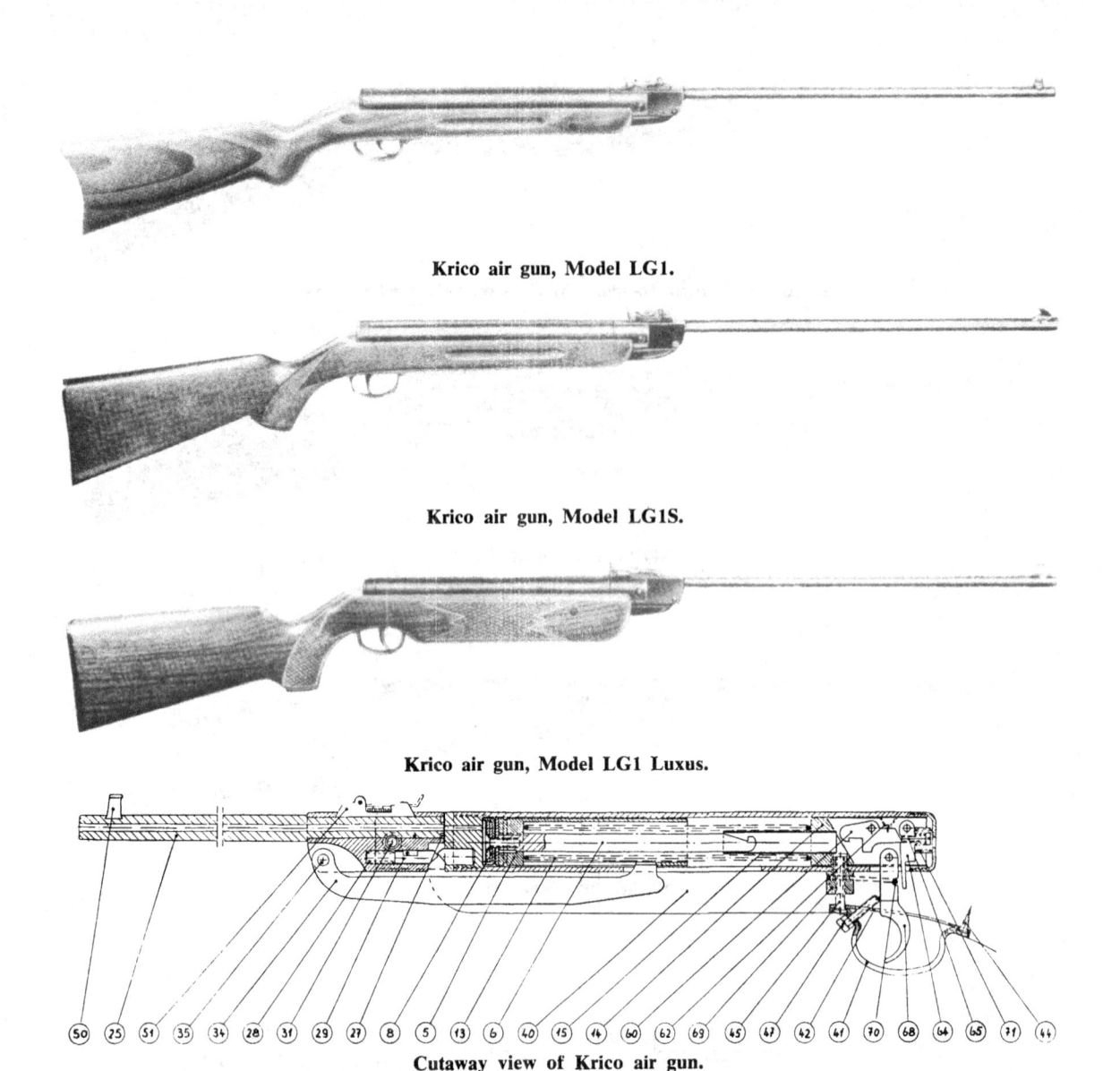

Krico air gun, Model LG1S.

Krico air gun, Model LG1 Luxus.

Cutaway view of Krico air gun.

KRICO AIR RIFLES

The Krico was one of the first air rifles to arrive on the market at the end of the war. Members of the American occupation forces who were shooting enthusiasts and were stationed near Stuttgart spent considerable time with the manufacturer of these rifles and many American soldiers overseas are thoroughly familiar with their uniformly fine quality.

The Krico appeared as the LG1 and the LG1S. These are sturdy barrel-cocking air rifles particularly noteworthy for the meticulous care in tempering parts and in finishing and fittting so that the rifles will give the utmost accuracy of which the type is capable. Calibers are standard .177 and .22.

The Krico-luxus is an advanced version of the same arm, mechanically being very much the same. It is made only in .177 caliber. It has however a heavy and specially fitted and finished stock, and better sighting equipment is available. These rifles are used today in certain 50-meter shooting contests in Germany according to the maker.

This firm today is also manufacturing a specially designed and built short-action Mauser to handle rifle cartridges of the type of the .222 Remington as well as other low- and high-power quality arms. The quality is maintained throughout. The manufacturer is Kriegeskorte Waffenfabrik, Hedelfingen, Stuttgart.

HEYM AIR RIFLES

The Heym factories were at Suhl before the war. This area is in the Russian Zone at this time and manufacture is now at Bayern in West Germany. While the Heym family has for generations been known primarily for fine custom guns, their name on any arm is a guarantee of high quality.

The Heym Model 100 is a typical barrel-cocking air rifle design. It has no particular distinguishing characteristics but is a good arm of its general classification. Entry into the air-arms field by Heym may be considered a "stop-gap" type of operation; as once again they have taken up production of high-quality, decorated rifles and guns on a custom basis.

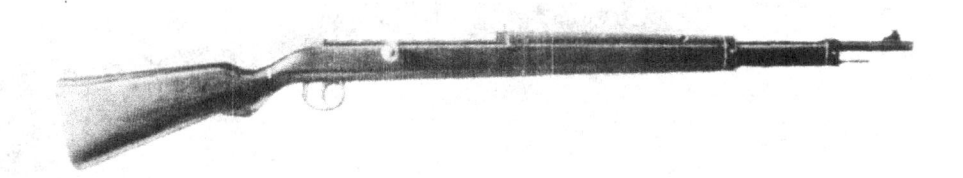

The Bonna repeating air rifle, Model 2.

THE BONNA REPEATING AIR RIFLE MODEL 2

This is another version of the rifles which resemble military design, operated by lifting and drawing back a bolt. Except that it is usable as a military trainer and has a large magazine capacity (75 precision balls), there is nothing unusual about the arm. Power is low and range short.

HAENEL AIR RIFLES

These arms are being distributed again through the firm of W. Schlumper of Dusseldorf.

As in prewar designs, the Haenels provide a line comparable to the Diana. That is to say, the various models accommodate all ages starting with the youngest and provide a continuous training group of air rifles preparatory to hunting or military-weapons handling. Some are toys. Some are precision arms.

The line of rifles manufactured includes the following:

Model X. This is a single-shot breakdown weapon of the toy variety for the youngest boys. It is of sheet-metal construction. This design has been widely copied throughout Europe and Japan.

Model XZA. This is second in the series. This type is of the more advanced breakdown construction with the barrel hinged further forward and operating through a lever. It has a wooden fore-end.

Models XX, XXX, and XXXX. These are all of the order of high-power barrel-cocking rifles resembling the early forms of the German and B.S.A. construction, in which the stock is attached to the action without benefit of a wooden fore-end. The designs, while unpleasing to the eye by modern standards, are efficient for low-cost types.

Model 45. This is an improved and heavier version of the earlier X models. It is a barrel-cocking rifle of the serious order.

The entire Haenel line listed above all represent pre-

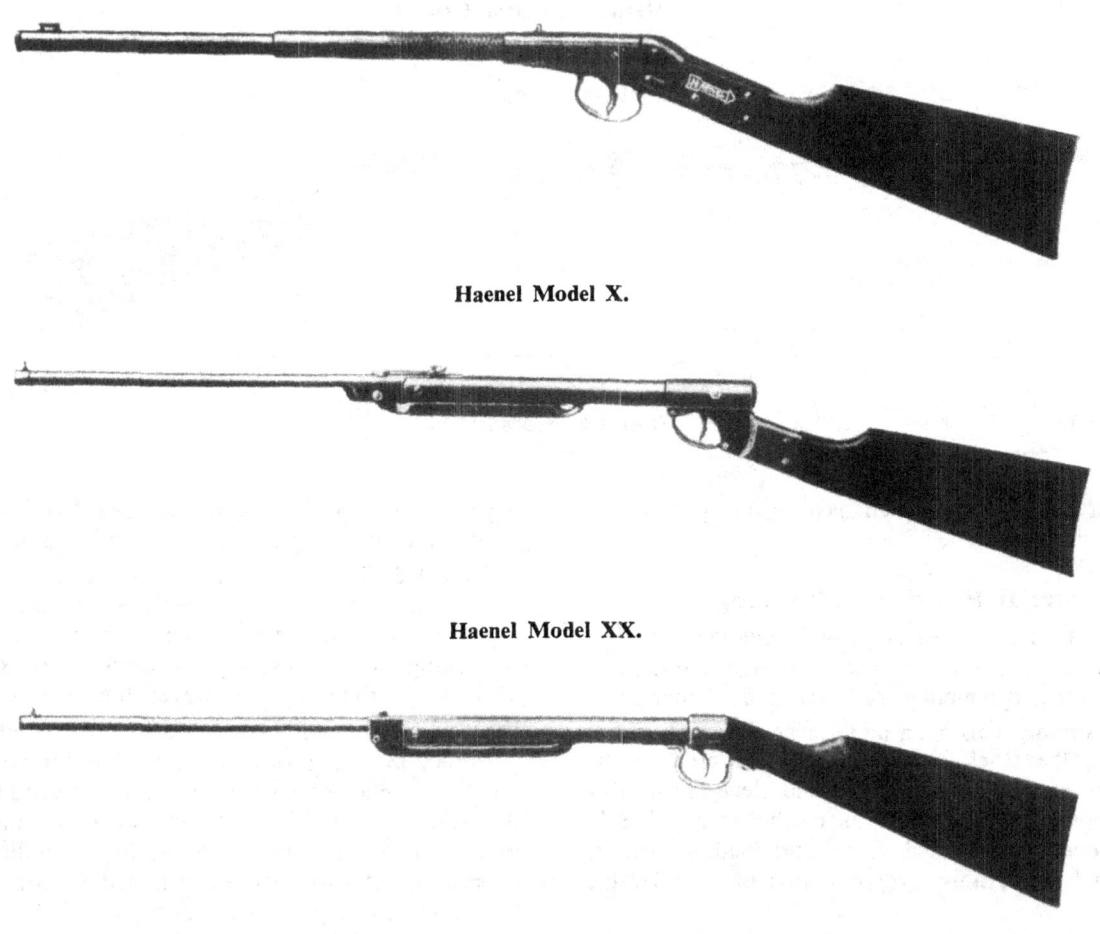

Haenel Model X.

Haenel Model XX.

Haenel Model 45.

Haenel New Model I.

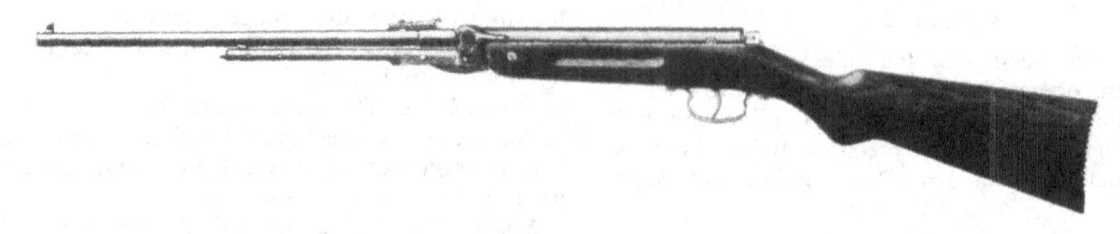

Haenel New Model V Junior.

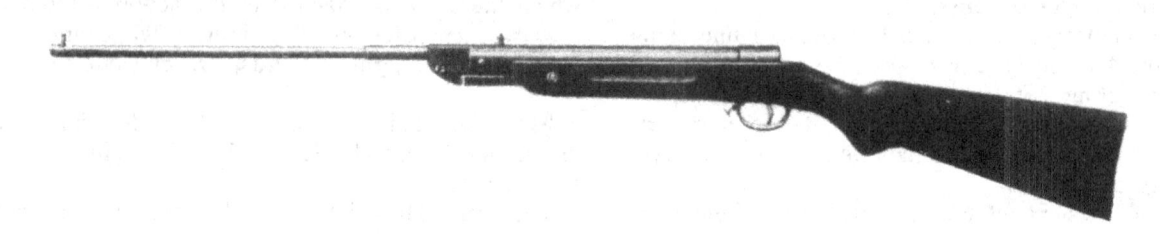

Haenel New Model II.

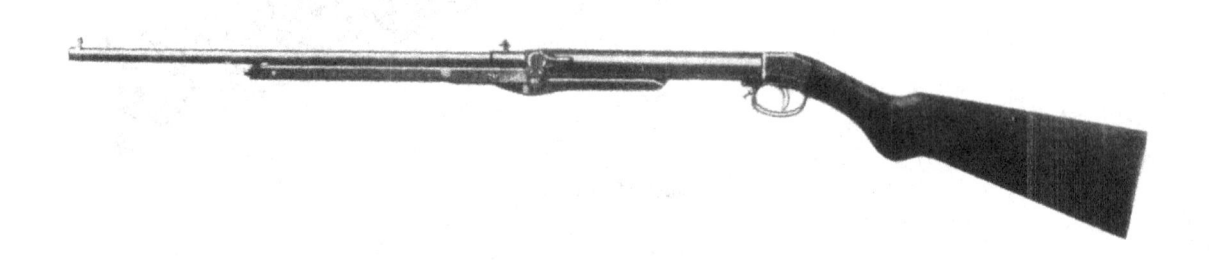

Haenel New Model IV.

war types of manufacture which have again appeared on the world export market.

Postwar II Haenel Air Rifle Designs

Model 1. This is an elementary barrel-cocking rifle. However as in most modern postwar design a one-piece stock is provided, the metalwork being housed therein.

Model V Junior. This is an underlever rifle of the same general type, the stock being the same as used in the Model 1, however. This leaves the underlever projecting forward beyond the stock line as in the earlier B.S.A. rifles. This design with fixed barrel and loading port or tap actuated by a turning lever is a rifle of considerable power.

Model 2. This is merely an improved form of the earlier Model 1 in this series. The basic improvement relates mostly to sights and to an adjustable trigger.

Model 5. This is a heavy-duty rifle of the underlever construction but again is a reversion to the early B.S.A. types in which the stock is an appendage to the end of the spring-compression tube. Underlever cocked, it has a standard loading port. However the rifle is well manufactured and is capable of good match shooting.

Model 33. This turn-bolt-action repeater, which is based on the Schmiesser patents, is again in production. Both this rifle and the 33 Junior are noted not only for their military lines and their relation to the military type of operation, but also for the fact that they carry their round bullets in *box* magazines (inserted from below in the rifle) instead of in the customary tubes or discs.

New Haenel Model 33.

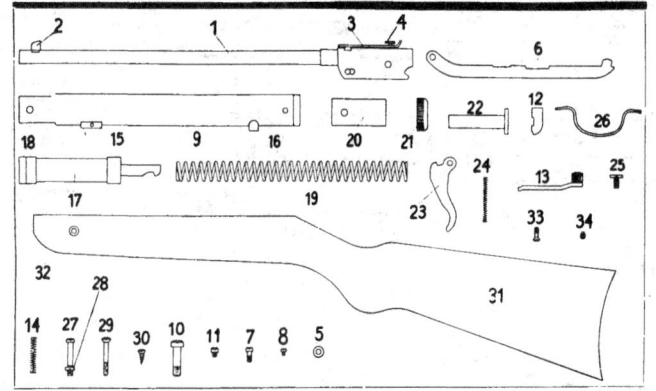

Haenel Model I.

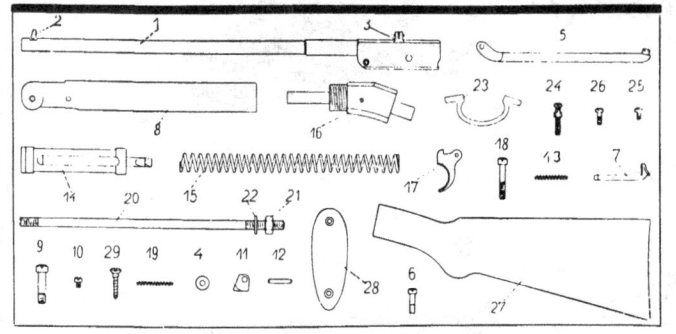

Haenel Model II.

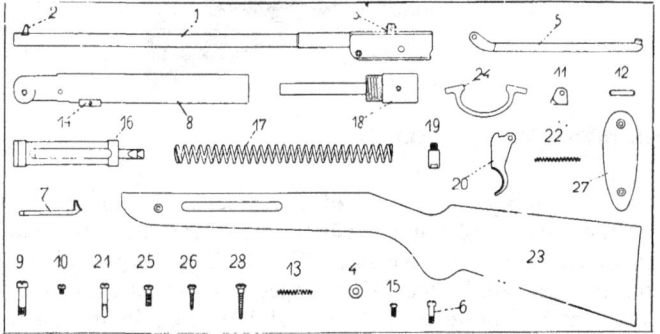

Haenel Model III.

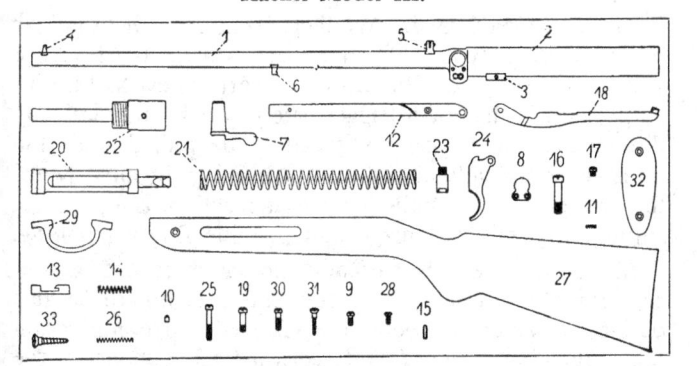

Haenel Model V.

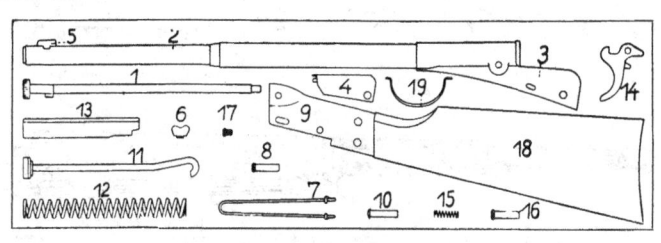

Haenel Model X.

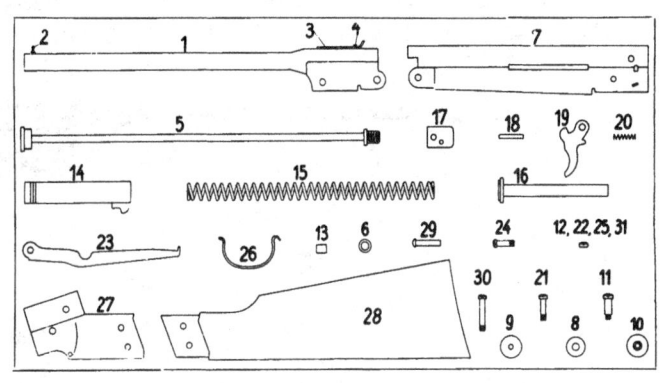

Haenel Model 15.

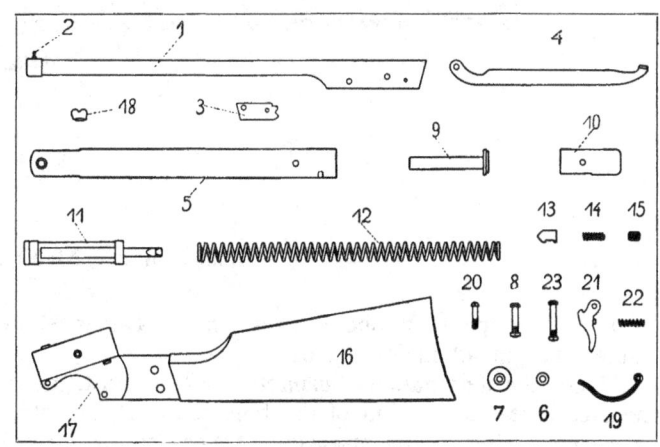

Haenel Model XX.

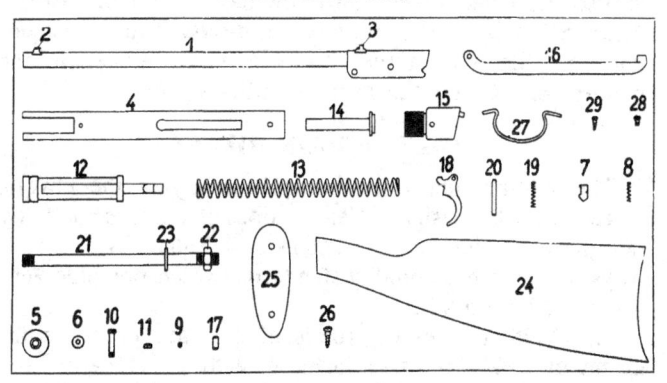

Haenel Model 45.

143

Haenel Model 33.

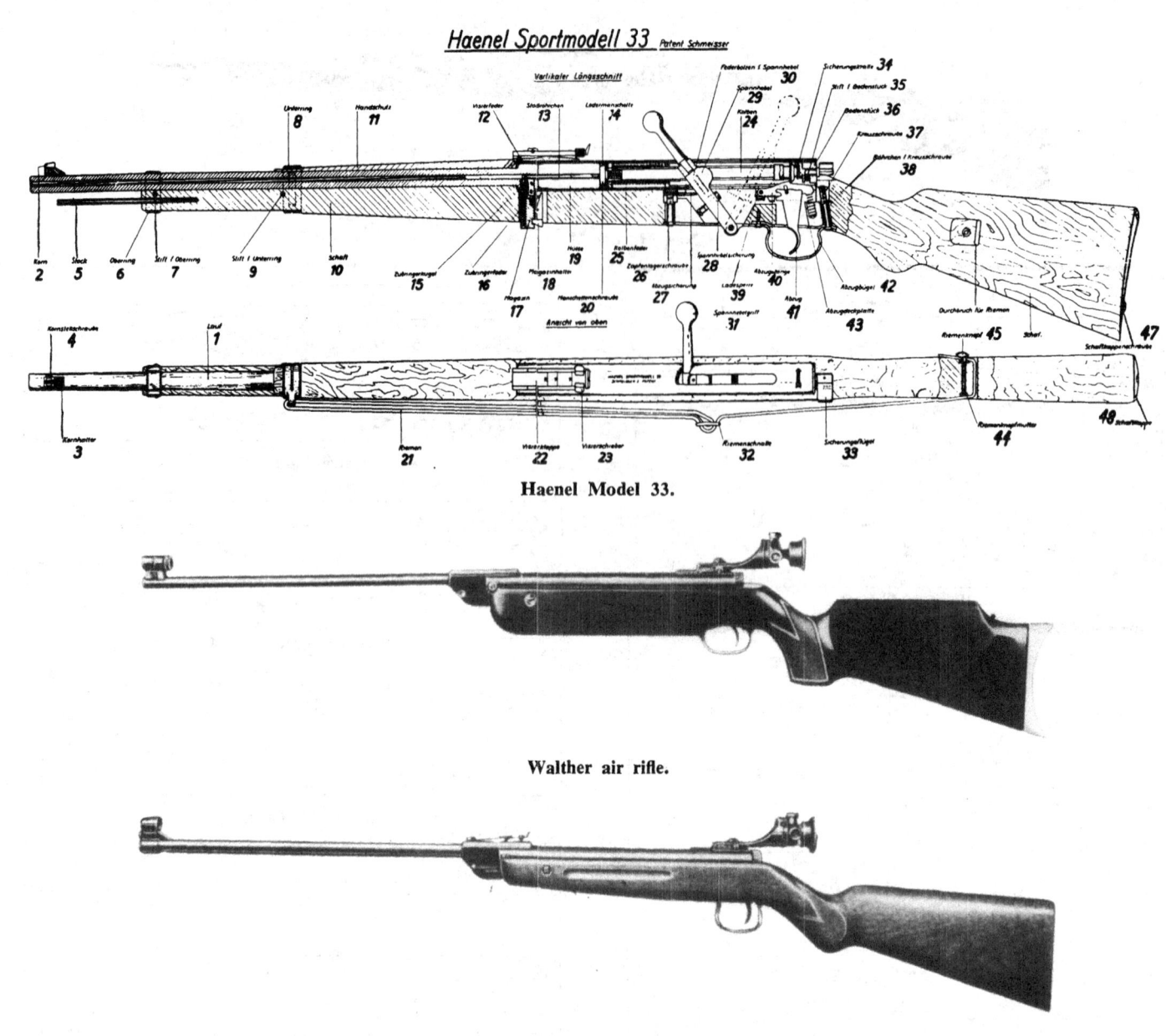

Walther air rifle.

Walther air rifle, Model LG53ZD, caliber .177 (4.5-mm.)

The accompanying photographs and drawings show these rifles in all major details.

Under the designation *Sportmodell 49,* a short, modified, carbine-type version of the bolt action is available, handling 6 slugs in its magazine. A very similar design is also marketed under the trade designation of "Blitz." These rifles have the military wing-type safety protruding from the rear of the rifle, which is operated in the manner of that on the Mauser military rifles.

WALTHER AIR RIFLES

The Walther line does not include any of the lowest-priced air rifle designs. Neither does it embrace the toy designs as in the case of Diana and Falke. Walther always works to high-quality standards, which preclude very low-priced products.

All Walther rifles regardless of cost are precision instruments and are manufactured with great care from the finest materials. Differences in price depend largely on the quality and types of the stocks and sights and on the amount of hand finishing and fitting, together with special triggers and the like. The basic quality is always the highest within the price range, however. In air rifles, Walther has adhered to classical barrel-cocking designs except for details.

Model LG51Z is the Walther version of the familiar barrel-cocking type with one-piece stock. Its leverage system is very good. The most noteworthy new feature incorporated is that of a trigger safety which automatically disconnects the trigger so it cannot be pulled until the barrel is completely closed ready for firing. In most types, the trigger can be pulled while the action is open, resulting in possible damage and possible finger pinching.

Model LG53ZD is basically the same as a 51Z, except for stock and sighting equipment as noted. In this design, however, is found the grooved top compression tube, allowing *forward and rearward* adjustment of the receiver sight. This has become a characteristic of the higher-priced sporting and target German air rifles, as it allows a maximum of individual sight adjustment for the shooter. (Note: Most serious air rifle shooting is by adults, many in age groups where special eye conditions exist.)

The Model 53M or Marksman rifle is still a further advance of the 53ZD design. Again the differences are principally in refinements such as fine stocks and in the sighting equipment provided.

The added quality of the Walther is discernible only on actual examination in comparison with other models. In addition to such new technical developments as the

It must be noted that this design does NOT lend itself to *feeding* the Diabolo type of 4.5-mm. pellet. However, if the magazine is removed and is replaced with a special device provided therefor, (a blank head), Diabolo pellets may be used in standard single-shot fashion, inserting each one directly into the firing chamber before closing the action ready to shoot.

All these rifles have excellent set triggers, which are adjustable from below. To prevent casual tinkering with trigger adjustments (something which nearly every novice tries when handling a new rifle not his own!) the trigger on this model can be adjusted only by first removing the

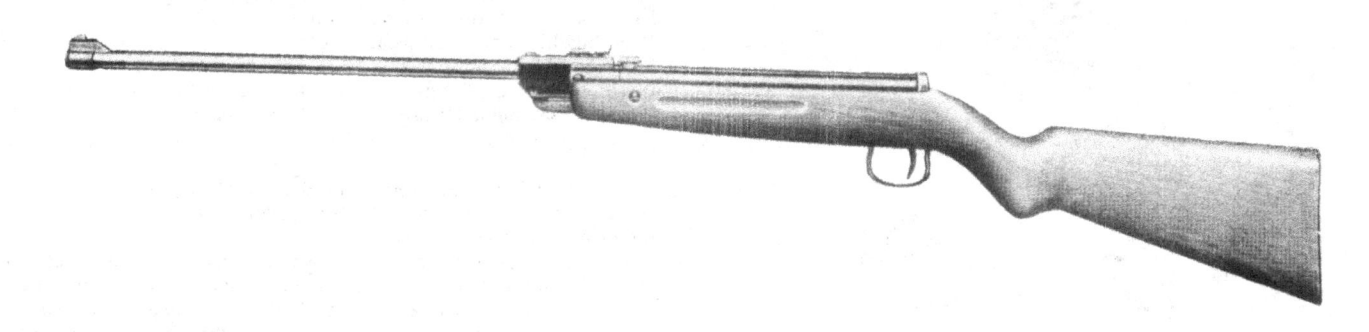

Walther magazine air rifle, Model LG54MG, caliber .177 (4.5-mm.).

special trigger safety-lock, the matter of special precision sights has been given particular attention by this firm.

The photographs and drawings herewith detail many of the highlights of the unusual features of this fine line of air rifles. The sighting equipment available for the higher-priced models permits the enthusiast to get the most out of the accuracy factors built into these Walther air rifles.

New Walther Magazine Air Rifles

Walther has introduced an improved repeater magazine in the Model LG54, where it is applied to the barrel-cocking type of air rifle.

While simple, it is quite efficient and makes it unnecessary to individually load the small 4.5-mm. round balls into the rifle.

In essence, it is a small circular magazine into which 5 round bullets are inserted and forced into place against spring pressure. The circular magazine has a *plexiglass top,* which shows at all times the number of bullets contained therein. This is a decided advance over any similar device thus far to be marketed. Earlier repeaters have been notorious for accidental firing due to inability of the shooter to check the magazine loads easily and visually.

There are flanges on the sides of the magazine which are fitted into corresponding slots in the top of the rifle and the magazine is then turned to the right to lock.

When the barrel is turned down to cock the gun and compress the firing spring, the first ball from the magazine falls automatically into place. As the gun is closed ready for firing, the magazine is in position to await the next opening movement, when it will again feed a ball into the firing chamber.

rifle mechanism from the stock.

The accompanying data sheets and photographs give a good general understanding of the appearance and construction of these arms; but only an examination of the arms themselves can disclose the real craftsmanship involved.

WALTHER LG55M, MASTER AIR RIFLE MODEL
(Walther Best Grade)

Manufacturer: Carl Walther Sportwaffen-fabrik, Ulm, Donau, Germany.
U.S. Distributor: International Armament Corporation, Washington, D. C. (Note: Air arms to order. Not stocked.)
Overall Length: 41 inches.
Weight: 9 pounds approximately. (Sights and stock, beech or walnut, alter weight.)
Caliber(s): .177 (4.5-mm. or No. 1 bore). This is the match caliber.
Type(s) of Ammunition Used: .177 German precision pellets (or British or U.S. equal).
Rifled: Yes. Walther small-bore precision rifling.
Operating System: Spring-air. Barrel cocker.
Cocked & Spring Compressed By: Breaking down barrel in classical fashion.
Loaded: Directly into breech of barrel when action is open and cocked.
Number Rounds: Single shot only.
Stock Type: Heavy Olympia design. Checkered pistol grip. Target butt plate.
Front Sight(s): Hooded front. Three interchangeable insert sights.
Rear Sight(s): On rear of barrel, or special receiver micrometer.
Velocity (Approximate): 550 f.p.s.
Normal Accurate Range: Standard air ranges.
Normal Maximum Range: Normal for this design.

REMARKS

The Walther name is always a guarantee of the finest materials and craftsmanship. Only really new feature is the trigger

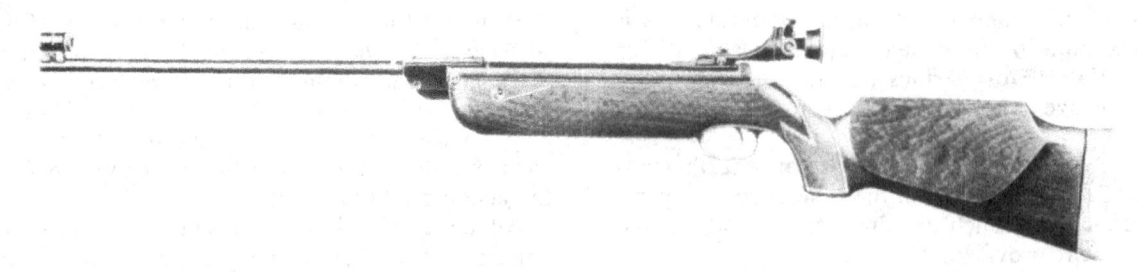

Walther master air rifle, Model LG55M, caliber .177 (4.5-mm.).

Front sight base and sight protector for Model LG55.

Post front sight and aperture for Model LG55M.

Hensoldt-optic
peep-sight disc with adjustable aperture
and Zeiss-Umbral or Uropol filters.

block which prevents firing unless gun is closed. This is seldom found in air rifles. Special attention has been paid to providing optical sights for those desiring them. Excellent trigger system, adjustable.

The barrel-cocking system has been in use so long that improvements which can be made are very few indeed. The test of superiority, therefore, lies in the materials and workmanship and the accuracy provided. In the observation of the author, Walther has no superior judged by these standards, though shooters may prefer other good makes because of personal preferences in stock, sight, or operating designs.

WALTHER LG54MG (MAGAZINE) MODEL AIR RIFLE

Manufacturer: Carl Walther Sportwaffen-fabrik, Ulm, Donau, Germany.
Overall Length: 41 inches.
Weight: 6 pounds approximately.
Caliber(s): .177 (4.5-mm. or No. 1 bore). (German match caliber.)
Type(s) of Ammunition Used: 4.5-mm. round shot only in magazine. Diabolo for single shot. .177 German precision Diabolo-type pellets or equal.
Rifled: Yes. Walther quality rifling.
Operating System: Spring-air. Barrel cocker.
Cocked & Spring Compressed By: Breaking barrel down on its hinge, standard procedure.

Loaded: See magazine-loading data below. .177 Diabolos may be singly loaded only.
Number Rounds: Magazine, 5 round balls. Will not feed Diabolos.
Stock Type: Conventional one-piece with pistol grip.
Front Sight(s): Front post on ramp.
Rear Sight(s): Screw adjustable rear.
Velocity (Approximate): 450 f.p.s.
Normal Accurate Range: Average for type.
Normal Maximum Range: Standard for type.

REMARKS

This model was evolved from the LG51 Series. As a single-loader it is a conventional barrel cocker, but of Walther manufacturing quality in its price range.

Its magazine feature is an advance over previous similar (Haenel-type) systems. The detachable magazine is circular with a plexiglass top which allows checking the number of rounds at a glance. Five round balls are inserted through the underside against spring opposition. There are flanges on the underside of the magazine to engage in mating cuts in the receiver top to rear of breech. The magazine is slid in and turned to lock. Each time the rifle is cocked the magazine spring brings a ball into loading position and it is fed into the breech by gravity. Note that the device will NOT feed waisted (Diabolo-type) pellets. By removing the magazine and installing a blank filler, it is possible to use the rifle as a standard single-shot type, feeding in waisted pellets in customary single-shot fashion.

WAGRIA AIR RIFLES

This line of moderate-priced high-power air rifles is based entirely on the barrel-cocking principle.

In addition to the Wagria-Standard Models *M50* and *M56,* the following designs are also currently manufactured:

Scout Model M55. This is intended for children. The caliber is 4.5-mm., the barrel is smooth bore. Either pellets or darts may be used in this design. The rear sight is adjustable and the trigger is of the two-stage military type. The rifle has a beech stock. The overall length is 39 inches. The weight is about 4 pounds.

Aero-Sport Model M58. This has the same type of action but is built of heavier components. It, too, will shoot either pellets or darts. Its overall length is 41 inches. Its weight is about 6¾ pounds. Model M59 of the same design is in the standard 5.5-mm. (.22) caliber.

Wagria-Rapid. This is a barrel-cocking design known as the "160." The caliber is 4.45-mm. round pellets. The magazine holds 10 of the round shot. At each breakdown of the rifle barrel for cocking, a pellet drops into the chamber so long as there are any left in the magazine. This rifle is of a type commonly used in shooting galleries in Germany where powder rifles are not normally permitted.

The Wagria-Rapid Model M61, also in caliber 4.45-mm. for round balls, is fitted with a 50-shot magazine.

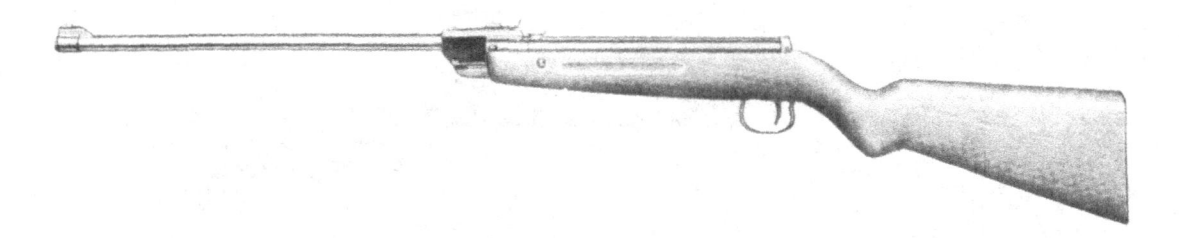

Walther LG54MG Model.

While used in shooting galleries also, it is a favorite for outdoor club shooting at close ranges. The length is about 39 inches; the weight about 5.25 pounds. This entire line of rifles may be obtained with smooth barrels or rifled barrels as specified. Using darts in the rifled barrel is likely to injure the rifling very quickly as we have already pointed out.

The Wagria line is manufactured by Maschinen und Appartebau, G.m.b.H., "Wagria," Ascherberg, Holstein.

WISCHO AIR ARMS

None of these rifles are of the toy variety. In all designs they are well constructed and have considerable power. Most, however, are standard barrel-cocking types.

In addition to the standard Model L60, a break-down type in both .177 and .22 calibers, which is 40 inches overall and weighs about 6¼ pounds, the following are offered:

The Media. This rifle is a medium-weight design incorporating the quality design of the Model L60 with that of the stock and general weight of the Junior types.

It, too, is of the barrel-cocking variety. The length is about 38 inches. The weight is 5½ pounds.

The Junior. Caliber again is .177 or 4.5-mm. The design and construction is similar to the other Wischo barrel-cocking rifles, except that it is lighter and not as powerful, being intended for youth training.

In addition to the above, the Wischo line has recently added two powerful underlever-cocking rifles with mechanisms reminiscent of the Webley Mark III.

These are identical except for the stocks and sights. The operation is by movement of an underlever extending forward of the fore-end below the barrel. These are solid fixed-barrel rifles, with loading taps to feed a pellet directly into the breech. These rifles all use the standard Diabolo type of pellet. This manufacturer incidentally also supplies his own pellets in the standard .177 and .22 calibers.

These rifles (and also air pistols of barrel-cocking design) are manufactured by "Wischo" K. G., Wilsker & Co., Erlangen.

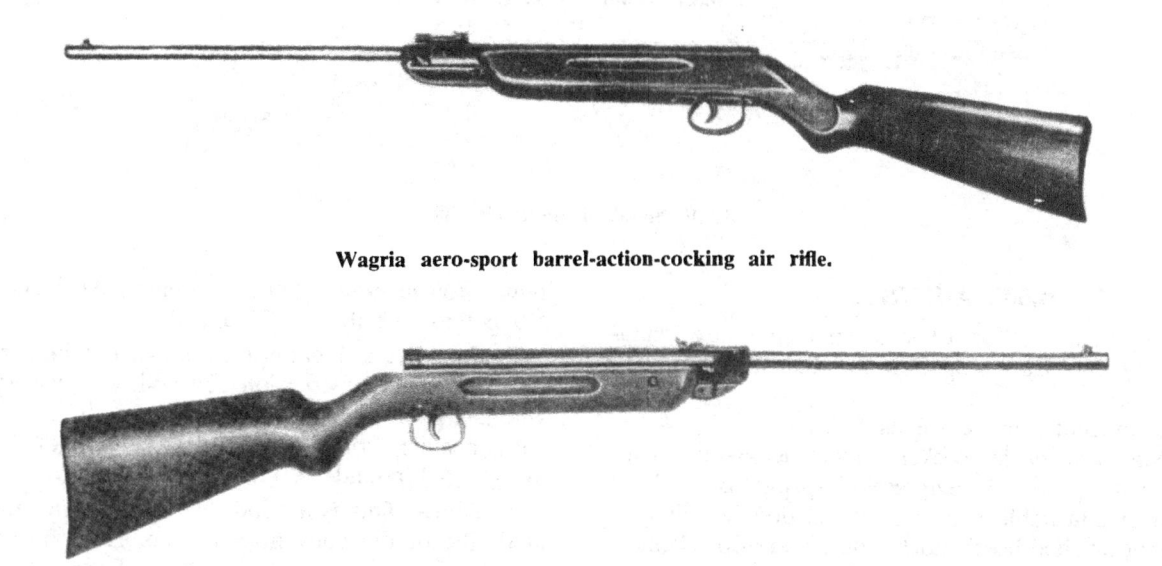

Wagria aero-sport barrel-action-cocking air rifle.

Media Wischo air rifle, caliber 4.5-mm.

Wischo German heavy-duty underlever match rifles.

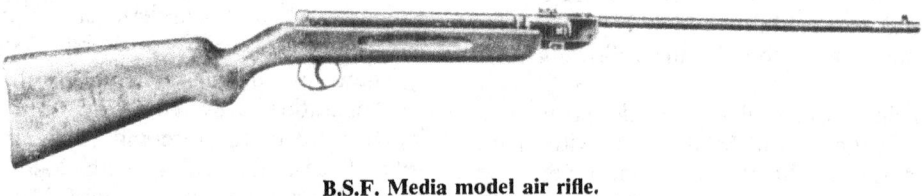

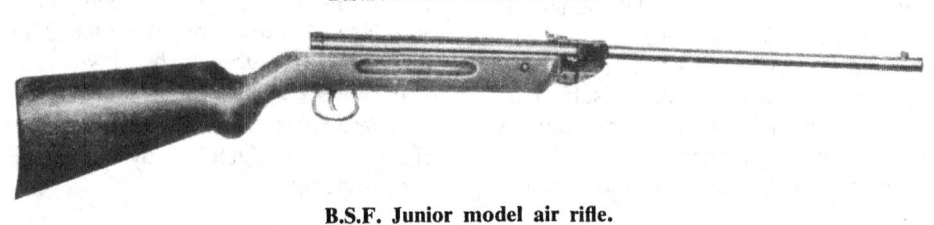

B.S.F. Model S60 air rifle.

B.S.F. Media model air rifle.

B.S.F. Junior model air rifle.

B.S.F. Standard model air rifle.

B.S.F. AIR RIFLES

These rifles, as well as a line of air pistols, are manufactured by the Bayer Sportswaffen-Fabrik, G.m.b.H., at Erlangen.

Models currently made are as follows:

S60. Standard barrel cocker. Good heavy-duty construction with powerful compression spring. Bead front sight, barrel adjustable rear. Adjustable double-pull trigger. Walnut finished beech stock with pistol grip. Calibers .177 and .22. Length 44 inches. Weight 6.6 pounds.

Media. Lighter-weight version of above with lower power for teen-age shooters. Length 41 inches. Weight 5.9 pounds. Calibers .177 and .22.

Junior. General pattern as above but lighter and still less powerful construction for still younger age groups who do not have the strength to easily cock the guns with heavier compression springs. Length 39 inches. Weight 4.4 pounds. Caliber .177 only.

Standard. This is a good, heavy-duty, *underlever*-operated rifle of the conventional type. Has powerful spring and cocking leverage. Loading tap at breech. Fixed barrel. Adjustable trigger. Special sliding-type rear sight on bar-

B.S.F. Bayern model air rifle.

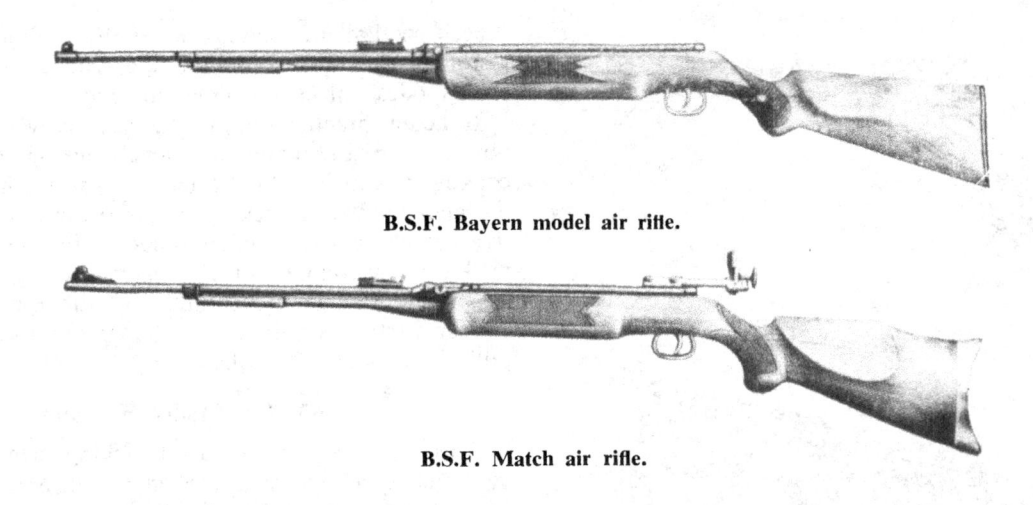

B.S.F. Match air rifle.

rel. Walnut finished pistol-grip stock. Calibers .177 and .22. Length 45 inches. Weight 7.4 pounds.

Bayern. This is the same as the STANDARD above mechanically. It has a good walnut stock, checkered, and a Bavarian-type cheekpiece. Rear sight may be micrometer peep. Weight 7.92 pounds. Length 46 inches.

Match. Mechanically the same as above underlevers. Heavy walnut stock of Swiss target design with target butt plate. Has interchangeable front sights, barrel rear and in addition removable receiver micrometer peep combination. Length 47 inches. Weight 8.36 pounds. This model is built specially for match shooting as done in air rifle matches in Germany and Switzerland, and is an excellent rifle of its type in all respects.

They are not currently available in the United States.

CURRENT GERMAN SPRING-AIR PISTOLS

Several manufacturers in Germany are making low-priced smooth-bore single-shot "toy" air pistols comparable in general to the American Daisy. These may be used with either 4.5-mm. air-rifle shot or with darts in some instances. While they are not serious arms from the standpoint of either velocity or accuracy, they do have certain pre-training value and use for parlor games, and do fall therefore into the general classification of spring-air arms.

The Diana Model 2 pistol system consists of a barrel and compression spring so mounted within the tubular receiver that when pushed back it telescopes within the receiver. Pulling the trigger drives the barrel ahead to its forward limit. In the Daisy equivalent, cocking is by pushing back the barrel, but there is no telescoping action. The barrel is spring-returned when cocking pressure is released. On trigger release, only the internal piston moves ahead.

The Heym, the H. S. Luftpistole, the J.G.A. (for J. G. Anschutz, noted small-arms maker), and the Koma LDP 3 are other varieties of this type of low-priced pistol. Koma Model 4 is a better version with a barrel-break cocking system.

B.S.F. Pistol

These are all very simple and sturdy versions of the B.S.F. barrel-cocking rifle. The receiver is welded to the spring tube. The barrel, in turn, together with its cocking lever, operates off the front of the compression-spring tube as in common barrel-cocking air rifles. Barrels are all held closed by spring detents. Breaking the barrel down on its hinge forces the attached cocking lever to thrust the piston back in the compression tube and compress the piston spring. The pellet is loaded directly into the barrel breech and the barrel snapped shut. The "knee action" cocking lever has a double cam action which eases cocking considerably over some other types. Standard model is the S20, with overall length of 14 inches, weight 2.4 pounds, caliber .177, and a rifled barrel. The "Match" model is the same except for the addition of a good micrometer receiver sight on a tube extension, which adds 1 inch to the length and a few ounces to the weight.

The pistol is provided with a sear and a trigger adjusting screw which permits excellent pull. Because of the design, the line of sight is exceptionally good. The adjustable rear sight is attached to the top of compression tube at the rear extremity of the pistol. Power, as in all such designs, is adequate for good target shooting at ranges up to about 40 feet. Quality and finish are good. This is a serious target type, not to be confused with the toy varieties.

(Note: In tests by the author, the B.S.F. with H&N pellets gave higher velocity than any other pellet pistol regardless of make or firing system.)

Diana No. 5 Pistol

This pistol is the Diana version of the serious target air pistol. Basically it is merely a pistol variety of Diana's form of barrel-cocking rifle. It has its spring, compression

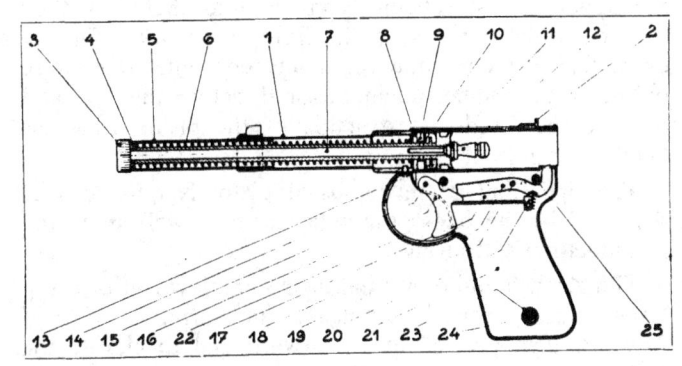

German B.S.F. air pistol. A very high-power (relatively) barrel cocker. This is actually a modern spring-air rifle cut down to large pistol size. The barrel is held closed by a heavy spring detent. When it has been started open, the actual cocking action is reasonably easy for the power involved because of the excellent leverage system. This is a highly accurate pistol. In comparative tests it consistently showed a higher velocity than any air pistol made, domestic or foreign.

chamber, and piston in the tube above the receiver, the barrel being hinged at the forward end of the tube and broken down for cocking and spring compression in standard fashion. Note that this differs radically from the Haenel system which it superficially resembles.

The breech is held closed by powerful spring-supported wedges, which serve as detents in standard fashion.

Firing contact is from trigger to sear, a screw adjustment being incorporated. Like all Diana products, it is a good value in its class. Caliber .177, rifled.

The EM-GE "Zenit" Pistol

This design was a product of Moritz and Gerstenberger Waffenfabrik at Zella Mehlis before the war. This area in Thuringia is now in Russian zone. Some of these pistols are apparently still being manufactured there, as they are appearing at times on the European market. In any event this pistol is quite commonly encountered because of the large numbers manufactured before the war and because the sturdy construction of the pistol itself has kept thousands of them in use.

The operation of this unusual pistol is quite clearly disclosed by the photographs herewith as well as by the manufacturer's drawing.

The Zenit is quite unusual in the employment of a top lever which is raised to unlock. The barrel is first slid forward, then pivoted at its forward end to elevate the breech section for loading, while the cocking spring and piston in the tube section to the rear of the barrel are forced back through compound levers.

In actual practice the pistol gives relatively little higher power than the common barrel-cocking type, though cocking is considerably easier. It is superior to many of the cheaper barrel-cocking types however in that a positive breech seal is definitely effected by the forward and backward movement of the barrel during actuation to open and close the breech and cock the arm. The trigger-to-sear contact is quite good, allowing an excellent trigger pull. Caliber is .177, rifled.

EM-GE Model Herkules

This pistol is also a barrel-cocking arm of the conventional type, the compression spring and piston being housed in a tube above the line of the stock, with the barrel hinged at the forward end of the tube extension.

The breech is held closed by the conventional sliding spring-impelled wedges forming a detent which must be overcome by downward pressure on the barrel in order to elevate the rear breech section for loading and to thrust the pivoted lever back to cock the piston and spring within the tube. The sear and trigger contact is such as to afford a reasonably good trigger pull, but the sight line is short, the rear sight being mounted conventionally above the barrel breech. Caliber is .177, rifled.

The Falke Model 33

This pistol has much in common in external lines and to a certain extent in design with the EM-GE Zenit.

It differs however in that while the barrel elevates for loading, and spring compression and cocking is effected through levers, actuation here is by a *triggerguard* lever.

The Zenit had a top lever which was rather unsightly and could be a point of trouble because of its exposure. The Falke utilizes the triggerguard, forming also the front-end grip section of the butt as in the British Abas-Major. A catch is provided at the toe of the butt. When released it permits the triggerguard lever, which is pivoted full forward at the front end of the receiver section, to raise the barrel and operate the lever to compress the spring for firing. An exceptionally long and well-pivoted sear allows very good trigger pull in this design. The rear sight is also better positioned than in the EM-GE as a result of the design. The power however is not materially greater than that in the elementary barrel-cocking designs, though

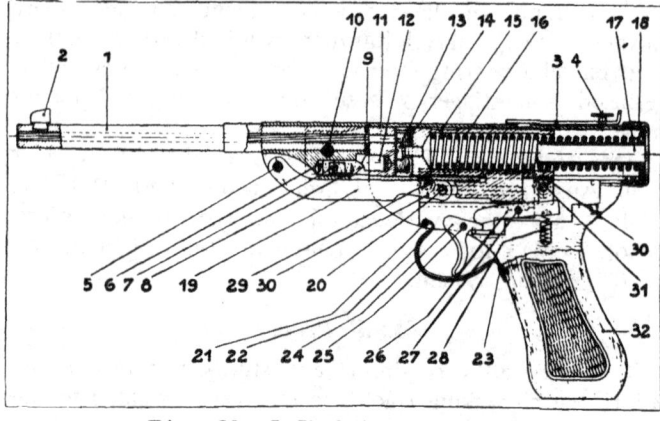

Diana No. 5. Typical barrel cocker.

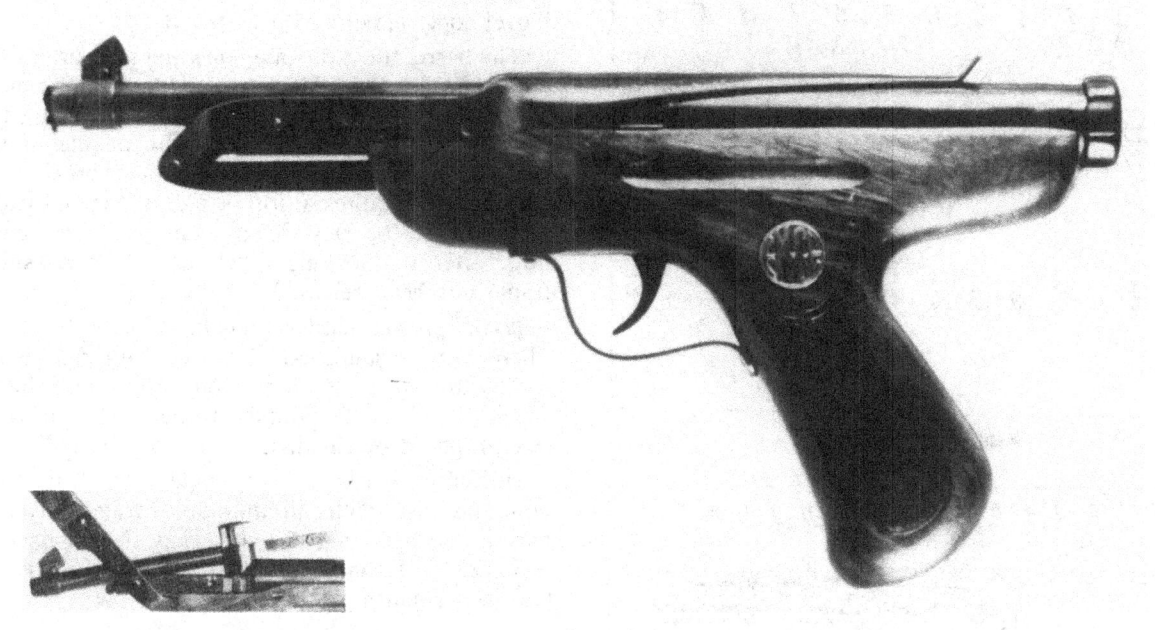

German EM-GE (for Moritz and Gerstenberger) single-shot Zenit, spannhebel air pistol. Was made both rifled and smooth bored, caliber .177. (Note: A modification of this pistol, the Krone model, had a top magazine holding 10 pellets. Except for the feed mechanism, the models are the same. Insert is Krone repeater.)

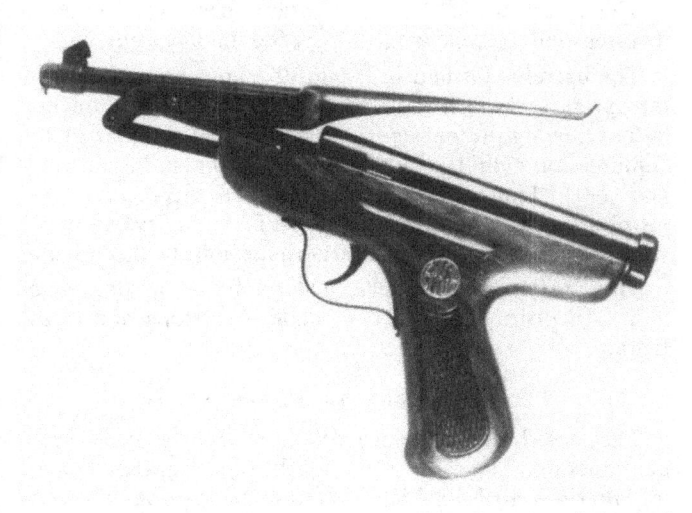

German Zenit by EM-GE. Lifting lever moves barrel forward away from breech washer, thus breaking the hermetic seal. Continued lever lift elevates barrel breech for loading.

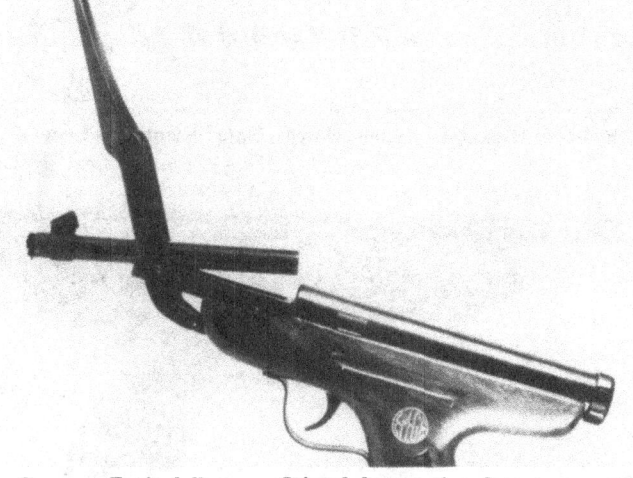

German Zenit full open. Jointed knee-action levers compress the powerful mainspring and cock the piston (or plunger) in the compression tube as lever on top is raised. Note that tip of cocking lever forms the rear sight.

the breech closure is much more positive and likely to hold air very much longer without attention to washers or seals.

An important feature of the gun's design is that the trigger is disconnected when the cocking lever is being actuated, thereby preventing injury to the fingers by the lever flying back or causing a disturbance through discharge of the air during the period of compression while the arm is open for loading. Caliber is .177. Barrels may be either smooth bore to shoot darts and .177 pellets, or precision-rifled for pellets only, giving maximum accuracy.

Haenel Air Pistols

While manufacture of this brand name is controlled in the Russian Zone, some models of the prewar pistols are again in distribution in Europe. These include the Model 100, a cheap 100-shot smooth-bore toy-type pistol; also the Models 26 and 28 DRP of the barrel-cocking serious variety.

The prewar Haenel repeating pistol is not however in production.

Haenel Model 28 Air Pistol

It will be noted that the design in appearance is a general approach to that of the external lines and balance of the German Luger, which was the official pistol of the German armed forces when this Haenel was introduced.

This design differs radically from most of the other air pistols. The barrel itself is conventionally hinged to the frame. The action of opening it to load, however, is in no way connected with the cocking and compression

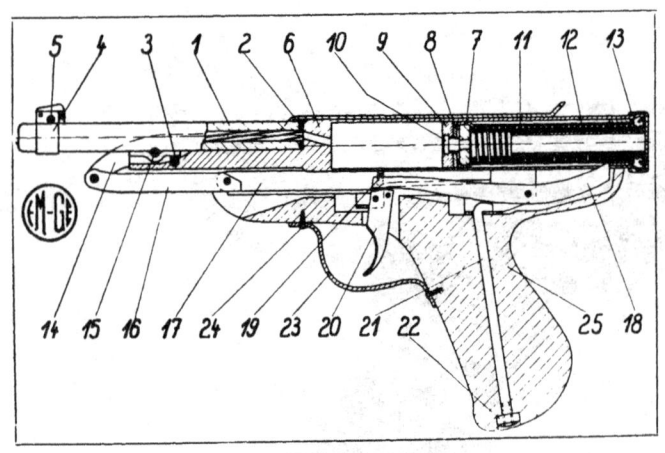

Zenit pistol cocked.

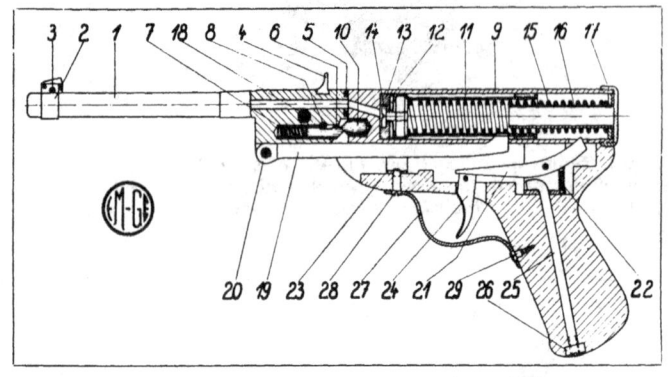

EM-GE Herkules. Action closed. Note detent-bolt system.

The Falke Model 33.

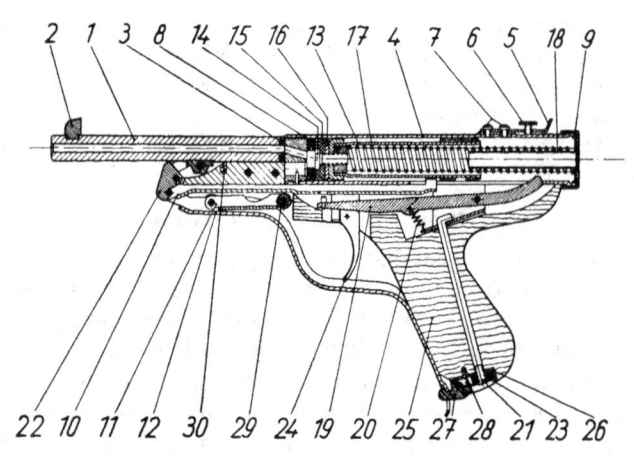

German Falke pistol. Action closed. Uncocked.

of the spring and valve as in common forms of breakdown barrel construction, such as the B.S.F.

The barrel turns down against the pressure of the spring detent for loading. This action does NOT compress the spring for operating the piston and for cocking the pistol. This is accomplished by using the handle of the pistol as a lever and requires a separate "breaking" action. This in turn requires a firm grip on the cylindrical receiver section while bearing down with the other hand on the butt, after the locking catch on the right side of the frame has been released.

As in prewar models, the barrel is 4.25 inches long. There are 12 lands and grooves with right-hand twist; widths are equal. Rifling is one turn in 18 inches. The weight is about 2 pounds 6 ounces. Barrels may be smooth-bored or rifled. Calibers may be .177 or .22.

Haenel pistols have been made with all-steel construction and also with all-aluminum frame, receiver, and barrel, and brass barrel liner. They do not have the ease of cocking of some other designs. Velocity is relatively low. Workmanship is good.

The J.G.A. Air Pistol

This pistol, while of the toy variety, has several unusual features and is somewhat surprising in its accuracy.

The barrel is pushed back into the housing to compress the spring to furnish the air power. The breech is opened by unscrewing the projecting lock screw at the rear of the compression cylinder. A pellet or a dart may be inserted, and the locking screw is then returned to position. The pistol is now ready for firing. While clumsy by most similar standards, the power perhaps offsets this failing.

This system, incidentally, will be found in dozens of makes of pistols of this style made in Europe and Great Britain.

Walther Air Pistols

The noted firm of Carl Walther, as we have seen, manufactured precision arms of the finest grades including air rifles at Zella Mehlis before the war. At the conclusion of hostilities the area in which their plant was located was ceded to the Russians.

The Walther organization undertook to develop their old arms manufacturing pursuits outside Germany during the period when no German factories were permitted to produce firearms. Specifically, Walther firearms designs were manufactured in a specially constructed factory in Turkey. Also, their famous P.P. and P.P.K. pocket pistols are still being manufactured at Mulhouse in France by the Manhurin organization under license.

The fine Swiss firm of Hämmerli at Lenzburg is currently making .22 Olympia target pistols on license from Walther.

The Walther firm was first allowed to re-enter the field of arms manufacture by producing precision air rifles at a new plant at Ulm-Donau a few years ago. They have since developed a precision air pistol originally marketed as the Model 53. This pistol in every respect is equal to the finest quality workmanship in Germany, something one has come to expect from the Walther family with

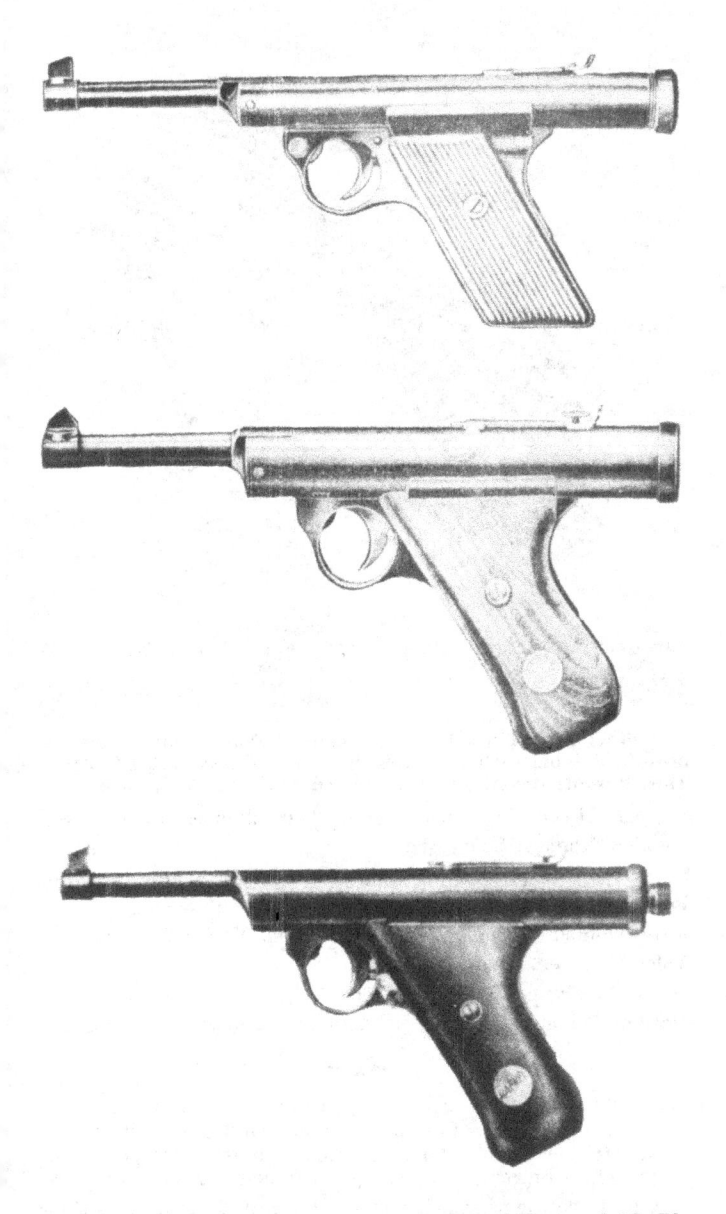

German Haenel single-shot air pistols, Models 26 and 28. The M28 is a more powerful type. The barrel breaks down for loading on hinge at forward end of compression tube. The mainspring is cocked by a separate movement. Holding the end of the compression tube with one hand, break down the grip section with the other. The repeating Haenel shown in insert does not load via barrel breakdown, but by a plug projecting from compression cap.

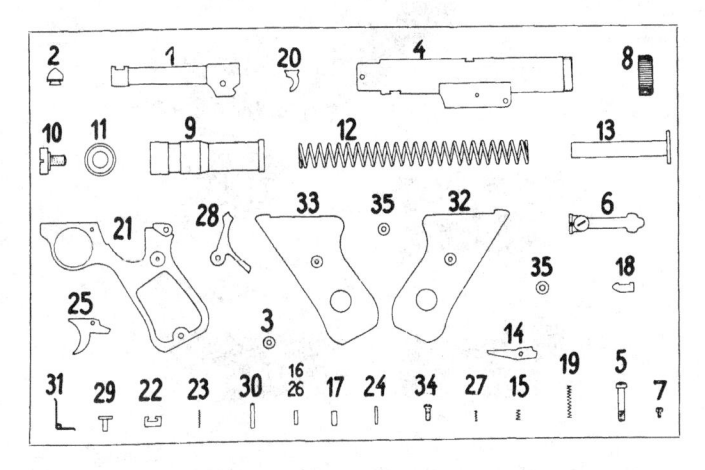

Haenel M28 parts drawing.

their high degree of engineering and manufacturing efficiency.

The Walther air pistol is actually in a class by itself. There is no standard in any air-pistol manufacture by which it can be the subject of comparison as to design. It has been truly stated that *it is not really an air-pistol design but is actually a high-grade target pistol* adapted to the use of a spring-air compression system to serve as a trainer for standard .22 caliber cartridge shooting Olympias. (Note: Its *manufacturing quality* is fully equalled by the British Webley alone. For all-around *air-pistol* use, the Webley is preferred.)

It is designed along the familiar lines of the famous Walther Olympia .22 target pistol. The specially posed pictures disclose the general construction in considerable detail. It will be noted that it has a barrel which is hinged to a standard firearm pistol-type receiver, not to the cheap tube construction normally encountered in air pistols.

In order to simulate as closely as possible the actual recoil effect of the standard Walther cartridge pistol, Walther incorporated two driving springs to operate a piston housed in the grip. As a result, the *nature of the recoil* as the springs are unleashed by the trigger pull to allow the piston to thrust up and compress the air follows closely that of the typical powder pistol. The Walther is entirely original in this concept from a *production* standpoint; though Jeffries patented the system in England years ago.

It must be pointed out that the pistol is intended entirely as an air-type trainer. It gives the illusion, because of its magnificent construction, of being a very powerful pistol. It is not. It is not so intended. This arm was designed for shooting the finest possible small group targets at short air ranges, and is strictly a trainer for the .22 caliber Walther target pistol, which is its general counterpart in appearance. Its best range is about 6 meters.

In order to get the necessary leverage to effect compression of the springs, it is necessary to provide a wood cocking block which is slipped over the muzzle to protect the front sight (and also the operator's hand!) in cocking. Unless this block is used, the thrust necessary to open the pistol and compress the springs in the grip is very difficult to achieve.

The idea of a piston in the butt, as we have pointed out, is not original with Walther. It has appeared in various British patents, notably those of Jeffries shortly after World War I. Walther, however, has made a most unique application of the idea, and its design is a *modification,* not a *copy* of the Jeffries—which, incidentally, was never produced for mass sale.

The trigger disconnector, which prevents pulling the trigger except when the action is closed, is merely an adaptation of the familiar semi-automatic pistol system. It is a most desirable feature in an air arm, though few makers incorporate it. A formal barrel-release lock would ease the cocking action; but aside from this deficiency the Walther is a remarkable, if low-powered, design.

German Walther Model 53 air pistol, caliber .177 only. Right side view. This is a trainer for use with the Walther Olympia auto pistol, caliber .22. Mainsprings (2) are housed in the grip and are compressed as the pistol is opened on its hinge. The wood cocking block is slipped over the muzzle to protect the front sight and the shooter's hand when cocking the strong springs. Due to limitations of spring power because of the cocking design, this pistol is not as powerful as the British Webley.

WALTHER AIR PISTOL, M53

Manufacturer: Carl Walther Sportswaffen-fabrik, Ulm, Donau, Germany.
U.S. Distributor: Currently, Thalson Company, San Francisco, California.
Overall Length: 12.25 inches.
Weight: 2 pounds 10 ounces.
Caliber(s): .177 ONLY.
Type(s) of Ammunition Used: .177 German (or equal) Diabolo-type pellets.
Rifled: Yes.
Operating System: Spring-air. Barrel cocker.
Cocked & Spring Compressed By: Breaking down barrel against opposition of detent.

German Walther Model 53. Left side view. Action opened to full cocking stroke. Triggerguard forms the direct cocking-lever under-action of the barrel. Note resemblance of this system to the old British Jeffries. Cocking block has a brass plug to enter muzzle without injury to rifling when cocking.

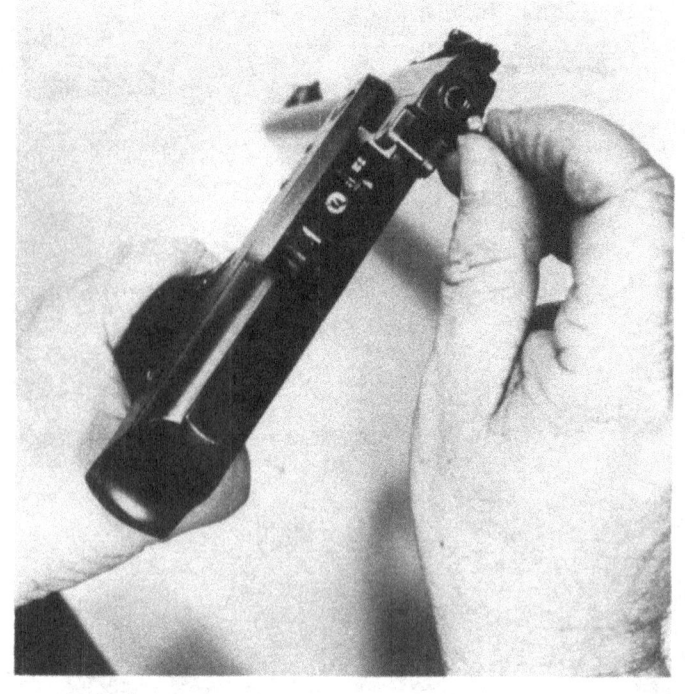

Walther Model 53. Loading chamber. Note solid, automatic-pistol type construction of this air pistol. Disconnector is rising. This prevents the trigger being pulled while action is open.

Loaded: Directly into barrel breech when action open and cocked.
Number Rounds: Single shot only.
Stock Type: Grip, close approximation of Walther Olympia pistol.
Front Sight(s): Blade on ramp.
Rear Sight(s): Wheel, adjustable elevation. Windage in slide.
Velocity (Approximate): 300 f.p.s.
Normal Accurate Range: 30 feet.
Normal Maximum Range: Standard for design.

REMARKS

Features adjustable trigger, heavy-duty, firearms-quality construction throughout. Two compression springs in butt to approximate powder-arm type of recoil. Auto-pistol type disconnector which prevents firing except when action is closed.

A wood cocking block is required for easy cocking. This slides over the muzzle to protect the front sight and shooter's hand.

Finest Walther quality throughout.

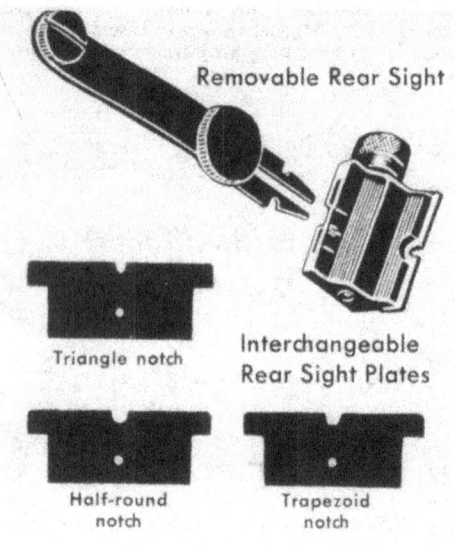

Walther P53 rear sight construction.

CHAPTER 11

Other Foreign Spring-Air Guns

THE area which is now **Czechoslovakia** has a considerable history of its own in the field of early air-gun manufacture. Many of the "wheel lock" air guns encountered in fine collections abroad were made by Christopher Hintz at Prague. Like many of the later "flintlock" patterns, at a glance these arms are always accepted as gunpowder weapons.

In 1881 a gunmaker named Sekyra produced experimental bellows guns at Podebradech, substituting iron side plates for the customary leather. The system permitted faster wall compression and did increase power, but arms of this type had little commercial value at that rather late date.

In addition to the commercial air rifles originally distributed by Kovo, Limited, and now being offered through Omnipol, bolt-action military training air rifles have been produced which differ considerably from their German counterparts in design, though their purposes were identical.

VZ35 AIR RIFLE

The small arms works at Strakonice was apparently the design center for these air arms also. The first was this fact, the rifle would pass muster as a fine Czech Mauser service rifle when first seen.

Loading may be single ball through the top of the receiver by lifting the cover of the loading port; or, the gun may be gravity fed from a tubular magazine which has a capacity of 20 balls.

The bolt handle is raised to unlock. Pulling it back to the end of the stroke (it requires quite a tug!) compresses the firing spring. When it clicks, the sear will hold the piston back ready for firing. If it is used as a magazine loader, the forward bolt thrust will drive the pellet into the chamber. (Note that since the muzzle must be tilted to allow the cocking pull necessary, the balls feed down the magazine tube by gravity without benefit of spring.)

Pulling the trigger releases the piston and spring. The power source is the standard type—the forward moving piston compresses the air in its path in the chamber and forces it through a small vent behind the bullet and down the barrel. It is a true spring-air type.

A safety operating on the Mauser 3-stage turning pattern is located on the receiver forward of the bolt-handle position.

A later, cheaper model was produced in 1947. These

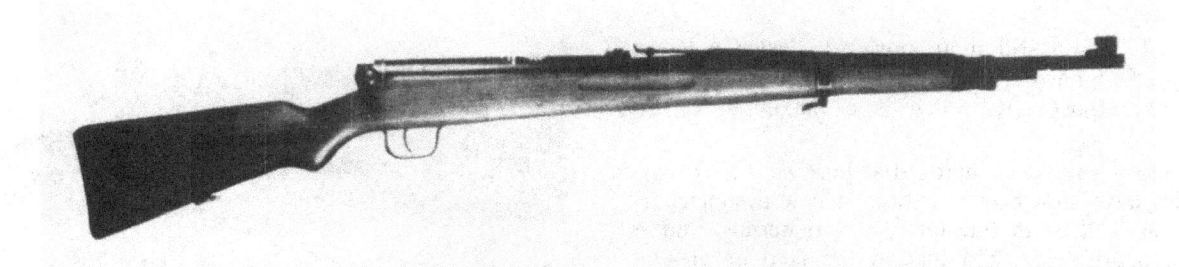

Czech VZ army air-rifle trainer. In practically every outward aspect it is a duplicate of the justly famous Czech Mauser service rifle. It can be fitted with the standard Czech service bayonet. The velocity is very high for its type. Using steel ball bearings of about .177 caliber it develops about 500 feet per second. A quality rifle of the finest type. The current production under Russian occupation and influence is very much poorer than in this prewar-made type.

apparently the VZ35, a precision-built arm in the finest Czech manufacturing tradition—which is high praise indeed!

The overall appearance, weight, and length are very close to that of the official Czech Mauser-pattern bolt-action service rifle. (Turn-bolt design, fine finish, barrel turned to standard dimensions, even equipped to allow mounting the standard bayonet! It weighs a little over 9 pounds and is 43 inches long.)

The bolt handle is positioned at the end of the receiver tube because of design requirements. Except for

are stamped "Ceska Zbrojovka, Narodni Podnik, Strakonice, V.Z. 47." This translates "Czech Armory, National Establishment, Strakonice City, Model 47."

While the VZ35 was a highly creditable service trainer, the later model has been considerably cheapened. Its bolt handle has been lengthened to give better leverage, however.

The rifles, while quite different from the German types made on the Schmeisser patents, have much in common with those currently being marketed in Germany under the "Blitz" trade-mark.

Czech service Mauser, showing bolt lifted to unlock action and drawn back to full-cock position to compress the firing spring.

CZECH SPORTING AIR RIFLES

These air rifles manufactured at Prague are elementary barrel-cocking designs with no unusual features of special interest. Specimens examined have been average for their type of manufacture, but are completely outdistanced by those of the better German and English makes in the matter of new design features.

They are made by Kovo, Limited, Praha, Czechoslovakia. Model 519T is a smooth bore which will use Diabolo pellets or round balls. Caliber is .177.

Model 522T is of heavier construction and has a trigger safety.

Model 523T is a still more powerful design with an accurately rifled barrel. However its power is indicated by the sight adjustment, which is a maximum of 20 meters.

In passing it should be noted that postwar Czech cartridge rifles have shown imagination in new design characteristics as well as in fine quality of materials, and it is a little surprising to find that in the field of air-gun design they have merely picked up where prewar models left off.

MISCELLANEOUS SPRING-AIR ARMS MANUFACTURE

Austria

The Tyrol Arms Company manufactures a small line of barrel-cocking air rifles. These are all elementary types on the low-priced German Diana pattern. They are more costly than the comparable German and are not as well made.

Italy

Manufacture here is limited to a rather weird type of low-efficiency design based on some of the cheap prewar

Czech VZ35 top views showing magazine loading port open and closed. It is merely necessary to spill the round balls into the opening. Feed is by gravity, no springs or followers being employed. This model is finest high-grade rifle quality throughout. Current production and similar German types are not as well made. Up to 30 feet, this is one of the finest precision trainers ever encountered by the author.

Haenels. Most are single-shot barrel cockers made at Milan. Basically these guns are made from stampings as in our Daisy air rifles and have tube barrel liners. They differ from the Daisy pattern in being breech loaders in the manner of the better German and English made barrel cockers.

The few better-grade types available are basically only minor variations of the lower-grade German Diana barrel cockers.

156

This is the only type of sporting rifle currently manufactured in Czechoslovakia.

Japan

The major producer of serious high-power air rifles in the Orient is the Kawaguchiya Firearms Company, Limited, of Tokyo and Osaka. The firm is a major dealer in all types of sporting and military arms and accessories, as well as military and industrial explosives. Founded in 1887, K.F.C. entered the export-import field in 1926, and today is again in the export field, while it also supplies 80 percent of the Japanese market for air rifles, shotguns, hunting goods and accessories, and ammunition.

Their air-rifle production currently consists of two basic types using the standard Diabolo waisted pellets. Their design, oddly enough, are very minor modifications of the East German (Russian Zone) Haenel air rifles, both in barrel cocker and underlever designs. The quality of a few specimens examined approached that of the German popular standard, though far short of the Walther or Krico in fitting and finishing.

The Asahi Model, made in caliber .177, is a typical barrel cocker with a long compression tube in prolongation of the barrel. The barrel is steel, and well-rifled. It has open sights. The wood buttstock is the customary ungainly design found in such rifles and common to the British prewar designs. It is husky, well-built, and relatively easy to cock for a rifle of its power. It weighs 6¾ pounds and measures 44.7 inches overall. The rear sight is barrel-mounted, giving a short sight line. The trigger is adjustable by the standard exposed adjusting screw.

Two models are produced with the underlever cocking system and fixed barrel. Model S.K.B. M3 uses the buttstock and compression tube of the Asahi model, but has a fixed barrel with standard loading plug operated by left side lever to open the breech for pellet loading. The underlever is the standard pattern hinged below the loading plug and extending forward below the barrel. When actuated it thrusts back the compression lever. A hooded-ramp front sight and a receiver-mounted adjustable rear sight are features. This model weighs about 7½ pounds and measures about 45 inches overall. It is produced in both .177 and .22 calibers, both rifled.

Model S.K.B. M53 is basically the same as the M3 above, except that it has a modern one-piece wood stock and fore-end into which the metal parts are dropped as a unit, giving it something of the look of a Webley Mark III at first glance. It is slightly shorter than the M3 because the butt is shorter since it does not have to be affixed to the compressing tube, but the rifle weighs about one-half pound more because of the additional wood in the fore-end section. This is a modern-appearing, efficient design of good quality.

K.F.C. claims an "effective" range of 60 yards with all these rifles, a figure which in the light of extensive tests by the author is exaggerated very considerably. Based on our own tests on three checked electronic chronographs here in the United States, as well as on RWS tests for Krico in Germany, it is an established

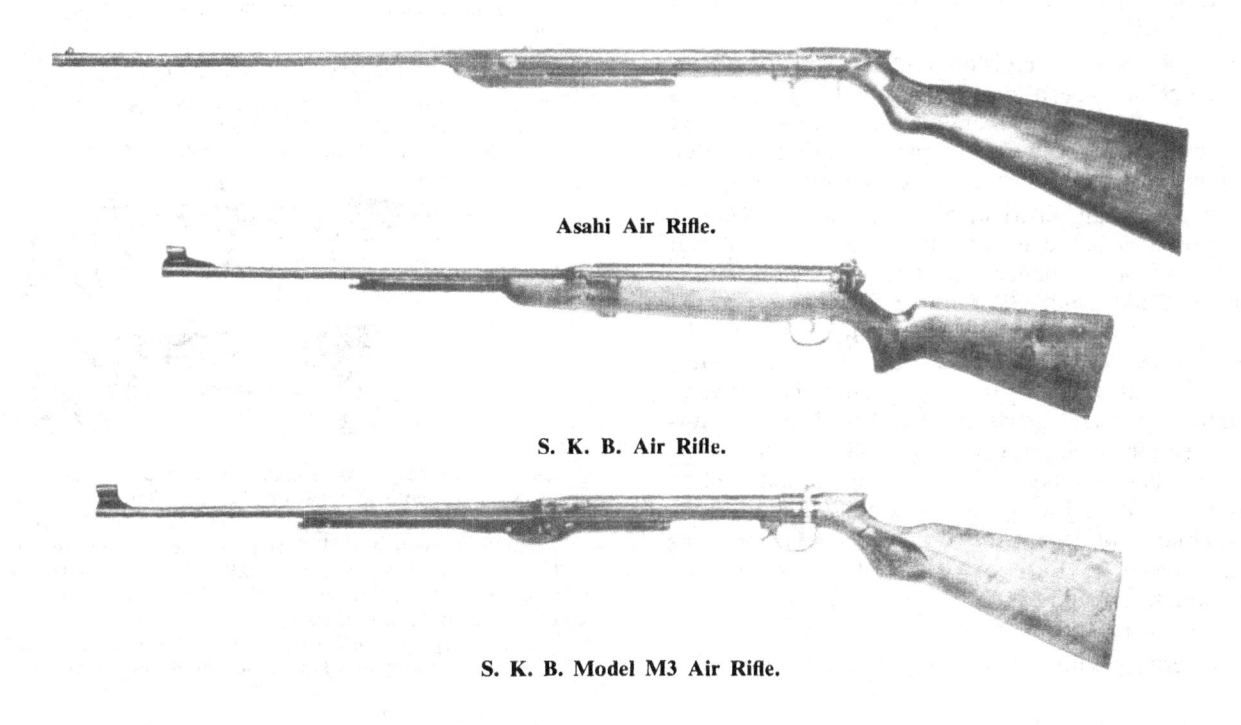

Asahi Air Rifle.

S. K. B. Air Rifle.

S. K. B. Model M3 Air Rifle.

fact that the very lightweight Diabolo air pellets lose velocity so rapidly after passing the 20-yard range that resultant bullet drop makes controllable accuracy very difficult beyond 30 yards range. The heavier .22 pellet even when starting at a velocity of about 600 f.p.s. (a very high velocity in a spring-air rifle of any make) will normally fall and deflect so far from the control screens that they cannot be checked at 50 yards with any degree of regularity. Occasional pellets which can be tracked average about 270 f.p.s. at that range.

This Japanese firm produces a fair quality of Diabolo pellets in both .177 and .22 calibers, packed 500 in a cardboard box under the trade name White Eagle.

As of the time of this writing, K.F.C. rifles have not been imported into the United States in quantity.

Spain

Some low-priced barrel cockers of standard German Diana type have been made at Eibar, the center of the Spanish mass gun industry. None have any features or quality worthy of particular note here.

U.S.S.R. (Russia)

The author utilized the services of experts familiar with the Russian language in an endeavor to locate any data of value to this work in connection with pneumatic arms. Since there has never before been a book published in the United States on the subject, it was not surprising to learn that none had been published in Russia, and the only historical or technical references located were those commonly found in the not very accurate French encyclopedias and reference works.

As has been pointed out elsewhere, Daisy toy-pattern air rifles have never been permitted to enter Russia. A few "Russian" rifles of this type encountered by the author proved to be of German manufacture and doubtless represented guns which had been brought home by privileged travelers.

Many 19th century air pistols and rifles bearing Russian markings have been encountered, but most seem to be of French or Austrian manufacture. Doubtless there were some Russian custom-built pieces during this era, though none are known which indicate native design.

The only generally distributed information in Russian on this subject is found in the latest issue of the official *Soviet Encyclopedia* under the headings (translated) "Pneumatic Rifle" and "Pneumatic Weapon." In the former is a statement not touched upon in any of the documented sources published in English, French, German, Greek, Italian, or Spanish; viz., that the blowgun is mentioned in the legends of the American Iroquois Indians! Doubtless the statement is taken from some Russian or Siberian folklore dealing with the old idea of the settling of America by Siberian natives who came here over land bridges which sank beneath the seas before the dawn of European exploration. No French sources, which are the reliable ones on matters of the Iroquois, make any mention of the blowgun.

The modern "pneumatic weapon" described is an elementary German-pattern barrel cocker, as both the description and the line drawings establish.

Many air rifles, particularly of the bolt-action army type that the Germans somewhat whimsically call "Sport Models," are currently being made in the East German (Russian Zone) area about Suhl. Despite the Russian language markings, all examples encountered by the author have been merely German prewar patterns made with German tooling.

PNEUMATIC RIFLE
(Translation from the Russian)

The ancestor of this type was mainly used for birds and very rarely used for military purposes. It represents a pipe about 1½ to 3 meters, usually inserted into another larger pipe.

Miniature arrows, coated with plant poison were thrown out of the rifle by pressure of air, which was blown by the shooter out of the opposite end of the tube. The arrows flew a distance of 30 or 40 meters.

The primitive type of pneumatic rifle is still in existence in the depths of the Islands of Sumatra and Borneo and in the tropical forests of the Straits of Malacca and of South America.

In the past, this form of pneumatic rifle was used to a much greater extent. It is known for example that "Prokezes" (North America Iroquois) have some legends which you can interpret as an indication of its existence in the far past and use by some people of West Siberia and in the Ural Mountains.

The present sportsmen's weapon works on the same principle, that is, by movement of the piston which creates pressure inside of the barrel, the shot is produced under the action of compressed air. The caliber is 4.5 mm.

The pneumatic rifle of the old type had a smooth surface inside of the barrel. The new type rifles are rifled (up to 12 grooves).

The barrel is placed tight toward the air chamber which is located on the shank. In the chamber there is a piston with a very strong spring.

The rifle is charged with the lead bullet or with a sharp very short arrow with a brush on the end. You press the trigger; the piston on the spring goes forward fast and under the pressure of the air the bullet leaves the barrel. The distance of the shot is up to 30 meters. The pneumatic pistols have the same construction and action.

The pneumatic pistols are intended for sport shooting in closed galleries.

PNEUMATIC WEAPON

The pneumatic weapon is a certain type of sport weapon in which the bullet is thrown out by force of compressed air. The shooting from the pneumatic weapon is done by special lead bullets or small, sharp arrows (a small, sharp piece of pin with a brush on the end). There is in existence a pneumatic rifle and pistol. The maximum range of the pneumatic weapon is 150 steps or nearly 100 meters. The [range of the] weapon of small caliber for shooting in a room is 10 steps. Caliber of bullet [is] from 2 to 3 (shot size) up to 10 to 11 millimeters.

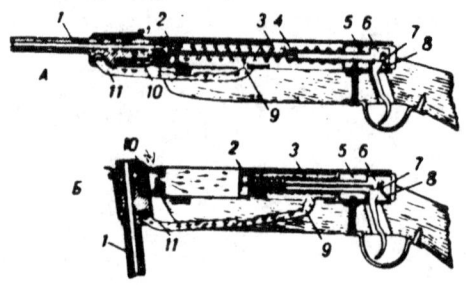

For charging, the barrel is turned downward, the same way as in shotguns. This time the lever moves back the piston and compresses the spring. When the piston is raised it is kept in position by the trigger mechanism. By pressing the trigger, the piston is released from the hold hook and under action of the spring it moves, springing forward, compressing the air in the cylinder; the compressed air going into the barrel pushes out the bullet or small arrow.

The use of the pneumatic weapon for military purposes did not get acceptance. Although in the end of the 18th century in Austria, France, and in some other countries, the pneumatic rifle with detachable stock and reservoir for compressed air, which was shooting 100 meters distance, was given to some regiments. This idea was abandoned in the beginning of the 19th century and pneumatic rifles were exchanged for effective types of firearms.

SWITZERLAND

The Hämmerli rifle trainer is an entirely new concept in the field of air-rifle training. It is *not* an independent rifle. It is a complete barrel, magazine, cocking, and power mechanism which can be inserted in a specified rifle (or pistol) without tools and without alterations to the original powder weapon. An explanation of its application to the Swiss Kar. 31 (the current official Swiss high-power service rifle) will cover in detail its general design and functioning.

The Makers. This device was designed and is manufactured by the Hämmerli organization at Lenzburg, Switzerland. This firm is noted as the manufacturers of many of the finest small arms ever produced. While all phases of their products from materials to workmanship are of ultimate quality, Hämmerli is most noted for the supreme accuracy they build into their arms.

Hämmerli match rifles are known throughout the world anywhere shooters gather. Made in both small- and large-bore calibers, their precision rifles sell from $400 to $500 and expert shooters gladly pay these prices.

The Hämmerli .22 caliber single-shot match pistol costs about $300 in this country. This pistol is used by champions in 39 different countries. Our own Sergeant H. L. Benner, coach at West Point, won the Olympic free pistol championship at Helsinki by defeating champions of 48 contesting countries using one of these Hämmerli pistols.

The factory is small, relatively, its single-shot pistol production being of the order of some 500 pistols a year. BUT—no Hämmerli is allowed to leave the factory until it scores 100 points on a standard target when fired from a machine rest!

The German firm of Carl Walther a few years ago entered into an agreement to allow Hämmerli to manufacture their .22 Olympia auto pistol design in the full confidence that of all the European gunmakers only Hämmerli could maintain the original Walther quality. These Hämmerli-made Walthers sell from $225 to about $300 here.

To sum up, the name Hämmerli on any firearm product is the finest hallmark of quality. You may buy arms which will shoot as accurately as Hämmerlis—you will never buy any that will excel them, regardless of advertising claims. In the final analysis, such superb accuracy is achievable only at considerable expense. You pay well for Hämmerlis. But you get what you pay for.

Design. This new Hämmerli development is a brand new approach to instructing in the handling of a rifle, and in training for its use in target shooting, hunting, or service. In essence it is a simple idea: merely adapting the prewar German ERMA .22 conversion system and the postwar close-fulcrum air-gun lever principles to make a quick insertable and equally quick removable device for converting a standard high-power rifle to an indoor precision air rifle which will use all the original rifle elements except the bolt and magazine mechanism. The idea itself

Right side view of Swiss Kar. 31 (official service rifle) with Hammerli air trainer installed. The stock overhang is necessary because of the air-compressing system. It does not interfere with holding or shooting.

Right side view of the trainer overall with top locking clamp raised.

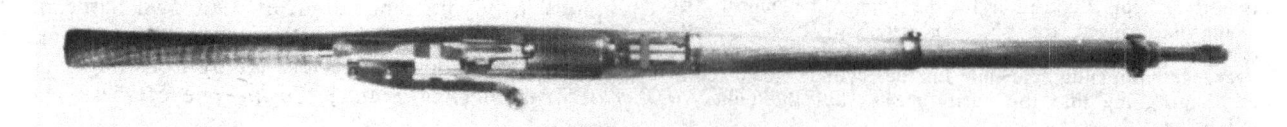

Top view of Hämmerli trainer installed.

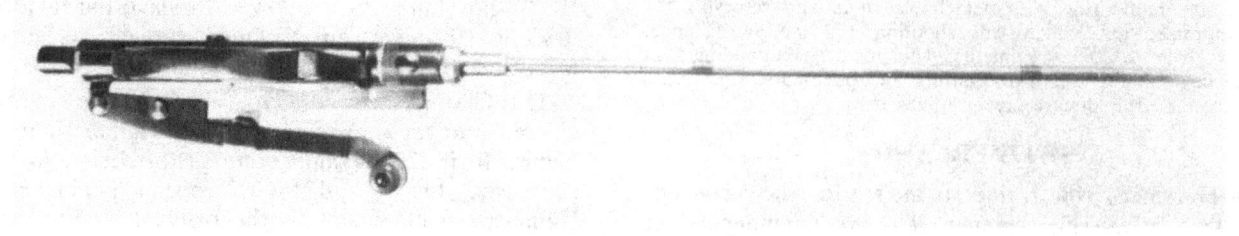

Top view of trainer. Note position of pivot and leverage points.

Left side view showing details of attachment lock.

is simple. The way Hämmerli worked it out is a remarkable mechanical achievement, indeed.

The original German ERMA .22 conversion consisted of a breech and firing mechanism, barrel, and magazine, which could be inserted in a regular Mauser rifle by withdrawing the bolt. In theory it was fine. In actual practice the author has never seen one used successfully because of fragile construction, variable accuracy, and sighting problems; and in any event, since it used a regular powder cartridge, its use was confined to that of any regular .22 rifle with regard to range requirements. A .22 powder rifle is pretty potent anyway you construct it. Its use calls for formal range facilities or plenty of space.

The Hämmerli conversion, on the other hand, is a *deliberately* low-powered conversion. However, it has built into it the accuracy for which Hämmerli is famous, even though in this case it is necessarily a short-range accuracy. At distances up to 15 feet, in comparative tests this rifle consistently shoots groups which are not excelled by any spring-air, compressed-air, or CO_2 rifles made anywhere; and it actually outshot most of them in the personal tests undertaken by the author. The remarkable factor here is that the test shooting was done with the standard Swiss service rifle open sights!

At the time of writing, the device is made only for Mauser sporting rifles and the Swiss Kar. 31 (service rifle). The latter was used for testing and for the accompanying explanatory and illustrative photographs and drawings.

Prototypes have been built for various other rifles, and for the Walther Olympia and the Walther PP auto pistols, among others.

(Note: The design has also been adapted to a CO_2 gas system, using the common metal CO_2 small capacity cylinders.)

HAMMERLI AIR-GUN TRAINER
(Individual Models for Various Arms)

Manufacturer: Hämmerli Hunting and Sporting Arms Factory, Incorporated, Lenzburg, Switzerland.
Overall Length: Trainer only—about 28 inches. (Swiss Kar. 31 is 43 inches long.)
Weight: About 1 pound.
Caliber(s): Air-rifle shot (.175 inch).
Type(s) of Ammunition Used: Round steel precision balls, bearing type.
Rifled: No.
Operating System: Spring-air by pulling out and back on right side lever. Utilizes trigger mechanism of original rifle.
Cocked & Spring Compressed By: Lever-arm engagement with spring-driven piston.
Loaded: Breech, top of rifle. Turn sleeve right to expose loading port.
Number Rounds: Six.
Stock Type: Unit is inserted in barrel and action of standard rifle.
Front Sight(s): Utilizes regular rifle sights.
Rear Sight(s): Utilizes regular rifle sights.
Velocity (Approximate): 250 f.p.s.
Normal Accurate Range: 5 to 6 meters (approximately 19.5 to 23.5 feet).
Normal Maximum Range: 125 feet.

Top view. Trainer ready for insertion.

REMARKS

The accompanying drawings showing left side and top cutaway views of the device give a clear picture of its nature. It consists of a smooth-bored barrel of highest precision quality, a throating plug and stop to seat in the barrel chamber of the rifle itself, a cylindrical receiver, a spring-driven air piston assembly, and a gravity magazine.

At the forward end of the receiver is a serrated collar which encloses the loading port and magazine area. When this collar is turned to the right, it exposes the port, and 6 steel balls can be dropped into the magazine well. There is no spring—the balls are fed by gravity as the muzzle of the rifle is tilted up during the cocking operation.

Within the receiver to the rear of the magazine is housed a formal piston and coil spring. A cocking lever, double jointed for maximum leverage is positioned on the right side of the receiver. It is pivoted at the extreme end of the receiver and operates through a toggle action not unlike the familiar Luger pistol to draw back the piston and compress the mainspring when the lever handle is pulled out (to unlock) and drawn full back (to cock). A sear face on the underside of the piston travels in a receiver slot, and at the end of the rearward stroke it is held by the regular rifle trigger ready for firing. At that point the side lever is pushed forward to locked position and to chamber a ball.

Unlike earlier cartridge conversion units, this one requires no barrel fixing nut or similar forward lock unit. The barrel is shorter than the standard (18.7-inch) Swiss service barrel and is wrapped at two forward points with fishline for forward support when inserted.

The unit-lock itself mechanically is old, but its application is quite new. It is shown clearly in the drawings and photos. It is a simple dual sheet-metal spring clamp design, the front piece engaging the forward lip of the rifle receiver bridge, and being drawn tight under spring pressure as the rear lifting section is snapped down into position over the rear of the receiver bridge.

Inserting the Device. The bolt is first removed from the rifle. In the case of the Kar. 31, it is merely necessary to press down the long spring catch below the cocking handle, hold it down, and pull the bolt out. (In the Mauser, of course, the left side catch is operated while the bolt is withdrawn.)

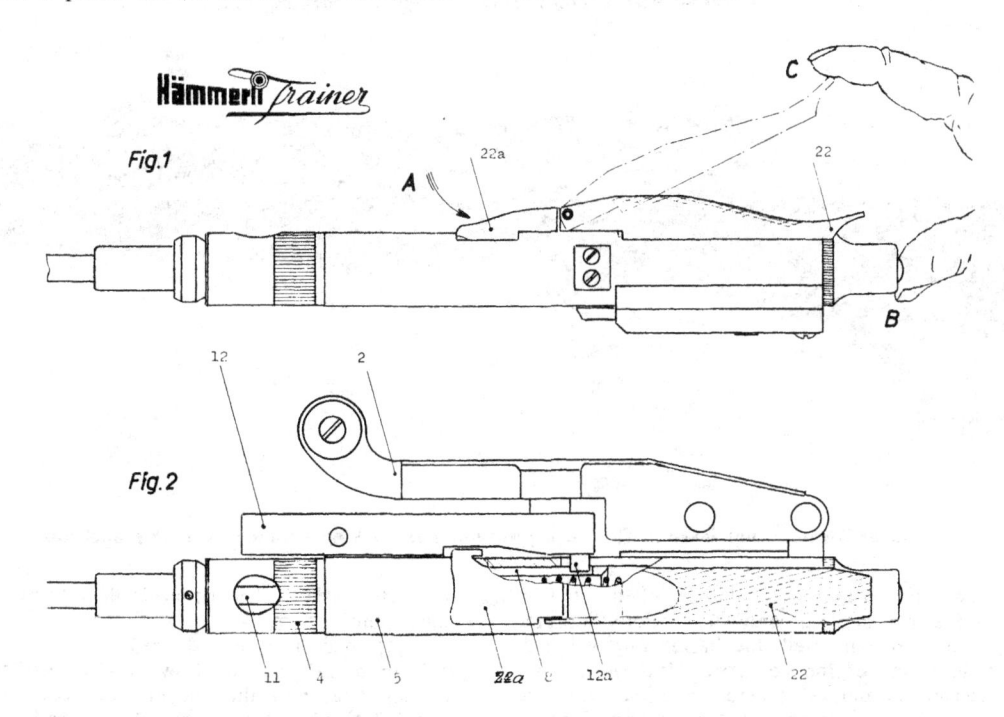

Trainer drawings. Upper: "A" is front lock hook which engages over front end of receiver. "C" is rear clamp section, when pressed down against spring it draws front section tight and locks down into rear of receiver bridge. "B" is end cap.

Lower: Top view cutaway. 11 is loading port. 4 is knurled sleeve turned to right to open loading port. 5 is receiver of device. 2 is cocking lever. 12a is cocking tip on lever which pulls back piston and compresses mainspring as lever is operated.

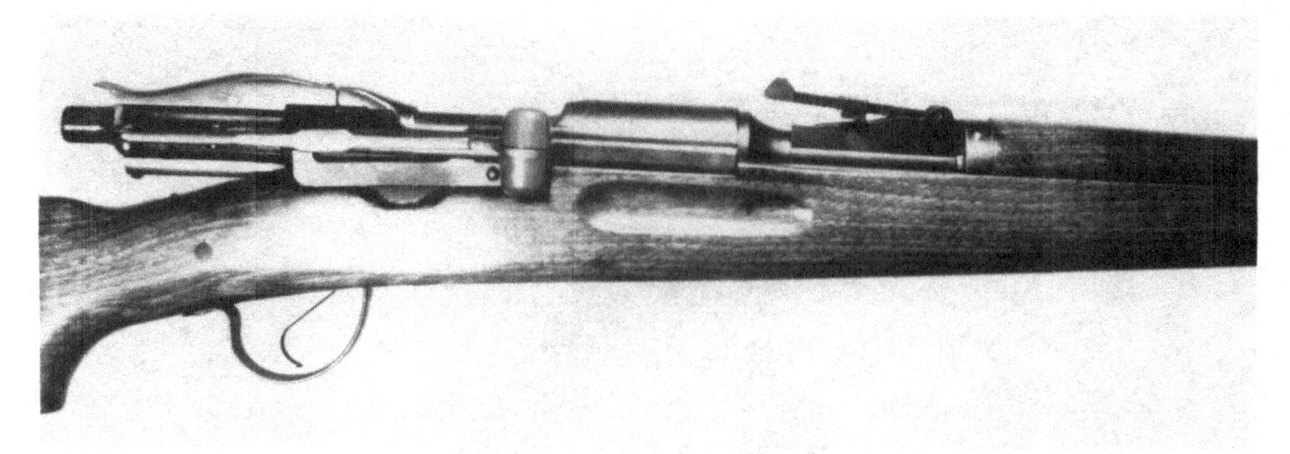

Trainer with action closed.

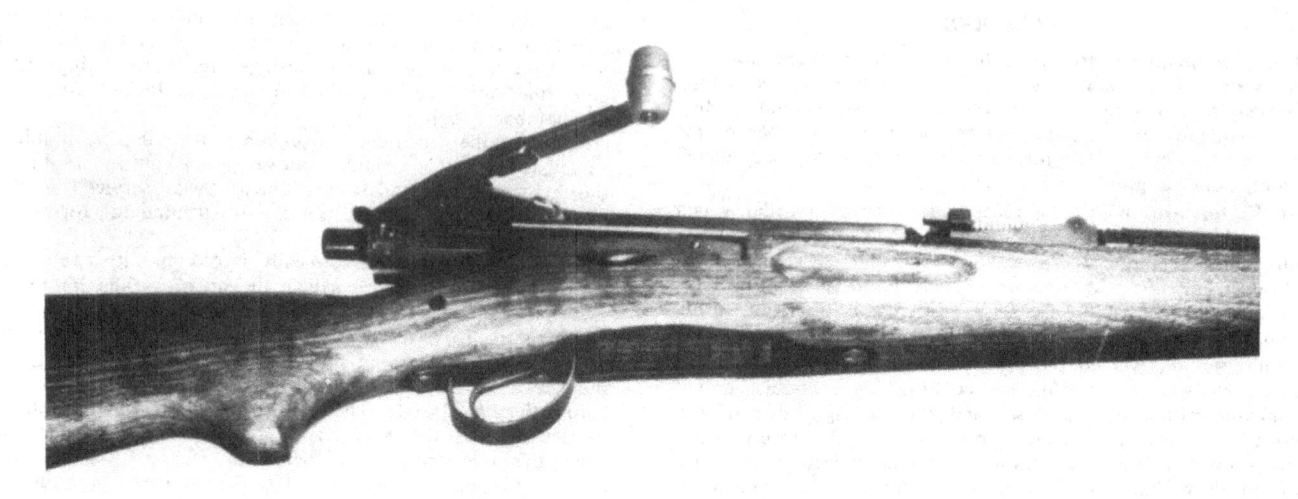

Trainer with action uncocked ready for cocking pull.

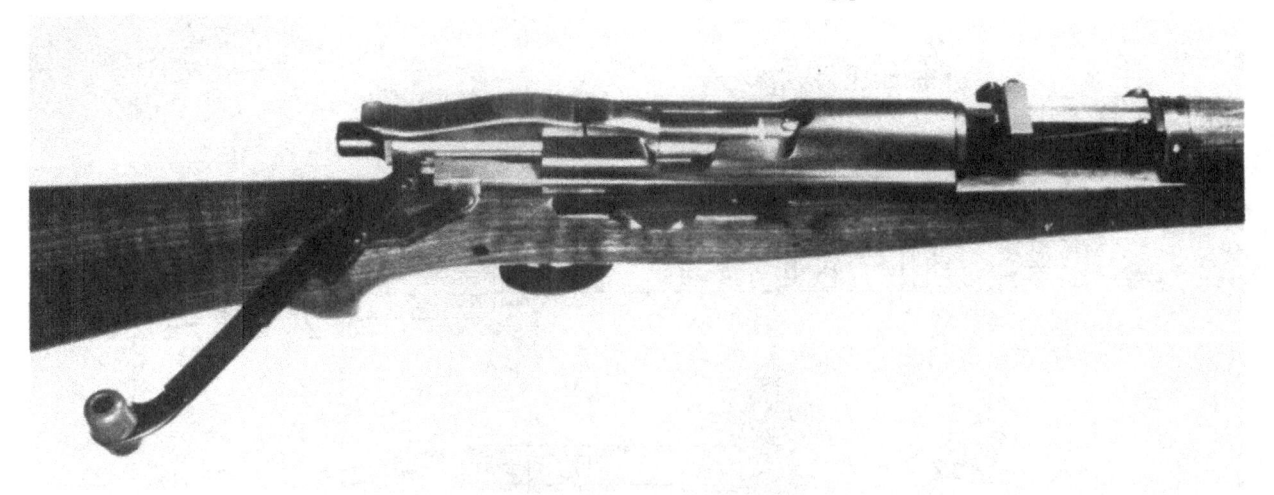

Trainer with cocking lever at full cock position. The cocking action is a toggle operation.

The device follows the engagement contours of the bolt it replaces, so it is necessary only to insert it carefully into the receiver opening. When fully inserted, the barrel stop will halt travel. The front hook end of the conversion lock is snapped down over the receiver lip and held there while the rear lock unit is pressed down into locking position against opposition of its support spring.

The trigger is half cocked as the device is inserted. In this position the gun cannot be full cocked. Pull the trigger to release the piston mechanism.

The magazine collar is now turned to the right and 1 to 6 balls dropped in. The collar is then turned to the left to close the opening.

Sights may now be adjusted.

With muzzle up to allow gravity feed of the first ball into feeding line, pull the cocking lever out to the right. This is merely an unlocking action and requires little effort. The cocking tip of the lever is now engaging the piston at its rear. Pulling back on the cocking lever will now draw back the piston and compress the spring. The trigger will catch and hold the piston sear point at the end of the stroke.

Push the cocking lever ahead to closed position to chamber

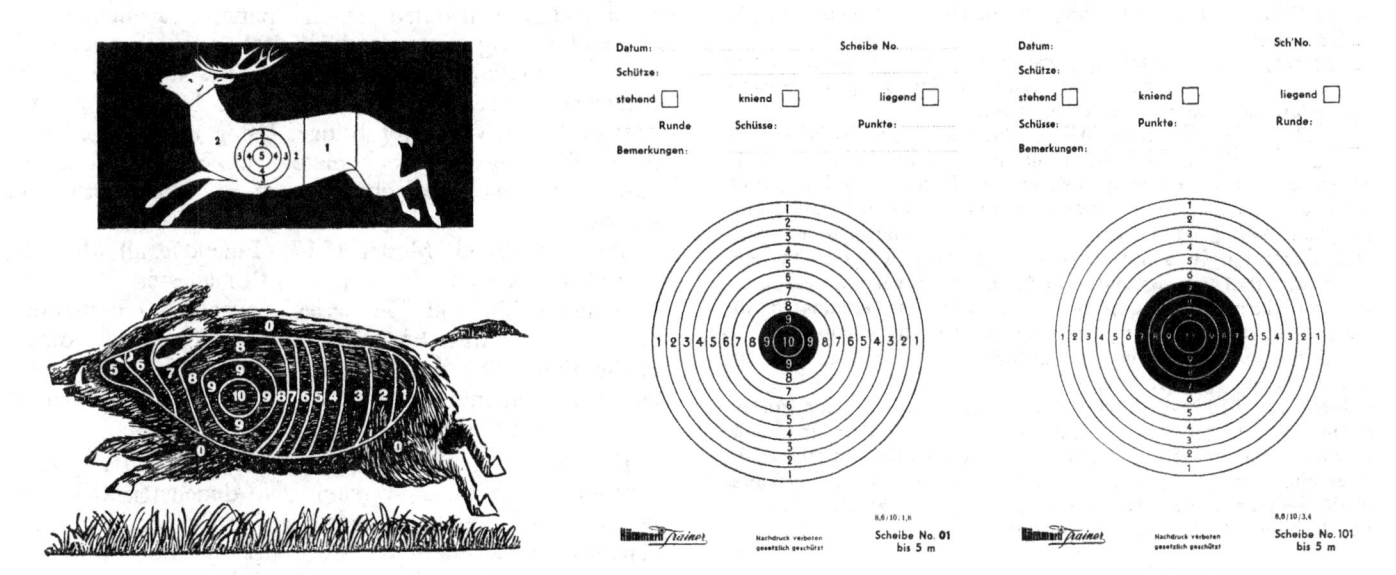

Typical scaled-down targets to simulate long-range game and target shooting at 5-meter ranges.

the ball and lock the lever. When the trigger is squeezed off, the piston will be freed and the unleashed spring will drive it ahead in the air cylinder. The air compressed in its path will be forced through the small air vent behind the ball to drive it out the barrel.

The trigger should not be pulled until the lever is fully closed, just as in any standard air rifle. Also, it must be remembered that the *one opening stroke of the lever gives full power*. There is no sense pulling the lever back until after firing, as such action will merely double-feed the action and will not increase power.

Application to Other Rifles. Since each type of bolt rifle has a different design or dimension of receiver bridge (the "bridge" being the section of the receiver directly behind and above the cartridge head position of the formal magazine in a bolt-action rifle), obviously a different locking device and receiver length are required. Thus a Hämmerli trainer which will enter a Swiss Kar. 31 cannot be used in a Mauser action. As presently constituted, this device cannot be applied to rifles like our M1 (Garand) because there is no opening at the rear of the receiver to allow its insertion. It can be used on Springfields, Enfields, Mausers, Winchester 70's, Remington 721's, and similar rifles where the bolt mechanism is readily withdrawn through the rear of the receiver—though a different lock detail is required for each of these types.

(Note: "Kar. 31" is the official Swiss designation for the "karabiner" or short rifle adopted in 1931. It is a straight-pull bolt design, in which pulling back on the bolt handle first unlocks the action and then draws the bolt back for ejection of the fired case. Like the Springfield, the entire bolt mechanism can be withdrawn to the rear by releasing a simple holding catch.)

A further complication concerning widespread American use of this device will be encountered where the rifle has scope mounts or special receiver sights which may interfere with either the device's locking operation or the line of sight. However, for owners of rifles to which the device may be made applicable, it has more practical value than any training device the author has ever encountered.

The Hämmerli system as designed to use a CO_2 cylinder, on the other hand, is readily adapted to, and inserted in, Springfields, Mausers, and Enfields because of the compact design possible where long spring compression and moving piston are not involved.

Shooting with the Hämmerli Trainer. While formal short-range bull's-eye targets are provided for the true precision shooter, the Hämmerli scaled-down animal targets make shooting more interesting for the average gun owner.

In a rifle where the standard sights are used, the device actually enables a very high degree of precision shooting—particularly under rapid-fire conditions—which simulates long-range game shooting most effectively. Here you have the feel, hang, trigger pull, weight, and sights of the rifle you will use

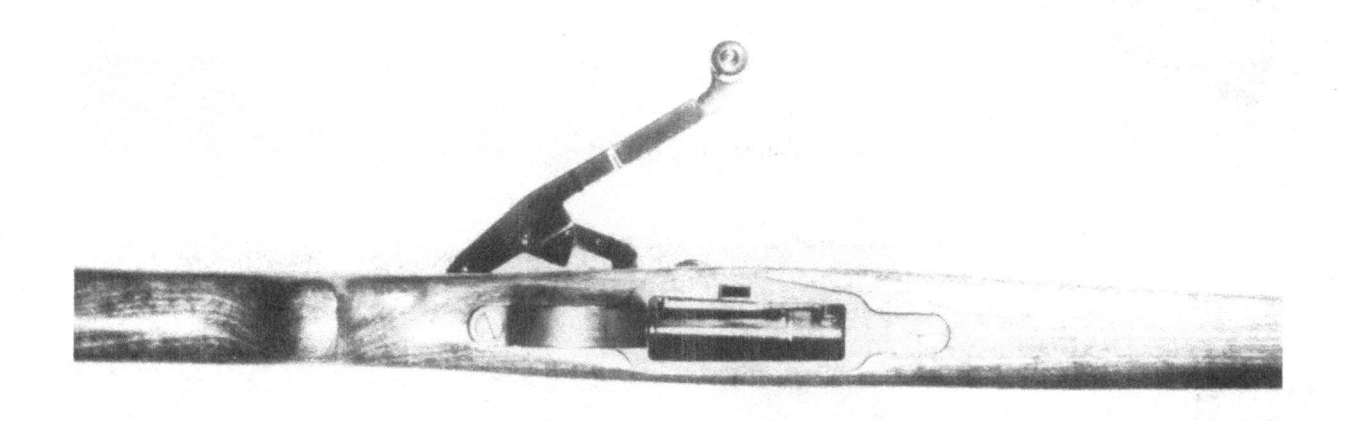

Trainer, bottom view, right side, showing details of cocking leverage system.

163

in the field. In short, everything except the recoil, noise, danger, and expense.

Accuracy. The unusual accuracy which characterizes this device stems from the combination of design, workmanship, dimensions and tolerances, barrel—AND ammunition.

The balls do not touch the regular rifle barrel at any point during their flight, so there is no possible injury to the rifle. Their velocity is relatively low, and so is their striking power. They are intended for accuracy training, NOT for penetration or game killing. You can shoot sparrows, starlings, or pests with them; but it is not recommended. They just do not have the wallop that true air and gas rifles have. By keeping the power low but beautifully controlled, Hämmerli has eliminated the violent forward slamming encountered with heavy-duty spring-air rifles, so there is no aim disturbance. In this respect the trainer equals the compressed-air and CO_2 guns. The target holder furnished has provision for a suspended leather curtain behind the target which cushions the shock after the balls penetrate the cardboard targets. An examination of the balls after shooting indicated that they could be re-used many times if the leather curtain was hung in place so that the balls did not hit the wood backstop directly.

Carbon Dioxide (CO_2) Arms

In addition to the quick-insert attachments for converting standard military and sporting rifles *of some types* to air-rifle trainers, a subject already dealt with at some length herein, authorization has been extended by the Hämmerli firm to include in this book, in advance of general release, pictures, drawings, and data which will give the reader some idea of the extent of that firm's research and development in the pellet-gun field.

These developments in the CO_2 field include not only conversions for certain military and sporting high-power rifles and automatic pistols to allow their use as indoor and short-range trainers, but also a line of *completely new* CO_2 precision pistols, which will be followed in due course by a series of automatic CO_2 rifles.

CO_2 Rifle Conversions

As an example, consider the common German Mauser Kar. 98 pattern of high-power military rifle—still the most widely distributed military pattern. By merely lifting and pulling back on the bolt handle, the action is opened. Holding out the catch on the left side of the receiver permits the bolt mechanism to be drawn out the rear of the rifle receiver bridge. Using a cartridge bullet point, the magazine floor plate can be sprung and the entire magazine assembly drawn out of the bottom of the rifle.

The Springfield, Model 1917 (Enfield), all Mausers, Mannlichers, Arisakas, Nagants, Winchester 70 series, Remington 720 and 721 series, Savage 340 bolt-action series, most British Enfield models, and a host of others in the high-power field are stripped of bolt and magazine assemblies on minor variations of the Mauser principle, and just about as easily.

Each of these varying types, of course, will require a *different* Hämmerli conversion as to dimension and lock-in system, since each varies dimensionally. However, conversions for the major types are already underway which make allowance for these factors in the device itself.

Reverting now to the Mauser as the basic pattern CO_2 Hämmerli conversion unit: Shown herewith are pictures of a standard service German Mauser of modern pattern, and with it a picture of the same rifle with the CO_2 Hämmerli conversion installed. The bolt has been replaced by the combined subcaliber barrel, magazine, sear, and striker unit which is merely inserted in place of the bolt and retained by the formal Mauser bolt-lock catch. The magazine has been replaced by the combination CO_2 cylinder and chamber (the cylinder or "gas cartridge" is the standard one obtainable in drugstores), complete with the common valve assemblies and impact release. This is compressed into an area which permits housing it within the magazine well with only a pleasing projection below the stock line. The barrel section, of course, is inside the standard 7.92-mm. (.308) rifle barrel.

The drawing shows the assembly working mechanism, but gives little idea of the engineering ability and ingenuity which went into its design. Note that when the as-

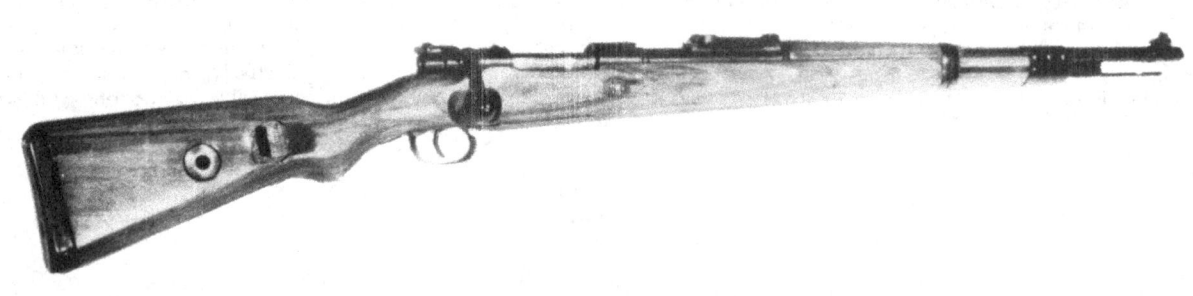

Mauser Rifle, Kar. 98.

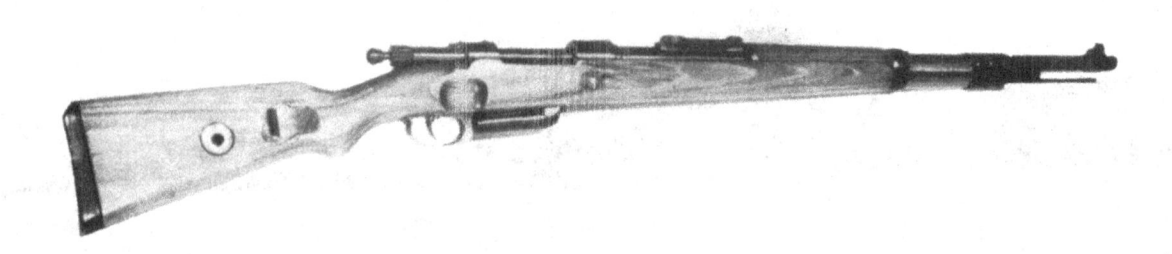

Mauser rifle with Hämmerli CO_2 conversion unit installed.

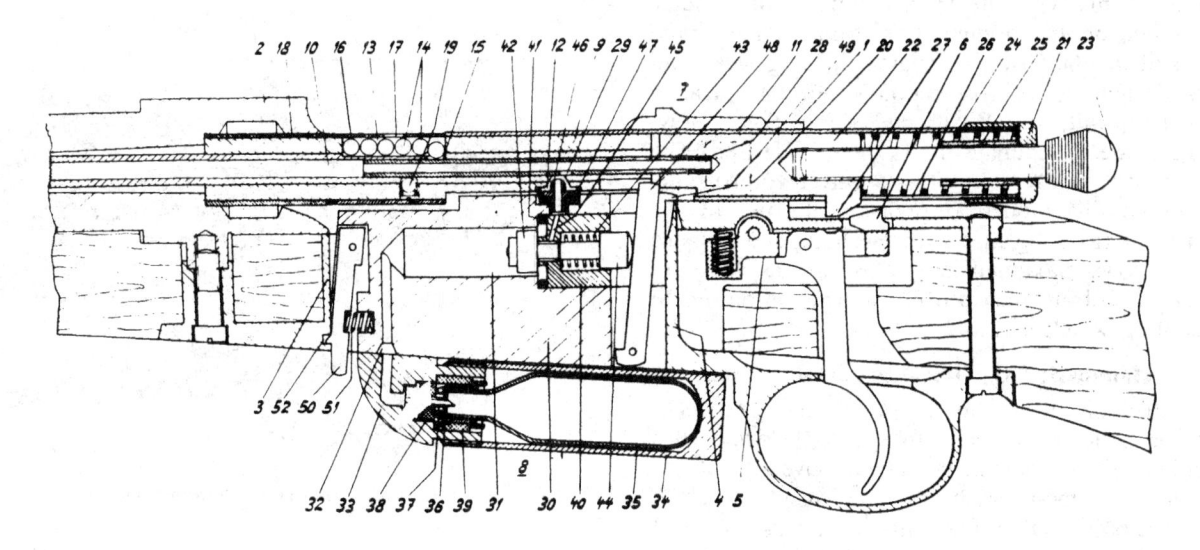

Working mechanism of the Mauser K98 with CO_2 conversion unit in place.

sembly is cocked, its sear operates off the Mauser sear, so that the trigger pull you get using this assembly for training is the same as when firing standard high-power cartridges. Likewise, the original sights on the rifle are used, since it is possible to adjust them to simulate long-range firing. The magazine holds in this case 6 steel bearing-quality balls of .1725-inch diameter. Feed is by gravity as the muzzle is elevated slightly during actuation. When used, as the loading rod is brought back, a ball falls in front of it, where it is held in position by the rising ball detent. As the rod goes forward to move the ball into line with the gas discharge flow, it overrides the detent.

Note that the formal magazine catch is utilized to retain the lower gas assembly. The all important thinking behind these developments was that insertion and use of the trainer must be done without *in any way altering the original weapon*; and with a maximum of speed and a minimum of skill, knowledge, and effort on the part of the average shooter.

All these devices combine fine workmanship, close tolerances, and a very high order of engineering skill and ingenuity.

Hämmerli Auto Pistol CO_2 Trainers

These have been developed on the same broad thesis as the rifle trainers. The photos below afford a graphic illustration of the general principles. While they are shown here on a war-model German P38 pistol, similar devices are in preparation for our Government Model .45 Auto and can be produced for any type of pistol (such as the S&W 9-MM. Auto, Luger, Browning, Beretta, Star, Neuhausen, etc.) in which the hammer and trigger mechanism remains in the grip section when the barrel and slide assemblies are removed. Naturally, only where a substantial market exists will it be advisable to manufacture for special pistols, as tooling expenses are considerable. However, one will be made for the .45 Auto in due course. As to the P38, it might be mentioned in passing that this pistol, originally designed by Walther and officially adopted by Germany in 1938 as a service pistol to replace the Luger (P08), is again under manufacture in a somewhat improved form by Walther in a new factory under the designation P54, and the device will also be adaptable to this model.

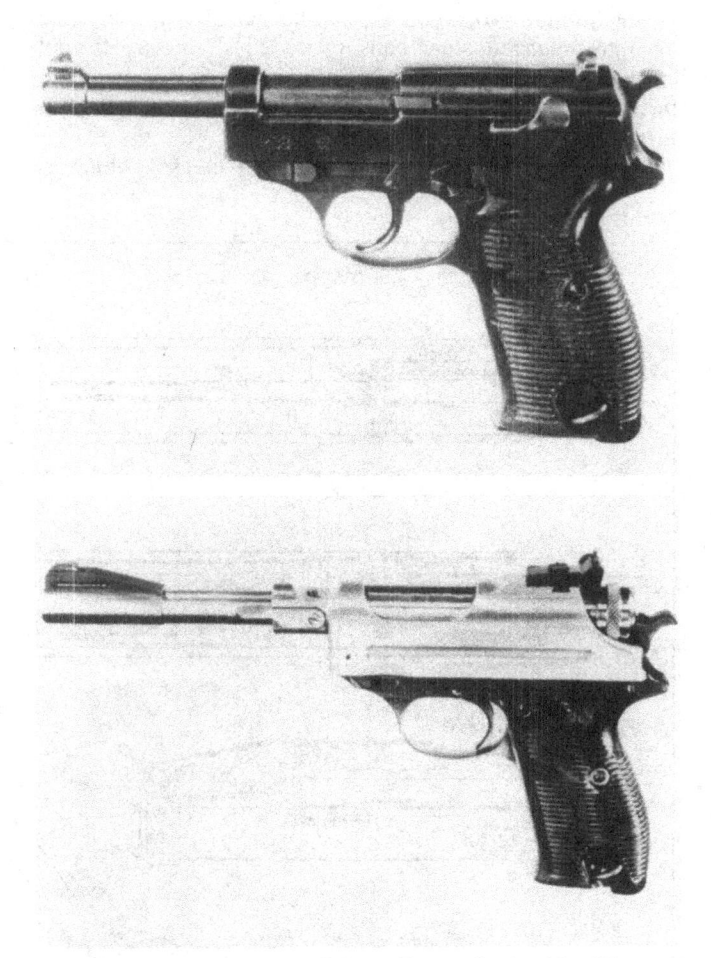

The slide and barrel assemblies of the P38 system are easily slid off the front of the frame section by merely turning down the thumb lever seen at the forward end of the frame and pulling the units ahead.

Above: War-model P38. Below: Same pistol with CO_2 conversion device in place.

In pistols of this type, the trainer consists of a frame which will slide on the original grip-frame runners, and can be locked in place by the original locking lever and bolt. This design, of course, requires not only frame, barrel, and CO_2 unit, but also its own sights. Sights however can be made to simulate the original if desired. The lever shown just to the rear of the barrel controls the loading plug in this model. Here again the use of the original firing trigger, together with the hang and balance of the arm, allows maximum indoor use at low cost and without danger and furnishes a training arm without equal for the pistol on which it is used.

Hämmerli CO₂ Quickfire Pistol

As an indication of the advanced thinking and technology in the pellet field today, the photo below of this newest Hämmerli development should give the trade something to think about! With only one exception, which cannot be disclosed at this time, this represents the most remarkable advance in short-range and trainer shooting since the introduction of the CO_2 system.

The tubular projection below the barrel is a magazine for high-precision steel balls of .1725 diameter. It will hold five and can be made to hold more. It is, of course, spring and follower fed from below, as in a standard cartridge magazine.

This is the first pistol ready for the market which is designed along lines which allow maximum use of efficient CO_2 power principles, all previous efforts having been merely conversions from compressed-air arms. It must be stressed that it is not designed for Diabolo waisted pellets, as feeding these fragile units is too much of a problem. By utilizing precision steel balls, feeding troubles are eliminated and maximum accuracy is still obtainable at distances up to roughly 35 feet.

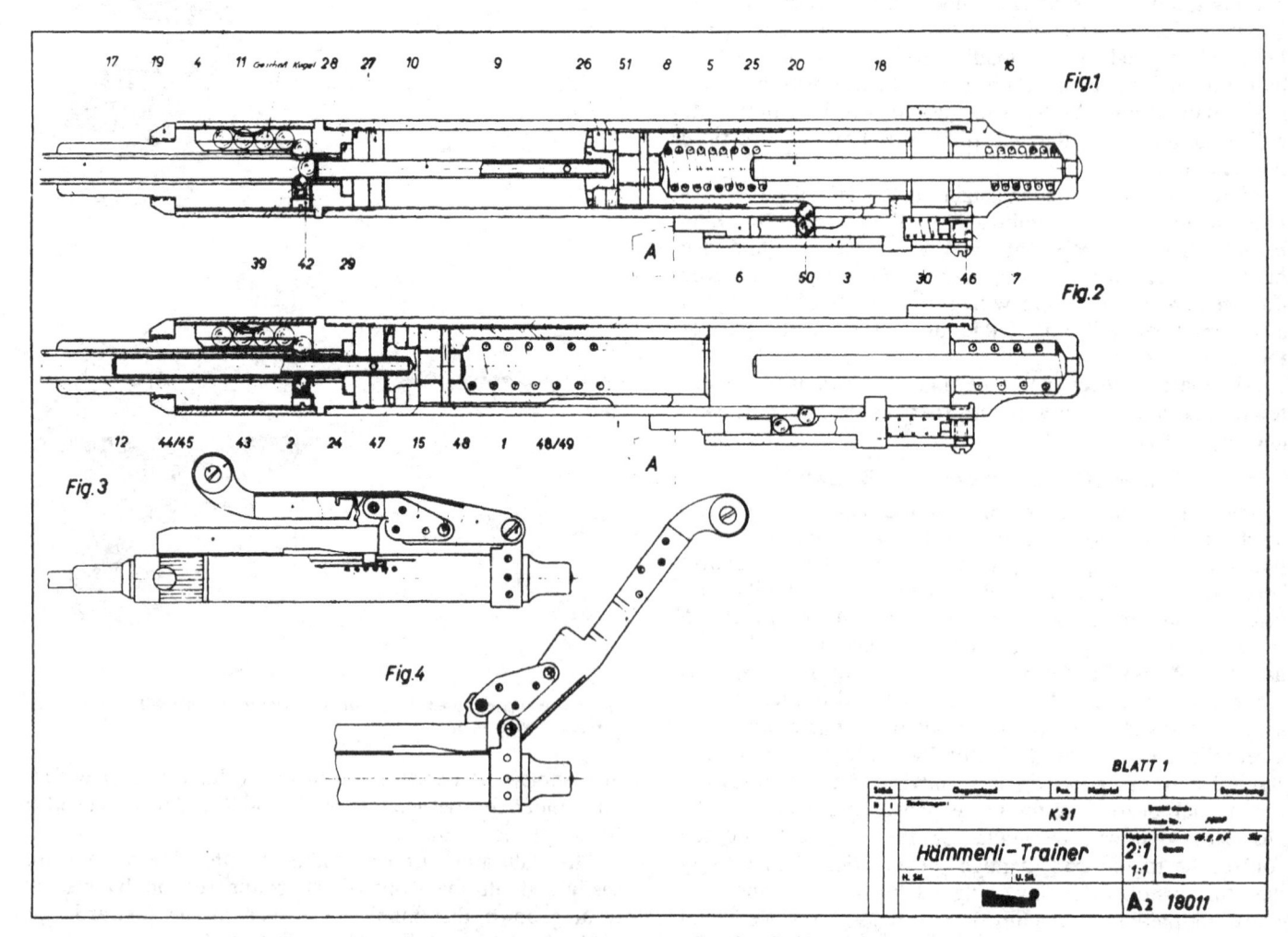

Hämmerli miniature bobbing target.

Hämmerli spring-air trainer magazine conversion for Swiss straight-pull Kar. 31.

166

Hämmerli CO₂ Quickfire Pistol.

The standard gas cartridge will give about 60 shots, due largely to the proper design and positioning of the valving system. As currently being readied for production it is modeled after the Walther Olympia as made by Hämmerli under license, using the same grips and having the same balance. When one remembers the success the Olympia has achieved as a .22 target pistol, this addition as a trainer presages new records in the CO_2 field.

This Quickfire pistol, incidentally, is the basis for a mechanism which will eventually appear as an automatic CO_2 rifle, and as a trainer for automatic arms if the plans of the factory are effectuated. While the author, as a result of experience, has many mental reservations here, the fact remains that the basic designs do lend themselves to developments long overdue in this field.

Other Hämmerli Developments

The application of the Hämmerli trainer to spring-air (not as erroneously claimed "compressed air" usage) has been dealt with herein. In all cases it is superior to the CO_2 system from the standpoint of low cost and long life; for in the exhaustive series of tests conducted by the author it has been established that no valve-using gas system can hope to be as trouble free as the spring-air system.

The cost and convenience differences are self-apparent. You can use the spring-air arm anytime you have projectiles; the CO_2 requires gas cartridges in addition. On the other hand, the air trainers as made by Hämmerli are rated as usable with accuracy up to a maximum of 20 feet, while the CO_2 versions extend the distance to about 35 feet, the basic reason being that dimensional limitations prevent spring usage which will give maximum velocity in the experience of Hämmerli. It might be noted in passing, however, that systems have been encountered by the author which permit far better use of springs than currently used and contemplated, so the spring-air system may be capable of overcoming this particular handicap.

Hämmerli Bobbing Targets

While there are scores of ingenious low-cost targets for both plinking and target work on the market—British, German, and American—the one developed by Hämmerli for use with the Quickfire pistol is by far the best the author has encountered, which is to say the best of probably 200 designs!

A photo of this new Hämmerli silhouette target gives an idea of its value. It is, dimensionally, a 6-yard target, which exactly simulates shooting at the standard 25-meter international target! What you can do on this at 6 yards with the Quickfire you should be able to do on the international 25-meter with a .22 match auto target pistol. Everything about it from the overall size of the target on down is proportionally reduced as required. It can be operated manually or by electricity. It can be set for repeating cycles of 4, 6, and 8 seconds, and for the desired "hold" periods in between. Here is a development long overdue, and one quite as important in its way as the pistol for which it was developed.

World Interest

While still in the almost unknown stage to the general public, these various devices have recently attracted considerable attention in world military and precision-shooting circles.

This photo shows a group of military attachés, including U.S., studying and test shooting at the Hämmerli factory at Lenzburg, Switzerland. They are shown shooting the Swiss Military Kar. 31 with the Hämmerli trainer installed.

When expert shooters of the caliber of these men are impressed with Hämmerli trainer results, the average marksman cannot help but be interested.

CHAPTER 12

Current Compressed Air (Pneumatic) Arms

(Note: All current compressed-air arms are of American manufacture.)

A COMPRESSED-AIR GUN (or rifle or pistol) is an arm in which the air which furnishes the force to propel the pellet (or ball, bullet, dart, or spear) is compressed in a chamber, which may be housed within the arm or may be attached directly to it.

A COMPRESSED-AIR DESIGN differs from a SPRING-AIR DESIGN in that the former has the air *already stored under compression* when the trigger is pressed; while in the latter type the air is *compressed during movement of the spring-driven piston* after release of those elements by trigger squeeze.

The only COMPRESSED-AIR ARMS currently being manufactured are the Benjamin, Crosman, and Sheridan. These are all made in the United States. Regulatory laws, or fear of them, have been the basic reason for failure of the British and European air-gun makers to undertake compressed-air design.

An official of one large manufacturing group put it this way: "We know that were we to lift the velocity of our large air rifles . . . we should immediately run into trouble with the Home Office who are in a position *administratively to declare* the air rifle producing such a velocity a *firearm,* whereby it would require the owner to be in possession of a firearm certificate before purchase. This, of course, would considerably reduce the volume of our (home) sale."

Since compressed-air types are capable of developing far more power than the common spring-air variety, obviously their production would invite regulatory action. Hence all standard British and European types are spring-operated with factory-set power limitations built into them which do not materially exceed 600 f.p.s. In Britain penetration is the deciding legal factor. Any air gun which will exceed the penetration currently acceptable, can be arbitrarily classed as a "firearm" by the Home Secretary.

TYPES OF COMPRESSED-AIR ARMS

Without exception, all the above mentioned current types have *built-in air chambers*. These are pumped up as required by a pump which is an integral part of the arm itself. The number of pumping strokes determines the variable power, which can considerably exceed European police regulations. (See under Sheridan for an example.) All current production types are designed *to release the entire pumped-up air charge on one pull of the trigger.*

These appear as:

(1) Single-shot types, where the gun must be pumped up and the individual projectile hand-inserted in the breech for each shot. The entire air charge is released by each trigger pull.

(2) Magazine types, which require pumping up for each discharge, but where the pellets are contained in a tubular magazine, commonly of the gravity type. The muzzle is elevated slightly to allow the pellets to feed down and the cocking of the action feeds them in one at a time without manual insertion for discharge.

(3) Rifles, guns (not rifled), pistols, and miniature shotguns.

Calibers are air rifle shot or .175, .177 (4.5-mm. European designation and No. 1 bore British designation), .20 (or 5-mm.), .22 (5.5-mm. or No. 2 bore), and obsolete types occasionally encountered such as .25 caliber (British No. 3 bore). (The American Apache also had a .250 caliber, but this is not currently made.)

ADVANTAGES OF COMPRESSED-AIR DESIGNS

Advantages over the spring-air types are many. They may be summarized as follows:

(1) Lack of Disturbing Recoil. This leads to better shooting by the beginner. The trigger merely releases the valve to allow air already compressed to enter the chamber behind the pellet. (Note: Spring-air guns all have noticeable recoil which, unlike powder rifles, starts well before the bullet is out of the barrel. The recoil varies according to the spring-piston and air-chamber design.) (See under Spring-air arms for a detailed description.)

(2) Shorter Overall Length. Compressed-air chambers are normally *below the shot barrel,* allowing compact design, an important factor to beginners and youths. (Note: Spring-air rifles of modern design and target power all house their pistons and compression springs in a tube *to the rear* of the barrel and in prolongation of it. Many spring-air *pistols* are design exceptions, for like the compressed-air types, they often house their power units below the barrel or, alternatively, around the barrel or in the grip. Many common German designs, however, are merely shortened versions of their standard spring-air rifles.)

(3) Lighter in Weight. The shorter overall length, lighter parts, and absence of shock factors found in spring-air types all serve to allow weight reductions in com-

First Benjamin repeater. Called the Automatic, Model 600. Length 36 inches. Barrel 20 inches. Trigger safety and slip-trigger firing mechanism. Push-piston type. BB. Magazine on right side of receiver.

pressed-air types. Since there is no appreciable recoil, weight is not a desirable factor in a compressed-air arm, as it may be in other types requiring weight for stability.

(4) Greater Power. Air chambers and valves are designed to handle *variable amounts* of air, depending upon the compression produced by the number of pump-up strokes. This permits far greater velocity and penetration *under maximum compression* than is customary with spring-air arms. (Note: While it is actually possible to use springs which will give air compression of a higher order than customary, this is seldom done. See under spring-air arms for description. The maximum power which will still allow easy cocking, plus low weight, plus regulatory factors, have decided the approximate maximum power of European types.)

(5) Variable Power. Power may be varied for indoor or outdoor shooting depending upon the number of pump strokes. Spring-air patterns on the other hand have preset springs, giving (usually) constant and not controllable power.

(6) Chamber Charge. Compressed-air arms may be kept pumped up ready for instant cocking and loading with pellet without damage to the mechanism. (Note: Spring-air types are subject to damage and spring injury through spring settings if left for any appreciable length of time with the spring compressed ready for loading and firing.)

(7) Ease of Operation. The pumps in current arms are all pivoted near the muzzle, allowing maximum leverage and ease of operation, a most important factor to the young shooter. (Note: By comparison, most of the breakdown and underlever spring-air patterns are clumsy, awkward, and relatively difficult to compress.)

DISADVANTAGES OF COMPRESSED-AIR ARMS

(1) They Require Two or More Pump Strokes. While the strokes are easier than the single-cocking action of a spring-air type, more strokes still are required to equal that power. This however is a relatively minor factor in actual use. One stroke will seldom seal off the valve and will normally result in a bullet sticking in the barrel. The normal minimum is 2 strokes, but these are fast and easy.

Five or seven strokes will usually *equal* the power of any spring-air type. Eight to ten should normally be the maximum number used if the valves are in good condition.

(2) They Require More Attention for Constant Shooting Qualities. Strokes must be balanced. That is, one must consciously use the *same number* of strokes, made at *about the same speed* for best results. All strokes should be to the full extent of the pump movement. Varying the length of the stroke or its rhythm will somewhat vary the amount of air compression resulting. Thus compressed-air arms need more conscious attention in use than do spring-air patterns.

(3) Energy Loss in Air Compressing. First let it be stated that for all *practical* purposes, this loss has little effect on shooting. Nevertheless, it is a scientific fact that all pump-up arms regardless of type are in the isothermic class, meaning that changes in pressure or volume will take place in charging the air chamber.

All air pumping, of course, generates heat which is simply wasted effort and energy. This heat energy is lost through conduction before the arm is discharged. Some of the energy used in pumping up the chamber will thus be diverted into useless heat rather than usable air pressure. Each degree centigrade of heat developed during pumping will expand the volume of air by one two hundred and seventy-third, and as the heat dissipates, there will be a corresponding loss of volume and of accompanying pressure. In addition, there is always a certain (small) amount of air seepage, much as in automobile tires. Valving requirements for handling high pressure really make this a desirable characteristic so long as it is controlled.

(Note: Spring-air arms also have deficiencies which offset their efficiency comparison factors. For instance, friction varies in relation to piston-washer or ring wear, lubrication, etc.)

POWER COMPARISONS: COMPRESSED-AIR VS. SPRING-AIR TYPES

Here we must make a distinction between rifles and pistols.

Figures given by manufacturers invariably indicate results obtained under optimum conditions, naturally. They know their product, know how to get best results from it. Their data in general are to be depended upon. However, it must be kept in mind that in the hands of the *average* user, many variables will arise. In the observation and individual tests by this author, making controlled comparisons on the most modern scientific testing equipment available, results generally bore out pretty well the general claims on velocity and power made by manufacturers, although there were exceptions, of course.

Data on individual makes will be discussed in relation to those herein where manufacturers have made checkable data available.

Where no checked data are mentioned, the manufacturer in question, for reasons best known to himself, failed to submit data *for impartial comparative testing*.

The finest spring-air pistol made *from a weapons standpoint* is probably the Walther 53. It not only looks like a target auto pistol, it also is designed to *recoil* like one. However, the spring compression, while strong enough for maximum accuracy within short-range limits, is not enough to give much striking power or penetration. This is a special purpose design (see under Walther).

In comparison tests, the Webley Senior was the most efficient and accurate pistol of overall air-pistol usage.

BENJAMIN COMPRESSED-AIR ARMS

The Benjamin Air Rifle Company is the oldest firm continuously in the business of manufacturing compressed-air rifles and pistols. Benjamin developed the first successful modern, low-priced air rifles and pistols.

Walter R. Benjamin was granted original patents for a compressed-air rifle in the last century at a time when Quackenbush was busy developing spring-air patterns. Because the design, while very simple in essence, required precision manufacture and fits, Benjamin worked out a manufacturing deal with the Wissler Instrument Company of St. Louis, Missouri, a firm then turning out quality surveying instruments and doing fine general machine work.

The Wissler organization made the first "Benjamin pump" rifle in 1882. The principle was simple, operating like the common single-stroke bicycle pump. Below the

COMPRESSED-AIR RIFLES (comparison of strokes to f.p.s.)

Make	Model	Number of Strokes	Velocity (Approximate)	Ammunition Used
Crosman	140	6 pump strokes. Minimum, 2 strokes. Maximum, 12 strokes.	450 f.p.s. at muzzle. 350 f.p.s. at muzzle. 700 f.p.s. at muzzle.	Cal. .22 Crosman pellet, Diabolo pattern.
Sheridan	"Silver Streak"	6 pump strokes. Minimum, 2 strokes. Maximum, 12 strokes.	620 f.p.s. at muzzle. 400 f.p.s at muzzle. 770 f.p.s. at muzzle.	Cal. .20 (Sheridan Special) Sheridan bullet, bantam, pointed.

(Note: Disparity in above comparisons may stem from differences in bullet weights and types more than from the rifles.)

SPRING-AIR RIFLES

Make	Model	Operation	Velocity	Ammunition Used
BRITISH:				
Webley	Mark III	Underlever	Approximately 540 f.p.s. at muzzle.	Cal. .22 (standard No. 1 bore) Webley pellets, Diabolo pattern.
B.S.A.	Airsporter	Underlever	Approximately 520 f.p.s. at muzzle.	Cal. 22 (standard No. 1 bore) B.S.A. pellets (Pylarm), Diabolo pattern.
GERMAN:				
Diana	Peerless 35E	Underlever	411 f.p.s. at muzzle.	Cal. .22 (standard 5.5-mm.) RWS "Hornet" pellet, Diabolo pattern.
Weihrauch	HW35M	Special breakdown	430 f.p.s. at muzzle.	Cal. .22 (standard 5.5-mm.) Diabolo pattern—RWS "Hornet."

(Note: These spring-air rifles are all heavy and require considerable cocking-power effort. The underlevers are actually easier to cock than powerful breakdown types of the order of the Wiehrauch.)

POWER COMPARISONS—COMPRESSED-AIR VS SPRING-AIR PISTOLS

Make	Model	Number of Strokes	Velocity	Ammunition Used
COMPRESSED AIR:				
Crosman	(Series)	6 pump strokes. (Up to 10 strokes allowable.)	Approximately 300 f.p.s. at muzzle.	Cal. .22 standard Diabolo pellet.
SPRING-AIR:				
Webley	Senior	Cocking completed, 1 stroke. (No additional power possible.)	320 f.p.s. at muzzle.	Cal. .22 standard Diabolo pellet.
Hy Score		Cocking completed, 1 stroke. (No additional power possible.)	Approximately 365 f.p.s. at muzzle.	Cal. .22 standard Diabolo pellet.

(Note: While Webley has a better cocking leverage principle, the American Hy Score pistol has the advantage of a longer barrel and greater spring compression, the spring being around the barrel. These two factors help account for the higher muzzle velocities.

Hy Score oiling recommendations result in utilizing "diesel effect" much more than does Webley. This factor tends not only to *increase* velocity but to hamper *uniformity* of velocity, which can adversely affect accuracy.

All German makes currently in production and available for test are in .177 (4.5-mm.) caliber, so comparisons are not made here. However, in nearly all such designs either the leverage, the spring compression, or the barrel length—or all three factors—are inferior to both the Webley and the Hy Score. Results of checks on these individual pistols will be found under data on the individual arms.)

171

Pumping up the air chamber, Benjamin 300 Series.

shot barrel a barrel of larger diameter was positioned, which was actually a pump tube. From the tube projected the flanged head of the pump rod. The rod was pulled out to its stroke limit. The rod head was placed against the floor, a tree, a wall, or other solid object. The rifle was pressed down or forward quickly. A traditional leather plunger at the inner end of the rod compressed air in the tube after passing the air inlet. The compressed air forced open the air inlet valve into the air chamber (or reservoir), the spring valve closing automatically at the end of the pump stroke. The rod could be pulled out and pushed in repeatedly to store more air and build up progressively higher pressures in the air chamber just as was done in a bicycle tire. With a shot in the barrel, pulling the trigger caused that member to rock and depress a pin which opened the chamber outlet valve. The contents of the air chamber blew violently through and propelled the missile out of the barrel. The outlet valve was spring returned ready for the air chamber to be re-charged.

The better accuracy, absence of practical recoil, and particularly the very considerable penetration obtainable (as much as 1 inch in soft pine) quickly established the rifle as being superior to the spring-air guns of the time. It was a short-range weapon usable at low cost and without the use of powder cartridges. Various attempts at competition failed because very few organizations at that time could work to the required fits and tolerances; and the economic and social conditions in the 1880-1890 period did not provide a very wide market for serious air arms as is the case today. The interest then was basically at the toy level, as in the case of the Daisy.

However, the public acceptance of the rifle soon induced Wissler to take a financial interest in the project. In 1900 Walter Benjamin sold out his entire interest to Wissler. He entered the toy manufacturing business with considerable success.

Since the name was well established and the rifle widely accepted, the Wissler Company continued manufacture of Benjamin pump guns until the time of the death of the owner of the firm in 1926. At that time A. P. Spack, Sr. arranged to purchase the entire Wissler business from the heirs. Mr. Spack had worked in the firm for over 14 years and was aware of its possibilities. At the time of this writing Mr. Spack is still active as president and general manager of the organization.

Spack sold out the surveying instrument business in 1927 to concentrate on the manufacture of air rifles, and at that time incorporated the new business under the name of the "Benjamin Air Rifle Company."

The depression of the 1930's, which destroyed so many small firms, was a severe setback to the Benjamin Company, and only the personal drive and energy of Mr. Spack kept Benjamin in business.

In 1933 Benjamin introduced their first pump-up Benjamin air *pistol,* quite a notable achievement in this field. The early models used the pull-out-push-in piston-rod system of the original Benjamin design, but these were later replaced with the current pump-lever system.

Every competitor who followed Benjamin borrowed to a greater or lesser extent from that firm, a fact that was inevitable because the basic patents had long since expired and variations could be made of later details.

Unfortunately, there are no very clear historical details on the very early Benjamin models. In addition to the current line, however, details, photos, and drawings of all the important models which were sold in large quantities will be found herein, together with the author's photos of several of the early unlisted ones, which, incidentally, are still in good working condition after 50 to 60 years of use and standing in collections!

With the national interest in this pellet-shooting field expanding (both in compressed-air and CO_2 designs), Benjamin is working to improve its current lines and to develop new ones. The manufacturing firm is under the control of Mr. Spack and his sons, a fact which has much to do with the maintenance of high product quality for the price.

Benjamin Rifle Notes

As an accuracy index, Benjamin expects its rifles to target as follows:

Smooth Bore Using Air-Rifle Shot (Round). Fired from machine rest, may keep all shots in a 3-inch pattern (if pump-up and quality of ammunition is standard) at 15 to 20 yards. Note that accuracy is the same with either single-shot or magazine smooth bore. Using .177 pellets, this same gun because of the tighter air seal provided by this style of bullet, should group about 2 inches.

Rifled Models Using Either .177 or .22 Pellets. Under the same conditions as above, these rifles will normally keep all shots within a 1-inch pattern, according to the manufacturer.

Exceptional marksmen who know their rifles and their ammunition may often make much smaller groups, of course. The above figures are stated as average.

For accuracy at the above ranges, the lighter and hence faster traveling .177 pellet will be somewhat better than the heavier and slower-moving .22. The .22 of course hits somewhat harder. The light Benjamin trigger pull is an aid to accurate shooting.

The Benjamin Company tests each rifle and pistol by pumping up and firing several shots before final inspection.

When trouble occurs with a new Benjamin compressed-air gun, it is usually because of a lack of knowledge on the part of the owner. Common troubles are:

(1) Safety is not put "off," and gun can't be fired; or safety is set and trigger pulled with it on, resulting in a need for recocking the hammer as described.

(2) Trigger assembly is not fastened securely to the gun barrel, and must be tightened.

(3) Gun has been over-pumped and is "air locked." Usually this can be remedied by firing without loading to drop air pressure.

(4) A pellet may be stuck in the barrel. This happens when an occasional poor pellet sticks, or a re-used one wedges in the barrel; or when the rifle is discharged without sufficient air having been pumped up to expel the bullet. (Note that *any* compressed-air arm needs a minimum of 2 strokes because of sealing needs and pressure requirements.) Bullet should be pushed out of barrel with a rod if it does not respond to pressure from 8 or 10 pumps.)

(5) Valves may be unseated, allowing leakage, or oil (which should never be used) is put on valves. Valves can be corrected with special valve tool. In many cases, however, they can be seated merely by pumping to get pressure into air chamber.

(6) Bolt screw guide may be lost or battered and should be replaced. This failure is an obvious one.

(7) Bolt-lock cam can be out of adjustment, allowing air to escape at breech. This is not dangerous. It can be corrected by lifting bolt handle about halfway, then loosening the cam screws, pushing the cam piece forward until tight, then tightening the screws.

BENJAMIN AIR RIFLES, 300 SERIES, MODELS 310, 312, AND 317

Manufacturer: Benjamin Air Rifle Company, St. Louis, Missouri.
Overall Length: 35 inches. (Barrel 23 inches.)
Weight: About 4 pounds.
Caliber(s): M310, air-rifle shot .175; M312, .22 Diabolo; M317, .177 Diabolo.
Type(s) of Ammunition Used: Steel round air-rifle shot, .177 and .22 waisted, respectively.
Rifled: M310, smooth bore. M312 and M317, rifled.
Operating System: Compressed air. Underlever pump-up. Single discharge system.
Cocked: Raise and pull back bolt handle as in common bolt action.

Loaded: M310, shot placed in bolt nose cavity. Others, standard.
Number Rounds: Single shot only. Must be pumped up and loaded each shot.
Stock Type: Walnut, one-piece. Separate pump handle also wood.
Front Sight(s): Standard post type.
Rear Sight(s): Usual barrel type V, adjustable windage and elevation.
Velocity (Approximate): Varies with number of pumps. (Tests indicate 250 to 700 f.p.s. range.)
Normal Accurate Range: Maker claims 1 inch at 15 to 20 yards.
Normal Maximum Range: Standard for pellet type.
Approximate Retail Price: $18 to $20 average. Higher-priced stocks available.

REMARKS

Description. These are compressed-air rifles with built-in pumps below barrel. The pump lever is pivoted near the muzzle. It folds under the barrel forward of the stock.

In common with all compressed-air devices, these rifles utilize a piston which works back and forth in an air cylinder. The jointed pump lever operates this piston (or plunger) to make pumping easier.

When the lever is pulled away from the body of the rifle, it draws the piston out past an air-intake hole. When the lever and the rifle proper are pushed together to close, the piston is thrust down in the air cylinder (tube) and compresses the air in its path, forcing it through an intake valve into the air chamber. The valve is seated to hold air pressure. A powerful valve spring closes the valve at the end of the pumping stroke. Strokes should be continuous and positive once started.

(Note: Over-pumping can buckle or strain the pump lever, may damage both intake and outlet valves, and can even result in pulling the shot barrel loose from the pump barrel. More than 10 or 12 pumps are never advisable. If the gun doesn't achieve maximum power on that number, then the valves are probably defective and should be replaced. This applies to any pump-up design of this pattern regardless of manufacturer.)

Late models use Hycar pump washers. These are a neoprene-like material, self-expanding, with positive sealing when in good condition. One or two pumps should be left in the air chamber when the rifle is not in use to maintain sealing qualities. This pressure will keep the valves firmly seated.

When the rifle has been pumped up as desired, turn bolt handle up and pull back until trigger and hammer engage, when a click will be heard. This is the end of the rear stroke on the bolt.

Loading Model 310. End of the bolt in this model *is bored out*. Press a ball into the bolt cavity. Push bolt handle forward to chamber shot, and turn it down to lock. Very little pressure is needed to close, as the design does not require it because of the relatively low chamber pressures involved.

Note that in this model the standard .177 *waisted pellet* may also be used if desired. Because of design and tight fit, it will shoot more accurately than the air-rifle shot, which is a round ball. If pellets are used, they should be seated directly into the barrel chamber until flush.

.177 darts may also be used, since the barrel is not rifled. Push these in pointed end first until the tail is clear of the bolt. Then close bolt and lock.

Loading Models 312 and 317. Instead of the hollow bolt end as required for round shot in Model 310, these have shaped projections at the end of the bolt. Merely place the correct caliber pellet in the breech opening, solid end to the front. Push the bolt forward and the front end of the bolt will properly seat the pellet in the rifling. Turn the bolt handle down and the gun is ready to fire.

Safety. The safety should always be applied except when ready to fire. The trigger should not be pulled when the safety is applied, as the hammer may then press against the safety and make it necessary to pull the bolt back to recock the hammer before gun can be fired. (Note that this is not a very satisfactory safety design in this respect. It is the principal unsatisfactory feature of the Benjamin arms.)

When these guns are very hard to pump up, either the pump cylinder is too dry, which is seldom the case and which requires just a very little oil in the air hole; or more probably, the gun is being pumped against a maximum-loaded air chamber. Firing without using pellets will correct this condition by gradually letting off air pressure until the point is reached where the air release mechanism will function.

It should be noted, also, that since there is a difference in the suppleness of pump washers, different rifles may require a different number of pumps to achieve the same power. Hence the owner should test his individual rifle to learn how many strokes are required to do the kind of shooting he personally wants to do. Remember, too, that any over-pumped (air-locked) gun, if it functions, will have lower, not higher, power, because the air pressure in the air chamber will be too great, and the hammer blow which opens the outlet valve will not be great enough to overcome the additional pressure. This prevents release of the entire air charge at one hammer blow, which in turn means less power and useless air remaining in the air chamber.

Photographs and drawings below show all details of construction and operation of this series. It must be kept in mind that all must be individually pumped up for each shot, since the air reservoir is emptied at each trigger pull if the gun is in proper order; it also must be individually loaded for each shot, since it has no magazine.

BENJAMIN MODEL 720 AIR RIFLE

Manufacturer: Benjamin Air Rifle Company, St. Louis, Missouri.
Overall Length: 35 inches. (Barrel 23 inches.)
Weight: About 6.5 pounds.
Caliber(s): Steel air-rifle shot ONLY.
Type(s) of Ammunition Used: Round steel air-rifle shot ONLY (.175 inch). Lead not recommended.
Rifled: Smooth bore only.
Operating System: Compressed air. Underlever pump. Single discharge system.
Cocked: Standard turn-bolt action.
Loaded: Magazine tube. See details below.

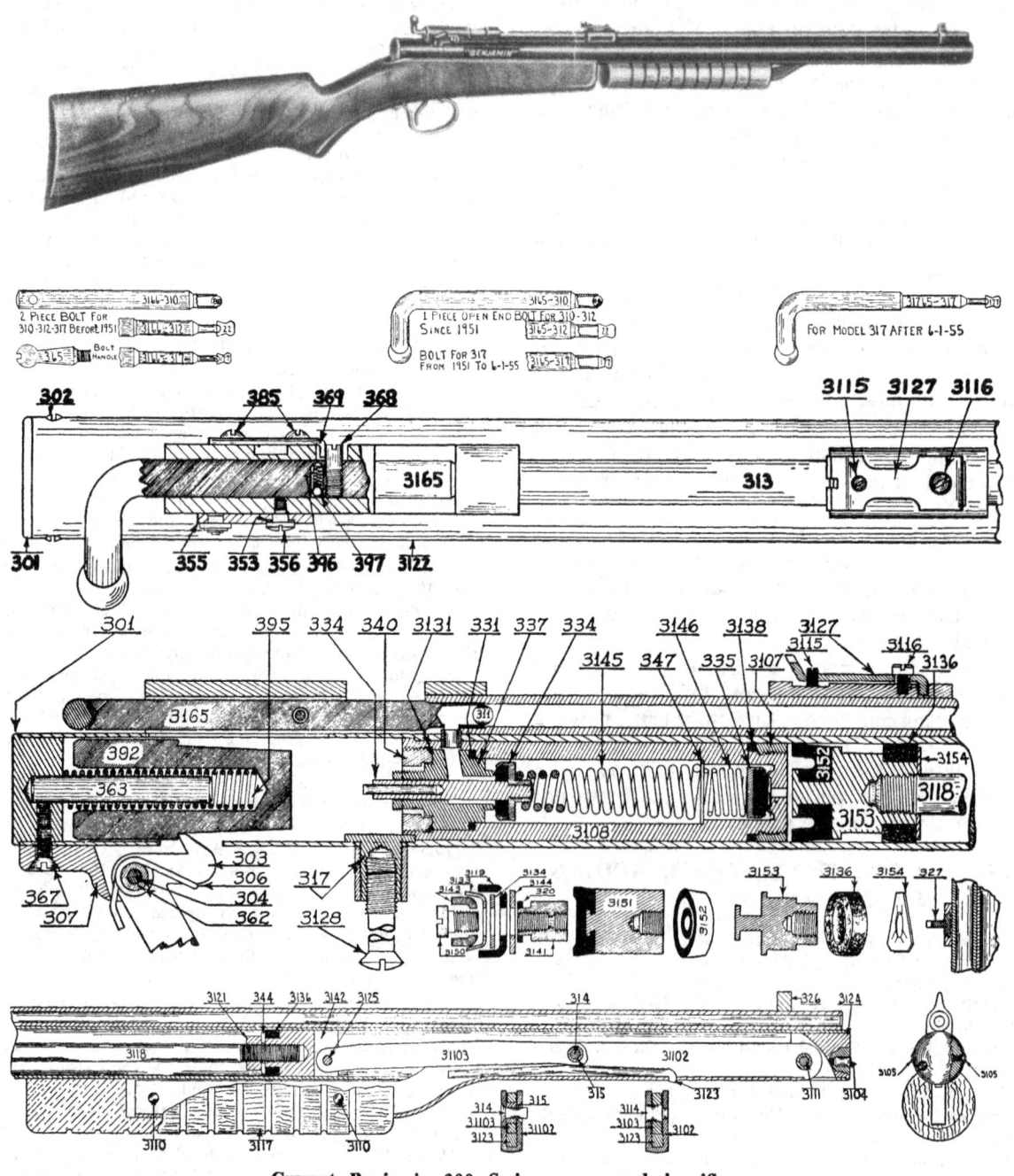

Current Benjamin 300 Series compressed-air rifle.

Number Rounds: 25. (Note that the magazine feeds each time bolt is operated.)
Stock Type: Same as Benjamin 300 Series design.
Front Sight(s): Same as 300 Series.
Rear Sight(s): Same as 300 Series.
Velocity (Approximate): Tests indicate 280 to about 540 f.p.s., according to pumps.
Normal Accurate Range: Maker claims 3-inch group at 15 to 20 yards from rest.
Normal Maximum Range: Standard for type.
Approximate Retail Price: $30.

REMARKS

This is an improved form of the earlier Model 710, the *magazine system* being adapted from the Model 700, which model used a push-pull-rod pump design. The 720 uses the pump-lever system as in the new single-shot rifle described. Note that while it *feeds* automatically, it MUST BE PUMPED UP FOR EACH SHOT.

This model is made to shoot steel air-rifle shot only, waisted-type pellets are too difficult and fragile for a satisfactory feed in this design.

Operation. The magazine feed tube is on the right side of the barrel. It may be loaded before or after pumping the gun up. A projecting feeder handle is provided on the tube. When the magazine is loaded (it will take 25 shots), the handle is released gently.

Then lift bolt handle to unlock. Pull handle all the way back to cock. The magazine spring will feed a shot into line. Push the bolt handle forward and the shot will be chambered. Turn handle down to lock breech ready for discharge.

Note that the last shot serves as a magazine follower and is not expelled from the gun. Incidentally, the bolt should not be opened once the chamber is loaded until it has been discharged. If it should be, then the chambered shot will roll out when the breech is opened and the next round will be fed in. The last shot may be removed when the breech is open by tilting the muzzle up.

This model just as the single-shot models is designed to exhaust all its air on each trigger pull. Each shot fired requires 4 to 5 pumps for average velocity, and 7 to 12 for maximum. In any event, remember that this smooth bore model is not designed for best target accuracy. For real accuracy of the target order, use the models with rifled barrels. The only advantage offered by this type of magazine is that chamber loading is easier and faster. It makes an excellent "plinking" gun.

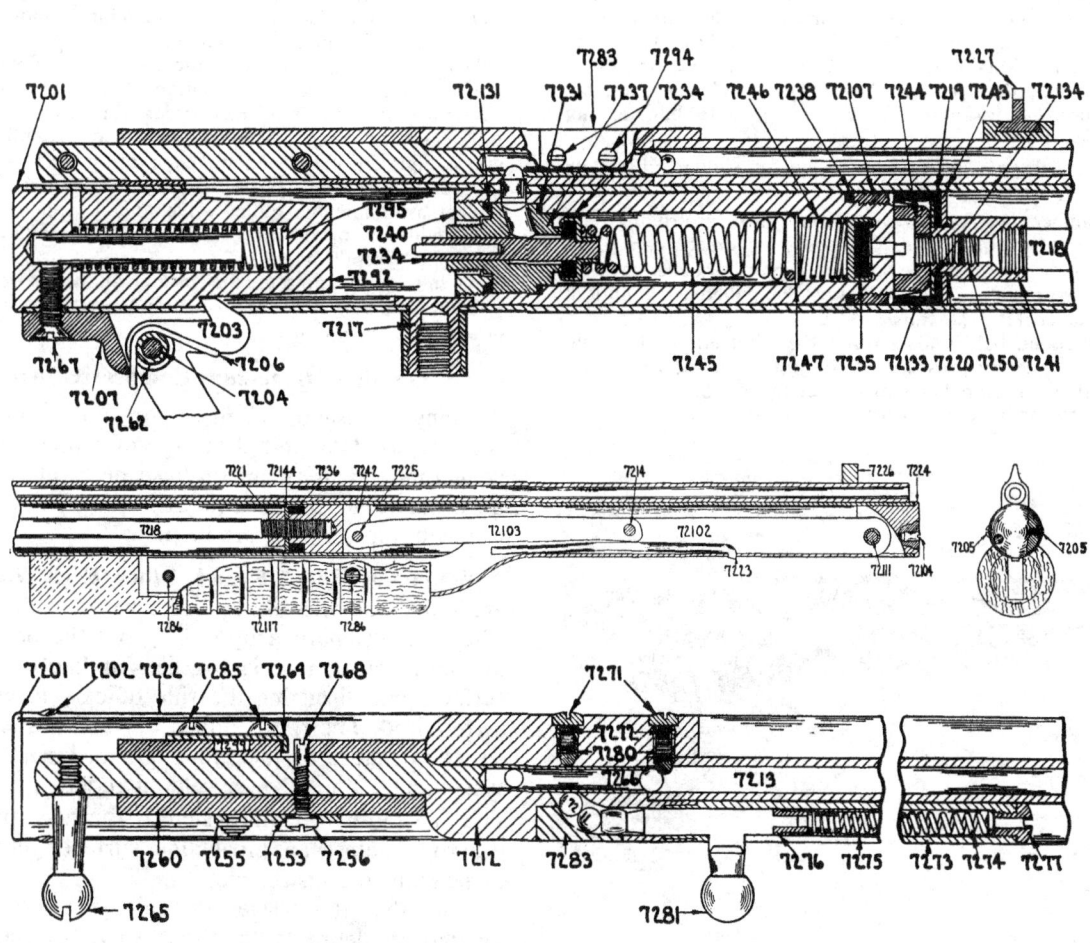

Current Benjamin M720 magazine rifle, round shot only.

BENJAMIN SUPER SINGLE-SHOT TARGET PISTOL, SERIES 130, MODELS, 130, 132, AND 137
(Identical Except As Noted)

Manufacturer: Benjamin Air Rifle Company, St. Louis, Missouri.
Overall Length: 11 inches. (Barrel length 8 inches.)
Weight: 1.75 pounds.
Caliber(s): M130, air-rifle shot (.175); M137, .177; M132, .22.
Type(s) of Ammunition Used: M130, round air-rifle shot, steel or lead; M132, .22 Diabolo-type lead pellets; M137, .177 Diabolo.
Rifled: M130, smooth bore. M132 and M137, rifled.
Operating System: Compressed air. Underlever pump. Single-discharge system.
Cocked: Turn bolt button to unlock. Pull back.
Loaded: Same as in rifle.
Number Rounds: Single shot only.
Stock Type: Well-pitched grip with plastic stocks. Dual thumbrests.
Front Sight(s): Fixed standard post.
Rear Sight(s): Adjustable stamped design. Placed to rear of frame.
Velocity (Approximate): Tests indicate 200 to about 380 f.p.s., varying with number of pumps.
Normal Accurate Range: Average for type. About 30 feet.
Normal Maximum Range: Average for type. About 30 feet.
Approximate Retail Price: $18 to $20.

REMARKS

These are the pistol equivalents of the Benjamin rifles. Smoothbored M130 is expected to group 2 inches at 30 feet. Rifled Models 132 and 137 group 1 inch at 30 feet, according to the manufacturer.

Operation. Pump up by holding pistol firmly in one hand and pulling pump lever out as far as it will go with other hand. Bring the two sections together smartly, taking care not to pinch fingers. Normal power takes 5 or 6 strokes, which are not usually hard. Maximum power takes 10 to 12 strokes, if pistol is in good order. (When valves or piston elements are not in good order, many more strokes are possible but do not produce added power.)

In pumping, observe all precautions as for similar rifles with regard to overpumping, care, etc.

When chamber has been pumped up, turn protruding bolt button at rear of pistol until its pin clears the breech cap below it. This unlocks the breech. Now pull bolt straight back to cock and to expose chamber. Bolt must be pulled back until it clicks into its cocking notch.

The M130 round ball is loaded into the front end of the bolt, where there is a cavity provided for it, just as in the rifle. With M132 and M137, load pellet into the chamber.

Push bolt button to close. Turn it down to lock.

Benjamin 130 Series compressed-air pistol.

Keep safety applied at all times except when ready to fire. Do not press trigger except when ready to fire, as safety is not a positive trigger block.

BENJAMIN SUPER 8-SHOT TARGET PISTOL, MODEL 160

Manufacturer: Benjamin Air Rifle Company, St. Louis, Missouri.
Overall Length: 10.12 inches approximately. (Barrel length 6 inches.)
Weight: 1.75 pounds approximately.
Caliber(s): Air-rifle shot (round .175) ONLY.
Type(s) of Ammunition Used: Steel air-rifle shot, round, .175 ONLY. (Lead may jam.)
Rifled: Smooth bore.
Operating System: Compressed air. Underlever pump. Single discharge system.
Cocked: Turn bolt button up and pull back.
Loaded: Magazine as for corresponding rifle.
Number Rounds: 8.
Stock Type: Standard pistol design.
Front Sight(s): Post.
Rear Sight(s): Elevating by screw adjustment. Sight line 9 inches. On rear of pistol.
Velocity (Approximate): Varying with number of pumps. Tests indicate 260 to 400 f.p.s.
Normal Accurate Range: Maker states it will group 2 inches at 30 feet.
Normal Maximum Range: Average for type.
Approximate Retail Price: $30.

REMARKS

Operation. This is the pistol equivalent of the Benjamin 720 Rifle and is operated in the same manner. Bolt button and pin substitute for rifle bolt handle. Magazine holds only 8 but is otherwise same system. Being but a compact version of the M720, the magazine is loaded in similar fashion.

Air reservoir must be pumped up for each shot as in the rifle or the single-shot Benjamin air pistols. Five to six strokes are required for normal shooting. Maximum should be about 12 strokes if pistol is in good order. Entire air reservoir capacity is released as trigger is pulled. If the air chamber (reservoir) is not completely exhausted on each firing in this model, stretch the hammer spring. This will increase the weight of the hammer impact as it hits the outlet valve, thereby making sure that the valve will stay open long enough to let all contained air be used for pellet propulsion.

At maximum pump-up this pistol will penetrate about ¼-inch of soft pine at 5 feet. Drawings and photos show all details of design and operation.

Obsolete Benjamin Compressed-Air Rifles

Many thousands of these are still giving satisfactory service, so data and drawings of value and interest to collectors and users are supplied herewith, covering those most likely to be encountered. Note that *none* of the following are now in production.

Benjamin Model F and Other Early Designs. These are quite complicated by comparison with later models. They are all charged by pulling out the pump rod below the shot barrel, resting the flanged knob against a solid surface, and thrusting the rifle quickly forward or down as required. The rod is pulled out and pushed in for each stroke. Because of the full-length piston allowed by this system, maximum power seldom requires over 4 strokes. The one fault with this system is the necessity for resting the rod against an unyielding surface, and the danger of bending the piston rod.

Note that the trigger on early models like this one pivoted to depress the outlet valve to release the air. This system required a *fast pull* on the trigger, in order to get complete and efficient air release. This poor feature was improved in the Model G, but not remedied.

Benjamin Model G Rifle. As the operational drawing shows, this was a vast improvement in valving, valve spring system, and valve release. This rifle operated on the pressure system also, but was a big improvement over the earlier "F."

Pulling the trigger forced a striker (or firing pin) ahead to open the valve. Here again it was necessary to pull the trigger *fast* to get best air-release results.

About 2 or 3 strokes gave average power, and 5 was about the maximum that could be pumped up when the gun was in good condition. (Pressure at times could be pumped up as high as 2,000 pounds; but because of the bullet used, the pressure was never worth the effort.)

Benjamin Models 300-317 and 322. Except for caliber and loading data on the 300, these were the same rifles. They were the forerunners of the current series, except that charging was still accomplished by the pull-push-rod system instead of by the modern lever.

Note, however, that these used the hammer "impact" system of valve release. Loading, firing, and other details have altered little since this series was first introduced. The valving system has been improved, but is still the hammer impact type. This system, of course, does away with the necessity for fast trigger pull, and since the arm can be sighted and discharged in match-rifle style by slow pull-off on the trigger, accuracy was easier to achieve than with earlier models.

CAUTION: When charging any of the pull-push chargers, care must be taken to see that the stock is *firmly* screwed to the barrel before the charging motions are started, as otherwise the pressure involved is so great that stocks can be broken during charging, the stock wobbling and the physical thrusting pressure cracking it.

Benjamin Model 600 Magazine Rifle. This is the early version of the current 25-shot, smooth-bore magazine rifle. Charging is on the pull-push-rod pump system.

Magazine system is an early version of the current one. It holds 25 shots. The firing system is on the trigger pressure release idea, though of modified design. This type still required a fast trigger pull which interfered with best accuracy.

In this design, as the trigger pull started, a shot was automatically placed in line for firing, while the continuing pressure resulted in valve release. Thus if the pull was started and not completed, double feeding could happen on the next pull.

The breech cap could be removed to give access to a nut, which, when turned to the left, shortened up the trigger movement, and, when turned to the right, increased it. This gave either lower power and more shots, or higher power and correspondingly greater power by lessening or increasing the opening movement of the valve. This "regulated power" was another Benjamin development of this type.

Like later models, it could be pumped up heavily and would then allow firing 4 or 5 shots before velocity fell off to the point where a few more strokes were required. In other words, within limits it was a true repeater as to charging as well as to feeding.

Benjamin Model 700 Magazine Rifle. The pull-push-charging pump system was still used in this repeater also, but the magazine system was similar to the current one except for minor details.

The firing system was an impact hammer type, how-

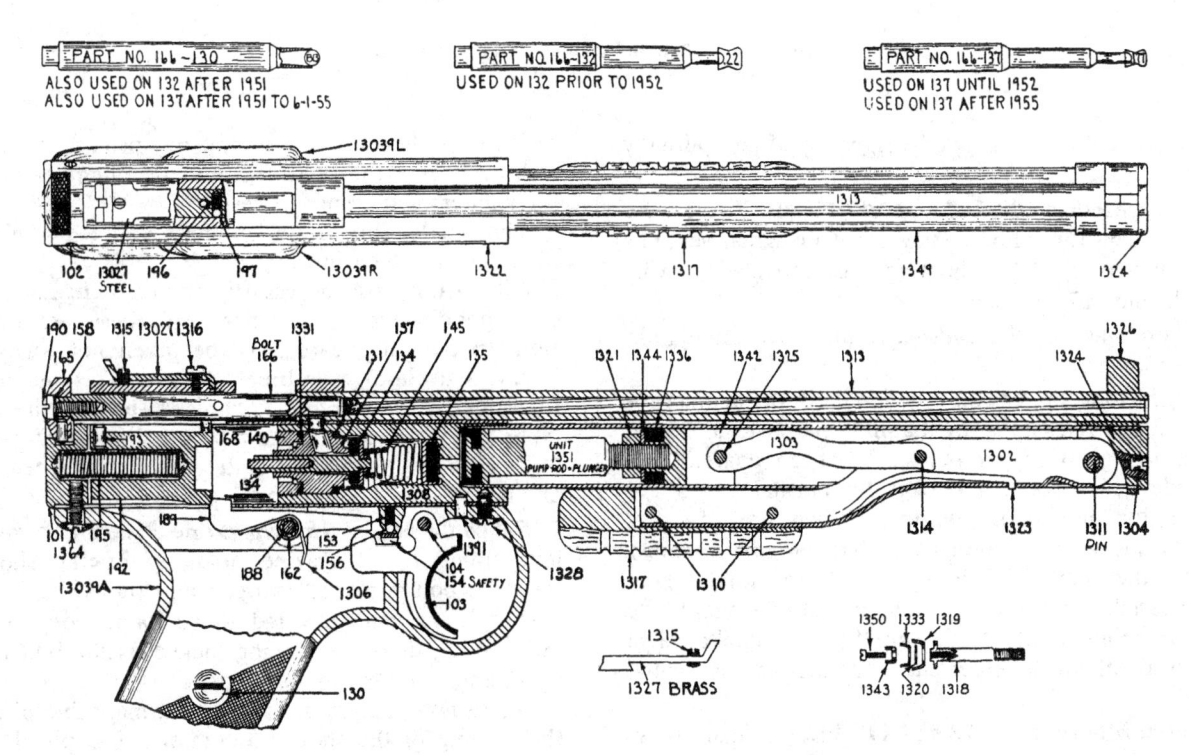

Drawing of Benjamin Super Single Shot Air Pistol.

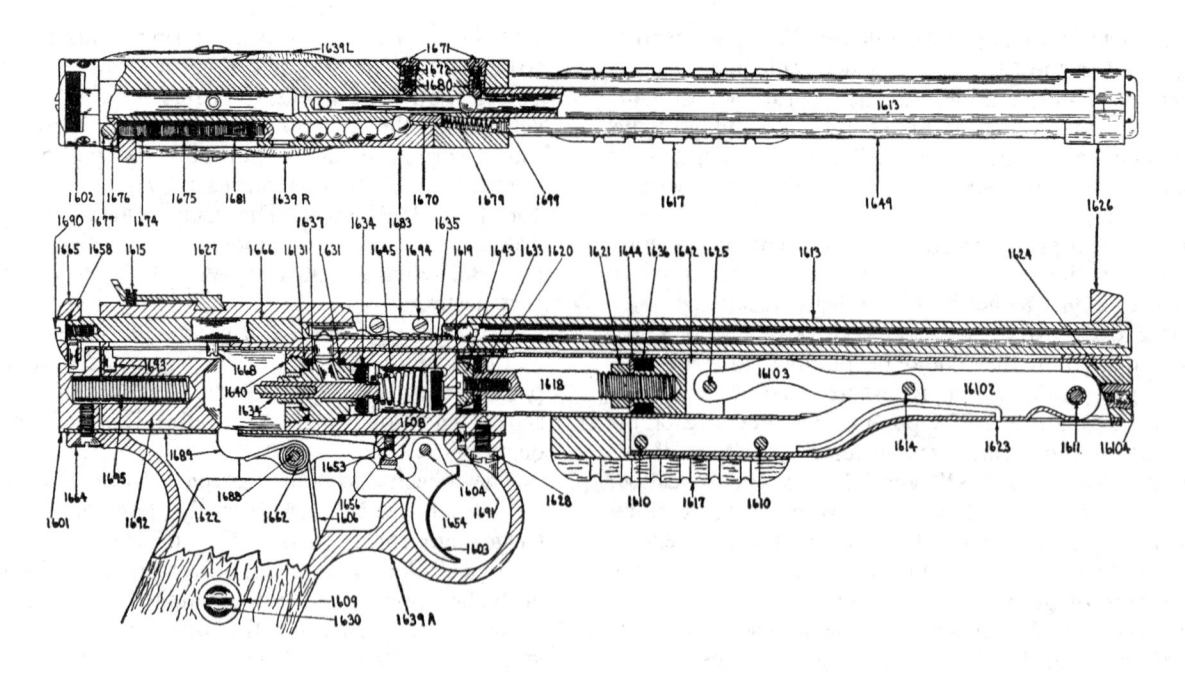

Drawing of Benjamin Super 8-Shot Air Pistol.

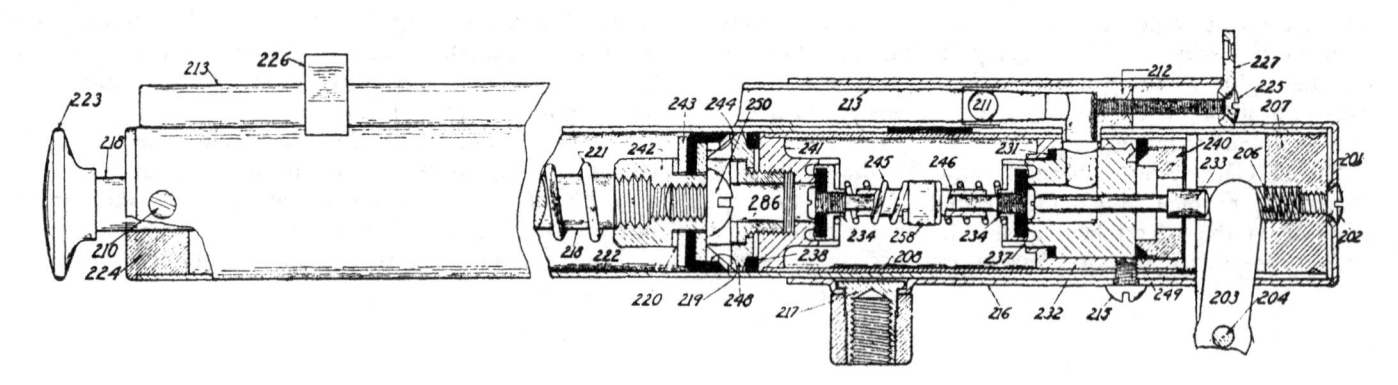

Drawing of Benjamin Single Shot Model "G"

ever, which allowed a good trigger pull as already discussed.

Benjamin Models 100-102 and 107 Pistols. These were the same except for caliber. They are the original versions of the current models, shooting, respectively, air-rifle shot, .22, and .177 pellets.

Pump-up was on the *pull-push pump-rod* Benjamin system, however.

Safety, loading, and firing are standard Benjamin procedure. Valve release is by hammer impact, a design which allows good trigger pull as has been pointed out. This model takes about 4 strokes for normal and about 6 strokes for maximum pump-up. When pressure gets heavy, the air which cannot be forced into the chamber will blow the pump rod back past the air-intake hole when released. To avoid this, the last stroke should be held down momentarily to be sure that the intake valve has allowed all air to enter the chamber and is seated properly.

Benjamin Models 110-112 and 117 Pistols. Again these are the same except for caliber and similar details. This series uses the pump-lever system, instead of the earlier pull-push rod for charging the air chamber. It is the forerunner of the current series.

The safety should be applied before pumping as a precautionary measure.

All pistols are necessarily more delicate than the corresponding series of rifles, and these are no exception. In pumping, care must be taken not to overdo it. You can strain or even break the pump pistons, levers, or fulcrums on any compressed-air pistol by sheer abuse. Note that any additional air pressure so obtained is useless practically, since the outlet valve can't open for long enough to use the additional power.

Benjamin Model 150 Magazine Pistol. Charging is by lever pump-up. Magazine holds 8 air-rifle shot. Each time the bolt is turned to open and pulled back to cock, a shot is automatically fed to be loaded on the closing bolt stroke, the breech being locked as the bolt is turned by pressure on its pin.

Again note that as on the current magazine pistol, only the feeding of the shot is automatic. The pistol must be pumped up for each individual discharge because of the

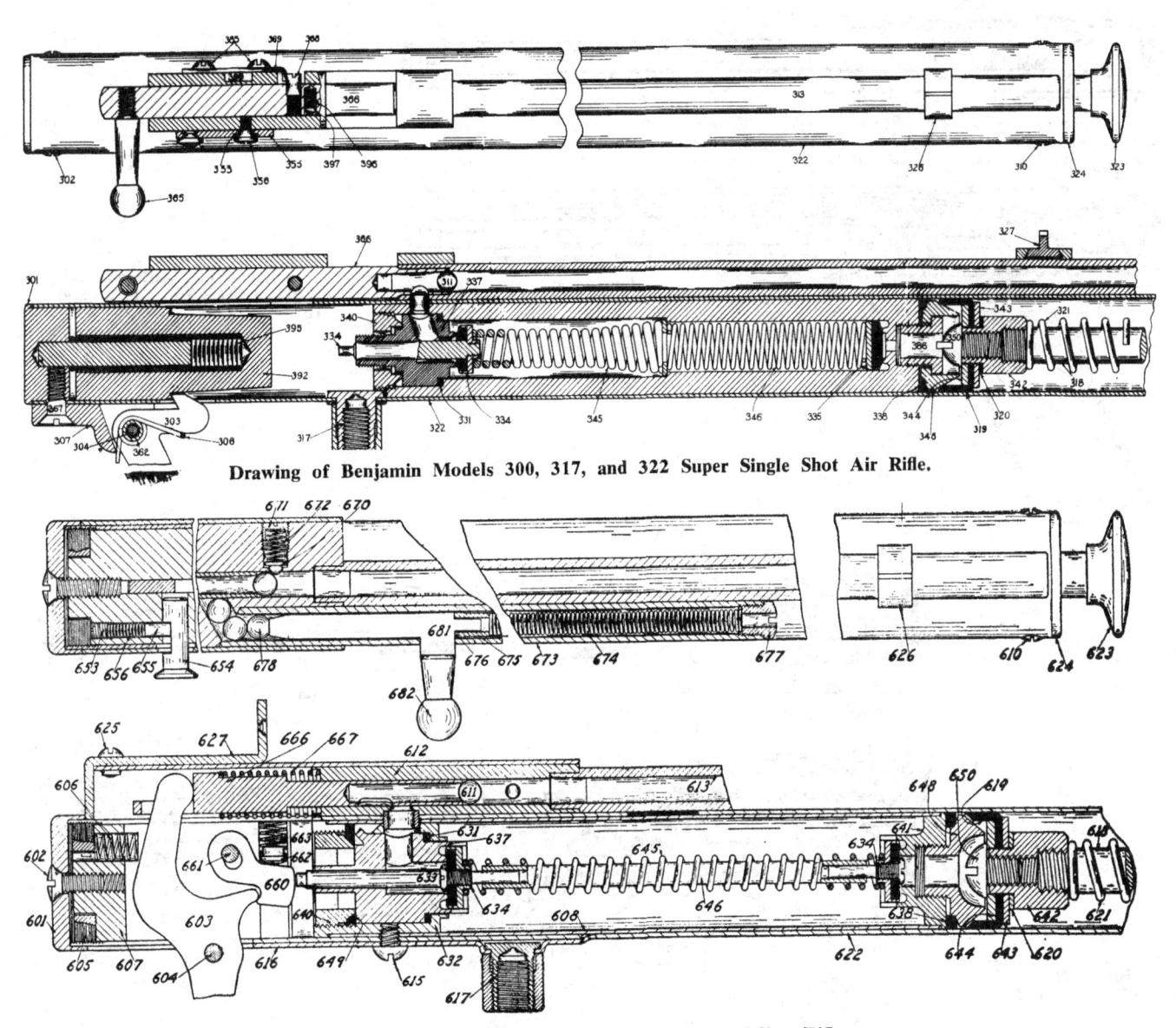

Drawing of Benjamin Models 300, 317, and 322 Super Single Shot Air Rifle.

Drawing of Benjamin Model 600 Automatic 25-Shot Rifle.

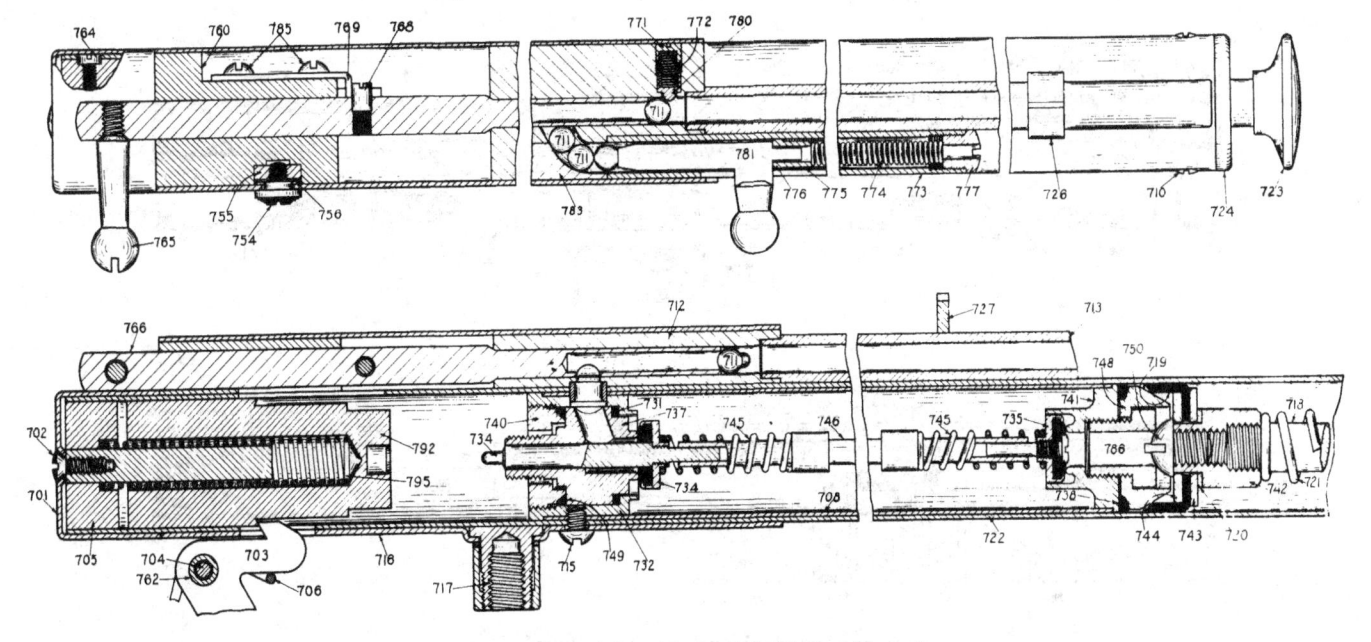

Drawing of Benjamin Model 700 25-Shot Repeater.

179

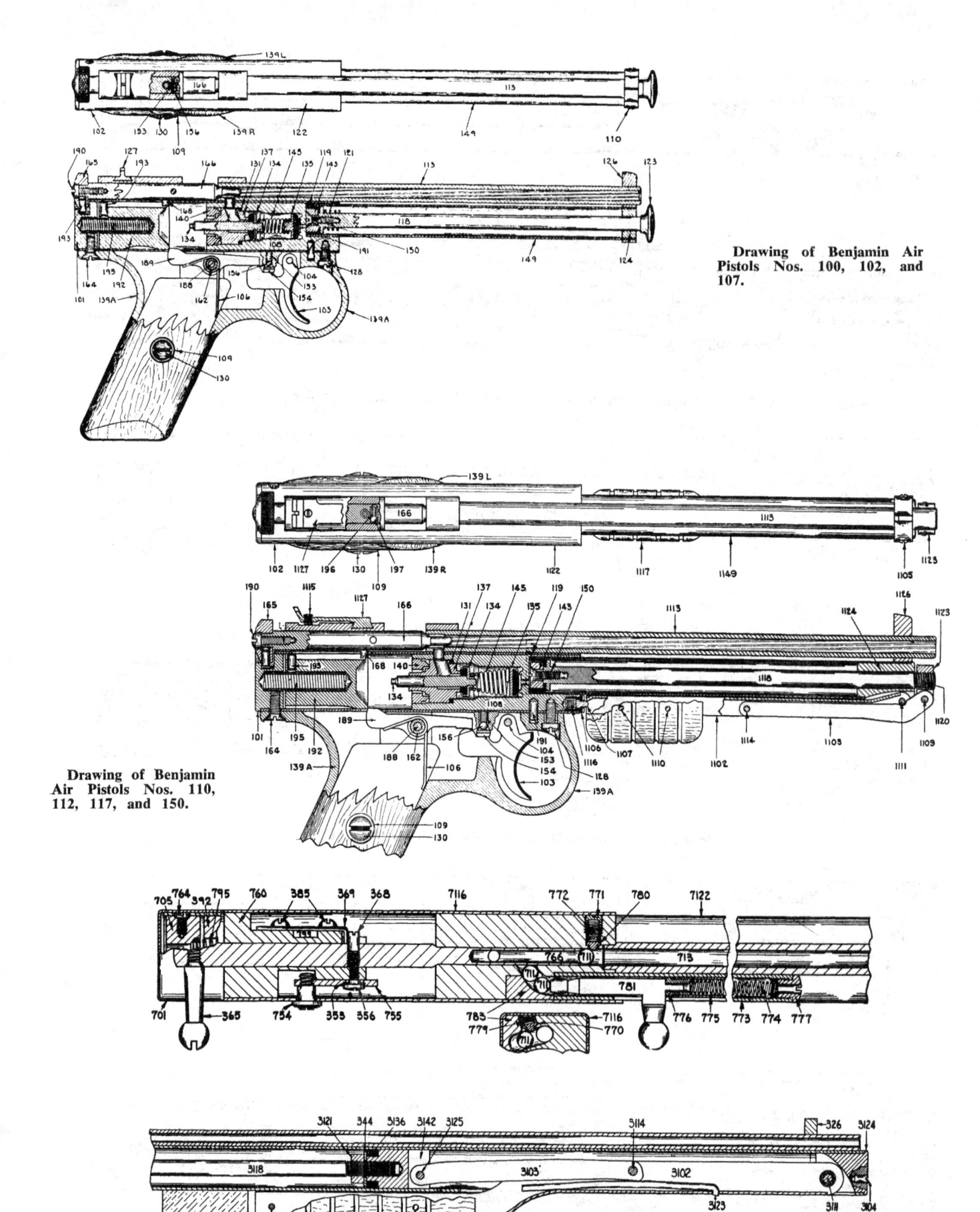

Drawing of Benjamin Air Pistols Nos. 100, 102, and 107.

Drawing of Benjamin Air Pistols Nos. 110, 112, 117, and 150.

Top view Benjamin Magazine Pistol.

180

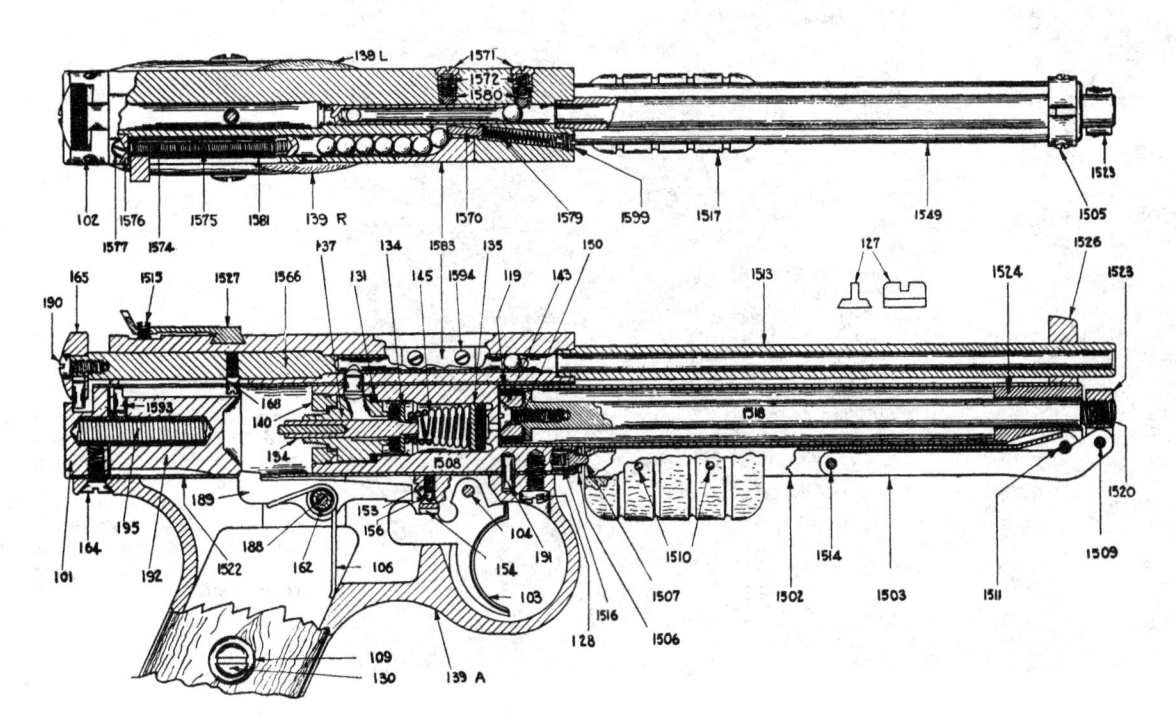

Drawing of Benjamin Model 150 Magazine Pistol.

small capacity air chamber and relatively light leverage possible within pistol length and weight limits.

Benjamin Model 710 Magazine Rifle. This model uses the standard 25-shot magazine and the same loading system as earlier and later magazine models. It has the firing mechanism of the Model 310 single-shot type.

UNLIKE Model 700, the 710 charges with the current type of pump lever.

LIKE Model 700 (and UNLIKE the current Model 720), the air chamber is designed to hold enough air on about 12 pump strokes to fire 4 or 5 shots before needing additional pumping strokes. This distinction is important.

Model 710 does NOT require pumping up after each shot as does the current 720. On the other hand, it must be pointed out that the added value of this system is gained only at the expense of very serious physical pumping effort.

In short, Model 720 is to be preferred.

CROSMAN ARMS COMPANY, INCORPORATED

The Crosman Arms Company was founded in 1925. It is now located in its own plant at Fairport, New York. It was named for the Crosman family of Rochester, New York, owners of the Crosman Seed Company. They formed the corporation originally to produce a compressed-air gun on the pump-up principle invented by William McLean, a chauffeur for the Crosman family.

The initial design used the pull-push piston-rod system of air charging as used in the Benjamin of that period.

Philip Y. Hahn, Sr., now president of Crosman Arms Company, and the husband of a member of the Crosman family, joined the firm on its incorporation in 1925 and was sales manager until 1930, when he resigned because of differences in company policies.

The rifle as originally manufactured was efficient but entirely too costly for the price at which rifles of this type can be sold in volume in the United States market, even today.

Manufacture and sales were practically dormant during the 1930 to 1940 period. Hahn purchased the corporation in 1940 for the sum of $5,000.

Government production controls made it all but impossible to manufacture during the war period. However someone in the O.S.S. (Office of Strategic Services) conceived the idea of purchasing 2,000 Crosman compressed-air rifles for an unexplained use. Maybe some bright planner with an exceptionally fervid imagination and the all too often limited knowledge thought these rifles could be used as "silent executioners" by the ultra-

Philip Y. Hahn, Sr., president of Crosman Arms Company, Inc., shown with Rudolf Merz, chief engineer, who is holding a Crosman 160 CO_2 "Pellgun."

The fast-rising field of American precision high-power pellet-gun shooting owes most of its development and success to these two men and their staff.

secret O.S.S. Perhaps they were intended for distribution in the Far East, in Malayan areas in particular, as silent arms to be used for foraging purposes. The record does not state. Then as now, the strength as well as the weakness of intelligence services was in the fact that they were not accountable to anyone.

Whatever the ultimate rifle disposition, Phil Hahn and a friend, a Swiss with an unusual flair for mechanics and engineering, Rudy Merz, undertook with some other little help at nights and weekends, the assembly of 2,000 rifles from parts on hand and parts that could be specially made when required. It was a considerable task, but aside from the money involved, they felt they were making a contribution to the war effort.

From this most unlikely beginning stems the actual rise of the Crosman Arms Company to its position today as the largest manufacturer in the field of compressed-air and CO_2 guns in the world! With Hahn, a salesman of exceptional drive, and Rudolf Merz, the mechanic, to marshal the mechanical development and production as chief engineer, Crosman Arms was developed to the point where today it has a new factory complete with the most modern equipment required for this type of business which this autror has ever seen. Approximately 125 people are employed. The new factory covers 100,000 square feet. The sales volume is currently of the order of $2,000,000. The Crosman development is a success story in the best American tradition.

Because of manufacturing efficiency and highly specialized production design, both in the arms themselves and in the methods of manufacturing them, the Crosman weapons are today exceptional values for the dollar judged by any gun standards anywhere.

The manufacture of compressed air and CO_2 guns is a very highly specialized business. It is not directly analogous to true firearms manufacture, although it parallels it in many ways. Fits and tolerances are actually often closer in compressed-air gun design, in order to keep the chambered air properly under control and also for release, than comparable powder arms.

Special automatic stock-turning equipment is required for low-cost production, and the fact that Crosman has such equipment while its competitors do not, gives it a decided edge in this department alone. Possession of its own 6-spindle automatic screw machine equipment and scores of specially designed, compressed-air-controlled machines and drills enable Crosman to keep the major bulk of its manufacture captive within its own plant. This is one of the true reasons for its success, since it is not dependent for most of its important sub-assemblies on outside manufacturers who must add their profit to the manufacturing costs, and whose delivery delays can cause trouble in production schedules.

Crosman is by far the most efficient manufacturing organization of its type that this author has ever seen, whether here, in Great Britain, or in Europe. No foreign manufacturer could possibly compete with the Crosman Arms Company on manufacture of arms of their peculiar type. It must be kept in mind that in this field, expendability is greater than in Europe.

Years ago Hahn foresaw that the population changes in the United States and the building involved, restricting as it did hunting and target shooting areas, must inevitably lead to a greater popularization of short-range shooting, such as has been common in Great Britain and in Germany since the turn of the century. While compressed-air guns have long been a major item in the Crosman manufacture, the greatest sales volume has

Representative views of the Crosman Arms Company plant at Fairport, New York. The ultra-modern equipment includes air-feed machine controls, automatic multi-spindle electronically controlled stock-carving machinery, giant 6-spindle Gridley screw machines and many automated machine units. All arms are individually tested for operation and grouping.

been developed since the introduction of the line of CO_2 pellet pistols and rifles. The reason stems directly from normal American psychology, of course.

We are ever searching for and receptive to any development which will lessen physical effort, whether in the form of automatic shifting on our automobiles or even use of gas power in our pellet guns! A European would say that we are lazy and extravagant in this respect, since it is possible with a pump-up compressed-air gun to develop higher velocities than with a CO_2 cartridge, without the expense of the CO_2 charge and entirely through use of a little elbow grease. In fact, some European manufacturers have repeatedly insisted to this author that the *spring-air gun alone* is the ultimate design in that it requires merely *one* manual operation to charge and can produce a velocity approximating that of even the CO_2 gun as currently manufactured.

The fact remains that the average American likes to do it the easy way, and it is considerably easier to insert a CO_2 cartridge in its chamber than it is to continually pump up the arm to achieve equal velocity over a number of shots; or even to make one heavy cocking pass on powerful spring-air rifles. Furthermore, we have a highly specialized situation in that CO_2 gas is a common item encountered in every city, town, and village in our fortunate country, something which cannot be said for any other place in the world today. Thus the matter of providing power is never a very difficult one for the CO_2 arms user.

Still another important factor in the development by the Crosman Arms Company of the CO_2 guns was its initiation of a policy of dealer repair services across the country. Since these guns are commonly purchased by or for people with very little training in arms handling, the number misused is very high indeed. So long as the weapons had to be returned to the factory with the inevitable delays in shipping and handling, there could be no really widespread development of CO_2 gun sales. Again, Phil Hahn must be given much credit for initiating the development of repair stations which made it possible for the person encountering some minor trouble in his gun to take it to a local source for adjustment or speedy repair, thus developing further confidence in this type of arm.

The Crosman organization has been by far the most active in its field in steady development of shooting interest among industrial concerns, Legion posts, summer schools and camps, and even by affiliation with the National Rifle Association. Organizational work of this caliber takes time, effort, and money. Other members of the industry have not been financially strong enough to equal the Crosman efforts along this line, although they too benefit both directly and indirectly from what the Crosman group has achieved.

The groundwork having been well laid, and the importance of pellet-gun shooting now becoming recognized, it is inevitable that eventually some of the larger firearms companies will interest themselves in this field. This same statement applies also to the great mail-order houses which control specialized manufacturing organizations. However, there is no substitute for long experience, and regardless of any competition which may arise, the Crosman project is now well organized and established. With Crosman's manufacturing and sales efficiency, it will require a considerable effort indeed for any of the major organizations to encroach unduly into its field.

American pellet guns are not built to last the way European spring-air guns do. American types sell at a fraction of the price of the better European types; and they are offered and purchased as reasonably expendable arms. Crosman compressed-air (and CO_2) arms must of course be considered in relation to these facts.

Types of Crosman Compressed-Air Arms

Current Model Production. The only pneumatic arms now in manufacture by Crosman are the series 140 and 147 rifles and series 130 and 137 pistols. These are both pump-up, single-shot designs.

The Model 140 rifle is .22 caliber. Model 147 is the same except that the caliber is .177. Model 130 pistol indicates .22 caliber, pump-up design. Model 137 indicates the same pistol but in caliber .177.

All current models of Crosman arms eliminate brazing, soldering, and welding, and replace these assembly procedures with pins and screws. This is a very considerable advance, allowing proper servicing and repairs when required with a minimum of effort and specialized tools and fixtures. Seals where required are accomplished through the use of modern rubber compounds.

At the end of this section will be found photographs and such comment as is necessary and valuable to owners, repairmen, designers, and collectors on all obsolete Crosman models.

CURRENT CROSMAN COMPRESSED-AIR (PNEUMATIC) RIFLES, MODELS 140 AND 147

(Identical Except for Caliber)

Manufacturer: Crosman Arms Company, Fairport, New York.
Overall Length: 35.5 inches. (Barrel length 19.5 inches.)
Weight: 4 pounds 10 ounces approximately.
Caliber(s): M140, .22. M147, .177.
Type(s) of Ammunition Used: .22 or .177 Diabolo type as required. (Crosman Pells).
Rifled: Yes. Six grooves. Twist, 1 in 16 inches.
Operating System: Compressed air. Underlever pump. Single discharge system.
Cocked: Special self-cocking action (see below). Turn-bolt operation.
Loaded: Raise bolt and withdraw. Insert pellet in breech.
Number Rounds: Single shot only.
Stock Type: Good one-piece wood design. Pump-lever handle blends in.
Front Sight(s): Blade on matted ramp.
Rear Sight(s): Adjustable on rear of barrel.
Velocity (Approximate): Tests indicate 300 to 770 f.p.s. in caliber .177 and 300 to 650 f.p.s. in caliber .22, depending on number of pumps.
Normal Accurate Range: Standard for type.
Normal Maximum Range: Standard for type.
Approximate Retail Price: $17.

REMARKS

Operation. These models have several outstanding new design characteristics. The pumping principle is the same as in other makes, naturally. The forearm conceals the pump lever when the rifle is closed. Pulling the forearm and the rifle in opposite directions pivots the pump lever, and the piston is withdrawn within its tube under the barrel for the compressing stroke.

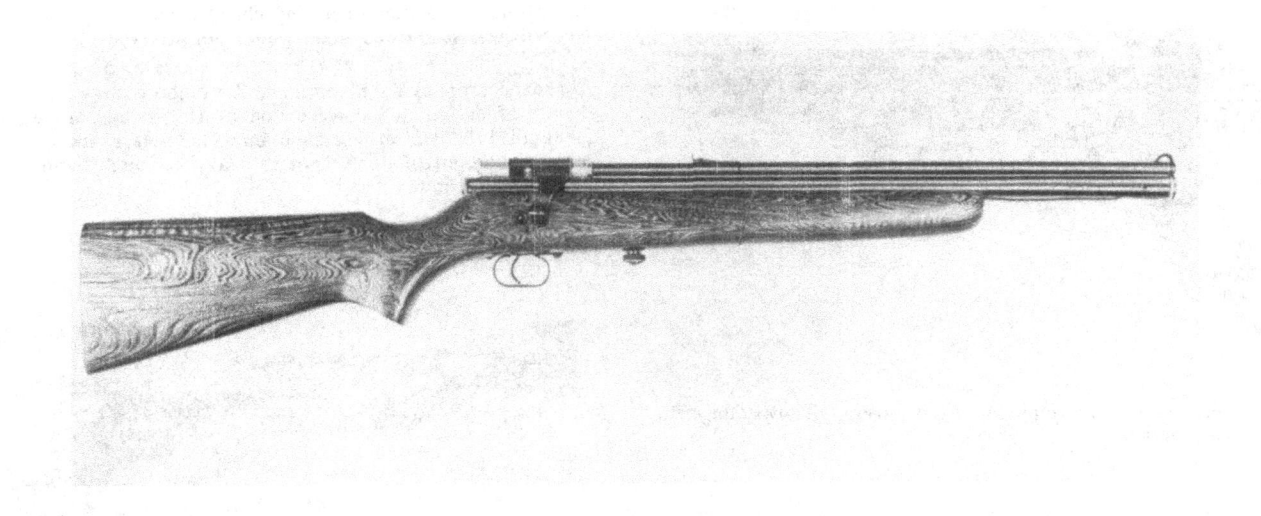

Current Crosman pump (compressed-air) rifle.

Bringing the two sections together smartly forces the pump piston to compress air within the storage chamber. Three to five pump strokes are normally used. Six strokes customarily equal a velocity average of about 453 feet per second. Not over 10 strokes is recommended at any time. When the rifle can be pumped up beyond this point, there is danger of injury to the valve. If it can be easily pumped up beyond 10 strokes, then there is definite air leakage and the gun is in need of repairs.

The basic differences and improvements over previous models start with the cocking and loading. The turn-bolt system is used. However it incorporates in it a metal breech cover which slides over the breech to completely encase the chamber when in locked position, thereby giving complete protection from dirt, leaves, or other foreign matter entering when the rifle is ready for firing.

Because of the incorporation of an entirely new valve mechanism, the original bolt on this system also features actual *fingertip cocking.* (In the latest models, the design is actually *self-cocking* as explained below.)

Valve Seal. The exhaust valve is sealed by a cap section which engages the end of the valve body and seals through action of a quad-ring. This cap is retained in engagement by the sear block. As the trigger is pressed it actuates and releases the sear from engagement. As the air in the compression chamber is released by opening the valve, *the cap blows off,* completely emptying the compression chamber. The cap and sear are instantly returned to cocked position *by spring action,* thereby giving a complete self-cocking feature to the mechanism.

Aside from the factor of a self-cocking design, the valve system is extremely important in preventing "air locks."

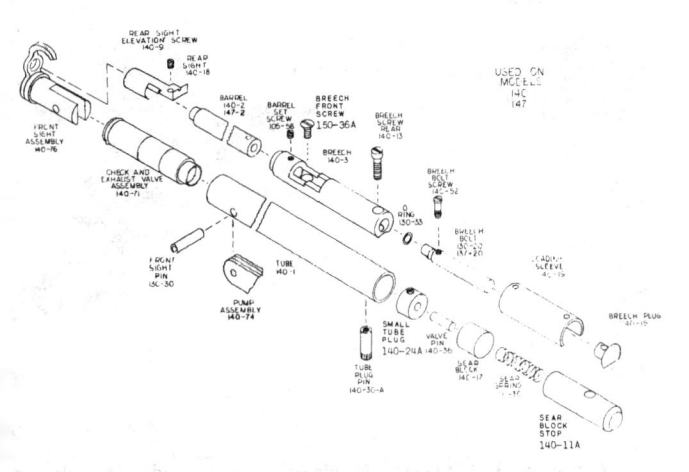

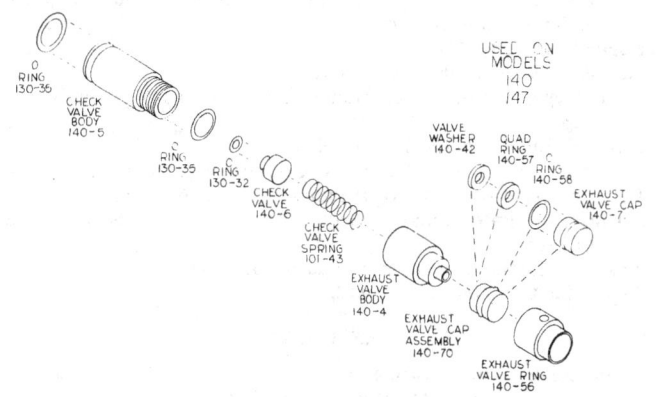

Check and exhaust valve assembly for models 140 and 147 pump rifle.

In all previous Crosman designs and in competing designs, the valve may "lock" when the chamber has been over-pumped. This is a condition often encountered when too much air has been pumped in, and where the air valve is released by *impact* of a moving striker or hammer. *An air lock occurs where the air pressure in the storage chamber is too great for the spring of the valve air-release mechanism to overcome it.* Such a condition renders the rifle unusable until leakage has lowered the compression chamber pressure to the point where it can be overcome by the normal impact against the valve.

(Note: The early models of the 140 and 147 types did not have a complete self-cocking unit as described above. In these early models the escape valve was closed by pushing forward a button on the left side of the rifle, which closed the valve. The valve was held closed by the sear block however.)

The phantom photographs presented herewith of the Model 130 pistol, show also the action of the Models 140 and 147 rifles. The isometric drawings show the new rifle design in detail, the parts being laid out in approximation of their position in the rifle for assembly and disassembly.

CURRENT CROSMAN COMPRESSED-AIR (PNEUMATIC) PISTOLS, MODELS 130 AND 137

(Identical Except for Caliber)

Manufacturer: Crosman Arms Company, Fairport, New York.
Overall Length: 11.5 inches. (Barrel length 8 inches.)
Weight: 1 pound 4 ounces approximately.
Caliber(s): M130, .22. M137, .177.
Type(s) of Ammunition Used: .22 or .177 Diabolo as required. (Crosman Pells.)
Rifled: Same as Crosman rifle.

General assembly used on new pump rifle, models 140 and 147.

185

Improved "blow-off" type air valve pistol. Allows fingertip self-cocking action.

Operating System: Compressed air. Underlever pump. Single discharge system.
Cocked: Same as M140 rifle, except breech cover button instead of bolt handle to turn.
Loaded: Same as M140 rifle.
Number Rounds: Single shot only.
Stock Type: Well-designed frame like target auto pistol. Plastic grip.
Front Sight(s): Unique hollow blade.
Rear Sight(s): At rear of pistol to give long sight line. Adjustable.
Velocity (Approximate): Tests indicate 250 to 640 f.p.s.
Normal Accurate Range: Standard for type. Groups 1 inch at 30 feet.
Normal Maximum Range: Standard for type.
Approximate Retail Price: $12.

REMARKS

Operation. These two pistols are identical except the 130 Model is .22 caliber and the 137 is .177.

The mechanical functioning of these pistols is the same as the Model 140 and Model 147 rifles. These represent probably the most advanced design in pneumatic pistols on the market today. The breech cover is not fitted with a bolt handle as in the case of the rifle. The cover itself is turned up to unlock and drawn back to expose the chamber. When closed, however, it serves exactly the same function as the Crosman bolt-handle designs, completely enclosing the firing chamber and excluding dirt and foreign matter.

The self-cocking design and the new air-valve system described for the Model 140 rifle is the same for this pistol. In a series of independent tests conducted by the author, this pistol proved to have somewhat less power than earlier Crosman models, due primarily to manufacturing changes required to lower costs. Nevertheless it showed good power for its type.

* * *

The accompanying phantom and isometric drawings show all details of design and construction of this pistol. Made to retail at about $12, it is an excellent buy in its class, though in some respects its construction is not as heavy as rough handling might normally demand.

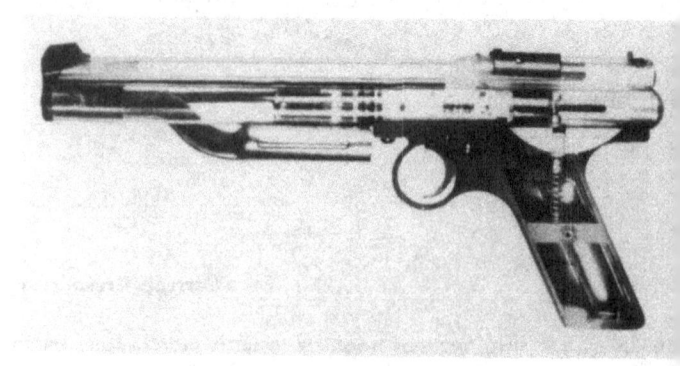

1. Crosman 130 Series air pistol. Piston full forward.

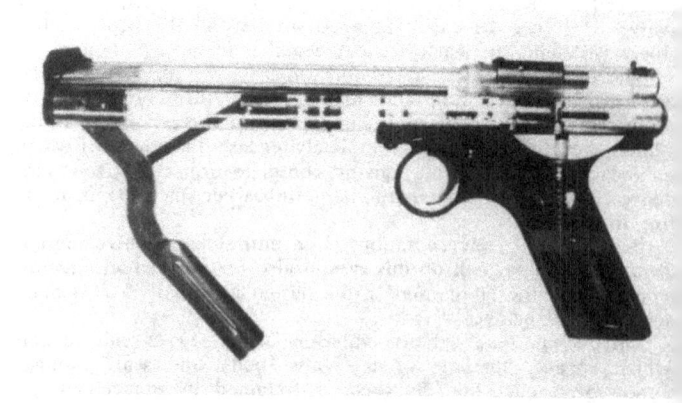

2. Crosman 130 Series air pistol. Piston partly opened for charging.

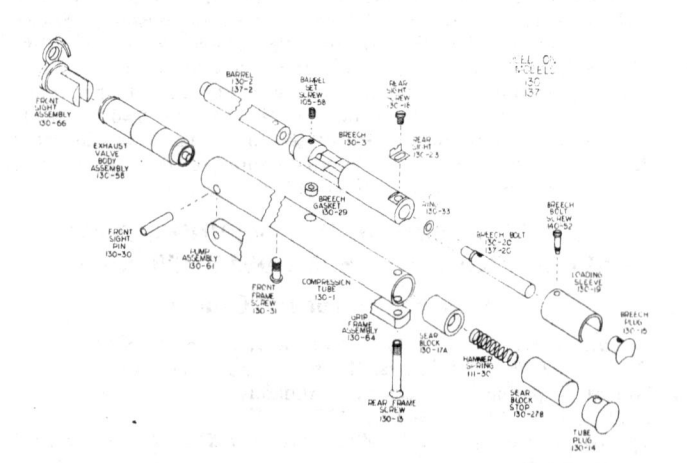

General assembly of pump pistol, models 130 and 137.

3. Crosman 130 Series air pistol. Piston ready for closing (compression) stroke.

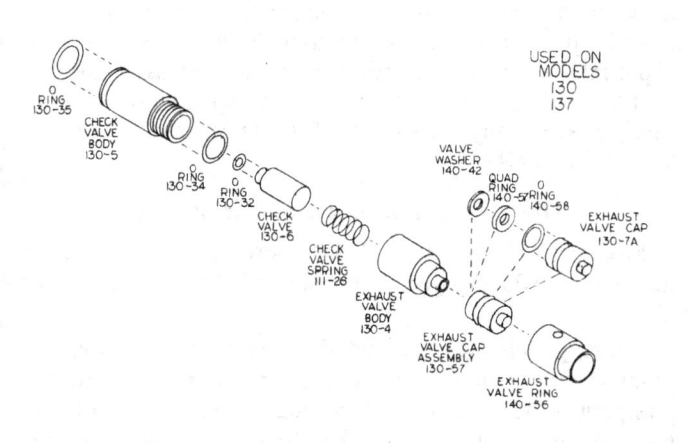

Check and exhaust valve assembly for pump pistol, models 130 and 137.

it fed down by gravity. The rifle, since it had to be pumped for each individual firing, normally involved elevation of the muzzle which automatically fed a pellet into a slide. This was cam-actuated by the bolt movement to line the pellet up for loading into the breech by thrust of the bolt when closing. This was one of the early forms of production magazine development using this type of pellet. It is a very simple matter to feed *round balls* on such a principle, but quite difficult with shaped bullets of the Diabolo type.

Rifle Models 107 and 108. The only difference in these two was in the caliber, 107 indicating the .177 caliber and 108, the .22.

The introduction of this rifle marked probably the beginning of Crosman as an advertising factor in the pellet-gun field. The rifle was developed to retail at a rather

Model 109, .177 and Model 110, .22 Town and Country Junior pump rifle. Replaced Models 100 and 101. Discontinued January 1953. Replaced by Model 120 which is an improved version of same.

Obsolete Crosman Compressed-Air Rifles

Models 100 and 101 Rifles. These models were the same except for the caliber, the first being .177 and the second, .22. These were single-shot, forearm-lever pump-up type air rifles, and were the forerunner of all the later Crosman designs. Well built and heavily constructed, they were unduly expensive to manufacture and were not true production-type arms.

The barrels of these early models were made of brass. Because of the difficulty of producing such barrels at a reasonable price in the United States at the time, they were imported from Germany. In 1925, rifling in particular was a very considerable "trade secret" and the manufacturers of firearms were not particularly inclined to give any cooperation to new organizations along that or any other technical line. As a result, in order to stay in business, the Crosman Arms Company was compelled to purchase barrels from Germany.

This series was discontinued in July 1951.

Models 102 and 104 Magazine Rifles. These were magazine-type air rifles, the former being .22 caliber and the latter, .177 caliber. These were magazine modifications of the earlier models 100 and 101.

The valve assemblies used to receive, store, and expel air, were identical in both groups. So were the hammer assemblies whose function was to release air by impact when the trigger was squeezed. Breech bolt assemblies were modified as required for the repeating design. The magazine was a tube on the left side of the rifle. Loaded from the front end with standard pellets,

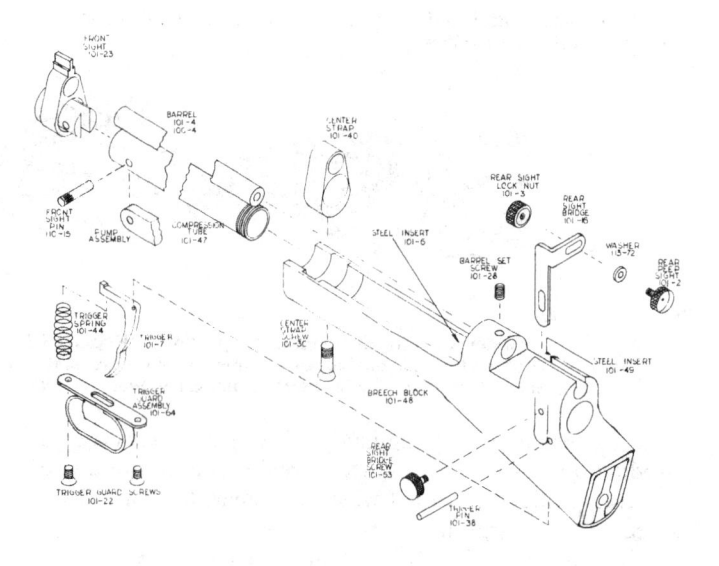

Pump-trigger and sight assembly for early model pump rifle. Used on models 100 and 101.

high price, $34. It was given a name, "The Town and Country." It featured dual front sights which could be swung in or out of position to give either peep or open sights. This design was discontinued in 1949, further advances in low-cost design having been made.

Models 109 and 110 Rifles. These, again identical except for caliber, were modifications to permit lower cost production of the compressed-air design. The effect

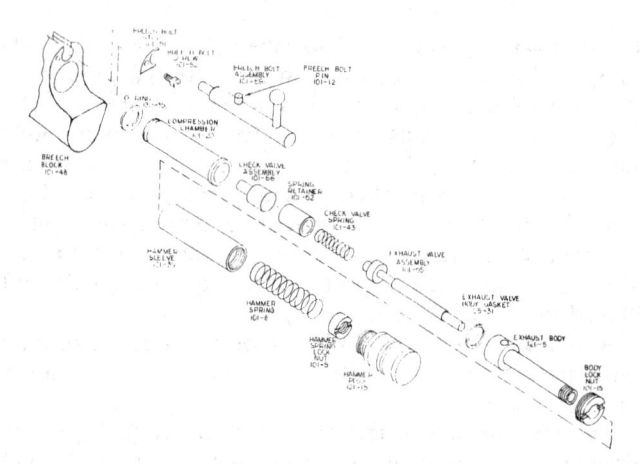

Valve, hammer and breech bolt assembly for old style pump rifles. Used on models 100, 101, 102, and 104.

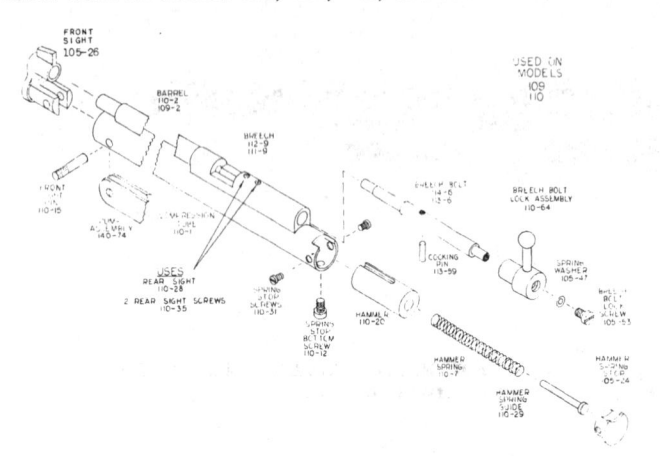

Front sight, breech bolt and hammer assembly used on models 109 and 110 pump rifles.

tests, including chamber pressures in excess of 2,500 pounds per square inch, without failure. Nevertheless, experimentation was continued in an endeavor to find a still more efficient valving system which would definitely prevent any possibility of air lock; and this led to the current 140 series.

Obsolete Crosman Pneumatic Pistols

Models 105 and 106. These were the first Crosman air pistols; 105 designated caliber .177 and 106, caliber .22.

These pistols operated on the *pump-up principle,* the pump being actuated by a lever positioned below the pumping tube and hinged at the forward end of the tube. A unique feature of the design was the fact that the pumping lever was made to resemble the familiar triggerguard lever of the conventional *rifle* of lever pattern. This gave considerably more purchase and provided easier operation than competing models. The grips were pitched at a good angle and furnished with a thumbrest as in the best automatic pistols. The general hang and balance was that of a good target model pistol.

The cocking knob was turned and withdrawn to expose the chamber for loading. The power was about average for arms of this design, and in this connection it may be stated that entirely too much in the way of power is expected from such pistols by the average purchaser. They are decidedly limited by the amount of pumping which is reasonable in connection with the type of air cylinder which can be incorporated in such a design. Within the limits of weight required, the pump must be relatively fragile.

Model 120 air rifle—impact-type valve. Replaced Models 109 and 110. Pump lever was made sturdier and front sight was brazed onto tube to increase stability. This gun had a gauge frazed into the chamber and under test over 2,500 pounds pressure was put into the chamber.

was a considerable streamlining as well as a lowering of production costs. This series is really the beginning of the two production forms which Crosman has since marketed in very large numbers.

This rifle was discontinued in January 1953.

Model 120 Rifle. This single-shot pump-up type rifle was produced only in caliber .22.

Replacing the earlier models 109 and 110, its pump lever was made much heavier. A front sight was brazed onto the tube to give increased support and sturdiness. Very serious engineering efforts went into the development of this rifle. From this point on the manufacturing development rested as much on intelligent engineering as on general production and sales efforts. For example, a gauge was frazed into the chamber of a model of this rifle. The rifle was then subjected to many

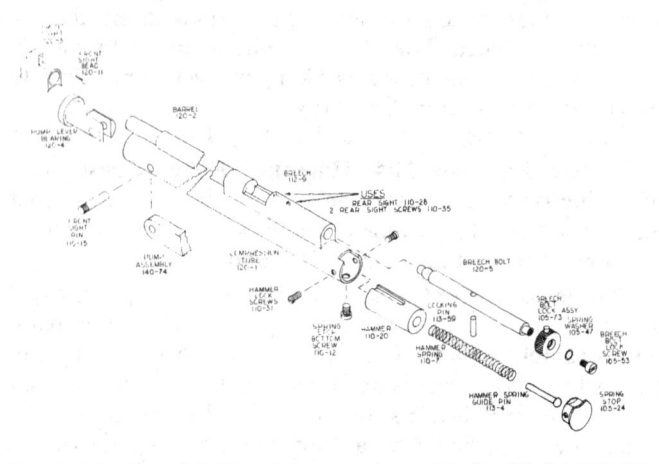

Front sight, breech bolt and hammer assembly for Model 120 rifle.

Model 105, .177 and Model 106, .22 pump pistol. First Crosman air pistol. Discontinued July 1952. Impact-type valve. Replaced by Model 130 ("blow-off" valve).

This design which used the impact type of valve with its consequent limitations, was replaced by the Model 130 which is described and pictured in detail above as current production. The Models 105 and 106 were discontinued in July 1952.

The current models are not as heavily constructed as the 105 and 106, but from the standpoint of improved design represent better values for the average shooter.

The cutaway photograph of this model herewith gives a clear indication of its internal construction and operation.

The differences in this design and in the current Models 130 and 137 will be evident when a comparison is made of the internal photographs.

THE SHERIDAN PNEUMATIC RIFLES

These rifles are manufactured by Sheridan Products Incorporated, Racine, Wisconsin. The name "Sheridan" has no bearing whatever on the designer or manufacturer of the rifle personally.

The name "Sheridan" was selected because it was that of a prominent street in the city of Racine near the homes of E. R. Wackerhagen, the founder of the corporation, and of I. R. (Bob) Kraus, the engineer who did most of the ultimate design and production work on the Sheridan rifles.

Sheridan is the youngest of the successful manufacturers of pneumatic arms. The corporation was founded in 1947. Sheridan rifles cost more than competing makes. They are the quality products of this particular arms field. They are, on a basis of independent and unbiased tests, well worth the additional money they cost for the serious rifle shooter who is interested in finest quality and long life.

Mr. Wackerhagen has been a shooting enthusiast, and a most proficient one, since boyhood. When he decided

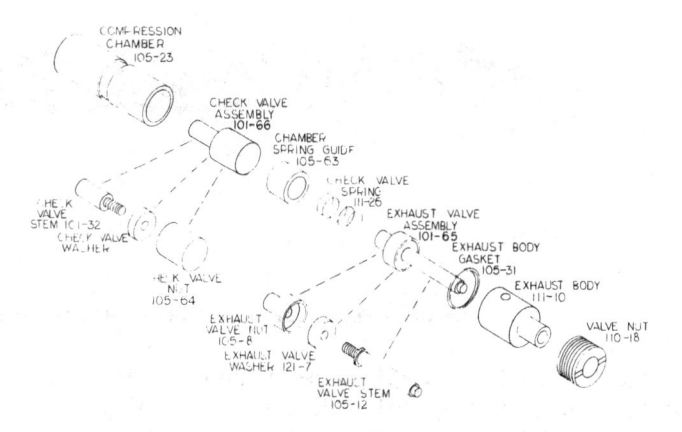

Valve assembly for pump pistols. Used on models 105 and 106.

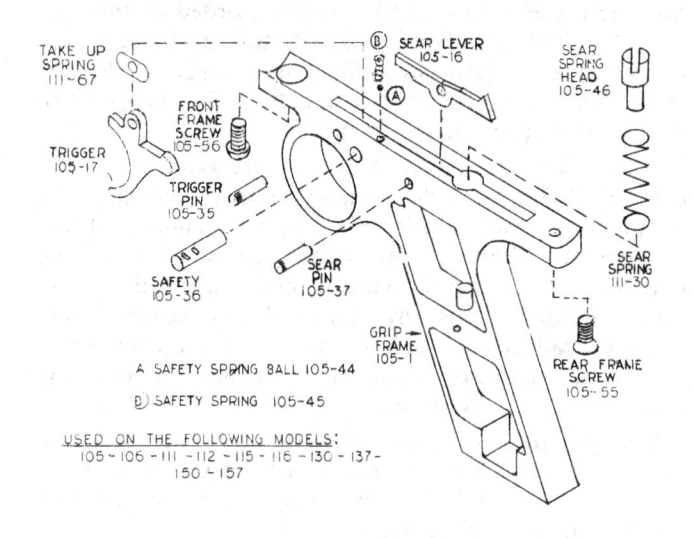

Pistol frame assembly.

to develop a compressed-air rifle which would be cheaper to use for training, short-range target, and vermin shooting than the standard powder rifle, he set up standards which would make his rifle the "Cadillac of the pneumatic arms field."

In spite of an impressive background in manufacturing expediting, Mr. Wackerhagen soon found the actual production of a rifle of the type he visualized called for constant professional engineering, supervision, and gunmaking attention beyond his personal capabilities. He was fortunate at the time in associating with Mr. I. R. Kraus, whose engineering and production ability finally produced the new air rifle in 1947.

Called the "Super Grade," the rifle in relation to all competition was exactly that. The design was standard— a pump-up system is a limited creative field. The finest materials, the closest tolerances, the most rigid inspection, and the most thorough testing standards conceivable were, however, set up by these two men, who are shooting perfectionists. The result was the finest pneumatic sporting rifle ever produced in quantity. Stocks were of the finest walnut. The ball-valve seats were of chrome alloy steel. The pump cylinder was made of a special lead-bronze alloy which provided self-lubrication. The head of the piston after much experimentation was made of

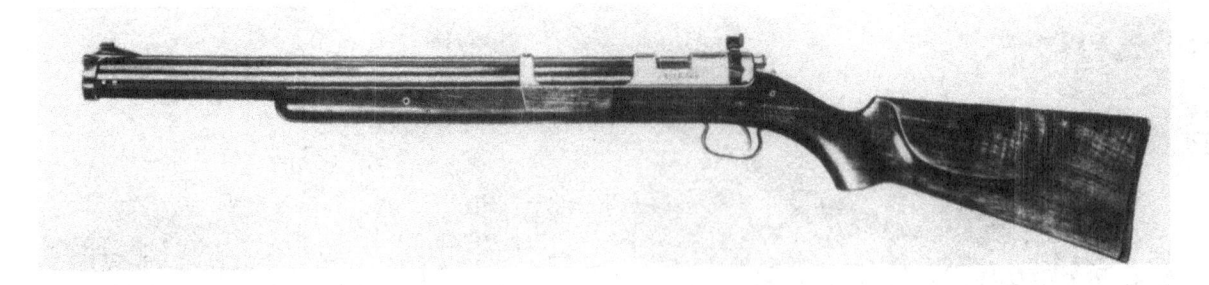

Sheridan Super, the finest and most expensive United States production air rifle yet made.

Hycar, a special variety of synthetic rubber of the neoprene species with special sealing qualities capable of retaining to a maximum, air held in a chamber under pressure. On mechanical testing apparatus it was shown that there was no measurable wear recorded in this system after half a million (500,000) strokes of the pump! (Other makers have since adopted it, incidentally. Hy Score, for example, found it a better and cheaper seal than expensive metal piston rings.)

The 9-inch piston stroke and air reservoir (or chamber) of 1/3-cubic-inch capacity gave opportunity for building up power with 8 strokes to approximately 1,000 foot-pounds. While 1,500 pounds or more could be pumped into the air chamber without injury, this is an excessive pressure at any time and was never recommended. Ballistically, with any pellet projectile the extra air pressure just isn't worth the extra physical pumping effort and the parts strain.

The pump handle and lever were of the strongest construction and very thoroughly engineered to seat below the barrel and give an excellent line to the rifle without unsightly protrusions.

The air chamber was a phosphor-bronze cylinder having a ball valve. A powerful striker system enabled the ball to be unseated momentarily when the trigger was pressed, releasing all the air stored in the chamber to power the pellet in the barrel.

The compression chamber and valve were developed *as a unit*. The unit was removable, so that in the event of difficulty from this source (the weakest point in any pneumatic gun) the entire unit could be returned to the factory for replacement or adjustment required. In normal procedure it is necessary to return the entire rifle mechanism, a factor which can cause shipping complications, delays, and general annoyance.

Any sudden release of air from a compression chamber with the resulting expansion produces intense cold. In damp areas, rust will set in rapidly unless the materials employed are such as to prevent it.

With this idea in mind the Sheridan people made their barrels of phosphor-bronze. (Note: Steel tubing is the normal barrel material in the lowest priced compressed-air rifles.)

While broaching steel is comparatively simple, handling the bronze alloys is an entirely different matter. It was necessary for Mr. Kraus to develop a special broaching technique to produce the rifling in this barrel and to give it a mirror-like surface. This enabled him to absolutely minimize the friction of the bullet passing down the barrel, thereby increasing power and velocity and eliminating the possibility of lead piling up in the rifling grooves.

When tests with the customary .177 and .22 type of Diabolo pellet did not satisfy their own accuracy ideas, a special bullet was developed of a lead alloy, which in combination with the phosphor-bronze barrel gave an absolute minimum of friction, both because of the material and because of the bullet design. The caliber of .20 was decided upon as being the best intermediate which would have the maximum velocity combined with the maximum striking power for the type of design desired.

The caliber designation is .20. Land diameter is .195 inch. The barrel is rifled with 3 grooves of .0025 inch. The twist is right hand. After extensive testing with various leads (or twists) varying from 12 to 26, Sheridan finally settled on a specification of one complete turn in 12 inches as giving the maximum average performance with the design and power available in their rifle and with their special projectile.

The weight of the bullet was set at approximately 15.5 grains. The front diameter is .195 inch. However a narrow rotating band of .200 inch is provided at the rear to take the rifling and give a positive air seal.

The rifle had a bolt handle of the positive locking variety. When the handle is lifted and pulled back it cocks the striker. The bullet is inserted in the barrel chamber and the bolt pushed forward and turned. This chambers the bullet and locks the breech. A safety of the shotgun push type was provided.

When ready for the market the new rifle was a short, man-sized job of superlative design and balance. Its quality showed in every line. With its 20-inch barrel it measured only 37 inches overall. It weighed 5 pounds 14 ounces.

A true "variable power" rifle, it established a velocity of 400 feet per second on 2 movements of the forearm pump and stepped up to about 770 feet per second on 12 pumps. It must be noted here that *any* pneumatic rifle is relatively easy for the first 4 strokes, but becomes increasingly difficult to pump up beyond that point. This Sheridan Super, by the way, showed a velocity of about 510 feet per second on 4 strokes of the pump. On standard indoor ranges, with 3 strokes, the Sheridan provided enough power to consistently register "possibles," or 100-score accuracy.

When used outdoors where the wind must be bucked, an additional 2 strokes would compensate for this factor. While the truly practical target ranges are below 75 feet,

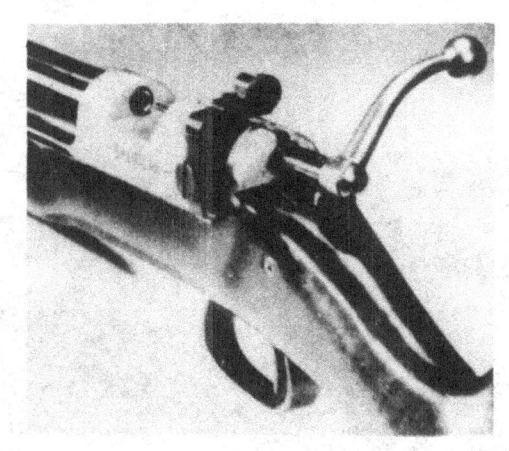

Sheridan. Action open. Very easy to load the small pellet.

pests or vermin can be killed as much as 60 yards or 70 yards distance from the muzzle. The Sheridan has been used as a rat exterminator on the Los Angeles dumps, as a hog stunner for slaughtering on farms, and for killing trapped foxes; but exceptional uses such as these, while recognized, are not recommended by the makers.

There was only one thing wrong with the Sheridan thinking! Quality costs money! And not too many Americans recognize that fact. While a quality rifle like a quality automobile has a market, the increased price necessary to produce the *finest* quality must be reflected in the selling price. Now it happens that in the air-gun industry the trade discounts are high. The maker gets less than 50 percent of the *retail* price for a rifle of this type, because sales must pass through a sales representative, to a jobber, to a retail outlet before reaching the customer. It will be understood, therefore, that the selling price of $56.50 was really phenomenally low for the quality product involved when what the manufacturer received is considered.

Unfortunately, in the United States it is only recently that people have come to realize that a compressed-air rifle is an entirely different item than the toy type of air gun with which we have been familiar. The Sheridan "Super" was ahead of its time. Finding the price unacceptable in the air-gun market, the manufacturers, while still retaining their basic quality, produced a lower-priced rifle without many of the refinements of finish to sell under the name of the "Sporter" for $35. Much of this price reduction came out of the manufacturer's legitimate profit, the rest out of production capital investment.

Since other compressed-air rifles were selling under the $20 price, Sheridan was compelled to still further redesign to bring its price more nearly into line while still maintaining all possible quality.

The result was the current line of Silver Streak and Blue Streak Sheridan rifles, selling in the neighborhood of $24 retail. This price is actually too low to allow a proper manufacturing profit, in the opinion of this author.

The new designs incorporate practically all the fine features of the original, but have replaced the ultra expensive phosphor-bronze barrel with a hard, red brass barrel which is still far superior in a compressed-air rifle to steel tubing. It was necessary also to replace the ultra expensive ball valve system with one of the more common impact types. As manufactured by Sheridan, with careful attention to close tolerances and the use of the finest materials possible at their price level, double seals on the valve guide and high-grade material for valve seats, the Sheridan is still the aristocrat of pneumatic rifles manufactured anywhere.

Further data on the current models will be found herein.

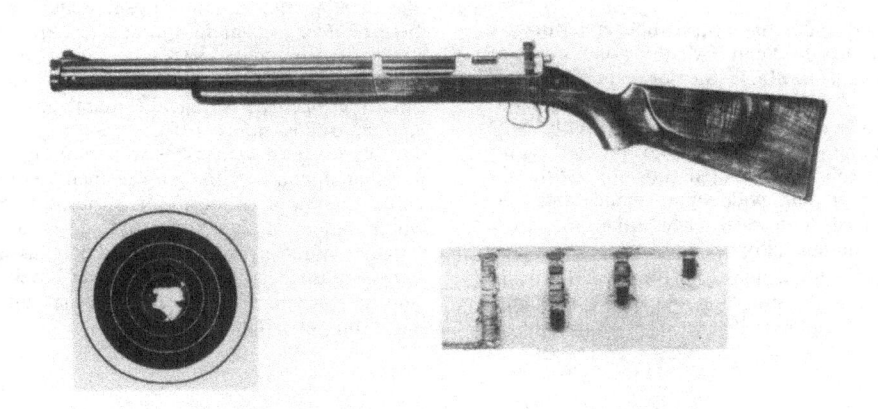

Target and penetration capabilities of the Sheridan.

SHERIDAN COMPRESSED-AIR (PNEUMATIC) RIFLES, SILVER STREAK AND BLUE STREAK, MODEL C

Manufacturer: Sheridan Products Company, Racine, Wisconsin.
Overall Length: 37 inches. (Barrel length 18.5 inches.)
Weight: 4 pounds 10 ounces approximately.
Caliber(s): .20 (5-mm.), Sheridan Bantam only.
Type(s) of Ammunition Used: Special Sheridan pointed bullet, caliber .20.
Rifled: Yes. Three grooves. One turn in 12 inches.
Operating System: Compressed air. Standard underlever pump. Single air discharge system.
Cocked: Turn-bolt action. Cocks on opening stroke.
Loaded: Standard, but pellet insertion is very easy.
Number Rounds: Single shot only.

Stock Type: Walnut. Simulated Mannlicher full-length design, with pump handle blending into line.
Front Sight(s): Blade front.
Rear Sight(s): Open adjustable rear. (Receiver sight available.)
Velocity (Approximate): Tests indicate 300 to about 800 f.p.s., depending on number of pumps.
Normal Accurate Range: Better than common standard—about 40 feet.
Normal Maximum Range: Slightly more than Diabolo-type pellet guns.
Approximate Retail Price: $24 (in either finish).

REMARKS

This gun on test has been pumped up to give greater penetration than any other standard gun of its type. This is partly due to bullet design, which is intended not only for accuracy but also for penetration.

By contrast, note that Crosman, for example, modified the head of their regular Diabolo-type waisted pellet to deliberately lower penetration, since their gun is intended for training purposes where too much penetration is not desirable.

The current Sheridan Silver streak and Blue Streak rifles are identical, except that one is silver finished and the other finished in blue.

Operation. Turn up the bolt handle and draw it back slightly until it is stopped against the mainspring. Now pull the bolt handle back hard against the powerful spring until the sear engages. A click will be heard. (Note: A powerful spring is needed in a compressed-air rifle of any conventional design, much more so than in a powder rifle, because the spring furnishes the power to trip or release the valve to permit the compressed air in the chamber to escape violently and thus propel the bullet.)

Note also that the rifle should always be cocked before the pump is operated. This insures that the exhaust valve is tightly closed.

Hold rifle with right hand about the piston tube area forward of the triggerguard. Grasp the fore-end (which is the pumping arm) as far down as convenient. Raise the lever to the entire length of stroke *at all times*. This is important in any pneumatic. Best efficiency is achieved by not trying to pump only with the left hand. While pushing the lever in with the left hand, simultaneously force the rifle into closed position with the right hand. With elbows high and wide apart, hands opposed, the two parts may be pushed toward each other to effect maximum leverage with minimum effort.

Use the *same number* of pump strokes each time for the same type of shooting. If you are shooting indoors, 3 or 4 pumps are normally the maximum required. The strokes should be as nearly the same as possible for each operation in order to get the most stable effects in velocity.

When ready to shoot, open bolt and place bullet with nose to the front in the breech end of the barrel. Push the bolt home and it will automatically chamber and seat the bullet. A taper on the forward end of the bolt will act as a needle valve and seal the breech. A locking cam plate on the left side is provided with screws which permit it to be moved forward against the locking lug in the event any looseness develops at the breech. This is standard procedure in design.

These new model Sheridans have an *automatic* safety, which rises on the tang of the stock *when the rifle is cocked*. As the rifle is gripped for firing, the thumb must deliberately push down and hold this safety before the trigger may be released. There is something to remember and nothing to forget in this design. It is analogous to the Government Model .45 auto pistol grip safety in that it is normally spring-supported in "safe" position; but it differs in that you must consciously depress the Sheridan.

This safety incidentally also acts as a cocking indicator. It can be pushed down out of trigger-block position only when the gun is cocked. The special photographs of a cutaway model show this in detail.

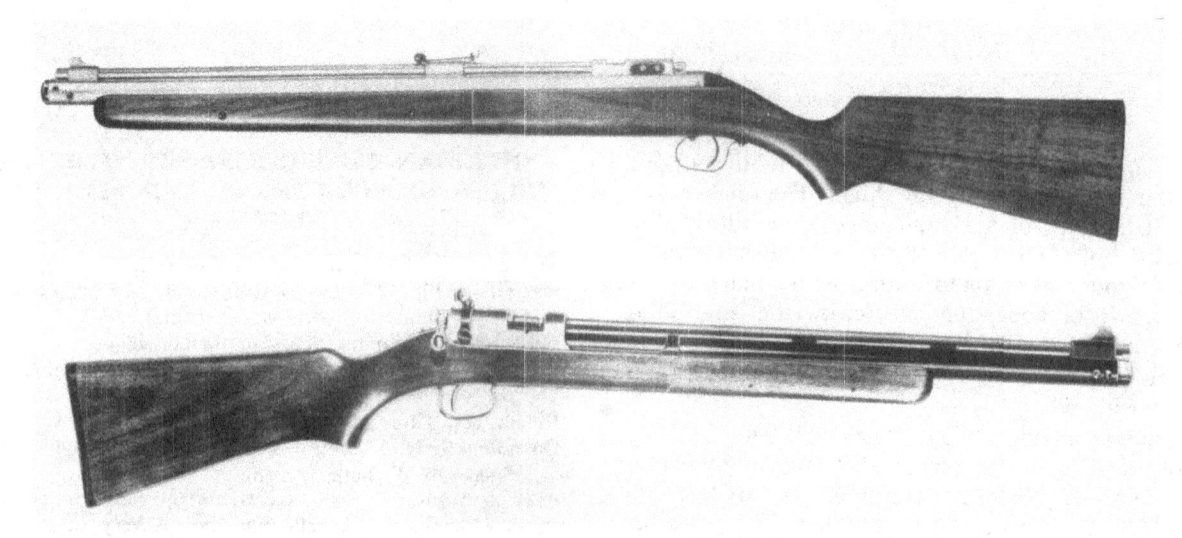

Close-up of bolt. Notice thumb safety which must be held down as trigger is pulled. This is an excellent safety, particularly for boys. Safety is also a cocking indicator, as it cannot be depressed unless rifle is cocked.

Sheridan Blue and Silver Streak Models are same except for finish. Sights are optional, extra cost for peep.

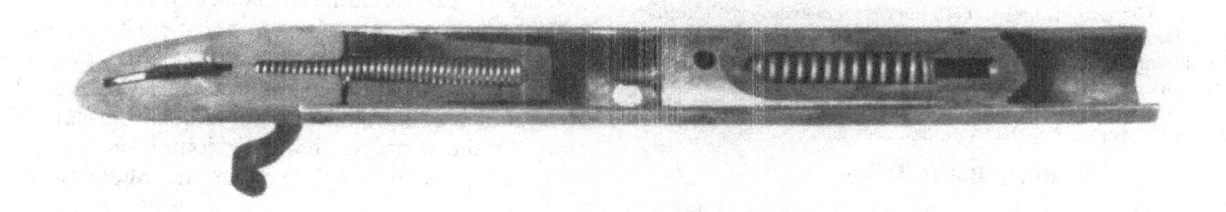

Sheridan Blue and Silver Streak Models action cutaway. The striker is shown cocked, with the mainspring compressed within. Details of the valve stem, air port, valve spring, and air-compression chamber may be seen. Pressing the trigger pivots its forward end out of contact with the holding face on the underside of the striker. The striker is driven forward to hit the valve release, driving it in against its spring far enough to allow the compressed-air charge to pass through the port into the chamber behind the projectile. The safety seen at top rear is blocking the trigger when action is cocked, and must be deliberately held down by the thumb of the firing hand before the trigger can be pulled to disengage the striker.

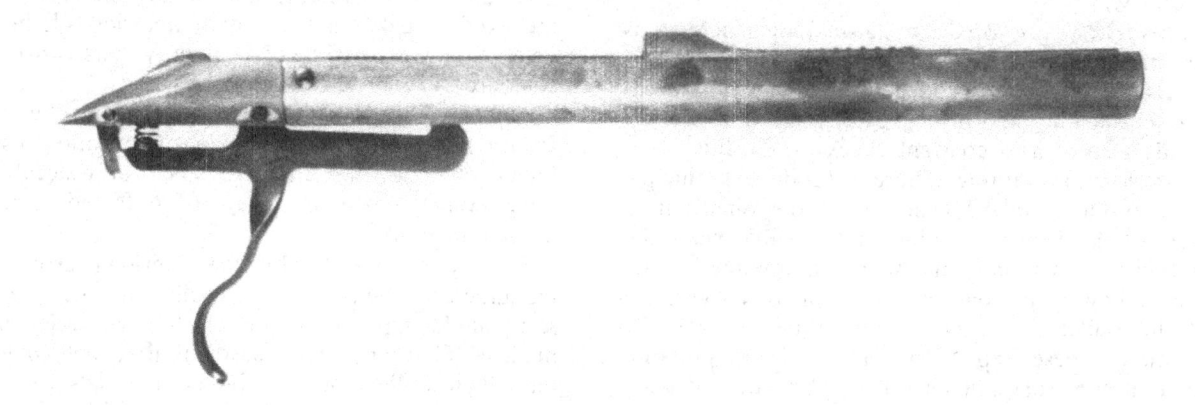

Side view of Sheridan Silver and Blue Streak Models cutaway. The action is not cocked. When it is cocked, the safety spring pivots the rear of the safety into engagement with the rear of the trigger extension. The gun can be fired only when the safety is depressed and held down so that its lower projection is held out of the path of the trigger extension, thereby allowing the trigger to move up at its rear while its forward end is lowered out of striker engagement.

An intrinsic part of the Sheridan design is to make all moving parts so they will have to "wear in." This is a sound engineering principle, making tight fits which wear in instead of loose ones which become looser. A rubber bumper is provided in the pump arm, for instance, which holds the fore-end slightly out from the stock when the rifle is new, but which compresses with use and finally becomes a flush joint.

Very little oiling is necessary. A light body oil of good cold test properties is all that is necessary. It should be one which will not gum. The front bearing of the piston rod (called the "cross head") is made of an oil impregnated powder metal alloy which is self lubricating. Oil is seldom if ever required where such material is used. An occasional drop or two of oil in the long slot in the pump lever, where the end of the toggle link is in contact with the spring, and an occasional drop of fine oil in the air-intake hole in back of the long slot in the tube will be all the lubrication normally necessary. Safety, striker, and trigger should be lubricated only when dry and required.

It should be noted that in *all* compressed-air rifles of these pump-up types, no shooting is attempted with only one stroke of the pump. The air thus compressed is seldom enough to drive the tight-fitting bullet down the barrel with safety. Very often a bullet will jam under these circumstances. Two strokes are the normal minimum. Only a *hard* valve seat will hold tight compression. Sheridan rifles are built to stand all but absolutely insane pump-up pressures which are completely unrealistic both ballistically and from the standpoint of physical effort required.

Note on Dry Firing. A pneumatic rifle should not normally be "dry-fired"; that is, fired without a pellet in the chamber.

The reason for this is that a pneumatic rifle requires a much higher spring pressure and harder hammer blow than any powder rifle because of its impact action on the valve. This necessarily subjects it to greater strain. Another thing to avoid is over-pumping. Under all normal conditions the maximum number of full stroke pumps should be 10. If more than this are employed, tremendous pressure will be needed to achieve the compression and there is a possibility of pressure cutting or heat scorching the valve seats. An air lock may be produced.

The term "air lock" in a pneumatic arm indicates a condition which exists when pulling the trigger either does not release or *completely exhaust* the air in the compression chamber. This means lower velocity and power, since some air remains in the chamber, which is ineffectual for any further use; or in extreme cases, the valve may not open at all until air has leaked enough to drop the pressure.

One other factor must be kept in mind: Each pump stroke must be *complete,* that is to the maximum opening and to the complete closing. It is possible otherwise merely to go through the motions of pumping without actually compressing any additional air in the chamber. If very short strokes are taken, instead of pumping up air you are merely getting exercise. This applies equally to *any* compressed-air arm. One unusual factor taken into consideration by the manufacturers of this rifle is the providing of *average dimensions* at various points to control *average uses* of the rifle and give best results. Specifically for instance, tests indicated that the normal best procedure (and that most commonly used by shooters) is 4 or 5 pump strokes. The gun was engineered within that range to give necessary velocity for all practical target shooting within practical distances for any air arm, and at the same time provide the necessary striking energy for anything except long-range pest and vermin shooting. If desired or required, the lever may be pumped several additional times as indicated.

Since additional pump strokes mean additional air compressed, and that in turn means increased velocity, the Sheridan engineers decided upon a rifling turn of one in 12 inches because that rate of twist produced the best *average accuracy* with pump strokes ranging from the lowest to the recommended maximum. This can be an extremely important point where so apparently elementary an item as the quickness of the rifling turn is concerned. It is but one indication of the thought, care, and engineering which went into the Sheridan designs.

Sheridan Bullet Design

The Sheridan is an individual, not a *standard* bullet and caliber. This has advantages and disadvantages.

The Sheridan bullet tolerance as well as design are a considerable factor in the extreme accuracy achieved with Sheridan pneumatic rifles. The bullets are held to a tolerance of between .186 and .189. In actual practice, the machine operator continually gauges samples coming off the bullet-making machine and holds the tolerances *on the low side*.

The operational rate of the bullet-making machines is 168 per minute. In other words over 72,000 of these ultra-precision bullets are produced in an 8-hour operation of one machine, and a high percentage of these are individually gauged as a constant check on die life.

The Sheridan is entirely different in bullet principle from that of the standard Diabolo. In the Sheridan, a large area of the forward section of the bullet rides the rifle lands very consistently and with a minimum of friction. The hollow in the base and the thin rear oversized wall of the bullet is very carefully gauged to actually allow complete base expansion under the air pressure developed in the Sheridan air rifles. Thus the "driving band" effect of this bullet is to furnish a complete air seal during the travel of the bullet down the barrel. The design is such that no bullet "cocking" is possible because of the large forward bearing surface. The Diabolo design, on the other hand, with its hourglass design, is intended to have its narrow forward end ride the rifling lands. The wider rear skirt section which is very thin, is intended to fit snugly into the rifling to provide the air seal. In actual practice, however, because of the slight support given to the forward end of the bullet, the Diabolo when not carefully inserted is not always fully centered and may be cocked slightly because of the dual dimensions involved and the inadequate bearing surfaces required for friction reduction. As a result, when air pressure is applied in the hollow base, the sudden base expansion may start the pellet off in an already deformed condition by upsetting it enough so that the soft metal does not bite *uniformly* into the grooves.

Expert marksmen knowing this are very careful in micrometering each pellet and in carefully starting it into the rifling, when using the Diabolo for precision match shooting. For "plinking" this is not much of a factor, however.

The Sheridan by its intrinsic design and bearing surfaces, plus extremely close tolerances, completely avoids any such deformation of bullet as is often encountered in the Diabolo design. Also, compressed-air designs automatically seat the bullet as the action is closed, a condition which does not obtain in European spring-air systems.

In this condition it must be pointed out that while the pointed air-gun bullet of general design resembling the Sheridan has been in manufacture in Germany since the turn of the century, it has seldom been brought to the state of perfection achieved in the Sheridan bullet.

Note On Sheridan Caliber

One note must be made with reference to the .20 Sheridan caliber. While as has been stated it is an excellent ballistic compromise between the .177 and the .22 Diabolo, it nevertheless presents a certain amount of hazard to the average purchaser. The standard Diabolo-type pellets are used internationally in very many weapons and are obtainable almost anywhere that air guns are sold. Regardless of manufacturing claims, in an emergency most makes of Diabolo pellets can be used in standard .177 or .22 air arms.

On the other hand, the .20 Sheridan caliber is manufactured *only* by the Sheridan organization itself. The bullets will not be found in stock in general distribution, though they may always be obtained directly from the manufacturer.

It may be asked why the Sheridan group did not manufacture their style of bullet in the .22 caliber, since similar types although ballistically inferior have been made in Germany. The reason is that they matched not only their bullets but the bullet materials to the barrel material used to obtain the finest possible friction coefficients in their overall bullet and rifle design. If they manufactured the bullets in the standard .22 caliber, they would inevitably be used in rifles designed for the Diabolo type of bullet. Many, in fact *millions* of such rifles particularly of the spring-air type are in existence. Regardless of manufacturers' claims, only the best of these have sufficient air compression on the stroke of their piston to properly propel a very tight-fitting expanding-band bullet of the Sheridan type. Sheridan did not manufacture in this caliber because of the possibility of their ammunition receiving bad notices through jamming in barrels of other manufacture.

In the Diabolo bullet, only the very thin and light skirt at the rear of the bullet engages the rifling. The resistance therefore is very small if the bullet is properly seated. On the other hand the base of the Sheridan bullet is hollow and the rear of the bullet is wider than the nose to form a driving band. The expansion of the rear of the bullet to grip the rifling gives much greater friction in the customary barrel made of steel tubing in which the Diabolo pellets are shot.

Anyone purchasing a Sheridan rifle for use outside of the United States, therefore, should be certain to purchase a sufficiently large quantity of ammunition to last.

CHAPTER 13

American Spring-Air Arms

A spring-air arm is one in which the released power of a heavy, compressed spring is used to drive a piston in a compression tube, the tight-fitting piston compressing the air in its path and forcing it through a very small vent to drive the pellet down the barrel. The difference in size between the small vent and the large piston (or plunger) head, together with the heavy spring power, determines the air force.

AMERICAN MANUFACTURERS

There is only one serious production arm being made in the United States at this time on this principle—the Hy Score *Pistol*. (Note: Hy Score imports the spring-air *rifles* sold under its name.)

The Daisy air rifles and pistols, classed as toys but actually usable as arms trainers for boys, come under this classification because of mechanical design. The National Rifle Association of America conducts Junior qualification courses for spring-air rifles on official N.R.A. 15-foot targets. Pneumatic (pump-up) air rifles may not be used at this course. (Note: There is a separate N.R.A. classification for higher power "pellet" rifles.)

Daisy rifles are included here even though they are not in the high-power category because of (1) mechanical design and (2) use under N.R.A. auspices as indicated above.

While various "toy" air rifles appear from time to time, examination of various types shows clearly that they are exactly as classified—toys. The Daisy (and German Diana and Falke boy's models) are the only ones in this category which are quality- and precision-built to serve as acceptable youth target trainers.

HY SCORE

Hy Score Spring-Air Pistol

This pistol is manufactured by the Hy Score Arms Corporation of Brooklyn, New York. It is manufactured in a single-shot and also in a repeating variety. It is produced in calibers .177 and .22. Long- and short-barreled types are available. The basic design is common, however.

The Hy Score Arms Corporation imports Diana low-priced barrel-cocking air rifles. These are *merchandised* under the name of the Hy Score Arms Company, but it must be understood that, unlike the pistol, they are *not* manufactured in the United States.

Externally this pistol somewhat resembles the Luger's lines as adapted by Hy Score from the familiar German prewar Haenel. It was developed by Mr. Andrew Lawrence about 1938. Lawrence had an engineering background in automotive work, but not in firearms. He undertook development of a production-type air pistol to meet United States pricing requirements. This entailed making a pistol which would be a composite of the better existing design features, plus some improved features; the whole designed for mass production.

His approach was diametrically opposed to that of the European manufacturers. All serious foreign air pistols had been produced by *gunmakers*. They followed the normal course of firearms manufacture, utilizing the forging and milling processes of production which resulted in good but inevitably high-priced products. Pistols of the Haenel and Webley types, for example, were basically fine pieces of gunmaking manufactured on a *relatively* small scale and therefore commanding a relatively high price on the open market. Such other pistols as were then generally manufactured either fell into the toy category or were very poorly and cheaply designed.

Lawrence obviously made an intensive analysis of the various types on the market. Any study of the Hy Score pistol will disclose at once its similarity to the various types which were its forerunners in Europe. However, it is a definite improvement on most of those from which it was developed. Designed for basic stamping and tubing manufacture, it costs less than most equivalent imports.

Lawrence passed over the idea of the *pump-type* pistol, even though it could be brought up to a higher power than the spring-actuated type, because of the physical effort necessary to produce the requisite air storage to give this added power. He concentrated on developing a *spring-air* actuated pattern which would be superior in the velocities commonly developed and simpler to manufacture than most of the German pistols which had theretofore been marketed. (Note: This is not true of all German postwar pistols.)

By fixing on the established concentric design, he was able to produce a particularly efficient pistol of its type. Note that the British Acvoke, the British Abas-Major, and several European types had already utilized this principle. However, the Hy Score adaptation was actually a simplification and a more efficient operation than most of these earlier pistols.

The important feature in the concentric design is that the barrel runs almost the entire length of the pistol—10 inches in the case of the largest Hy Score model. This compares with an average 5-inch barrel permitted by the

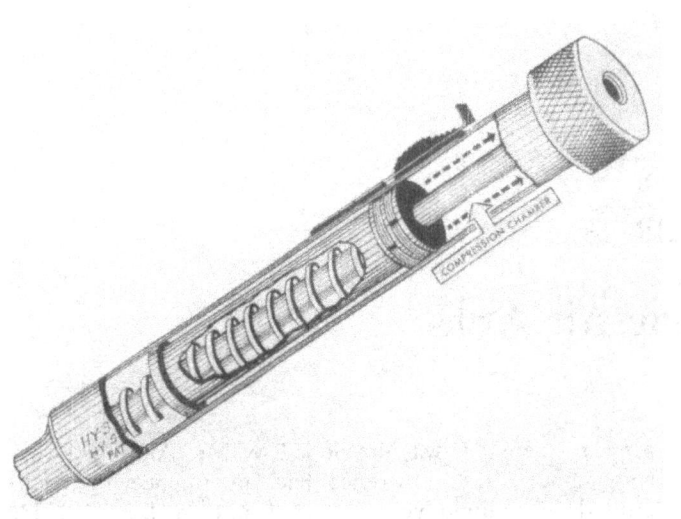

Hy Score compression system.

Diana and Haenel designs where the spring is in a tube *to the rear* of the barrel and 7½-inch in the Webley design where the spring-compression tube is below the barrel. (Note: Webley offsets this advantage, however by better cocking leverage and by being shorter and more compact.) The greater barrel length adds something to velocity in normal usage. It also has the advantage of giving a better sight line. The design has a major disadvantage, as we must in fairness point out; it is not as easy or as satisfactory to *load* as the Haenel or Webley.

In the concentric design, the spring and piston which form the pump elements are mounted around the barrel within the casing. (The barrel serves as a guide for the piston and spring.) This system allows the use of longer compression springs. The compressed pressure of the Hy Score is given as about 95 pounds, which is unusually high. The springs furthermore are specially heat-treated to prevent taking a "set." This form of heat treatment may give an effective added spring valve of as much as 15 percent. With the relatively low pressures involved in arms of this design, 15 percent can be a very considerable factor where it exists.

The Hy Score was designed along lines to utilize automotive-valve, tube-drawing, and stamping techniques. Thus the barrel casing is a specially drawn tube. The barrel itself is a piece of elementary seamless tubing. Lawrence utilized the then common European system of rifling in which a swaging "button" is drawn through the barrel to compress the rifling into the metal, rather than to rifle-cut or broach as in customary barrel-rifling systems in use until quite recently in the United States. This type of rifling eliminates the possibility of ragged edges in the rifling which may tend to slow up the very lightweight and soft bullets used in air arms. It is faster and cheaper than cutting, and quite as satisfactory as broaching when used in soft-metal barrels of the air-gun type.

According to the designer, 8 models were built before the final design was settled. The pistol uses a maximum of stamping and tube parts, and a Tenite molded-plastic grip. The grip incidentally is counterweighted to afford balance, the Colt Woodsman pistol having been used as standard for comparison. This was required because the Hy Score does not have the heavy-unit grip frame of the Haenel and Webley type designs.

All elements subject to shock-loading strains were heat-treated. This is familiar practice in all good European air-gun manufacture today, but was not at the time Lawrence initiated it. For a time the Hy Score pistol used automotive-type piston rings of cast iron. Later the two rings were supplanted by one. However because of the excessive amount of machining and close tolerance holding required, these have been supplanted in recent manufacture with neoprene O rings. These are quite as effective and efficient. In this connection it might be noted that the best European practice still utilizes either metal rings or a leather cup at the piston end (depending upon the design pattern) to provide the most efficient of all seals with a minimum of close tolerance holding. Leather will wear and need replacement. The cups may be damaged easily and the oil is subject to drying out, thereby destroying the effectiveness of the air seal. Various forms of chemical synthetic rubber are increasingly being used for such rings and will probably supplant leather in the not-too-distant future in most designs.

The early forms of spring-air arms suffered from excessively heavy trigger pull because the compressed spring and *piston pressure* bore directly on a trigger element. In such designs even where a sear is incorporated the friction *involved will often require* a 10 or 12-pound pull to overcome it.

One original feature designed and patented by Lawrence to give a good trigger pull was a form of servo-mechanism which is under a light spring load and which is cocked automatically as the gun is closed. This gets around the necessity for a direct contact made through the full cocking stroke and allows a 3-pound trigger pull to release the

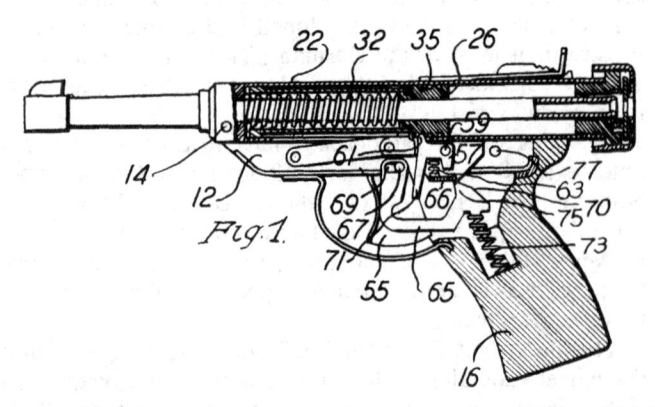

Patent drawings showing original trigger mechanism. Pistol is cocked.

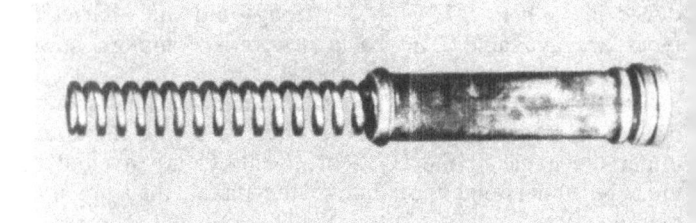

Hy Score piston and powerful compression spring.

sear. In effect this mechanism is actually a *double set-trigger*. It has the added advantage that for "dry" firing it is possible to open the pistol slightly and then close it, thereby cocking it so that the trigger can be pulled, but *not* compressing the powerful spring with the possibility of resultant damage to the piston when firing against an empty chamber. This firing while empty is a hazard in all spring-air rifles and pistols. Unless there is a pellet in the chamber to cushion the shock the moving piston face can be damaged by impact against the breech when "dry-fired" too often.

The accompanying photographs and drawings show the design construction quite clearly. Pistols of the Haenel type have about one-half the cocking stroke of the Hy Score, yet require greater effort to cock because of the necessity for pulling against the triggerguard. (Haenel barrels break down for loading only.) The Hy Score by utilizing the entire grip as a cocking point, permits maximum spring compression with a minimum of effort for the hinge design used. The manufacturers state that a single complete opening and closing movement of the pistol provides spring power to the equivalent of 7 to 10 pumps of the typical compressed-air pistol. The muzzle velocities obtained by the author on a comparative electronic test basis generally bear out this drastic statement. While there are better leverage linkages than the Hy Score, Mr. Lawrence did an excellent job in design compromise. The Hy Score pistol can be manufactured for a fraction of the cost of the comparable Webley. It is also better adapted to mass production.

The pressure developed is stated as of the order of 400 pounds per square inch. Some accuracy tests show groupings of 1 inch from a machine rest at 30 feet. It should be possible to do good shooting with this pistol once one has become accustomed to its hang, balance, and peculiar recoil. It has the basic pointing qualities of the Haenel and Luger designs, the balance of the weight being above the firing hand. Some shooters like this design, some do not. It is a matter of individual taste. Compression thrust, as in the Webley, is to the rear as the pistol is discharged.

In controlled tests by the author, velocity was found to be related directly to the diesel effect in this pistol, meaning high *average* velocity with poor *uniformity*. This adversely affected accuracy at times, though the floating barrel design also was a probable factor here.

The *repeating* model is the single-shot model with an adaptor at the rear operating somewhat on the loading principle of the camera shutter. It must be turned manually to allow each successive pellet to drop into the breech by gravity, the pistol muzzle being pointed down during loading.

Again as in the case of all air pistols, too much stress cannot be laid upon the necessity for perfect ammunition to get best results from the Hy Score, particularly from the repeater. Ammunition sold by the manufacturer, in theory at least, should give the best shooting results. It must be remembered that deformed ammunition or incorrectly sized ammunition can be a hindrance to velocity because of slow starting through friction or wedging action in the barrel, and also through possible keyholing in flight. As has already been pointed out, the correct fit of the bullet in a pistol of this type can be a major factor in both velocity and accuracy. Care should be taken when loading to avoid bullet deformation.

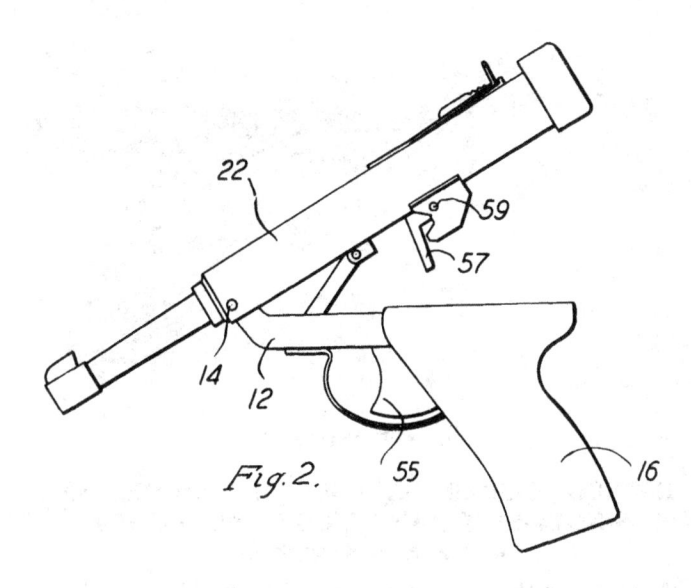

Hy Score original patent drawing showing cocking system.

Hy Score Air Rifles

The Hy Score spring-air rifles listed as models 801, 805, 806, and 807 are the old Diana air rifles imported and sold under the Hy Score name. The so-called Model 807 is fitted with one variety of trigger design of the Diana make which allows an excellent adjustable trigger pull. Actually, the trigger is a unique two-stage system which while not Diana's best is still good. Either a single- or a two-stage military-type pull is possible with this design.

The compressed spring of the Diana of this type is of the order of 165 pounds. An excellent line for their respective prices, these Dianas are not the quality found at higher prices under the "Peerless" name, but in velocity and accuracy they at times excel the more costly models.

Hy Score Pellets

The Hy Score Diabolo pellets are manufactured in Great Britain by Imperial Chemical Industries. They are of good quality and well manufactured. However they are subject, as are all soft-lead pellets, to deformation through rough handling. This factor should always be kept in mind when attempting precision shooting. Deformed pellets will jam the repeating loading mechanism also.

The .177 Diabolo pellets are sold under the Hy Score brand name in boxes of 500 at $1.75 per box. They weigh approximately 7.75 grains each.

The .22 pellets weigh 14 grains, and are packed 500 to the tin box to sell at $2.15. Darts are 50 cents a dozen for the .177 and 60 cents a dozen for the .22. (Note: darts should not be used in rifled barrels.)

In the author's tests, German-made pellets gave better velocity on an average than did the Hy Score brand in the "Hy Score" Diana rifles. This is understandable since German pellet makers work closely with German rifle makers.

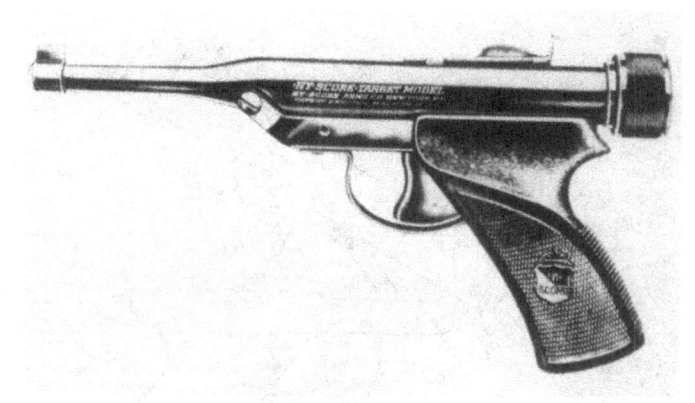

Hy Score single shot.

HY SCORE SPRING-AIR PISTOLS, MODEL 800, SINGLE-SHOT, AND MODEL 802, 6-SHOT
(Same Except as Noted)

Manufacturer: Hy Score Arms Corporation, Brooklyn, New York.
Overall Length: 10.25 inches. (Barrel approximately same.)
Weight: M800, 30.5 ounces. M802, about 42 ounces.
Caliber(s): Choice air-rifle round shot, .177 or .22 Diabolo.
Type(s) of Ammunition Used: Air-rifle shot, .177 or .22 Diabolo as required.
Rifled: Yes. Swaged, 6 grooves, shallow.
Operating System: Spring-air. Hold barrel casing, break down grip section on hinge.
Cocked & Spring Compressed By: (1) Release lock catch. (2) Hold tube and break grip down.
Loaded: M800, turn knurled loading head; insert pellet; close head. M802, see below.
Number Rounds: M800, single shot. M802, six-shot but individual loading manipulation required.
Stock Type: Pistol grip. (Not frame type.) Plastic.
Front Sight(s): Patridge.
Rear Sight(s): Stamped design. Adjustable elevation and windage; 8-inch sight line.
Velocity (Approximate): Maker claims 450 f.p.s. for .177 and 350 f.p.s. for .22. Tests indicate some velocities even higher.
Normal Accurate Range: Standard for type, about 30 feet.
Normal Maximum Range: Standard for type.
Approximate Retail Price: M800, $20 to $25, blue or chrome. M802, $23 and $28, blue or chrome.

REMARKS

Cocking Both Models. (1) Push release catch on right side of pistol. (2) Hold knurled cap firmly and break grip down as shown in accompanying photographs. Note that the spring is very strong.

To Cock for Dry Firing. (1) Release catch. (2) Raise tube clear of frame but not enough to start mainspring compression. (3) Close. Trigger may now be pulled for practice. Note that the mainspring is not compressed at this point, and the pistol must not be loaded.

Loading the Hy Score Repeating Pistol. (1) Push lock button on right side of pistol frame forward slightly and open gun.

(2) Break the gun open until it clicks, indicating it is at full cock.

(3) Turn the two ears on magazine clockwise until red indicator reaches hole marked "load here." Then turn it one more position to expose the loading port.

(4) With muzzle pointing down, drop first pellet (head down) into the loading port. Then turn the magazine ears one position and insert the next pellet. Continue this until six pellets have been loaded. Red indicator now appears at loading port.

(5) With muzzle still down, again open breech. This allows the first pellet to drop in when the knurled cap is turned counter clockwise. Should the pellet stick, move the cap slightly back and forth until the pellet drops in. Close the breech. Turn cap clockwise, which will close the shutter and tighten it. Small ring on the shutter will show in center hole when it is properly closed. You are now ready to fire.

(Note: The manufacturer cautions that while pellets may be forced into breech, if they are deformed they will jam the mechanism.)

(6) To fire additional shots, repeat the cocking motion for each firing, as the cocking spring must be compressed each time. Advance the magazine by one position and repeat opening and closing of the shutter.

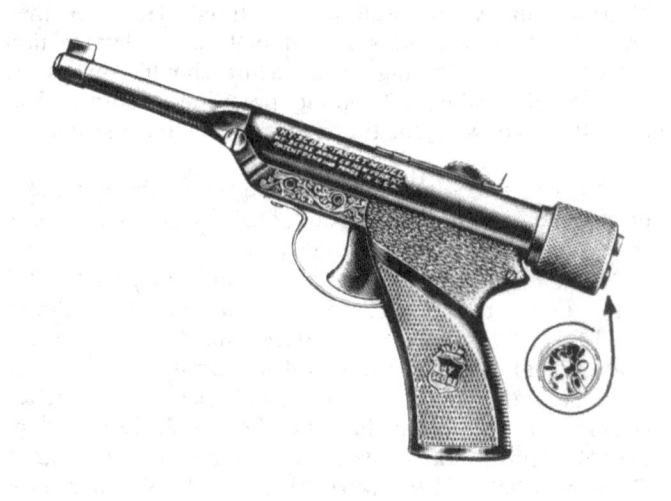

Hy Score repeater.

Loading for single shot.

(7) To use as a single loader, insert pellets one at a time through the center hole, opening and closing the shutter.

(8) For "dry" firing open gun slightly to cock the trigger mechanism and close without cocking the mainspring. This valuable feature allows practicing trigger pull without the physical effort of compressing the heavy spring each time; and it also prevents injury to the piston by slapping against an empty, uncushioned chamber.

(Note: Except for the magazine system, the single-shot and magazine models are alike.)

Figure 1.

Figure 2.

Figure 3.

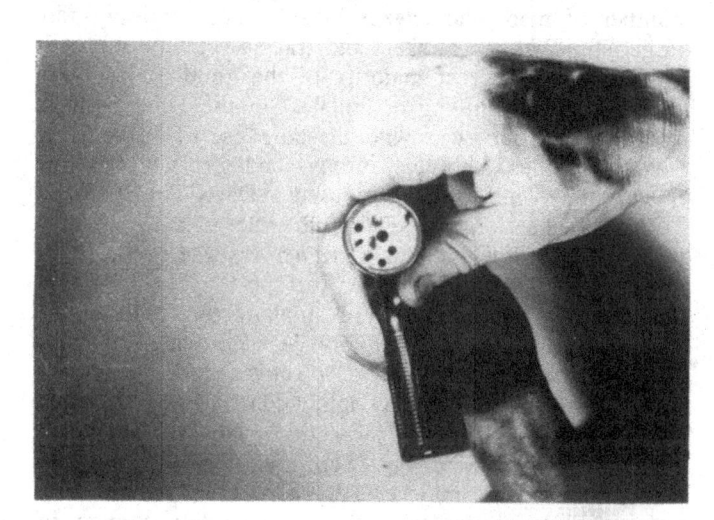

Figure 4.

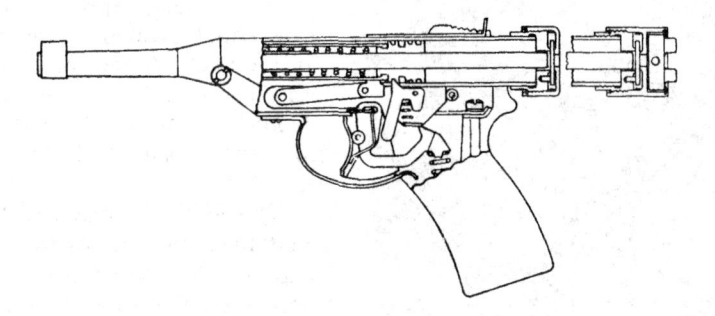

Hy Score pistol. Details of single shot and end view of repeating device.

DAISY AIR RIFLES
The Daisy Story

Daisy air rifles have been an important factor in the development of American youth for nearly 75 years. Very few people have any idea just how important a factor they actually have been! To do more than briefly outline the matter would require a full-sized book in itself!

"The boy," so the maxim goes, "is father to the man." Just how important shooting training is to boys can be gauged by data just released by the U. S. Fish and Wildlife Service after a nationwide survey. In 1955 11,784,000 hunting licenses were sold in the United States! For ammunition and for travel and living expenses to and from shooting areas, these men and women spent $936,867,000 —an average of $79.49 each! The figures do not include the cost of weapons.

When we add to this startling figure, the tremendous number of men who engage in small-bore and big-bore target shooting and in skeet and trap target shooting, it is obvious that the vast majority of the adult males (with more than a sprinkling of females) in the United States are directly concerned with the *safe* use of firearms.

Most of these shooters as boys and girls at one time or another owned or at least used a Daisy air rifle.

By classification, the Daisy air rifle is a *toy*, not a weapon. Nevertheless it is a *trainer* for use in the later handling of weapons, whether for sport or war. And in common with arms generally, its manufacture requires the highest degree of precision tolerances to provide the training factors which are its main objectives.

Its power, for instance, is rigidly controlled by scientific manufacture and constant inspection to make sure that it *remains* in the power range where it can provide adequate target effectiveness and accuracy to warrant its use as a trainer, while at the same time staying low enough in power that it will do no injury except under most extreme conditions. A thrown baseball is more dangerous than the average Daisy air rifle!

Mr. E. C. Hough pumping the original Daisy Model 25. The inventor Mr. Charles F. Lefever is holding a current Model 25. Well over fifteen million Model 25's have been used to train American youth in the safe handling of the familiar sporting pump gun system.

Boys taught to shoot by using the Daisy air rifle automatically learn the *proper* handling of firearms, unquestionably the finest preventative to any possible future accidents. Accidents and deaths by firearms use are really very minor in relation to most other forms of accident and death causes. Three times as many people die each year in the United States by drowning as through firearms use, whether accidental or in the course of police or criminal procedures. Three times as many die of accidental burns. Nearly ten times as many die of accidental falls. And about seventeen times as many die from motor accidents!

From these figures it will be seen that the factor of firearms accidents and deaths is not quite as drastic as the unthinking newspaper reader often is led to believe, not to mention the unthinking legislator. On the other hand, early training of the boy in proper handling of firearms can still further minimize these relatively very low rates.

Hunting and shooting are a part of the national heritage of every American boy. One might almost say of every boy everywhere. And in giving direction to the energy of youth in this direction, Daisy has performed a remarkable achievement in American manufacture and in our national sporting life.

Origin of the Name "Daisy"

The first air rifle of this make was presented to the board of The Plymouth Windmill Manufacturing Company in 1888 by Clarence J. Hamilton, the inventor, the original "man who hated wood"! At that time the company was manufacturing windmills of iron because Hamilton had conceived one which was better than one made of wood. All air rifles then in manufacture were of wood, and Hamilton characteristically had conceived one entirely of metal! Later he embarked on a manufacturing enterprise of his own, this time to manufacture a cartridge rifle which again had no wood in it. It was all metal, also! But we are here concerned only with Hamilton's air rifle.

The vice president and general manager of the company at that time was Lewis Cass Hough. After examining the all-metal rifle, he turned to Hamilton and said, "Clarence, that's a daisy!" The story came down from Lewis Hough to his son, the present treasurer of the company, who told it to the author.

In the slang expression of that time, the highest praise you could give anything was to call it "a daisy." The name stuck. A few years later the same board of directors changed the company name to the "Daisy Manufacturing Company"; and the manufacture of wildmills was soon abandoned for the sole manufacture of "wind" guns!

The first salesman was Charles H. Bennett. Mr. Bennett liked to recount that in those early days, traveling through the countryside in a buggy to solicit orders, he was often able to exchange rifles for overnight accommodations of board and lodging, a fact which in its time gave rise to very many salesmen's jokes! His first large order from a Chicago jobber took care of the entire year's production of Daisy, a quantity gigantic in those days but equal today to about one week's production.

Charles Bennett, late president of Daisy Manufacturing Company, aiming the first Daisy rifle.

One of Bennett's remarkable achievements was opening up a Chinese market for Daisy air rifles. While most of us tend to think of China as one vast mass of people without money, then as now there were tremendous groups of merchant or ruling classes who could and did purchase the good things of life for their families, at least.

When it was originally presented in China, the Daisy ran into legal trouble because of its resemblance to a rifle. When Bennett insisted that even though fairly accurate, it was nevertheless not basically a weapon and was not lethal, a Chinese official to whom the decision was left insisted on Mr. Bennett allowing himself to be used as a target to prove or disprove his statements!

As told in polite society early in the century, the shooting was done at Charlie's "extended hand." However, in view of the relatively low accuracy above 10 yards, it is more probable that the story he himself told is the correct one, since a larger target was obviously required! He was requested to turn and bend over, while the mandarins tested both the accuracy of their own aim and the stinging power of the Daisy against the seat of his trousers! While he did not get much opportunity to sit down comfortably in the next few days, he did achieve a sales victory. At one time 30 percent of the Daisy export business went to China!

The one time that "Uncle Charlie" Bennett's judgment slipped it was not on air rifles. It was on automobiles! In 1903 he met the late Henry Ford while in Detroit buying an automobile. Ford offered him 49 percent of his company's stock if he would provide enough money to make 250 cars. He passed up the offer, but in 1904 he bought 50 shares of Ford Motor Company for $5,000 and in 1907 congratulated himself when he sold them for $35,000 as a result of a disagreement with Ford Company policies. In later years, of course, the stock was worth millions, but Mr. Bennett lived out his life selling air rifles with few regrets.

Under the management of Lewis Cass Hough, the Daisy business soared until his death in 1902. He was replaced as treasurer by his son, Edward C. Hough, who still functions in that capacity.

It is to the business acumen of Edward C. Hough that the company owes much of its tremendous growth during the first four decades of this century; and to

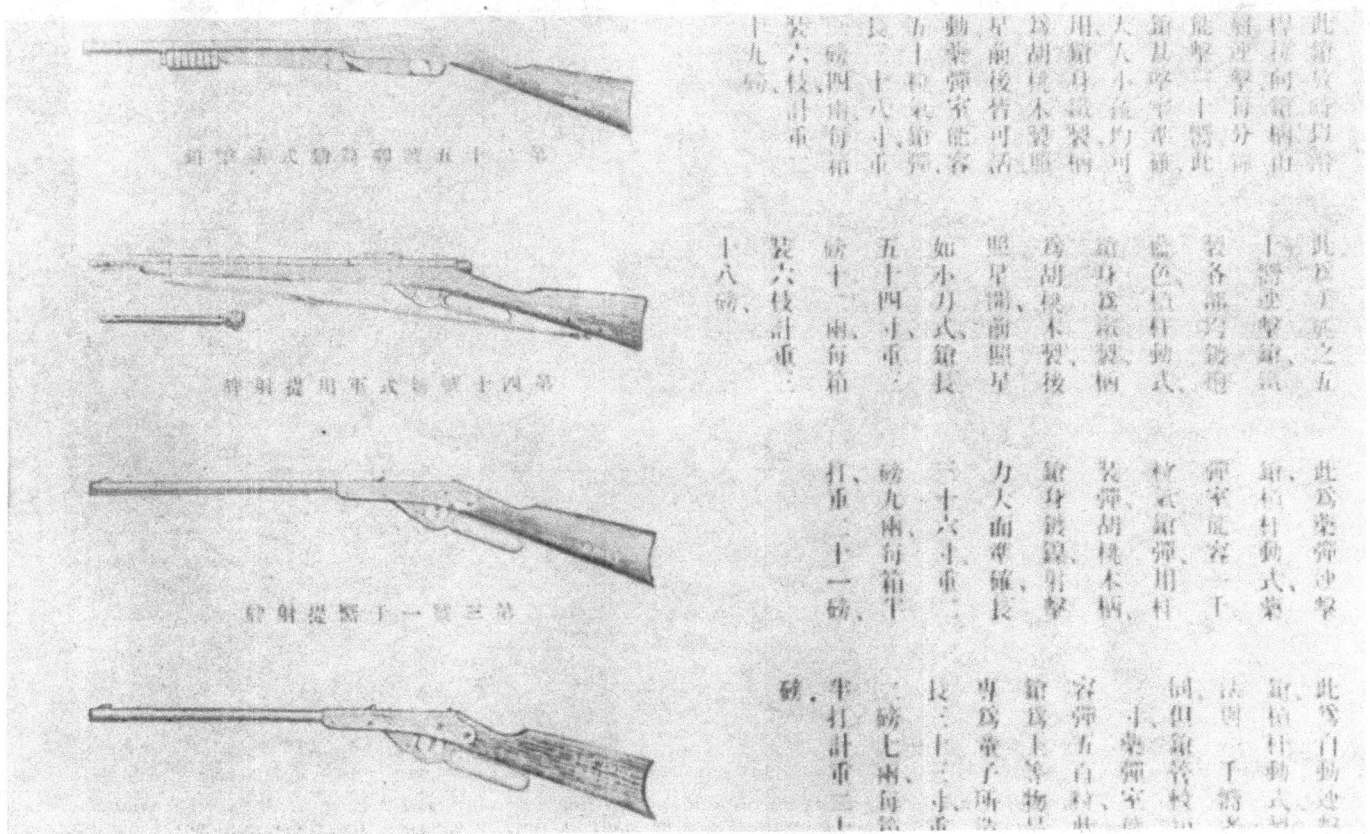

Daisy rifles (from Chinese catalog).

Representative views of automatic shot-making department, and of air-rifle assembly and testing at the Daisy Manufacturing Company plant at Plymouth, Michigan. Although its products are basically in the toy category, the Daisy company holds precision fits and tolerances equalling, and often surpassing, those of many large firearms manufacturers. The near-monopoly enjoyed by this firm stems equally from its high sense of business ethics, its progressive sales policies, its fine research facilities, and its amazingly efficient plant.

the sales wisdom of the grand old man of the air-gun trade, Daisy's president from 1912 until he passed on a short time ago at the ripe old age of 93, Charles H. Bennett.

The Daisy "25" Repeating Air Rifle

The original Daisy break-open air rifle was joined by the underlever type in 1901, a design patterned after the famous Winchester lever-action rifle of the great West.

By the year 1912, the great trend in American sporting bird shooting had produced the slide or "trombone"

Edward C. Hough made a trip to St. Louis. He spent one evening at Mr. Lefever's home, where he examined the design of the new air rifle. He recognized instantly in the design the possibilities of development of a youth training arm which would prepare boys *for the handling of the pump shotguns,* which even then were becoming a major factor in firearms production in the United States, and which today are the number one selling design.

Mr. Hough made a deal not only to buy the gun design but to have Mr. Lefever and his wife move to Plymouth, Michigan, to work in the Daisy factory on its general production.

Daisy current Model 25 repeating pump gun with improved easy-operating pump mechanism.

action shotguns. The most popular of the earlier models were the Winchester and Marlin, which had exposed movable top actions. As the slide was operated, the breechblock was unlocked and was then pushed back directly into line of eye of the shooter.

Charles F. Lefever, a member of the famous Lefever family of American shotgun manufacturers of that era, had worked for the Union Arms Company at Toledo, Ohio, where he developed a semi-automatic revolver along the general lines of the British Webley-Fosbery, had done some work on the Reifgraber automatic pistol which that company manufactured, and had also developed a *solid top,* 6-shot repeating shotgun with a trombone action. Other manufacturers recognized the value of an enclosed breech action, wherein the breechblock would move within a solid steel casing when actuated. The Union Arms Company about that time ran into financial difficulties and was dissolved. Lefever moved to St. Louis, where he went to work as a gunsmith for a major gun jobber.

As Mr. Lefever himself tells the story, while looking over some air rifles he conceived the idea of adapting the general outline of the popular Winchester inclosed breech hammerless pump gun into a repeating air-rifle design. He made a rough model and wrote to the Daisy Manufacturing Company concerning it.

When it became apparent to the St. Louis employer that he was going to lose Lefever, he offered him an increased salary to stay. Just how gigantic the increase was Mr. Lefever (now 84) would not state. Since however it was that employer's policy to grant the fine bonus of $10 at the end of each year provided gunsmiths had worked without unusual vacations or layoffs, it may be taken for granted that it was not too alluring!

Mr. Lefever and his wife moved to Plymouth, intending at the most to stay about 6 months. They arrived in the middle of a storm and for a time contemplated returning to St. Louis immediately. However, like the proverbial man who came to dinner, Mr. Lefever stayed on at Plymouth. Working conditions suited him, and year in and year out he stayed on until the period of his retirement. During those years from 1914 to 1952, he was granted over 60 patents for designs and improvements on various air and toy guns. He developed the first really successful toy water pistol, a toy item which created a tremendous stir throughout the trade. This in one form or another is still a very important item in toymaking throughout the entire world.

However, it was for that original pump rifle that the youth of America owes so much to Mr. Lefever. In the years between, nearly 15,000,000 of these Model 25 repeating pump air rifles have been sold by Daisy!

203

The current version of this famous rifle as redesigned by Daisy technicians is very much easier to operate than it was originally. It has been redesigned for greater efficiency of manufacture and for easier operation by boys. However, in essence and in principle, it is still Lefever's brain child.

Daisy Today

Merchandising changes like everything else, of course. The era of the moving picture and television introduced the great West again and new "interplanetary" heroes through the personalities of Buck Jones, Buck Rogers, Buzz Barton, Red Ryder and their ilk. Western and interplanetary heroes of film and cartoon swayed to a great extent, and still do, the purchasing habits related to youth. New blood, as always, was needed for new merchandising.

The present active head of Daisy, a grandson of the original Mr. Hough, entered sales at this point. Cass S. Hough, now executive vice president, was elected a director of the company in 1934. During World War II he spent 4 years in the service, emerging as technical director of the Eighth Air Force in England with rank of full colonel. For his services he was given the Congressional Medal of Honor. In passing it might be mentioned that many of the important members of the sales and technical staff left Daisy at the same time to enter active military service with him.

While adhering to the original Daisy concept that their air rifles should be merchandised as character builders, contributing to the eyesight, nerves, and health development of boys, Cass Hough also took advantage of changing times and tied his merchandising into the spirit of the period. Sales mounted steadily.

Today sales requirements are again changing. With the necessity for safety programs in every sport from swimming to shooting being recognized, Cass Hough again has been the principal figure in the toy field in generating interest in such training and safety programs.

Through affiliations with the National Rifle Association, the Boy Scouts of America, and various hunter training programs in schools and camps, with emphasis laid on adult training and supervision, the Daisy Manufacturing Company has again established itself as an important factor in American life.

The Daisy Manufacturing Company was founded on the American ideas of integrity and principle. Its products have always been intended to fill an elemental need in the community. That objective has never for a moment been lost sight of. Its dominant place in the industry is an excellent example of just how far a manufacturer can go when he places integrity above any immediate profit possibilities. The story of Daisy has been a story of growth as well as a story of American business. Competitors by the hundreds have come and gone since the origin of the Daisy Manufacturing Company. On the principle that someone can always make something cheaper and poorer, the Daisy products have been imitated both here and abroad over many years.

None of these have ever been truly successful. While one might steal a design, it is not possible to steal sound and honest business principles. In advertising and sales,

Daisy's problem is the fabrication and assembly of precision parts at extremely high production rates. The "chain reaction" of a minor change on just one small part is examined by, from left, Research Director Ciro Scalingi, Executive Vice President Cass Hough, and Factory Manager John J. McHenry.

in manufacturing quality and methods advancement, in public and labor relations, and in recognition of duties and obligations to the public weal generally, many manufacturing firms throughout the country might profitably study the story and the success of the Daisy system.

DAISY AIR RIFLE, MODEL 98 WITH SCOPE
(Toy Trainer Type. Mechanically Other Models Are Similar)

Manufacturer: Daisy Manufacturing Company, Plymouth, Michigan.
Overall Length: 35 inches.
Weight: About 2 pounds.
Caliber(s): Air-rifle shot (commonly called "BB").
Type(s) of Ammunition Used: Steel air-rifle shot, round, .175.
Rifled: No. Not required for short range.
Operating System: Spring-air by triggerguard-lever spring compression.
Cocked & Spring Compressed By: Operation of triggerguard lever as for sporting rifles.
Loaded: From magazine by gravity. (See below.)
Number Rounds: About 850 shot. (Other models 350 to 1,000.)
Stock Type: Sporting lever-action type with fore-end.
Front Sight(s): Ramp-type blade.
Rear Sight(s): Auxiliary open sights. Telescope with adjustable cross-hairs.
Velocity (Approximate): 280 f.p.s.
Normal Accurate Range: 20 feet or more.
Normal Maximum Range: About 100 feet.
Approximate Retail Price: $12.95 with telescope. (Note: Scope and mount are plastic with genuine optics.)

REMARKS

The telescope actually functions and is not merely a toy. It can be used to instruct in scope shooting.

Loading. Open "lightning loader" at muzzle and pour in shot; 850 is normal, but as many as 1,000 may be accommodated. NOTE THAT UNLIKE THE MODEL 25 PUMP, the lever-actions are NOT force-fed by spring follower. They feed by gravity in this design. Close loader.

Operation. Pull triggerguard lever out as far as possible. This retracts piston and compresses mainspring. At end of stroke, the hook end of piston will be caught by trigger. Pull lever back to full closed position. Pressing trigger will release piston and spring and discharge shot in chamber. Gravity will feed another pellet as the lever is manipulated for next cocking stroke when normally used.

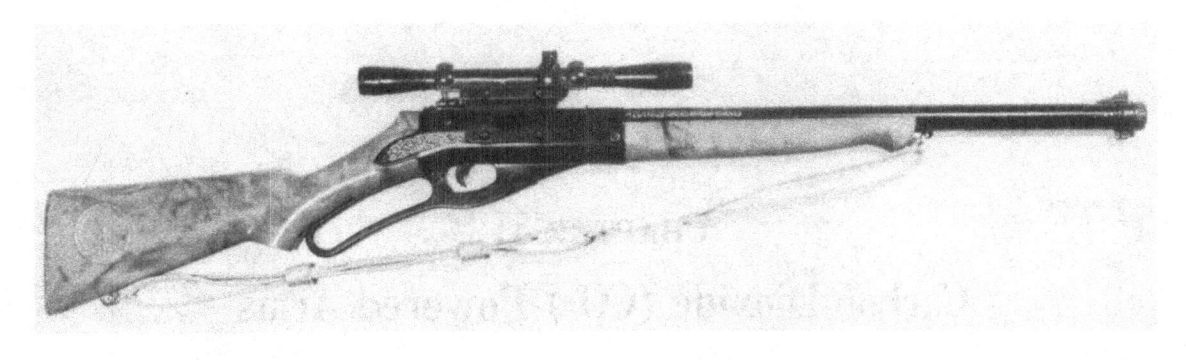

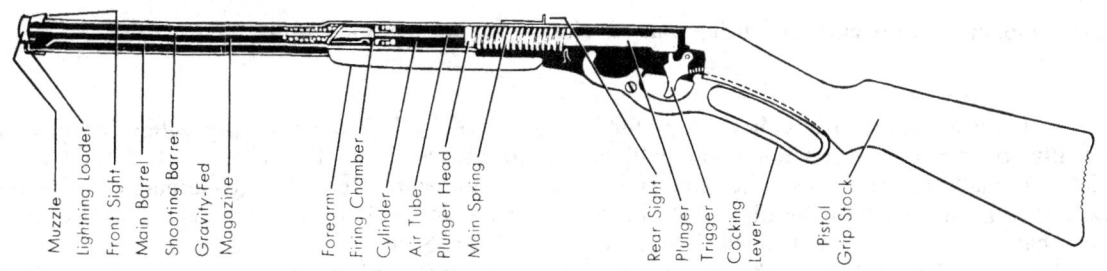

Daisy Air Rifle with 2-power telescope which has ground optics and functions exactly like expensive rifle scopes.

DAISY AIR RIFLE, MODEL 25, PUMP-ACTION REPEATER

Manufacturer: Daisy Manufacturing Company, Plymouth, Michigan.
Overall Length: 37 inches.
Weight: About 2¼ pounds.
Caliber(s): Air-rifle shot (commonly called "BB").
Type(s) of Ammunition Used: Steel air-rifle shot, round, .175.
Rifled: No. Not required for short-range training.
Operating System: Spring-air by forearm-lever spring compression.
Cocked & Spring Compressed By: Operation of hand-pump type lever below barrel.
Loaded: From force-feed magazine as explained below.
Number Rounds: 50.
Stock Type: Pistol-grip sporting as in pump shotgun or pump rifle.
Front Sight(s): Ramp-type front blade.
Rear Sight(s): Combination folding peep and open. Adjustable elevation and windage.
Velocity (Approximate): 340 f.p.s.
Normal Accurate Range: 20 feet.
Normal Maximum Range: About 100 feet.
Approximate Retail Price: $9.50.

REMARKS

This rifle operates on the same spring-air system as high-priced European precision rifles. Operating the pump lever forces back piston and compresses mainspring. Piston is caught and held back by trigger at end of compression stroke. When trigger is pressed, spring and piston are released. Piston is driven forward in tight-fitting tube and compresses air in its travel path. The air vent (or outlet hole) behind the pellet is very small, and the difference in size between it and the large head of the moving piston is responsible for the relatively high air pressure developed.

Loading. Unscrew and withdraw shot barrel from end of rifle. Slide shot follower forward to notch and pour 50 (or less) shot into the shot channel therein. Release shot follower, and its spring will force the first shot into the discharge chamber. Put shot barrel back in and screw down tightly. (Note that this magazine feeds automatically by spring pressure and is not dependent upon gravity.)

Operation. (1) Pull fore-end straight back as far as it will go. The cocking levers will move the cocking arm and force the piston back until it hooks over top of trigger, its spring being compressed meanwhile.

(2) Note that this "toy trainer" has a safety feature not commonly found on high priced precision air arms! Should you pull the trigger accidentally in this rifle with the action open, a built-in safety bar prevents the gun from firing. ONLY when the action is completely closed is the bar out of blocking position. (NOTE: In serious European air arms with few exceptions, you can pull the trigger with the action open, and the action will slam shut violently and may injure the rifle and the shooter's fingers.)

(3) Press trigger to release piston and spring, and discharge the shot in the chamber.

(4) For additional shots, merely work fore-end lever back and forth and pull trigger for each shot.

Sights. The open and peep sights are available as desired by turning the leaf. This permits use of open sights for quick shooting and the peep for shooting at formal paper targets and the like.

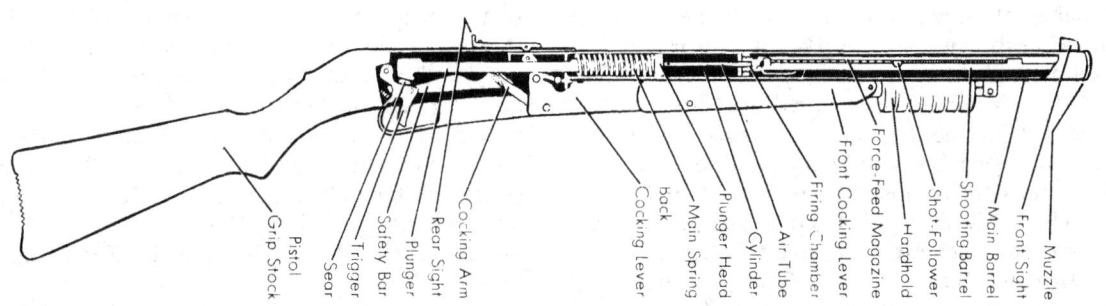

Daisy Model 25 pump cutaway showing construction and operation.

205

CHAPTER 14

Carbon Dioxide (CO₂) Powered Arms

(Note: All production arms currently using carbon dioxide gas as a propellant are of American manufacture.)

CARBON dioxide arms (popularly called CO₂ guns) are currently (or recently) production manufactured as pistols, rifles, or small-bore shotguns. They fire pellets or small shot which are loaded into the discharge chamber of the shot barrel. The missile is propelled by a jet of carbon dioxide gas released behind the pellet when the trigger pull results in momentary opening of a gas-outlet valve from an accumulator area or gas chamber.

All *current* models are charged by inserting a non-refillable, low-cost disposable metal "cartridge" in a tube or "barrel" below the shot barrel or in the pistol grip. Earlier models still in use are charged either (1) from a large-capacity metal CO₂ cylinder into a sealed and valved tube below the shot barrel, the tube gas providing power until refill is needed; or (2) from a large-capacity (normally 10-ounce) heavy-steel refillable cylinder which is screwed into the gas tube reservoir below the barrel, and which is replaced and refilled when necessary; or (3) in certain shooting-gallery types by direct hose feed from a large CO₂ gas cylinder to the discharge reservoir.

The only CARBON DIOXIDE ARMS currently being manufactured on a production basis are the Benjamin and Crosman lines of pistols, rifles, and smooth-bore pellet-type arms and the Carbo-Jet pistol.

British and European manufacturers have not yet entered this field for various reasons. The most common answers given by foreign pellet-gun makers when queried by the author are these: (1) Spring-air arms have reached such a high degree of perfection and shooter acceptance abroad that CO₂ manufacture would not be profitable to the manufacturer. (2) Shooting costs are lower with spring-air guns, since the propelling force is developed by springs alone. (3) There is no such accessiblity to CO₂ supplies abroad as is common in the United States. There are many other reasons, but they are too subject to controversy for attention here, as for instance: Spring-air guns are capable of much more accurate shooting—a statement which in the author's observation and testing is true when you are comparing our CO₂ guns (all of which are extremely low in price as required for large scale American sales) with the *fine and expensive order* of British and German air rifles with heavy precision barrels, costly and intricate sight equipment, finely-bedded stocks, and extra weight. This does NOT hold true when the two systems are shot against each other in *reasonably comparable price brackets*. Here the CO₂ guns will do anything that the lower-priced air guns will do both as to penetration and accuracy, while being infinitely easier to use as a youth trainer and a plinker. (Note: For comparison a really good German air rifle costs a minimum of $35 in the United States, while CO₂ rifles sell for $16.50 to $22.)

As this book went to press, Hämmerli, the noted Swiss gunmaking firm, was preparing to market precision arms and devices in the CO₂ field. Other European makers have been studying designs for possible export markets, but none are as yet in production.

TYPES OF CARBON DIOXIDE ARMS

As already listed, all current designs use low-cost "throwaway" steel CO₂ tubes commonly called cartridges or Powerlets. These have the advantage of being easy to store, to transport, and to use. They have the disadvantage of having relatively small capacity, though this is not a serious factor in a trainer or home-use item, such as these are designed to be.

All current Benjamin and Crosman designs are single shot. Ammunition is the same as for their air arms. Pellets must be individually loaded. However, the *power supply* is adequate for many shots depending upon the individual "cartridge" used, the arm in which it is used, and the power adjustment employed (most types have either a dual or a multi-range adjustment built in). Since both of these old-line makers have produced compressed-air designs with magazines which fed in the projectiles as the action was manipulated, it is inevitable that in due course both will introduce magazine CO₂ arms.

The Carbo-Jet made by Swanson Manufacturing Co., on the other hand, has a somewhat rudimentary magazine built into the top of the pistol, which automatically feeds balls into the breech as the action is operated ready for discharging.

(Note: In the course of preparing this book for publication, the author has found that many new developments in the CO₂ field are under intensive experimentation both here and abroad. Any which are not confidential will be described further on in this text.)

Benjamin manufactures its carbines (short rifles) and pistols to shoot standard .177 or .22 caliber air-type pellets of Diabolo pattern. The Benjamin name is HC, for high compression. Darts may also be used, even though all barrels are rifled, as the Benjamins use bronze barrels.

Crosman likewise manufactures all models of its rifles

and pistols to shoot standard .177 or .22 caliber air pellets of Diabolo pattern. The Crosman name is Super Pells. Darts are not recommended by Crosman. All barrels are rifled steel tubing.

CO_2 ADVANTAGES OVER COMPRESSED-AIR DESIGNS

For American use, advantages exceed disadvantages. They may be summarized as follows:

(1) Easier to Operate. This is an important factor. Once the gun has been gas-charged (a very simple operation), it is only necessary to load and, where required, manipulate the cocking mechanism in order to discharge a succession of shots.

(2) Closer Resemblance to Firearms Handling Procedure. Since CO_2 loading procedure most nearly approximates that of loading true firearms, it follows that in addition to the avoidance of physical pumping, *this operational similarity makes firearms training easier than with the compressed-air type.*

(3) Better Uniformity of Velocity Within Normal Handling Limits. Until pressure begins to drop off seriously, CO_2 arms will give reasonably consistent velocity without any direct attention on the part of the shooter. Compressed-air arms, conversely, require the shooter to count the number of pump strokes and also to control the *type* of stroke in order to maintain consistent velocity, something which can easily be done by the expert, but which is difficult for the beginner and the plinker.

(4) Better Average Accuracy by the Average Shooter. On observational tests it can be easily demonstrated that *the physical effort* of pumping up for 10 or more target shots with a compressed-air arm in a limited period of time will result in poorer scores than will be registered by the same shooter using a CO_2 arm where the physical effort is avoided. Note that the accuracy here is attributable not to any inherent qualities in the weapon, but to the fatigue and psychology of the average shooter. (To a lesser degree, this applies also to comparisons with spring-air arms.)

(5) Increased Speed of Fire. The elimination of need for individual shot pump-up speeds up "firepower" to an astonishing rate, of course. This is valuable for group training in particular.

DISADVANTAGES OF THE CO_2 DESIGN

(1) Increased Cost of Shooting. While CO_2 "cartridges" are low in cost, this may be a factor in some instances, particularly if full-power shooting is done or if "dud" cartridges are encountered. For most purposes, and particularly for training use, the added cost of CO_2 shooting is more than neutralized by the ease and pleasure it adds to pellet-gun shooting, however.

(2) Higher Maintenance Cost. The CO_2 gun will be used more. Also, its gas chamber will be under pressure more than the pump-up type arm. Its valves and seals will normally be affected more quickly than those in a compressed-air design.

While CO_2 designs are essentially simpler than the corresponding pump-up types, and have fewer parts, for the foregoing and other reasons it is to be expected that their life will not be as long without attention as the air designs. (Note: Both Benjamin and Crosman have servicing arrangements in areas of major sales. What is more important, these arms are all sold at such low prices that they may be considered "expendable" anyway. A $20 trainer cannot be expected to last a lifetime without attention. Again it may be stated that the higher maintenance cost is offset by the ease, pleasure, and consistency it adds to pellet-gun shooting.

(3) Lower Penetration. The penetration is *entirely adequate for pellet-gun uses;* but it must be conceded that if one wishes to put in the physical pumping effort required, the compressed-air pattern will develop somewhat more velocity and penetration. It must also be recognized that the CO_2 gun will lose velocity and penetration as the cartridge charge loses pressure, while the air design can be maintained if the effort is put into it. Again this is a matter of compromise, and in any event is not a serious practical factor: If you want real penetration, get a firearm, not a pellet gun of any type!

COMPARISON OF CO_2 AND SPRING-AIR SYSTEMS

Here again the CO_2 design *from an American standpoint* is superior on the average. The spring-air design by comparison is slower to operate (though not nearly so much so as the compressed-air designs). GOOD spring-air guns are much more costly than CO_2 guns.

Spring-air designs of good makes will give more consistent velocity than CO_2 guns, of course, since their spring powers are relatively constant. Velocity of a high-priced air gun will approximate the *average* (not the highest) velocity obtainable from a CO_2 gun; but the price differentials and physical operating efforts must be weighed in the balance.

Any good spring-air arm will obviously be cheaper to operate and maintain than a CO_2 gun, since the former employs no valves and uses only springs for power generation. They have fewer and sturdier parts. They have been in production and use longer and their major "bugs" have long since been eliminated or discounted.

When all the factors are weighed, for training and plinking purposes the CO_2 designs emerge as the most practical compromise in the field of pellet-gun types *for use in the United States.* They were designed for specific purposes for ease of operation, safe short-range shooting, firearms training, and to be sold at low cost. They do all these things superbly well, everything considered.

Compared to small-bore firearms and to imported spring-air guns, the current American CO_2 guns are a far better value.

Considered from the standpoint of indoor shooting, or for short-range shooting for fun or training in settled areas, the CO_2 arms are the nearest approach yet made to the "perfect" type.

(Note: During the course of preparing this book, the author has encountered several spring designs which are more efficient by far and nearly as easy to operate as the best CO_2 designs. However, no production is currently contemplated by owners of such designs.)

207

CARBON DIOXIDE GAS AS A PROPELLANT

Carbon dioxide gas is the nearest approach to a perfect projecting force for short-range pellet guns that has yet been developed. It is colorless, non-toxic, and odorless. It won't burn. On the contrary, it is commonly used as a fire extinguisher. (Note: Some European gas guns now appearing employ ether-type gases.)

It is a chemical anhydride—a compound from which water has been extracted. It is easily liquified, relatively speaking, the required pressure being only 36 atmospheres or about 540 pounds per square inch. Hence it is cheap to produce and to purchase. Because of its relatively low pressure it is easy and safe to store if normal precautions are taken not to expose it to too much heat. If we remember that it is the gas used in every soda fountain for charging water, the very factor of its widespread use is an assurance of its inherent relative safety. Like compressed gases generally, of course, it can be expanded by increased temperatures, and all manufacturers caution against storing either the gas "cartridges" or the charged gun itself in a hot place; but these precautionary measures are entirely normal.

Let us for a moment compare CO_2 gas and air as propellants.

If we draw power from a cylinder of compressed air, we *automatically reduce the pressure at each discharge*. Thus in old model pump-up guns where one charge fired many rounds of bullets, each bullet had a definitely lower velocity than the one before it. In practical use this did not always impair accuracy until 20 or more shots had been fired; but for precision target shooting it was, and is, a factor. (Note that in current American compressed-air guns, the *entire charge* of air is intended to be used up for each shot; hence a dependable repeating system is not practical.)

If, on the other hand, we draw power from a container of liquified carbon dioxide, *we do NOT necessarily reduce the pressure of each discharge*. This is the important consideration, and to understand it we must know something of the nature of liquified CO_2 gas.

Carbon dioxide is a liquid-vapor power supply as it comes in "cartridges" or cylinders. If you rock the container back and forth, you will note that the heavy liquid within moves back and forth much as mercury will. The container is never filled to liquid capacity. There is space in which vapor (CO_2 gas) is present. The *vapor pressure over the liquid gas remains the same for any given temperature so long as any liquid remains in the container*. This CO_2 pressure at normal room temperature is approximately 900 pounds per square inch. However, if the gas is bled off into a large accumulator, naturally pressure will be reduced.

So long as there is any *liquid* gas remaining in the direct supply line, the *vapor pressure* remains constant. When there is no more liquid but only vapor (or gas), the pressure drops off sharply and bullets will keyhole and possibly stick in the barrel. When the drop-off occurs, it is immediately noticeable in the report made, so there is actually no excuse for the shooter delaying too long replacing a nearly expended cylinder. (Note that the action should be cocked and fired repeatedly without pellets at this point to almost completely exhaust the gas before opening the gas tube in the gun; otherwise the retaining plug may still be blown out of the fingers when

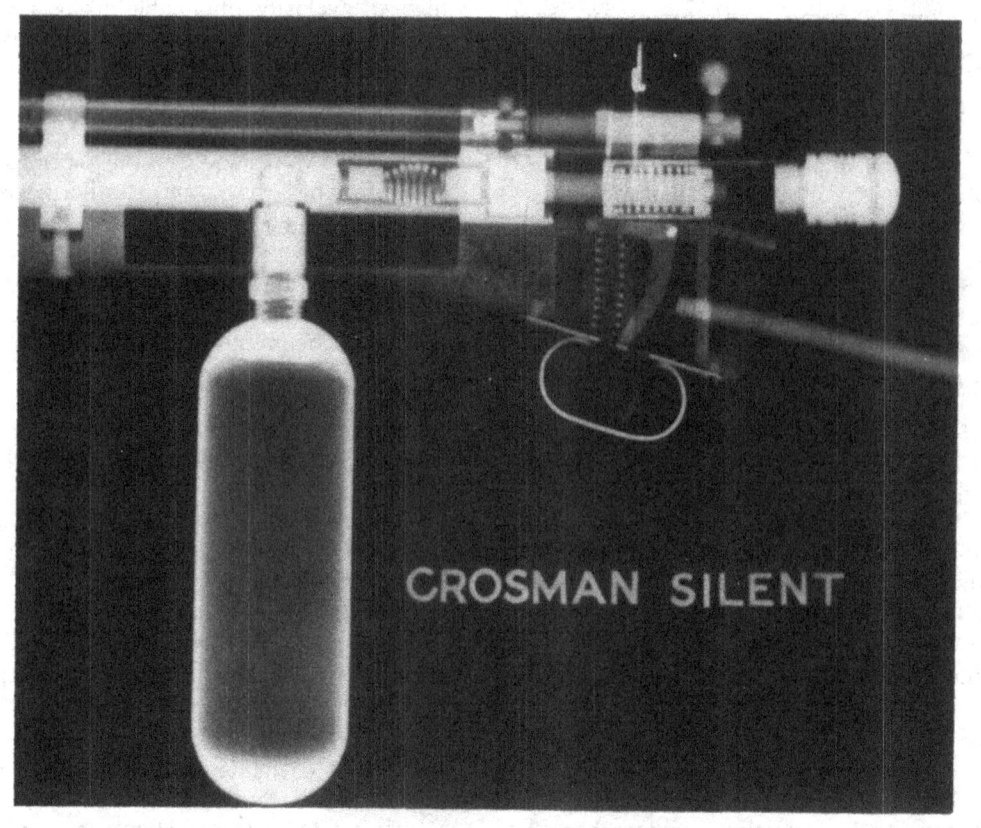

Model 122 (X-ray photo), obsolete Crosman. Shows internal construction and liquid-gas system. Current models all use small expendable gas container in fore-end.

unscrewing it, unless an automatic "bleed" is incorporated.)

The operation of the gun itself is quite simple once the gun has been charged. When you push in the valve stem on a bicycle or automobile tire, air will spurt out under pressure. It will stop when you release the pressure as the spring reacts to re-seat the valve. Similarly, when the hammer, striker, or equivalent element in a CO_2 gun strikes and releases the stem of the valve leading into the power supply, a portion of the vapor head is suddenly released to drive the pellet out of the barrel.

Standard gas capsules hold 9 to 19 grams of CO_2. However, the oversized "cartridges" or "Powerlets" used by Crosman are much more practical for pellet-gun use because the greater capacity means that liquified gas is present for a much longer time than in the drug-store gas tubes, which means in turn not only more shots but more powerful ones over a longer average tube life.

Since all expanding gases produce cold, naturally there is a "refrigerating" effect at each discharge. Because of the extremely small amount of CO_2 gas used for each shot (usually not over 0.0009 pound!) this cold is normally not enough to affect operation appreciably. However, in warm temperatures it may produce a slight rust at the mouth of gas cartridge and interior of the gun gas tube. This can be prevented by slightly greasing the tube at time of insertion when the condition shows itself.

Now if considering the chemical and physical factors involved in normal CO_2 usage were all there were to CO_2 gunmaking, it would follow that we would get *the same pressure and the same velocity* for all shots right up to the last few.

Unfortunately, it doesn't work that way. In actual practice many variables enter into the matter. Not only temperature and gas supply, but also spring and valve actions, parts tolerances, friction coefficients, accumulator areas, and a score of other factors are encountered. Some can be discounted by the manufacturer. Some can't.

It would be very simple to write an engineering thesis on this aspect of CO_2 guns; but it would be both a thankless and profitless task so far as this author is concerned.

So without going into specific technical "whys," just let it be said that, regardless of chemical gas facts, *in a CO_2 gun you will NOT get uniform velocity* right down to the last few rounds you can fire from the gun. Very, very far from it. But you will get a highly satisfactory average.

What can you actually expect in average performance? In chapter 16 will be found results of a series of very recent tests. Some were conducted by an independent ballistics research laboratory, others by the author. The figures, velocities, accuracy notes, and general data will establish the value of the arms tested.

It must be stressed that velocity and similar data were developed by the latest and finest accepted electronic testing equipment; and that all arms tested were subjected to equal tests.

CURRENT BENJAMIN CO_2 RIFLES AND PISTOLS

Current Benjamin CO_2 rifle (or carbine) production is limited to one series. Model 362 designates the .22 caliber version and Model 367 designates the .177 caliber in the series. Benjamin calls them "carbines" because of their short length—35 inches overall. Two stages of power adjustment are provided.

Similarly, current Benjamin CO_2 pistol production is limited to one series. Model 262 designates the .22 caliber version and Model 267 designates the .177 caliber in the series. Again, two stages of power adjustment are provided. The pistols mechanically are very closely allied to the carbines as to parts and operational design.

Carbines and pistols use the same ammunition. They also are powered with the same Benjamin No. 2500 non-refillable CO_2 "cartridges."

BENJAMIN M362 AND M367 SUPER CO_2 CARBINES
(Same Except for Caliber)

(Note: The term "carbine" indicates a short rifle.)

Manufacturer: Benjamin Air Rifle Company, St. Louis, Missouri.
Overall Length: 35 inches. (Barrel 23 inches.)
Weight: About 3¾ pounds.
Caliber(s): M362, .22. M367, .177.
Type(s) of Ammunition Used: Required caliber Benjamin HC pellets (or equal).
Rifled: Yes. (Note: Darts may be used if shanks have no burrs.)
Operating System: CO_2 gas from non-refillable tubes (No. 2500 Benjamin CO_2 cartridges).
Cocked: Turn bolt button and withdraw bolt.
Loaded: Insert pellet in breach. Push bolt forward and turn to lock.
Number Rounds: Single-shot loading ONLY.
Stock Type: Short walnut, carbine type.
Front Sight(s): Blade, fixed.
Rear Sight(s): On barrel. Open type. Adjustable for elevation and windage.

Benjamin Super CO_2 carbine.

Benjamin Super Rocket 260 Series CO$_2$ Pistol.

Velocity (Approximate): At full power, 700 f.p.s. maximum.
Normal Accurate Range: 15 to 20 yards. Average for type and ammunition.
Normal Maximum Range: Average for type and ammunition.
Approximate Retail Price: $16.50.

REMARKS

(Note: Manufacturer advises the following precautions: (1) Keep safety "on" at all times until ready to fire. (2) Never expose charged gun or cartridges to sun or other heat. (3) Do not put rifle away with CO$_2$ gas or pellet in it. (4) Never remove knurled fore-end until all gas has been completely exhausted. To empty gas chamber, discharge gun without pellets until empty.

To Charge. Unscrew and remove knurled metal fore-end. Drop CO$_2$ cartridge in, neck first. Replace fore-end with "O" ring in position. Tighten to snug fit. (Overtightening will jam thread.) Turn bolt button up to unlock. Pull back until it clicks into cocked position. Next push bolt forward and turn to lock. Pull trigger, being sure there is no pellet in the chamber. THIS FIRST FIRING MOTION IS NECESSARY TO PIERCE THE GAS CARTRIDGE EVERY TIME A NEW "CARTRIDGE" IS INSERTED.

Loading. Turn up and pull back bolt button to unlock and cock action. Insert pellet in breech. Push bolt button forward and turn down to lock and seal breech. Push safety off, if ready to fire.

Firing. Press trigger. It will pivot and release internal hammer. Spring will drive hammer forward to hit outlet valve stem. Valve will be opened and allow a high pressure jet of CO$_2$ to pass through into chamber behind pellet. Valve spring will react and re-seat the valve.

(NOTE: Should trigger be pressed while safety is "on," it is necessary to recock before safety can be raised to allow firing.)

Caution. (1) Valve may lose elasticity if not frequently used. Valve and packing may have to be replaced because of loss of elasticity if gun is laid away for a long period.

(2) "O" sealing ring may swell when fore-end is removed due to gas affecting it. It will return to normal size after about 15 minutes.

(3) Never use oil on valve or allow oil to enter gas chamber. External surfaces and bearings should be oiled as needed for lubrication and rust prevention.

(Note: These carbines are stated to be capable of grouping 5 shots in 1 inch at 15 yards from machine rest. Penetration at full power as much as ¾-inch in soft pine.)

BENJAMIN MODELS 262 AND 267 SUPER ROCKET CO$_2$ PISTOLS

(Same Except for Caliber)

Manufacturer: Benjamin Air Rifle Company, St. Louis, Missouri.
Overall Length: 9.25 inches. (Barrel 5¾ inches.)
Weight: About 2.5 pounds.
Caliber(s): M262, .22. M267, .177.
Type(s) of Ammunition Used: Benjamin HC pellets, .22 or .177 (or equal).
Rifled: Yes.
Operating System: CO$_2$ gas from non-refillable, low-cost Benjamin No. 2500 CO$_2$ cartridges.
Cocked: By opening of bolt mechanism as for carbine.
Loaded: Insert pellet in open breech. Close and turn bolt mechanism.
Number Rounds: Single-shot loading ONLY.
Stock Type: Molded plastic grips with dual thumbrests.
Front Sight(s): Post front.
Rear Sight(s): Stamped screw-adjustable rear.
Velocity (Approximate): At full power, about 500 f.p.s. maximum.
Normal Accurate Range: Standard for type. One inch at 10 yards from rest claimed by maker.
Normal Maximum Range: Standard for type.
Approximate Retail Price: $15.

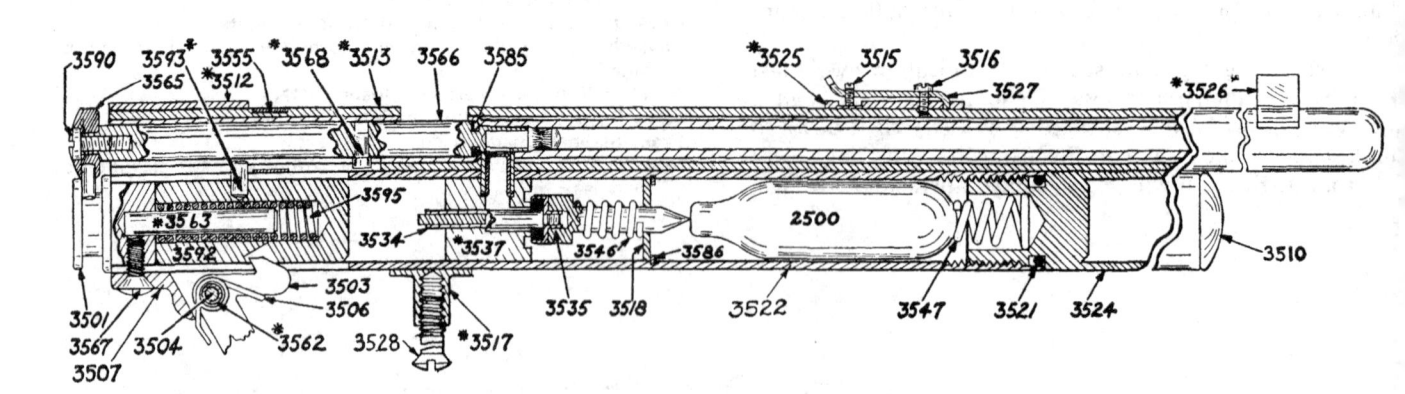

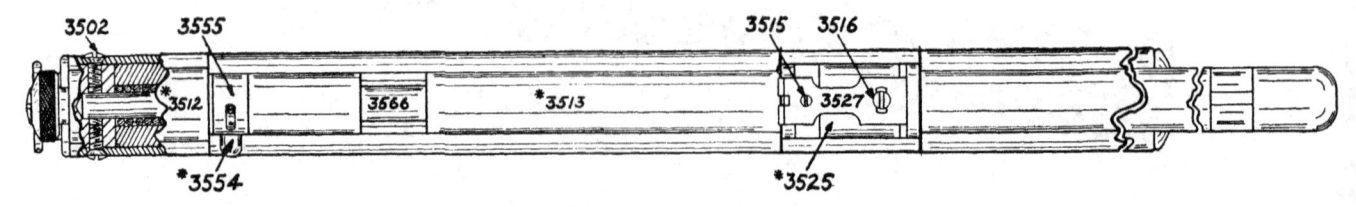

Drawing of No. 352 Benjamin Super CO$_2$ Carbine.

210

REMARKS

Operation. This CO_2 pistol is a modification and improvement in some ways over the earlier series. It was introduced late in 1954. In either .177 or .22 caliber it sells at $15 retail. One gas bulb, or cartridge, and a sample supply of pellets is packed with each pistol.

To prepare for firing, remove screw cap at muzzle end of gas reservoir tube Insert gas cartridge, narrow end first. Screw cap back on. Turn protruding knob of bolt to unlock and pull back to full cock. Push bolt forward, turn and lock. Press trigger and internal hammer will fall and puncture the gas cartridge, allowing controlled gas to enter pressure chamber.

With the insertion of each new gas cartridge (which may fire 25 or more shots according to power utilized), it is necessary to repeat these motions, as the initial hammer fall *breaks the seal on the fresh gas cartridge.*

For actual firing thereafter, each shot requires only that the bolt be turned and pulled back to cock, pellet be inserted in breech, bolt pushed forward to seat pellet, and turned to lock breech. Trigger safety should be applied if pistol is not to be fired immediately.

The cocking bolt draws back an internal hammer when pulled back. This bolt also functions as a *power selector* affording *two* power stages. The first click and stop (if bolt is released) is low power; but a continuing pull, which requires considerable effort to overcome the heavy spring, will halt on the second click ready for *increased* power. This action is standard. The *hammer travel* determines the extent to which the valve is opened, but only the two stages of opening are provided for.

There is a considerable variation in the amount of released gas (and consequent pressure) between these two power stages, and sights must be adjusted for the stage in use. Naturally, the low stage will give more shots per cartridge used, and the high stage will give maximum velocity and penetration but fewer discharges.

Because of the power stages, the trigger pull is not as good as in the earlier single-stage models. However, plastic molded grips with right and left thumbrests on the Crosman pattern are an addition to the new models.

Several items should be noted about the design. It has a fair cross-type trigger-block safety of standard pattern. For best results, it is wise to apply this safety *after each firing,* and not to push it off until you have loaded and are ready for the next shot.

The reason is simply this: If the bolt is merely pushed forward to chamber a pellet, and *not turned to lock* as often happens with the new shooter, the arm can still be discharged by pulling the trigger. Part of the energy provided will drive the bullet out, but with reduced power the backward thrust of the expanding gas will blow the breech open. A puff of gas will be visible at the breech when this happens, though it must be noted that there is no danger to the shooter when the pistol is being handled in standard fashion with arm extended. Another small engineering fault is that the trigger may be pulled *with the bolt fully open*—the gas evacuating from the breech if no pellet has been loaded; and if the chamber has been loaded, the bullet will usually still leave the muzzle with some force. This could possibly cause minor mishaps and is to be avoided.

* * * * * * *

Maximum power and accuracy are about the same as for the earlier models. While with reduced power accuracy is still good at 10 yards, the customary range for shooting of this type, many more shots can be discharged. The quality of the workmanship and finish are in line with past products of Benjamin, good for the selling price. The design, while undistinguished, is simple, husky, and efficient for its type except for the failings mentioned which are not inherently dangerous to the shooter, but are not good safety design either.

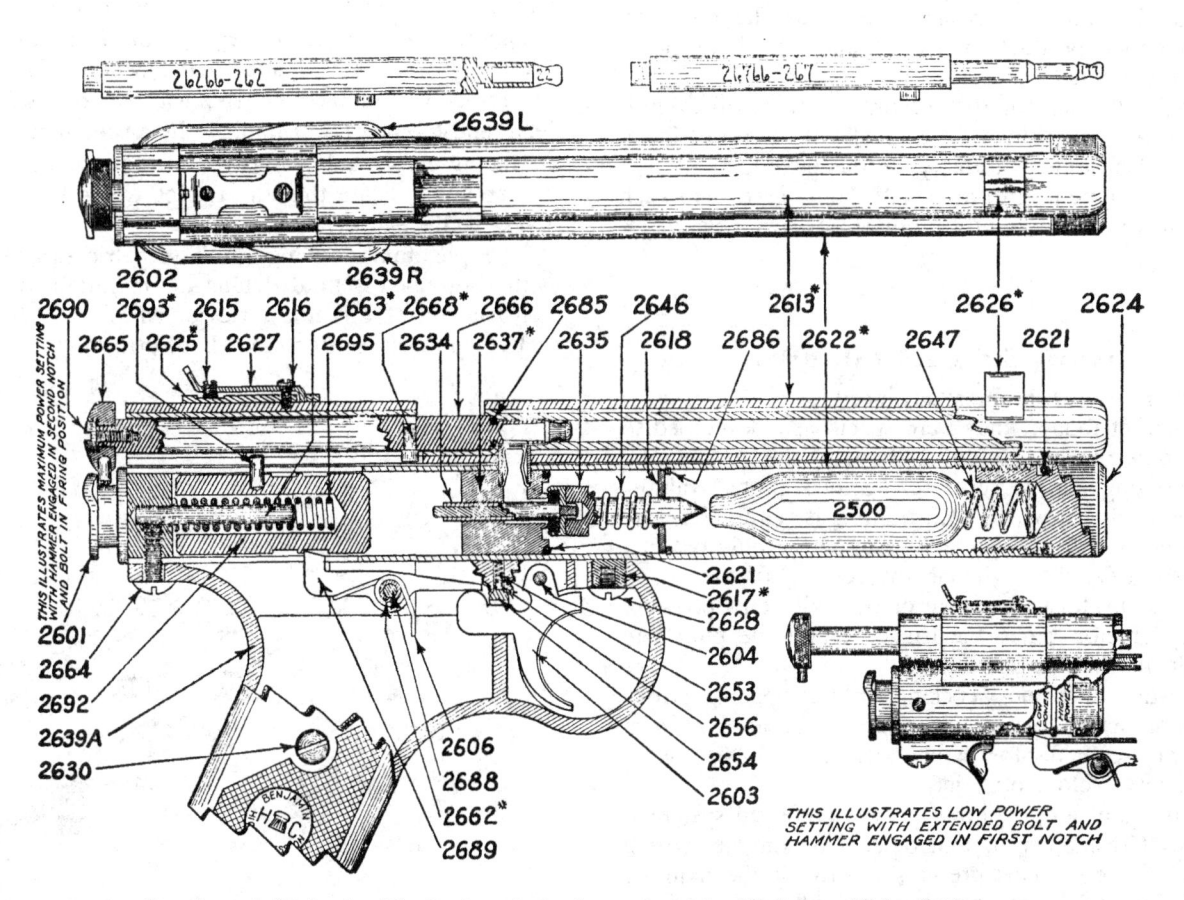

Drawing of Benjamin CO_2 Rocket single-shot gas pistol with 2-stage Hi-Lo Jet Power.

Crosman Pellgun rifle. Current Models 160, .22 caliber; and 167, .177 caliber. Originated July 1955.

CURRENT CROSMAN CO$_2$ RIFLES AND PISTOLS

Current Crosman CO$_2$ rifle production is limited to two series, the 160 Model in .22 caliber (Model 167 designating .177 caliber); and the 180 Model in .22 caliber (Model 187 indicating .177).

The only CO$_2$ series pistols currently produced by this firm are the 150 (the designation 150 indicating .22 caliber and the designation 157 indicating .177 caliber).

A minor modification of the series 180 rifle is currently being manufactured by Crosman under the trade designation of "J. C. Higgins," for Sears, Roebuck and Company.

The foregoing qualifications are necessary in view of the large number of designs which Crosman has introduced from time to time. Earlier models had a gas reservoir below the barrel. This was charged from liquid carbon dioxide cylinders which held 10 ounces of the liquified gas by weight. One rifle, Model 118, was fitted with a detachable tube magazine which held 10 of the standard .22 caliber "Crosman Pells" as the company designates their production of the familiar Diabolo, hourglass pattern bullets.

Undoubtedly this enterprising organization will eventually produce a magazine CO$_2$ type rifle of improved form. There is also some possibility of the introduction of a CO$_2$ shotgun-type arm to fire small-shot charges. No such arms however are currently produced or available.

Crosman Series 160 CO$_2$ Rifles

These are by far the most advanced form of CO$_2$ rifles on the market today. They were specifically developed to form a part of the 25-foot National Rifle Association range shooting and to serve for various hunter training programs in States where such training is required before the issuance of a new license. These are the only production model CO$_2$ rifles wherein the cocking of the action is produced by forward stroke of the bolt. This provides a "safety" factor, since the trigger cannot be pulled to fire when the breech is open.

In powder-type rifles, cocking on the opening stroke of the bolt-action system is preferable because of cam action, which makes for easier cocking, and because of design safety factors built in.

In pellet-gun designs, however, the preferred system is as in this Crosman arm, that of cocking on the *closing* stroke of the bolt. This prevents release of the hammer and bolt by accidental or purposeful pull on the trigger while the breech is open. As has been previously pointed out, in arms where this can happen, the propelling gas can escape at the breech and may result in low power behind the pellet, causing it to lodge in the barrel. This foolproof factor is of very considerable importance in a design of this type.

The late General Merritt Edson, then head of the National Rifle Association, was responsible for the incorporation of still another feature in this design—if the safety is in its "off" position as the breech is opened, it automatically goes on "safe." Design features such as these are extremely important in CO$_2$ arms, where inadvertent operation of bolt or safety may result in wastage of the CO$_2$ charge.

A questionable feature of this design is the incorporation of a charging principle in which *two* Crosman CO$_2$ gas cylinders ("Powerlets" as they call them) allow somewhat more power than is obtainable in the standard single-charge CO$_2$ cylinder used in other arms. This Crosman "Powerlet" has a larger gas charge than normal commercial cartridges to begin with. It is also used in Model 180 series rifle and in the Model 150 pistol. In the series 180, unlike the 160 which takes two "Powerlets" end-to-end, the 180 like the pistol takes only *one* in the reservoir below the barrel. Independent tests by the author indicate that the two-cartridge system is relatively inefficient.

The phantom drawings and isometric drawings herewith show all essential details of operation, design, and construction of this fine series of rifles.

Use of these self-contained, disposable CO$_2$ cylinders

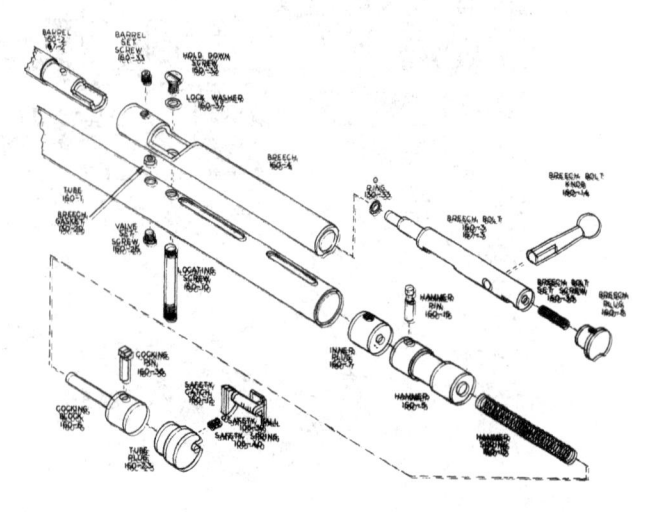

Breech end of Crosman CO$_2$ rifle. Used on Models 160 and 167.

does away with the necessity for a charging service such as was required on earlier designs. For average home or training use, the advantage of a self-contained metal cartridge which may be inserted in the rifle, over the principle of having to charge a section of the rifle from an independent cylinder can be readily seen. This is the latest evolution in this line, but further development is obviously desirable.

It may be expected that advances on this system will be developed in time. As of the current writing, however, these rifles represent the foremost of their type in production.

CROSMAN MODELS 160 AND 167 CO_2 PELLGUNS (RIFLES)
(Same Except for Caliber)

Manufacturer: Crosman Arms Company, Fairport, New York.
Overall Length: 35.5 inches.
Weight: 5 pounds 10 ounces.
Caliber(s): M160, .22. M167, .177.
Type(s) of Ammunition Used: Required caliber Crosman Pells (or equal standard Diabolo type).
Rifled: Yes. Crosman standard.
Operating System: CO_2 gas from non-refillable Crosman Powerlet large-size gas cartridges.
Cocked: By operation of bolt, standard action.
Loaded: Pellet loaded into breech when action is open.
Number Rounds: Single shot only.
Stock Type: One-piece wood, pistol-grip design, sporting type.
Front Sight(s): Blade on matted rib.
Rear Sight(s): Open adjustable rear on barrel, sporting type.
Velocity (Approximate): Full power, about 600 f.p.s. maximum.
Normal Accurate Range: Standard for design; 15 to 20 yards at full power.
Normal Maximum Range: Standard for design, about 300 feet.
Approximate Retail Price: About $22.

REMARKS

These models are charged with *two* (2) Powerlet gas cartridges.

Operation. Unscrew gas-plug cap below barrel. Drop first Powerlet in, neck first. Then drop second Powerlet in, wide-end

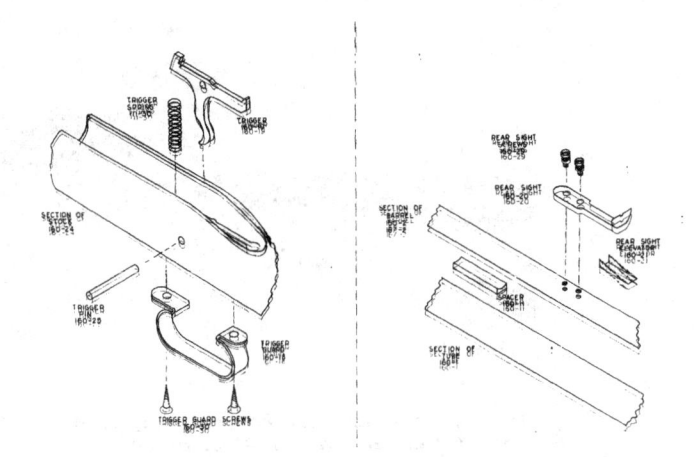

Left: stock and trigger assembly. Right: rear sight assembly.

first. The "neck" ends are designed to be punctured when the action is cocked (after Powerlets have been inserted and the plug screwed in tightly). Cock rifle by opening and closing bolt in standard fashion. Pull trigger. Striker will pierce first seal and power will drive the second Powerlet back enough for its seal to be pierced. (See drawings herewith.) Open action, load, and fire.

(Note: The two Powerlets will give about 40 average shots at full power.)

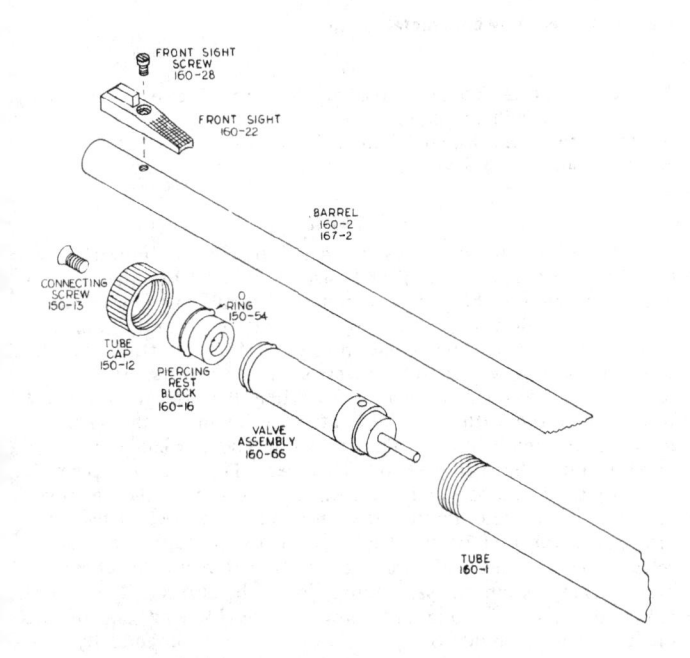

Crosman Series 180 CO_2 Rifles

As already pointed out, these are essentially the Model 160 type using one gas cylinder instead of two, resulting of course in lower power output with shorter range. The weight and length are substantially less than that of the 160 series. These shorter and lighter designs, somewhat simplified, are intended primarily for training of boys and women.

In slightly modified form, these are the rifles now being sold by Sears, Roebuck under the designation "J. C. Higgins."

CROSMAN MODELS 180 AND 187 CO_2 PELLGUNS (RIFLES)
(Same Except for Caliber)

Manufacturer: Crosman Arms Company, Fairport, New York.
Overall Length: 34 inches.
Weight: 4 pounds.
Caliber(s): M180, .22. M187, .177.
Type(s) of Ammunition Used: Crosman Pells of required caliber (or equal Diabolos).
Rifled: Yes. Crosman standard.
Operating System: CO_2 gas from one non-refillable Crosman Powerlet.
Cocked: Initially by standard bolt action. Fingertip action only required after firing.
Loaded: Directly into open breech.
Number Rounds: Single shot only.
Stock Type: Short carbine type for youngsters.
Front Sight(s): Blade on ramp.
Rear Sight(s): Open adjustable on barrel.
Velocity (Approximate): 40 shots at 450 f.p.s. from single Powerlet.
Normal Accurate Range: Factory-claimed to group ¾-inch at 25 feet.
Normal Maximum Range: 300 feet.
Approximate Retail Price: $18.

REMARKS

Safety. As in M180, a push-type cross safety showing red when "off." Trigger lock.

Muzzle end of CO_2 rifle as used on Models 160 and 167.

This model uses only one Powerlet (CO$_2$ cartridge). With minor modifications, this rifle is sold by Sears, Roebuck & Company as their J. C. Higgins.

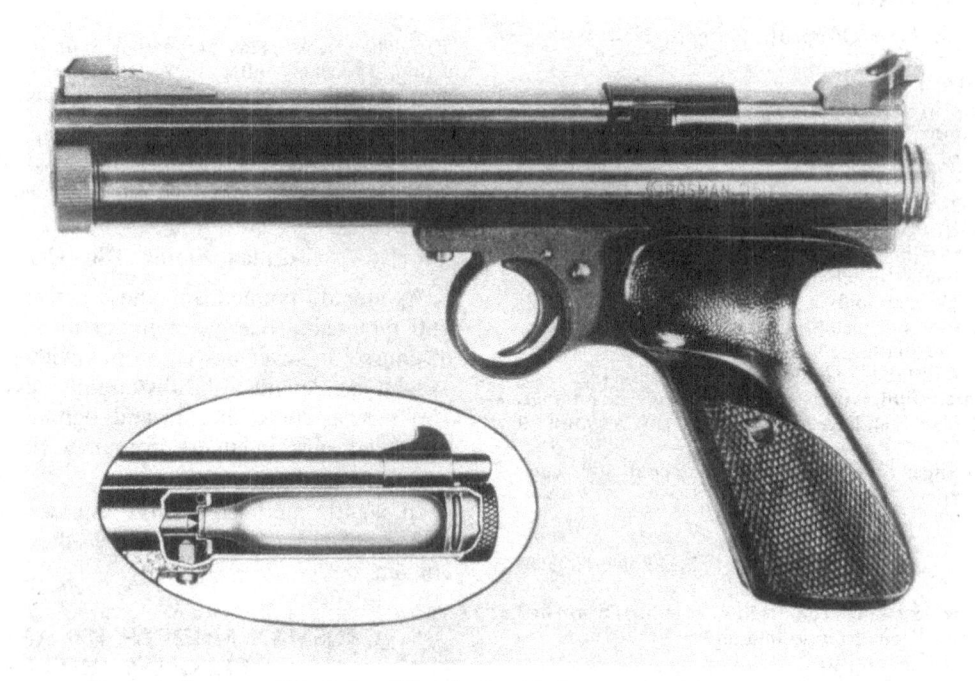

Current Crosman 150 Series CO$_2$ pistol with improved powder metal sights.

Fingertip Cocking. As detailed under M180, opening action firing is confined to actually unlocking and drawing back bolt, though trigger engagement is complete only when action is closed. This makes operation very easy.

See detailed drawings and photos.

CROSMAN MODELS 150 AND 157 CO$_2$ PISTOLS

Manufacturer: Crosman Arms Company, Fairport, New York.
Overall Length: 10 inches. (Barrel 6 inches.)
Weight: 1 pound 10 ounces.
Caliber(s): M150, .22. M157, .177.
Type(s) of Ammunition Used: Crosman Super Pells (or equal Diabolo type).
Rifled: Yes. Crosman standard.
Operating System: CO$_2$ gas from one Powerlet. About 50 shots at full power.
Cocked: Pull back on projecting cocking knob.
Loaded: Turn up and draw back breech cover. Insert pellet. Close breech.
Number Rounds: Single-pellet loading ONLY.
Stock Type: Well-pitched grip. Stocks over frame. Thumbrests.
Front Sight(s): Blade on ramp.
Rear Sight(s): Adjustable rear.
Velocity (Approximate): 370 f.p.s. at full power, average.
Normal Accurate Range: Standard for type. Factory states will group ¾-inch at 25 feet.
Normal Maximum Range: Standard for type.
Approximate Retail Price: $15.

REMARKS

Operation. In this series the gas cylinder, or "Powerlet" as Crosman designates the special size necessary for their pistol and produced for them, is inserted in the compression reservoir or chamber below the barrel, by removal of the end cap. The cap is screwed on by hand pressure after insertion of the cylinder, narrow end first. The cocking knob projecting at the rear of the breech is drawn back. When the trigger is pressed for the first time after insertion of a gas cylinder, the resulting hammer movement pierces the gas bulb. The gas can now enter directly into the compression chamber. The breech cover is then rotated to unlock and is drawn back to expose the chamber. A pellet is inserted. Pulling the knob back to cock, leaves the arm ready for pull of the trigger to work through the sear to release the hammer and discharge the bullet from the chamber. The cocking knob is self-rebounding. The breech cover encloses the chamber area and prevents gas blowing out of the breech. The amount of gas released, and consequently the amount of power developed behind the pellet, can be controlled

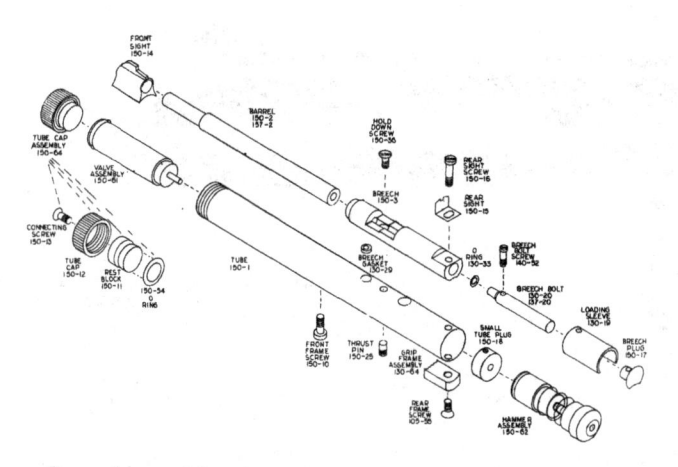

General assembly of CO_2 pistol using Powerlet cartridge.

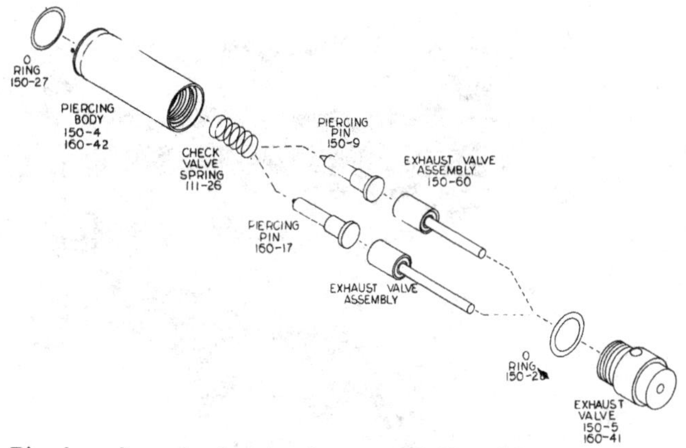

Piercing pin and exhaust valve assembly for CO_2 pistol and rifle.

Crosman 150 CO_2 pistol. Action open for loading. This is a self-cocking valve design, but bullets must be loaded individually.

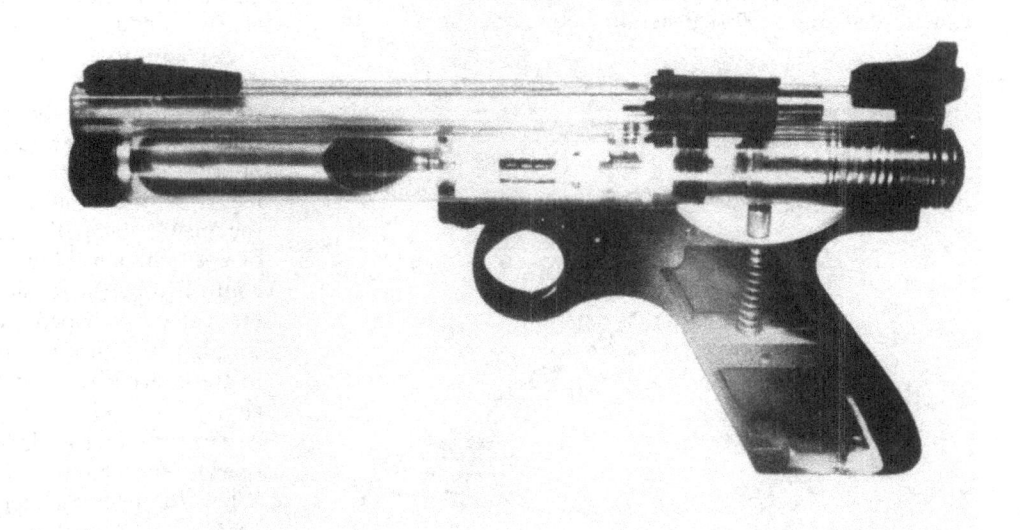

Crosman 150 Series plastic model. Breech cover closed. CO_2 Powerlet cut away to show gas flow into power chamber.

Models 115, .177 caliber, and 116, .22 caliber. Six-inch barrel. Placed on market about one year after Models 112 and 111 because of requests from consumers and tradesmen for a shorter barrel pistol. Other features same as Models 111 and 112.

in this design. When the cocking knob is turned full right, maximum power allowable is developed. Turning it to the left gives it immediate power until at the extreme of the left-turning movement the load power is developed. Fifty shots are normally expected from a gas cylinder with maximum power set, while as many as 100 may be fired in the lower-velocity ranges.

The author's phantom photographs as well as the isometric drawings herewith show all essential design and operation details of this pistol.

DISCONTINUED CROSMAN CO_2 RIFLES AND PISTOLS
Models 111 and 112

The next CO_2 pistols to appear after the Schimel reached the market were the first Crosman models. These were tooled and styled generally along the lines of the successful air pistols of this maker, while mechanisms followed the pattern of their CO_2 rifles.

Instead of the insertable gas bulb, as in the Schimel, these Crosmans had a gas *reservoir* below the barrel, replacing the air cylinder of the pump-ups. Loading was unique. As in the rifle, a 10-ounce gas cylinder (re-fillable) was furnished with each pistol.

To load, the end cap was unscrewed from the muzzle end of the reservoir to expose the intake valve. The gas cylinder was screwed on to the threads on the reservoir muzzle. The valve wheel on the cylinder was turned and left open for 5 seconds, then shut off. Unscrewing the cylinder and screwing on the end cap, left the pistol ready to cock, load, and fire. A cylinder would give about 800 shots at full power. The pistol reservoir held enough gas for about 30 shots at each loading.

An adjusting screw at the rear of the pistol increased or decreased the amount of gas released. Turning it to the right progressively altered the tension on the coil spring which operated the release valve. There was an internal straightline hammer which was cocked by drawing back the knurled head projecting from the rear of the pistol above the gas-adjustment screw. The strength of the hammer blow delivered to the valve, which was controlled by the tension adjustment, determined how long the valve was open, hence how much gas was allowed through. It's all quite simple in theory, but proper valving in these arms is the most important feature in their success or failure!

The motion of drawing back the cocking knob also opened the chamber for loading. A pellet was inserted. When the cocking piece was pushed ahead, it closed the breech and thrust the pellet into its seat ready for discharge.

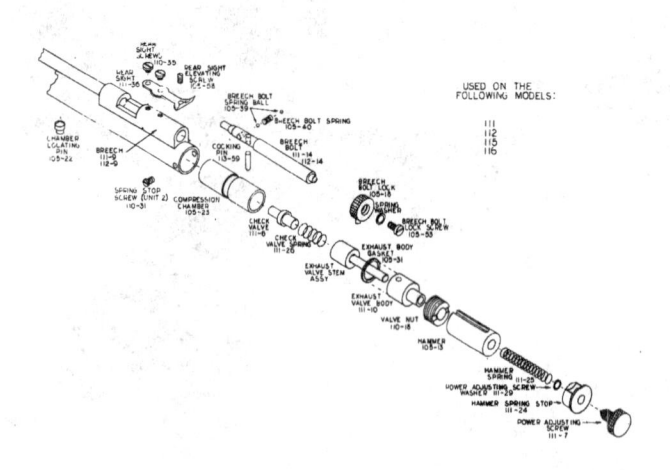

CO_2 gas pistol breech block and tube components.

Filling head assembly.

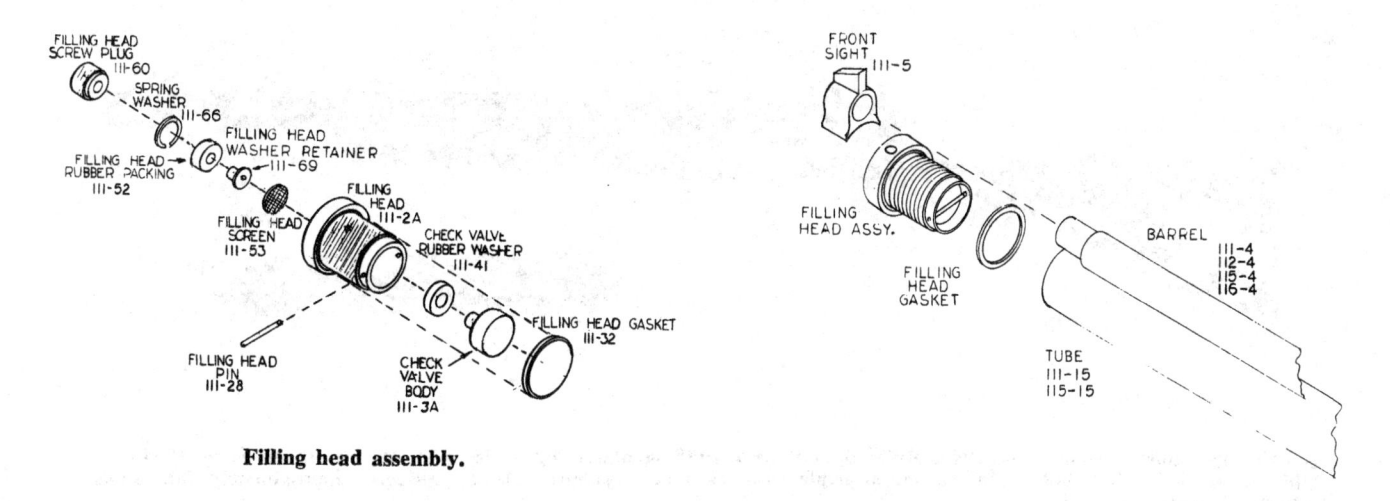

Labels:
- FILLING HEAD SCREW PLUG 111-60
- SPRING WASHER 111-66
- FILLING HEAD RUBBER PACKING 111-52
- FILLING HEAD WASHER RETAINER 111-69
- FILLING HEAD SCREEN 111-53
- FILLING HEAD 111-2A
- CHECK VALVE RUBBER WASHER 111-41
- FILLING HEAD PIN 111-28
- CHECK VALVE BODY 111-3A
- FILLING HEAD GASKET 111-32

Front sight and filling head assembly.

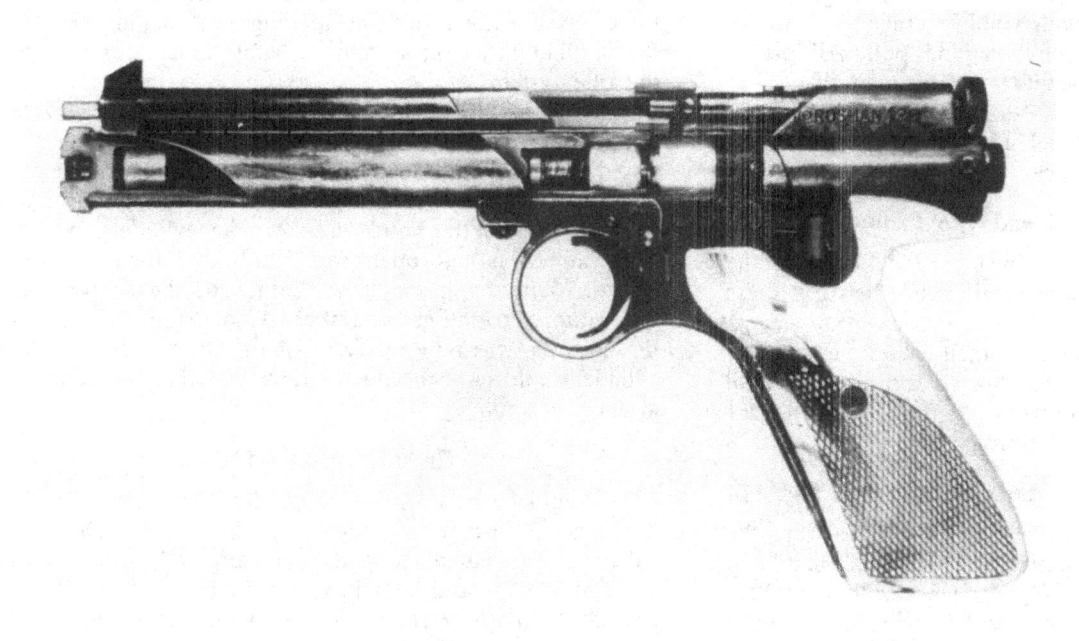

Labels:
- FRONT SIGHT 111-5
- FILLING HEAD ASSY.
- FILLING HEAD GASKET
- BARREL 111-4, 112-4, 115-4, 116-4
- TUBE 111-15, 115-15

Crosman 111 and 150 CO$_2$ series. Charged from container. Cut away to show mechanism. Breech closed and locked.

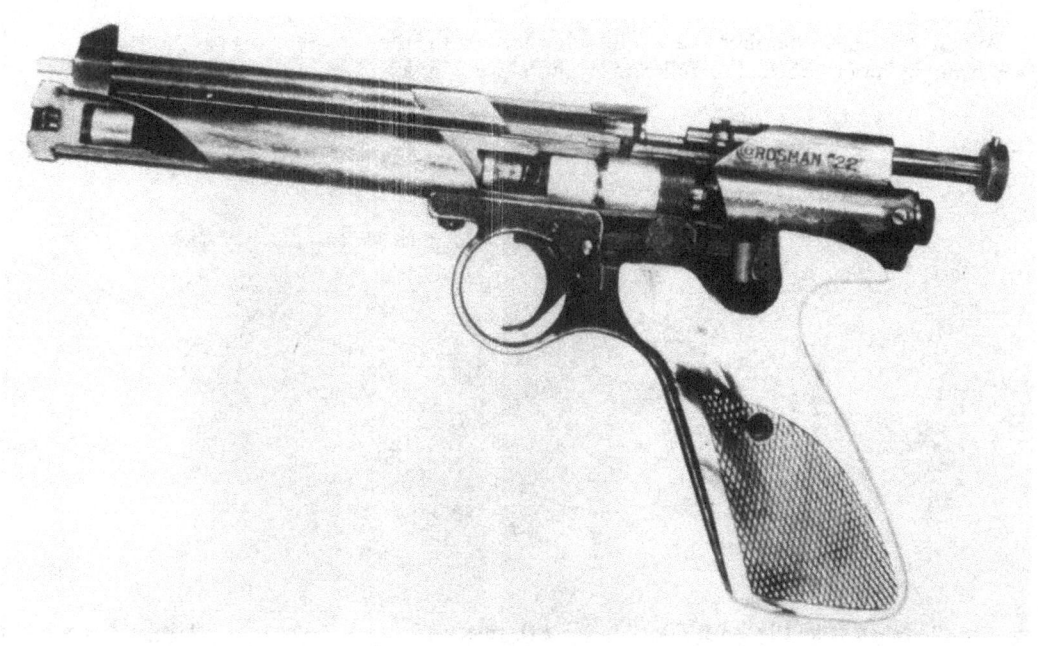

Crosman 111 and 115 series, cutaway mechanism. Breech unlocked ready for loading. Obsolete.

217

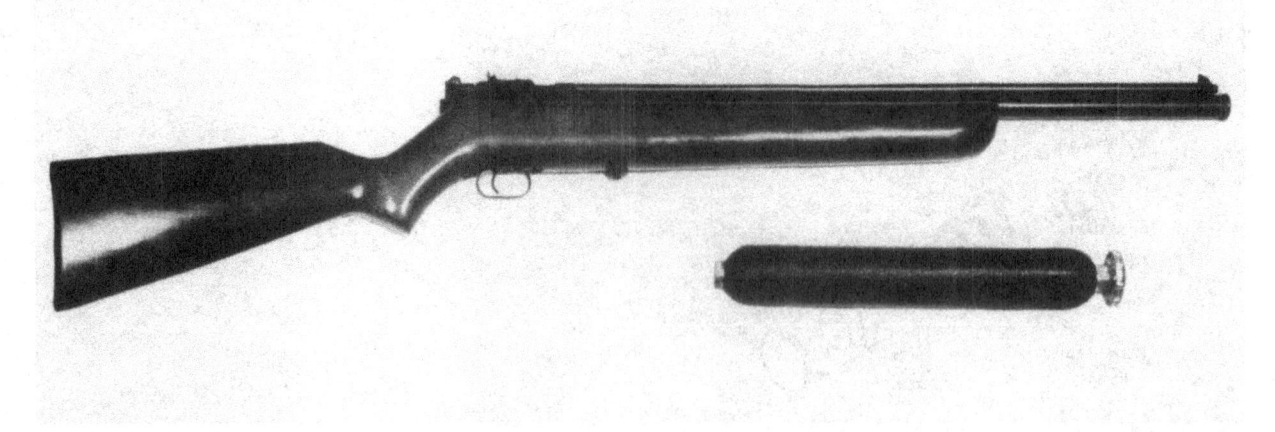

CO_2 gas guns introduced in 1949. Rifles discontinued 1955—replaced by Series 160. Pistols discontinued 1954—replaced by Series 150. Both used transfer principle from 10-ounce cylinder. Pistol produced approximately 800 shots from 10 ounces of CO_2.

These designs had push-type trigger-blocking safeties behind the trigger. Sears with good leverage were incorporated and provided reasonably good pull. All pistols were rifled to same specifications as Crosman rifles.

These initial models had 8-inch barrels. Model 111 was .177 caliber, and Model 112, .22 caliber. Except for caliber they were identical.

CO_2 Models 115 and 116 Pistols

Except that the Model 115 was .177 caliber and the 116 was .22 caliber there was no difference between these two pistols.

These models were merely 6-inch-barrel versions of the Models 111 and 112. The shorter barrel and overall length was furnished in answer to a trade demand for a shorter and more compact pistol.

Crosman CO_2 Discontinued Rifles, Models 113 and 114

The first of the series of Crosman CO_2 rifles were the Models 113 and 114, respectively .177 and .22 calibers.

These were single-shot CO_2 gas rifles with chambers below the barrel *which were charged from a 10-ounce cylinder.*

When the gas chamber was fully charged from the separate cylinder, about 70 full-power shots were available. The pellets of course had to be inserted individually for each shot however. The loading and cocking was by the familiar turn-bolt system. A safety catch was part of the rifle system.

To charge with CO_2, the rifle was held with the muzzle up and the end cap unscrewed and removed. This exposed an inlet valve leading into the gas chamber below the barrel. The independent gas cylinder was then screwed to the rifle and the hand valve on the cylinder opened. The valve was left open for 5 seconds, then screwed closed. With the gas cylinder removed, the screw plug was returned to the gas chamber. After loading and cocking, the rifle was now ready to shoot. On an average, the cylinders hold enough CO_2 to refill the rifle gas chamber about seven times.

Crosman Model 118

It should be noted that the Model 118 was originally designed for use in amusement parks and for shooting galleries, very much along the line originally used about 1912 in Sweden and later in Germany by the "Excellent" gas rifles. In this form a special high-pressure hose ran

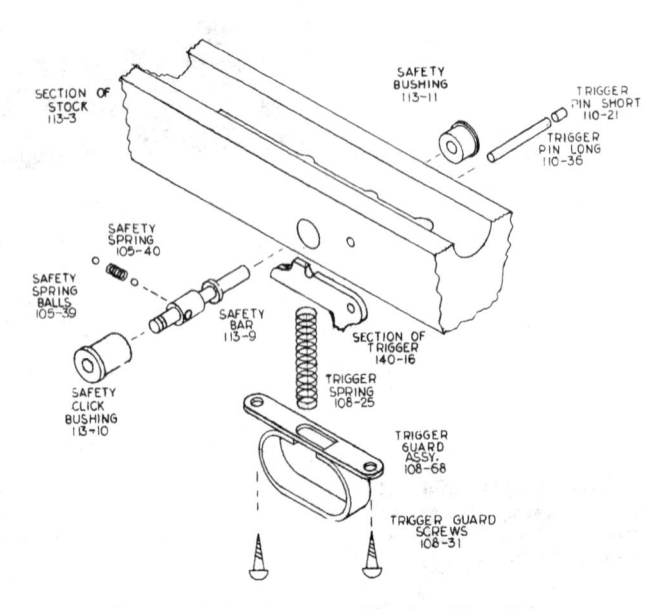

Breech bolt and hammer assembly for CO_2 rifle.

Trigger and safety assembly for CO_2 rifle.

This rifle was originally developed for use in amusement park galleries, the gas supply coming directly from a 50-pound tank, attached to gas feed pipe with a special high-pressure hose. Ten-shot repeater with removable clip. Converted in 1952 to refillable type (10-ounce cylinder) for regular market due to requests. Marketed for $34.50.

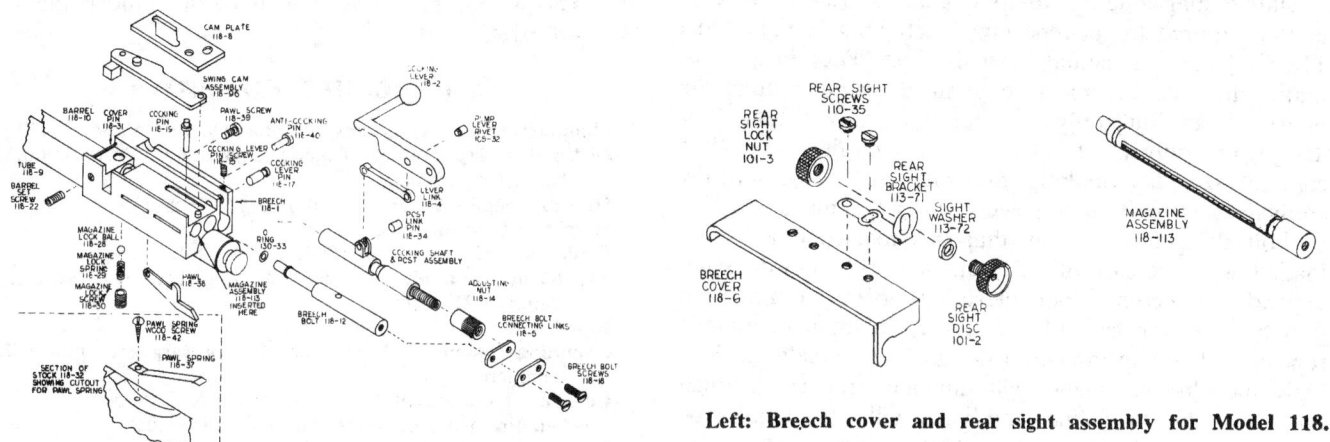

Breech bolt and feed assembly for Model 118 repeater rifle.

Left: Breech cover and rear sight assembly for Model 118.

Right: Magazine assembly for Model 118.

Fig. 3C

Fig. 3B

Fig. 3A

Fig. 5

Fig. 4

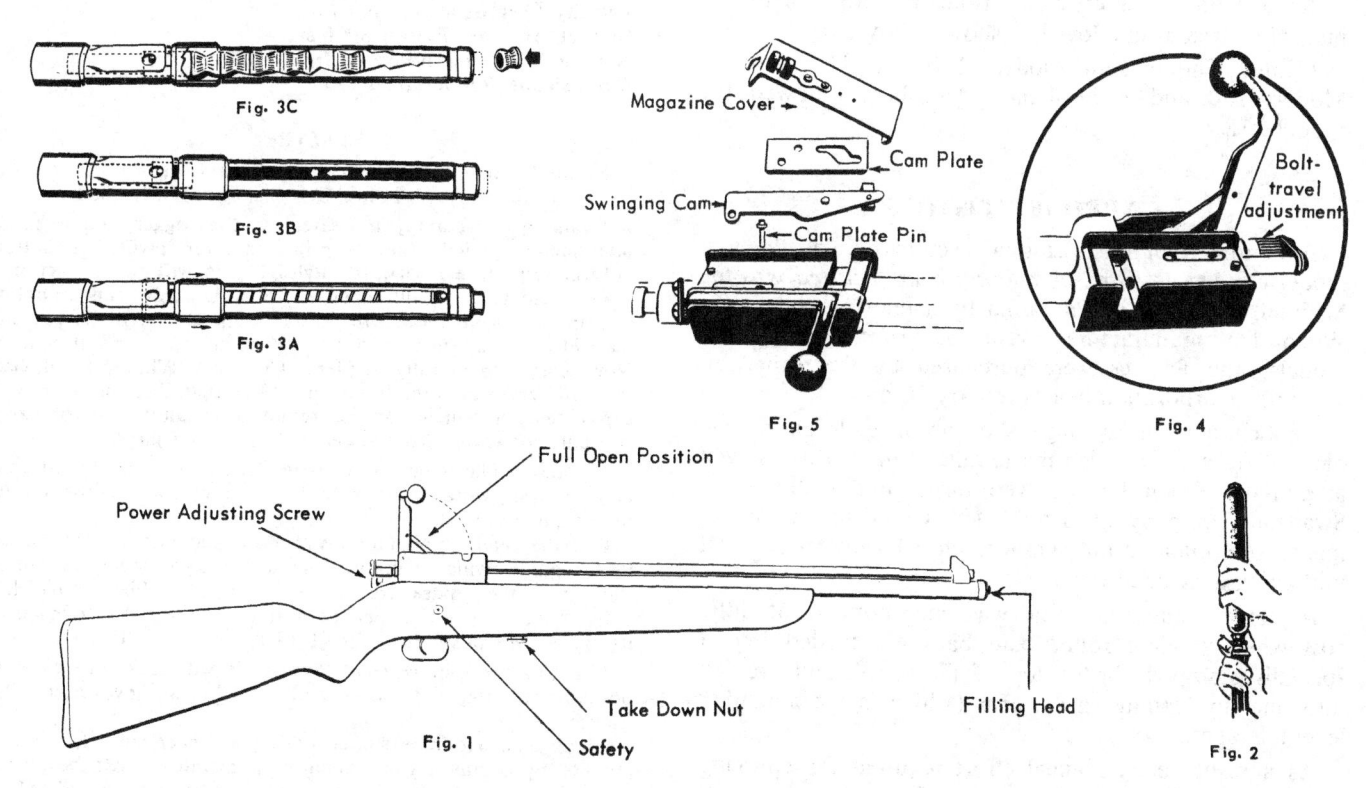

Fig. 1 — Power Adjusting Screw, Full Open Position, Take Down Nut, Safety, Filling Head

Fig. 2

Details of the CO_2 power cylinder Crosman repeater.

219

from the rifle to a 50-pound tank of CO_2 liquified gas.

This rifle as supplied for gallery use had a 10-shot removable pellet clip, incidentally.

It was converted to the refillable type for individual use and sale (using the 10-ounce cylinder) in 1952 as a result of popular demand. The original selling price was $34.50.

A few notes may be of interest in connection with this Model 118 *magazine* rifle. It differed from the single-shot version in that cocking was accomplished as the bolt handle was lifted, instead of by pulling back the bolt. The detachable 10-shot tube magazine held the standard-type waisted pellet. Operating the bolt fed the pellets directly into the breech. If there was already a pellet in the breech, an automatic double-loading eliminator prevented another pellet from being fed in.

Unlike magazine pump-up pneumatic rifles, the only action required to get repeating functioning in the Model 118 CO_2 gun was actuation of the bolt. Thus in a pneumatic, the chamber must be pumped up each time, the magazine resulting only in faster feeding. With the CO_2 design, not only the feeding but the charging was taken care of, thereby making the rate of fire practically equivalent to that of a powder cartridge magazine rifle of bolt design. Note, too, that this magazine is spring loaded as in the case of a .22 cartridge rifle and does not depend for feeding upon elevation of the muzzle and gravity as in the case of the earlier Crosman pneumatic repeaters. Feeding in such a design is extremely ticklish. Only the Crosman pellet will function properly through this particular magazine, and jams will occasionally be encountered with them also. Air-gun type pellets are very sensitive to load because of light weight and a thin "skirt" section.

As a point of interest, an isometric drawing of the magazine system employed is shown above.

(Note: The current Models 160 and 167 and the Models 180 and 187, already described, followed the Model 118.)

CARBO-JET PISTOLS

As outlined in the historical section herein, the first modern CO_2 arm to be *production manufactured* was the Schimel, produced in California by a man of that name. When the manufacturer went bankrupt, tools, dies, models, and fixtures were purchased by the American Weapons Corporation headed by Hy Hunter.

The Schimel was a single-shot pistol built on a zinc die-cast frame, for which the familiar Luger pistol served as a model. When the tools were turned over to the A. C. Swanson Company of Sun Valley, California, improvements were made in the (unsatisfactory) valve, a one-seal unit being developed for it.

A clever magazine idea was incorporated at little cost whereby eight round lead balls are loaded into a specially stamped clip on top of the pistol, and are fed into line for feeding as the grip (which is the actuating lever) is operated.

As a result, each manual effort required for charging the pistol (or any other CO_2 arm) is here utilized also to feed a .22 caliber ball so long as any remain in the magazineway.

The valving system lends itself to furnishing more direct power than in some systems where gas is first fed into an accumulator. The design is very ingenious. The power output can be readily adjusted.

The first models of this repeater were marketed by Hy Hunter and the American Weapons Corporation under the name "American Luger." The trade name "Luger" is controlled by the Stoeger Arms Corporation of New York, who formerly imported the Luger cartridge pistols from Germany. Stoeger compelled the manufacturer and distributor to desist in use of the name—though the external pistol lines could not be protested since this pistol has been made in many countries and under many designations.

The 8-shot model is now marketed under the name "Carbo-Jet."

CARBO-JET CO_2 PISTOL

Manufacturer: A. C. Swanson Company, Sun Valley, California.
Distributor: Hy Hunter, American Weapons Corporation, Burbank, California.
Overall Length: 9.5 inches. (Barrel 5¾ inches.)
Weight: 2.5 pounds.
Caliber(s): .22 round ball ONLY.
Type(s) of Ammunition Used: .22 round ball (will NOT handle standard Diabolo .22).
Rifled: Yes.
Operating System: CO_2 standard-size or large-size non-refillable commercial tubes.
Cocked: Operation of back-strap lever as described.
Loaded: From 8-shot magazine as described below.
Number Rounds: 8.
Stock Type: Luger pistol form.
Front Sight(s): Luger pattern blade.
Rear Sight(s): Stamped open type, adjustable.
Velocity (Approximate): 360 f.p.s.
Normal Accurate Range: 30 feet.
Normal Maximum Range: Standard for type.
Approximate Retail Price: $25.

REMARKS

Formerly sold under name "American Luger."
This is the only repeating CO_2 pistol currently made.

Charging. First apply the safety so the trigger cannot be unintentionally pulled. Rear of grip is a lever, pivoted at bottom. Push grip (lever) forward slightly. This will unlock action. Pull grip back to full open position. Unscrew cap at bottom of grip (a 50-cent piece will do it). Remove cap. Insert gas bulb (cartridge), small neck end first. Push in as far as it will go. Now screw cap in fully to pierce CO_2 bulb. When pierced, back the cap screw off one full turn. (Note that there is a screw-in cap extension which can be removed to allow use of larger size bulb, however Crosman Powerlets are too large.)

Magazine. The magazine is a simple, stamped-metal feed guide and follower with spring held in place by two screws on top of the pistol frame.

Pull the small knob (follower) back and turn it into the cut in the guide, which will hold its spring under compression. At this point, the guides are cut to allow .22 caliber round lead balls to be dropped in one at a time. Release the follower so its spring can push the balls (1 to 8) ahead for loading.

Firing. Push grip (lever) forward. It will lock and can't be opened until trigger has been pulled to fire. Remove safety. Pull trigger.

(Note: The action is simple once you understand it, but it is "tricky" by common gun standards. Remember it can be pushed forward only a slight distance *when it is not cocked*. (If it won't go forward, then it is already cocked.) It can be pulled back thereafter an inch or more for the loading stroke. When next pushed closed, it is breech-locked ready to fire.)

Additional Firing. Repeat the push-pull-push action and pull trigger. The back-strap lever is positively locked in forward position *when the arm is cocked*. It cannot be opened without first pulling the trigger to allow the hammer to fall.

The retaining cap in the bottom of the butt must never be moved so long as there is any pressure remaining in the CO_2 cylinder. If it is desired to remove the cylinder, which is pierced at the top, the screw cap should be backed off *very slowly* to permit a gradual gas escape before the cap is completely removed.

By turning the screw in the bottom of the rear of the back strap clockwise, the power output is decreased. Turning it counter-clockwise increases the power. The maximum power variance is about 5 turns of the adjustment screw.

Trigger pull may be adjusted by use of the screw forward of the safety button.

The single seal valve is designed to afford, in theory at least, maximum *direct* power release of the CO_2 liquid gas directly behind the bullet. However it still makes two 90° bends.

Manufacturer claims 20 to 30 shots from a single standard-size CO_2 bulb and up to 50 shots at reduced power.

Balance and hang are good. The magazine mechanism is rather delicate and should not be abused by fast, slamming action; and being exposed on top of the frame it must be handled with enough care to prevent injury to it. The basic pistol is a zinc-base die-casting, giving the weight, balance, and general feel of the true Luger. It is a much more impressive looking pistol than the typical tube-and-stamping product commonly encountered. The insert seamless tube barrel is well rifled. Sights are adequate. The valve system is sound in theory, but has not as yet been subjected to enough production and field testing to make it entirely reliable, if one may judge by test results conducted with one pistol bought in the open market and a second provided by the sales organization distributing the pistol.

Carbo Jet repeating pistol. Gas cylinder is in the grip.

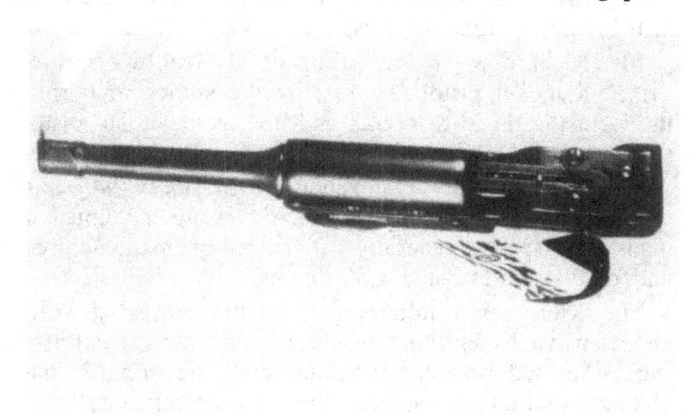

Carbo Jet pistol. Top view showing exposed repeating mechanism.

Carbo Jet pistol with power capsule and .22 round balls. Action is drawn back to start cocking and loading stroke.

221

HEALTHWAYS PLAINSMAN CO$_2$ SEMI-AUTOMATIC PISTOL

During the preparation of this book the author unearthed several good semiautomatic carbon dioxide pistols in prototype, both in the United States and in Europe. One by Hämmerli of Lenzburg, Switzerland, is pictured herein because manufacture is expected shortly after the initial printing of this book is released for sale. Most of the others cannot be described at this time because the developments are still of a confidential nature.

This brings us to the latest commercial United States development in this field: A very low-priced pistol which will use round air-rifle shot, now in manufacture by Healthways, one of the world's largest sporting-goods distributors, in Los Angeles, California.

Mr. Richard M. Kline, president of Healthways, furnished a model pistol for tests by the author to permit its inclusion in this book, and the commercial pistol should be generally available to buyers in the near future.

Healthways is an organization which since 1945 has specialized in a steadily advancing group of unusual items for sports generally. It currently manufactures and/or distributes some 1,500 items.

Mr. Kline, an outdoors and health enthusiast with an extensive background in sports and physical culture, was connected with the distribution of the original line of single-shot compressed-air rifles and shotguns marketed under the trade name of Plainsman, which are discussed elsewhere in this book.

Impressed with the indicated sales potential of CO$_2$ and air arms because of population expansion, shooting-cost increases, and other considerations which are also dealt with herein, Mr. Kline in 1952 turned his attention to the development of a new line of CO$_2$ arms which would feature semiautomatic (that is, self-loading) characteristics and allow the shooter to more nearly approximate true pistol shooting than he could with the current-pattern CO$_2$ single-shot pistol.

Working with Kenneth Pitcher, a designer who had a considerable background in CO$_2$ valve development, Kline worked out the details of the current pistol, which is to be marketed under the name of Plainsman and is not to be confused with any of the earlier arms under that name and dealt with herein, all of which are obsolete.

This pistol will be followed by a rifle of similar design and in all probability by a shotgun in due course. As of the time of this writing, however, only the pistol is in actual manufacture.

The Healthways Plainsman Pistol

This arm rates as a remarkable achievement in its field. It has many advantages over earlier forms. It also has limitations, most of which derive directly from the fact that it is designed and built to sell at a very low price—initially $12.95 retail.

It shoots only standard steel air-rifle shot, the same as used in the Daisy-type spring-air guns. Lead shot cannot be used successfully because the feed includes a magnetic feature which requires use of a suitable projectile of the Daisy type. Since manufacture of this type of ball (see under Daisy) precludes perfect sphericity, *extreme* accuracy is never possible, regardless of advertising claims. If, on the other hand, ball-bearing-type steel projectiles, such as are used in Hämmerli pistols, are available, this new Plainsman is capable of a very good degree of comparative accuracy up to 20 feet, even when measured against expanding-base "Diabolo" type slugs. Such quality steel balls, it must be noted, are considerably more expensive than the Daisy type and hence are of interest only to serious target shooters. For all reasonable practice and plinking shooting at close ranges, this new pistol is adequate for the beginner.

Appearance and General Design

This Plainsman is built to the general lines, balance, and appearance of the Colt .22 Woodsman pistol. Note that its lines are an approximation only, not an exact duplicate.

For example, the internal firing and feeding systems are such that the grip area to the rear of the trigger is a distortion of the classic Colt lines. Our detailed description of the operation of the pistol will explain this detail, since the feed and hammer mechanisms are unique.

The low selling price of the pistol is possible largely through the design, which was developed specifically for low-cost precision die-casting in the main. The overall frame, receiver, and barrel housing consists of a single Zamak (zinc alloy) casting, which requires very little finishing as it comes from the casting machines. Since there are no critical pressure points in the casting, zinc alloy provides an entirely acceptable tensile strength,

The new Healthways Plainsman autoloading CO$_2$ pistol with the gas cartridge and steel air-rifle shot it uses (caliber .175). This is a die-cast design. When the magazine door and rear-sight unit is slid up, about 100 shot may be poured into the opening. The CO$_2$ cylinder is inserted in the grip. When ready for firing, it is necessary only to pull the trigger once for each shot as long as gas and missile supply lasts. Feed is gravity and magnetic. Each pull on the trigger indexes a ball for firing, raises and drops the hammer, which opens poppet valve. Pistol has three-power adjustment.

while allowing cast-in details which in a powder-cartridge pistol would often require costly machining or bushing, or replacement by an expensive high-tensile aluminum forging.

The barrel, a piece of steel tubing, is cast in place with the zinc-base barrel housing, providing a smooth heavy-duty interior surface, which the steel projectiles will not wear down rapidly. (The barrel is not rifled, but this is merely a detail when using nonprecision ammunition for short ranges.)

Loading and Firing

The magazine will hold approximately 100 round, steel air-rifle shot. In the author's experience, Daisy's so-called "BB's," which are copper-flashed balls (plated thinly), functioned best.

Magazine Loading. The magazine well is in the frame above the hammer and behind the manifold. A combination loading door and rear sight at the rear of the pistol is held in position by its spring and by friction. When this door is slid upwards, the loading port is exposed and balls are poured in. The door is then slid down to closed position.

Gas Charging. (1) Unscrew and withdraw plug in the bottom of the grip. (2) Insert gas cartridge (large end first) in the steel tube within the grip. The CO_2 cartridge used is the standard size sold in most drug, hardware, and sporting-goods stores. (Note. The Crosman Powerlet is too large to enter. The Benjamin CO_2 cartridge worked best in the author's tests, giving many more shots than unbranded makes, which would indicate that the Benjamin suppliers work to better specifications, at this time anyway.) (3) Screw plug back into grip socket. (4) NOTE: In order to prevent momentary gas escape through the valve before the released gas pressure builds up sufficiently in the reservoir to force the valve closed, HOLD TRIGGER ABOUT HALFWAY BACK WHILE TURNING THE CAM LEVER ON THE PLUG WITH A COIN. The cam forces a piercing needle into the nose of the CO_2 cartridge, which incidentally in this pistol is inserted (large end first) into the grip—the direct opposite of the Crosman, Benjamin, and other systems currently used. Rotating the cam causes the needle to pierce the neck of the CO_2 cartridge and release the gas into the reservoir. (5) The cam (the heavy screw in the plug) is then returned to position.

Power Adjustment. By turning the control screw, which is a three-position cam, three different tensions can be applied to the hammer spring. Since the strength of the hammer blow determines the degree to which the light valve spring (which is a poppet type) is overcome, the volume of gas released to project the missile can be controlled to a considerable degree. In cam position 1, the manufacturer claims approximately 100 shots at low power. In cam position 2, the claim is about 60 shots at medium power. In cam position 3, the claim is approximately 40 shots at high power for maximum range and penetration. (Note. In the author's test, maximum shots were, respectively, 80, 51, and 29. However, it is to be remembered that the test was conducted with only one pistol, and that a production model in its early stage.)

Firing. This pistol has a hammer-and-trigger firing system roughly similar to that found in so-called "hammerless" double-action revolvers, where the hammer is enclosed within the frame. The firing system operates like that of a double-action revolver when fired entirely by trigger pull. Note that there is NO HOLDING NOTCH on the internal hammer. Pressing the trigger progressively drives the hammer to full cock and slips it to hit the poppet-valve stem to release gas from the reservoir into the manifold area behind the projectile in the barrel. Just as the trigger movement in a double-action revolver also actuates a connected pawl to rotate the cylinder, in this Plainsman pistol a vertical slide attached to the trigger feeds and indexes a ball to the breech end of the barrel on each movement before the hammer falls.

Note therefore that the feeding mechanism is NOT strictly semiautomatic in the sense that a cartridge pistol is, since the power impulse plays no part whatever in the feeding. Feeding and loading are strictly MECHANICAL; but are nevertheless semiautomatic in the sense that no individual, conscious manual action is required from the shooter— All he does is pull the trigger for each shot, releasing it to allow the mechanical elements to re-engage for the next shot, just as is required in a cartridge pistol.

(NOTE ON THIS "DOUBLE-ACTION-TYPE" FIRING SYSTEM: It is not, of course, possible to get as good a trigger pull with this "slip" system as it is where the pull has only one function; i.e., to release the hammer. However, anyone with experience in double-action shooting can do reasonably good plinking with this type of firing mechanism. Except for the true specialist, however, precision shooting can seldom be undertaken with any double-action-type firing mechanism; but it must be remembered that this Plainsman pistol is made—and priced—for the plinker, NOT for the targeteer.

This pistol can be fired as rapidly as the trigger can be pulled, released to return, and pulled again. All other U.S. CO_2 arms currently available *commercially* require mechanical manipulation to reload for each successive shot, although Crosman will soon introduce theirs as indicated.

Manual Safety. The safety is a slide on the left side of the frame to the rear of the trigger. Pushed down to OFF position, it leaves a clear path for trigger travel. Pushed up to ON position, a lug on the safety forces the trigger link up, thus preventing the link from engaging the hammer-link pin required for the cocking action.

Operation and Functioning

This revolutionary pistol breaks down into five major assemblies as follows:

(1) The Frame Group. The steel barrel tube is cast in place. The magazine cover and its spring are part of this assembly.

(2) The Gas-Reservoir Group. This embraces the valve-seat assembly, the steel CO_2 cartridge tube, and the plug assembly with its nut.

(3) The Trigger Group. This comprises the trigger assembly with its link and return spring and the feed-slide spring.

(4) The Manifold Group. This consists of the manifold and slide assembly, exclusive of the slide spring.

Operational Details. When the trigger is pulled, it rotates on its pivot pin. The attached trigger link pushes the hammer back until the hammer-spring pin and lower link surface make contact. Continuing pressure on the trigger causes the hammer-spring pin to force the link off the hammer-link pin. This releases the hammer.

The falling hammer hits the projecting stem of the poppet valve, thereby releasing a metered amount of gas from the reservoir to propel the missile. The released gas blasts through the manifold outlet, which is to the rear of the missile, hence drives it down and out the barrel. The valve, of course, closes in standard automatic fashion as its spring reacts.

When the trigger is released, its spring returns it to firing position for the next shot, and simultaneously pushes the rear end of the link down for the next hammer contact.

There is a permanent magnet positioned in the upper end of the feed slide. This facilitates the steel ball entering the slide opening from the magazine area. It also acts to prevent the ball from rolling down and out of the barrel in the period between the indexing of the ball for firing and the hammer fall which releases the gas-propelling charge. (Note. While this system is not as entirely reliable as the mechanical holding systems used in the Hämmerli, for instance, it is much cheaper to install and is a factor in enabling the manufacturer to offer this pistol at such a low price.)

The slide spring is intended not only to synchronize the feeding of each ball with the hammer fall but also to prevent damage to the manifold and slide in the event a defective ball should jam the mechanism.

The slide spring normally acts with the trigger through the center-trigger travel movement, which corresponds to the entire travel distance of the slide itself. After the slide halts at the end of its stroke, however, the trigger continues on for a few additional degrees. This added travel results in a slight flexing of the slide spring, thereby assuring ball entrance into the slide and providing for complete ball line-up with the barrel breech as the hammer falls on the valve stem. If a ball is jammed, the trigger, when moved to either end of its travel limit, encounters only the force of the completely deflected slide spring on the slide, thus preventing damage.

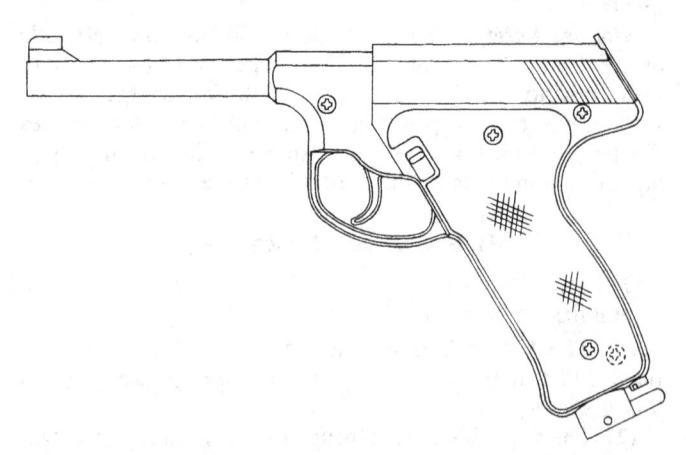

Left side view of new Healthways Plainsman CO$_2$ pistol. Combination rear sight and upward sliding magazine door at top rear. Manual thumb safety to rear of trigger prevents trigger and hammer contact for firing when pushed up to ON position.

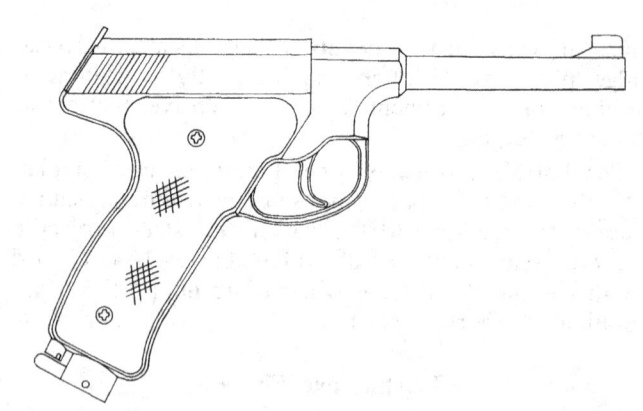

Right side view of new Healthways Plainsman CO$_2$ pistol. Gas retainer plug and power-adjusting screw shown at bottom of grip.

Evaluation

No mechanical device is 100 percent failure-proof, and no missile-projecting device is any more consistent than the sum of its own elements together with the projectiles used, the power supply, and the *general characteristics* inherent in all these when combined.

Thus the number of shots per CO$_2$ cartridge will always vary considerably with varying cartridges. Penetration varies correspondingly also.

Thus, too, accuracy will be affected not only by the gas charge, but much more so by variations in the quality of the missiles used. Steel air-rifle shot as made by Daisy, for instance, is the ultimate in low-cost projectiles, but it is neither intended nor represented by the makers as being suitable for *precision* shooting. Keeping that qualification in mind, the accuracy performance of this pistol is very good.

Failure to feed will be encountered in some instances. Round balls tend to bunch up as they enter the feed channel of this pistol. In such instances, the characteristic fizz of the escaping gas warns of the feed failure, since the propelling charge is merely exhausted down the barrel.

When this condition is encountered, if the pistol is shaken or tilted muzzle down to jar the balls in the feed channel, the jamming will clear without much difficulty. If a good quality ball is used, size and sphericity are adequate for very good operation. However, *used* shot may be deformed enough to interfere with proper feeding, and such use is not advisable, unless you are prepared to face jams without blaming the pistol.

Velocity is of the general order of 350 f.p.s. at full power, a speed which is entirely adequate for the short-range plinking and training for which this pistol is designed and for the missiles which it uses. In the considered opinion of the author this arm should *not* be used for small-game shooting.

As an advance in the field of CO$_2$ arms, this new Plainsman is a most worthwhile development. At the price at which it is retailed it is a real achievement in manufacture of this type. However, it has, as has been pointed out, limitations as well as advantages. Its resemblance to a common form of .22 cartridge pistol both in appearance and handling is a distinct advance over any CO_2 pistol thus far marketed. It constitutes a tremendous value for the money invested. It is still, however a "BB" type missile pistol, not to be confused with the "pell-gun" type. Its feed mechanism does not lend itself to handling the formal type of pellets which are capable of base expansion to seal off the gas behind the missile for utmost power and accuracy.

This Healthways Plainsman is important as a new entry into this field of shooting; and if the manufacturers follow up on its development as they have on sporting items in other fields which they have pioneered, future CO_2 arms from this source will rapidly make a place for themselves in this fast-growing field of shooting.

THE HARRIS MARKSMAN SPRING-AIR PISTOL

This pistol is by far the best value and design in its field. It is not to be confused with the strictly toy classes of stamped spring-air pistols, such as the Daisy line on the one hand, nor with the ultra-accurate (and correspondingly costly) machined target pistols of the Webley, Walther, and B.S.F. class on the other.

This Harris MARKSMAN is a precision-engineered training and plinking pistol which, while selling slightly above the toy-pattern pistols (currently $6.95 retail), has design and accuracy factors built in which make it as desirable at ranges up to 20 feet as the most costly serious domestic and imported spring-air pistols for training purposes.

The general outline of the arm is that of our Government Model .45 service auto pistol, and it has considerable value as an indoor trainer because of its appearance, hang, weight and balance. It is yet another example of America's unmatched ability to combine the best in mass-manufacturing techniques (in this case die-casting) with precision-engineered parts to produce outstanding values for the general market.

Description and Operation. While considerably less powerful than the far more expensive pistols of the Hy Score, Webley, and B.S.F. types, the MARKSMAN still has sufficient power to develop a velocity high enough to give maximum spring-air pistol accuracy at standard indoor range distances up to 20 feet; and it is far easier to cock and load than any of the others. Its piston and spring design are the most ingenious of the type.

The front sight has an extension within the barrel housing which serves as a breech lock. Pull the sight forward and the lock is released, permitting the barrel section to hinge down in the front end of the frame section. This common American "tip-up" action allows a standard round air-rifle shot, a .177 dart, or any standard .177 Diabolo or waisted expansion pellet to be inserted directly into the barrel chamber. The barrel section is then snapped back into firing position where it locks automatically.

The exceptional ease of cocking, which is quite remarkable for the power generated, is achieved by a combination of spring pressures which allow partial spring compression as the "slide" area is pulled back in standard auto-pistol fashion, and completion by thrusting the slide home against spring opposition. This compound spring system, of course, also explains the ability of the design to develop such unusual power within the overall limits imposed by the length of a military pistol of standard proportions.

An element which externally resembles the manual (thumb) safety of the Government Auto .45 is, in this pistol, actually a part of the mechanical cocking system. It is pushed into engagement before starting the cocking strokes. The barrel is not rifled, since the pistol is designed to use all available styles of .177 air-gun missiles, including darts.

This is a breech-loading single-shot pistol which for accuracy and *usable* power will rank with the finest made anywhere for practical air-pistol target work at short ranges. Trajectory and velocity at such ranges compare most favorably with those of all expensive pistols tested. Used with waisted pellets, which provide a good air seal, accuracy and power compare very favorably with longer barreled, harder cocking, far more expensive patterns.

It is generally agreed that because of light weight and low striking energy NO common air pistol should be used against even small game—the one possible exception being small birds of the nuisance class. At ranges substantially over 20 feet it has been established that precision air-pistol target shooting is more a matter of luck or skill than of spring-developed power; and the power of the MARKSMAN is entirely adequate for any practical use which can be made of an arm of this pattern.

For beginners in particular, this pistol can be most highly recommended. It has no competition in its class.

CHAPTER 15

Other Gas Systems

IN 1954 a German firm introduced a "booster" or gas adapter to be used on high-power spring-air operated rifles. The system is very old in concept, as has been outlined in the historical section. The current system "Barakuda," however, is an unusually good and relatively stable utilization of the "explosion" system.

It is merely an application of the well-known "diesel effect" encountered in high-power spring-air arms, but in this case the makers supply a very highly volatile gas of the ether group instead of the low-volatile lubricating oil which occasions normal diesel action in spring-air arms.

When this effect occurs *normally,* it is the result of small quantities of grease or lubricating oil in the spring-compression chamber being atomized and combined with the heated air caused by friction of the tight-fitting, spring-powered piston moving down the tube at a very high speed and compressing the air in its path. Since the air vent is minute, the air-compression rate (and resulting heat generated) is high as the piston is thrust ahead in the large compression tube.

When the mixture of air and petroleum gases is thus suddenly compressed, the projecting force is actually a combination of normal air-compression thrust *plus* the explosive force of the mixture. In normal usage, this will greatly increase the velocity, and if fired in a darkened room, flash will be perceptible at the muzzle.

It is possible to induce this condition by the simple expedient of putting a single drop of very light machine oil directly into the compression tube, firing with chamber empty to vaporize the oil, then cocking and firing again *with* a pellet in the chamber. It won't do the pistonhead or the compression spring any good to use this system. The shock of hitting against the breech without the slowdown effect achieved when there is a pellet in the chamber will soon batter the piston (or plunger) head and can produce spring-set. The major factor in air-gun performance is the combination of tight pistonhead fit, vent size, and spring power; and nothing should be done to injure these elements or their relationship.

THE GERMAN "BARAKUDA" SYSTEM

In 1954 Barakuda-Gesellschaft of Hamburg introduced a diesel-pattern "booster" device on high-power spring-air rifles manufactured by Herman Weihrauch of Mellrichstadt, Bayern (Bavaria).

It must be understood that the inventor and owner of the system is the *Barakuda firm.* The device itself could be mounted on ANY high-power spring-air arm of comparable type. It just happens that Barakuda uses it on Weihrauchs.

The Weihrauch Model HW35 (which is described and pictured with drawings in another section of this book) is a heavy-duty barrel-cocking design with a locked breech. Instead of the customary holding detent (latch) system to keep the barrel in closed position, the HW35 has a positive lock which must be pushed manually and held while the barrel is broken down on its hinge to unlock and start the cocking motion.

A short underlever attached to the barrel actuates a straightline cocking lever as the barrel is broken down. The main cocking lever has an arm extending through a cut in the underside of the compression tube which picks up the piston and forces it and its spring back to let the sear catch and hold the piston at the end of cocking stroke.

The Barakuda Attachment

When the Weihrauch (or any other) spring-air rifle using the Barakuda attachment is cocked and breech-loaded with proper ball, it can be fired like any ordinary air rifle. In this case, since the rifle with attachment uses a 5.6-mm. round ball instead of the familiar 5.5-mm. Diabolo pellet, neither the accuracy nor the power will be quite as good as standard. HOWEVER, A GUN FITTED WITH THE DEVICE CAN BE USED AS A REGULAR AIR GUN.

Note in this connection that the 5.5-mm. Diabolo must not under any conditions be used with the attachment in operation! If the gas-air combination is used, it will normally expand the thin Diabolo at its waist, completely deform it, blow a hole through the Diabolo head, and leave the pellet stuck in the barrel! The back pressure won't do the lock area any good, either!

The attachment consists of a tube which is a valved gas-expansion chamber mounted on the right side of the rifle compression tube. It has a sliding charging handle on its side which allows an individual charge of its ether-type gas to enter the spring-compression chamber each time the handle is pulled back and released. It has its own return spring. Only one charge of gas will stay in the compression chamber regardless of the number of times the handle may be operated, a necessary factor for safety of course.

Advantages of the Barakuda Gas System

This does make a "dual purpose" rifle within limits. You can use it on air power alone for indoor-target and short-range shooting. Even using the round ball, it will still shoot very good groups at about 50 feet—though

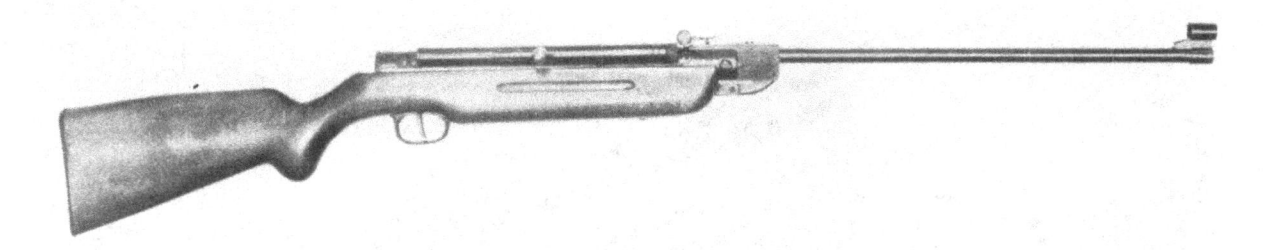

German "Barakuda." This is a high-power Weihrauch air rifle (barrel cocker, locked breech) with an ether-gas attachment. It may be used as an air rifle without using the gas "booster" if desired.

The Barakuda attachment.

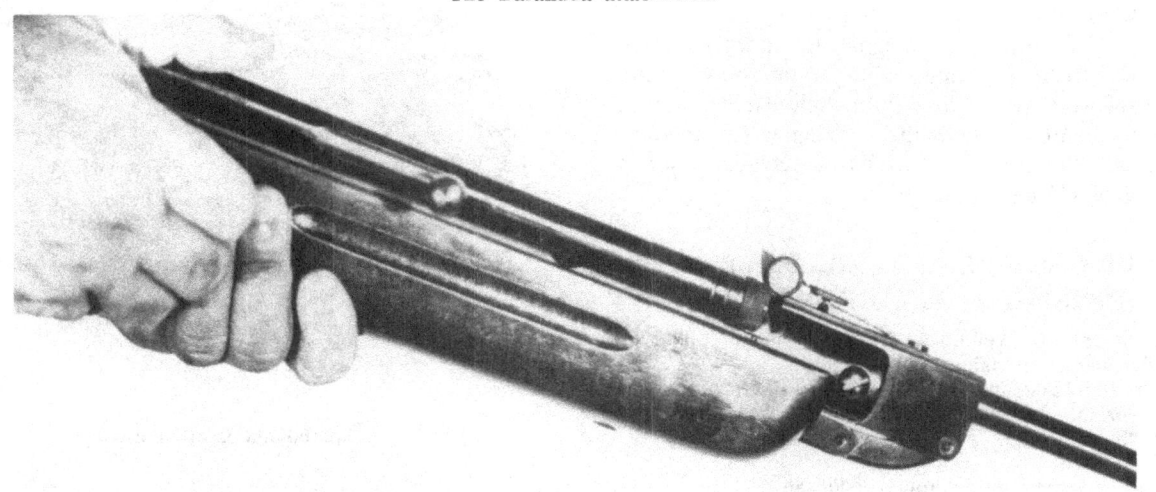

Barakuda. Note ether-gas charging handle full forward ready for action.

it won't do the kind of precision shooting the Weihrauch or any equivalent precision spring-air rifle will, using Diabolo pellets. Up to 50 feet, however, it will shoot better than the *average* shooter can hold. It has enough power for its type, though again penetration isn't as great as a Diabolo pellet gun.

Used with the ether charge, it is in a class with the .22 short powder cartridge *for short-range work.* The reader must note the emphasis carefully!

The Barakuda will, with an ether-air charge and its round ball, punch a hole through a 1-inch pine plank pretty consistently at 50 feet. Usually it will tear out a piece of wood—not leave a clean hole. For ranges up to 20 yards it is an excellent vermin killer.

However, the ball has neither the weight, shape, nor power behind it to give it ballistic coefficients to put it in a class with the .22 powder cartridge beyond very short ranges.

As a "backyard" rifle for vermin shooting where you must limit the carrying distance of the design, it has certain uses. In short, it may *complement* the .22 cartridge rifle for some uses; *but it is in no way a substitute for it!*

Disadvantages

(1) Its Power Supply. Ether is highly volatile, flammable, and explosive. Because of its fire hazards, anaesthetic and poisonous properties, dangers in storing, and similar deficiencies, its general use in the United States would undoubtedly induce both police and fire regulatory actions. As such it is a hazard to both firearms and airgun manufacturers.

(2) Short Range. Equivalent penetration can be obtained with good pump-up guns if the shooter has the energy; while for longer range, powder arms are necessary.

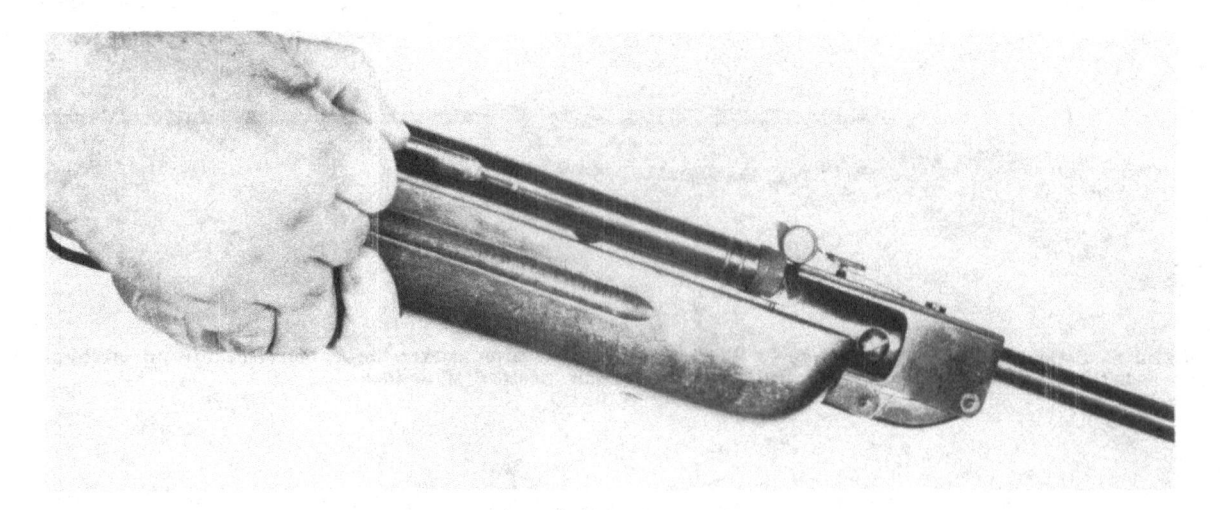

Pulling back to operate gas charger.

(3) Operation. From an American (not a European) standpoint, this is a difficult gun to shoot consistently. The first shot or two are fine. BUT—consistently breaking down the barrel to cock a weapon with the heavy spring necessary to produce enough heat to ignite these gases is a job the average American won't like. It's a lot easier to use a CO_2 gun for short-range and training work; and a .22 powder cartridge rifle for longer range and hunting vermin.

(Note: Various other gas designs are under development. Some which the author has seen show future promise. However, since no combustible-explosive arm can hope to compare with the efficiency of powder-cartridge arms, the utilization of gases such as ether is not practical in United States usage.)

BARRACUDA MODEL EL54 AIR RIFLE WITH ETHER-GAS ATTACHMENT

(Note: Current rifle is Weihrauch HW35 spring-air rifle with Barakuda (Barracuda) special gas attachment.)
Manufacturer: Barakuda-Gesellschaft, Hamburg, Germany.
U.S. Distributor: Stoeger Arms Corporation, New York City.
Overall Length: 45 inches.
Weight: 7.5 pounds.
Caliber(s): .22 (5.6-mm.) special round lead ball.
Type(s) of Ammunition Used: Special 5.6-mm. ONLY. (Cost, $3 for 500.)
Rifled: Yes.
Operating System: Spring-air by barrel cocking. Plus gas attachment when desired.
Cocked & Spring Compressed By: Break down barrel. Gas, additional motion of pulling back and releasing cocking handle.
Loaded: Directly into chamber.
Number Rounds: Single shot only.
Stock Type: One-piece sporting. Pistol grip. Uncheckered.
Front Sight(s): Hooded (globe) front.
Rear Sight(s): Adjustable barrel type. All Weihrauch combinations available.
Velocity (Approximate): Air, approximately 411 f.p.s. With gas added, about 629 f.p.s. Averages are based on author's electronic velocity tests.
Normal Accurate Range: Air, 40 feet. Gas, about 60 feet.
Approximate Retail Price: $50. (Note: Gas ampules cost $2.50 for box of 10.)

REMARKS

For details of the rifle itself, see under Weihrauch HW35.
This is the regular model drilled for mounting attachment and neoprene seal fittings.

Special ammunition used.

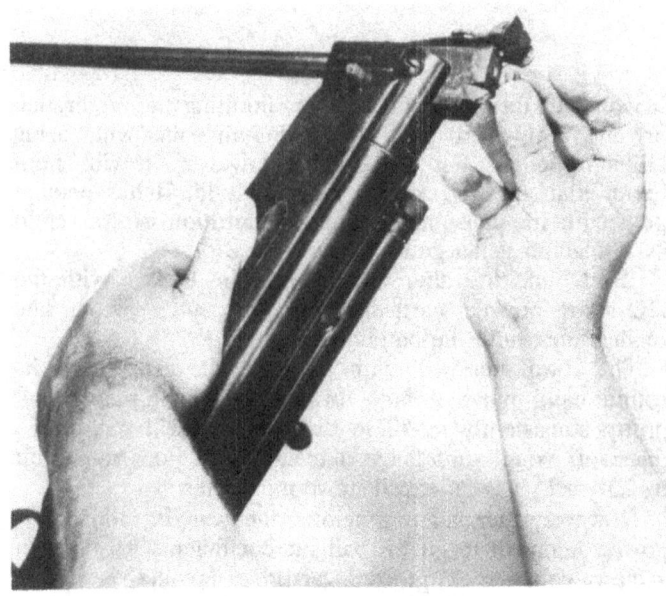

Loading pellet into chamber.

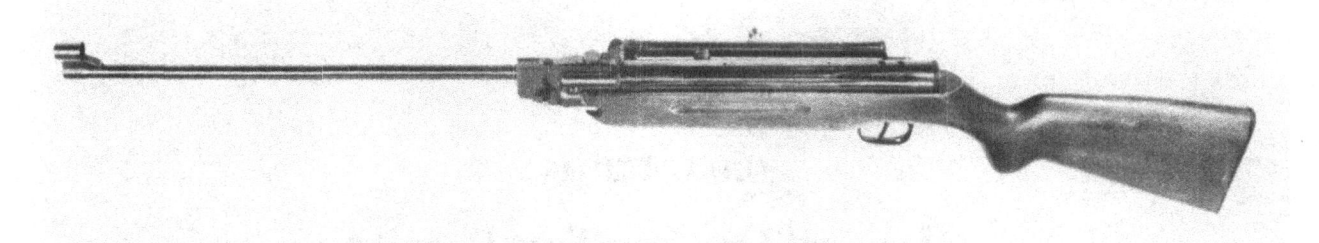

Sold under name "Barakuda" (Barracuda in the United States), only the attachment is of special design.

Charging the Auxiliary Barakuda Gas Chamber. Individual medical-type glass ampules of ether provide the charging power. These come packed 10 to a small box. Each is expected to give about 100 ether gas-power charges.

(1) The retaining cap at the forward end of the Barakuda tube is unscrewed.

(2) The tip is broken off an ether ampule, and the liquid contents are poured into the Barakuda gas tube. The retaining cap is immediately screwed back on tightly. The cap, naturally, has a gas-seal ring. Now dispose of the glass ampule.

(3) Push the barrel lock catch and break the barrel down on its hinge to full cock position. The spring is powerful. Be sure you complete the cocking stroke.

(4) Insert the special 5.6-mm. round lead ball into the chamber. (Don't use Diabolo waisted pellets. They will only be expanded in the bore, causing trouble.)

(5) Snap the barrel closed. It will lock automatically under pressure of the lock catch spring.

(6) Draw back to full stroke the cocking handle which projects from the side of the Barakuda gas tube. This will compress the spring behind it, just as in an auto-loading .22 rifle. This action will open a special vent leading into the spring compression tube forward of the cocked piston. When the cocking handle is released, a graduated charge of ether gas will be forced into the spring-compression chamber as the cocking-handle plunger goes forward, and more gas will be sealed off. (Note that if the cocking handle is manipulated more than once, each opening stroke will merely evacuate the gas already fed and replace it with a new charge. In other words, more than one stroke does not increase power; it just wastes gas.)

(7) Press trigger.

Action. Pressing the trigger actuates the sear and releases the piston. The spring drives the piston forward, travelling at very high speed. The heat generated as the large pistonhead compresses the ether-gas-air mixture in the compression tube ahead of it will *explode* the mixture.

Note that this is not, as in the case of air compression, merely using the expanding force of air for propulsion—in this system you have *combustion*, which acts exactly like gunpowder (though to a lesser degree) and produces a very high volume of gases as a result.

If you fire this arm in a darkroom, you will observe the same characteristic flash as when firing .22 powder cartridges.

Examples of test results on Barakuda rifle as a simple air gun and as a gas gun.

CHAPTER 16

Air- and Gas-Gun Test Results

IN the course of visiting factories where air and gas guns are made, the author observed that no manufacturer either here or abroad possessed collection, library, or research facilities which could in any way be compared with those of the major firearms manufacturers such as Winchester or Remington Arms.

No one knew very much about his competitors' products. Very few had adequate modern scientific testing equipment to check the actual performance of their own products as measured by the standards applied in other metal-working industries.

Some statements of product performance seemed questionable. In view of the manufacturing methods and facilities observed, as well as the tests to which the products were submitted, it was apparent to the author that some claims were reasonable, some were unrealistic, and (a very few) were just not possible.

No manufacturer knew the history or background of his type of product. Indeed, few except where they were the founders knew very much about the history of their own products or even their own companies!

In view of this situation it was decided that truly scientific tests should be set up to check on manufacturers' claims, not with the idea of producing negative, destructive data, but rather for furnishing for the first time a clear picture of what air and gas arms are and are not—what they can and can't do—and for indicating ways in which the industry may move to improve products in this rapidly expanding field of manufacturing.

The entire course of this investigation has been constructive in approach. Any product in any field can always be improved upon. Any product and any manufacturer may at some stage be the object of healthy criticism which, if acted upon intelligently, can benefit both the maker and the buyer. An attempt is made here to present the actual *average* performances of most of the items in this field purely as a form of constructive suggestion.

It must be stressed that no part of this book has in any way been subsidized by any manufacturer or industry. It represents solely the work of the author and the publisher as conducted at their own expense. It is strictly impartial. Manufacturers who make a number of items have, naturally, been given more space than those who manufacture a more limited line. The same would hold true for books prepared on any subject. For example, in a thorough coverage of automobiles, more space would have to be devoted to General Motors or Ford products than to Nash or Studebaker.

These tests cost thousands of dollars in money and a tremendous investment in knowledge, contacts, and time—which after all is the same thing. Wherever it was found that manufacturers had paid outside qualified testing organizations to subject their products to scientifically controlled tests, and where the manufacturers offered access to their files without qualification, the author utilized such test data to *supplement his own findings*. All such instances, however, are clearly labeled for what they are.

Just as in the firearms field, air and gas gunmakers fall into common classifications. Some are just salesmen, some are frank and open, some are secretive to a stupid degree, some are completely cooperative, some cooperate to a limited degree, some are evasive. However, regardless of classification, all have been treated impartially in this book. If impartial, scientific tests bore out their claims, it has been so stated regardless of their degree or type of cooperation. If the tests did not bear out the claims, that too is stated. In some instances findings are fairly conclusive. In others, the findings are subject to alteration as improvements or changes may later be made in the products presented.

While to a limited degree the tests were developed to show the *maximum performance* which may be obtained with a given arm or type of arm, real emphasis was placed on finding what the *average* shooter could expect from the *average* arm of the type discussed as it came off the dealer's shelf. In the field of .22 powder-rifle shooting, as a basis for analogy, the true expert, shooting a specially tuned-up Remington Model 40X or an equivalent Winchester 52 with special match ammunition, will shoot rings around any *average* shooter with any *average* .22 rifle and ammunition. So, too, an expert with a tuned-up air or gas gun of one make using specially selected, weighed, and micrometered pellets may shoot scores or get other performances which for advertising purposes may be fine, but which in no case indicate even remotely what the *average* shooter can hope to equal.

This book is concerned primarily with the average buyer—since he constitutes some 99.94 percent of the air and gas gun users. If he wants to equal the experts, he will find herein hints which may help him; but most of all he will find what he can honestly expect in the way of average performance from the arm he buys from a production factory.

One closing note: There will be some who wonder why the author does not offer many solutions for problems or shortcomings encountered in products tested. The answer is simple. Such data would not help the average buyer of this book, who is a shooter. And at the manufacturing level the author has long since learned that the more backward the manufacturer is, the less he is inclined to act on information for which he doesn't have to pay.

TESTING METHODS USED

The original research done in preparation of this book included an examination of all related patent abstracts of importance in the field. It also embraced the contact of museums, manufacturers, and important collectors to check specimens.

For actual testing, representative samples of current production were sought on either a purchase or lend basis from the manufacturers. In all instances sample arms came from warehouse stocks waiting to be shipped, so that each represented the item the buyer might expect to receive from a dealer. The same system was applied to ammunition, oils, and (in gas guns) power supplies.

The next step was to purchase in the open market from dealers' shelves duplicates of all the more common and best-selling types for comparison tests. This meant that the products of each maker tested represented different manufacturing dates at the factory, giving an indication of relative performance not otherwise obtainable.

On a very few items of interest (but of limited sale or availability), where they could not be obtained by the above methods, the author borrowed specimens from collectors or used those available in his own collection.

Every effort was made to see that all arms were average and representative of the regular production.

The maker's literature as enclosed with the arms or ammunition was studied, and tests were designed to check those claims, as well as to make our own comparison checks under rigidly controlled conditions which would show the performance of one brand as it related to a competing brand product of similar type and classification.

It is to be noted that all testing was done with individual arms as they came from sealed factory cartons and were handled as prescribed by the maker. NO ARM WAS DISMANTLED OR OTHERWISE TAMPERED WITH MECHANICALLY UNTIL *AFTER* VELOCITY, ACCURACY, GROUP, AND PENETRATION TESTING HAD BEEN COMPLETED This is a very important factor to be considered; as except for sight setting, no mechanical checking is expected (or recommended by the maker) as the gun is unboxed and prepared for shooting. Since no two shooters have exactly the same vision or hold, or shoot under identical circumstances, every arm of any type will require either sight adjustment or hold compensation as it comes from the factory.

Velocity Testing

The first tests undertaken were for velocity as stated by the maker at distances he specified. Later, velocity tests were conducted at similar distances from muzzle and screens, under known atmospheric conditions and temperatures, for all types, so that true comparisons were obtainable. The reason was simple: Regardless of the use of the term "muzzle velocity," some makers test at 5 feet, some at 10, a few at longer ranges; and while the differences are merely a matter of feet, the author wanted both types of tests to: (1) check the maker's own claims; (2) obtain as nearly a true comparative basis with others as was possible.

At this point it should be noted that in the firearms industry, as well as in the air-gun industry in the United States, velocity testing except by the largest makers is pretty much conducted on a hit-or-miss basis. Only a few makers have modern Potter counter electronic equipment for testing velocity. In fact, few have even outdated mechanical equipment. Most depend upon the ammunition makers, on mathematics, or guesswork, or on other inconclusive methods. In the United States, for instance, the ONLY air or gas gunmaker equipped to make regular spot checks of each lot on their own premises is the Daisy Manufacturing Company—whose products are in the "toy" category!

The author therefore arranged to have all velocity testing done on the most modern testing equipment available—the Potter counter chronograph with interval timer. To check the findings made under his own supervision, two independent testing laboratories with Potter equipment were engaged to make spot checks of several makes under identical conditions.

The Counter Chronograph. A ballistic chronograph is used to determine the length of time it takes a projectile to travel from one point to another. The "counter" chronograph or interval timer is the most modern electronic instrument for determining this length of time. It is a lineal descendant of the Geiger counter in many ways. Its performance verges on the fantastic, breaking a second of watch time down in 100,000 parts for purposes of time travel determination.

Looking rather like a small telephone switchboard, it has a series of jacks and switches on its face, as well as four columns of ¼-inch neon tubes which blink on and off 100,000 times per second. It is operated somewhat like a stopwatch as the pellet (or bullet) flies.

When the instrument is set to operate, the gun is fired through a suitable port. The projectile passes over a photoelectric cell set at a predetermined point from the muzzle. When fired outdoors or in unroofed structures, the light source which activates the cells is the sky and such photocell units are called "skyscreens." When the testing is in a dark indoor range, a tubular light is mounted above each photocell.

Everyone is familiar today with the common use of photoelectric cells in restaurants, railway stations, and the like as door openers—as you walk through the first light beam you cut off the light source, thereby activating the mechanism to open the door.

In the counter chronograph, similarly, the bullet or pellet passing over the first photocell breaks the light reaching it and starts the counter working; and when the missile passes over the second photocell, which is set up at a predetermined distance ahead, the counter is stopped. It is just as simple—and as electronically complex!—as that.

The counter chronograph has within it a counterpart in some ways of the human heart—a quartz crystal and an oscillator which "beats" at the rate of 100,000 times per second. Serving as a balance wheel, the crystal, which

Taking Potter chronograph readings at the H. P. White Laboratory.

is about the size of a ten-cent piece, controls a continuous series of electrical impulses delivered by the oscillator to a switch attached to the counter. The switch is closed to admit pulses to the counter when the pellet passes over the first photocell; and is opened as the pellet passes over the second photocell to halt the recording.

The "scaling circuit," as the electronic brain is technically known, records impulses which are far too fast for any ordinary electrical device. On the face of the counter chronograph there are four different columns of neon bulbs. The scaling circuit uses only the figures 1, 2, 4, and 8, each represented by an appropriate bulb. Each of the four columns carries these numbered bulbs.

The pulses entering the counter as the switch closes travel at incredible speed. They enter No. 1 column, the first pulse lighting up the No. 1 bulb there. The second pulse puts out the No. 1 bulb and lights up No. 2. The third pulse relights No. 1 bulb, and No. 2 bulb stays lit, thereby counting a total of three pulses. The next (fourth) pulse puts out 1 and 2 bulbs and lights up No. 4. The fifth relights No. 1 and leaves No. 4 bulb still lit. Thereafter each additional pulse selects the correct light (or combination of lights) until reaching the total of nine which is maximum column capacity, indicated when both 8 and 1 remain lit.

When the tenth pulse enters the counter, all the bulbs in column No. 1 are put out. No. 1 bulb in the SECOND column is lit up. Each time from there on that column No. 1 totals another 10, an additional number is automatically added to column No. 2. When column 2 hits capacity, it carries over to column 3. Thus, each pulse starts in the first column, but moves progressively from 1 to the next.

It will be seen that as a matter of elementary mathematics, when the full four banks of bulbs have been lighted, we can count a *total* of 9,999 pulses. In time measurement on the counter, this equals .09999 second, which is approximately 1/10 second. It is hardly conceivable that any bullet will ever be designed which cannot be measured on this electronic marvel—which, by the way, was developed by the Army's Ordnance Department during World War II.

The term "muzzle velocity" is a very loose term in this electronic age. As measured on any chronograph, the velocity measured is not actually at the muzzle—it is really measured *over an interval* forward of the muzzle. In high-power arms where there is heavy muzzle gas blast, the first photocell (or screen) is usually about 3 feet ahead of the muzzle. In gas and air guns, the author obtained best results usually at an average distance of 5 feet from the muzzle. 0 and 10 feet are good with air guns. Thus the average velocity between the screens represents approximately the velocity at a distance midway between the screens. The velocity is the time it takes the pellet to cover the distance between the two screens divided by the distance traveled.

A look at one of our reports (table 1) may simplify an understanding of the Potter velocity test procedure. It must be remembered that only four columns of figures show on the counter, and that a zero placed before the figures, and which is itself preceded by a decimal, gives the actual time interval of the recorded flight. Thus the reading on the counter when its operation is electronically halted as the pellet passes over the second photocell or screen may read 1808. *This represents .01808 second as the time of bullet flight between the start and stop photocells.*

Accuracy and Group Testing

In every case where the manufacturer claimed a given group accuracy at a stated distance, our tests for minimum of two 10-shot strings were made at those stated distances. Later these same arms were tested in competition at ranges which would give an index to the *comparative* accuracies of various comparable makes, systems, and calibers.

Accuracy testing took two forms: (1) Firing from machine rest. Here the arms were vised-in to prevent any upward or side movement in standard practice. Shooting was indoors with controlled temperatures, preventing any wind from affecting pellet flight. (2) Firing from bench rest in standard practice, also indoors, using muzzle and elbow rests.

Standard N.R.A. targets were used for some accuracy tests. Group tests were commonly made on plain paper X'd to furnish an aiming point. In all cases each shot was checked with spotting scope.

Some testing was also done while chronographing for velocity. This enabled us to check the impact point of each pellet against the velocity characteristics involved. A trained technician looking at the chronograph readings can often predict the rise or fall of the pellet above a normal line, since the trajectory of the bullet's flight is directly related to its velocity, among other factors.

Each type of arm operation (spring-air, pneumatic, gas, or combination) has different factors involved in the ac-

TABLE 1

Sample Velocity Test With Hy Score Spring-Air Pistol

Shot number	Time interval (in seconds)	Velocity (in feet per second)
1	.01808	277
2	.02217	226
3	.02928	170
4	.02580	194
5	.02432	206
6	.01725	290
7	.02024	247
8	.02363	212
9	.02015	248
10	.02022	247
11	.02564	195
12	.01996	251
13	.01941	257
14	.02154	233
15	.01957	255

15-shot average velocity: 234 f.p.s.

Note 1. Single-shot model; range 5 feet—2.5 center shots; Potter screens and interval timer; shots fired 4 inches above photocells; average range temperature—71 degrees; pellets—Hy Score.

Note 2. Velocities above were obtained with standard Hy Score pellets as taken from container, following the maker's instructions in loading. No attempt was made to select, micrometer, or size pellets, since no such instructions were given by the maker. (See separate data sheet for pellet alterations which increased the average velocity to 297 feet per second.)

Note 3. Above is a record of a Hy Score pistol made in 1949. 1956 production models tested showed much higher velocities (see text).

H. P. White Laboratory chronograph screens on indoor range. The gun port with machine rest is at the right.

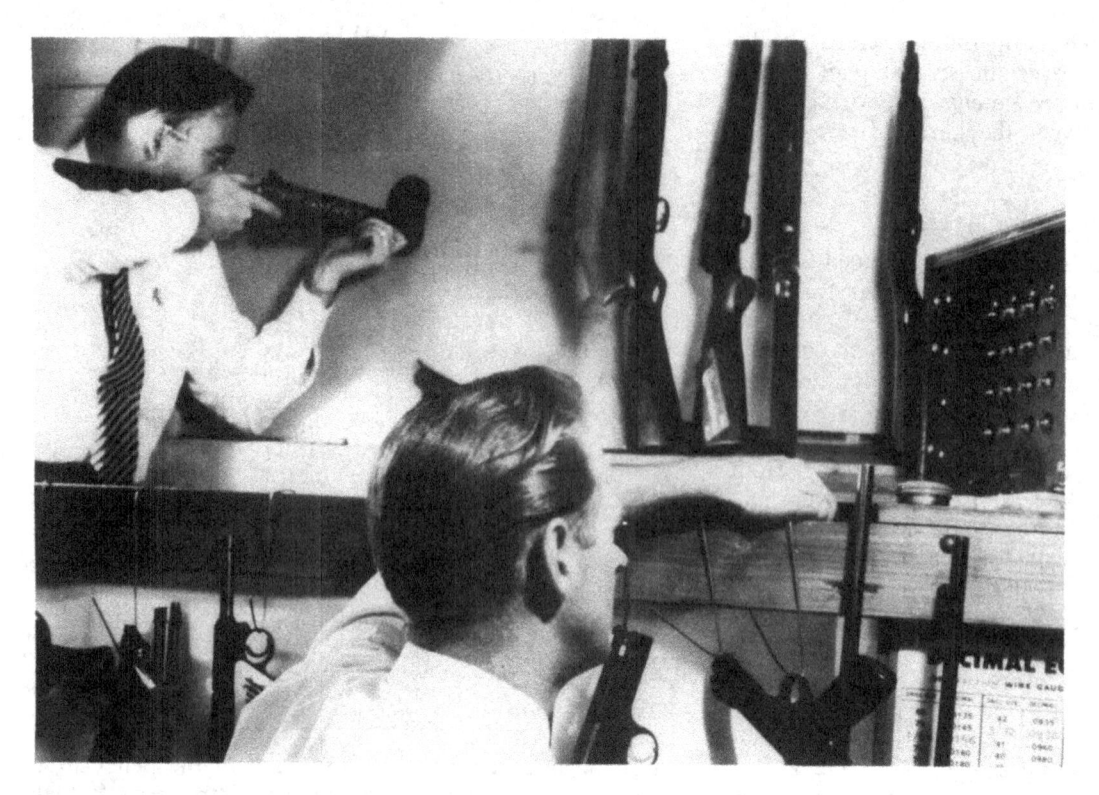

Firing through gun port in velocity test.

curacy of that particular system, all of which are treated herein under their proper headings. For instance, powerful spring-air-arms have a definite lunge and recoil as the piston is driven forward to compress the air, the recoil starting while the pellet is traveling down the barrel. *This does not occur in pneumatic and gas guns.* Pneumatic arms, on the other hand, have problems deriving from the number and type of pump strokes and the valving. These conditions, conversely, do not occur in spring-air arms. Gas arms, as a further illustration, have problems deriving from valving, from power source (gas cartridge) variations, and from decreasing pressures as the power supply diminishes. These are but a few illustrations.

Some tests were conducted to establish as nearly as possible what *ultimate,* rather than *average,* accuracy could be obtained from certain types of arms. These tests involved micrometering and weighing pellets; checking the exact depth of insertion into the chamber; starting the pellets in the rifling; checking oil distribution on pistonheads, etc. With such match-procedure techniques, improved performance was obtainable with practically all types. However, the tests on the whole, as stated above, revolved around finding the accuracy the average shooter could expect with the average arm and ammunition, if he followed the maker's instructions.

Penetration Testing

Penetration is not necessarily a true test of power. The shape, weight, and design of the pellet; the barrel and ammunition coefficients; lubrication; power consistency; rifling, and a host of other factors can affect pellet-gun penetration.

In England and Europe generally, testing for penetration is commonly done by firing at ranges from 5 to 20 feet against a number of 3/64-inch-thick strawboards placed ½ inch apart—strawboard being a very coarse yellow board made from compressed straw pulp. Webley arms, for instance, are thus checked at 20 feet. Such tests stem from official test methods set up by the Home Office, which has control of arms licensing. In the opinion of the author such tests are too variable for true penetration comparisons, not only because of variations in the strawboard itself, but because moisture or dryness factors will slow down or make easier the pellet's travel through such material.

Tests against wood are also far from conclusive because of grain structure, moisture content, and similar factors. It is only by shooting against selected, planed planks of soft pine or fir wood, at the same session, and under the same conditions, that true wood comparisons are possible. (Note: Such "deal" planks are often used abroad for penetration tests.) A few tests of this sort were conducted to test indications of penetration.

Another common European test is against steel "splash plates." Pellets are fired against a smooth steel plate. A comparison of the flattened lead pellets thus fired gives a far better idea of the power (and hence to a considerable degree of the penetration) of arms being tested than does any other method commonly available to the average shooter or manufacturer. A really powerful rifle will usually drive its pellet hard enough to knock the edges off, the degree of fragmentation giving a good index for comparisons. A few shots from each of several air arms at an old Manhattan telephone directory will also tell a lot about power and penetration comparisons.

Perhaps the most accurate penetration comparisons for air arms is that made by shooting through Kirkman's soap. All types of general tests were undertaken, but to a limited degree.

While certain air arms are usable against vermin and small game, such use is so limited that in the opinion of the author detailed penetration studies were not of sufficient value to warrant the great expense necessary to establish true comparisons.

Mechanical and Design Tests

Upon the conclusion of velocity, accuracy, group, and penetration tests, all arms used were dismounted, studied, and analyzed—the only exception being a few designs which were so welded, brazed, or riveted as to make examination impracticable by complete dismounting procedure. These were in a small minority.

Important good and bad features encountered are presented for the reader's information where they are considered to be of value to him.

A great deal of information thus derived, however, has not been listed or discussed since it is of technical and research value only.

Ammunition

Every commonly available type of air- and gas-gun ammunition was included in these tests. Representative samples were checked for weight, measurements, tolerances, consistency, and to some degree as to metallurgy.

By using competing ammunition in the arms of all major makers—or distributors—comparisons of pellet makers' claims were possible. Many of these findings are described.

In justice to the makers or distributors, however, it must be pointed out that all pellets (like any other ammunition) can vary from lot to lot—as tools and manufacturing dies wear in, for instance. No such manufacturing is ever necessarily static. It is possible that by closer inspection or better attention to tolerances, pellets of any *medium-quality brand* may be improved to give better performance.

DAISY PATTERN SPRING-AIR ARMS

The air "rifles" and pistols manufactured by the Daisy Manufacturing Company are, as has been stated, in the "toy" category, both as to design and price. In that category no similar products made anywhere approach their degree of quality as missile-projecting arms.

Since they have never been offered with any claims of extreme accuracy or penetration, and since their recommended user bracket is the 6- to 15-year-old groups, they cannot be considered in any but a most general relation to serious spring-air arms intended for, or claimed to be capable of, use for any form of *precision* target shooting.

However, on the theory that any form of air arm which has engaged the serious attention of the National Rifle Association of America and the Boy Scouts of America is important enough to warrant coverage in a serious work of this nature, the author gave considerable attention to Daisy products.

These arms have all the general operational characteristics of expensive precision-type spring-air arms. They differ in that their manufacture is limited largely to stamping and diecasting procedures required by their very low selling price; also their ammunition, while held to extremely close manufacturing tolerances, is not offered as precision-type projectiles.

However, the research organization headed by the director, Ciro R. Scalingi, and assistant director, Richard Daniels, has carried research in the spring-air field to a point where the performance of their products actually excels that of several high-priced foreign makes! The author knows of only two precision German firms, one Swiss, and one British whose products and performance indicate equivalent study and knowledge of compression-spring, piston-friction, and oiling factors; while in the field of pellet study, the Daisy research has been excelled only by two old-line German ammunition makers.

In spite of the tremendous Daisy production, all these "toy" guns are subjected to target and function tests; and are regularly spot-checked for velocity. The deliberate intent of the makers is to provide as much accuracy as is feasible and usable, and at the same time *to control range and penetration within limits considered safe for use by boys.*

The velocities involved, averaging 280 f.p.s for the lever-action and 345 f.p.s. for the pump-action types, are entirely adequate for really accurate shooting at the official N.R.A. 15-foot junior range. While both ammunition and barrels are held to very close tolerances, the combination cannot, of course, be compared with high-priced precision shooting products. Still, the accuracy is all the average young shooter is capable of utilizing. When he gets too good for the Daisy, it is time to move him on to a higher priced pneumatic or spring-air arm which has been developed for true accuracy.

As to penetration, the Daisy can be safely used indoors with a simple backstop consisting of any available corrugated cardboard carton of the standard grocer's pattern stuffed with folded newspapers. It is necessary only to stuff the carton fairly firmly, then pin, paste, or scotch-tape a target on the outside. Any of the commercial short-range target backstops or bullet catchers can be used, of course. In spite of the relatively high velocities involved, the pellets can be stopped by a few thicknesses of corrugated cardboard, since the first one penetrated slows the pellet down with a fast snubbing action.

The Daisy spring-air pistol uses special small shot and has a very much lower velocity. Its use should normally be confined to about 10 feet if any degree of accuracy is hoped for. Aside from its value as a "plinking" toy, this pistol has been used to instruct adults in fast-draw and quick-point pistol shooting with considerable success. It has finger serrations at the rear of the receiver which enable it to be cocked like a standard automatic pistol by pulling back with the fingers of the left hand, and releasing so the compressed spring returns the barrel section to firing position. The gravity magazine feed requires merely tilting the muzzle up during the cocking stroke to feed a shot into the firing barrel. Thus used against a man-sized target at distances up to 20 feet, it is a very effective means of teaching draw and point firing for close-quarters shooting, as a preliminary to the use of a cartridge pistol.

Some mention must also be made in passing of the Daisy 303 Bulls-Eye Scope. Again remembering that

235

this is a "toy type" accessory sold at a commensurate price, the device is quite remarkable. Retailing at around $4, it is a plastic rifle-type telescope using genuine optics. Its four lenses are molded in optically ground cavities to give good target definition. The mount is detachable. Adjustment knobs are spring-loaded and definite clicks are heard as the cross hairs are adjusted for elevation or windage. The adjustment indexing is positive, the magnification is 2X. It is a technical achievement of some magnitude to get two-power magnification with four lenses in the short overall length of 11 inches. Issued complete with guard caps, this toy scope is not only an interesting plaything for the boy, it is a realistic and practical low-cost unit for instructing in the use of the common rifle telescope, which is rapidly becoming a "required" accessory on many American plinking and sporting rifles.

The Boy Scouts of America is the largest democratic youth training organization in the world. It embraces a membership of some 850,000 Boy Scouts, 375,000 Explorers, and 1,000,000 Cub Scouts. Marksmanship merit badges may be earned for spring-air rifle shooting at the 15-foot range. In the face of the interest of this great organization in teaching safe-shooting procedures under proper guidance and control, it is obvious that the acceptance of the spring-air gun, and eventually pellet guns generally, will increase in this country as time goes on.

PRECISION-TYPE SPRING-AIR ARMS

United States manufacturers have completely ignored or overlooked this field with the sole exception of the Hy Score pistols. There seems to be a number of reasons for this, the most important being the relatively limited market which has existed for any expensive air arms here until recently; the American concern with getting maximum power in everything from guns to automobiles, whether usable or not; and the relatively high cost of designing and tooling suitable new products in this field.

As has been noted, the market is now steadily increasing due to population pressures, hard-to-reach firearms shooting areas, need for short-range precision training arms, high ammunition costs, and similar factors. In short, the conditions which started the German and British interest in precision air-gun shooting some 60 years ago have finally caught up with us—though not necessarily for the same reason! Our crowded shooting conditions result not alone from tremendous population increase, but also from economic advances which have decentralized so much industry and made well-to-do suburban districts out of what used to be free-shooting areas. Where the last generation could use long-range .22 rifles without much trouble, today's youth must turn to the short-range precision air arm for first rifle training.

As to the "power" factor in air arms, that is something the Benjamin pneumatic has been plugging in its advertising for over three-quarters of a century, hence when Sheridan, Crosman, and others came along, they saw no chance of achieving sales except on a basis of equal or superior power. The natural trend, therefore, was towards the *pneumatic* rifle rather than the *spring-air* design, which in the mind of the average American was just a toy. Now it happens that most good foreign spring-air arms will give as much power on one loading stroke as the best pneumatic will on 5 or 6, and very few shooters will consistently pump up 8 or 10 strokes to utilize the higher potential power of the pneumatic. However, it is a lot easier to sell Americans on the superior power available if wanted, than it is to convince them that they will use or need that power so seldom that it is often just not worth the physical work involved! So all American manufacturers since Benjamin have avoided spring-air design and stayed with the pneumatic principle. It so happens that this author is familiar with model spring-air rifles with which a relatively light single stroke can actually give velocity higher than the best available pneumatic or CO_2 guns; but none are available commercially. And that brings us to the last consideration mentioned: The design alone of such an arm is a technical achievement of a very high order. The cost of tooling for and producing it to satisfactory standards so it could be sold at a competitive price would call for an investment which would scare off most manufacturers at this time.

As has been pointed out in our text, European and British makers are subject to legal controls if they materially exceed the performances of their current production where velocities very seldom surpass 600 f.p.s. Also, since most of them manufacture *to firearms standards,* their costs are too high to allow them to export to the United States and sell in competition with domestic pneumatic rifles, though that condition may change.

So much for the "reason why" American firms don't manufacture spring-air precision rifles!

Operating Consistency of Spring-Air Arms

In theory spring-air arms give consistent velocity with attendant accuracy. In actual practice, as electronic velocity tests clearly demonstrate, there are many variables involved, despite the fact that only one equal-effort stroke is required to prepare the arm for firing each time. Washer wear, spring fatigue, piston friction, lubrication, sear-contact-surface-hardness, and other factors, together with the almost inevitable diesel action which will occur from time to time, all work to some extent to interfere with true consistency of velocity in any compression-type system where the power is generated by spring-propelled moving parts after trigger release. A most important factor, also, is ammunition consistency. The finest air rifle made won't perform properly with variable ammunition, any more than the finest Cadillac could perform when powered by indifferent grades of gasoline.

Certain ammunition factors will be considered separately as a result of test findings. As to operation of the arms themselves, it is the old story of getting what you pay for. An air gun made to better rifle standards, utilizing forgings, properly selected and hardened metals for contact surfaces, which is precision reamed and has a rifled barrel, and is hand fitted where required, costs money to make. Almost any of the heavy-duty air rifles or pistols made in Germany and England will give good service for the price paid, and will be entirely adequate for the requirements of the average user. However, the better and costlier grades are worth the additional price to the serious shooter. As a rule, relatively low-priced air

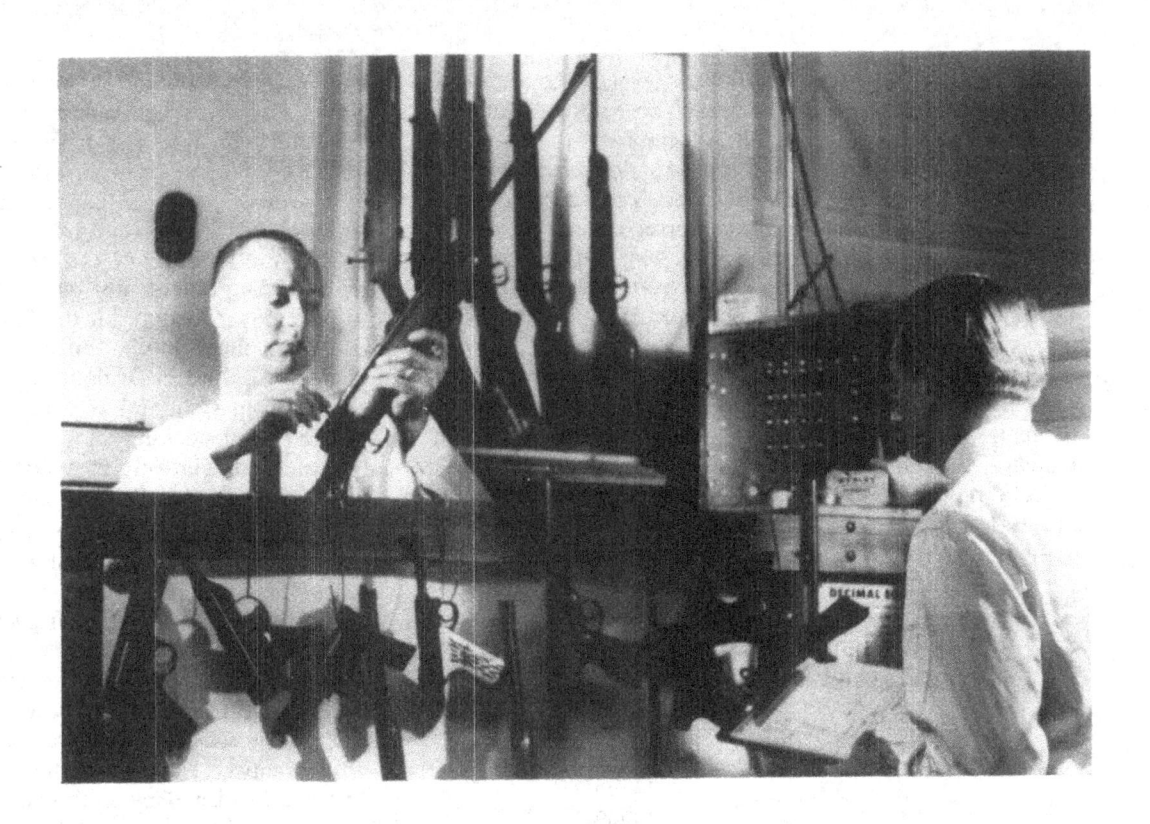

Velocity testing Crosman CO₂ rifle.

arms will usually be nearly equal in power *on an average* to the higher priced lines. But in consistency of operation, accuracy, and shooting qualities they will not compare on an average and over a period of time.

It is necessary to stress these facts because velocity, penetration, and similar data do not by themselves give a true picture of the value involved. Indeed a poor rifle with good ammunition will often give better velocity and penetration than a fine rifle with inferior pellets.

No manufacturer of spring-air arms gives any specific loading data, for example, yet proper or improper loading can affect the velocity as much as 200 feet per second by actual tests! There is enough variation in manufacturing tolerances of pellets to require actually seating the pellet before firing if you want best results. It is understandable perhaps that makers of barrel-cocking or other hinge-frame air arms do not stress that fact. In such an arm, regardless of the make or quality, the precision shooter (even when he "mikes" the pellets) should *start* them into the rifling. In a pneumatic or CO₂ arm, normally the forward thrust of the bolt takes care of this matter of positioning. The average man loading a barrel-cocking pistol or rifle will merely insert the pellet in place, close the action, and feel he has done all that is necessary. The European match shooter, on the other hand, after dropping the pellet into the breech will use a nail or stiff wire bedded in a wooden handle to thrust the pellet directly in for about a half inch, so that the rifling cuts into the skirt of the pellet. This action not only sizes the pellets with maximum uniformity, but by overcoming much of the starting friction, allows utilization of the air entirely for pellet propulsion. In the case of the underlever air rifle or other arm with the "tap" or "loading-plug" loading system and fixed barrel, the pellets should be pressed to the bottom of the tapered hole in the plug to size them uniformly. The fact that the pellets cannot be forced into the rifling here marks the one big difference between these two loading systems. While in Great Britain match shooting is normally done with underlever rifles and "miked" pellets, in Europe match shooting is more commonly done with barrel-cocking designs in which the pellets are seated into the rifling.

In the matter of oiling, the shooter should as a general rule follow the instructions of the maker. Oil on the pistonhead, for example, can be a major help or hindrance in the matter of velocity when serving purely as a lubricant. In actual tests it has been found possible to cut the velocity of a .177 air rifle down from 600 to 410 feet per second merely by varying the type of light machine oil used as a lubricant!

On the matter of "diesel action," the general substance has been set forth in the text where relevant. This action, which is the actual combustion of oil vapors in the compression tube, is not normally controllable. The best makers try to avoid dieseling because it interferes with consistent velocity. An occasional manufacturer recommends oiling which encourages the diesel effect, since by so doing he achieves a higher *average* velocity, though a highly inconsistent one. When high velocity is thus achieved, accuracy is sacrificed regardless of the advertising claims made to the contrary.

LEADING SPRING-AIR PISTOLS OF THE WORLD
Germany

Both in the toy and precision field of spring-air pistols, Germany is the producer of the widest variety. All the important types are described in the text. Pistols of the Heym, J.G.A., and Diana 2 types fall in the classification *somewhere between* toys and precision arms.

This last class is uniformly of the spring type where the barrel casing is forced in to compress the powerful spring, the breech screw, which then projects, is removed, the pellet or dart inserted, the breech screw then replaced. In order to cock this type, it is necessary to place the muzzle against a solid surface and bear down heavily.

As these pistols fire there is a very considerable jump as the powerful spring and the barrel casing whip forward. On tests, curiously enough, it was found that even though they were uniformly cheap stamped pistols with smooth barrels, reasonably good accuracy was possible after you became accustomed to the jump. At 20 feet, which is about maximum for any kind of accuracy with these designs, it was possible to shoot 2-inch groups. At 30 feet, groups from rest occasionally averaged about 4 inches, though this was not consistent.

As a representative example of velocity, the time intervals for the Heym .177, firing a 10-shot group with Benjamin pellets is of interest (table 2).

TABLE 2
GERMAN HEYM PISTOL VELOCITY TEST

Shot number	Time interval
1	.....
2	.02117
3	.01895
4	.01787
5	.01769
6	.01771
7	.01866
8	.01682
9	.01708
10	.01775
Total	.18163

(Equals 275 f.p.s. average velocity.)
Note. Shot No. 1 was oversized and did not emerge.

From the foregoing it is evident that these very low-priced pistols are not in the toy category. While they cannot be recommended for serious shooters, they are suitable for casual plinking at close range. Darts may also be used in most arms of this design, but because of relatively high velocity and consequent deep penetration, they should not be fired into any holding materials such as wood. Darts are expensive and since pliers are required to withdraw them from a plank or tree, such usage usually deforms the dart.

All pistols of this design, whether German or British, are borderline arms. The materials and general construction are of the toy variety, but the spring-air power is far beyond the toy classification and verges on that of the serious spring-air pistol.

B.S.F. Spring-Air Pistols. These pistols are currently available in the United States. They are imported by the Hoffritz Cutlery Company of New York City and are sold in retail stores controlled by that organization and by a jobbing subsidiary.

The better grade, known in Germany as the "Modell Match" was selected for testing. The somewhat cheaper Model 20 is the same design and caliber as the Match, but of somewhat lower power and with less efficient sights and trigger.

This model and design is actually a cut-down version of the formal barrel-cocking rifle, fitted with a bulky wood grip. The workmanship throughout is of a very high order. The sturdy rear sight is adjustable for both elevation and windage, and is positioned at the extreme rear of the cylindrical receiver tube. As a result, the sight line is unusually long, a factor making for more accurate shooting by the average man.

Like most pistols of this type, the barrel is held closed by a holding detent, not by a formal lock. It is necessary to bear down heavily on the forward end of the barrel to overcome the combination of close barrel fit and spring-loaded bolt, and in so doing it is possible to cut the hand on the front sight unless care is exercised. It is desirable to use wood cocking block as does Walther (see text) for safe and relatively easy cocking of the B.S.F., though the makers do not furnish one.

In tests on operation it was found that cocking can be eased considerably by breaking it down into two operations—first, while holding the pistol by its grip (with firing finger outside the triggerguard), with left hand press sharply down on muzzle area just to *open* the action; then, second, exert pressure with both hands simultaneously to bring the barrel down full length until the sear clicks into cocking engagement with the piston. With a little practice, because of the excellent type of cocking leverage furnished by a knuckle joint, the cocking stroke is not too difficult in relation to the exceptional power of this pistol.

While the general construction with spring chamber in prolongation of the barrel does not permit use of a very long barrel, as in the case of grip-housed spring (Walther) or concentric spring (American Hy Score), it does permit offsetting advantages. The spring positioning and type gives considerably more power than does the Walther, though tests indicate that for practical precision target shooting the added power is not an important factor. This pistol is simple to dismount and repair when this may be necessary, all the metal units being removable from the wood stock as a self-contained unit. The trigger adjusting screw is simple and efficient.

Like the Walther and various other barrel cockers, it is the most efficient type to load. .177 precision pellets are very small and easily battered. In this loading system the pellet is placed visibly directly into its barrel seat. For best accuracy and velocity the pellet should be forced into the rifling to a depth of about ½ inch as previously discussed.

The velocity and accuracy tests all indicate that this pistol will function best with either the German H-N Pellets sold by Hoffritz or the German RWS pellets. Note that all tests shown in table 3 are average. All were made without deep seating or micrometering the pellets. In short, these tests reflect what the average shooter should encounter with a new pistol using pellets from an average box and merely finger-loading them.

As to average accuracy, from machine rest this pistol very closely approaches the German Walther and the British Webley Senior, and in the hands of a match air shooter might be expected to equal their performance. At 30 feet with good German or British Webley ammunition a group of about 1 inch at 30 feet is possible. With other brands of pellets, while groups are good, too many "flyers" were encountered to allow small group averages.

TABLE 3
Example of Pellet Velocity Comparison Tests

H-N PELLETS		BENJAMIN PELLETS		CROSMAN PELLETS		WEBLEY PELLETS	
Shot number	Time interval	Shot number	Time interval	Shot number	Time interval	Shot number	Time interval
1	.01209	1	.01476	1	.01406	1	.01228
2	.01185	2	.01490	2	.01397	2	.01265
3	.01189	3	.01494	3	.01389	3	.01225
4	.01175	4	.01721	4	.01398	4	.01236
5	.01184	5	.01614	5	.01359	5	.01196
6	.01159	6	.01462	6	.01433	6	.01211
7	.01153	7	.01347	7	.01225	7	.01346
8	.01191	8	.01397	8	.01337	8	.01218
9	.01170	9	.01315	9	.01345	9	.01220
10	.01173	10	.01406	10	.01215	10	.01202
Total	.11788	Total	.14722	Total	.13504	Total	.12347
(Equals 425 f.p.s. average.)		(Equals 339 f.p.s. average.) (Note: Pellets tight fit.)		(Equals 370 f.p.s. average.)		(Equals 405 f.p.s. average.)	

As to top velocity obtainable, when H-N or RWS pellets were "miked" and carefully started in the rifling, this pistol gave the highest velocity of any air pistol made; 472 f.p.s. In this respect only the American Hy Score approached it. Again it should be stressed that achievable higher velocity in this caliber is not much of a factor in accuracy at maximum effective air-pistol ranges.

While this pistol rates as probably the highest powered spring-air weapon of its type, it must be kept in mind that it gains its power largely by virtue of its oversize design. It is not a compact, truly portable pistol by comparison with other lower powered, but equally accurate makes. Its bulk and large grip make it an excellent practice arm for grown men, but it is not a practical pistol for the average boy.

Diana No. 5, Wischo, Jung Roland, M.G. Herkules Pistols. These German pistols are all very much the same in basic design and in velocity, penetration, and accuracy. All were tested in caliber .177. They may be loosely classed as minor, and poorer, versions of the B.S.F.

All are barrel cockers of standard spring-air construction, the barrel being held in place by the familiar detent system of camming bolt and spring support. The Diana proved to have the most efficient leverage system for cocking. The Herkules was slightly more powerful than the others. All are merely pistol versions of respective barrel-cocking rifles. Compression springs housed in a tube to the rear of the barrel gave fast, direct piston-power thrust. The added power thereby gained, however, was somewhat offset by the longer barrels used in other systems. Sear operation was uniformly fair, the Diana giving the best trigger let-off of the samples available for testing.

The Diana was also superior in that the rear sight, while a cheap stamping, was positioned far back on the receiver tube and thus gave a greater sight line, which allowed rather better accuracy in bench rest shooting. The other models have a cheap stamped sight mounted on the barrel itself just forward of the breech. All pistols have a completely contained metal assembly, which is housed in a one-piece wood stock, screw or bolt retained. The Wischo barrel was rather better rifled than the others, but no appreciable increase in accuracy was apparent.

These pistols are all of relatively good construction, though the Wischo showed evidence of better attention to materials used. By good pistol standards all are relatively clumsy and ungainly, but hang, balance, and pointing qualities are adequate. The Diana weight distribution was better and allowed rather better instinctive pointing for fast plinking. All models tested had rifled barrels.

These pistols do not approach the B.S.F. Match for quality of materials, finish, fitting, or accuracy. On the other hand, they cost less and are all more nearly true pistol size than the B.S.F. They are entirely adequate for plinking and as an air pistol for beginners.

Velocities. In view of the relatively small number of these pistols in the United States, velocity testing was confined to use of German H-N pellets. The Diana No. 5, 10-shot average was 311 f.p.s. Wischo average was 299 f.p.s.; Jung Roland, 286 f.p.s.; Herkules, 328 f.p.s.

Accuracy. All these pistols about averaged out on bench-rest shooting tests at about 2.5-inch groups at 30 feet, though the Wischo was the most consistent.

Oiling is a very important factor in all pistols of this design, and velocities could be lowered considerably and built up a little by viscosity of oil and regularity of application. The Herkules in particular was subject to dieseling which increased velocity but impaired accuracy, a condition apparently produced by greater spring compression.

Falke Model 33 Spring-Air Pistol. From the standpoint of manufacture, materials, hardening, finish, and design, this is one of the best spring-air pistol types. While it is a grip-lever cocker, it has most of the advantages inherent in the barrel-cocking system with several added advantages. It is rather surprising that this design, which is priced well under other German match pistols, has not been more generally accepted. It is not currently imported into the United States.

Pulling out the underlever which has a locking action, also draws the barrel ahead out of engagement with the forward extension of the compression tube. Continuing the forward lever movement elevates the barrel breech for loading directly into the breech, then forces the cocking lever back to compress the mainspring. Holding the pistol in the right hand while pulling out to the left with the left hand allows application of excellent leverage and easy cocking with the spring employed. However, since the design is held within reasonable pistol dimensions for overall length, the compression-tube length limits spring power, and the resultant velocity obtainable (see table 4) was relatively low, though entirely adequate for maximum accuracy at air-pistol ranges. The breech seal, while theoretically more efficient than that of the standard barrel cocker which depends upon breech fits, detent, and washer exclusively, actually wears in rather fast. However, with adequate neoprene-type barrel seals, there is no mechanical reason why it should not outlast the barrel-cocking designs in hermetically confining the compressed air during firing.

While there is some possibility of pinching fingers while closing the cocking lever, this is readily prevented if reasonable care is taken. Sights were the poorest and cheapest feature of the pistol tested. Caliber was .177. The barrel was well rifled.

TABLE 4

GERMAN FALKE PISTOL TEST—VELOCITY AVERAGE WITH RWS PELLETS

Shot number	Time interval
1	.01627
2	.01597
3	.01721
4	.01832
5	.01571
6	.01742
7	.01644
8	.01659
9	.01670
10	.01889
Total	.16984
(Equals 296 f.p.s. average.)	

Accuracy was about the same as for B.S.F., several groups averaging 1 inch at 25 feet, 9 out of 10 grouping 1 inch at 30 feet on several targets, a fact which again indicates that under 30 feet, velocity is not a particularly important factor in air-pistol shooting so long as it is in the 300 f.p.s. range. At greater distances the very light weight of the .177 pellet (under 8 grains average) neutralizes any added velocity.

Walther Air Pistol. This pistol really belongs in a class by itself. It is an example of the finest gunmaking art applied to an air-pistol trainer. It is the most expensive of all the air pistols. Its power is relatively low, but its accuracy in tests was equalled only by the British Webley. It must be kept in mind that this pistol was developed by Walther to simulate their famous .22 Olympia target auto pistol. In materials, fittings, finish, and design it is equalled only by the Webley, a pistol which also is a product of fine gunmakers rather than of air-rifle makers.

This pistol has only two minor points which merit professional criticism: (1) The rear sight, while fully adjustable and adequate for air-pistol shooting, is not the husky construction found in the B.S.F. Match Model, for example, and is a somewhat jarring note on an otherwise ultra-high-quality arm. On two models tested, the rear sight platform worked loose from the sheet-metal spring base. The flat spring and adjusting screw elevation system is at variance with the otherwise fine gun quality of this arm. (2) The breech is held closed by spring detent as in formal barrel cockers, rather than by positive lock as in the American Hy Score and the British Webley. This means that added leverage must be exerted in the opening movement before cocking action starts.

Everything else about this pistol is on the positive side for its type of design. The barrel hinge point and barrel length and construction permit relatively easy cocking when the wood cocking block provided is used. Note that the pistol can be cocked without use of this device, but the average shooter will have to exercise considerable care not to injure his hand or the rugged front sight in so doing. Still another factor to be guarded against is to avoid hand pinching when *closing* the action, since the cocking lever also forms the triggerguard and front grip. (See Walther photos in text.)

In adapting the old British Jeffries cocking system, Walther has been able to utilize the normally objectionable jump of the pistol as the unleashed compression spring drives the piston ahead of it to compress air for power. The dual springs in the grip, the piston, and gasket construction tend to give a simulation of the normal recoil *of a powder arm,* a valuable factor where the air pistol is intended as a trainer for cartridge-arm use.

By incorporating an elementary trigger disconnector of the automatic pistol order, Walther has also evaded another trouble found in most air pistols—the danger of accidentally pressing the trigger and releasing the action while the pistol is open. In the Walther, only when the pistol is fully closed and the underside of the breech is depressing the disconnector can the piston be released by trigger pull. Only a few other pistols have this feature, and in none is it as fully developed as in the Walther.

The barrel is, again like the Webley alone, a fine-quality forging, which is deep-drilled, reamed, and rifled. While the author has handled many individual air arms using precision drawn tubing which shot as well as the Walther or the Webley, it is a fact that none would do so with quite the consistency. However, as an expression of personal opinion based on experience and observation, it seems more likely that the care in watching and holding dimensions, and particularly care in sizing the bore and rifling, are more important here than the matter of use of tubing or forgings.

The Walther sights are worthy of special attention. The front sight is retained in the ramp by a screw. Three varieties of front sights are furnished to allow the user to select the style best suited to his personal vision and sighting preferences, and they may be readily interchanged by merely removing the screw, lifting the sight out of the base and replacing it with an alternate. This sight is husky, sturdy, and beautifully designed. The rear sight by comparison is fragile in the ordinary air-pistol manner. Its sight base is a spring metal stamping. To elevate, press the sight down and turn the large flathead adjusting screw to allow the spring to rise higher. Windage is efficiently controlled, on the other hand, by the formal side-screw adjustment in the sight platform. All adjusting marks on this pistol indicate a movement of 3 millimeters (.117 inch approximate) at 6 to 8 yards, the standard range at which the pistol is intended to be used.

Velocity. Velocity was stated by Walther to the author as about 110 meters (358 feet) per second. In tests with two pistols, using RWS and H-N pellets, author's velocity was substantially lower, averaging about 305 f.p.s. Accuracy, on the other hand, agreed substantially with the maker's claim and enclosed targets.

As an average example, the interval timer record in table 5 is indicative of findings.

TABLE 5

WALTHER PISTOL TEST—H-N PELLETS

Shot number	Time interval
1	.01600
2	.01598
3	.01634
4	.01702
5	.01741
6	.01649
7	.01707
8	.01591
9	.01652
10	.01535
Total	.16909

(Equals 305 f.p.s.)

Note 1. 1 foot equals 0.3048 meter.
Note 2. Whether used with RWS or H-N pellets, penetration was rather low, not that this is of any importance in a pistol intended purely for target shooting. The usual .177 pellet penetration at 10 feet is of the order of ¼ inch in soft fir or pine. Many of these pellets would not penetrate deeply enough to stay in the plank, and unless hit head-on would occasionally glance off.

Accuracy. In machine-rest shooting only the Webley *consistently* equalled the Walther. In off-hand and arm-supported (bench-rest) shooting equal scores occasionally were made by the above and by the Falke and B.S.F.

Unlike other makers, Walther encloses in each box with the pistol an actual target shot at 6 yards with that particular pistol to indicate its 5-shot group possibilities. While it does not necessarily follow that the average shooter with average ammunition can regularly duplicate the target, it does indicate what the specific pistol is capable of doing. Three-quarter-inch groups are possible with reasonable consistency, and at times the pistol will shoot ½-inch groups at 6 to 8 yards. Most other pistols, regardless of advertising claims, will not on an average approach this record. In passing it might be noted that it is much easier to shoot 5-shot groups, and that such are probably a fairer test of an arm's reasonable capabilities than the 10-shot strings used by the author.

Haenel Model 28. While these pistols are offered for sale in Europe as new manufacture, the only specimens obtainable by the author were in every respect identical with prewar construction. Generally speaking it is possible to spot postwar (Russian Zone) German manufacture. The only obtainable Haenels were definitely prewar quality. Steel and aluminum models were encountered.

This design, while interesting, and embodying several good characteristics, is not as efficient as most of the current types. It has some of the good and bad features of the typical barrel cocker—though the Haenel itself is NOT barrel cocked. Thus the barrel breaks down at the breech *for loading,* the only pressure needed, however, being that to overcome the spring detent. The design allows simulating the lines and balance of the Luger, for those who like that design, and also permits direct piston thrust since the mainspring is housed in the tube in direct prolongation of the barrel. This system of course gives a relatively short barrel in relation to the overall length, and also limits the length and power of the mainspring.

By using a formal locking catch rather than a heavy spring-loaded camming bolt to lock the grip and cocking mechanism to the receiver, the Haenel permits the start of the cocking operation (breaking the grip down on the hinge) to be easier than is customary. However, the leverage provided is inferior to that of pistols like the Hy Score, which is a variant of this cocking system, and the velocity is considerably lower than in pistols with more efficient cocking systems which allow longer and/or more powerful springs.

The all-aluminum frame and barrel-casing type is very light by comparison with the standard steel construction, but due to the Luger-pattern weight distribution, the shooting qualities are not adversely affected, though the jump is rather more pronounced than in competing makes.

Velocity was relatively low for .177 rifled pistols. The chronograph interval timer readings in table 6 were the *best* obtained, the average being about 25 f.p.s. lower.

TABLE 6

HAENEL PISTOL TEST—RWS PELLETS

Shot number	Time interval
1	.01817
2	.01778
3	.01877
4	.01820
5	.01861
6	.01825
7	.01883
8	.01822
9	.01836
10	.01889
Total	.18408

(Equals 273 f.p.s. average.)

Accuracy was only fair by comparison with most other makes, machine-rest tests at 30 feet never averaging below 2-inch groups for 10 shots. This pistol, while one of the most impressive in appearance, proved to be inferior in performance to most of the better grades of competitive air pistols.

Great Britain

While there are several makes of spring-air pistols made in Great Britain, only the Webley series can be classed as serious precision types.

The Diana series as made by Millard Brothers is the same as the German types made by the originators of the designs as detailed in the text.

Of the Diana 2, Thunderbolt, and Gat pattern, all of

which are but minor modifications of the original German Diana No. 2, and the I.G.A. and Heym patterns, only the Gat is sold in the United States. It is a borderline design, being constructed of sheet metal on the toy pattern, but having power well above the toy average because of its powerful spring.

The Gat is imported into the United States and sold here by J. Galef and Son of New York City.

The Webley Series.

The Junior. While the basic operating system of this model is the same as that of the other two, the construction is lighter. A study of the photos in the Webley section will immediately show the basically lower cost lines of the pistol, though the quality of the workmanship itself is uniformly high.

The sights are fixed. The barrel is smooth-bored. The pistol is made in caliber .177 only. The lock is the old original Webley serrated spring-supported sliding catch above the barrel at the breech end. The construction is lighter and the spring power substantially lower than in the other models.

This pistol was specifically designed for teen-agers, though it must be said that the cocking effort required is still considerable. It is, nevertheless, a quality product not to be confused with the Gat type of pistol.

Webley states a velocity of approximately 290 f.p.s. for this pistol at a 20-foot range. On a runthrough of a routine Potter 10-shot test at that range to conform to the maker's standards, using Webley pellets, the average velocity was 288 f.p.s. With German RWS pellets, the average reached 298 f.p.s. On an average, all Webley claims were more closely borne out by tests than those of any other spring-air pistol maker.

The Mark I. The current model as tested provides an interesting commentary on the basic soundness of the Webley design, as it is merely an improved form of the first pistol ever made by this firm.

Its cocking stroke is similar to that of the Junior, being accomplished by releasing the same type of barrel-lock catch, lifting the barrel at the breech end through the same style linkage and the same arc. It differs in that it is made on the basic forged frame of the heavier model, has a standard screw-adjustable trigger projecting from the front of the triggerguard, and is fitted with an elevating rear sight. While it is made in both .177 and .22 calibers (barrels may be interchanged in the same pistol), all barrels are precision rifled. Darts are not advised in barrels rifled to Webley quality because of danger of injury to the rifling caused by occasional steel dart heads which may be oversized or battered.

Because of weight, sights, rifling, and trigger pull, this pistol is capable of a very high degree of accuracy. In his *Textbook of Revolvers and Pistols*, published in 1935, Major General Julian S. Hatcher lists velocity then obtained with the Webley Mark I of that period as 273 f.p.s. in caliber .22 and 367 f.p.s. in caliber .177 in his own tests. Commenting on accuracy possibilities despite the peculiar jump induced by the compression system, he tells of having seen a group shot at 25 feet which could be covered with a dime—which is to say approximately ¾-inch.

The present author testing 1956 manufactured models of the Mark I developed 309 f.p.s. with the .22 caliber (manufacturing average states 314) and 381 f.p.s. for the .177 (manufacturer average states 350) using Webley pellets. As to accuracy, machine-rest tests were about 1 inch, a fact which indicates that a qualified shooter with this pistol should often shoot ¾-inch or slightly less, since in actual practice it is found that a trained marksman with any type of arm learns to compensate automatically for recoil factors in particular, to a degree not achieved by a fixed mechanical rest. In short, the history of impartial tests through the years attests to quality maintenance by Webley.

The Senior. The quality of materials and workmanship in this pistol is equalled only by the German Walther. It is approached only by the German B.S.F.

Its velocity is exceeded by the American Hy Score (which see), but the added velocity was not found to affect shooting qualities in any way at air-pistol distances.

This pistol is made to best firearms manufacturing standards, a fact which is reflected in its accuracy and consistency. The manufacturer tries to control diesel firing by advising lubrication on a limited basis and with suitable oil, as diesel firing increases velocity but tends to produce "fliers" which increase group size when shooting for accuracy. As has been previously pointed out, it is possible to increase velocity substantially in this design, but the manufacturer has held it within limits which give maximum accuracy possibilities at air-pistol ranges while still holding it within the power ranges which would invite British legislation.

The entire Webley line is sold throughout the world. Abercrombie & Fitch import them to the United States for sale here. However, the bulk of factory sales is still in areas covered by British legal requirements.

The Webley cocking system provides, in its original form, perhaps the most efficient air-pistol leverage ever commercially produced. However, the linkage from the barrel, which is the lever, to the rim of the pistonhead, which is drawn forward to compress the mainspring in the tube under the barrel, is relatively fragile; and only the superb hardening of materials and the close fitting done by Webley permits successful use of this system.

The Senior Model because of the double linkage obtained through a toggle action instead of the direct, single pull of the earlier models, is *mechanically* substantially easier to cock, the action taking place over a much longer arc. However, in the observation of the author, this extra long throw seemed to make cocking somewhat more difficult for several young men and adults to whom it was handed for cocking. The difficulty stemmed from the fact that the added length of throw was just not suitable physically for the average user—the distance was too great to permit *continuity* of maximum continuous pull. Cocking usually took two grip stages.

Nevertheless the manufacturer when queried about this aspect stated that the acceptance of the double joint had been so satisfactory that alteration of other models to this system was under contemplation.

While granting that the double-lever cocking permitted *starting* of compression easier than in the Mark I system, users observed by the author found it easier to *complete* the cocking stroke in a continuous movement with the single lever. As an experiment, the author made a barrel and barrel-lock alteration which proved easier to cock than the long-throw double lever. It might be added that these experiments were undertaken as a check on claims by other makers who, while admitting the basic superiority of the Webley cocking principle, still sought to gloss over the advantage.

One other claim made against the Webley by a competitor was the danger of bending the barrel when it served as a lever. In very rugged actual tests, it was determined that only deliberate misuse would do this, and that similar or equivalent misuse would ruin any air pistol made.

Velocity tests on the .22 caliber ran slightly lower than the maker's averages, though they were conducted at somewhat shorter ranges to get a fair comparison with other makes. Velocity tests on the .177, on the other hand, ran somewhat higher. The average for the .22 was 320 f.p.s. and that of the .177, 381 f.p.s. These differences are negligible, actually, and could be accounted for on many bases ranging from lubrication to ammunition differences.

The outstanding feature was the *consistency* achieved, a factor which appeared to be related directly to manufacturing qualities.

At 25 feet and at 30 feet, the Senior targeted well in a 1-inch circle. Only the Walther equalled this consistency, though both the B.S.F. and the Hy Score would on occasion make similar groups. The Webley system of rifling (very wide lands with narrow grooves) appeared to be a factor here, judged by the rifling prints on the skirts of pellets recovered after passing through a paper target into a cotton backing. Deliberately seating the pellets for sizing and starting into the rifling (by forcing them ½-inch into the open breech with an awl) increased the velocity slightly, but did not produce any appreciable increase in accuracy. Yet in every other pistol or rifle tested except the Walther, accuracy thus achieved was noticeably greater.

Once the shooter has learned to compensate for the individual jump, lunge, or recoil characteristics of any spring-air arm (none occurs in pneumatic or CO_2 weapons), if the pellets are of good quality and properly seated, accuracy appears to be controlled more by the quality of the barrel and the rifling than by any other single factor, assuming proper lubrication and trigger pull of course. In the matter of barrel manufacture, Webley has no superior in the field of air arms judged by tests and inspections conducted on an impartial basis.

Any air pistol will eventually need replacement of pistonhead and gaskets whether through use, abuse, or lack of use. Since no valves are employed in the spring-air system, such designs can be made to permit dismounting and overhaul by the owner or by an average gunsmith, since factory parts are available and basically interchangeable. In this respect, too, Webley is superior on an overall average, though the continued use of close-fitted metal piston rings might be questioned in the face of the success of the neoprene-type materials. If care is exercised in removing and replacing the ring, the Webley may be repaired by any average mechanic when necessary—which should not be very often. This is possible because of the design and materials used. Other pistols utilizing stampings must be returned to the factory or scrapped when any considerable replacement work is required.

United States

Hy Score Spring-Air Pistols. These pistols are the subject of considerable misunderstanding in many places visited by the author. Many dealers insist—and believe—that they are of European design and manufacture, and that Hy Score merely imports them. This is not correct, and the misapprehension doubtless stems from the fact that the principals of the Hy Score Corporation with whom the dealers have come in contact are naturalized Americans of European origin; together with the fact that Hy Score does import German air rifles—which curiously, some other dealers insist on classing as American made —and that the pistols in general outline resemble the familiar German Haenel air pistol and the Luger pistol.

Hy Score pistols are among the most powerful air pistols made. In impartial competitive testing by the author, only the German B.S.F. Match Model pistol, made only in caliber .177, consistently outranked it in velocity, and that by a very small margin. It was the most powerful of all currently mass-manufactured spring-air designs in .22 caliber.

All spring-air pistols currently made are relatively difficult to cock, though when compared with pneumatic pistols it must be remembered that spring-air designs require only one stroke to achieve a power which calls for a large number of strokes with a pneumatic. The easiest cocking designs found were the obsolete British Abas-Major with underlever and ratchet and the obsolete German Zenit, closely followed by the current German Falke underlever. However, none of these pistols had the power of the comparable caliber (.177) Hy Score.

The Hy Score is relatively easy to cock because of two basic factors: First, it is fitted with a breech-lock catch (as in the Webley and Haenel) which is manually disengaged, hence does not require the user to overcome a heavy detent spring as in the B.S.F. and similar designs. Second, by using the entire grip as a cocking point while pulling upwards against the overlapping receiver head, maximum effective leverage is applied within the maximum arc through which it can be applied with a single *continuing* manual operation. You do not, as in the Webley, have to grip the fingers ahead of the latch area, but have complete freedom to lift from the extreme rear of the pistol.

The very high velocity achieved is a product of several factors, some good and some not considered desirable by most makers. First is the concentric design. Since the barrel forms a guide shaft for the piston, it is possible to get an extremely long barrel for the overall length of the pistol, while still retaining pistol dimensions and appearance. This is an excellent feature, affording not only maximum barrel length but also maximum piston stroke. Second is spring material and construction. In all the arms tested, only Webley and Walther demonstrated an equivalent (or somewhat better) usage of spring technology. This, combined with the use of low-cost, easy-fitting neoprene O-rings instead of more expensive metal rings, serves to give above-average air compression for

243

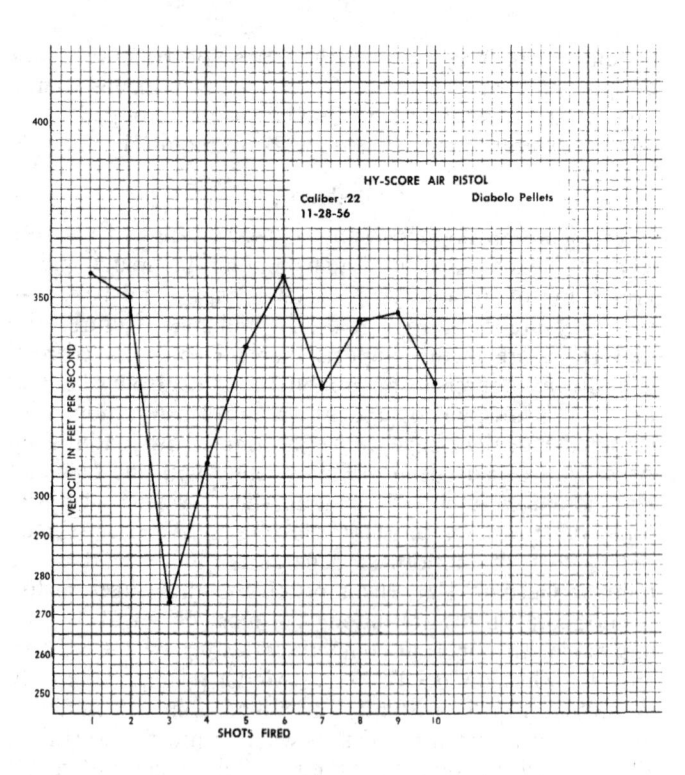

the stroke factors involved. Finally, and in author's tests not too desirable, is the rather deliberate buildup of the diesel effect to achieve added power. If the piston is lubricated about every 100 shots, velocity will appear at its maximum. If, for instance, the pistol is fired without pellet (not a desirable thing to do because of danger of piston injury, but something which is a common occurence), then fired with a pellet in place in a dark room, sparks will be noted at muzzle as the pellet emerges. Here is clear indication that the propulsion is actually by the mild explosive effect of the oil and air mixture in the compression chamber, not merely of the compressed air. While all spring-air arms will do this at times, none were as noticeable or regular as the Hy Score. It was, for the type of explosion induced, relatively consistent; but occasionally the effect would vary enough to give a velocity differential of 90 feet or more per second between shots in a string.

The accuracy achieved was good for a stamped pistol but not consistent. When fired with pellets taken directly from the box furnished by Hy Score, it did not in machine-rest tests begin to approach the 1-inch grouping claimed for it. However, when pellets were "miked" and weighed for consistency and forced into the rifling with a loading awl, 1-inch groups were achieved fairly often at the 30-foot range specified.

Jump was like the pattern found in the Webley, since both operate on a rearward piston thrust, but was much more violent and difficult to control. The barrel in this design actually floats and is not rigidly locked as in the Webley.

The trigger mechanism which allows cocking merely by opening and closing the action without compressing the mainspring is an excellent feature of the Hy Score. In all other pistols the arm can be "dry fired" only by completing the cocking stroke, and snapping very often without a cushioning pellet in the barrel will injure the piston. This is avoided by the Hy Score design, of course.

It should be noted, however, that when the pistol is open and cocked, the downward protruding sear *can* be released to let the piston go forward and the action close violently. Granted that no sensible shooter should do this, amateurs to whom the pistol was handed *did* do it on several occasions, hence this warning. It is an unusual commentary that only Walther has had the foresight to install a simple disconnector to entirely prevent this happening.

Without the special trigger system the Hy Score would require a 10- or 12-pound pull for piston release, but with the system employed which pre-sets the trigger as the action is opened, you get the effect of a hair trigger, which results in a good, light pull, very near to the 3 pounds claimed for it.

Single-Shot Models. The loading system consists of turning a shutter to expose the barrel, dropping the pellet, then closing the shutter before firing. The shutter should be completely closed before firing, but it is possible to fire without complete closure. However, there can be only a malfunction resulting therefrom, not injury to the shooter. If pellet happens to be burred, oversized, or defective, the shutter may not be closable, as the fit is very tight. Very little trouble of this nature was experienced.

Repeating Models. In two specimens tested, these did not work too well on feeding. Judging by the manufacturer's instructions which accompanied the pistols, others also have had trouble with consistent feeding. This must always be expected in ANY repeating mechanism using a fragile, shaped, thin-skirted pellet of the Diabolo design. The author has used several air pistols and rifles with very efficient feed systems, both gravity and spring types, for loading *ball*-type ammunition. With the sole exception of the complicated and fragile slide system once used by Crosman rifles, no repeating system examined has been found even reasonably reliable for feeding Diabolos.

"If," says the Hy Score instruction sheet, "the pellets are badly deformed, it may be necessary to push them into the breech with a nail." In tests it was found necessary to force them in when pellets were OK to eye inspection, but actually had oversized skirts. In pistols with accessible barrel breeches, such as the B.S.F., Walther, and Webley, slightly oversized pellets could be forced in with the fingers far enough for the action to be closed. With the Hy Score when such a condition was encountered, a loading awl was used to force the pellet in, but no further difficulty was encountered.

It must be kept in mind when using this repeater that the pellets feed from the revolving magazine ONLY by gravity. The pistol muzzle must be held down to allow this, and if there is trouble feeding them into the magazine itself, then another box (or brand) of pellets should be used.

Another magazine "don't" supplied by the manufacturer should be well heeded: "Don't turn the magazine until the pellet in the center is shot out." Double-loading this pistol will foul it up.

Finally, if you have any trouble with a Hy Score pistol

remember the maker warns: "Do not dismantle any part of the gun. Our 60-day guarantee is void if gun has been tampered with." This pistol was designed for production stamping-type manufacture, and if you tamper with it you will only compound the troubles. Pistols made by arms makers such as Walther and Webley are designed and intended to be treated like firearms, and may be safely disassembled by any competent mechanic. The Hy Score was not designed by a firearms firm, and it was never intended to fit completely into the firearms scheme of things. It is a precision product *of its type;* but its repair or replacement is a matter for the manufacturer only.

If you follow carefully the instructions given, this pistol will give very little trouble during its lifetime. Barring the occasional dud which can turn up in any product wherever made, or by whom, if you have trouble with the Hy Score which requires disassembling, the chances are that you are personally responsible.

Note that this does not apply to the matter of ammunition. This maker also warns that the guarantee is void if you use any but Hy Score pellets. Exhaustive tests by the author in his own pistols show that Hy Score on an average sells very good pellets. These are not manufactured by Hy Score, but are purchased in England from I.C.I., Britain's largest ammunition maker. The quality in general is above reproach. However, many other pellets worked just as well in the Hy Score as those sold under its trade name, while Diabolo pellets made in Germany quite consistently gave better results than any others. Some average velocity results given in table 7 are indicative.

SPRING-AIR RIFLES OF THE WORLD

Austria

One specimen of the Tyrolean Arms Company air rifle was tested. This elementary barrel cocker is a very minor variation of the common Diana patterns, though it is priced very much higher. Caliber .177 is rifled. The testing was limited, as nothing about either the design or the manufacturing quality warranted particular attention. This rifle is not currently sold in the United States.

Average velocity was about 360 f.p.s., the spring being relatively weak.

Czechoslovakia

Kovo—Commercial. The only Czech commercial rifle available was the Kovo. This is an elementary barrel cocker not varying in any important aspect from the common German Diana from which it was copied. The barrel was well rifled. Caliber, .177. Fitting and finish were both about average, not of the quality associated with the customary Czech firearms by any means.

Velocity averaged about 481 f.p.s., low for a heavy spring-powered rifle in this caliber. Accuracy was about average with the middle-priced Diana lines.

VZ35—Military. This is one of the finest quality and best designed air rifles encountered. (See text for description.) It is a repeater using lead or steel ball-bearing-type projectiles of 4.5-mm. caliber. (The balls "miked" an average of .1725-inch.)

Cocking is relatively easy, particularly when compared with the effort required in many of the German Falke and similar patterns. The magazine works perfectly, being the easiest loading system encountered, gravity fed. It is, of course, suitable only for round balls, however, not for Diabolo pellets.

Accuracy up to 25 feet is exceptional. This rifle does do what many others only advertise they do—make ¾-inch groups. The velocity, while relatively low in relation to average heavy-duty barrel-cocking .177's, is entirely adequate as a military trainer where its purpose is to simulate cartridge-rifle training on a subcaliber basis, and is high in relation to the cocking effort involved.

No Czech-made ammunition was available for testing, but the two tests listed in table 8 give a good average picture of the velocity capabilities of this superior rifle.

VZ47. This rifle, a much cheapened version of the VZ35, was somewhat easier to cock because of a lengthened lever handle. Velocity was of the order of the VZ35, but accuracy was not nearly as good on an average.

TABLE 7

HY SCORE PISTOL COMPARISON TESTS

.22 HY SCORE PELLET		.22 RWS PELLET		AMERICAN PELLET "X"	
Shot number	Time interval	Shot number	Time interval	Shot number	Time interval
1	.00929	1	.01261	1	.01485
2	.01422	2	.01404	2	.01726
3	.01697	3	.01382	3	.01619
4	.01368	4	.01359	4	.01649
5	.01395	5	.01408	5	.01504
6	.01401	6	.01400	6	.01738
7	.01417	7	.01346	7	.02042
8	.01407	8	.01352	8	.01644
9	.01422	9	.01425	9	.01608
10	.01348	10	.01422	10	.01637
Total	.13806	Total	.13759	Total	.16652
(Equals 362 f.p.s.)		(Equals 363 f.p.s.)		(Equals 302 f.p.s.)	

Note. Hy Score claims 350 f.p.s. average for its .22 pistol. With both German and British made pellets, this velocity was achieved regularly. Using British-made Webley pellets, which are to somewhat different specifications, velocity was lower by about 48 f.p.s. Conversely, Hy Score pellets as made in England by I.C.I. would not always fit in the Webley pistols without sizing.

TABLE 8

CZECH MILITARY TRAINER TESTS

U.S. LEAD AIR-RIFLE SHOT		SWISS HAMMERLI STEEL AIR-RIFLE SHOT	
Shot number	Time interval	Shot number	Time interval
1	.01109	1	.01044
2	.01123	2	.01039
3	.01134	3	.01060
4	.01222	4	.01059
5	.01057	5	.01043
6	.01102		
7	.01021	Total	.05245
8	.01196	(Equals 477 f.p.s.)	
9	.01259		
10	.01020		
Total	.11243		
(Equals 445 f.p.s.)			

Note. U.S. lead balls not a satisfactory fit. Swiss steel balls extremely uniform.

Germany

Diana. While the entire German-made Diana line was examined and studied, tests were run only on the important models where the time and expense could be justified. The entire line, covering all stages from toy varieties through precision barrel cockers and underlevers, represents good buys for the prices asked.

In the field of expensive precision air rifles, several German and British makes have forged ahead of the Diana in design and to some extent in performance. In the intermediate class of medium priced "plinking" air rifles, the Diana line provided the best average performances.

(Note: Four models of the Diana are sold in the United States by the Hy Score Arms Corporation. The importer retails them at approximately $9, $15, $20, and $30, designating them Hy Score Models 805, 806, 801, and 807 respectively. Only one, the so-called 807, has any precision capabilities. This is the Diana M27, probably the best buy in the Diana line, under whatever name it may be sold.)

Two model types, the Diana 35 and 50 series, are sold in the United States by the Stoeger Arms Corporation, who have their imports roll-stamped with their own trade brand Peerless. These models sell from $35 to $85, and except for the lowest priced model which has fixed sights, all are in the better class of air rifles capable of match target use.

The entire "Diana" line sold in Great Britain and manufactured in Scotland by Millard Brothers is but a duplicate of the earlier German Diana patterns. (See text for details.) Spot-checking and testing of the British-made line indicates that quality of models made is about the same as the German.

Diana Model 15. This is a borderline construction of barrel cocker, made of sheet metal and fitted with a cheap barrel liner. Velocity average on tests ran 286 f.p.s. Shooting qualities about in a class with the Daisy toy variety. This is a smooth-bore single-shot design. In Germany, where it serves as a trainer for the boy whose next gun will be a better grade of barrel cocker, it doubtless has its place, but it is not a good value by comparison with the Daisy line. Caliber is .177 only.

Diana Models 22 and 23. These are boys' pattern barrel cockers of low cost but more satisfactory construction. Barrels are of steel tubing, well button-rifled. They are made only in caliber .177. These models have been imitated in Austria, Italy, and Spain. They are relatively easy to cock, as their spring power is comparatively low.

One velocity test with rifled-barrel Model 23 averaged 372 f.p.s. Routine machine-rest group indicated good barrel, as 10 shots at 30 feet were under 1 inch. Trigger pull was poor.

Diana Model 27. This heavier version of the M25 tested out as the best buy in the Diana line. (It costs 48 marks with a rifled barrel from the distributor G. Genschow at Hamburg.)

The adjustable trigger system employed has been copied or used as a basis for design by many of the better grade air-rifle makers throughout the industry. Parts are well designed and properly hardened. The adjusting screw permitted pull down to 3 pounds, quite a remarkable achievement to hold a 165-pound spring compression in leash.

Two series of tests were run with this Diana model, one on a gun imported directly, the other with a gun obtained from Hy Score Arms Corporation. Both models were caliber .177. The best average velocity groups are shown in table 9.

TABLE 9
DIANA M25 AND M27 RIFLE TESTS

HY SCORE PELLETS		GERMAN H-N PELLETS		U. S. PELLET "X"	
Shot number	Time interval	Shot number	Time interval	Shot number	Time interval
1	.00837	1	.00825	1	.00791
2	.00798	2	.00816	2	.00966
3	.00988	3	.00946	3	.01067
4	.00915	4	.00757	4	.01111
5	.00903	5	.00762	5	.01109
6	.01000	6	.00933	6	.00842
7	.00972	7	.00802	7	.00896
8	.00997	8	.00880	8	.00847
9	.00844	9	.00707	9	.00954
10	.00813	10	.00903	10	.01083
Total	.09067	Total	.08331	Total	.09666
(Equals 551 f.p.s.)		(Equals 600 f.p.s.)		(Equals 518 f.p.s.)	

Note 1. Hy Score pellets are British-made by I.C.I.
Note 2. Control test with German RWS pellets averaged 596 f.p.s.
Note 3. Control test with U.S. pellets, brand "Y," averaged 556 f.p.s.

It should be pointed out that this Model 27 series is very close to peak power for any spring-air gun currently manufactured, and that maximum power *in all German-made* guns without exception was achieved with *German-made* pellets.

The combination of well-rifled barrel, excellent trigger system, and spring power provided better than average accuracy with this rifle in its price class. Because the rear sight is mounted on the barrel, the sight line is short, about 16 inches.

Diana Model 35 Series. This rifle is currently sold in .22 caliber only as the Peerless Model 35 by Stoeger Arms Corporation at a retail price of $35. It has "fixed" sights in the sense that they are barrel-mounted, but the rear sight is adjustable. This is a larger and heavier version of the Diana 27 (Hy Score 807), being 4 inches longer and about 2 pounds heavier. The finish of the two is almost identical, but for the serious shooter the Model 35 is a much better buy at the Stoeger price.

On actual velocity and machine-rest tests the M35 series proved to have no more deliverable power than the M27, but accuracy was of a considerably higher order on an average. The M35 ranked quite high among the .22 caliber group, averaging 496 f.p.s. with German-made pellets and 481 with British and one U.S. make. Groups were not appreciably lower than with the M27, but grouping was *more consistent,* a factor probably attributable largely to weight and vibration factors.

Under the trade name Peerless Model 35B, the rifle is the same except it is fitted with special receiver sights (see text). Price is $46. (Note: In Germany this model is also available with special diopter sights and with special Olympic match stocks for precision shooters.)

Diana Model 50 Series. These are underlever cocking

TABLE 10

DIANA (STOEGER "PEERLESS") M35 COMPARISON TESTS

GERMAN RWS PELLETS		U.S. PELLET "X"		U.S. PELLET "Y"		GERMAN H-N PRECISION BALLS	
Shot number	Time interval	Shot number	Time interval	Shot number	Time interval	Shot number	Time interval
1	.00983 (509 f.p.s.)	1	.01535 (326 f.p.s.)	1	.01121 (445 f.p.s.)	1	.01665 (300 f.p.s.)
2	.01056 (473 f.p.s.)	2	.01795 (289 f.p.s.)	2	.01166 (429 f.p.s.)	2	.01942 (257 f.p.s.)
3	.01093 (456 f.p.s.)	3	.02243 (223 f.p.s.)	3	.01113 (448 f.p.s.)	3	.01933 (258 f.p.s.)
4	.01458 (372 f.p.s.)	4	.01484 (337 f.p.s.)	4	.01063 (470 f.p.s.)	4	.01661 (300 f.p.s.)
5	.00954 (525 f.p.s.)	5	.01237 (405 f.p.s.)	5	.01179 (424 f.p.s.)	5	.01881 (252 f.p.s.)
6	.01095 (456 f.p.s.)	6	.01897 (264 f.p.s.)	6	.01487 (336 f.p.s.)	6	.01715 (291 f.p.s.)
7	.00973 (514 f.p.s.)	7	.02126 (235 f.p.s.)	7	.01456 (344 f.p.s.)	7	.02147 (232 f.p.s.)
8	.01226 (407 f.p.s.)	8	.01619 (309 f.p.s.)	8	.01461 (342 f.p.s.)	8	.02017 (248 f.p.s.)
9	.01450 (347 f.p.s.)	9	.01547 (324 f.p.s.)	9	.01365 (366 f.p.s.)	9	.02148 (232 f.p.s.)
10	.00993 (504 f.p.s.)	10	.01862 (268 f.p.s.)	10	.01549 (323 f.p.s.)	10	.02066 (242 f.p.s.)
(Average equals 466 f.p.s.)		(Average equals 298 f.p.s.)		(Average equals 392 f.p.s.)		(Average equals 261 f.p.s.)	

Note 1. Pellet "X" gave better averages in Weihrauch rifles than above.
Note 2. Pellet "Y" coincided with performances of this pellet in most European air guns.
Note 3. Precision balls were slightly oversize.

rifles with fixed barrels and manually operated loading plugs (also called taps). Stoeger under the brand name Peerless imports two versions of this model: The 50E, with adjustable rear sight mounted to the rear of the loading plug at $50, and the 50M with special stock and special receiver sights at $85.

The 50 series are the finest of the Diana line. In workmanship, materials, and fittings they are the equal of any air rifles currently made.

In velocity, curiously enough, these apparently powerful underlever rifles did not approach the power of their British opposite numbers, the Webley and B.S.A.! Cocking effort was about the same throughout, but the spring compressions were lower for the Diana.

Velocity tests conducted with varying brands of pellets (table 10) again established that the close liaison between German ammunition makers and the air-gun manufacturers results in better performances when German ammunition is used with these guns.

Machine-rest tests on accuracy did not on the specimens available for testing bear out accuracy claims of many shooters. (Note: The Diana *manufacturers* do not publish any accuracy claims. The author was unable to extract any statements from them regarding accuracy. Similar type rifles, specifically the Webley Mark III are stated to group 1 inch at 20 yards, and in author's test several 1-inch groups were obtained.) No Diana rifle tested was as accurate as the Webley Mark III.

On 5 independent tests with the Diana 50 using RWS Diabolo pellets and 5 tests using H-N precision balls, the accuracy attained at 50 feet under controlled indoor-range conditions is shown in table 11.

TABLE 11

DIANA M50 ACCURACY GROUP TESTS

10-shots	RWS Diabolo pellets	H-N precision round lead balls
	Inches	Inches
Test No. 1	1.1250	1.250
Test No. 2	1.750	2.250
Test No. 3	0.875	2.000
Test No. 4	1.250	2.250
Test No. 5	1.000	2.000

Falke. Various Falke rifles examined were basically counterparts of the Diana in a similar range of styles and approximate prices.

Only the most expensive model, the M90, was considered important enough for comparison testing. Except for the stock, this is the same as the Model 80. The range of sight equipment available is similar to that offered by all the leading German makers, more particularly Diana and Weihrauch.

Except in the 80 and 90 series, these arms are not appreciably different from their Diana equivalents, and in price they run a bit lower. (Such rifles with micrometer sights and diopter cost about 100 to 110 marks from the German sales outlets.)

Falke M90. This is an underlever cocker with rifled barrel. Specimen tested was caliber .177, though it is also made in .22 caliber. The lever, unlike that of the Diana 50, is built into a short fore-end and acts to pull rather than push the piston back when operated. Whether it was copied from the current British B.S.A. system, the German manufacturer would not state, but the similarity is marked.

In actual practice this newly positioned lever is an advance over the earlier patterns and affords easier cocking for the spring power involved. However, the more important new feature is the loading-plug system which opens *automatically* as the lever is pulled down and back to cock (all others except the B.S.A. require manual opening and closing of the plug to load), and which automatically closes as the lever is returned to its housing. The adjustable trigger is one of the best of the German designs. The weight, flexible sights (see under Falke in text), and sling swivels all indicate the rifle should have maximum capabilities as a precision arm.

However, average velocity tests produced only 585 f.p.s., and groups shot at 50 feet were never lower than .875-inch from machine rest. While it is recognized that this velocity is entirely adequate for match use up to 60 feet, the powerful spring, oversized compression tube and sights, trigger, and weights seemed to indicate that the rifle is much more powerful than it actually is, and that it might perform at much longer ranges. Average of 5 groups at 50 feet was 1.250 inches.

Krico LG1 Luxus. The manufacturers of this rifle are a postwar concern in this field, and are currently specializing in finely crafted and extremely accurate powder-cartridge rifles. Specimens of their various arms show the highest quality of workmanship. The only air rifles they manufacture are variants of the Model 1.

While these rifles are merely another version of the Diana system, they are distinguished by their quality and finish and by beautifully rifled barrels. Mechanically they are elementary barrel cockers in caliber .177, but they use one of the best trigger systems available.

Only one rifle was available for testing. Average velocity with RWS pellets was 615 f.p.s. With U.S. pellets "X," 515 f.p.s. With U.S. pellets "Y," 575 f.p.s. With British Webley pellets, 577 f.p.s.

From machine rest this rifle grouped very consistently at 25 and 30 feet, 9 of 10 shots making one hole with German pellets. At 60 feet it averaged 1.35-inch groups, a figure bettered very slightly only by the German Walther 53 and the British Webley Mark III.

The superiority of the rifle to most others in accuracy apparently stems from the fact that as precision cartridge rifle makers, Krico is more aware of shooting standards and possibilities than the average air-rifle maker. Except for fits and finish, there is no constructional reason why air rifles made by firearms makers should be more accurate or consistent than those made by general air-gun or machinery firms.

Walther. All air rifles made by Walther are merely modifications of their original M51 series, the arm with which they reentered the field of arms manufacture after the close of World War II.

Two models were available for testing, M51ZD and MLG53. The latter model is considerably more expensive (128 marks as against 80 for similar equipment), but velocity and machine-rest accuracy were practically identical. (Note: No attempt was made to evaluate triggers or sights for usage, since different shooters will always have individual preferences.) Triggers were inspected and tested for adjustability and let-off, but firing tests were machine-rest, where quality of sights and trigger pull are not affecting factors.

Velocity average as stated by Walther to the author is 175 meters per second, which would be about 574 f.p.s. (1 meter equals 3.2808 feet.) No specific accuracy claims could be extracted.

The author's velocity tests with RWS, and also H-N German-made pellets, gave somewhat better averages than claimed, 592 and 602 f.p.s., respectively, indicating that the ammunition makers have found that in a .177 an approximate velocity of 175 meters per second is optimum.

As to accuracy, the two Walthers were about equal in machine-rest performance, doing slightly better than the German Krico and the British B.S.A. and equalling the British Webley Mark III. At 25- and 30-foot ranges the Walthers would place 5 shots consistently in one hole (averaging about ½ inch), would usually duplicate the performance with 9 shots, and would occasionally group all 10.

The better makers all endeavor to minimize diesel effect and try to control air-power generation within relatively narrow limits to get relatively consistent velocity and hence trajectory. In their efforts in this direction, Walther uses no welding or soldering, as in similar types of barrel cockers made by non-firearms makers to cut manufacturing costs. Forgings are used where others rely on stampings. It would require long and expensive metallurgical research to tie down with any exactness just *why* the air guns made by firearms makers tend to develop better accuracy, but the fact itself is apparent in any unbiased tests properly controlled.

In its advertising RWS features targets shot with Walther air rifles in which 50 shots are grouped in a single hole. At no time and with no rifle has this author been able to duplicate this feat; and an examination of the mass of time-interval and f.p.s. readings reported herein, made on checked chronographs, and with control tests, will indicate the velocity variability commonly encountered.

While these Walthers are mechanically only advanced forms of the cheaper barrel cockers, they do unquestionably have built into them to as high a degree as is attainable in a spring-air arm, the materials, engineering, and experience which has placed Walther products high in the scale of quality arms.

Weihrauch. Two examples of this line were available for testing, one HW35 in caliber .22, the other a Model 55 Meisterstützen in caliber .177. Weihrauch, incidentally, has long been noted for super-accurate fall-block .22 cartridge match rifles.

These air rifles are barrel cockers, but they differ from other modern manufacture, such as the Walther, in having a formal barrel lock rather than merely a spring-detent barrel-support system. When the lock lever on the left side at the breech is pushed ahead, the barrel is free and will normally swing down on its hinge of its own weight, thereby easing the *initial* pressure required to start the cocking action. On closing, the locking bolt has a camming face which allows the action to be closed without reference to the barrel lock—in short, the action is similar to that of a standard double shotgun, you must manually operate a lever to open the action, but it can be snapped shut without any attention to the opening lever. This feature will ease considerably the cocking action of *any* barrel-cocking rifle and is a desirable design feature. It has an added advantage in that the position of the barrel when the cocking action is started is such as to allow good grip and leverage.

The trigger mechanism is equal to any on the market. Finish is excellent. Sights range from the simple barrel open type to the most elaborate modern sliding-receiver patterns, with optical lenses if desired. The barrel is precision steel tubing, well rifled. All general features of this rifle indicate capabilities of extreme power and accuracy in a spring-air design. The compression tube, for example is extra long and large in diameter, measuring about 11.75 inches from cap to barrel-contact face (side arms extend further ahead to give side support to the barrel housing in jaw fashion), and is of 1 5/16-inch diameter. The *decompressed* spring pressure is some 40 pounds, if the rifle is dismounted it is a considerable job for the average mechanic to replace the spring in its tube. The barrel housing is a steel monobloc with the barrel press-fitted.

Trigger adjustment on the HW35 is through a hole in the underside of the trigger. (Note: Except for details of finish, stocks, and sights, there is very little difference in the various models.)

This is by far the most difficult spring-air gun to cock encountered by the author. It would seem to have been designed on the principle that the larger the spring and piston assembly, the greater the power. However, airgun power development is considerably more complex than that! In actual comparisons under test conditions it was established that rifles with smaller springs and pistons, shorter compression strokes, and which require far less cocking effort actually exceeded these heavy-duty rifles in velocity and penetration!

Accuracy with the .177 was very good, approaching the Walther and the Webley. From a machine rest it is possible to shoot 1-inch groups at 60 feet—a quite remarkable achievement. While it is claimed that these rifles are usable in matches at 50 meters, no accuracy whatever was obtainable in machine tests at 50 yards. Neither Diabolo pellets nor round balls would consistently even hit a formal air-range target at such distances. It is conceivable that some shooters with picked rifles, ammunition, and shooting conditions may do such shooting. However, the tests conducted indicate that the average shooter with the average rifle and ammunition cannot.

Regardless of type of ammunition used—and as usual RWS proved to be the best and most consistent performer in this German rifle—the highest average velocity obtained was 590 f.p.s. The highest *individual* shot was 626 f.p.s. With most brands of ammunition, the velocity was in the 560 f.p.s. average range.

As to the .22 caliber, the smallest 50-foot group obtainable with best ammunition was 1.250 inches. This, it might be added, is a very good showing, but is a far cry from the type of accuracy claimed by some enthusiasts.

Velocity comparisons are indicated by the average figures given in table 12.

Great Britain

B.S.A. Guns Limited. B.S.A. rifles have been a standard in this field since the turn of the century. On tests using pre-World War II B.S.A. underlever rifles, the author was able to get better accuracy but lower velocity than with two samples from current production. All rifles tested were in No. 2 bore (.22 caliber), using the maker's pellets. The prewar type gave an average 10-shot velocity of 440 f.p.s. The rifle had been thoroughly overhauled and was in like-new condition mechanically. At 50 feet this model will consistently group 5 shots in 1 inch, and at the shorter, standard air-rifle distances will give "possibles," but only with a shooter who knows how to compensate for the spring surge. Experts with firearms who could make "possibles" at 25 feet with compressed-air rifles could not equal the performance with the B.S.A. because of the peculiarities of the spring-air action. (This of course holds true of ALL spring-air arms.)

The postwar underlevers (Airsporter .22's) are mechanically superior to the prewar design. They are better looking, better balanced, have better trigger systems, and are somewhat easier to cock because of the new close-in lever and fulcrum employed (see in text). Average velocity was 480 f.p.s., a figure somewhat below that stated by the manufacturer, but considerably *above* that actually encountered in competitive German air rifles, and exceeded slightly in this field only by the British Webley Mark III.

A very valuable feature in the new line is the automatically opening breech, the loading plug being rotated as the underlever is pulled down and back to cock the action. The fit of the plug, an important sealing factor in this type design, was excellent. In general, however, it must be stated that the overall fitting and finish was below the standards of the Walther, Krico, and Webley rifles. Since the last war B.S.A. has become a diversified giant, as British corporate manufacturing bodies go. It has carried on very considerable methods research, which is apparent in all its new arms, whether air or cartridge type, resulting in new materials, new methods, more machine operations, and less handwork. The resulting end product is always satisfactory to the *average* buyer, but the serious shooter will miss many evidences of handwork which appeared in earlier designs and which invariably reflect in the top, though not necessarily in the average, performance.

Thus in machine-rest tests above 30 feet, the B.S.A. did not equal some others.

The only claim made by B.S.A. regarding accuracy is that the rifle "is expected to group 1 inch at 20 yards." At least, that is the extent to which the author was able to get a checkable commitment.

TABLE 12
WEIHRAUCH SPRING-AIR RIFLE VELOCITY TESTS

RWS PELLETS		U.S. PELLET "X"		U.S. PELLET "Y"	
Shot number	Time interval	Shot number	Time interval	Shot number	Time interval
1	.01124 (444 f.p.s.)	1	.01889 (264 f.p.s.)	1	.01244 (401 f.ps.)
2	.01128 (443 f.p.s.)	2	.01705 (293 f.p.s.)	2	.01213 (411 f.p.s.)
3	.01120 (446 f.p.s.)	3	.01767 (283 f.p.s.)	3	.01282 (390 f.p.s.)
4	.01163 (430 f.p.s.)	4	.01392 (358 f.p.s.)	4	.01194 (418 f.p.s.)
5	.01164 (430 f.p.s.)	5	.01918 (261 f.p.s.)	5	.01233 (405 f.p.s.)
6	.01112 (499 f.p.s.)	6	.01503 (332 f.p.s.)	6	.01171 (416 f.p.s.)
7	.01172 (426 f.p.s.)	7	.02177 (230 f.p.s.)	7	.01146 (436 f.p.s.)
8	.01178 (424 f.p.s.)	8	.01719 (291 f.p.s.)	8	.01268 (394 f.p.s.)
9	.01040 (480 f.p.s.)	9	.01506 (332 f.p.s.)	9	.01160 (430 f.p.s.)
10	.01197 (411 f.p.s.)	10	.01375 (364 f.p.s.)	10	.01196 (417 f.p.s.)
(Average equals 438 f.p.s.)		(Average equals 300 f.p.s.)		(Average equals 411 f.p.s.)	

Of two Airsporters tested, accuracy was not up to the factory's "expectations." Tested at 50 feet from the muzzle they were nearly parallel with the German Diana underlever, running from .875- to 1.625-inch groups of 10 shots. Three strings from rest at 20 yards with B.S.A. Pylarm pellets grouped an average of 1.65 inches. This is really quite a good performance by any air-gun standards incidentally, and indicates that inch groups can be gotten, but hardly by the average good marksman with average ammunition.

In handling, appearance, and general performance the Airsporter is one of the most desirable spring-air rifles made today, and it is regrettable that because of mass-production methods its precision-target performance has apparently been allowed to slip somewhat in comparison with prewar models.

Webley Mark III. This rifle and the Walther were the only spring-air rifles tested which accented quality manufacture to the utmost, and which performed on a high general average to the claims of the makers. Tested in .22 caliber only, the velocity was the highest of any rifle of its class and caliber, yet was well within British legal limits. Average was 505 f.p.s. when the pellet was merely dropped into the plug, and reached 530 when the pellet was forced down into the taper.

The loading plug in this design must be manually operated both to load the plug and to close the breech, in which respect it is not as desirable as the B.S.A. The underlever cocking mechanism, while not as readily accessible, was still simple and efficient to cock. The cocking took somewhat greater force than in the Diana 50, but the spring compression and velocity produced were much higher.

RWS pellets gave 535 f.p.s. velocity in this rifle, and just about equal shooting performance. I.C.I. pellets under the Hy Score brand name, curiously, were too large to chamber properly unless deliberately forced in.

A shooter familiar with the lunge and recoil can consistently shoot possibles at 25 feet with this rifle. At 50 feet in competition with others it gave consistent 1-inch groups of 5 shots, and regularly would place 9 out of 10 in the 1-inch ring. When shooting was spaced to attempt averaging the friction and heat factors in the compression tube, all 10 could be placed in the 1-inch circle, one group measuring .750 and one measuring .800 out of the 2 groups fired.

The quality and style of the Webley rifling, attention to piston fit, close tolerances in the loading plug, and superior spring technology would appear to be the reasons for the consistently fine performance of this rifle; always remembering that *average* rifles were tested, with average ammunition, under test controls. It is conceivable that experts may do as well with some other makes under special circumstances, but based on averages this Webley and the German Walther emerge as the finest spring-air guns made today.

Italy

No Italian air rifles were encountered which were worthy of extensive (and expensive) testing for the purposes of this work.

The entire Vittoria series (see text) were sheet metal patterns with smooth-bored tube barrel liners of the borderline toy pattern not adapted to serious air-rifle use. Routine tests indicated velocities of from 230 to 310 f.p.s. for the various models, but accuracy was of the Daisy gun order only. All were single-shot barrel cockers.

The barrel-cocking Italian Compretta rifle using .177 Diabolos is merely an adaptation of the familiar low-priced Diana 23 Model. Velocity averaged 375 f.p.s. which is good for the spring power and cocking effort involved. No groups of under 1 inch were obtained at 30 feet, the normal average being 2.5 inches at that distance.

Author's Note on Spring-Air Design Rifles

Despite all claims, the Walther 53 and Webley Mark III emerged as the most consistently accurate spring-air rifles tested. The Webley produced the highest velocity.

The author has seen and tested both lever and barrel-cocking *experimental* rifles which are easier to cock and which give more velocity with standard Diabolo pellets than any rifles currently manufactured.

However, tests indicate that with the ammunition available, velocity above that currently available does not result in added accuracy at usable air distances. The only gain is in possibly better consistency of groups and in better penetration. It is not believed that increased penetration is particularly desirable, since except at the closest distances or under special circumstances air arms should not be used for small-game shooting.

Regardless of the weight involved, so long as it leaves the rifle portable, spring-air rifles all have peculiar firing characteristics which can be overcome only by practice on the part of the shooter. For instance, when the striker in a firearm is released by trigger pull, it travels only a fraction of an inch in a match rifle, and when it hits the primer the resulting explosion comes so fast that the bullet is usually well out of the barrel before the shooter begins to feel the effect of the recoil, for which he can brace himself. In a spring-air gun, when the piston is released by trigger pull it must lunge forward, compressing air in its path, hence the forward pull is an *immediate* affecting factor. Usually the pistonhead hits and rebounds from the face of its compression tube while the pellet is still in the barrel. These and various other factors cannot be sensibly compensated for except by the individual shooter himself. This is the basic reason why the pneumatic (pump-up) or CO_2 gun, which merely releases stored power—instead of generating it by a moving piston—is easier for the average shooter to learn to use. Another difficulty, that of proper pellet seating, has been overcome only by bolt-action spring-air guns on the same system as the CO_2 guns, and cannot be sensibly achieved in formal systems.

It may be assumed, therefore, that the spring-air design has about reached the perfection of its form. However, combination systems utilizing the good spring-air characteristics of a single cocking stroke, combined with an air storage chamber giving the good release characteristics of the pneumatic type, offer considerable possibilities for future development, as the interest in these arms and their form of shooting increases.

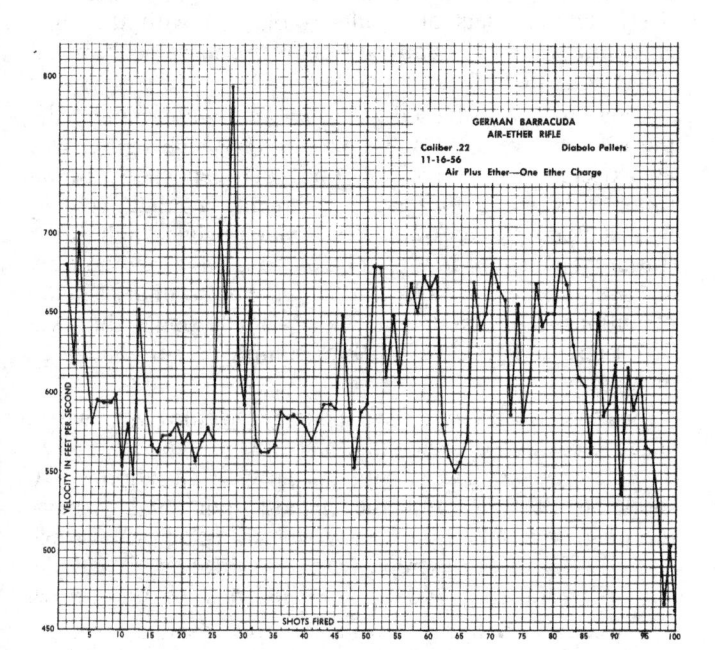

EXPLOSION GAS SYSTEM (AIR AND ETHER BOOSTER)

The only rifle currently available on this system is the Barracuda (German: Barakuda), which is merely the Weihrauch .22 Model 35 adapted to use a special gas "booster" attachment (see under Barracuda).

The manufacturer supplies the liquid gas in capsules (ether) and also a box of special .22 round, lead precision balls made by H-N. These balls, incidentally, are a very tight fit in the bore. Rifle-bore diameter measured .213 inch, groove diameter .219 inch. The balls ran .002 to .003 inch oversize for these dimensions, obviously to give gas sealage.

As usual in most cases, it was found impossible to get any specific claims of performance from makers or distributors on this system. "Better than usual velocity as an air gun" was one generalized claim. Scientific tests did not bear this out unless in an average performance you include all the *low-priced* rifles. In the price bracket of this rifle, its velocity was *exceeded* by both British makes and several German makes. Accuracy and velocity figures obtained by the author tell their own comparative story. In the matter of penetration, claims were justified when used with gas attachment.

As an air gun, this arm can (and should) be used preferably with Diabolo-type pellets, preferably German. The round balls supplied by the producer will not *at all times* leave the barrel due to tight fit and resultant friction, which the air power alone is insufficient to overcome, though it is true they can be used.

Used as an ether-air gun, performance is highly erratic. It will be affected by a wide range of variables, despite the good workmanship of the device and the attempt at precision metering of the charge. For instance, it will perform differently depending on the number of shots in the string; on the individuality of the charging stroke, the performance of the gas-closing spring, the oiling of the pistonhead, the ammunition, and a host of other variables.

Author's Tests

A very large amount of money, time, and effort went into the author's testing of this rifle as a new production pattern—though the system itself is old. At no time does the rifle begin to approach the efficiency of the common .22 short powder cartridge, though at times it surpasses the performance of currently available carbon dioxide arms. Because of the fire hazards and physiological dangers of ether generally, it is far from a desirable design.

It should be understood that the author is writing from a purely American standpoint. In areas where .22 powder rifles are not generally or legally available, the system has its uses. In the United States, however, it is not a desirable pattern, since it is not as accurate nor as powerful at full power as, for instance, an American Sheridan pump-up rifle. The cocking effort, though confined to one stroke, is very considerable, and very few "teen-agers" could repeatedly cock this arm more than a few times, and then with difficulty. If used as a gas gun, it of course requires a separate charging movement in addition to the air-cocking stroke.

Being a chemically explosive arm, it flashes at the muzzle and gives nearly as loud a report as the common .22 short. No missile designed for such rifles can be compared ballistically with the .22 short. Experiments with oversized balls indicated that high pressure could blow the barrel gasket out and leave the ball in the rifling. Tests with various Diabolo pellets showed that except with the finest grades there was always danger of the pellet either being blown apart inside the barrel, or having holes blown right through it and the pellet itself expanded in the barrel, which would necessitate forcing it out with a rod.

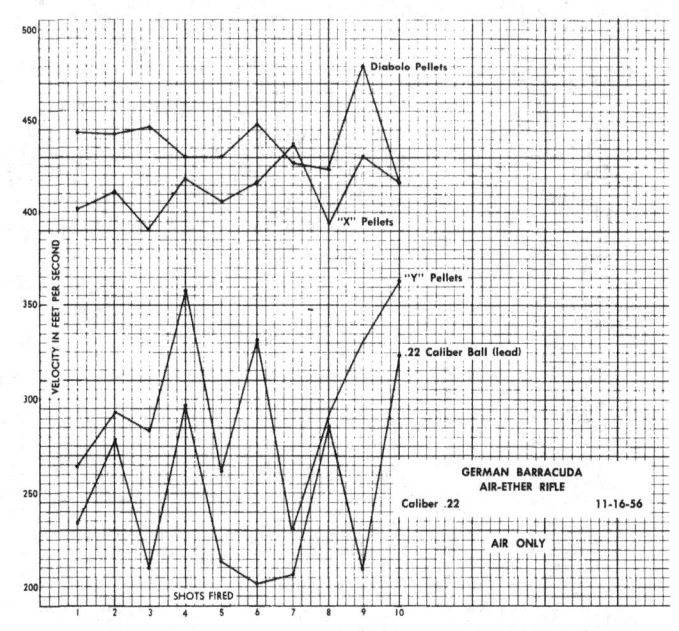

Used as a gas-air gun this rifle with round ball has considerable penetration and shock effect at close range, and in this respect is a better close-range pest gun than any type below the firearms group; but even this effect is evidently due more to the shape and weight of the ball than to the power factor, an item which is offset by the ballistic inefficiency of the ball design after passing 50 feet. The ball used, incidentally, is obviously a compromise missile, since it will occasionally stay in the barrel when only air is used.

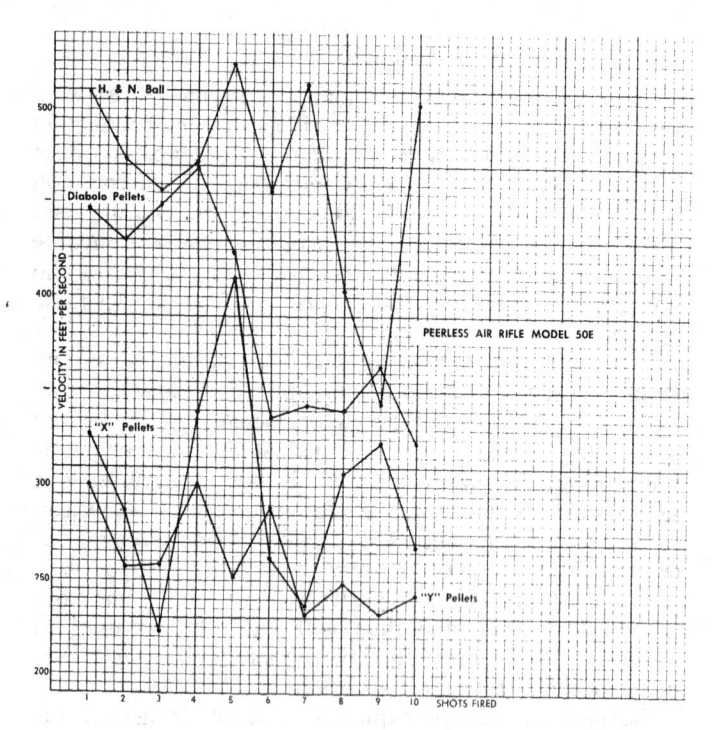

As a gas-air gun, this design is subject to extremely erratic performance, as has been pointed out. So much variation was encountered that *three* different chronographs after checking for calibration and for correctness with known arms and ammunition, still gave three entirely different sets of results (table 13) with the same rifle and with balls and pellets from the same box—all range conditions being equalized.

Thus on one test used as an *air gun* with round balls, the velocity averaged 433 f.p.s.—a very high figure, with an extreme variation of 46 f.p.s. between shots. In the same tests using the gas attachment, average velocity was stepped up to 629 f.p.s., which while high for a spring-air gun was low in relation to *a good compressed-air gun or a good CO_2 gun at full power* under similar conditions! The maximum velocity for a single shot was 701 f.p.s., a figure well below compressed-air and CO_2 maximums.

In other tests using RWS pellets, Diabolo type, where heads blew out occasionally, the average velocity as an *air* rifle was 438 f.p.s., with an extreme variation in 10 shots of 69 f.p.s. and the highest individual velocity reaching only 480 f.p.s. As a *gas* air rifle, the average was 613 f.p.s., the extreme variation 146 f.p.s., and the most powerful shot 700 f.p.s. *on the first 10 shots fired*.

On continued firing up to 125 shots, the gas-air combination performed so erratically that some later 10-shot strings, if isolated, would show a much higher velocity, while other earlier ones, if isolated, would show a much lower velocity. Very seldom, however, did any individual shot reach a velocity of 700 f.p.s. This, remember, was with relatively lightweight Diabolo pellets, NOT the heavier round balls.

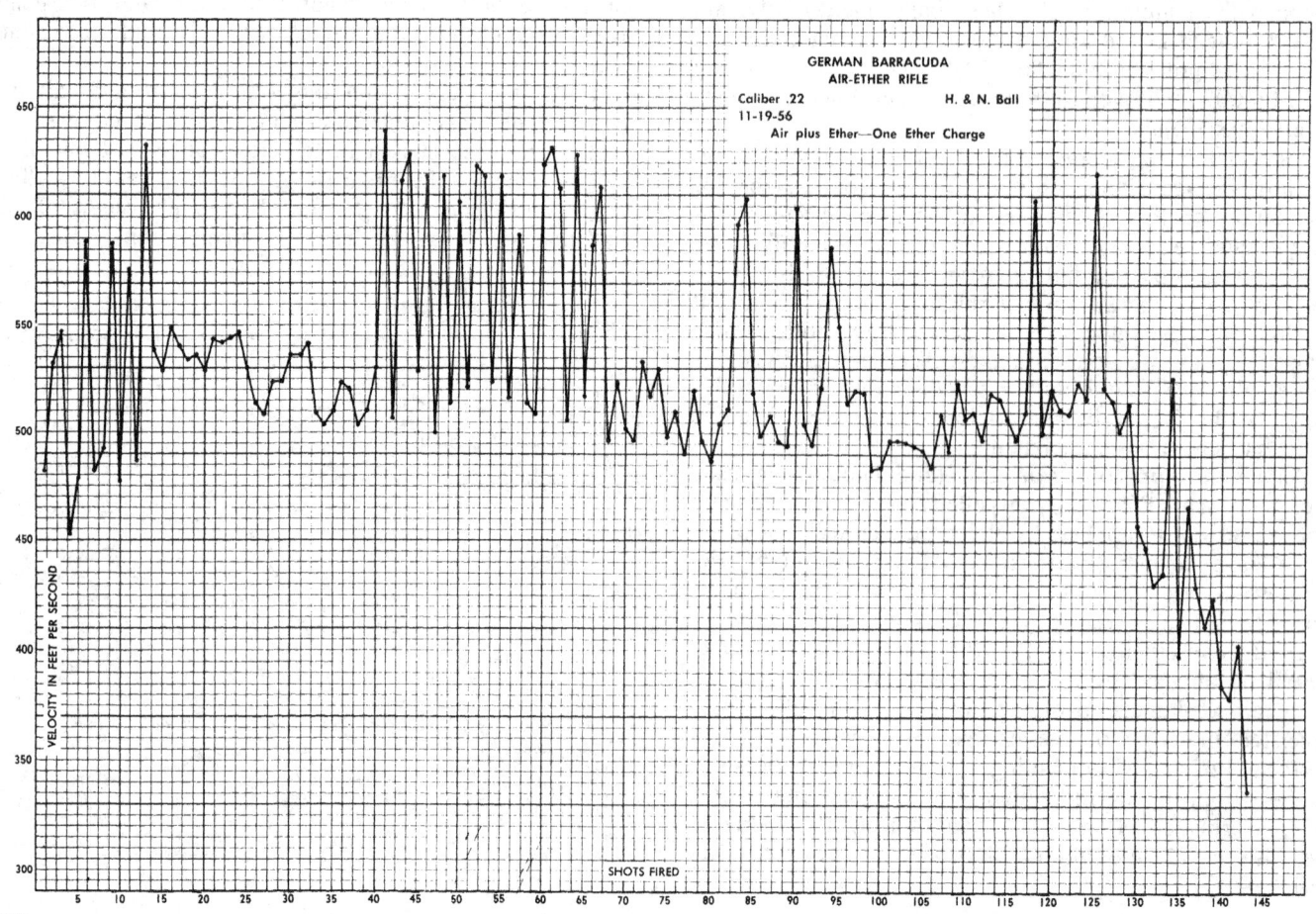

U.S. pellet "X" used with the gas attachment gave an average velocity of only 465 f.p.s. for 10 shots, ranging from a low of 392 to a high of only 572 f.p.s.

U.S. pellet "Y" was even worse, averaging only 101 f.p.s. In these pellets either the heads blew or the pellet was blown into fragments in the barrel, though unlike the German, none stuck in the barrel.

In other tests, of *125 shots* fired using the gas attachment and lead balls supplied by the manufacturer, the maximum velocity attained was 640 f.p.s.; the minimum velocity was 452 f.p.s., and for the first 10 shots fired, the average velocity was 511.5 f.p.s.

Velocity Conclusion. Based on tests of two guns, new, using gas and ammunition accompanying the guns, and with tests conducted on three checked chronographs, it is not believed that any *true average velocity figure* can be stated or maintained for this ether-air system as presently constructed.

In general, the pneumatic system as applied to rifles proved to be capable of better penetration than any other pellet-gun system; and in one make (Sheridan) capable of equalling the accuracy rating of any pellet gun encountered. Its most important characteristic, however, was the reliable, relatively constant, variable power factor.

The sole drawbacks of this system were: (1) The effort necessary to pump up pressure, 4 strokes being about the minimum which would give satisfactory performance, and 6 being necessary to equal the velocity range of many single-stroke spring-air and CO_2 guns. (2) Servicing due to relatively delicate mechanism. Unlike spring-air arms, no pneumatic rifle can be repaired satisfactorily by the average user.

No current rifle tested failed at any point during tests.

TABLE 13
GERMAN BARAKUDA GAS-AIR RIFLE
ACCURACY TESTS (10-SHOT GROUPS)—50 FEET

Target number	Barakuda air (Diabolo pellet)	Barakuda air (round ball)	Air plus ether (Diabolo pellet RWS)	Air plus ether (round ball H-N)
1	1.750 inches	1.625 inches	1.750 inches	2.000 inches
2	1.250 inches	1.250 inches	1.125 inches	2.250 inches
3	1.125 inches	1.125 inches	1.750 inches	2.000 inches
4	1.500 inches	1.000 inch	1.375 inches	2.250 inches
5	1.500 inches	0.937 inch	1.000 inch	2.000 inches

Note. 1-inch groups or slightly under at 30 feet. Three out of ten on 8- by 10-inch targets at 150 feet.

Penetration. At 30 feet with air alone, the ball would usually, but not always, imbed itself 1 inch in a soft-pine packing-case plank. At the same range with gas, the ball would penetrate 9 times out of 10, and in ball-missile fashion would usually splinter wood above the emerging point.

Author's Note on Gas-Air System

In the opinion of the author, there are entirely too many variables which can affect this ether-air system in consistent functioning to warrant extended use. It is quite possible to utilize the diesel effect of common SAE-40 grade oil in a spring-air arm to produce increased velocities comparable to the averages developed by the ether system, the author having seen and tested several such development models. However, it is highly questionable whether consistency of performance or the results achieved are worth the effort, as the added velocity thereby attained using standard air-rifle missiles has little practical trajectory value at practical air-rifle ranges. While it is obviously simpler to release explosive gases from ether than from lubricating oil, the fact remains that with the ram efficiency available in a properly constructed spring-air rifle it can be done satisfactorily, and without recourse to dangerously flammable ether.

PNEUMATIC (PUMP-UP, COMPRESSED-AIR) RIFLES

There are currently only three firms making such rifles on a production basis. All are United States manufacturers. These are: Benjamin Air Rifle Company, Crosman Arms Company, and Sheridan Products, Incorporated.

However, there is no question that over a period of time any arms on this system will require more attention than the related spring-air design; and valves and seals, while not as critical as in CO_2 arms, are likely eventually to require expert attention.

Records of various makes which are no longer manufactured are listed for general interest, for possible performance comparison values, and for research value.

The absence of recoil in this system is doubtless a big factor in the superior accuracy of which it is capable, as demonstrated by the Sheridan. (This is also a factor in the CO_2 power system.) The *flexibility of power* is a very useful factor to those who want to use a pellet gun for indoor, outdoor, and pest shooting, since each of these uses requires different velocities for satisfactory performance. The spring-air system allows only one power normally, and is therefore a compromise operation. The CO_2 system while theoretically permitting adjustment to increase or decrease power, in actual practice is affected by its valve operation and its gradually diminishing power supply, and does not in any way approach either the consistency or the flexibility of power range found in the pneumatic guns.

Sheridan Blue Streak and Silver Streak Models

Sheridan is currently making only one type of compressed-air rifle. With blue barrel it is designated "Blue Streak." With the barrel plated to give a silver-satin finish, it is designated "Silver Streak." Regardless of finish, the price is the same—currently $23.95. The only "extra," if desired, is a Williams receiver sight, which costs $5.00 extra, plus a mounting charge of $2.50.

The caliber is special with Sheridan. It is .20 (5-mm.) "Sheridan Bantam." This is a conventional bullet-shaped pellet, not a ball or Diabolo waisted type. (Note: See under Sheridan for complete Sheridan data.)

Sheridan Pump-Stroke and Velocity Tests (See Table 14).

TABLE 14
SHERIDAN BLUE STREAK MODEL PUMP-STROKE AND VELOCITY TESTS

Number of strokes	Average velocity (f.p.s.)
1	265
2	391
3	468
4	532
5	580
6	611
7	632
8	661
9	675
10	704

Note 1. Firing point temperature—70 degrees F.
Note 2. First 3 pumps easy and smooth; difficult after 7; very difficult after 10. Pumping done slowly and in rhythm.

Comparison With Earlier Sheridan Tests. For comparison, data in table 15 is supplied. It indicates the quality maintenance by the manufacturer. This test was made on a Potter chronograph by a research group on December 20, 1948, using the Sheridan Super Grade then being made. This test is quoted directly and in context:

TABLE 15
SUPER GRADE SHERIDAN 5-MM. (.20 CALIBER) CA (COMPRESSED-AIR) GUN—(USING SHERIDAN PELLETS)

Number of strokes	Average velocity (f.p.s.)	Number of strokes	Average velocity (f.p.s.)
1	277	1	618
2	412	2	640
3	480	3	676
4	545	4	682
5	589	5	712

Writing in the *American Rifleman Magazine* of April, 1947, of the Sheridan Super Grade, Major General Julian S. Hatcher reported velocity tests at 10 feet from muzzle as shown in table 16.

TABLE 16
HATCHER'S SUPER GRADE SHERIDAN TESTS

Number of strokes	Velocity (f.p.s.)
2	400
4	510
6	620
8	707
10	750
12	770

Comment On Velocity Tests. Original models had phosphor-bronze barrels 19.75 inches long. The Super Grade sold for $56.50. Current models have hard, red-brass barrels 18.5 inches long. The relatively slight differences in velocities shown could stem from barrel length, friction factors in barrel material, bullet metal, or a dozen other factors, varying from temperature conditions to pumping methods and firing time. The velocity consistency shown is a very considerable achievement in any type of arm, and is outstanding in the field of pellet guns.

Accuracy Tests.

Target: Sheridan indoor. One-inch-diameter black bull with inner 9 and 10 rings. The 10 ring is one-half-inch diameter.
Range: 25, 30, and 35 feet, indoors, from bench rest.
Sights: Standard Sheridan blade front and open rear.
Strings: 10 shots at each distance after sighting in.
Results: At 25 and 30 feet from the rifle muzzle, all shots in 10 ring. At 35 feet, 9 shots in 10 ring and 1 in 9 ring.
Number of pump strokes: 3 at 25- and 30-foot ranges. 4 at the 35-foot distance.

Comment On Accuracy Tests. No other American pellet gun currently approaches the accuracy of the Sheridan. No foreign pellet rifles tested exceeded its accuracy, though the British Webley Mark III and the German Walther M51 equalled it. Both models are more expensive than the Sheridan.

Reasons For Superior Accuracy. Since all pneumatic arms today are basically very much alike, considerable attention was devoted to determining the reason for the Sheridan's superior accuracy showing.

On a basis of the author's personal study and observation of all types, it would seem that the materials used, extreme attention to details, and above all the careful fitting and inspection are the most important factors. Sheridan is the smallest of all the air-gun producers, and the owners are men long interested in precision shooting. Their rifles are built to an approximation of very high quality small-bore powder rifle standards—which means to much higher standards than the average powder rifle you can buy for the price of the Sheridan, incidentally.

Qualified writers on arms of the caliber of Major General Julian S. Hatcher of the *American Rifleman* and Lucian Cary of *True Magazine* are on record as to the superior accuracy of the Sheridan; and the independent comparisons of this author, conducted under scientifically controlled conditions, bear out their findings. Cary, for instance, in commenting on his own shooting with various pellet guns stated that "No other air rifle I tried proved as accurate;" and concluded that "If you miss a dime with the Sheridan at 35 feet, it is your own fault." General Hatcher writes of it: "The accuracy of this gun is superb. . . . Here is a gun which is capable of real target shooting, is deadly on small pests, and is a real pleasure to shoot."

The relationship of the Sheridan accuracy to the combination of barrel and pellet has been dealt with extensively in the body of this book in discussing the Sheridan. One additional factor may be pointed out here, the care taken in bullet seating. All pneumatic arms are superior to most (not all) of the spring-air types in that closing the bolt automatically seats the pellet, a factor which means that added energy is available to propel the bullet. In the Sheridan, this seating was found to be more closely controlled than in competing makes, indicating that the pellet had less starting friction. Since the pellet design and barrel material of the Sheridan differ from its competitors', *exact* comparisons are not possible, but the chronograph and bench-rest tests tell the story.

Regardless of the materials and equipment used in air-gun manufacture, a high degree of strictly personal skills will always be involved where ultimate, not average, product performance is required. This, of course, is true in any field of arms, as evidenced by the fact that one can buy Winchester .22 rifles, for example, at prices varying from about $15 to about $150, un-ornamented. Each is worth what it costs, but the deciding factor is more the number of man-hours and special skills required for ultimate accuracy than the cost of the materials involved.

After a careful analysis of all the factors involved, the author is inclined to doubt that the Sheridan quality could be maintained on a quantity production basis without greatly adding to its cost. With the current relatively small production and overhead costs, plus the thorough and painstaking supervision of the owners, the Sheridan is by far the best buy in its type of air rifle; and on a basis of the skilled man-hours which go into its manufacture, the rifle is very much underpriced.

Crosman Current Pneumatic (Compressed-Air Pump) Rifles

Tests on Models 140 and 147. Crosman is currently manufacturing a single-shot pump-up rifle designated Model 140 in .22 caliber and Model 147 in .177 caliber.

As the relationship in performance between the two calibers is well known, the author concentrated current tests on Model 140, or .22 caliber, in order to permit reasonably accurate comparisons with other makes; and in view of the fact that in the United States the .22 is the preferred caliber. (In Europe, the .177 is preferred, air arms being used there extensively for precision indoor target work).

H. P. White Laboratory Tests. The Crosman organization proved very cooperative in opening their technical files for examination and study by the author. It so happened that Crosman had but recently submitted a full line of their arms to the H. P. White Laboratory of Bel Air, Maryland, for unprejudiced testing. The White group, one of the best-equipped ordnance engineering firms in the United States, conduct all the official small-arms tests for the National Rifle Association of America. Their professional and ethical standing is in itself a guarantee of the reliability of any reports issued by them.

Since the White testing equipment parallels that used by this author, Crosman's action in releasing the entire White test results on their arms permits the publication here of complete comparative data never before available. It should be noted that all H. P. White Laboratory data dealing with Crosman products was released directly to the author by Philip Y. Hahn and Rudolph Merz, respectively president and chief engineer of Crosman Arms Company, not by the White organization.

The author has known the principals in the H. P. White organization for very many years. As a complete check on his own facilities, he engaged White to run independent control tests—many of which are included in this test section. This was done to eliminate any possibility of error in tests conducted by the author or in tests conducted under his observation or supervision.

Crosman specified the tests they wanted run by White, but did nothing to influence the findings in any way. The author set up tests in many instances paralleling the instructions given to White on Crosman products; but no personnel or associates connected with his tests saw the White results until after testing had been completed. The following data, therefore, gives a complete and accurate picture.

Crosman's instructions to White on April 20, 1956, were to test Models 140 and 147 as follows:

Test at 5 and 25 feet from muzzle, using 2, 4, 6, 8, 10, 12, and 14 strokes.

Also test at 50 and 75 feet from muzzle, using 8, 10, 12, and 14 strokes.

When queried by the author regarding reasons for these unusual conditions, Merz wrote on October 1, 1956: "The spacing of the shots was to show me how the velocity would maintain itself. We know from tests made some years ago that the trajectory is the same at 50 feet when shooting at 900 pounds down to 350 pounds pressure . . . Distances selected were to answer customers' letters posing various questions, and to have comparisons between our models."

Results of these tests are shown in tables 17 and 18. It will be noted in these tests that the very light weight .177 pellets did not register on the chronograph in most instances after passing the 50-foot range. This indicates that the pellets had spread and dropped so much at 75 feet that no accuracy could be expected of the .177 at that range. This performance is at variance with European claims of accuracy with this caliber at 50 meters, since

TABLE 17
TESTS BY H. P. WHITE LABORATORY ON CROSMAN MODEL 140 (CALIBER .22)

	VELOCITY (F.P.S.)			
Number of strokes	5-foot range	25-foot range	50-foot range	75-foot range
2	329	304	...	...
4	455	419	...	...
6	487	453	...	...
8	565	520	505	444
10	602	551	528	440
12	634	581	543	456
14	651	598	583	483

TABLE 18
TESTS BY H. P. WHITE LABORATORY ON CROSMAN MODEL 147 (CALIBER .177)

	VELOCITY (F.P.S.)			
Number of strokes	5-foot range	25-foot range	50-foot range	75-foot range
2	454	417	...	...
4	561	511	...	...
6	645	591	...	...
8	702	634	587	526
10	764	691	645	...
12	776	709	653	...
14	773	703	639	...

average velocity of German high-power air rifles at muzzle has shown in author's tests to be well under 600 f.p.s. on an average.

With reference to these tests, White reported: "All velocities were measured by use of Potter Lumiline screens and Potter counter chronographs. The screens were placed 10 feet apart with the mid-point between the screens being at the ranges stated in the firing records. In some instances it was most difficult to obtain velocity readings at the longer ranges. If results were not obtained after two trials, further effort was discontinued. *All velocity records are based on a single shot rather than an average of a number of shots.*"

Author's Test On Crosman Model 140 Rifle (Caliber .22). This test (table 19) was conducted by the author on the Potter counter chronograph, using Crosman Super

tion, hence this rifle does not have (and is not expected to have) the longer range accuracy and the penetration of the Sheridan.

As an indication of the progress made by Crosman in pneumatic rifles, the comparison of velocity data given in table 20 is interesting.

Benjamin Model 312 Super Single-Shot Air Rifle (Caliber .22)

While all discontinued air guns in the Benjamin line were handled, shot, and examined, only the 312 was used for exhaustive testing. The tests made offered an opportunity to check performance against other makes in the higher priced .22 brackets, both domestic and foreign, pneumatic and spring-air patterns.

TABLE 19

Test by Author, Crosman Model 140 Rifle (Caliber .22), September 25, 1956

Shot number	1 pump stroke	2 pump strokes	3 pump strokes	4 pump strokes	5 pump strokes	6 pump strokes	7 pump strokes	10 pump strokes
1	.02342	.01456	.01190	.01052	.00971	.00907	.00840	.00781
2	.02687	.01477	.01228	.01055	.00947	.00810	.00860	.00765
3	.02527	.01456	.01164	.01064	.00923	.00886	.00849	.00760
4	.02337	.01425	.01155	.01019	.00930	.00935	.00852	.00762
5	.02617	.01477	.01192	.01054	.00966	.00897	.00845	.00779
6	.02326	.01489	.01163	.01090	.00950	.00889	.00848	.00751
7	.02675	.01435	.01174	.01058	.00951	.00887	.00819	.00758
8	.02540	.01473	.01222	.01044	.00962	.00877	.00846	.00753
9	.02154	.01508	.01203	.01048	.00966	.00898	.00839	.00760
10	.02520	.01456	.01214	.01061	.00960	.00902	.00843	.00765
Total	.24725 (Equals 203 f.p.s.)	.14652 (Equals 341 f.p.s)	.11905 (Equals 420 f.p.s.)	.10545 (Equals 465 f.p.s)	.09526 (Equals 525 f.p.s.)	.08888 (Equals 564 f.p.s.)	.08441 (Equals 593 f.p.s.)	.07634 (Equals 655 f.p.s.)

Pell pellets; shooting conditions were as set forth by White. The tests were run September 25, 1956.

Note that while velocities were taken only at the 5-foot range, each indicated number of pump strokes was tested for 10—not just 1—shots *to get an average velocity.* For the benefit of those who are interested technically, the individual *time intervals* are shown for each shot; each total of 10 shots is shown in both time-interval totals and in the average velocity indicated by the aggregate of the time-interval records.

Note On Crosman Velocity Tests. The author's graph herewith indicates that the rifle is very efficient in the ranges of power where the average air rifle is likely to be used. For practical air-gun target shooting at 30 feet, this rifle will produce adequate velocity (above 450 f.p.s.) with 4 strokes of the pump. While it is true that most German and British spring-air types will equal this velocity with just one action movement, this must be set against the fact that the spring-air type has a positive and often harsh recoil which must be compensated for in shooting; while the pneumatic does not suffer from that condition and hence is easier for the average man to sight and shoot accurately.

Crosman develops its pellets primarily for indoor target shooting, not for longer range shooting or extra penetra-

Models shooting common air-rifle shot were passed over because they are not materially more accurate or powerful than the toy Daisy patterns. This applies also to the Benjamin Model 720, a repeating air rifle of good design but with neither the velocity nor the accuracy to warrant expensive testing for a serious work of this nature.

The Benjamin has several points of superiority over the Crosman equivalent which are cancelled out by several points of inferiority. On an average, the Crosman products showed somewhat better performance results, though the superiority was not particularly marked; and if spread over a period of production checks, there is no reason technically why the two should not run neck and neck.

Somewhat better groups were made with the Benjamin than with the Crosman, though on an average the grouping was not as good as claimed by the maker. The use of a nonferrous rather than a steel barrel is probably a positive contributing factor here, not only in its freedom from moisture effects as the gun is fired (in a pneumatic, of course, this is a decompression effect with corresponding temperature lowering inside the barrel), but also in the frictional factors involved during bullet travel, bronze and lead being more nearly ideal in theory than bronze

TABLE 20

VELOCITY TESTS SHOWING PROGRESS ON CROSMAN
PNEUMATIC RIFLES

TEST BY AUTHOR, CROSMAN COMPRESSED-AIR RIFLE
(CALIBER .22) SEPTEMBER 25, 1956

Number of strokes	Velocity (f.p.s.)
1	203
2	341
3	420
4	465
5	525
6	564
7	593
10	655

Note 1. Difficult to pump after 6 strokes; very difficult after 10.
Note 2. Barrel 19.5 inches; pellet weight 14.2 grains.

TEST BY RESEARCH GROUP, CROSMAN COMPRESSED-AIR RIFLE
(CALIBER .22), APRIL 29, 1949

Number of strokes	Velocity (f.p.s.)
1	149
2	266
3	334
4	377
5	456
6	488
7	501
10	574

Note 1. Very difficult to pump after 10 strokes.
Note 2. Length of barrel 19.75 inches; pellet weight 14.2 grains.

and steel *in a pneumatic design*. An examination of the rifling indicated it to be considerably smoother than in the Crosman steel barrels of the specimens available.

However, as will be discussed later under the heading Pellet Testing, the author is inclined to believe that most of the slightly better accuracy encountered could be attributed to the Benjamin pellets, since regardless of what arm they were used in, Benjamin pellets showed better than average accuracy and velocity patterns.

The Benjamin on an average was somewhat better fitted than the Crosman, as might be expected from an old-line firm with a relatively small production and modest tooling where hand-fitting skills and assembly plays a considerable part in manufacture.

The Crosman safety, while merely an elementary trigger block, does lock the action safely against any misuse of the trigger. In this comparison the Benjamin is deficient, as pressure on the trigger while the safety is applied can set up a condition of potential danger or nuisance by allowing the striker to move out of trigger-sear engagement. The Benjamin instruction literature warns of this condition, in fact, which makes it doubly puzzling why the condition has not been corrected mechanically, since the makers know it exists.

The pumping mechanics of the two makes are the same in principle, of course, but on limited tests the Benjamin proved easier to pump for the first 6 strokes. After that the performances leveled out. At the other extreme, pump stroke for pump stroke the Crosman gave somewhat better velocity. Incidentally, for what the observation is worth, the Crosman developed better velocity with Benjamin pellets than the Benjamin rifle did with Crosman pellets.

The Benjamin was considerably harder to cock preparatory to loading than was the current Crosman, a condition produced by the difference in valving systems. The Benjamin uses the proven impact valve which requires a striker blow to open; the Crosman utilizes the newer blow-off valve released by trigger and air, hence does not require the effort necessary to cock a heavy striker spring as the gun is opened.

Benjamin does not release any velocity data, but the author's Potter counter chronograph figures given in table 21 show the picture there. For the Model 312 rifles tested, Benjamin claims a bench-rest accuracy group of "1 inch at 15 to 20 yards." Firing from a Modern-Bond machine rest—not a bench rest where human factors are involved—the author was unable with 10 separate group tests to equal the records claimed at 15 yards, much less 20. In fairness to the Benjamin Company, however, it must here be stated that such groups could not be made with the Crosman rifle either; while on the other hand, 1-inch groups were made at 20 yards with a British Webley underlever spring-air rifle and with a German Walther 51 breakdown barrel-cocking rifle. In short, such groups ARE possible with Diabolo-type pellets; though three Benjamins obtained in the open market would not shoot to those standards.

On the matter of penetration the Benjamin did make a good showing in the high-pump-stroke range. Benjamin pellets are designed to give better penetration than the Crosman. This is understandable as has already been pointed out, because Crosman is interested primarily in indoor shooting where penetration is not too desirable a factor. On the other hand, the Benjamin penetration did not in any sense compare with that produced by the special Sheridan pellet.

TABLE 21

TEST BY AUTHOR, BENJAMIN MODEL 312, SUPER SINGLE-SHOT
AIR RIFLE (CALIBER .22), WITH BENJAMIN H-C PELLETS
(AVERAGE OF THREE TESTS)

Number of strokes	Velocity (f.p.s.)
1	194
2	319
3	401
4	451
5	503
6	542
7	572
8	596
9	617
10	639

Note 1. Easy up to 5 strokes; difficult 7 to 10 strokes; very difficult after 10 strokes.
Note 2. Pellet (H-C) weight, 14.99 grains. (Weight is an average of 30 pellets, 10 from each of 3 boxes.)

Tests on Obsolete and Experimental Pneumatic (Pump-Up) Rifles

The following data is furnished for general interest and to indicate some possibilities in the field of pneumatic arms. As has been pointed out in the body of this book, literally scores of inventors and manufacturers have introduced compressed-air arms in the United States in recent years. Only three of these have been able to remain in business—excluding the Daisy Manufacturing Company, which up to this point has confined its activities to air arms in the toy category despite precision manufacture.

Many of those who failed were ahead of their time. Some were under-financed. Others had good designs but lacked manufacturing or sales know-how.

The data given below covers a few of the best types which were offered. Since they can no longer be serviced, it is not recommended that any of these types be purchased except for collections.

The Kessler Pneumatic Rifle. The Kessler, as has been discussed in our text, was financed by a group in Rochester, N. Y., after the Crosman Arms Company refused to sell out to them. Kessler later went bankrupt.

The Kessler was a typical pump-up in most respects. It weighed 6.5 pounds, measured 36.5 inches overall, used the standard forearm pump for air charging, and the typical turning bolt for single-shot breech loading.

Like the original Sheridan, Kessler incorporated an expensive ball-seat valve. The gun could be pumped up to about 1200 pounds pressure—a power which is not uncommon, incidentally. The striker moving ahead as the trigger released it hit the ball and unseated it momentarily, releasing the full air charge. When it is of precision design and manufacture, the ball-seat valve is an excellent fast-air-release system. Maintaining precision, however, in manufacture and assembly is likely to be too costly for use in a low-priced design. (The Kessler sold at about $16.)

Kessler for a time produced pellets rather like a Sheridan, bullet type with hollow base and driving band in both .177 and .22 calibers.

The test shown in table 22 was made with standard Crosman pellets, no original Kessler ammunition having been available at the time of test, but the rifle was in perfect condition. This fact is mentioned because Kessler claimed a velocity as high as 790 f.p.s. with their own pellets.

If compared with velocity figures on a Crosman of the same manufacturing period, the Kessler will be found to have been far less efficient. Ten strokes on the Crosman of that period developed 574 f.p.s. as against 496 for the Kessler, ammunition for ammunition.

The truly noteworthy feature was the relative ease of pumping. However, as evidenced by the failure to increase

TABLE 22
TESTS BY AUTHOR, KESSLER PNEUMATIC RIFLE, WITH CROSMAN PELLETS

Number of strokes	Velocity (f.p.s.)
1	118
2	263
3	326
4	373
5	417
6	437
7	462
8	483
9	490
10	496
11	503
12	504
13	507
14	503
15	506
16	506

Note 1. Quite easy to pump at all times, regardless of the number of strokes.
Note 2. Length of barrel—20 inches. Steel. Weight of Crosman pellet—14.2 grains.

TABLE 23
TESTS BY AUTHOR, PLAINSMAN COMPRESSED-AIR RIFLE

Number of strokes	Velocity (f.p.s.)	Number of strokes	Velocity (f.p.s.)
1	200	11	708
2	313	12	748
3	425	13	778
4	485	14	790
5	526	15	788
6	572	16	812*
7	587	17	833
8	646	18	828
9	668	19	811*
10	695	20	822*

Note 1. Additional tests were conducted at stages marked with an asterisk because the valves, while not air locking, were obviously not letting off all pressure during the interval of valve opening. The results were as follows:
At 16 strokes a second shot was fired with a velocity reading of 318 f.p.s.
At 19 strokes a second shot was fired with a velocity reading of 405 f.p.s.
At 20 strokes a second shot was fired with a velocity reading of 489 f.p.s.
Note 2. The rifle was very difficult to pump after 7 strokes, but the velocity achieved with 7 strokes was in itself quite remarkable.

pressure after 11 strokes, the valve work wasn't what it might have been.

One passing note for the collector: Kessler rifles were offered in 1949 by Klein's Sporting Goods Company of Chicago for $9.95 under the name of Rochester Air Rifle.

The Plainsman Pneumatic Rifle, .177 and .22 Calibers. Rifles, pistols, and even shotguns were produced under this brand name, as discussed in our text. Manufacture was at various points, and a few years ago the name was revived on a group of unsuccessful CO_2 guns.

The Plainsman line as originally produced was very well worthwhile. In many respects this design gave performance characteristics (table 23) surpassed even today only by the Sheridan. It, too, fell by the wayside because of the production cost to maintain quality and lack of adequate financing.

In 1948 these arms were made and distributed by the Challenger Arms Corporation of Los Angeles, California. Some were later sold, chiefly through mail-order firms, under the trade name "Challenger."

The most remarkable feature of this design, perhaps, was the attempt to make it a "repair-it-yourself" design. Like the Sheridan Super, the Plainsman featured a self-contained valve unit in the form of a sealed valve chamber which could be replaced much as you would replace a dry cell in a flashlight. Pump cups and washers were also designed to be owner-replaced without having to ship the rifle to the factory. In practice, however, it was soon apparent that quality of this sort could not be maintained in a rifle to sell at a low price ($14.95 retail in 1948). Other details of the arm, which is essentially the same in pistol, shotgun, and rifle mechanism, will be found in the body of this work.

The Simco Pneumatic Rifle, Caliber .177, Round Ball. This rifle, also made in California in the late 1940's, was made as a repeater, the spring-fed system being a forerunner of that found in the current Carbo-Jet CO_2 pistol. Details of the arm will be found in the text.

TABLE 24
Tests by Author, Simco Compressed-Air Rifle

Number of strokes	Velocity (f.p.s.)	Number of strokes	Velocity (f.p.s.)
1	220	11	820
2	436	12	846
3	536	13	869
4	607	14	869
5	641	15	872
6	705	20	907
7	726		
8	764		
9	789		
10	815		

The round shot used was standard air-rifle shot. Considering the fact that such shot does not give an effective air seal, by comparison with expanding base types which are forced into the rifling, the velocities shown in table 24 are truly remarkable.

The rifle itself was the standard scissors-pump design, and was very difficult to pump after 7 strokes. Incidentally, the scissors handle failed after 20 pump strokes.

British Teddington Experimental Pneumatic Rifle. This experimental rifle was built by the noted British Teddington firm with the idea that while it would be too powerful for sale in England, it might be made and sold in the United States. More details of it will be found in the text. The test results are shown in table 25.

This rifle was made with interchangeable .177 and .22 barrels. It used Webley Diabolo-type pellets.

TABLE 25
Research Bureau Tests, Teddington Compressed-Air Rifle

CALIBER .177		CALIBER .22	
Number of strokes	Velocity (f.p.s.)	Number of strokes	Velocity (f.p.s.)
1	327	1	0*
2	466	2	396
3	530	3	481
4	606	4	554
5	657	5	607
6	705	6	652
7	745	7	671
8	792	8	739
9	816	9	743
10	836	10	772

* Bullet did not emerge.
Note 1. Very difficult to pump after 6 strokes.
Note 2. Normal maximum velocity to stay within legal air-rifle sales limits in Great Britain is about 550 f.p.s. for caliber .22 and about 600 f.p.s. for caliber .177.

American Vincent Experimental Pneumatic Rifle. This gun is pictured in the text. Fewer than 100 were made, incidentally. It is of passing interest to the collector and the technician as one of the modern forms of repeat-charge compressed-air arms. That is, while most types are designed to evacuate all air when the trigger is pulled, an occasional one like the Benjamin 720 and the Vincent is intended to allow a number of shots (with constantly decreasing velocity, of course) to be fired before it is necessary to pump the rifle. However, in such designs the chamber must be loaded either manually or by movement of a feeding mechanism.

The results of tests by the author with this gun are shown in tables 26 and 27.

TABLE 26
Tests by Author, Vincent Compressed-Air Gun (Caliber .177)

	VELOCITY (F.P.S.)				
	Number of strokes				
Shot number	20	50	100	150	200
1	282	539	699	723	763
2	256	509	673	720	785
3	177	496	652	634	761
4	168	455	620	690	720
5	...	401	597	600	672
6	...	375	581	600	675
7	...	253	556	593	629
8	...	226	521	590	644
9	...	172	502	554	580
10	...	81	459	570	600
11	...	...	...	511	567
12	...	...	...	483	523
13	...	...	...	466	548
14	...	...	...	448	483
15	...	...	...	425	476
16	...	...	...	360	413
17	...	...	...	365	376
18	...	...	...	335	381
19	...	...	...	209	347
20	...	...	...	177	347
21	...	...	...	180	...
22	...	...	...	0	...
23	...	...	...	...	278
24	...	...	...	...	194
25	...	...	...	...	94
26	...	...	...	...	84

TABLE 27
Velocity Drop In First 10 Shots, Vincent Compressed-Air Gun (Caliber .177)
(See Table 26 Above)

Number of strokes	Velocity drop (f.p.s.)
50	458
100	240
150	153
200	165

Note. From the above figures it is apparent that this multiple air-discharge pump-up system is not practicable. It was used in early 19th century air guns of various types, including the Austrian Girardoni. The accurate electronic tests to which the Vincent was subjected give a clear picture of the amount of effort required to give any semblance of sustained power such as is required for even a mild form of accuracy.

Discontinued Apache Air Rifle. The California-made Apache rifle had much in common with the Plainsman. However, it was supplied with a rifled barrel of .250 caliber (British No. 3 bore) for which round shot were supplied. The ball weighed approximately .22 grains. No. 4 buck would fit.

The forward stroke of the bolt seated the ball in the rifling, so that (as in the case of the current German Barakuda rifle which uses a round ball in a rifled barrel) a narrow band of lead was exposed on fired bullets, indicating clearly that the ball took the rifling. This compression of course gave an effective air seal and prevented power loss behind the bullet.

Since the pump system and air-chamber capacity were of the same order as the current types, velocity was considerably lower than with the current .22. However, the bullet weight and type gave good shock power against pests.

An extra barrel, smooth-bored, was supplied with the Apache. It was to be inserted in the .250 barrel and was held by a threaded nut. It used air-rifle shot, .175, and would take any of the .177 pellets because of the bolt-thrust seating. Accuracy was poor.

One of the principal causes of trouble in this rifle was the plastic stocks used. This design was not considered worth spending time and money testing, since few are in use and the design is impractical.

Care of Pneumatic Rifles

Only normal lubrication and rust protection is recommended. No average shooter or mechanic should tinker with ANY compressed-air arm. Only a light-body, neutral oil with good cold-test properties should be used.

One note of warning; NEVER USE ANY OIL CONTAINING SOLVENTS IN ANY AIR OR CO_2 RIFLE. Never use powder solvents or metal-fouling solvents on such arms. Pump and valve mechanism can be injured very easily by use of solvents or inferior grades of oil.

Points which may be given an occasional drop of oil are: air-intake hole to the rear of the long slot in the piston tube (this takes care of the moving parts in the compression chamber). The pump lever where the toggle link contacts the spring. Pivots of the trigger, safety, and striker, if they are dry. And very occasionally only, the front bearing on the piston rod.

Do not "dry fire" excessively. While snapping on an empty chamber occasionally won't do any harm, it must be remembered that pneumatic rifles differ greatly from powder rifles, in that most utilize very hard striker blows to operate the valve release, and these heavy blows when the air chamber is empty won't do the firing mechanism any good.

It is also not advisable to use reclaimed pellets.

If you have failed to pump up sufficient pressure and the pellet lodges in the barrel, merely pump up 5 or 6 strokes and try to blow it out. NEVER try to drive out a stuck pellet with another one, however. If the air pressure won't dislodge it, chances are you have a defective pellet (this applies to any air arm). In that case insert a suitable rod and tap it gently and regularly until the pellet is punched out.

If you are the type that insists on taking things apart, even at the risk of ruining them, you can remove the piston assembly as follows: drift out the pins; tap off the muzzle cap; line up the piston assembly until you can push the toggle-link pin out; and withdraw the piston assembly. In any event, leave the valves alone! Without special tools and knowledge you are just asking for trouble in thus dismounting any type or make of pneumatic arm.

If you remove ANY air gun from its stock, check your sights after reassembly, as changes in screw tensions alone can cause changes in impact point of pellets.

Storing. If you do not intend to use a pneumatic arm for some time, it is well to put one or two pumps of air into it to protect the air chamber against moisture, dirt, or excessive dryness. Oil vapor is always present; and if it mixes with dirt or dust, it can sludge up and cause air seepage, since it keeps the delicate valves from seating perfectly. If you have too much moisture present, sooner or later something will rust or corrode—though in some makes there are fewer parts which can be affected than in others. If, at the other extreme, the gun is too dry, oils present will tend to gum up.

Pneumatic Rifle Grouping Comparisons

While the author's research and controlled firing tests produced a vast amount of comparative accuracy data, it is recognized that manufacturers are steadily working to improve their products, both arms and ammunition; and in view of this fact all accuracy data in particular must be considered as being subject to revision as products are improved.

As a general indication of what adequate research by manufacturers could develop in this field, sampling test statistics on *smooth-bored vs rifled barrel accuracy* may be of interest (table 29) as well as a sampling test of the

TABLE 28
AUTHOR'S PELLET ACCURACY COMPARISON TEST WITH PNEUMATIC RIFLE BY MAKER "A" (PURCHASED FROM DEALER)

String No. (pellet "A")	Spread of group (inches) 10 of 10	Best 9 of 10	String No. (pellet "B")	Spread of group (inches) 10 of 10	Best 9 of 10
1	.812	.812	1	.625	.625
2	.875	.875	2	.562	.562
3	1.250	.875	3	.562	.562
4	.687	.687	4	.625	.625
5	.937	.937	5	.562	.562
Averages (inches)	.9122	.8372	Averages (inches)	.5872	.5872
Maximums (inches)	1.250	.937	Maximums (inches)	.625	.625
Minimums (inches)	.687	.687	Minimums (inches)	.562	.562

Note 1. Caliber .177; range, 15 feet from muzzle; shots per string, 10 with rifle maker "A's" pellet and 10 with competitor's pellet ("B"); number of strings fired, 5 with each brand of pellet; firing control, muzzle and elbow bench rest; number of pump strokes, 6.
Note 2. Average velocity for 50 shots, rifle "A" and pellet "A," 623 f.p.s.; average velocity for 50 shots, rifle "A" and pellet "B," 625 f.p.s.
Note 3. Similar tests on above with locked machine rest gave groups comparing very closely to all the above figures.

use of a competing maker's pellets vs the pellets of the rifle manufacturer (table 28).

Note that all the above comparison tests were run by the same technicians under equivalent conditions. Velocities were almost identical, but pellet shapes varied and the weight of the "B" pellet was somewhat heavier than for rifle maker "A's" pellet. In short, if the velocities were "weighted" to allow for the heavier pellet, the "B" velocities would have been higher than "A's."

The important factor, however, is that the tests show quite definitely that in "A's" gun, his competitor's pellets actually gave not only far better groups, but also far more *consistent* groups than his own ammunition! Note also that a higher velocity was obtained with a rifled barrel whether used with pellet "A" or "B" than with a smooth-bored barrel. However, whether using pellet 'A" or "B," accuracy was better, and all average, minimum, and maximum group sizes *were better with the smooth-bored than with the rifled barrel at the 25-foot range.*

MODERN PNEUMATIC SHOTGUNS

The Plainsman shotgun, as mentioned and pictured in the text, is the only modern arm of this type to be generally distributed. The manufacturer failed.

However, it is known that Crosman has been considering a shotgun with either a pneumatic or CO_2 power system, hence some tests were run of the Plainsman shotgun to indicate what the shooter might expect in the way of performance.

As to accuracy and pattern possibilities, the three illustrations below are reduced from 8½ by 11 target sheets. They were shot at 6, 9, and 15 feet from the muzzle, respectively, at the center aiming point.

Both pattern and penetration tests indicated that such "air shotguns" do not have enough real value to recommend their use except at small-bird specimens at extremely close range.

Incidentally, at least 10 pump strokes are required to get any semblance of penetration.

TABLE 29
SMOOTH-BORED AND RIFLED-BARREL COMPARISON TEST USING PNEUMATIC RIFLE BY MAKER "A", PURCHASED FROM DEALER
(SEE NOTE 1)

	Spread of group (inches)	
	10 out of 10 shots	9 out of 10 shots
Average with rifled barrel	2.125	1.625 (pellet "A")
Average with smooth-bored barrel	1.375	1.275 (pellet "B")
Maximum group with rifled barrel	2.50	2.00 (pellet "A")
Maximum group with smooth-bored barrel	1.50	1.375 (pellet "B")
Minimum group with rifled barrel	1.75	1.25 (pellet "A")
Minimum group with smooth-bored barrel	1.25	1.125 (pellet "B")

Note 1. Pneumatic rifle by maker "A" was purchased from dealer with rifled barrel. Same weapon was tested with rifled barrel *replaced by smooth-bored barrel from the same manufacturer*. This was done to assure that pump and valve factors would remain constant, as such factors can vary from gun to gun in production manufacture.
Note 2. Caliber .177; range, 25 feet from muzzle; shots per string, 10 with rifle maker "A's" pellet in rifled barrel and 10 with competitor's pellet ("B") in smooth-bored barrel; number of strings fired, 5; firing control, muzzle and elbow bench rest; number of pump strokes, 3.
Note 3. Average velocity of pellet "A" in rifled barrel, 483 f.p.s.; average velocity of pellet "B" in smooth-bored barrel, 459 f.p.s.

TESTS ON CURRENT PNEUMATIC (PUMP-UP) PISTOLS

The only pneumatic pistols currently being manufactured are the American Benjamin and Crosman lines (which see in text). For purposes of tests the author used only the Benjamin Model 132, rifled, .22 shooting pellets; and the comparable Crosman Model 130, also rifled and shooting pellets. In both instances it is possible to relate the performances of the accompanying .177 rifled models. Benjamin claims group accuracy of 1 inch at 30 feet, Crosman claims group accuracy of ¾ inch at 25 feet for its .22 models as listed.

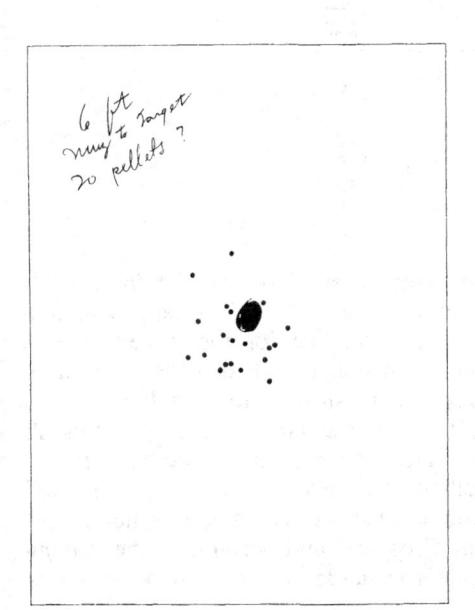

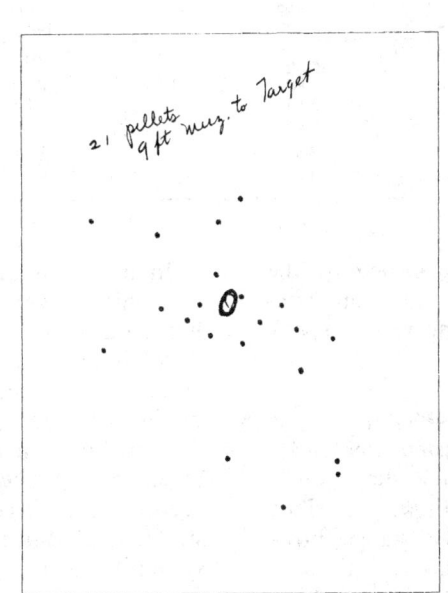

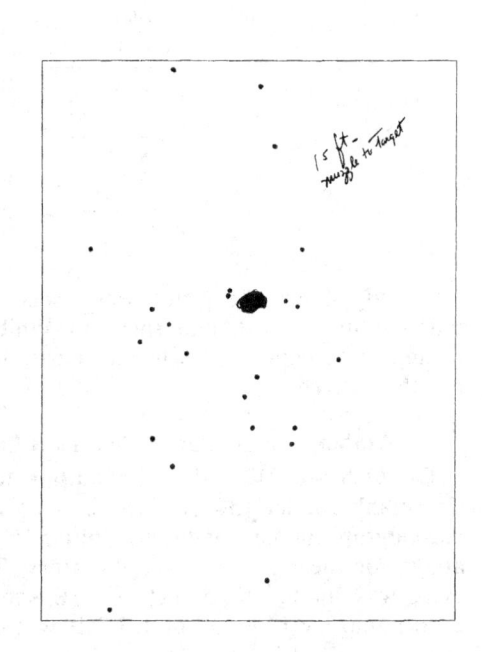

Since other model Benjamins use air-rifle shot, which is not precision ammunition and on which the makers claim group possibles of 2 inches at 30 feet, accuracy tests were not considered valuable enough to warrant the time and expense involved. More velocity can be obtained from these pistols since they use smaller and lighter weight shot, but accuracy is suitable only for general plinking.

The manufacturers offer pneumatic pistols for their variable power and because they "have no heavy springs to cock." In the considered opinion of the author, neither one of these claims is particularly valid *in a pistol,* though they have considerable validity from the power standpoint in a pneumatic *rifle.*

The outstanding value of the pneumatic pistol over the spring-air type lies almost entirely in the fact that it does not have the lunge or recoil factors of the spring-air pistol, hence is easier to learn to shoot. Impartial tests indicate quite clearly that in a .22 pellet-type air pistol best air-range *accuracy* requires a muzzle velocity of about 300 to 350 f.p.s. Higher velocity gives better penetration, but at air-pistol shooting distances does not materially improve accuracy. Any of the serious spring-air pistols will develop these velocities; and granted that many are difficult to cock, the fact still remains that they require only *one* leverage movement to produce that velocity and the velocity is relatively constant. Some spring-air pistols can be built up to produce over 400 f.p.s., if desired.

To produce average velocities of 300 to 350 f.p.s. with a pneumatic requires a minimum of 6 to 8 strokes, and may require 12. The first 3 or 4 are not difficult, but to pump up much beyond that point when the pistol is in good condition requires considerable effort.

H. P. White Tests

The tests shown in table 30 were made by H.P. White Laboratory for the Crosman Arms Company, and the author is indebted to the president and chief engineer of that organization for making the results available for this study. Since the pistol tested was furnished by the manufacturer direct, and since all White tests are conducted on a controlled scientific basis, the results speak for themselves.

Authors Tests (Potter Counter Chronograph)

On October 24, 1956, the author tested (table 31) Crosman's Model 130 (caliber .22) on a Potter counter chronograph under conditions similar to those prescribed above for the H. P. White Laboratory. The range, however, was limited to 5 feet and 10 shots were fired at each pump level instead of 1. (This was done to establish complete averages, to check uniformity of air-valve release, etc.)

The pistol tested by the author was supplied by Crosman, but a second one purchased from a dealer gave approximately the same results on controlled tests. In making comparisons between author's test results and those by White, two factors must be considered: (1) Individual pistols, whether air or powder types and regardless of make, can vary within the limits shown in all normal production manufacture. (2) The rugged tests of the author were designed to test average performance under the most strenuous normal-use conditions, and the heat and friction produced in firing *long strings of shots,* as opposed to firing *one* for each varying number of pump strokes, can in itself account for some of the lower velocities encountered. The differences in time intervals will tell those qualified much of interest about performance. Pellets used were Crosman make.

The special valve system and superior crosslock trigger safety are features of these pistols. True the safety is only a trigger block and under abuse the firing mechanism can be jarred off; but anyone so abusing any mechanical item should not own it in the first place.

Benjamin Model 132 Tests

Benjamin does not release anything but the most generalized data on their arms, and no velocity claims could be obtained from them for comparison. Two of their pistols were purchased from dealers' shelves and submitted to comparative tests. The data in table 32 indicates that on an average the current Benjamin is slightly more powerful than the current Crosman. (Note: It must be kept in mind that the Crosman is a high-production pistol which retails at $9.95 at time of this writing, while the Benjamin retails for $20.)

TABLE 30
H. P. White Crosman Tests (Potter Counter Chronograph), May 18, 1956

	CROSMAN MODEL 137, CALIBER .177			CROSMAN MODEL 130, CALIBER .22	
Number of strokes	Velocity (f.p.s.) 5-foot range	25-foot range	Number of strokes	Velocity (f.p.s.) 5-foot range	25-foot range
2	253	245	2	201	192
4	316	316	4	240	238
6	329	314	6	312	294
8	372	352	8	360	331
10	390	364	10	379	365
12	408	370	12	397	372

In line with the higher cost of the Benjamin, the fits and finishes were better than in the Crosman. Benjamin has always made a good product for the price and this pistol is no exception. In common with other Benjamin arms it is well made and finished within the limits of its pricing. Trigger pull is particularly good, and this in conjunction with the lack of recoil in a pneumatic pistol, together with a well-rifled bronze barrel, makes for good accuracy for all common usages. The safety is not as desirable as that in the Crosman; and because of the valving system used, the pistol is harder to cock than the Crosman.

TABLE 31
AUTHOR'S TESTS, CROSMAN M130 COMPRESSED-AIR RIFLE

2 strokes		3 strokes		4 strokes		5 strokes		6 strokes		7 strokes		8 strokes	
Shot number	Time interval	Shot number	Time interval	Shot number	Time interval	Shot number	Time interval	Shot number	Time interval	Shot number	Time interval	Shot number	Time interval
1	.04709	1	.02651	1	.02123	1	.01952	1	.01773	1	.01575	1	.01523
2	.03780	2	.02604	2	.02229	2	.01802	2	.01772	2	.01690	2	.01593
3	.03737	3	.02542	3	.02249	3	.01973	3	.01693	3	.01612	3	.01546
4	.03750	4	.02615	4	.02145	4	.01886	4	.01701	4	.01632	4	.01594
5	.04362	5	.02856	5	.02149	5	.01879	5	.01712	5	.01613	5	.01554
6	.04799	6	.02582	6	.02174	6	.01893	6	.01730	6	.01644	6	.01532
7	.03132	7	.02465	7	.02149	7	.01854	7	.01756	7	.01617	7	.01593
8	.04485	7	.02579	8	.02093	8	.01871	8	.01691	8	.01609	8	.01597
9	.04974	9	.02631	9	.02110	9	.01857	9	.01751	9	.01643	9	.01554
10	.04128	10	.02382	10	.02025	10	.01798	10	.01739	10	.01654	10	.01565
Total, .41856		Total, .25907		Total, .21446		Total, .18765		Total, .17318		Total, .16289		Total, .15651	
(Average velocity 120 f.p.s.)		(Average velocity 194 f.p.s.)		(Average velocity 228 f.p.s.)		(Average velocity 265 f.p.s.)		(Average velocity 289 f.p.s.)		(Average velocity 307 f.p.s.)		(Average velocity 319 f.p.s.)	

9 strokes		10 strokes		11 strokes		13 strokes		15 strokes		20 strokes	
1	.01522	1	.01481	1	.01422	1	.01406	1	.01378	1	.01308
2	.01494	2	.01487	2	.01389	2	.01424	2	.01413	2	.01312
3	.01491	3	.01518	3	.01433			3	.01401	3	.01297
4	.01550	4	.01524	4	.01448			4	.01408	4	.01352
5	.01520	5	.01488	5	.01508			5	.01480	5	.01341
6	.01504	6	.01509	6	.01546			6	.01384	6	.01318
7	.01540	7	.01495	7	.01517			7	.01474	7	.01296
8	.01565	8	.01515	8	.01509			8	.01420	8	.01309
9	.01553	9	.01480	9	.01468			9	.01402	9	.01320
10	.01560	10	.01477	10	.01492			10	.01398	10	.01303
Total, .15299		Total, .14974		Total, .14732		Total, .02830		Total, .14158		Total .13156	
(Average velocity 327 f.p.s.)		(Average velocity 334 f.p.s.)		(Average velocity 339 f.p.s.)				(Average velocity 353 f.p.s.)		(Average velocity 382 f.p.s.)	

Velocity Records

In the course of making these tests, every available pistol of recent manufacture (within the past 20 years) was examined and tested where conditions warranted. No pistol tested could be pumped up to exceed the velocity found in the Benjamin. (Pistols included earlier model Benjamin and Crosman types, Plainsman, and Apache).

.22 calibers tended to get in the 400 f.p.s. range on about 10 strokes with the pistol in good working order, and no leaks were detectable by water-submersion tests. None would go much past the 425 f.p.s. level, regardless of the number of pumps, tending to flatten the trajectory curve between 13 and 15 pumps, and picking up somewhat on 20 pumps to reach the 425 f.p.s. level.

This, of course, does not mean that it is impossible to develop a pneumatic pistol which will considerably exceed this velocity. Indeed the author is acquainted with several experimental models which will do so. However, in view of the overall pistol length factors, which limit the length of the piston stroke, and the type and operation of levers required for pumping, it is questionable whether any production pistol for sale at a popular price will ever be made to exceed the current power.

Any modern air pistol is strictly a short-range arm for indoor-target or for mild plinking use, 25 feet being about the limit of true accuracy except in the hands of a real expert. For longer ranges or for use against small game, the .22 powder-cartridge pistol should be used.

An analysis of all current pneumatic arms indicates there may well be possibilities of developing more powerful and more easily operated *rifles* on this system; but mechanical limitations are a definite inhibiting factor in improving usable power in pneumatic pistols. Edwards (Pete) Brown, currently gun editor for *Sports Afield Magazine*, while on the staff of *The American Rifleman Magazine* in 1949, conducted a series of tests with the Crosman air pistol of that year. On Potter chronograph tests he established that the .177 caliber started at about 235 f.p.s. on 2 pump strokes, reached 300 f.p.s. between 4 and 5 strokes, hit 425 f.p.s. between 8 and 9 strokes. The curve flattened at about 11 strokes.

Pete's tests on the .22 showed a starting velocity of about 200 f.p.s. with 2 pump strokes. They hit 325 f.p.s. at 6 strokes, reached 400 f.p.s. at 8 strokes, curved to about 425 f.p.s. on 15 strokes, and flattened at about that point so that no additional pumping increased the velocity.

The *current* Crosman pistol was designed for a low selling price in its field, and in comparative tests by the author did not achieve the velocity of earlier Crosman

TABLE 32
TESTS BY AUTHOR, BENJAMIN MODEL 132, CALIBER .22, WITH BENJAMIN H-C PELLETS

Number of strokes	Velocity (f.p.s.) at 5-foot range
2	215
4	252
6	331
8	386
10	407
12	429

models. In any event, authenticated data between 1948 and 1956 support the conclusions stated as to pistol power and accuracy in the pneumatic field.

CARBON DIOXIDE (CO_2) ARMS TESTS

As a result of a long series of closely controlled tests of all current and many recent, but no longer made CO_2 arms, it is possible to draw several generalized conclusions. Ease of operation is by far the most important advantage the CO_2 system possesses in the pellet-gun field. When these arms are tested for precision accuracy against the best pneumatic and spring-air designs, they are invariably on the low side. However, for the *average* shooter or plinker, the accuracy is entirely adequate; and the absence of the lunge and recoil factors found in the spring-air system makes them much better arms trainers. New shooters in almost every case will be able to make better scores with a CO_2 pistol or rifle than with the corresponding spring-air weapon. Though the shooting cost is somewhat higher due to the CO_2 cartridge cost, the CO_2 designs on an average also make better trainers than the pneumatics, for while the pneumatics do not have the lunge faults of the spring-air systems, the physical effort in pumping up a number of shots rapidly is a definite deterrent to best accuracy. Thus, particularly for rapid-fire work, the CO_2 system is to be preferred for the beginner. (Note: As always, of course, there are exceptions. Low-power but heavy spring-air operated arms such as the Czech VZ35 rifle and high-power rifles equipped with the Hämmerli spring-air device are equally rapid to operate and the spring lunge is not noticeable.)

The tests detailed below bear out statements in the text regarding velocity, operational consistency of CO_2 systems, and accuracy. They completely dispel the recurrent myth of "absolute" equal pressures with resultant completely consistent trajectory and accuracy which has heretofore clouded the true facts about the CO_2 system.

The current CO_2 arms are good arms—on an average well worth the prices asked for them. Individual specimens under individual conditions will produce higher velocities, better accuracy, and longer "cartridge" life than some of the test results produced under averaging controls. On the other hand, still other individual specimens will produce lower velocities, poorer groups, and shorter "cartridge" life than shown herein. These results listed herein are what the average shooter may expect from the average arm he will buy and use.

As a matter of test experience it can be stated also that there is considerable opportunity for design improvements in all types. This applies particularly to the matter of power supply and valving. The present CO_2 cylinders obviously are not large enough for maximum efficiency, as a glance at the carefully prepared graphs herein will show. Nor is the dual-cartridge system the answer, since it produces only about 10 percent greater efficiency than the single cartridge and gives fewer shots. There is considerable room for improvement in the matter of valving, as evidenced by the often erratic pressures and sudden "bleed-offs." The author has encountered several experimental valve systems superior to those in use, though in all fairness it must be stated that the present valves when properly fitted, installed, and timed are capable of performances far better than the average. Here again the economic factor enters the picture, of course. There is a limit to the amount of hand-fitting time and testing which can be given to any relatively low-priced product, and the CO_2 arms available are all a lot of value for the dollar expended.

Another contributing factor to varying performances in CO_2 arms is the regularity and correct seating of the pellet during the closing action. When this factor was carefully checked, it was observable that the optimum efficiency was obtained where the pellet was driven in far enough for the rifling to cut into the pellet tail, thereby releasing more energy for pellet driving and equalizing the pressure application behind each pellet. While not critical, this loading factor has a definite influence on both velocity and accuracy in any type of pellet gun.

The type and nature of the rifling is of very considerable importance, and it is a source of considerable surprise to the author to find how relatively little is known in the air and CO_2 gun field about this very important factor. It was found possible to increase accuracy to a very marked degree by substituting a properly made (by good firearms standards) barrel for the CO_2 barrel in all arms tested.

Temperature changes, both external and within the arm, can considerably affect CO_2 gun operating efficiency. Best accuracy and velocity results are obtained when the gun is not fired until a minimum of 5 minutes after piercing the cartridge, and when a minimum of 1 minute is allowed to elapse between shots to dissipate the barrel and valve cooling effects produced by the decompression which follows the trigger pull. It is possible to "rig" tests with a CO_2 gun to produce relatively very high velocity merely by raising the temperature of the gun or cartridge; and it should be noted that all tests listed here were conducted under temperature controls in order to develop true averages, not freak performances. Thus velocity in winter or in a cold climate will be considerably lower than in summer or a warm climate; but since it will be relatively constant, this factor can be compensated for by sight adjustment in relation to the place and time of use. (This same type of factor, of course, affects firearms also, though not to as marked an extent because of the vast difference in even minimum powers.)

And finally there is the matter of ammunition. Some aspects will be covered under Pellet Tests. Just as the octane rating of a given gasoline will affect motor efficiency, so pellet fit, materials, tolerances—and even design—will affect, for better or worse, the performance of any arm, whether pellet type or firearm, but again it is much more noticeable in pellet arms because of the ballistic factors involved.

With regard to the much advertised factor of "variable power," tests indicate rather clearly that despite the American mania for "high power," so far as a CO_2 gun is concerned, the normally provided lower range is on an average more efficient than the higher. This was established by testing all 3 makes of American CO_2 pistols in both power ranges. Used with Diabolo pellets, the maximum single-shot velocity at high power was only about 15 percent higher than that for the low-power range;

while the fall-off in the higher power was so rapid that the number of reasonably effective shots produced was only about 50 percent of the low-power range. The high-power range for about 40 shots in a pistol, for instance, does have justification if you are shooting at pests or small game; but shooting at targets within normal ranges for such a pistol, it does not produce enough additional accuracy to warrant the extra gas usage. Also, because of valving factors, the "low" power adjustment will often give better velocity than the "high"!

Pistols

Benjamin Model 262 CO_2 Pistol. This manufacturer releases only fragmentary data on his products. No velocity claims are made. About the only checkable statements are regarding penetration and accuracy, which are simply stated as ⅜-inch in soft pine and 1-inch groups at 10 yards from rest, and "up to 50 shots" from the CO_2 cartridge.

In tests, penetration of ⅜ inch was quite regularly achieved at full power with this .22 caliber pistol, though not regularly at low power. At 10 yards, 5-shot groups were often made from rest, but 10-shot groups were considerably more difficult to obtain. However, the Benjamin consistently made slightly smaller groups than its competitors. The principal reasons for this seemed to be the combination of a well-rifled bronze barrel liner and a very good, soft lead (Benjamin) pellet. It was noticeable, for instance, that while better velocities (by a small margin) were obtainable with other pellets, this was seldom reflected in an accuracy increase except by RWS pellets, where again the group differences were marginal.

Best groups from rest with this pistol were .875 inch for 5 shots. Average groups were about 1.40 inches. In common with all current CO_2 pistols, where standard ammunition direct from the package without "miking" was used, occasional flyers threw 10-shot groups way out of average.

Benjamin CO_2 cartridges (smaller than the Crosman) gave consistently better performance than unmarked brands—this, remember, is a standard-size CO_2 cartridge. The number of shots from a Benjamin cartridge varied between 35 and 60, as compared with 15 to 25 from common brands. In other words, Benjamin's CO_2 purveyors are more reliable than the average.

In the matter of velocity, the Benjamin at full power fell below the Crosman with the latter's larger cartridge and slightly above the Carbo-Jet using a standard cartridge but a heavier (ball) missile. Maximum velocity achieved was 334 f.p.s. (Note: This velocity is entirely adequate for pellet-pistol performance at realistic ranges, maximum 30 feet.)

As in all CO_2 arms, at times a cartridge would fizzle out after 10 rounds or so, and although it was always difficult to establish whether the cause was a defective cartridge or valve operating movement, it was more probably the latter.

The performance of this pistol followed rather closely experience with the Benjamin Model 262 CO_2 Carbine (which see), allowance being made for barrel-length differences.

Crosman Model 150 (and 157) CO_2 Pistols. This manufacturer, quite unlike his American competitors, provided a vast amount of checkable research data to the author. As a result it was possible to set up comparative tests and control tests to determine to an extent never before attempted just what the potentials of the CO_2 system really are. The coverage given to Crosman products herein stems from this fact, not from any predilection on the author's part for this particular manufacturer. Crosman just provided more claims which could be scientifically analyzed.

This data is rated as of particular value to those interested, even when it doesn't agree with certain of the maker's advertising claims, because it reflects not only the author's personal tests and research, but also those of the H.P. White Laboratory which did much of the testing which the Crosman organization was unable to do in its own research department.

It might be added that the testing done for this book goes far beyond that undertaken by either the White organization for Crosman, or Crosman on its own behalf; and at some points where the tests may not appear to agree, the differences stem in part from individual weapons tested, and in others from the fact that testing for purposes of this book was done on a far larger scale.

H. P. White Laboratory Tests. The test conditions for these, as explained in a previous section, were set up by Rudolf Merz, chief engineer for Crosman, to determine velocity characteristics of these pistols at varying distances (from 5 to 70 feet) and at varying stages in usage of the power supply. All velocities shown indicate speed of that particular projectile at the distances indicated.

On comparative tests, the author's graphs show in general an interesting degree of relationship. As against White's maximum with the .22 of 383 f.p.s. at 5 feet, for instance, and a velocity of 368 f.p.s. on the 56th shot, we started at about the same level, scaled up to 415 f.p.s. maximum, stayed above 368 for 45 shots, and dropped off to 299 on the 56th. The differences in number of usable shots can reasonably be laid to valving or cartridge variances. Tests indicate that the Crosman Powerlet, an oversized CO_2 cartridge, will give roughly 50 shots at full power and 80 to 120 at low power, when used in this pistol.

CAUTION: These White tests should *not* be read across as indications of *continuing* velocity of the missile indicated in the 5-foot-range column. While it *is* possible to take the velocity of a powder missile at several points in its flight by use of additional screens, the trajectory of CO_2 pellets makes this course difficult, so White set up *separate* tests for each range rather than continuing tests on the same missile over several ranges.

These tests were made as follows: (1) First the pistol was loaded, the cartridge pierced, and firing delayed for 5 minutes. Then, starting with the first shot, each successive 5th shot was chronographed and the individual velocity recorded. This was carried on through the 71st shot after which power was unusable. (2) The gun was recharged and firing delayed 5 minutes. The chronograph screens were set to register at the 25-foot range. Starting with shot one, each 5th shot thereafter was recorded until the 56th after which at that range recording was diffi-

.22 CALIBER

TEST NO. 3 - CROSMAN MODEL 150 PISTOL

Full Power - 1 Powerlet

Shot No.	Range Ft.	Velocity F.P.S.	Shot No.	Range Ft.	Velocity F.P.S.	Shot No.	Range Ft.	Velocity F.P.S.
1	5	371	1	25	351	2	30	394
6	5	357	6	25	338	3	30	351
11	5	373	11	25	351	4	35	333
16	5	381	16	25	362	5	35	343
21	5	367	21	25	344	6	40	313
26	5	374	26	25	351	7	40	333
31	5	376	31	25	352	8	45	325
36	5	375	36	25	351	9	45	329
41	5	383	41	25	356	10	50	329
46	5	378	46	25	356	11	50	-
51	5	382	51	25	357	12	55	327
56	5	368	56	25	346	13	55	314
61	5	344				14	60	328
71	5	287				15	60	331
						16	65	320
						17	65	326
						18	70	279
						19	70	285

.177 CALIBER

TEST NO. 4 - CROSMAN MODEL 157 PISTOL

Full Power - 1 Powerlet

Shot No.	Range Ft.	Velocity F.P.S.	Shot No.	Range Ft.	Velocity F.P.S.	Shot No.	Range Ft.	Velocity F.P.S.
1	5	415	1	25	397	2	30	405
6	5	423	6	25	405	3	30	402
11	5	419	11	25	399	4	35	404
16	5	436	16	25	416	5	35	392
21	5	423	21	25	405	6	40	389
26	5	434	26	25	413	7	40	397
31	5	441	31	25	415	8	45	337
36	5	423	36	25	404	9	45	415
41	5	423	41	25	403	10	50	411
46	5	409	46	25	395	11	50	393
51	5	391	51	25	384	12	55	398
56	5	370	56	25	377	13	55	390
61	5	337				14	60	392
71	5	212				15	60	-
						16	65	340
						17	65	353
						18	70	320
						19	70	317

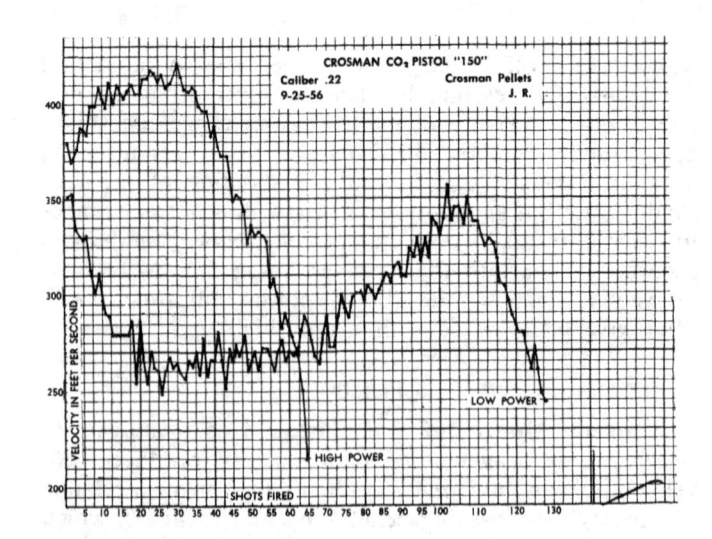

cult. The remaining charge was then exhausted. (3) The pistol was again charged and laid aside for 5 minutes after cartridge piercing. The first shot was not recorded. Shots 2 and 3 were fired with screens set for 30 feet, shots 4 and 5 were fired and recorded with screens set at 35 feet, etc., as indicated.

As an index of the potentially erratic performance of CO_2 arms (without necessarily interfering with accuracy performance at pellet-pistol range!), note that in test 1 at 5 feet, White's No. 1 shot registered 371 f.p.s.; at 25 feet, then using the same gun but a different CO_2 cartridge, the first shot registered 351 feet; while on the 2nd shot at 30 feet still another CO_2 cartridge registered 394 f.p.s.!

Author's Tests. The accompanying velocity graphs represent a good average test covering both the "full power" and "reduced power" ranges of a Crosman Model 150, caliber .22. Tests with another pistol of the same type produced about the same performance. Note that while these tests prove out better than the Benjamin, the factor of CO_2 cartridge size must be taken into consideration.

In comparative velocity tests at full power, penetration *only* equalled the Benjamin, apparently the somewhat heavier (14.99 against 14.20 grains average) Benjamin pellet offsetting the Crosman added power average. Groups were about ¼-inch larger on an average at 10 yards than the Benjamin from machine rest.

Carbo-Jet CO_2 Repeating Pistol. (Also listed as American Luger Model HV 822.) This is the only CO_2 repeating pistol currently available. It is much more impressive in appearance than its competitors. In hang and balance it more nearly approaches a firearm than any other pellet pistol.

In order to produce it as a repeater, the makers found it necessary to use lead ball ammunition instead of the Diabolo waisted pellets used by competing pistols. Feeding a Diabolo through any magazine mechanism is a trouble breeder, as the very thin skirt section which takes the rifling is easily damaged. (Note: This pistol appeared originally as a single shot under the name "Schimel" which would use either ball or Diabolo pellets.)

The ball used weighs 15.91 grains average (average was developed by weighing up units of 10 from manufacturer's boxes.) The round ball is capable of just as good accuracy as the Diabolo, as established by our tests, at ranges up to 25 feet—the distance at which most pellet-pistol target shooting is done. This however presumes a good barrel and best sphericity and dimensions in the ball. Even the best of the German precision lead balls did not prove capable of best accuracy, however. In fact, the only truly uniform balls found were the steel ball-bearing type made by Hämmerli in Switzerland, and the caliber was too small (.1775) to test in this pistol.

One sample tested gave quite remarkable consistency in velocity, though always on the low side. The valve was good, though hardly as revolutionary as claimed, but the particular factor evident was the close tolerances to which the valve system was held. From an engineering standpoint there may be some question as to the life term of the tolerances. In any event, when properly handled, the pistol performed well and gave consistent velocity. Penetration was unusually good with the ball punching through nearly ½ inch of pine and breaking splinters off the back of the plank as balls will do.

Accuracy left something to be desired. At 30 feet the *best* group obtainable was 1¾ inches. Balls were shot into cotton waste to recover them, and on examination showed the irregular line about the circumference usually found where a ball has taken the rifling too tightly and not too uniformly.

If valve tolerance life can be maintained, this pistol as a single shot adapted to Diabolo pellets should be capable of as good accuracy as any other CO_2 pistol, and in view of the comparative velocity consistency, might be expected to shoot very good groups.

The loading and manipulation of this pistol requires more knowledge of its operation than is contained in the maker's instruction leaflet. Several people who commented unfavorably on it, when handed one by the author to load and fire, quickly demonstrated that they were not really familiar with its operation! (See text for instructions.)

As a matter of record and comparison, the results of a typical test (table 33) for velocity with this pistol are set down here, together with the graph produced from this particular test series. It is interesting to note that despite the small size of the standard CO_2 bulb used, 40 usable charges were produced. The velocities shown were made at approximately full power, since previous tests with other ball-shooting arms had pointed up the fact that unless power is relatively high, with any pellet-gun system firing balls, oversized ones may be expected to stick in the barrel, and punching stuck balls out of a pistol of this design is a bit troublesome.

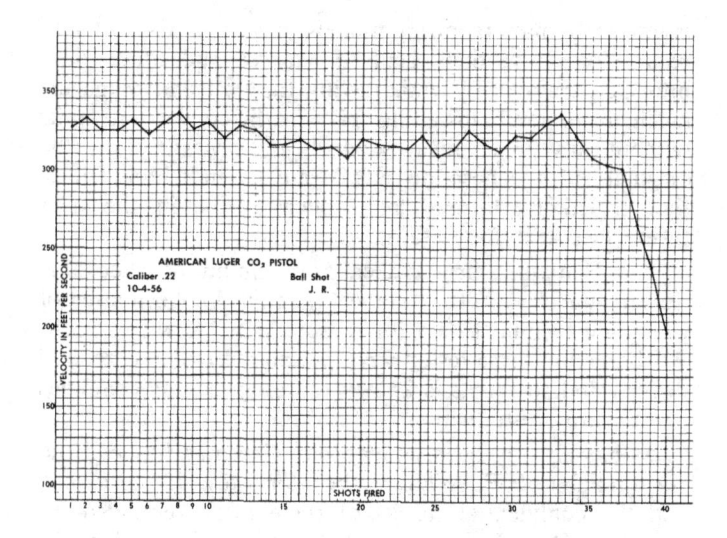

Carbon Dioxide (CO_2) Rifles

The only CO_2 rifles currently in production manufacture are:

(1) Benjamin Model 362 in caliber .22 and its counterpart in caliber .177, listed as the Model 367. These use *standard size* CO_2 cartridges; in tests, it should be noted, those bearing the Benjamin Super imprint functioned better than unmarked brands.

(2) Crosman 180 series using a *single* oversized gas cartridge common to all Crosman current models under the designation Powerlet.

(3) Crosman 180 Special, marketed by Sears, Roebuck and Company under their trade designation J. C. Higgins. This is a minor modification only of the standard Crosman 180 above.

(4) Crosman 160 series using *two* Powerlets inserted as detailed in the text. (Note: The Swiss Hämmerli firm

TABLE 33
AUTHOR'S VELOCITY TESTS, CARBO-JET CO_2 REPEATING PISTOL

Shot number	Time interval	Shot number	Time interval	Shot number	Time interval	Shot number	Time interval
1	.01578 (327 f.p.s.)	11	.01555 (321 f.p.s.)	21	.01575 (317 f.p.s.)	31	.01556 (321 f.p.s.)
2	.01493 (331 f.p.s.)	12	.01525 (328 f.p.s.)	22	.01581 (316 f.p.s.)	32	.01516 (330 f.p.s.)
3	.01536 (325 f.p.s.)	13	.01530 (326 f.p.s.)	23	.01593 (314 f.p.s.)	33	.01487 (336 f.p.s.)
4	.01537 (325 f.p.s.)	14	.01575 (317 f.p.s.)	24	.01549 (323 f.p.s.)	34	.01351 (322 f.p.s.)
5	.01506 (332 f.p.s.)	15	.01577 (317 f.p.s.)	25	.01618 (309 f.p.s.)	35	.01619 (309 f.p.s.)
6	.01545 (323 f.p.s.)	16	.01560 (320 f.p.s.)	26	.01587 (315 f.p.s.)	36	.01644 (304 f.p.s.)
7	.01511 (330 f.p.s.)	17	.01584 (315 f.p.s.)	27	.01532 (326 f.p.s.)	37	.01653 (302 f.p.s.)
8	.01483 (336 f.p.s.)	18	.01590 (314 f.p.s.)	28	.01575 (317 f.p.s.)	38	.01880 (266 f.p.s.)
9	.01531 (326 f.p.s.)	19	.01628 (307 f.p.s.)	29	.01603 (312 f.p.s.)	39	.02094 (239 f.p.s.)
10	.01511 (330 f.p.s.)	20	.01555 (321 f.p.s.)	30	.01543 (323 f.p.s.)	40	.02519 (198 f.p.s.)
						41	.03731 (134 f.p.s.)
Total,	.15231	Total,	.15679	Total,	.15756	Total,	.17319
						(excluding shot 41)	

Note. Average velocity 40 shots full power from 1 cartridge; 41st shot worthless.

is currently manufacturing models of various CO_2 *attachments* for converting standard Mauser and other rifles into CO_2 trainers by withdrawing the bolt and magazine mechanisms and installing Hämmerli conversion units without any mechanical work being necessary on the original rifles. These do NOT rate as individual rifles, though Hämmerli may make such a rifle in the near future (see text for details).

The Benjamin firm makes a minimum of checkable advertising claims. It is not cooperative in the matter of providing technical data for reasons best known to itself. All Benjamin arms tested were purchased from accredited dealers and so far as is known represent average samples of this firm's production.

As has already been pointed out, Crosman has had the very reliable H.P. White Laboratory test its products; and the confidential results of these tests were also released by Crosman to the author for checking and publication use.

Since Crosman makes more models and has done far greater basic research into its products, the author was able to make verifying checks—also to carry experimentation far beyond that done by Crosman. This explains the added space given to Crosman products. The author has no axe to grind, and the test results speak for themselves.

With regard to Hämmerli, this group has always been most cooperative with the author. However, at this stage they are not far enough advanced on production to permit release of much detailed information at this time. In fairness to both Benjamin and Crosman, it should be stated that the present direction of the Hämmerli developments is not along comparable lines; and despite various foreign developments which also cannot be disclosed at this time, for all practical purposes there will be no foreign CO_2 rifles of the American low-cost variety available for quite a long time.

Benjamin CO_2 Carbine (Short Rifle) Model 362. Three models of this arm purchased in different areas of the country from accredited dealers, all in caliber .22, were examined and tested. Control testing was done at two independent points on similar testing equipment. The figures and graphs shown are the best results produced, all being much alike; and may be taken as a fair average picture of the capabilities of this line as currently produced.

The velocity peak and general average is about the same as for the Crosman series. A high of 563 f.p.s. at 5 feet is what can normally be expected using a single CO_2 cartridge under test conditions which cover: (1) Potter electronic chronograph with screens set for 5-foot tests, with a dry-bulb temperature of 68 degrees, a wet-bulb temperature of 60 degrees, a relative humidity of 62 degrees, and shooting on an indoor range. (2) A delay of 5 minutes after cartridge piercing before firing the first shot. (3) An interval of 1 minute between shots to allow the barrel and valve to normalize and thus produce the best pressures.

The downward velocity range is about average for type, but the number of shots definitely is considerably lower than Crosman, due to differences in gas-cartridge size. In passing, it might be noted that standard-size gas cartridges are neither economical nor capable of producing the best results. Valving is a factor of course.

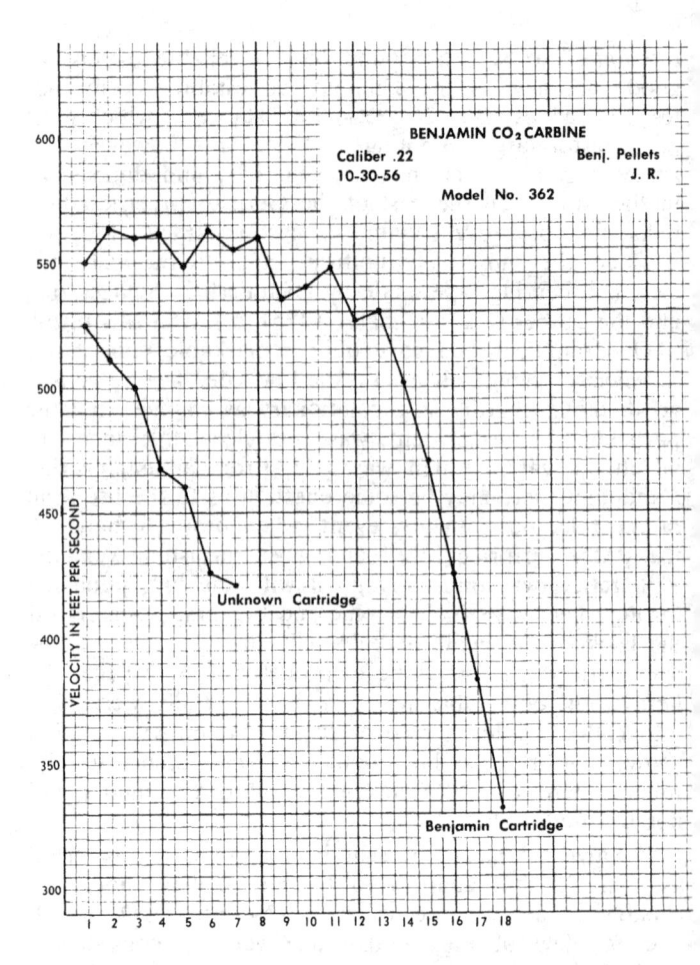

The price differences between this model and the Crosman 160 amount to about $3.50 retail. A comparison of photos and text data will enable the reader to form his own conclusions on appearance data.

Mechanically the Benjamin adheres to the tested impact-valve system. While not as efficient in theory as the newer blowoff pattern, in actual usage at this stage there is not too much difference in observable performance between the two so far as valving is concerned. On the other hand, hand-cocking the powerful spring necessary to actuate the hammer which opens such a valve calls for considerably more physical effort than is involved in the other type, which is, in effect, self-cocking. Despite this fact, however, the trigger pull in all carbines tested was acceptable.

The combination of well-rifled barrel of bronze and good-design lead pellet gave this carbine a somewhat better accuracy group for a limited number of shots; but on an overall average based on gas-cartridge life, the average fell behind the Crosman.

The maximum range at which any effective target work can be done with this general design is about 50 feet, while 30 feet is much more practical.

The "safety" is unsatisfactory. Instead of the elementary trigger block found in other types, which mechanically prevents any trigger movement, in these guns it was found that the following conditions exist: The gun was charged and barrel loaded. Safety was applied as for carrying. The trigger was pulled—as can inadvertently

TABLE 34
Author's Comparison Tests, Benjamin CO_2 Carbine

BENJAMIN SUPER CO_2 CARTRIDGE						UNBRANDED CO_2 CARTRIDGE (SAME SIZE)	
Shot number	Time interval		Shot number	Time interval		Shot number	Time interval
1	.00909 (550 f.p.s.)		10	.00929 (538 f.p.s.)		1	.00954 (525 f.p.s.)
2	.00899 (563 f.p.s.)		11	.00916 (546 f.p.s.)		2	.00978 (512 f.p.s.)
3	.00893 (560 f.p.s.)		12	.00950 (526 f.p.s.)		3	.01000 (500 f.p.s.)
4	.00891 (561 f.p.s.)		13	.00944 (530 f.p.s.)		4	.01048 (467 f.p.s.)
5	.00913 (548 f.p.s.)		14	.00997 (501 f.p.s.)		5	.01084 (460 f.p.s.)
6	.00892 (562 f.p.s.)		15	.01075 (465 f.p.s.)		6	.01170 (426 f.p.s.)
7	.00903 (554 f.p.s.)		16	.01174 (425 f.p.s.)		7	.01186 (421 f.p.s.)
8	.00993 (560 f.p.s.)		17	.01306 (383 f.p.s.)		8	.01432 (349 f.p.s.)
9	.00939 (533 f.p.s.)		18	.01507 (312 f.p.s.)			

Note. Eighteen shots at full power from Benjamin cartridge. Eight shots at full power from competing cartridge of the same size.

happen. The safety was still "on." When the safety was moved "off," the rifle fired. If you followed in detail the maker's instructions *and recocked the arm* before taking the safety "off," there was no trouble. If you put the safety "on" and pulled the trigger, the internal hammer moved out of engagement but could not fire. However, if without recocking, you took the safety "off," as the safety disengaged the hammer slammed home to hit the valve mechanism and fire. When queried by the author about why this condition has not been remedied through the years, the manufacturer ignored the inquiry, even though their instruction sheets indicate they are aware of the condition.

While the author's graphs herewith tell the story, detailed interval time and velocity translations are given in table 34 to afford a good average picture of results with Benjamin and an unbranded gas cartridge.

Crosman 180 Series CO_2 Rifles (Including J. C. Higgins Special).

H. P. White Tests. The following White tests on the Crosman Model 180 (caliber .22) were conducted as follows:

Twenty-eight shots (as numbered) out of 45 fired were recorded for velocity at a 5-foot range. The velocity given is for that particular shot.

The gun was then recharged with a Powerlet. Six shots out of 25 fired were recorded in the order listed for averaging purposes, but figures given show individual velocities.

The gun was again charged. Shots numbered were checked for velocity at 30, 35, 40, 45, 50, 60, 70, 80, and 90 feet. At the 100-foot range, pellets had dropped too far to appear on the Lumiline test screens. In other words, while velocity remains good at 90 feet from the muzzle, the light pellet *drops so fast* that range limitations are apparent.

Note that maximum range is achieved when a rifle is fired at an angle of roughly 30 degrees, not 45 degrees as is commonly believed. Tests fired over water indicated that, on an average, pellets thus fired hit about 300 feet from the shooter. This is a very important advantage of the pellet rifle over .22 firearms from a safe-shooting standpoint. Pellet force, incidentally, is almost completely exhausted at the end of its maximum trajectory flight.

As an example of CO_2 power variation which can be due to several causes, note that shot No. 2 at 5 feet in the first test registered 438 f.p.s., while shot No. 2 in the third test at *30 feet* registered 495 f.p.s.! Other data is self-apparent. Since all shooting conditions here were controlled, variations can be pinned down to the following causes: gas-cartridge power, valve operation, ammunition—or a combination of these.

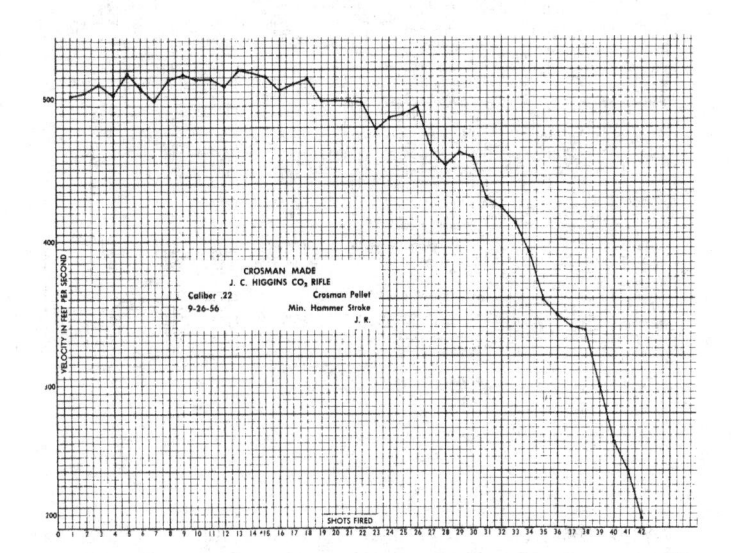

The results by any standards, however, are quite creditable.

Author's Tests on Crosman 180 Models. While adhering to the controls set up by White and using identical electronic equipment, our tests were much more comprehensive, covering use of both the standard Crosman 180 and the slightly modified J.C. Higgins (Sears) version. Furthermore, tests were run at both low and high power to establish performance averages.

Thus with the Crosman 180 on test we produced 45 usable shots on an average. Time intervals aggregated .10244 for the first 10; .10016 for the second 10; .10124 for the third 10; .11843 for the fourth 10.

With a minimum stroke, curiously, we again produced 40 usable shots and 3 too low for satisfactory use. The time interval for the first 10 aggregated .9657; the second 10, .9505; the third, .10115; and the fourth, .14017.

In other words, velocity was substantially higher in low power than in high, while the shots were about the same number, indicating (in this particular case) gas-cartridge variation. (Note: When a blowoff valve is operating properly, the valve stays open longer under lowering pressure.)

setting established as "low" was actually the more powerful. For a comparison, consider your automobile carburetor: Given the best fuel, there is a point at which it will give best performance on an average of both mileage and speed; but go beyond this point, and you will get a flooded carburetor with lower actual power and mileage delivered. Here was a similar case, repeated in three tests.

(Note: Continuing tests on the 180 and the J. C. Higgins models indicate that on an average (possibly due to power-cartridge differences) no positive claims can be made regarding either velocity or number of shots on high versus low power. There are two hammer-set positions; the first click is indicated as "low" and the second as "high" power, though only the Higgins' literature notes this power differential. One series of tests produced the same number of shots on "high" and "low" power thus: 40 shots ranging from 554 down to 235 f.p.s. on "high" and 40 shots ranging from 525 down to 353 f.p.s. on "low." Other tests produced 54 shots for each setting, the "high" running from 487 down to 361 f.p.s., while the "low" started at 493 and ranged down to 315 f.p.s.! Indications here are that the blowoff valves were working efficiently and *equalizing the pressure* to compensate for the pressure factors. This, of course, nullifies the "adjustable power" feature to a very considerable degree, much on the general principle of the thermostat.)

Crosman 160 Series. These rifles use two Powerlets (see text for details). In order to test their usability under all conditions the author conducted numerous independent tests not covered heretofore. These tests indicated that this model is by some 10 percent average the highest powered CO_2 arm on the market.

H. P. White Velocity Tests, Models 160 and 167. In each instance, the rifle was charged with two Powerlets and set aside for 5 minutes to allow pressure normalization. A 1-minute wait was made between shots, as in previous tests.

Test number 1 at the 5-foot measuring distance in each caliber, .22 (Model 160) and .177 (Model 167), consisted of firing the entire power charge and recording individual velocities of shots 1, 5, 10, 15, 20, 25, 30, 35, 37, 39, and in the case of the .22, of shot number 40. It will be noted that the power charges in both calibers maintained good usable velocity right up to the approach of the 40th shot; though the pressure drop on the whole was consistently steady as the charge diminished through

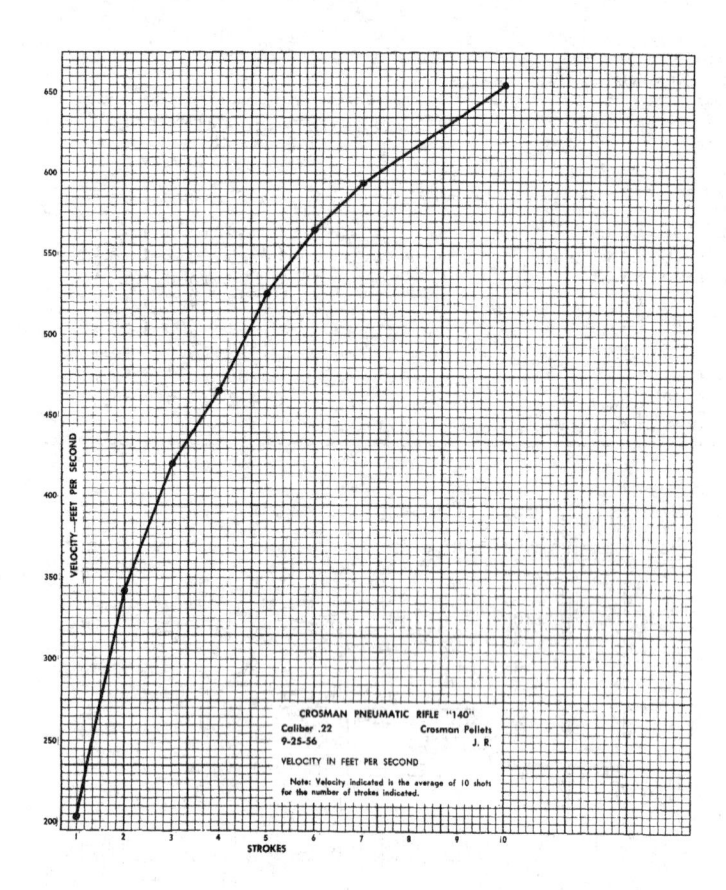

With the J. C. Higgins version on high power, 70 usable shots were obtained. Time-interval aggregates were for the first ten, .10116; for the second 10, .11171; for the third, .12208; for the fourth, .11408; for the fifth, .11438; for the sixth, .12032; and for the seventh, .15699.

On low power, the Higgins time-interval aggregates were: first 10, .9836; second, .9804; third, .10488; fourth, .14214. The performance given in table 35 shows very good consistency and is significant enough to tabulate as to velocity.

In other words, with the J. C. Higgins guns on low power, 42 usable shots were obtained, as against 70 on high power. Velocities on low were actually better than on high. This evaluation lead to a study of the valve structure. In this type of valve as mass produced, the

TABLE 35
AUTHOR'S CONTINUITY VELOCITY TESTS, CROSMAN M180 RIFLE

Shot number	Velocity (f.p.s.)	Shot number	Velocity (f.p.s.)	Shot number	Velocity (f.p.s.)	Shot number	Velocity (f.p.s.)
1	501	12	508	23	479	34	392
2	503	13	520	24	486	35	359
3	510	14	518	25	486	36	349
4	502	15	515	26	494	37	340
5	518	16	504	27	462	38	337
6	506	17	510	28	453	39	299
7	498	18	514	29	462	40	260
8	514	19	498	30	458	41	240
9	517	20	498	31	429	42	205
10	513	21	498	32	423	43	195
11	513	22	497	33	413		

.22 CALIBER

TEST NO. 2 - CROSMAN MODEL 160 RIFLE

Full Power - 2 Powerlets

Shot No.	Range Ft.	Velocity F.P.S.	Shot No.	Range Ft.	Velocity F.P.S.	Shot No.	Range Ft.	Velocity F.P.S.
1	5	605	1	25	551	11	50	469
5	5	605	5	25	544	12	55	467
10	5	618	10	25	544	13	55	452
15	5	584	15	25	535	14	60	442
20	5	552	20	25	496	15	60	441
25	5	524	25	25	477	16	65	438
30	5	513	30	25	476	17	65	437
35	5	476	40	25	330	18	70	427
37	5	414				19	70	-
39	5	400				20	75	425
40	5	347				21	75	-
						22	80	415
Note: After 40th Shot air charge lost suddenly.			2	30	625	23	80	412
			3	30	574	24	85	394
			4	35	560	25	85	390
			5	35	527	26	90	-
			6	40	503	27	90	361
			7	40	499	28	95	-
			8	45	492	29	95	355
			9	45	483	30	100	335
			10	50	474	31	100	328

.177 CALIBER

TEST NO. 1 - CROSMAN MODEL 167 RIFLE

Full Power - 2 Powerlets

Shot No.	Range Ft.	Velocity F.P.S.	Shot No.	Range Ft.	Velocity F.P.S.	Shot No.	Range Ft.	Velocity F.P.S.
1	5	673	1	25	635	11	50	544
5	5	667	5	25	627	12	55	534
10	5	654	10	25	617	13	55	528
15	5	650	15	25	604	14	60	519
20	5	648	20	25	601	15	60	510
25	5	639	25	25	594	16	65	509
30	5	612	30	25	581	17	65	504
35	5	554	40	25	522	18	70	486
37	5	439	45	25	432	19	70	482
39	5	409				20	75	479
						21	75	476
Note: After 39th shot air charge lost suddenly.						22	80	467
			2	30	588	23	80	457
			3	30	588	24	85	-
			4	35	587	25	85	454
			5	35	586	26	90	444
			6	40	583	27	90	-
			7	40	582	28	95	440
			8	45	571	29	95	423
			9	45	575	30	100	407
			10	50	548	31	100	392

use. Here is shown graphically the difference between *average* velocity and *individual* velocity through the life of the gas cartridges. It will be noted that despite the use of two Powerlets instead of the customary one, the number of usable shots at full power was confined to 40 in the .22 and 39 in the .177, quite a remarkable demonstration of valve uniformity in any CO_2 arm. The sudden dissipation of the remaining gas after all effective shots have been fired is, incidentally, an advantage not only in heading the shooter off from very poor accuracy and possible pellet stoppage in the barrel through low power; but also in assuring complete safety when preparing to recharge. (If pressure remains in the retaining cap at the forward end of the cartridge tube as it is unscrewed, there is danger of the cap being blown off violently in the hand.)

Test number 2 in each caliber started with a new power charge handled as before. Beginning with shots numbers 1, 5, 10, 15, 20, 25, 30, and 40, velocity was recorded at the 25-foot range. The velocity of the .177 at this range is sufficiently superior to the .22 to demonstrate why precision shooters prefer this caliber for match shooting at established air-range distances, as at that distance and when striking energy is not a factor, even the end velocity on the 45th shot was capable of match accuracy.

Test number 3 in each caliber started with new charges as before. Shots were individually recorded as indicated starting with numbers 2 and 3 at 30 feet, and ranging through 30 and 31 at 100 feet. (Note: Dashes indicate pellets which did not record on screens. In view of the remaining velocity, such instances are usually attributable to individual pellet faults.)

These tests, of course, established definitely that CO_2 weapon power diminishes in relation to power uses, though under certain optimum *laboratory* conditions it stays constant so long as any liquid CO_2 remains. In arms of this type, *as currently designed,* full use is not made of the gasifying characteristics of the CO_2 class of gases.

As to accuracy, the White tests indicated groups of 1.5 inches at 50 feet during the above tests. This is a very high degree of accuracy for arms of this type at that range, though poorer than manufacturers' claims.

Author's Test On Crosman Model 160 Rifle. Our tests followed very closely the average pattern found by White. (Note that no technicians used by the author saw the White tests until after the completion of all tests and graphs.) However, at no point did these tests achieve the maximum velocity obtained by White. Differences, however, are such that they can be explained on several grounds, running from valve factors to ammunition supply and power charges. Since in most cases the power supply ended at 35 shots—as against White's 40—either valve and/or power supply are the more likely factors here.

The average tabulation shown in table 36 gives a good

271

TABLE 36
Author's Special Tests, Using Two Powerlets, Crosman "Super Pell" .22 Pellets, and Crosman M160 Rifle

Shot number	Time interval (velocity)	Shot number	Time interval (velocity)	Shot number	Time interval (velocity)
1	.00893 (560 f.p.s.)	13	.00932 (536 f.p.s.)	25	.01037 (483 f.p.s.)
2	.00894 (560 f.p.s.)	14	.00911 (549 f.p.s.)	26	.01063 (470 f.p.s.)
3	.00893 (560 f.p.s.)	15	.00899 (560 f.p.s.)	27	.01095 (456 f.p.s.)
4	.00915 (546 f.p.s.)	16	.00921 (544 f.p.s.)	28	.01074 (465 f.p.s.)
5	.00919 (545 f.p.s.)	17	.00932 (536 f.p.s.)	29	.01174 (425 f.p.s.)
6	.00900 (555 f.p.s.)	18	.00925 (546 f.p.s.)	30	.01180 (423 f.p.s.)
7	.00908 (552 f.p.s.)	19	.00939 (533 f.p.s.)	31	.01242 (402 f.p.s.)
8	.00919 (545 f.p.s.)	20	.00958 (523 f.p.s.)	32	.01296 (386 f.p.s.)
9	.00914 (546 f.p.s.)	21	.00949 (528 f.p.s.)	33	.01333 (375 f.p.s.)
10	.00917 (545 f.p.s.)	22	.00974 (514 f.p.s.)	34	.01477 (339 f.p.s.)
11	.00916 (545 f.p.s.)	23	.00972 (512 f.p.s.)	35	.01540 (324 f.p.s.)
12	.00915 (546 f.p.s.)	24	.00984 (508 f.p.s.)		

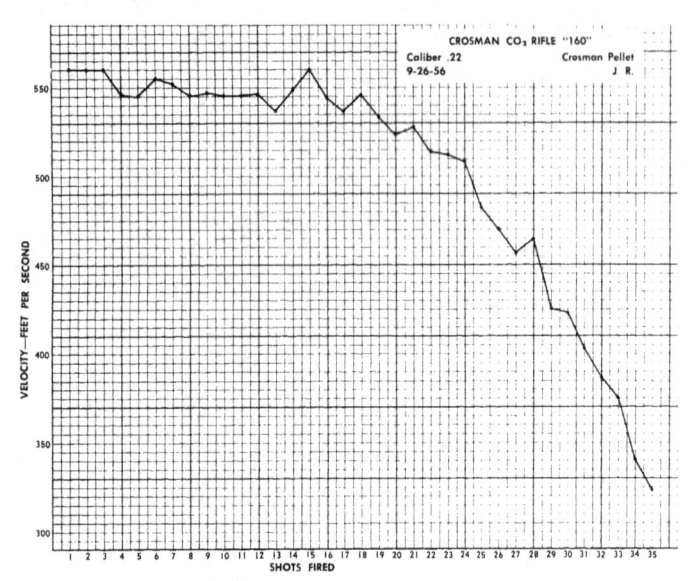

Note. Number of usable shots: 35.

picture of these strictly independent tests, conditions being the same as White's, except that the rifles used were right out of factory boxes prepared for retail sale.

TESTS WITH ONE (1) POWERLET IN MODEL 160

Among the various special tests conducted were those dealing with model comparisons. In the Crosman 180 and the J. C. Higgins, only *one* Powerlet is used. As already pointed out, this oversized cartridge is considerably more efficient on an average than the standard-sized gas cartridges used in other CO_2 arms.

As in all general CO_2 arms of modern construction, where one gas cartridge is used, the gas flow is from the piercing point in the forward cartridge into a relatively small gas chamber, just as in compressed-air-arm storage. This metering system is the simplest to control and in general the most satisfactory of any current type.

In an endeavor to gain power without introducing still another size gas cartridge, Crosman utilizes the two-Powerlet-charge system. The first gas cartridge (Powerlet) is inserted and pierced in standard fashion; the second is placed end to end with the first so that after its end cap is pierced, it releases gas into the retaining tube which serves as an accumulator. This definitely increases *power*, as shown by the relative velocities of the single-vs-double cartridge tests herein. However, there is not a *correspond-*

ing increase in the number of shots delivered, and in general the actual number will normally be no higher, if as high, as from a single gas cartridge.

Because of the large accumulator space, use of a single cartridge in these dual-cartridge types is completely uneconomical. The results of such tests speak for themselves when compared with the performance of the single-cartridge models.

Tests were conducted as follows: A loaded cartridge was inserted in the tube, followed by an expended one, the latter having been fired until empty. The gun was fired to pierce the loaded cartridge in standard fashion, then allowed to stand for 5 minutes. Shots were then fired at 1-minute intervals. The best result obtained was 18 shots itemized in table 37.

Exhaustive tests of the dual-cartridge system indicate that its sole value is added power, averaging about 10 percent above that of the similar single-cartridge model, with the added power having some value in obtaining better groups at target ranges. However, the basic value of the dual system lies solely in its use as a pest-shooting arm, where the added energy and penetration in the .22 caliber is justified.

PELLET TESTS

On all tests with German air arms, regardless of when made from 1905 to 1956, on an average all achieved higher velocity and better accuracy when used with German-made ammunition of current manufacture. It should be noted that when production was first started after World War II, German air pellets were not always good quality, a fact directly traceable in the author's observation to the use of reclaimed, junk lead, high in impurities. Even when the tolerances were closely held, metal impurities interfered with quality. That condition no longer exists. Measurements, weights, and metal purity of German-made pellets, is on an average of the highest consistency as appearing under the brand names of RWS, made by Dynamit-A. G., under the H-N mark, and under the trade name of Gustav Genschow & Company, the last being Germany's largest export house. The RWS brand is distributed in the United States by Stoeger Arms Corporation and the H-N brand by the Hoffritz Cutlery organization, both of New York.

It should be stated in all fairness to other makers that at no time did tests produce from machine rests any such degrees of accuracy as claimed by the German pellet makers. No arm tested was found actually capable of putting 20, much less 50, shots in the same hole at anything like 50 feet as is often claimed; nor did any from rest indicate the kind of 50-meter accuracy often talked about but never openly claimed by foreign factories.

However, at reasonable air ranges the German Diabolo pellets mentioned performed best in German arms. In British weapons, on an average, they equalled in accuracy, B.S.A. pellets in B.S.A. arms. In Webley arms, however, while German pellets often gave somewhat better velocity, they never quite equalled the accuracy of the Webley pellet.

In U. S. arms, the Sheridan, using an individual pellet, proved far more consistent than any other pellet type, but since it is bullet-shaped and not Diabolo and is of an individual .20 caliber, no exact comparisons are possible. No pellet or ball tested, incidentally, exceeded either the accuracy or the velocity of the Sheridan .20, regardless of the rifle in which it was used.

British pellets worked best in British arms, except as noted. Webley pellets on an average seemed better suited to their own arms than to any other make tested. (For instance, the British I.C.I.-manufactured .22 pellets sold here under the Hy Score brand name could not be inserted in our Webley pistols because of their oversized dimensions.)

In American arms generally, it was found that German ammunition on an average would shoot about as well as the average domestic brands. The most uniform American Diabolo pellet was the Benjamin, a fact which probably stems from the long contact and experience this firm has had dealing with Germany.

It must be stressed that different arms made at different times in the United States produced different results with various pellets. In Germany and Great Britain these pellets have been standardized, as have air arms, over a very long period. The Hy Score organization has benefited by drawing on British makers for pellets for their pistols. While the uniformity of these pellets is good, it is by no means superior. Thus we found that while better accuracy was at times achieved by using Hy Score pistols with their British-made pellets than with the best German; conversely in testing the German-made air rifles sold by Hy Score, better velocity and accuracy was uniformly obtained with German-made pellets.

To all intent and purposes, standard air-arm development in Britain and Germany has about reached a peak, so standards are possible of maintenance. In the United States, on the other hand, rifle and pistol models are being constantly tried, tested, and improved in both compressed-air and CO_2 patterns. Power variations, rifling-method changes, valving changes, materials substitutions —all these have been and are factors in pellet-gun manufacture here which require continued pellet experimentation and possible form and dimensional alterations. This fact cannot be stressed too highly.

As an example of the type of continuing check in this field by individual makers who must relate their arms to their product, consider the following tests conducted by one maker on March 8, 1956. The arm tested was a CO_2

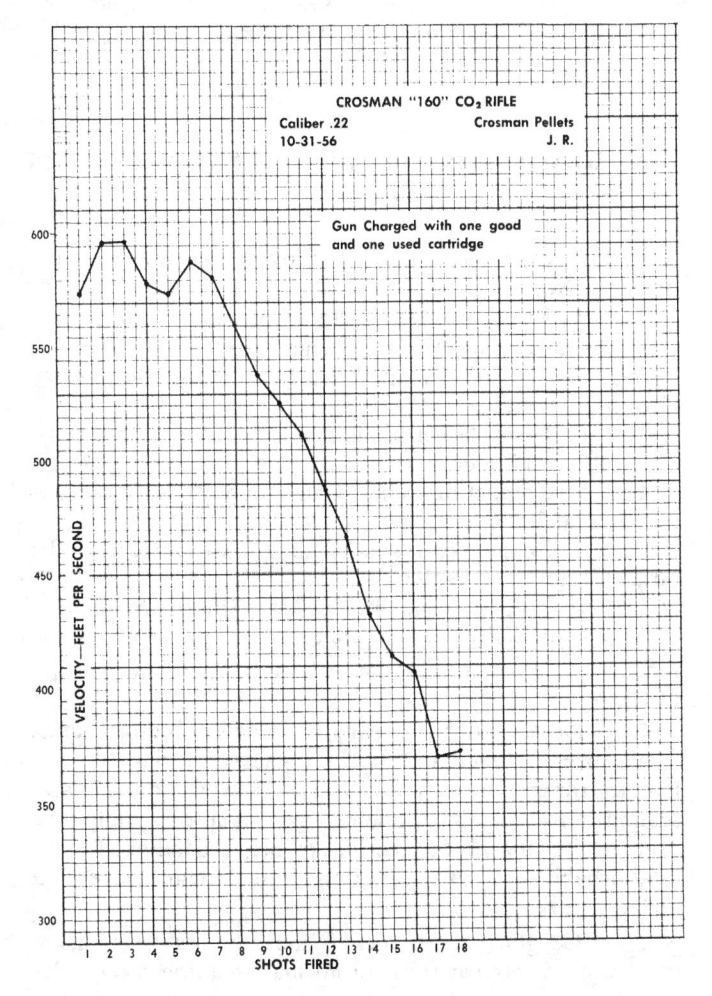

TABLE 37
AUTHOR'S SPECIAL VELOCITY CONTINUITY TESTS, CROSMAN M160 RIFLE

Shot number	Time interval (velocity)	Shot number	Time interval (velocity)
1	.00870 (574 f.p.s.)	10	.00950 (526 f.p.s.)
2	.00837 (596 f.p.s.)	11	.00974 (513 f.p.s.)
3	.00838 (596 f.p.s.)	12	.01027 (487 f.p.s.)
4	.00864 (579 f.p.s.)	13	.01074 (465 f.p.s.)
5	.00872 (573 f.p.s.)	14	.01154 (433 f.p.s.)
6	.00849 (589 f.p.s.)	15	.01208 (415 f.p.s.)
7	.00860 (581 f.p.s.)	16	.01227 (407 f.p.s.)
8	.00894 (560 f.p.s.)	17	.01350 (370 f.p.s.)
9	.00928 (538 f.p.s.)	18	.01343 (372 f.p.s.)

Note. Gas exhausted on 19th firing.

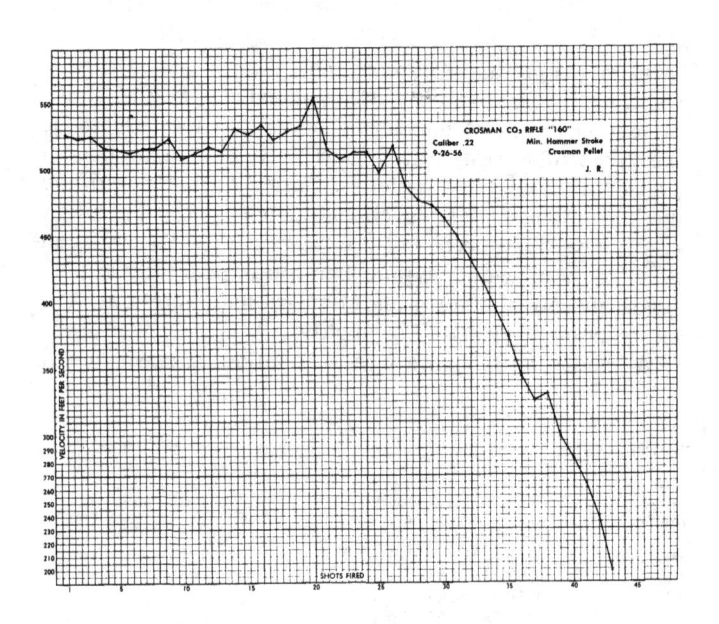

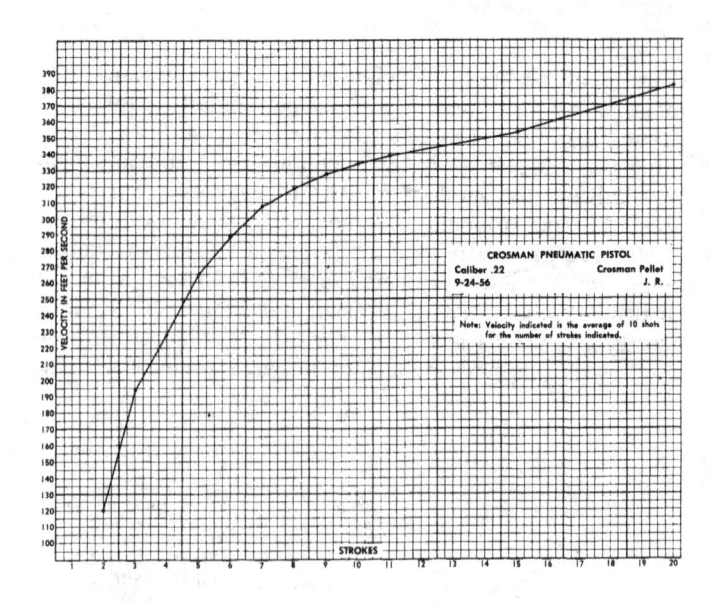

TABLE 38
AUTHOR'S TRAJECTORY TESTS, CO₂ RIFLES

	RIFLE NO. 1		RIFLE NO. 2	
Shots	Spread (inches)	Rifle position from center (inches)	Spread (inches)	Rifle position from center (inches)
1st 10 shots ..	2.25	Above center 1 5/16	3.00	Below center 1 3/16
2d 10 shots ..	2.50	Above center 1 3/16	2.75	Above center ¾
3d 10 shots ..	2.25	On center	1.75	Below center ⅛
4th 10 shots ..	2.75	Below center ½	2.50	Below center ⅛

Note. Ammunition and rifle were of the same manufacture and from current production. The gas cartridges bore the maker's imprint also.

rifle. Range was 38 feet, indoors. The rifle was vised solid.

Test 1: Current production. Group: 1⅛ inches (from machine No. 1).

Test 2: Knurl position changed to make small head and long skirt. Group: 2⅝ inches.

Test 3: Alteration to make long head and short skirt. Group: 1⅜ inches.

Test 4: Head larger than for test 2, but long skirt. Group: 2 3/16 inches.

Test 5: Competing pellet. One group ⅞ inch (following, 1⅞ inches).

Test 6: 3-mm. lead shot loaded into current pellet nose. Group: 1¾ inches.

Test 7: With current .177 pellet. Group 1¼ inches.

(Note: all except test 7 above used .22 pellets. Current production is best at this time pending further tests).

As another index of American pellet requirements, it has been pointed out that CO_2 tests starting at normal maximum pressure for CO_2 gas (900 pounds) and scaling down to 350 pounds gave approximately the same trajectory at 50 feet; tests being conducted with establishable pressures fed from a tank with valve and meter control.

Yet CO_2 guns at 30 feet in the author's tests, using the standard gas cartridge in normal shooting usage, developed the pellet trajectory data for the .22 rifle shown in table 38. Here is a graphic illustration of the difference between controlled laboratory tests and actual product tests on an average basis such as the shooter will encounter.

Ball Ammunition

Discounting Daisy round shot, for which no claims of precision accuracy are made, but which often still give groups no larger than some imported "precision" balls, the most accurate ball ammunition found was the new Swiss .1725 steel ball. These performed better both as to velocity and accuracy than any other round type, due to material, uniformity, and sphericity. Up to 35 feet, German precision lead balls were found to be, on an average, as accurate as Diabolo pellets when they were a proper fit. However, any tendency at all to be tight in the bore led to a stuck ball in the barrel. The pressure in the most powerful air or CO_2 arm is not enough to permit use of any missile which has a high friction factor; so on an average, the use of the Diabolo pellet was found best except in magazine arms where its fragile skirt invariably interfered with proper feeding.

On a basis of tests, it is obvious that in the field of CO_2 missiles in particular there is room for considerable improvement; and since this field is not currently of interest to any European manufacturers except the Swiss, it is basically a problem for American manufacturers. At least one of the major U. S. ammunition makers is currently conducting research into this problem now that the air- and gas-gun field shows indications of becoming large enough to warrant their attention, but lack of standards in either pellet arms or pellet making will prove a hindrance unless they work more closely than they have with the arms makers in this field. This is difficult since pellet profit is high and all makers of these arms are also making ammunition. When major companies become interested in the air- and gas-gun field, as they have abroad, the picture will change, of course.

Finally, plastic pellets are currently used to some extent abroad. They are not accurate beyond 20 feet because of their very light weight, but they will penetrate a standard paper target and present a great advantage in that they are difficult to deform and can be re-used.

THE PICATINNY AIR GUNS

The Picatinny Arsenal at Dover, New Jersey, is world famous as our Army's principal research center for artillery ammunition, bomb, and fuze development. As in all such successful centers, the technical staff is responsible for new and unique testing methods for each new project. The ingenuity involved is often fantastic, and since so many of the projects are necessarily secret because they involve top security in this uncertain day and world, their successes are seldom seen, heard of, or discussed in public.

One such outstanding achievement can be given passing mention here without violating security. It is the unique development and use of air "guns" which dwarf those of the fabled Vesuvius guns of the Spanish-American War, which are described in the historical section of this book.

These Picatinny air guns were not developed as wartime *projectile hurlers*—only specialized gunpowders and still secret and more powerful gas-generating and expansion compounds can do that efficiently today.

These monsters with 102-foot barrels were developed at Picatinny for testing such items as complete artillery rounds, rocket motors, the capabilities of new atomic munition assemblies, explosives, and artillery fuzes. They "fire" without noise, fuss, or recoil—and the results obtained save precious time and countless thousands of dollars. Many of the tests and much of the data obtainable through their use were not possible before the Picatinny Ordnance engineers produced these guns.

Let's take a look at the guns themselves for a moment. Two of them will handle ammunition up to 5 inches in diameter and one up to 2 inches! The big fellows have barrel extensions giving them an overall length of 102 feet, while little brother is 64 feet from breech to muzzle end.

The big fellow is a modification of the old 5/51 Navy gun of World War I, a rifle which was loaded by ramming in a shell and then punching in huge powder bags behind it. First, the rifling was bored and reamed out of the tube and a smooth-bore insert set in. Very heavy pipe was machine concentrically and affixed at the muzzle end to bring the overall length to 102 feet.

The guns are powered by compressed air. Both ends of the barrel are closed when firing. Cylindrical test carriages of heavy-duty aluminum bear the items to be tested for special data. The carriage is fastened to the gun breech. Air pressure in line with the item and the test requirements is shot into the gun, and the test carriage and its contents travel about 80 feet down the barrel before oscillating to a halt. The extra 22 feet? They are an engineering factor to give added protection.

The gun, for instance, allows a complete shell or its components to be tested *without firing the shell into a sand bank or other backstop,* which would deface and injure it.

Preparing to load one of the Picatinny giant air guns. The barrel is 102 feet long.

A laboratory view of the giant Picatinny air guns. Here our ordnance engineers solve big gun ammunition development problems without having to fire a single powder charge.

When tested in this air gun, the projectile is forced back to the breech by compressed air after firing, whereupon it can be removed and studied. The guns are so flexible that if (as is sometimes required for special-purpose study), the engineers wish to reverse fire, they can do so and actually shoot a steel-plated *target* at the object being tested.

Briefly, and as non-technically as possible, this gun simulates the *peak acceleration an artillery round or its components would encounter in actual firing of a weapon!* It can apply linear accelerations varying from 200 g's to 120,000 g's (Note: A "g" indicates a force equal to 1 time the weight of the projected object.) Take the normal round fired by a 90-mm. gun, for instance. The 90-mm. projectile reaches a peak linear acceleration of about 35,000 g's—or a force equal to 35,000 times its own weight! This air gun simulates perfectly for scientific study the force a 90-mm. shell would encounter being discharged at supersonic speeds in actual field firing— and without injuring the projectile being tested or making enough noise to disturb the mathematicians working alongside it.

It can be—and has been—used to check the capabilities of atomic ammunition assemblies. It permits checking a whole round for performance—the arming value and performance of the all-important internal fuzes which must explode the charge in the shell when it hits, or when it reaches its desired flight terminal, or approaches the point of proximity desired for detonation. It permits checks on metallurgy of the complex "guts" of a modern high-velocity shell, shows what component-parts performance will be under actual firing conditions, and establishes the required functioning characteristics of detonators under highest acceleration. In short, these giant air guns simulate in the laboratory at Picatinny every phase of the setback accelerations of all ammunition and components launched from weapons in the field.

Until these guns were developed, it was necessary to work on a strictly mathematical and firing basis and hope for the best on a thousand ballistic problems. When firing live rounds into a recovery barricade, the damage involved by impact had to be disassociated from the performance factors of the shell and its components, much as aviation experts have to piece together parts of a cracked-up plane and try and figure just what *did* happen, in order to design to prevent its happening again. These air guns eliminate guesswork, save valuable time in solving problems, and save tax dollars.

These compressed-air guns designed and developed at Picatinny are truly three "big guns" in the arsenal of Democracy. They are important scientific testing tools in the untold, little known story of those who work behind-the-scenes in the vanguard of our national-defense structure.

INDEX

A

Abas-Major Air Pistol, 57, 113
Abercrombie and Fitch, 242
Accuracy, air guns, 110, 233
Acouchi, 6
Acvoke air guns, 50, 56, 57, 109, 113, 114
Air canes, 42-46, 67
Air compared with powder as a propellant, 66
Air cylinder, 17
Air gun:
    As a military weapon, 24
    Bellows-spring compression type, 16
    Cautions for collectors, 46
    Definition of, 10
    Early American, 31
    Early British, 42
    Early European, 20
    Early history, 17
    Freaks, 16
    Foreign designations, 16
    Invention of, 16
    Later British developments, 47
    Legal problems, 67, 169
    Operating classifications, 17
    Operating principles, 10
    Pneumatic (pump-up) type, 13, 14
    Power potential, 67
    Spring-air compression type, 10-13
    Tests of, 230-276
    Training uses, 66
    Use in Spanish-American War, 64, 65
    Zoological uses, 111
Air pistol, definition of, 10
Air reservoirs, 24, 84
Air rifle, definition of, 10
Air rifle shot, 100
Air shotgun, definition of, 10
Alexandrian Library, 19, 20
Amazon Basin, 4
American spring-air arms, 195-205
Ammunition, air gun, 100-106, 109, 235
    European and American pellets compared, 104
    Testing, 235
Anacharsis, 17
Anson, E. J., 51
Apache air guns, 86, 259
Atlas Air Rifle, 41
Austrian air guns, 156, 245
Avery's patent, 19

B

Babcock & Wilcox, 62
Baker, W., 50
Ball air reservoir, 24, 43
Ball ammunition air gun, 273
Bancroft, H. H., 2
Bannerman, Francis, 64, 65
Barakuda gas system, 226, 227, 228, 229, 251, 253
    Model EL54, 228, 229
    Tests 251, 253
Barr, A. L., 70
Barrel-cocking system, 77
BB shot, 13, 100
Bedford, A., 37, 42
Beleopeacca, 62
Bellows, 17, 18, 23
Below-barrel push piston, 42
Benjamin CO_2 guns, 95, 96, 98, 206-211, 268, 269
    360 Series (carbines), 209
    260 Series (pistols), 210, 211, 265
Benjamin air guns, 42, 43, 84-88, 169, 171-181, 253, 257, 262, 263
    300 Series 173, 174
    720 Series 174, 175
    130 Series (pistols), 176
Benjamin pellets, (H. C.), 238
Benjamin, Walter R., 85
Bennett, Charles H., 40, 41, 200-203
Bent air cane, 43, 44
Birmingham Small Arms, 47-52, 79, 81, 84, 93, 101, 110, 113, 120-123, 171, 249, 272
    Airporter, 52, 120-123
    Cadet, 52, 120-123
    Cadet-Major, 52, 120-123
    Club, 52, 120-123
    Mark I, 48
    Mark 4, 52
Blitz Air Rifle, 83
Blowgun, 1-9
    Present-day uses, 8
    Umbrella type, 8
Bock, Carl, 7
Bolzenbuchsen, 24, 25, 71-73, 104
Bonna Air Rifle, 83, 141
Bontemps, 20
Borneo, blowguns in, 7
Bossu, 3
Bourgeois, Marin, 21
Breech loader, pneumatic, 34
Britannia Air Rifle, 48, 50, 113
British spring-air guns, 113-123
Brooks, R., 34
Brown, Edwards, 263
Buffalo, U.S.S., 66
Bugelspanners, 75, 76
Bunge, C., 73, 74, 76
BSF air guns, 148-150, 152, 238, 239
Butt flasks, 29

C

Caliber, air rifle ammunition, 101
Carbon dioxide (CO_2) arms, 89-99, 206-220, 264, 272
    Advantages and disadvantages, 207
    Comparison with spring-air arms, 207
    CO_2 as a propellant, 208
    Tests, 264-272
    Types, 206
Carbo-Jet Pistol, 98, 206, 220, 221, 266, 267
Carbonic acid guns, 69
Carbureted hydrogen gun, 69
Challenger Arms Corporation, 87, 99, 258
Chicago Air Rifle, 38
Chichimick Indians, 2
Choctaw Indians, 3
Chronograph, 231-233
Cochrane, Captain, 5
Cocking-lever arm, 77
Cocking systems, 71-83
    Types evaluated 79
Cohade, H. F., 69
Coke, E., 50
Compressed-air arms (See pneumatic arms)
Compressed-air projectors, 62
Compression, principles of, 84
Compretta Air Rifle, 250
Conical air bullets, 103
Contriner air gun, 14, 22, 28-31
Cortes, 2
Counter chronograph, 231, 232, 233
Crank guns, 17, 71-74
    Cocking system, 71
Crescentio, 21
Crosman air guns, 84, 86-88, 169, 171, 180-189, 253, 255, 256, 262, 263
    140 Models (rifles), 184
    130 Models (pistols), 185
Crosman CO_2 guns, 95, 96, 206-209, 211-220, 267-272
    160 and 180 Series (Pellguns), 213
    150 Series (pistols), 214-216, 265
Ctesibius, 18, 19, 62
Curare, 2, 4
Czechoslovakian air guns, 155, 156, 245, 246

D

Daisy Air Rifle, 38-42, 100, 101, 106, 107, 195, 200, 235, 236, 257
    Model 98, 204
    Model 25, 205
    Tests of 235, 236
Daniels, Richard, 23
Darts, 103, 104, 112
Davis, Richard Harding, 64
Decompression, principles of, 84
Defense stick, compressed-air, 34
Demmin, Auguste, 16, 20, 22, 24, 62
Denver Air Rifle Company, 70
Detent bolts, 77
Diabolo pellets, 101-103, 109
Diana air guns, 36, 77, 80, 81, 113, 124-133, 149, 150, 171, 195, 197, 237, 239, 246, 247, 272
Dickinson, 62
Diesel effect, 69, 84, 109, 110, 226, 253
Douson, 21
Drillings, 126
Dry ice (CO_2) gun, 70
Dumbler, Peter, 22
Dyaks, 7
Dynamit—A. G., 272
Dynamite gun, 62-64

277

E

Edington, C. H., 69
Edson, General Merritt, 212
Eisenwerke, 36
EM-GE, 150-152, 235
Endter, W., 125
Ether gas guns, 69, 226-229, 251-253
  Advantages and disadvantages, 227, 228
  Tests, 251-253
Excellent air gun, 77, 93

F

Falke air guns, 79, 127, 133-137, 150, 152, 239, 240
Firearms Act (British), 51, 113, 169
Fischer, G., 75
Flintlock air guns, 24
Flyers, 84
Fort Hamilton, 63
Foreign pellets, 102, 103

G

Galef, J., 238
Gallery rifles, 94
Gat air pistol, 113, 114, 241
Gas projection systems, 67
Genschow, G., 127
Gerard, M., 59
German air guns, 124-154
Gesellschaft, A. F., 125
Giffard, Paul, 34, 42, 89-94, 96, 104
Girardoni, C. G., 22, 28-31
Gomaro, Francisco, 2
Greener, W. W., 5, 43, 48, 56
Groups, testing, air guns, 233
Guiana (blowguns), 4, 5
Guter, 16, 18, 20, 21, 23
Gunn, G. P., 35, 36, 42, 47, 48, 76

H

Haenel air guns, 42, 83, 126, 141-144, 151, 153, 241
Hahn, Philip Y., 95, 96, 180-182
Hamilton, Clarence, 38-40, 200
Hammerli, 95, 152, 159-168, 206, 267, 268
  Rifle trainer, 159-163, 168
  Bobbing targets, 166, 167
Harris Marksman Spring-Air Pistol, 225
Hatcher, General Julian S., 242, 254
Haviland, Benjamin, 35, 36, 42, 47, 48, 76
Hawley air gun, 33, 34
HC (Benjamin) Pellets, 101, 105
Healthways Pistol, 222-225
Hebelscheiber verschluss, 76
Hebelspanner, 126
Hero of Alexandria, 18, 19, 20, 62
Herrera, 2
Hertzfeld's air cane, 42
Heym air guns, 126, 140, 237-239
Higgins, J. C. (Sears-Roebuck), 88, 212, 214, 267, 269, 272
Hoffritz Cutlery Company, 238
Hough, Edward C., 40, 200, 201, 203
Hough, Cass, 204
Hough, Lewis Cass, 40, 200, 201
Huhlman, 23
Humbolt, 5
Hunter, Hy, 220
Hunting with air guns, 111

Hycar, 190
Hyde's drum feed, 42
Hy Score guns, 80, 81, 107, 108, 113, 127, 130, 131, 171, 195-199, 236, 240, 243,
  Pistol, 195-199, 243-245, 246, 272
  Pellets, 102-105

I

I.C.I. pellets, 101, 197, 245, 273
Italian air guns, 156, 250

J

Jairy, M., 59
Japanese air guns, 157
J. G. A. air pistols, 152, 237
Johnson, Iver, 37, 42
Jung Roland rifles, 138, 139, 239

K

Kahn, H., 62
Kessler air guns, 87, 258
K. F. C. (Japanese), 157
King Air Rifle, 38
Kline, Richard, 222
Koes, Bartholomew, 21
Kovo Limited, 155, 156, 245
Kraus, I. R., 189, 190
Krico air rifles, 140, 248
Kürbelspanner, 73, 74

L

Lane-Fox, Colonel A. H., 5, 6
Langenhan, Fritz, 93, 124, 125, 138
Lawrence, Andrew, 195
Lefever, Charles, 200, 203
Lincoln-Jeffries, 47, 50, 51, 93, 113
Lobsinger, Hans, 21
Lock-breech systems, 78
Low, Hugh, 7

M

Machine of Ctesibius, 19
Madgeburg Air Rifle, 22, 24
Madgeburg spheres, 21
Malaya, 6
Marin gun, 24
Marks, E.T.C., 51
Markham, 38, 40
Marperger, Paul, 21
Martin gun, 24
Mauser system, 81
Mauserverschluss, 125
Mayer & Grammelspacher (see Diana)
Mayer, J., 50
McHenry, John J., 204
McGlashan air machinegun, 66
Mechanical and design tests, air guns, 235
Mefford, 62-64
Meisterschaftsbüchse, 138
Mendoza air gun, 41
Merz, Rudolph, 182
Miles, E. E., 51
Millard Brothers, 80, 113, 127, 241
Millita Air Rifle, 47, 48, 93, 124, 125
Monckton, E. H. C., 69
Monner, R. J., 70
Monroe effect, 64
Montezuma, 3

Morlet, Arthur, 2

N

National Air Rifle League (British), 108
Nichtheroy, S. S., 65, 66
N.R.A. qualification course, 106

O

Orinoco Basin, 4, 6
Ottomacs, 5

P

Papin, Denis, 22, 59
Parker & Hale, 51, 52
Patent problems, air guns, 48
Peashooters, 9
Peerless air guns, 80, 81, 127, 130, 132, 133, 246
Pellet tests, 238, 272
Penetration, air guns, 111
  Tests, 234
Perkins, Jacob, 59, 60
Philo of Byzantium, 18
Picatinny air guns, 274
Pitcher, Ken, 222
Plainsman Pistol (Heathways), 222-225
Plainsman air and CO_2 guns, 87, 99, 258
  Shotgun, 11, 104
Pneumatica, 19, 20
Pneumatic (compressed-air) guns:
  Advantages and disadvantages, 95, 169, 170
  Care of, 260
  History of, 85
  Legal problems, 85, 169
  Modern types, 84-88, 169-194
  Obsolete types, 14
  Power comparisons, 170
  Tests, 171, 253-264
  Velocity, 169
Poison arrows, 2, 4
Pope air gun, 33
Potter chronograph, 231-233
Powerlets, 212, 214, 215, 271, 272
Pucuna, 5
Pulverman air guns, 47, 48, 93, 124, 138
Pumps, air, 84
Push-lever lock, 76

Q

Quackenbush, H. M., 22, 33-37, 42, 47, 48, 76, 93, 124
  Slugs, 34
  1½ gun, 34

R

Rayner, Major John, 9
Recoil, air gun, 110
Reynolds, G. F., 63
Rivault, 62
Rifling, effect of, 109
Robin, Simon, 64
Rochester Air Rifle, 258
Ronnebeck, 69
Root, R. L., 39
Russian air guns, 158, 159
"Russian models" (pistols), 23

S

Sanderson, Ivan T., 111
Sarbacan, 6
Sars, 22

Scalingi, Ciro, 204, 235
Schmeisser, 33, 82, 83, 126
Schimel CO_2 pistol, 95, 96, 97, 98, 220
Sears-Roebuck guns, 87, 212, 214, 267, 270, 272
Searle, E. H., 50, 51
Shaw, John, 42
Sheridan air rifles, 67, 85, 86, 88, 169, 171, 189-194, 253-255
   Silver and Blue streak, 191-194
   Bullet design, 194
Shooting techniques, air guns, 110
Shooting with spring-air guns, 106-112
   European types, 108
   Maximum ranges, 108
Shot manufacture, 100
Shot shells, air, 104
Siebenkees, 20
Sight equipment, air guns, 110
Simco air guns, 86, 258
Sims, John G., 76
Sims-Dudley guns, 64, 65
Shlumper, W., 141
Skorzeny, Colonel Otto, 7
Spack, A. D., 172
Spanish air guns, 157
Sport Modell, 126
Spring-air rifle design, 250
Soviet air guns, 158, 159
Soviet air-rifle trainer, 83
Steam guns, 59, 67, 68
Steiglider, E., 125
Stocked air canes, 45
Stoeger air guns, 80, 81, 98, 105, 113, 127, 132, 133, 138, 220, 246
Suhl, 126
Sumpitan, 5, 7
Super Pells (Crosman), 101, 105
Swanson Manufacturing Company, 206
Swiss air guns, (See Hämmerli)

Syringe, air gun use, 17, 18, 20, 24, 42, 43

T

Taunery, 19
Teddington Air Rifle, 259
Tell, 125, 126
Tests, air and gas guns:
   Carbon dioxide (CO_2) arms, 264-272
   Explosion gas (ether) system, 251-253
   Methods, 231
   Pellets, 272-274
   Pneumatic arms, 253-264
   Precision spring-air arms, 236-250
Thevenot, 19
Thornton, Colonel, 24-26
Thunderbolt Air Pistol, 113, 114; 241
Thuringerwald, 126
Tomeang, 6
Tordesillas, Antonia, 2
Triggerguard spring-air cocking system, 74
Turn-bolt cocking system, 81

U

Underlever cocking systems, 75, 76, 78, 79, 80, 81

V

Valves, air, 84
Velocity, air guns, 110, 231, 232
Venuswaffenwerk, 73, 74, 125, 126
Vesuvius, U.S.S., 62, 63, 64, 66, 67
Vincent Air Rifle, 259
Vinci, Leonardo da, 59, 60, 67, 68
Vitruvius, 19
Von Guericke, Otto, 21
Von Murr, 20
VZ35 Air Rifle, 155, 156, 245
VZ47 Air Rifle, 155, 245

W

Wackerhagen, E. R., 189
Wagria air rifles, 146

Wagram, Battle of, 25, 28, 31
Walking-stick shotgun, 45
   CO_2 shotgun, 94
Walther air guns, 42, 73, 84, 109, 110, 113, 126, 127, 144-147, 152-154, 171, 240, 241, 248, 250
Warrior Air Rifle, 41
Wastl, Rochus, 46
Watterton, Charles 4
Weber, Paul, 22
Weber, M., 42, 45
Webley, Philip, 53
Webley & Scott, 11, 51, 53-56, 80, 110, 113-119, 240, 242, 250, 272
   Mark I pistol, 55, 114-119, 242
   Mark II pistol, 55
   Junior pistol, 55, 116, 118, 242
   Senior pistol, 55, 117, 242, 243
   Mark I rifle, 54, 55
   Mark II rifle, 54, 55, 111, 114
   Mark III rifle, 56, 118, 250
   Junior rifle, 56, 118, 119
Webley self-cocker, 54
Weihrauch air guns, 73, 79, 138, 139, 171, 226, 248, 249, 251
Werner, C. H., 24
Western Field air guns, 88
Westley-Richards air guns, 58, 113
White (H.P.) Laboratory tests, 9, 232, 233, 255, 262, 265, 268-271
Will Oscar, 73-75, 125, 126
Wischo air rifles, 147, 148, 239
Wissler Instrument Company, 85
Wourali, 2, 4,

Z

Zalinski, Edward L., 62, 63, 64
Zarabatana, 6
Zella Mehlis, 126
Zenit, 126, 150-152, 239
Zuendorf, John 75